FIRST CANADIAN EDITION

Advertising
& Promotion

An Integrated Marketing Communications Perspective

George E. Belch
San Diego State University

Michael A. Belch
San Diego State University

Michael A. Guolla
University of Ottawa

Contributors

Anne Marie Webb-Hughes
British Columbia Institute of Technology

Harvey Skolnick
Sheridan College

Toronto Montréal Boston Burr Ridge, IL Dubuque, IA Madison, WI New York
San Francisco St. Louis Bangkok Bogotá Caracas Kuala Lumpur Lisbon London
Madrid Mexico City Milan New Delhi Santiago Seoul Singapore Sydney Taipei

McGraw-Hill
Ryerson Limited

A Subsidiary of The McGraw·Hill Companies

Advertising and Promotion
An Integrated Marketing Communications Perspective
First Canadian Edition

ISBN: 0-07-0898588

1 2 3 4 5 6 7 8 9 10   TCP   0 9 8 7 6 5 4 3

Printed and bound in Canada.

Care has been taken to trace ownership of copyright material contained in this text; however, the publisher will welcome any information that enables them to rectify any reference or credit for subsequent editions.

Vice President, Editorial and Media Technology: Patrick Ferrier
Sponsoring Editor: James Buchanan
Developmental Editor: Sandra de Ruiter
Copy Editor: Michael Kelly
Production Coordinator: Mary Pepe
Marketing Manager: Kim Verhaeghe
Page Layout: Bookman Typesetting Co.
Photo Permissions: Alison Derry/Permissions Plus
Cover Design: Sharon Lucas
Cover Image Credit: Taxi: Micheal Simpson/EyeWire Collection/
Digital Vision/PhotoDisc
Printer: Transcontinental Printing

National Library of Canada Cataloguing in Publication

Belch, George E. (George Eugene)
   Advertising and promotion: an integrated marketing communications perspective /
George E. Belch, Michael A. Belch, Michael Guolla. — 1st Canadian ed.

Includes bibliographical references and index.
ISBN 0-07-089858-8

1. Advertising.   2. Sales promotion.   3. Communication in marketing.
I. Belch, Michael A.   II. Guolla, Michael Angelo   III. Title.

HF5823.B38 2003   659.1   C2002-904618-1

Dedicated to my wonderful family

Teresa, Louise, Daniel, and Nicholas.

About the Authors

Michael Guolla is an assistant professor at School of Management of the University of Ottawa. He completed his Ph.D. in Business Administration with a concentration in Marketing at the University of Michigan (Ann Arbor) and received his Honours in Business Administration from the Richard Ivey School of Business at the University of Western Ontario. Dr. Guolla has published articles in academic journals, proceedings of scholarly conferences, and management journals in the areas of customer satisfaction, innovation, marketing strategy, and business marketing. He has also written many cases.

Professor Guolla's most recent teaching includes promotion management, services marketing, and marketing research to undergraduate students and integrated marketing communications and customer satisfaction management to MBA students. He has previously taught at Richard Ivey School of Business, the Michigan Business School and at Queen's Business School.

Anne Marie Webb-Hughes—Contributing Author   Anne Marie Webb-Hughes is a faculty member with the British Columbia Institute of Technology. Since 1996, she has contributed to the Institute as a program head and instructor in the disciplines of marketing management, marketing communications, research, and entrepreneurial skills training. She is currently teaching e-marketing in the Information Technology Department and business development skills in the Venture Centre. As a previous contributing author in *Marketing Princi-ples*, Anne Marie is pleased to be able to contribute her research and authorship on the Canadian perspective to this text.

Anne Marie comes to BCIT with 20 years experience in retail management, having achieved the levels of general management, director of marketing, and vice president of stores with Canadian retail corporations. She has led creative teams to win the International R.A.C. award for "Best Magalogue" and the Canadian Creative award for "Best Newspaper Campaign." She received her Masters of Education in Adult Learning and Leadership from Simon Fraser University in Vancouver B.C. and has received her Certification of Internet Business Strategy through the University of British Columbia.

Harvey Skolnick—Contributing Author
Harvey Skolnick is a marketing professor in the School of Business at Sheridan College, and also currently teaches in continuing education at Ryerson University. He is the author of many articles that have appeared in *Marketing Magazine* and other business publications. He holds an MBA from the University of Toronto, specializing in marketing, and a B.Sc. from McGill University, specializing in psychology.

Professor Skolnick's most recent teaching includes introductory marketing, integrated marketing communications, direct marketing, and marketing management. He has also previously taught at York University and the University of Toronto.

Contents in Brief

Contents

Contents

Contents

x

Part Six
Implement, Control, and Monitor the IMC Plan

Chapter Sixteen
Organizing for Integrated Marketing
Communication   418

Chapter Seventeen
Measuring the Effectiveness of Integrated
Marketing Communications   448

Contents

Chapter Eighteen
Advertising Regulation and Ethical, Social, and Economic Effects of Advertising

Preface

The Changing World of Advertising and Promotion

Nearly everyone in the modern world is influenced to some degree by advertising and other forms of promotion. Organizations in both the private and public sectors have learned that the ability to communicate effectively and efficiently with their target audiences is critical to their success. Advertising and other types of promotional messages are used to sell products and services as well as to promote causes, market political candidates, and deal with societal problems such as the AIDS crisis and alcohol and drug abuse. Consumers are finding it increasingly difficult to avoid the efforts of marketers, who are constantly searching for new ways to communicate with them.

Most of the people involved in advertising and promotion will tell you that there is no more dynamic and fascinating a field to either practise or study. However, they will also tell you that the field is undergoing dramatic changes that are changing advertising and promotion forever. The changes are coming from all sides—marketers demanding better results from their advertising and promotional dollars; lean but highly creative smaller ad agencies; sales promotion and direct-marketing firms, as well as interactive agencies, who want a larger share of the millions of dollars companies spend each year promoting their products and services; consumers who no longer respond to traditional forms of advertising; and new technologies that may reinvent the very process of advertising. Currently, we are experiencing perhaps the most dynamic and revolutionary changes of any era in the history of marketing, as well as advertising and promotion. These changes are being driven by advances in technology and developments that have led to the rapid growth of communications through interactive media, particularly the Internet.

For decades, the advertising strategy for a national brand involved creating one or two commercials that could be run on network television, a few print ads that would run in general interest magazines, and some sales promotion support such as coupons or premium offers.

However, in today's world there are a myriad of media outlets—print, radio, specialty TV channels on cable and satellite delivery services, and now the Internet—competing for consumers' attention. Marketers are looking beyond the traditional media to find new and better ways to communicate with their customers. They no longer accept on faith the value of conventional advertising placed in traditional media.

In addition, marketers are changing the way they communicate with consumers. They know they are operating in an environment where advertising messages are everywhere. Consumers channel-surf past most commercials, and brands promoted in traditional ways often fail. New-age advertisers are redefining the notion of what an ad is and where it runs. Stealth messages are being woven into the culture and embedded into movies and TV shows or made into their own form of entertainment.

A number of factors are fueling this evolution in marketing communications. The audiences that marketers seek, along with the media and methods for reaching them, have become increasingly fragmented. Advertising and promotional efforts have become more regionalized and targeted to specific audiences. Retailers have become larger and more powerful, forcing marketers to shift money from advertising budgets to sales promotion. Marketers expect their promotional dollars to generate immediate sales and are demanding more accountability from their agencies. The Internet revolution is well under way and the online audience is growing rapidly throughout the world. Many companies are coordinating all their communications efforts so that they can send cohesive messages to their customers. Some companies are building brands with little or no use of traditional media advertising. Many advertising agencies have acquired, started, or become affiliated with sales promotion, direct-marketing, interactive agencies, and public relations companies to better serve their clients' marketing communications needs. Their clients have become "media-neutral" and are asking that they consider whatever form of marketing communication works best to target market segments and build long-term reputations and short-term sales.

This text will introduce students to this fast-changing field of advertising and promotion. While advertising is its primary focus, it is more than just an introductory advertising text because there is more to most organizations' promotional programs than just advertising. The changes discussed above are leading marketers and their agencies to approach advertising and promotion from an integrated marketing communications (IMC) perspective, which calls for a "big picture" approach to planning marketing and promotion programs and coordinating the various communication functions. To understand the role of advertising and promotion in today's business world, one must recognize how a firm can use all the promotional tools to communicate with its customers.

To the Student: Preparing You for the New World of Advertising and Promotion

Some of you are taking this course to learn more about this fascinating field; many of you hope to work in advertising or some other promotional area. The changes in the industry have profound implications for the way today's student is trained and educated. You will not be working for the same kind of communication agencies that have existed historically. If you work on the client side of the business, you will find that the way they approach advertising and promotion is changing dramatically.

Today's student is expected to understand all the major marketing communication functions: advertising, direct marketing, interactive media, sales promotion, public relations, and personal selling. You will also be expected to know how to research and evaluate a company's marketing and promotional situation and how to use these various functions in developing effective communication strategies and programs. This book will help prepare you for these challenges.

As a professor, I was, of course, once a student myself. In many ways, I am a perpetual student in that I am constantly striving to learn about and explain how advertising and promotion work. I share many of your interests and concerns and am often excited (and bored) by the same things. Having taught in the advertising and promotion area for a number of years, I developed an understanding of what makes a book in this field interesting to students. In writing this book, I tried to remember how I felt about the various texts I used throughout the years and to incorporate the good things and minimize those I felt were of little use. I tried not to overburden you with definitions, although I do call out those that are especially important to your understanding of the material.

I also remember that as a student I wasn't really excited about theory. But to fully understand how integrated marketing communications works, it is necessary to establish some theoretical basis. The more you understand about how things are supposed to work, the easier it will be for you to understand why they do or do not turn out as planned.

Perhaps the question students ask most often is, "How do I use this in the real world?" In response, numerous examples of how the various theories and concepts in the text can be used in practice have been provided. A particular strength of this text is the integration of theory with practical application. Nearly every day an example of advertising and promotion in practice is reported in the media. We have used many sources, such as *Marketing Magazine, Advertising Age, AdWeek, BrandWeek, The Wall Street Journal, Business Week, Fortune, Forbes, Marketing Tools, Sales & Marketing Management, Business Marketing, Promo,* and many others, to find practical examples that are integrated throughout the text. The benefit of hundreds of people discussing strategies and rationale behind the ads and other types of promotions we use as examples. Each chapter begins with a vignette that presents an example of an advertising or promotional campaign or other interesting insights. Every chapter also contains **IMC Perspectives** that present in-depth discussions of particular issues related to the chapter material and show how companies are using integrated marketing communications. **Global Perspectives** are presented throughout the text in recognition of the increasing importance of international marketing and the challenges of advertising and promotion and the role they play in the marketing programs of multinational marketers. **Ethical Perspectives** focus attention on important social issues and show how advertisers must take ethical considerations into account when planning and implementing advertising and promotional programs.

Each chapter features beautiful four-colour illustrations showing examples from many of the most current and best-integrated marketing communication campaigns being used around the world. Advertisements and examples of numerous other types of promotion, all of which were carefully chosen to illustrate a particular idea, theory, or practical application have been included. Please take time to read the opening vignettes to each chapter, as well as the IMC, Global, and Ethical Perspectives, and study the diverse ads and illustrations. These will stimulate your interest and relate to your daily life as a consumer and a target of advertising and promotion.

To the Instructor: A Text That Reflects the Changes in the World of Advertising and Promotion

The major goal for *Advertising and Promotion* was to provide you with the most comprehensive and current text on the market for teaching advertising and promotion from an IMC perspective. The focus is on the many changes that are occurring in areas of marketing communications and how they influence advertising and promotional strategies and tactics. This was done with an *integrated marketing communications perspective.* More and more companies are approaching advertising and promotion from an IMC perspective, coordinating the various promotional mix elements with other marketing activities that communicate with a firm's customers. A recent study found that an overwhelming majority of marketing managers believe IMC can enhance the effectiveness of their marketing communications efforts. Many advertising agencies are also developing expertise in direct marketing, sales promotion, event sponsorship, the Internet, and other areas so that they can meet all their clients' integrated marketing communication needs—and, of course, survive.

The text is built around an integrated marketing communications planning model and recognizes the importance of coordinating all of the promotional mix elements to develop an effective communications program. Although media advertising is often the most visible part of a firm's promotional program, attention must also be given to direct marketing, sales promotion, public relations, interactive media, and personal selling.

This text integrates theory with planning, management, and strategy. To effectively plan, implement, and evaluate IMC programs, one must understand the overall marketing process, consumer behaviour, and communications theory. This text draws from the extensive research in advertising, consumer behaviour, communications, marketing, sales promotion, and other fields to give students a basis for understanding the marketing communications process, how it influences consumer decision making, and how to develop promotional strategies.

While this is an introductory text, each topic is treated in some depth, with an understanding that marketing and advertising student of today needs a text that provides more than just an introduction to terms and topics. The book is positioned primarily for the introductory advertising, marketing communications, or promotions course as taught in the business/marketing curriculum. It can also be used in journalism/communications courses that take an integrated marketing communications perspective. In addition to its thorough coverage of advertising, this text has chapters on sales promotion, direct marketing and marketing on the Internet, and public relations. These chapters stress the integration of advertising with other promotional mix elements and the need to understand their role in the overall marketing program.

Organization of This Text

This book is divided into six major parts. In Part One, "Understanding Integrated Marketing Communications" we examine the role of advertising and promotion in marketing and introduce the concept of integrated marketing communications. Chapter 1 provides an overview of advertising and promotion and its role in modern marketing. The concept of IMC and the factors that have led to its growth are discussed. Each of the promotional mix elements is defined and an IMC planning model shows the various steps in the promotional planning process. This model provides a framework for developing the integrated marketing communications program and is

followed throughout the text. Chapter 2 examines the role of advertising and promotion in the overall marketing program, with attention to the various elements of the marketing mix and how they interact with advertising and promotional strategy. We have also included coverage of market segmentation and positioning in this chapter so that students can understand how these concepts fit into the overall marketing programs as well as their role in the development of an advertising and promotional program.

In Part Two, "Connecting Consumers to IMC," we cover the various theories and models to understand consumer behaviour in the context of marketing communications in order to perform a promotional program situation analysis. Chapter 3 covers the stages of the consumer decision-making process and both the internal psychological factors and the external factors that influence consumer behaviour. The focus of this chapter is on how advertisers can use an understanding of buyer behaviour to develop effective advertising and other forms of promotion. Chapter 4 examines various communication theories and models of how consumers respond to advertising messages and other forms of marketing communications.

These first sections of the text provide students with a solid background in the areas of IMC planning, marketing, consumer behaviour, and communications. This lays the foundation for the remaining sections as we discuss the development of the integrated marketing communication program.

In Part Three, "Articulate the Message," we consider how firms develop objectives for their integrated marketing communications programs and how to translate those objectives into meaningful messages. Chapter 5 stresses the importance of knowing what to expect from advertising and promotion, the different types of communication objectives, characteristics of good objectives, and problems in setting objectives. Chapter 6 discusses the planning and development of the creative strategy and advertising campaign and examines the creative process. In Chapter 7 we turn our attention to ways to execute the creative strategy and some criteria for evaluating creative work.

In Part Four, "Deliver the Message," we explore the various ways of getting the message to the target audience. Chapters 8 through 11 cover media strategy and planning and the various advertising media. Chapter 8 introduces the key principles of media planning and strategy and examines how a media plan is developed. We have also integrated the discussion of various methods for determining and allocating the promotional budget into this chapter. Chapter 9 discusses the strengths and limitations of TV and broadcast media, as well as issues regarding the purchase of radio and TV time and audience measurement. Chapter 10 considers the same issues for the print media (magazines and newspapers). Chapter 11 examines the role of out-of-home and support media.

In Part Five, "Strengthen the Message," we continue the IMC emphasis by examining other promotional tools that are used in the integrated marketing communications process. Chapter 12 examines the area of sales promotion, including both consumer-oriented promotions and programs targeted to the trade (retailers, wholesalers, and other middlemen). Chapter 13 covers the role of public relations in IMC. Chapter 14 looks at the rapidly growing areas of direct marketing. This chapter examines database marketing and the way by which companies communicate directly with target customers through various media. Chapter 15 provides a detailed discussion of interactive media and marketing on the Internet and how companies are using the World Wide Web as a medium for communicating with customers. We discuss how this new medium is being used for a variety of marketing activities including advertising, sales promotion, and even the selling of products and services.

In Part Six, "Implement, Control and Monitor the IMC Plan," we explore three issues for IMC program success. Chapter 16 describes how firms organize for advertising and promotion and examines the role of ad agencies and other firms that provide marketing and promotional services. A discussion of how ad agencies are selected, evaluated, and compensated, as well as the changes occurring in the agency business are included. Attention is also given to other types of marketing communication organizations such as direct marketing, sales promotion, and interactive agencies, as well as public relations firms. Whether responsibility for integrating the various communication functions lies with the client or the agency is also considered. Chapter 17 discusses ways to measure the effectiveness of various elements of the integrated marketing communications program, including methods for pre-testing and post-testing advertising messages and campaigns. The text concludes with Chapter 18, a discussion of the regulatory, social, and economic environments in which advertising and promotion operate.

Chapter Features

The following features in each chapter enhance students' understanding of the material as well as their reading enjoyment.

Chapter Objectives   Objectives are provided at the beginning of each chapter to identify the major areas and points covered in the chapter and guide the learning effort.

Chapter Opening Vignettes   Each chapter begins with a vignette that shows the effective use of integrated marketing communications by a company or ad agency or discusses an interesting issue that is relevant to the chapter. These opening vignettes are designed to draw the students into the chapter by presenting an interesting example, development, or issue that relates to the material covered in the chapter.

IMC Perspectives   These boxed items feature in-depth discussions of interesting issues related to the chapter material and the practical application of integrated marketing communications. Each chapter contains these insights into the world of integrated marketing communications.

Global Perspectives   These boxed items provide information similar to that in the IMC Perspectives, with a focus on international aspects of advertising and promotion.

Ethical Perspectives   These boxed items discuss the moral and/or ethical issues regarding practices engaged in by marketers and are also tied to the material presented in the particular chapter.

Key Terms   Important terms are highlighted in boldface throughout the text and listed at the end of each chapter with a page reference. These terms help call students' attention to important ideas, concepts, and definitions and help them review their learning progress.

Chapter Summaries   These synopses serve as a quick review of important topics covered and a very helpful study guide.

Discussion Questions   Questions at the end of each chapter give students an opportunity to test their understanding of the material and to apply it. These questions can also serve as a basis for class discussion or assignments.

Four-Colour Visuals   Print ads, photoboards, and other examples appear throughout the book. A number of ads, charts, graphs, and other types of illustrations are included in the text.

Changes to the Canadian Edition

A number of changes to the original U.S. edition have been undertaken in order to create a Canadian edition for Canadian students.

- **A Continuing Emphasis on Integrated Marketing Communications** The Canadian edition continues to place a strong emphasis on approaching the field of advertising and promotion from an integrated marketing communications perspective. It shows how the various elements of an organization's promotional mix are combined to develop a total marketing communications program that sends a consistent message to customers. More attention is also given to setting communication objectives for IMC programs. The importance of specific communication objectives for each target audience and the importance of unique messages that resonate for each target audience are given greater attention. This approach helps establish a unique brand position for each target audience while maintaining the overall market position of the brand. Collectively, these ideas allow for individual components of the IMC program, such as advertising or sales promotion, to have their own communication objectives that contribute to the overall communication objectives of the entire IMC program.

- **New Chapter Opening Vignettes** *All* of the chapter opening vignettes in the Canadian edition are new and were chosen for their currency and relevance to Canadian students. They demonstrate how various companies and advertising agencies use advertising and other IMC tools. They also provide interesting insights into some of the current trends and developments that are taking place throughout Canada.

- **New and Updated Perspectives** All of the boxed items focusing on specific examples of how companies are using integrated marketing communications are new or updated, and provide insight into many of the most current and popular advertising and promotional campaigns being used by marketers. The IMC Perspectives also address interesting issues related to advertising, sales promotion, direct marketing, and marketing on the Internet. Nearly all of the boxed items focusing on global and ethical issues of advertising and promotion are new.

- **Canadian Examples** The field of advertising and promotion changes very rapidly. Wherever possible, the statistical information presented in tables, charts, and figures throughout the text have been adapted. The most current Canadian trade literature was reviewed to ensure that this text reflects the most current perspectives on advertising, promotion, and the rapidly evolving area of integrated marketing communications in Canada. Many Canadian examples and ads throughout the book have been added. *Advertising and Promotion* is the most contemporary text on the market, offering students as timely a perspective as possible.

- **Fewer Chapters** The previous U.S. edition contained 22 chapters, which students and professors alike felt was too long. The text has been condensed to a more manageable length of 18 chapters. Some changes were quite simple as market feedback indicated a lessened need for chapters on personal selling and international advertising, so these have been deleted. Two chapters were merged into existing chapters. The previous "Source, Message, and Channel Factors" chapter was deleted, and some of the material was fit into this edition's chapters on creative strategy and creative tactics (Chapters 6 and 7). The previous "Regulation of Advertising and Promotion" chapter was deleted, and a section on advertising regulation in Canada was added to the existing chapter on social, ethical, and economical issues in advertising (Chapter 18). Overall, 18 chapters appears to be a more reasonable number to cover in one semester.

- **Clear Decision Focus** Chapter 1 features a clear planning framework and identifies the content of an IMC plan. This framework is followed more closely throughout the text. The major parts of the text are organized and given a title that corresponds to the steps in the IMC plan as noted in a previous section. Further, within many chapters, a clear distinction is made between the type of decisions that a marketer or advertiser makes versus the information they use to formulate the decision. This approach makes it easier for students to understand the key decisions that need to be made for a successful IMC plan.

Support Material

A high-quality package of instructional supplements supports this edition. We offer instructors a support package that facilitates the use of our text and enhances the learning experience of the student.

Instructor's Manual

The instructor's manual is a valuable teaching resource that includes learning objectives, chapter and lecture outlines, answers to all end-of-chapter discussion questions, and further insights and teaching suggestions. Additional discussion questions are also presented for each chapter. These questions can be used for class discussion or as short-answer essay questions for exams.

Test Bank

A test bank of multiple-choice questions has been developed to accompany the text. The questions provide thorough coverage of the chapter material, including opening vignettes and IMC, Global, and Ethical Perspectives.

Computerized Test Bank

A computerized Brownstone version of the test bank is available to adopters of the text.

Electronic Slides

A disk containing nearly 300 PowerPoint® Presentation slides is available to adopters for electronic presentations. These slides contain lecture notes, charts, graphs, and other instructional materials, written to accompany the U.S. edition.

Four-Colour Transparencies

Each adopter may request a set of over 100 four-colour acetate transparencies compiled for the U.S. edition, that present print ads, photoboards, sales promotion offers, and other materials that do not appear in the text. A number of important models or charts appearing in the text are also provided as colour transparencies. Slip sheets are included with each transparency to give the instructor useful background information about the illustration and how it can be integrated into the lecture.

Video Supplements A CBC video supplement package has been developed specifically for classroom use with this text.

i-Learning Sales Specialist Your *Integrated i-Learning Sales Specialist* is a McGraw-Hill Ryerson representative who has the experience, product knowledge, training, and support to help you assess and integrate any of the above-noted products, technology, and services into your course for optimum teaching and learning performance. Whether it's how to use our test bank software, helping your students improve their grades, or how to put your entire course on-line, your i-Learning Sales Specialist is there to help. Contact your local i-Learning Sales Specialist today to learn how to maximize all McGraw-Hill Ryerson resources!

Online Learning Centre

McGraw-Hill Ryerson content and the power of the Web combine to offer you Online Learning Centres—pedagogical features and supplements for MHR books on the Internet. Students can simply point-and-click their way to key terms, learning objectives, chapter overviews, exercises, and Web links. And professors profit from the instant access to lecture slides, Instructor's Manuals, test banks, and PowerPoint slides all in one place.

Acknowledgments

This Canadian edition represents a tremendous amount of work that would not have become a reality without the assistance and support of many other people. Authors tend to think they have the best ideas, approach, examples, and organization for writing a great book. But I quickly learned that there is always room for our ideas to be improved on by others. A number of colleagues provided detailed, thoughtful reviews that were immensely helpful in making this a better book.

I would like to thank the following reviewers who provided valuable feedback and helped shape the content of the first Canadian edition: Michael Basil, *University of Lethbridge;* Brad Davis, *Wilfrid Laurier University*; Dwight Dyson, *Centennial College;* Steve Finlay, *Conestoga College;* Stephen Janisse, *St. Clair College;* Mary Louise Huebner, *Seneca College;* Anne Lavack, *University of Regina;* John Milne, *York University;* Judith Nash, *SAIT;* Caroline O'Connell, *St. Francis Xavier University;* Elizabeth O'Neil, *University of Guelph;* Barbara Phillips, *University of Saskatchewan;* Harold Simpkins, *Concordia University;* Harvey Skolnick, *Sheridan College;* and Jim Swaffield, *University of Alberta;* Elaine Wilson, *Fanshawe College.*

I would also like to acknowledge the cooperation I received from many people in the business, advertising, and media communities. The Canadian edition contains several additional ads, illustrations, charts, and tables that have been provided by advertisers and/or their agencies, various publications, and other advertising and industry organizations. Many individuals took time from their busy schedules to provide us with requested materials and gave us permission to use them. A special thanks to all of you.

A manuscript does not become a book without a great deal of work on the part of a publisher. Various individuals at McGraw-Hill Ryerson have been involved with this project over the past year. My sponsoring editor, James Buchanan, provided valuable guidance and encouragement to complete the revision successfully. A special thanks goes to Sandra de Ruiter, my developmental editor, for her continuous hard work, friendly and helpful suggestions, and appropriate reminders to stay on schedule. Thanks also to Kelly Dickson for doing a superb job of managing the production process. I also want to acknowledge the outstanding work of Alison Derry for her help in obtaining permissions for most of the Canadian ads that appear throughout the book. I'd like to thank a couple of other people at McGraw-Hill Ryerson who participated in the initial stages of the project. Much appreciation goes to Lenore Gray Spence, who first approached me with the idea of contributing to the first Canadian edition, and Michael Ryan, who put in a "good word" for my involvement. Thanks to the other members of the production team for all their hard work on this edition.

I'd like to thank Anne Marie Webb-Hughes of British Columbia Institute of Technology, who made generous revisions to Chapters 14 and 15. Anne Marie was also a valuable colleague in providing feedback on my ideas for reorganizing the chapters and deciding upon the importance of some topics in the text. Much thanks goes to Harvey Skolnick of Sheridan College for developing some new Perspectives so that the text would have a strong Canadian flavour.

I would like to acknowledge the Dean of the School of Management at the University of Ottawa, Michael Kelly, who supported my involvement in this project right from the start. I have taught promotion at the University of Ottawa for 9 years, and I'd like to extend my appreciation to our former dean, Jean-Louis Malouin, who allowed me to hone my promotion skills in the classroom for these many years.

I'm grateful for the efforts of David Toeg, a previous student of mine. David offered a student's perspective on the book, helped identify good examples that students would enjoy reading, and contributed to a few of the chapter vignettes. I'd like to extend my appreciation to all my previous students who have given me the opportunity to develop my ideas. It is very gratifying to know that you enjoy my teaching and are using your new-found knowledge in the business world.

On a personal note, my kids, Louise, Daniel, and Nicholas, have been great during this time-consuming and hectic process of working on the text. To them, I owe a great big "Daddy hug"!! All my love and gratitude goes to my wife Teresa who helped me tremendously.

Michael Guolla

McGraw-Hill Ryerson
Online Learning Centre

McGraw-Hill Ryerson offers you an online resource that combines the best content with the flexibility and power of the Internet. Organized by chapter, the BELCH/BELCH/GUOLLA Online Learning Centre (OLC) offers the following features to enhance your learning and understanding of Advertising and Promotion:

- Online Study Guide
- Web Links
- Internet Exercises
- Quizzes

By connecting to the "real world" through the OLC, you will enjoy a dynamic and rich source of current information that will help you get more from your course and improve your chances for success, both in the course and in the future.

For the Instructor

Downloadable Supplements
All key supplements are available, password-protected for instant access!

PageOut PageOut
Create your own course Web page for free, quickly and easily. Your professionally designed Web site links directly to OLC material, allows you to post a class syllabus, offers an online gradebook, and much more! Visit www.pageout.net

Primis Online Primis Online
Primis Online gives you access to our resources in the best medium for your students: printed textbooks or electronic ebooks. There are over 350,000 pages of content available from which you can create customized learning tools from our online database at www.mhhe.com/primis

ning Centre

For the Student

Online Study Guide

Do you understand the material? You'll know after working through this comprehensive Online Student Study Guide. Try the Multiple Choice and True/False questions for each chapter to maximize your time spent reviewing text concepts. They're auto-graded with feedback!

Web Links

This section references various Web sites, including all company Web sites linked from the text. Find out more about the companies referenced in the text and stay current with industry news!

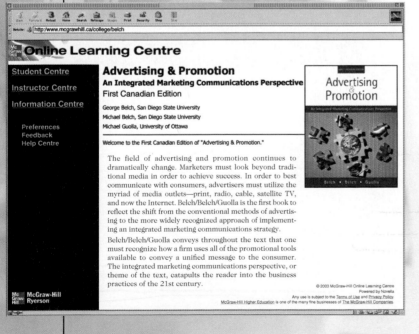

Your Internet companion to the most exciting educational tools on the Web!

The Online Learning Centre can be found at:
www.mcgrawhill.ca/college/belch

Chapter One

Integrated Marketing Communications

Chapter Objectives

- To review the various elements of the promotional mix: advertising, sales promotion, public relations, direct marketing, Internet marketing, and personal selling.

- To introduce the concept of integrated marketing communications (IMC) by considering its evolution, growth, and importance.

- To examine how various marketing and promotional elements must be coordinated to communicate effectively with the IMC perspective.

- To summarize a model of the IMC planning process and examine the steps in developing a marketing communications program.

Rebranding Using IMC in the Banking Industry

The TD Bank and Canada Trust merger of February 1, 2000, brought about one of the most ambitious marketing communication challenges ever witnessed in Canada. It needed to manage three different brands: Canada Trust, Toronto-Dominion Bank, and the newly formed TD Canada Trust with its own corporate logo. The success of this venture resulted in TD Canada Trust being recognized as Marketer of the Year by *Marketing Magazine* for the year 2001.

A key element of the marketing communication was the focus on customer service in all its promotional tools. Customer service was a hallmark differentiator for Canada Trust over the years as it had successfully carved out a niche in the competitive "banking" industry. A large, green, leather chair was the primary visual to capture the promise of this benefit, and the slogan "Banking can be this comfortable" reinforced the message and provided a simple reminder to consumers. As Dominic Mercuri, senior vice-president of advertising and marketing notes, "We are trying to drive home that, at TD Canada Trust, the customer, the individual, is our main focus and that they can count on comfort in their financial dealings with us."

Both the chair and the slogan became focal points of the in-print (magazines and newspapers) and television advertising. In fact, the two shades of green that signify TD Canada Trust and the chair were predominantly displayed on posters and floor decals in Toronto's Union Station. And these colours and the visuals from the print ads are reproduced on the first page of the company's website.

As part of the transition launch, a personalized direct-mail piece was sent to each of the nearly 4 million Canada Trust customers. The number of pieces and the customized nature of the message required 24-hour shifts of printing over 29 days! While a 20 percent increase in customer calls for clarification was expected, TD Canada Trust experienced only a 3 percent increase. Employee commitment and understanding was an integral part of the transition as TD Canada Trust launched extensive internal marketing communications campaign that featured a live presentation, video, and "Brand Library" packages for the more than 19,000 employees.

On October 27, 2001, public relations offered an interesting twist during the implementation of the transition. A short-term problem of the bank's computer systems not working due to an unusual hardware glitch resulted in TD Canada Trust immediately issuing an apology ad that appeared in major Canadian newspapers on October 29 and 30.

The marketing communications challenge faced a number of complications. One was the difficulty of communicating in four waves across four regions of Canada in the space of a few months. In May, the Atlantic Canada wave was just completing as the West wave (B.C. and Alberta) was starting. And at the same time, waves three (Saskatchewan, Manitoba, and Quebec) and four (Ontario) were at their critical pre-implementation stages. Another complication was the need for both sets of marketing departments, with differing orientations, to come together.

The rebranding efforts faced an uphill battle since they occurred during a particularly competitive year in the banking industry that featured many new marketing communications campaigns. CIBC attempted to position itself in their ads as a "responsive" bank for Canadians. The Royal Bank of Canada changed its name to RBC Financial Group and focused on the bank as a place for customers to fulfill their dreams, signified by a glowing yellow box in its television and print ads. One competitor jumped at the opportunity to take advantage of a realignment of products across the two merging firms. Scotiabank attempted to attract dissatisfied Canada Trust customers who could no longer use their MasterCard line of credit since TD was affiliated with VISA.

Sources: Lesley Young, "Taking Marketing to the Bank," *Marketing Magazine,* February 11, 2002; Lesley Young, "Comfort and Joy," *Marketing Magazine,* December 17, 2001; Chris Daniels, "Tech Glitch Forces Apology Ads," *Marketing Magazine,* November 5, 2001; Leslie Young, "Banks' Ads Pledge Customer Care," *Marketing Magazine,* October 8, 2001; *Marketing Magazine,* August 6 and 14, 2001.

As the previous discussion illustrates, many companies recognize that the way they must communicate with consumers and promote their products and services is changing rapidly. Developing marketing communications programs that are responsive to these changes is critical to the success of every organization. For example, in an effort to increase traffic during lunch and dinner, a major western Canadian franchisee of 25 Denny's Restaurants used advertising (i.e., radio, newspaper), sales promotion (i.e., featured menu prices, guarantee), and public relations (i.e., sponsorship of junior hockey) to increase sales by 15 percent during 2001.[1] Cadbury Trebor Allan communicated the crunch benefit of Crispy Crunch and Crunchie chocolate bars with a novel approach. It connected the "crunch" of the brands' names with the idea that the Toronto Raptors' Vince Carter "delivered in the crunch." Clearly a clever play on words, the campaign featured a special event called "Crunch Time" for the Raptors' home opener where fans received a poster and enjoyed various activities during the game. Print and TV ads communicated a contest to win tickets to the basketball game or a year's supply of bars. Special packaging and an employee tie-in with Vince Carter were other key connections between the brands and the star.[2] Thus, advertising and other forms of promotion will continue to play an important role in the integrated marketing programs of most companies. Each may take on a variety of forms, and each has certain characteristics.

Marketing Communications

Marketing is defined as "the process of planning and executing the conception, pricing, promotion, and distribution of ideas, goods, and services to create exchanges that satisfy individual and organizational objectives."[3]

The marketing function in an organization facilitates the exchange process and the development of relationships by carefully examining the needs and wants of consumers, developing a product or service that satisfies these needs, offering it at a certain price, making it available through a particular place or channel of distribution, and developing a program of promotion or communication to create awareness and interest. These four Ps—product, price, place (distribution), and promotion (marketing communications)—are elements of the **marketing mix.** The basic task of marketing is combining these four elements into a marketing program to facilitate the potential for exchange with consumers in the marketplace.

The primary focus of this book is one element of the marketing mix: promotion, or marketing communications. **Promotion** has been defined as the coordination of all seller-initiated efforts to set up channels of information and persuasion to sell goods and services or promote an idea.[4] While implicit communication occurs through the

IMC Perspective 1–1
Bell Canada Grows out West

Unleashing a stodgy monopolistic image is a significant marketing communications challenge, but the marketers at Bell (BCE), with their ad agency Cossette Communication Group, are doing the impossible with one simple word: GO! In all the years of its existence, Bell had never launched a national branding campaign until the fall of 2001. As chief strategist Bill Durnan exclaims, "We think it's quite an accomplishment to take such a very dramatic, all-encompassing company and get it down to a two-letter word."

With a wide variety of products and services directed towards both business and consumer markets, Bell envisioned "an inspirational invitation to Canadians to consider the technology and services that Bell has to offer that will help them enjoy more out of their business and personal lives," notes Durnan.

With expenditures in 2000 of $29.3 million for Bell Canada (local and long distance telephone service), $30.4 million for Bell Mobility (cellphones), $18.4 million for Bell Actimedia's Sympatico (Internet service provider), and Bell Expressvu (satellite television), BCE sought a common look to all the products and services with its simple and clever expression, "Go."

The campaign covers many promotional tools. "Go" is featured in television, newspaper, out-of-home media, and Internet advertising as the primary expenditures, but it is also prevalent on the Bell website, its sales promotion, and all public relations. In fact, Bell's inspirational leader Jean Monty showed the lead television ad, "Online Jam," when he accepted the Canadian Marketing Association's first-ever e-Visionary award.

Sources: Sarah Smith, "Go Kicks Off Bell National Campaign," *Marketing Magazine,* October 1, 2001; Stan Stutter, "Going Too Big," *Marketing Magazine,* October 8, 2001; Chris Daniels, "From the Word Go," *Marketing Magazine,* December 17, 2001.

---

various elements of the marketing mix, most of an organization's communications with the marketplace take place as part of a carefully planned and controlled promotional program. The basic tools used to accomplish an organization's communication objectives are often referred to as the **promotional mix** (Figure 1–1).

Traditionally the promotional mix has included four elements: advertising, sales promotion, public relations, and personal selling. However, in this text we view direct marketing as well as interactive media as major promotional-mix elements that marketers use to communicate with their target audiences.

Furthermore, while either term is suitable, promotion or marketing communications, many marketers are using the latter since the tools are linked to achieve specific communication objectives. In fact, marketers have recently begun to use the term *integrated marketing communications* (IMC) to recognize this connection among various promotion tools. Each tool plays a distinctive role within the marketing communications plan as seen by the opening vignette.

Advertising

Advertising is defined as any paid form of nonpersonal communication about an organization, product, service, or idea by an identified sponsor.[5] The *paid* aspect of

Figure 1–1   Elements of the promotional mix

The Promotional Mix

| Advertising | Direct marketing | Internet marketing | Sales promotion | Public relations | Personal selling |

5

this definition reflects the fact that the space or time for an advertising message generally must be bought. An occasional exception to this is the public service announcement (PSA), whose advertising space or time is donated by the media.

The *nonpersonal* component means advertising involves mass media (e.g., TV, radio, magazines, newspapers) that can transmit a message to large groups of individuals, often at the same time. The nonpersonal nature of advertising means there is generally no opportunity for immediate feedback from the message recipient (except in direct-response advertising). Therefore, before the message is sent, the advertiser must consider how the audience will interpret and respond to it.

Advertising is the best-known and most widely discussed form of promotion, probably because of its pervasiveness. It is also a very important promotional tool, particularly for companies whose products and services are targeted at mass consumer markets. More than 130 companies each spend over $100 million a year on advertising in the United States every year. Figure 1–2 shows the advertising expenditures of the 25 leading national advertisers in 1998.

There are several reasons why advertising is such an important part of many marketers' promotional mixes. First, it can be a very cost-effective method for communicating with large audiences. For example, during the 1999–2000 television season, prime-time network television reached 85 percent of Canadians on a daily basis. The cost per thousand households reached was around $14.00.[6]

Advertising can be used to create brand images and symbolic appeals for a company or brand, a very important capability for companies selling products and services that are difficult to differentiate on functional attributes. For example, since 1980 Absolut has used creative advertising to position its vodka as an upscale, fashionable, sophisticated drink and differentiate it from other brands. The advertising strategy has been to focus on two unique aspects of the product: the Absolut name and the distinctive shape of the bottle (Exhibit 1–1). Most of the print ads used in this long-running campaign are specifically tailored for the magazine or region where they appear. The campaign, one of the most successful and recognizable in advertising history, has made the Absolut brand nearly synonymous with imported vodka. While all other spirits sales have declined by more than 40 percent over the past 15 years, Absolut sales have increased tenfold, and the various Absolut brands have a combined 70 percent market share.[7]

Another feature of advertising is its ability to strike a responsive chord with consumers when differentiation across other elements of the marketing mix is difficult to achieve. Popular advertising campaigns attract consumers' attention and can help generate sales. These popular campaigns can also sometimes be leveraged into successful integrated marketing communications programs. For example, Eveready used the popularity of its Energizer Bunny campaign to generate support from retailers in the form of shelf space, promotional displays, and other merchandising activities (Exhibit 1–2). Consumer promotions such as in-store displays, premium offers,

Figure 1–2   25 leading advertisers in the United States in 1998*

Rank	Advertiser	Ad Spending
1	General Motors Corp.	$2,940.4
2	Procter & Gamble Co.	2,650.3
3	Philip Morris Cos.	2,049.3
4	Daimler-Chrysler	1,646.7
5	Sears, Roebuck & Co.	1,578.3
6	Ford Motor Co.	1,520.7
7	AT&T Corp.	1,428.0
8	Walt Disney Co.	1,358.7
9	PepsiCo	1,263.4
10	Diageo	1,205.7
11	Warner-Lambert Co.	1,104.3
12	IBM Corp.	1,079.3
13	Time Warner	1,077.3
14	McDonald's Corp.	1,025.4
15	Unilever	1,015.0
16	J.C. Penney	991.9
17	MCI WorldCom	948.4
18	Toyota Motor Corp.	939.2
19	Bristol-Myers Squibb Co.	923.6
20	Sony Corp.	879.6
21	Viacom	825.9
22	Johnson & Johnson	816.5
23	L'Oreal	806.3
24	Federated Department Stores	794.2
25	U.S. government	792.0

Note: Figures are in millions of dollars.
*Corresponding data for Canada is not publicly available.

Exhibit 1–1 Creative advertising has made Absolut a popular brand of imported vodka

Exhibit 1–2 Eveready used the popularity of its pink bunny campaign to generate support from retailers

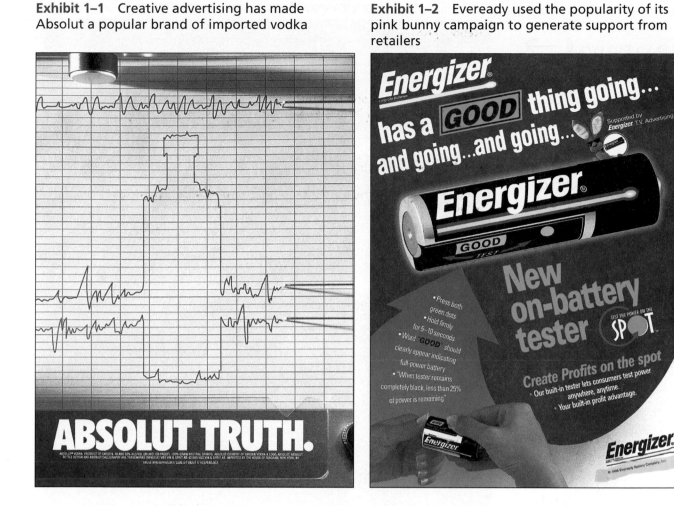

and sweepstakes feature the pink bunny. Pictures of the Energizer Bunny appear on Energizer packages to ensure brand identification and extend the campaign's impact to the point of purchase. Eveready has extended its integrated marketing efforts to include tie-ins with sports marketing and sponsorships.

The nature and purpose of advertising differ across industries (e.g., cars versus soft drinks), situations (e.g., new products versus established products, as in Exhibit 1–3), and target audiences (e.g., new customers versus loyal customers). We will illustrate these and other issues in Chapter 5 when communication objectives are discussed.

Exhibit 1–3 The goals of this milk campaign are to change the image of milk and increase sales of the product

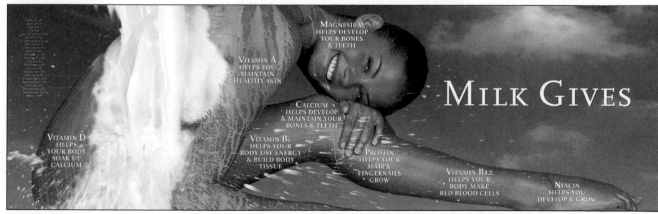

Figure 1–3 Classifications of advertising

[Handwritten notes:]
National →
Goal: image
awareness
front of mind

Retail/local →
↑ store traffic

Primary: ↑ demand product class

Selective: ↑ demand for specific brand.

- <u>Industrial goods</u>
- Office Supplys
- computers

- doctors
- professors

- retailers
- wholesalers

ADVERTISING TO CONSUMER MARKETS

National Advertising
Advertising done by large companies on a nationwide basis or in most regions of the country. Most of the ads for well-known companies and brands that are seen on prime-time TV or in other major national or regional media are examples of national advertising. The goals of national advertisers are to inform or remind consumers of the company or brand and its features, benefits, advantages, or uses and to create or reinforce its image so that consumers will be predisposed to purchase it.

Retail/Local Advertising
Advertising done by retailers or local merchants to encourage consumers to shop at a specific store, use a local service, or patronize a particular establishment. Retail or local advertising tends to emphasize specific patronage motives such as price, hours of operation, service, atmosphere, image, or merchandise assortment. Retailers are concerned with building store traffic, so their promotions often take the form of direct action advertising designed to produce immediate store traffic and sales.

Primary versus Selective Demand Advertising
Primary demand advertising is designed to stimulate demand for the general product class or entire industry. Selective demand advertising focuses on creating demand for a specific company's brands. Most advertising for various products and services is concerned with stimulating selective demand and emphasizes reasons for purchasing a particular brand.
   An advertiser might concentrate on stimulating primary demand when, for example, its brand dominates a market and will benefit the most from overall market growth. Primary demand advertising is often used as part of a promotional strategy to help a new product gain market acceptance, since the challenge is to sell customers on the product concept as much as to sell a particular brand. Industry trade associations also try to stimulate primary demand for their members' products, among them cotton, milk, orange juice, pork, and beef.

ADVERTISING TO BUSINESS AND PROFESSIONAL MARKETS

Business-to-Business Advertising
Advertising targeted at individuals who buy or influence the purchase of industrial goods or services for their companies. Industrial goods are products that either become a physical part of another product (raw material or component parts), are used in manufacturing other goods (machinery), or are used to help a company conduct its business (e.g., office supplies, computers). Business services such as insurance, travel services, and health care are also included in this category.

Professional Advertising
Advertising targeted to professionals such as doctors, lawyers, dentists, engineers, or professors to encourage them to use a company's product in their business operations. It might also be used to encourage professionals to recommend or specify the use of a company's product by end-users.

Trade Advertising
Advertising targeted to marketing channel members such as wholesalers, distributors, and retailers. The goal is to encourage channel members to stock, promote, and resell the manufacturer's branded products to their customers.

Marketers advertise to the consumer market with national and retail/ local advertising, which may stimulate primary or selective demand. For other markets, they use business-to-business, professional, and trade advertising. Figure 1–3 describes the most common types of advertising.

Sales Promotion

Sales promotion is generally defined as those marketing activities that provide extra value or incentives to the sales force, distributors, or the ultimate consumer and can stimulate immediate sales. Sales promotion is generally broken into two major categories: consumer-oriented and trade-oriented activities.

Consumer sales promotion is targeted to the ultimate user of a product or service and includes couponing, sampling, premiums, rebates, contests, sweepstakes, and various point-of-purchase materials (Exhibit 1–4). These promotional tools encourage consumers to make an immediate purchase and thus can stimulate short-term sales. *Trade sales promotion* is targeted toward marketing intermediaries such as wholesalers, distributors, and retailers. Promotional and merchandising allowances, price deals, sales contests, and trade shows are some of the promotional tools used to encourage the trade to stock and promote a company's products.

Sales promotion expenditures in the United States exceeded $240 billion in 1999 and accounted for more promotional dollars than advertising.[8] Among many consumer package-goods companies, sales promotion is often 60 to 70 percent of the promotional budget.[9] In recent years many companies have shifted the emphasis of their promotional strategy from advertising to sales promotion. Reasons for the increased emphasis on sales promotion include declining brand loyalty and increased consumer sensitivity to promotional deals. Another major reason is that retailers have become larger and more powerful and are demanding more trade promotion support from companies.

Promotion and *sales promotion* are two terms that often create confusion in the advertising and marketing fields. As noted, promotion is an element of marketing by which firms communicate with their customers; it is a term that is synonymous with all the marketing communications outlined in Figure 1–1. However, many practitioners use the term sales promotion to mean the incentives directed towards either consumers or the trade (retailers, wholesalers) to stimulate sales. We follow this logic in this book. Promotion is used in the broader sense to refer to the various marketing communications activities of an organization, and sales promotion is used refer to the incentives.

better definition

Public Relations

Another important component of an organization's promotional mix is public relations. When an organization systematically plans and distributes information in an attempt to control and manage its image, it is engaging in a function known as

Exhibit 1–4 Coupons are a popular consumer sales promotion tool

Four Seasons Hotel: A Rare Canadian Global Branding Success Story

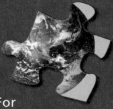

Susan Helstab says foreign contacts often do a double take when she tells them Four Seasons is a Canadian company. They think British-owned perhaps, maybe American. When she reassures them that she isn't joking, they then conclude that the luxury hotel chain's birthplace must be the secret to its success. "They think it is in our inherent nature as Canadians to offer a high level of personal service because we are kind and sensitive," says Helstab, Four Seasons' senior vice president of corporate marketing.

It's hardly surprising that the foreigners question the company's origin, given that Canada isn't noted as a hotbed of companies that are global leaders in luxury service. But make no mistake, Toronto-based Four Seasons Hotels and Resorts has emerged—under the Four Seasons and Regent brands—as the world's largest provider of upscale lodging for the rich and famous. Now its challenge is to maintain this status in a tough post–September 11 travel market, while expanding into more residential-style resorts.

"We're very discreet," explains Helstab, talking about the company's success. "There's an intimacy and residential feeling to our hotels, so someone who is, say, in the film industry and recognizable appreciates that discretion." For evidence of that discretion, look no further than the Four Seasons Hotel Toronto, which each year plays host to celebrities in town for the Toronto International Film Festival. Most recently, Tom Cruise stayed there while promoting his new film, *Vanilla Sky.* U.K. journalist Lynn Middlehurst, publisher of *The Gallivanter's Guide,* a newsletter for high-end travelers, said in a recent editorial that celebrities like it when Four Seasons treats them as ordinary people, and ordinary people like it when Four Seasons treats them as celebrities.

The key to this kind of service is great staff, and surprisingly, Helstab says the chain doesn't mind hiring employees with no prior hotel experience. "We want to hire people who feel serving another human being is their calling," she says. "No isn't part of their vocabulary." The chain's highly personalized service originated with Four Seasons' legendary founder Isadore Sharp. His goal was to create a group of medium-sized hotels with exceptional quality, and he's succeeded.

Source: Adapted from Chris Daniels, "A Room for All Seasons," *Marketing Magazine,* February 4, 2002. Used with permission.

public relations. **Public relations** is defined as "the management function which evaluates public attitudes, identifies the policies and procedures of an individual or organization with the public interest, and executes a program of action to earn public understanding and acceptance."[10] Public relations uses a variety of tools—including special publications, participation in community activities, fund-raising, sponsorship of special events, and various public affairs activities—to enhance an organization's image. Organizations also use advertising as a public relations tool. For example, Exhibit 1–5 shows a corporate ad for DuPont, which shows how the company uses science to make life better.

Publicity refers to nonpersonal communications regarding an organization, product, service, or idea not directly paid for or run under identified sponsorship. The message reaches the public in the form of a news story, editorial, or announcement about an organization and/or its products and services. Like advertising, publicity involves nonpersonal communication to a mass audience, but unlike advertising, publicity is not directly paid for by the company. The company or organization attempts to get the media to cover or run a favourable story on a product, service, cause, or event to affect awareness, knowledge, opinions, and/or behaviour. Tools used to gain publicity include news releases, press conferences, feature articles, photographs, films, and videotapes.

An advantage of publicity over other forms of promotion is its credibility. Consumers generally tend to be less skeptical toward favourable information about a product or service when it comes from a source they perceive as unbiased. For example, the success (or failure) of a new movie is often determined by the reviews it receives from film critics, who are viewed by many moviegoers as objective evaluators. Another advantage of publicity is its low cost, since the company is not paying for time or space in a mass medium such as TV, radio, or newspapers. While an organization may incur some costs in developing publicity items or maintaining a staff to do so, these expenses will be far less than those for the other promotional programs.

Traditionally, public relations and publicity have been considered more supportive than primary to the marketing and promotional process. However, many firms have begun making PR an integral part of their predetermined marketing and promotional strategies. PR firms are increasingly touting public relations as a communications tool that can take over many of the functions of conventional advertising and marketing.[11]

Direct Marketing

One of the fastest-growing sectors of the Canadian economy is **direct marketing,** in which organizations communicate directly with target customers to generate a

Exhibit 1–6 Energy uses direct advertising to promote its product line

response and/or a transaction. Direct marketing includes telemarketing and call centres, direct mail, mail-order catalogues, and direct-response ads in various broadcast and print media. Traditionally, direct marketing has not been considered an element of marketing communications since it had distinct objectives, strategies, and tactics. However, we view direct marketing as an important component of a firm's marketing communications program since it is connected to many other communication tools.

Direct-marketing tools are used by companies that distribute their products to consumers directly and by companies that distribute their products through traditional distribution channels or their own sales force. Companies spend large amounts of money each year developing and maintaining databases containing the addresses and/or phone numbers of present and prospective customers. They use telemarketing to call customers directly and attempt to sell them products and services or qualify them as sales leads. Call centres are used to respond to customer inquiries or concerns. Marketers also send out direct-mail pieces ranging from simple letters and flyers to detailed brochures, catalogues, and videotapes to give potential customers information about their products or services. Direct-marketing techniques are also used to distribute product samples and other promotional items. In addition, marketers use **direct-response advertising**, whereby a product is promoted through an ad (e.g., television or print) that encourages the consumer to purchase directly from the manufacturer (Exhibit 1–6).

Direct marketing has become very popular over the past two decades, owing primarily to changing lifestyles, particularly the increase in two-income households. This has meant more discretionary income but less time for in-store shopping. The availability of credit cards, toll-free phone numbers, and reliable delivery services has facilitated the purchase of products from direct marketing tools. This evolution has made shopping more convenient for consumers and has led to a tremendous growth of direct marketing.

Internet Marketing

We are experiencing perhaps the most dynamic and revolutionary change of any era in the history of marketing. These changes are being driven by advances in technology and developments that have led to dramatic growth of communication through interactive media, particularly the Internet. **Interactive media** allow for a back-and-forth flow of information whereby users can participate in and modify the form and content of the information they receive in real time. Unlike traditional forms of marketing communications such as advertising, which are one-way in nature, these new media allow users to perform a variety of functions such as receive and alter information and images, make inquiries, respond to questions, and, of course, make purchases. In addition to the Internet, interactive media also include CD-ROMs, kiosks, and interactive television. However, the interactive medium that is having the greatest impact on marketing is the Internet, especially through the component known as the World Wide Web.

While the Internet is changing the ways companies design and implement their entire business and marketing strategies, it is also a marketing communications tool in its own right. Thousands of companies, ranging from large multinational corporations to small local firms, have developed websites to promote their products and services, by providing current and potential customers with information, as well as to entertain and interact with consumers. Because of its interactive nature, it is a very effective way of communicating with customers. Many companies recognize the advantages of communicating via the Internet and are developing Web strategies and hiring interactive agencies specifically to develop their websites and make them part of their integrated marketing communications program. However, companies that are using the Internet effectively are integrating their Web strategies with other aspects of their IMC programs. The Internet is a medium that can be used to execute all the elements of the promotional mix. In addition to advertising on the Web, marketers offer sales promotion incentives such as coupons, contests, and sweepstakes online, and they use the Internet to conduct direct marketing, personal selling, and public relations activities more effectively and efficiently. For example, Exhibit 1–7 shows an ad for Land's End promoting the fact that consumers can now shop and purchase interactively through the company's website.

Personal Selling

The final element of an organization's promotional mix is **personal selling,** a form of person-to-person communication in which a seller attempts to assist and/or persuade prospective buyers to purchase the company's product or service or to act on an idea. Personal selling involves direct contact between buyer and seller, either face-to-face or through some form of telecommunications such as a telephone. This interaction gives the marketer communication flexibility; and the seller can see or hear the potential buyer's reactions and tailor the message to the customer's specific needs or situation. In this book, we do not devote any material to personal selling since many college/university programs have separate courses. An important point to keep in mind is that the message from sales people should be consistent with what is communicated from the other promotional tools.

Exhibit 1–7 Land's End uses a website as part of its direct-marketing efforts

Integrated Marketing Communications

For many years, the promotional function in most companies was dominated by mass media advertising. Companies relied primarily on their advertising agencies for guidance in nearly all areas of marketing communication. Most marketers did use additional promotional and marketing communication tools, but sales promotion and direct marketing agencies as well as package design firms were generally viewed as auxiliary services and often used on a per-project basis. Public relations agencies were used to manage the organization's publicity, image, and affairs with relevant publics on an ongoing basis but were not viewed as integral participants in the marketing communications process.

Many marketers built strong barriers around the various marketing and promotional functions and planned and managed them as separate practices, with different budgets, different views of the market, and different goals and objectives. These companies failed to recognize that the wide range of marketing and promotional tools must be coordinated to communicate effectively and present a consistent image to target audiences.

The Evolution of IMC

During the 1980s, many companies came to see the need for more of a strategic integration of their promotional tools. These firms began moving toward the process of **integrated marketing communications (IMC),** which involves coordinating the various promotional elements and other marketing activities that communicate with a firm's customers.[12] As marketers embraced the concept of integrated marketing communications, they began asking their ad agencies to coordinate the use of a variety of promotional tools rather than relying primarily on media advertising. A number of companies also began to look beyond traditional advertising agencies and use other types of promotional specialists to develop and implement various components of their promotional plans.

Many agencies responded to the call for synergy among the various promotional tools by acquiring PR, sales promotion, and direct marketing companies and touting themselves as IMC agencies that offer one-stop shopping for all of their clients' promotional needs.[13] Some agencies became involved in these nonadvertising areas to gain control over their clients' promotional programs and budgets and struggled to offer any real value beyond creating advertising. A task force from the American Association of Advertising Agencies (the "4As") developed one of the first definitions of integrated marketing communications:

> a concept of marketing communications planning that recognizes the added value of a comprehensive plan that evaluates the strategic roles of a variety of communication disciplines—for example, general advertising, direct response, sales promotion, and public relations—and combines these disciplines to provide clarity, consistency, and maximum communications impact.[14]

The 4As' definition focuses on the process of using all forms of promotion to achieve maximum communications impact. However, advocates of the IMC concept, such as Don Schultz of Northwestern University, argue for an even broader perspective that considers *all sources of brand or company contact* that a customer or prospect has with a product or service.[15] Schultz and others note that integrated marketing communications calls for a "big-picture" approach to planning marketing and promotion programs and coordinating the various communication functions. It requires that firms develop a total marketing communications strategy that recognizes how all of a firm's marketing activities, not just promotion, communicate with its customers.

Consumers' perceptions of a company and/or its various brands are a synthesis of the bundle of messages they receive or contacts they have, such as media advertisements, price, package design, direct marketing efforts, publicity, sales promotions, websites, point-of-purchase displays, and even the type of store where a product or service is sold. Integrated marketing communications seeks to have all of a company's marketing and promotional activities project a consistent, unified image to the marketplace. It calls for a centralized messaging function so that everything a company says and does communicates a common theme and positioning.

Many companies have adopted this broader perspective of IMC. They see it as a way to coordinate and manage their marketing communications programs to ensure that they give customers a consistent message about the company and/or its brands. For these companies, the IMC approach represents an improvement over the traditional method of treating the various marketing and communication elements as virtually separate activities. However, as marketers become more sophisticated in their understanding of IMC, they recognize that it offers more than just ideas for coordinating all elements of the marketing and communications programs. The IMC approach helps companies identify the most appropriate and effective methods for communicating and building relationships with their customers as well as other stakeholders such as employees, suppliers, investors, interest groups, and the general public.

Tom Duncan and Sandra Moriarty note that IMC is one of the "new generation" marketing approaches being used by companies to better focus their efforts in acquiring, retaining, and developing relationships with customers and other stakeholders. They have developed a communication-based marketing model that emphasizes the importance of managing *all* corporate or brand communications, as they collectively create, maintain, or weaken the customer and stakeholder relationships that drive brand value.[16] Messages can originate at three levels—corporate, marketing, and marketing communications—since all of a company's corporate activities, marketing mix activities, and marketing communications efforts have communication dimensions and play a role in attracting and keeping customers.

At the corporate level, various aspects of a firm's business practices and philosophies, such as its mission, hiring practices, philanthropies, corporate culture, and ways of responding to inquiries, all have dimensions that communicate with customers and other stakeholders and affect relationships. For example, Nike received a great deal of negative publicity from allegations concerning its use of youth labor and the working conditions in some of its factories in Southeast Asia that weakened its image among many younger consumers.[17] The company has had to engage in major public relations efforts to address these allegations and rebuild its corporate image with these consumers.

At the marketing level, as was mentioned earlier, companies send messages to customers and other stakeholders through all aspects of their marketing mixes, not just promotion. Consumers make inferences about a product on the basis of elements such as its design, appearance, performance, pricing, service support, and where and how it is distributed. For example, a high price may symbolize quality to customers, as may the shape or design of a product, its packaging, its brand name, or the image of the stores in which it is sold. Montblanc uses classical design and a distinctive brand name as well as a high price to position its pens as high-quality, high-status writing instruments. This upscale image is enhanced by the company's strategy of distributing its products only through boutiques, jewellery stores, and other exclusive retail shops.

At the marketing communications level, Duncan and Moriarty note that all messages should be delivered and received on a platform of executional and strategic consistency in order to create coherent perceptions among customers and other stakeholders. This requires the integration of the various marketing communication messages and the functions of various promotional facilitators such as ad agencies, public relations firms, sales promotion specialists, package design firms, direct response specialists, and interactive agencies. The goal is to communicate with one voice, look, and image across all the marketing communications functions and to identify and position the company and/or the brand in a consistent manner.

Many companies are realizing that communicating effectively with customers and other stakeholders involves more than traditional marketing communication tools. Many marketers, as well as advertising agencies, are embracing the IMC approach and adopting total communication solutions to create and sustain relationships between companies or brands and their customers. Some academics and practitioners have questioned whether the IMC movement is just another management fad.[18] However, the IMC approach is proving to be a permanent change that offers significant value to marketers.[19] We will now discuss some of the reasons for the growth of IMC.

Reasons for the Growth of IMC

The move toward integrated marketing communications is one of the most significant marketing developments that occurred during the 1990s, and the shift toward this approach is continuing as we begin the new century. The IMC approach to marketing communications planning and strategy is being adopted by both large and small companies and has become popular among firms marketing consumer products and services as well as business-to-business marketers. One example of the pervasiveness of IMC in Canada is the Canadian Marketing Association (CMA), a professional body for individual and company members. Previously known as the Canadian Direct Marketing Association, it changed its name and mandate because of the growth and convergence of all aspects of marketing communication and the increased importance of managing brands through communications. This may take some time, as a considerable amount of its professional activities still concern direct marketing. The Association of Canadian Advertisers (ACA), a professional body for about 100 member companies, claims it has always maintained a clear IMC perspective without a belief in the dominant role of any particular promotional discipline; however, it has not paid considerable attention to direct marketing. Whatever the future holds for these associations, it is clear that both are on an IMC path.[20] There are a number of reasons why marketers are adopting the IMC approach, notably, planning efficiency and effectiveness, consumer adoption of new technology and media, and innovative marketing practices.

Planning Efficiency and Effectiveness One reason for IMC growth is that marketers understand the value of strategically integrating the various communication functions rather than having them operate autonomously. By coordinating their marketing communications efforts, companies can avoid duplication, take advantage of synergy among various promotional tools, and develop more efficient and effective marketing communications programs. Advocates of IMC argue that it is one of the easiest ways for a company to maximize the return on its investment in marketing and promotion.[21]

Consumer Adoption of Technology and Media The move to integrated marketing communications also reflects an adaptation by marketers to a changing environment, particularly with respect to consumers, technology, and media. Major changes have occurred among consumers with respect to demographics, lifestyles, media use, and buying and shopping patterns. For example, cable TV and digital satellite systems have vastly expanded the number of channels available to households. Some of these channels offer 24-hour shopping networks; others contain 30- or 60-minute direct response appeals known as *infomercials,* which look more like TV shows than ads. Every day more consumers are surfing the Internet's World Wide Web. Online services such as AOL Canada provide information and entertainment as well as the opportunity to shop for and order a vast array of products and services. Marketers are responding by developing websites where they can advertise their products and services interactively as well as transact sales, such as at WestJet's website shown in Exhibit 1–8.

Even as new technologies and formats create new ways for marketers to reach consumers, they are affecting the more traditional media. Television, radio, magazines, and newspapers are becoming more fragmented and reaching smaller and more selective audiences. A recent survey of leading U.S. advertising executives on trends that will shape the industry into the next century identified the segmentation of media audiences by new media technologies as the most important development.[22]

In addition to facing the decline in audience size for many media, marketers are facing the problem of consumers being less responsive to traditional advertising. They recognize that many consumers are turned off by advertising and tired of being bombarded with sales messages. These factors are prompting many marketers to look for alternative ways to communicate with their target audiences, such as making their selling messages part of popular culture. For example, marketers often hire product placement firms to get their brands into TV shows and movies. MGM/United Artists created special scenes in the James Bond movie *The World Is Not Enough* to feature BMW's new Z8 sports car. BMW used the movie tie-in to develop a full-scale promotional campaign to launch the new car.[23]

Exhibit 1–8   Travelers can use WestJet's website to purchase tickets and reserve seats

Innovative Marketing Practices   The integrated marketing communications movement is also being driven by changes in the ways companies market their products and services.[24]

- *A shifting of marketing dollars from media advertising to other forms of promotion, particularly consumer and trade-oriented sales promotions.* Many marketers feel that traditional media advertising has become too expensive and is not cost-effective. Also, escalating price competition in many markets has resulted in marketers pouring more of their promotional budgets into price promotions rather than media advertising.

- *A movement away from relying on advertising-focused approaches, which emphasize mass media such as network television and national magazines, to solve communication problems.* Many companies are turning to lower-cost, more targeted communication tools such as event marketing and sponsorships, direct mail, sales promotion, and the Internet as they develop their marketing communication strategies.

- *A shift in marketplace power from manufacturers to retailers.* Due to consolidation in the retail industry, small local retailers are being replaced by regional, national, and international chains. These large retailers are using their clout to demand larger promotional fees and allowances from manufacturers, a practice that often siphons money away from advertising. Moreover, new technologies such as checkout scanners give retailers information on the effectiveness of manufacturers' promotional programs. This is leading many marketers to shift their focus to promotional tools that can produce short-term results, such as sale promotion.

- *The rapid growth and development of database marketing.* Many companies are building databases containing customer names; geographic, demographic, and psychographic profiles; purchase patterns; media preferences; credit ratings; and other characteristics. Marketers are using this information to target consumers through a variety of direct-marketing methods such as telemarketing, direct mail, and direct-response advertising, rather than relying on mass media. Advocates of the approach argue that database marketing is critical to the development and practice of effective IMC.[25]

- *Demands for greater accountability from advertising agencies and changes in the way agencies are compensated.* Many companies are moving toward incentive-based systems whereby compensation of their ad agencies is based, at least in part, on objective measures such as sales, market share, and profitability. Demands for accountability are motivating many agencies to consider a variety of communication tools and less expensive alternatives to mass-media advertising.

- *The rapid growth of the Internet, which is changing the very nature of how companies do business and the ways they communicate and interact with consumers.* The Internet revolution is well under way, and the Internet audience is growing rapidly. The Internet is an *interactive* medium that is becoming an integral part of communications strategy, and even business strategy, for many companies.

Importance of IMC

As noted, companies are changing the ways they market and promote their products and services. They can no longer be tied to a specific communication tool (such as media advertising); rather, they should use whatever contact methods offer the best way of delivering the message to their target audiences. A successful IMC program requires that a firm find the right combination of promotional tools and techniques, define their role and the extent to which they can or should be used, and coordinate their use. While this prescription sounds good, there are two compelling reasons why IMC has become very important for most firms.

Consumer's Point of View As a marketer, it is important to keep concepts distinct so that you can communicate with other people within your organization or other organizations when making decisions. For example, if you are planning a sales promotion, it is useful to refer to it as a sales promotion so that everyone involved can discuss its merits appropriately and allocate the sales promotion expenditure within the correct budget. Do we have the right sales promotion (i.e., coupon versus bonus pack)? Is the incentive strong enough to encourage the target audience to switch to our brand? Consumers, on the other hand, receive many exposures from many different brands, each using many different promotional tools. In fact, consumers receive so many exposures that they have the habit of often referring to any promotional tool as "advertising." Given this situation, the need for planning with an IMC perspective becomes imperative. All the elements of the promotional campaign have to be carefully linked in some manner so that the message is clear and does not misrepresent the brand.

The success of TD Canada Trust's rebranding illustrates the importance of having a well-planned and executed marketing communications strategy. However, it also provides an excellent example of how the roles of advertising and other forms of promotion are changing in the modern world of marketing. Today, many companies integrate their advertising efforts with a variety of other communication techniques such as websites on the Internet, direct marketing, sales promotion, publicity, and public relations (PR) and event sponsorships. They are also recognizing that these communication tools are most effective when they are coordinated with other elements of the marketing program.

The various marketing communication tools used by TD Canada Trust show how marketers are using an *integrated marketing communications* approach to reach their customers. TD Canada Trust runs advertising in a variety of media including television, radio, magazines, newspa-

Exhibit 1–9 Many non-profit organizations use advertising to meet their marketing objectives

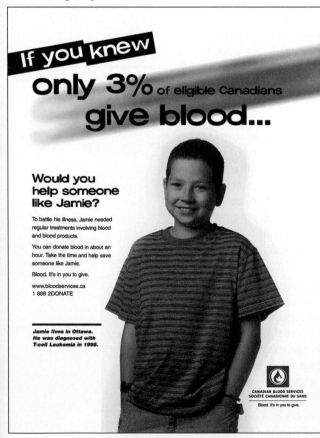

Exhibit 1–10 Dell Computer recognizes the importance of developing relationships with customers

pers, and billboards as well as on the Internet. Banner ads on the Internet and in other media encourage consumers to visit the TD Canada Trust website (www.tdcanadatrust.com), which provides updated information about the company's products and services. Publicity for TD Canada Trust is generated through press releases and PR activities. TD Canada Trust runs a number of sales promotions to generate extra sales. Recently it has offered cash prizes and cruises as prizes for engaging in various transactions.

Relationship Marketing   Today, most marketers are seeking more than just a one-time exchange or transaction with customers. The focus of market-driven companies—and many non-profit organizations (Exhibit 1–9)—is on developing and sustaining *relationships* with their customers. This has led to a new emphasis on **relationship marketing,** which involves creating, maintaining, and enhancing long-term relationships with individual customers as well as other stakeholders for mutual benefit.[26]

This relationship focus is generally more profitable since it is often more cost-effective to retain customers than to acquire new ones. Furthermore, these retained customers tend to buy more products or expand their purchases to other products that an organization offers. Marketers are giving more attention to the *lifetime value* of a customer because studies have shown that reducing customer defections by just 5 percent can increase future profit by as much as 30 to 90 percent.[27] Exhibit 1–10 shows an ad for Dell Computer, a company that recognizes the importance of developing long-term relationships with its customers. Relationship marketing makes IMC planning imperative as well. Marketers must recognize which tools within the promotional mix are enhancing the relationship. And since their customers are involved so closely with the firm, the need for consistency becomes even more critical.

In developing a promotional strategy, a company combines the promotional mix elements, balancing the strengths and weaknesses of each, to produce an effective promotional campaign. **Promotional management** involves coordinating the promotional mix elements to develop a controlled, integrated program of effective marketing communications. The marketer must consider which promotional tools to use and how to combine them to achieve its marketing and promotional objectives. Companies also face the task of distributing the total promotional budget across the

Planning for Integrated Marketing Communications

promotional mix elements. What percentage of the budget should they allocate to advertising, sales promotion, direct marketing, and personal selling?

Companies consider many factors in developing their promotional mixes, including the type of product, the target market, the buyer's decision process, the stage of the product life cycle, and the channels of distribution. Companies selling consumer products and services generally rely on advertising through mass media to communicate with ultimate consumers. Business-to-business marketers, who generally sell expensive, risky, and often complex products and services, more often use personal selling. Business-to-business marketers such as Honeywell do use advertising to perform important functions such as building awareness of the company and its products, generating leads for the sales force, and reassuring customers about the purchase they have made.

Advertising and personal selling efforts vary depending on the type of market being sought, and even firms in the same industry may differ in the allocation of their promotional efforts. For example, in the cosmetics industry, Avon and Mary Kay Cosmetics concentrate on direct selling, whereas Revlon and Max Factor rely heavily on consumer advertising. Firms also differ in the relative emphasis they place on advertising and sales promotion. Companies selling high-quality brands use advertising to convince consumers of their superiority, justify their higher prices, and maintain their image. Brands of lower quality, or those that are hard to differentiate, often compete more on a price or "value for the money" basis and may rely more on sales promotion to the trade and/or to consumers.

The marketing communications program of an organization is generally developed with a specific purpose in mind and is the end product of a detailed marketing and promotional planning process. As with any business function, planning plays a fundamental role in the development and implementation of an effective promotional program. The individuals involved in promotion design a **promotional plan** that provides the framework for developing, implementing, and controlling the organization's integrated marketing communications programs and activities. Promotional planners must decide on the role and function of the specific elements of the promotional mix, develop strategies for each element, and implement the plan. Promotion is but one part of, and must be integrated into, the overall marketing plan and program.

A model of the IMC planning process is shown in Figure 1–4. The remainder of this chapter presents a brief overview of the various steps involved in this process.

Review the Marketing Plan

The first step in the IMC planning process is to review the marketing plan and objectives. Before developing a promotional plan, marketers must understand where the company (or the brand) has been, its current position in the market, where it intends to go, and how it plans to get there. Most of this information should be contained in the **marketing plan,** a written document that describes the overall marketing strategy and programs developed for an organization, a particular product line, or a brand. Marketing plans can take several forms but generally include five basic elements:

1. A detailed situation analysis that consists of an internal marketing audit and review and an external analysis of the market competition and environmental factors.

2. Specific marketing objectives that provide direction, a time frame for marketing activities, and a mechanism for measuring performance.

3. A marketing strategy and program that include selection of target market(s) and decisions and plans for the four elements of the marketing mix.

4. A program for implementing the marketing strategy, including determining specific tasks to be performed and responsibilities.

Figure 1–4 An integrated marketing communications planning model

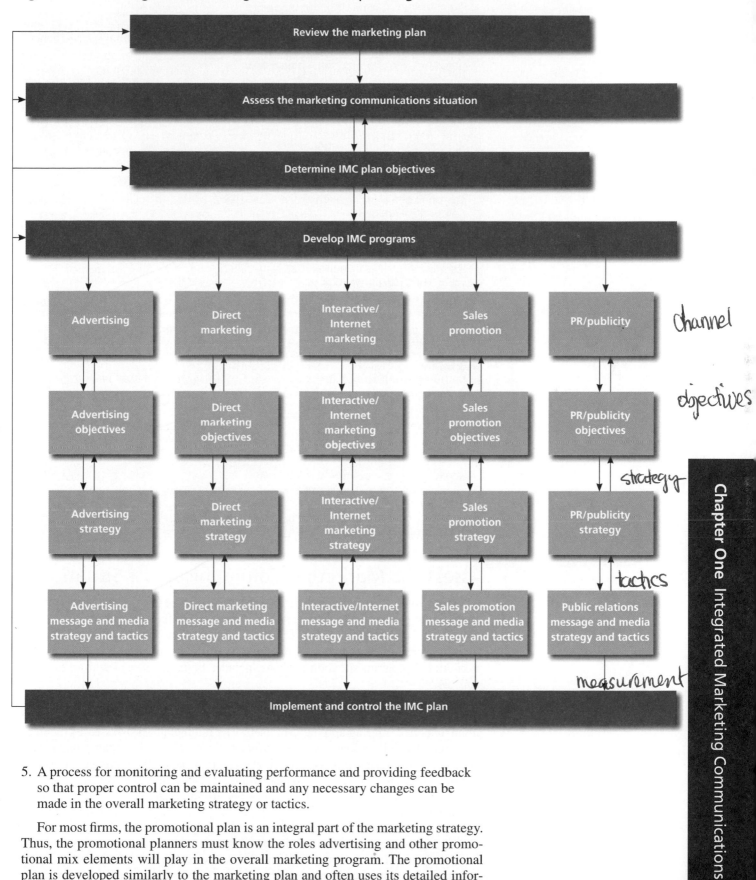

5. A process for monitoring and evaluating performance and providing feedback so that proper control can be maintained and any necessary changes can be made in the overall marketing strategy or tactics.

For most firms, the promotional plan is an integral part of the marketing strategy. Thus, the promotional planners must know the roles advertising and other promotional mix elements will play in the overall marketing program. The promotional plan is developed similarly to the marketing plan and often uses its detailed information. Promotional planners focus on information in the marketing plan that is relevant to the promotional strategy.

Figure 1–4   Concluded

Review the Marketing Plan
Focus on market, company, consumer, competitive, and environmental information
Examine marketing objectives, strategy, and programs
Understand role of promotion within marketing plan

Assess the Marketing Communications Situation
Internal analysis
   Relative strengths and weaknesses of products/services
   Previous promotional programs
   Brand image
   Promotional organization and capabilities
External analysis
   Customer behaviour analysis
   Competitive analysis
   Environmental analysis

Determine IMC Plan Objectives
Establish IMC communication objectives
Establish IMC behaviour objectives

Develop IMC Programs
For advertising, sales promotion, public relations, direct marketing, and Internet marketing:
   Set specific communication and behaviour objectives for each IMC tool
   Determine budget requirements
   Develop relevant message strategy and tactics
   Select suitable media strategy and tactics
Investigate integration options across all five programs

Implement and Control the IMC Plan
Design all promotional materials internally or with agencies and buy media space/time
Measure promotional program results/effectiveness and make adjustments

Assess the Marketing Communications Situation

After the overall marketing plan is reviewed, the next step in developing a promotional plan is to conduct the situation analysis. In the IMC program, the situation analysis focuses on those factors that influence or are relevant to development of a promotional strategy. Like the overall marketing situation analysis, the promotional program situation analysis includes both an internal and an external analysis.

Internal Analysis   The **internal analysis** assesses relevant areas involving the product/service offering and the firm itself. The internal analysis assesses the relative strengths and weaknesses of the product or service; its advantages and disadvantages; any unique selling points or benefits it may have; its packaging, price, and design; and so on. This information is particularly important to the creative personnel who must develop the advertising message for the brand.

Since the firm is planning a new promotional plan, it is imperative that a review of the firm's previous promotional programs is undertaken. Specifically, the objectives, budgets, strategies, and tactics of all promotional mix elements should be closely examined to understand the strengths and weaknesses. Furthermore, if the firm has utilized marketing research to track the results of previous programs, this information needs to be monitored.

Another aspect of the internal analysis is assessing the strengths and weaknesses of the firm or the brand from an image perspective. Often the image the firm brings to the market will have a significant impact on the way it can advertise and promote itself as well as its various products and services. Companies or brands that are new to the market or those for whom perceptions are negative may have to concentrate on their images, not just the benefits or attributes of the specific product or service. On the other hand, a firm with a strong reputation and/or image is already a step ahead when it comes to marketing its products or services.

Reviewing the capabilities of the firm and its ability to develop and implement a successful promotional program, and the organization of the promotional department, the analysis may indicate the firm is not capable of planning, implementing, and managing certain areas of the promotional program. If this is the case, it would be wise to look for assistance from an advertising agency or some other promotional facilitator. If the organization is already using an ad agency, the focus will be on the quality of the agency's work and the results achieved by past and/or current campaigns.

Figure 1–5 is a checklist of some of the areas one might consider when performing analyses for promotional planning purposes. Addressing internal areas may require information the company does not have available internally and must gather as part of the external analysis.

External Analysis   The **external analysis** focuses on factors such as characteristics of the firm's customers, market segments, environment, and competitors, as shown in Figure 1–5. An important part of the external analysis is a detailed consideration of customers' characteristics and buying patterns, their decision processes, and factors influencing their purchase decisions. Attention must also be

Figure 1–5   Areas covered in the situation analysis

Internal Factors	External Factors
Assessment of firm's promotional organization and capabilities	**Customer behaviour analysis**
Organization of promotional department	Who buys our product or service?
Capability of firm to develop and execute promotional programs	Who makes the decision to buy the product?
Determination of role and function of ad agency and other promotional facilitators	Who influences the decision to buy the product?
Assessment of firm's previous promotional programs	How is the purchase decision made? Who assumes what role?
Promotional objectives	What does the customer buy? What needs must be satisfied?
Promotional budgets and allocations	Why do customers buy a particular brand?
Promotional mix strategies and programs	Where do they go or look to buy the product or service?
Results of promotional programs	When do they buy? Any seasonality factors?
Assessment of firm or brand image	What are customers' attitudes toward our product/service?
Assessment of relative strengths and weaknesses of product/service	What social factors might influence the purchase decision?
What are its key attributes and benefits?	Do the customers' lifestyles influence their purchase decisions?
Does it have any unique selling points?	Do demographic factors influence the purchase decision?
Are the package and label consistent with the brand image?	**Competitive analysis**
	Who are our direct and indirect competitors?
	What key benefits and positioning are used by our competitors?
	What is our position relative to the competition?
	How big are competitors' promotion budgets?
	What promotion strategies are competitors using?
	Environmental analysis
	Are there any current trends or developments that might affect the promotional program?

given to consumers' perceptions and attitudes, lifestyles, and criteria for making purchase decisions. Often, marketing research studies are needed to answer some of these questions. A key element of the external analysis is an assessment of the market. The attractiveness of various market segments must be evaluated and the segments to target identified.

The external phase of the promotional program situation analysis also includes an in-depth examination of both direct and indirect competitors. While competitors were analyzed in the overall marketing situation analysis, even more attention is devoted to promotional aspects at this phase. Focus is on the firm's primary competitors: their specific strengths and weaknesses; their segmentation, targeting, and positioning strategies; and the promotional strategies they employ. The size and allocation of their promotional budgets, their media strategies, and the messages they are sending to the marketplace should all be considered.

Determine IMC Plan Objectives

An important part of this stage of the promotional planning process is establishing communication goals and objectives. In this text, we stress the importance of distinguishing between communication and marketing objectives. **Marketing objectives** refer to what is to be accomplished by the overall marketing program. They are often stated in terms of sales, market share, or profitability.

Communication objectives refer to what the firm seeks to accomplish with its promotional program. They are often stated in terms of the nature of the message to be communicated or what specific communication effects are to be achieved. The promotional planner must think about the process consumers will go through in responding to marketing communications. Communication objectives may include creating awareness or knowledge about a product and its attributes or benefits; creating an image; or developing favourable attitudes, preferences, or purchase intentions. Communication objectives should be the guiding force for the overall marketing communications strategy and the objectives for each promotional mix area. Behaviour objectives in terms of trial purchase or repeat purchase may be defined along with the communication objectives.

As these objectives are determined, some attention is given to the promotional budget. Two basic questions are asked at this point: What will the promotional program cost? How will these monies be allocated? Ideally, the amount a firm needs to spend on promotion should be determined by what must be done to accomplish its communication objectives. In reality, promotional budgets are often determined using a more simplistic approach, such as how much money is available or a percentage of a company's or brand's sales revenue. At this stage, the budget is often tentative. It may not be finalized until specific promotional mix strategies are developed.

Develop IMC Programs

Developing the IMC program is generally the most involved and detailed step of the promotional planning process. As discussed earlier, each promotional mix element has certain advantages and limitations. At this stage of the planning process, decisions have to be made regarding the role and importance of each element and their coordination with one another. As Figure 1–4 shows, each promotional mix element has its own set of objectives and a budget and strategy for meeting them. Decisions must be made and activities performed to implement the promotional programs. Procedures must be developed for evaluating performance and making any necessary changes.

For example, the advertising program will have its own set of objectives, usually involving the communication of some message or appeal to a target audience. A budget will be determined, providing the advertising manager and the agency with some idea of how much money is available for developing the ad campaign and purchasing media to disseminate the ad message.

Two important aspects of the advertising program are development of the message and the media strategy. Message development, often referred to as *creative strategy,* involves determining the basic appeal and message the advertiser wishes to convey to the target audience. This process, along with the ads that result, is to many students the most fascinating aspect of promotion. *Media strategy* involves determining which communication channels will be used to deliver the advertising message to the target audience. Decisions must be made regarding which types of media will be used (e.g., newspapers, magazines, radio, TV, billboards) as well as specific media selections (e.g., a particular magazine or TV program). This task requires careful evaluation of the media options' advantages and limitations, costs, and ability to deliver the message effectively to the target market.

Once the message and media strategies have been determined, steps must be taken to implement them. Most large companies hire advertising agencies to plan and produce their messages and to evaluate and purchase the media that will carry their ads. However, most agencies work very closely with their clients as they develop the ads and select media, because it is the advertiser that ultimately approves (and pays for) the creative work and media plan.

A similar process takes place for the other elements of the IMC program as objectives are set, an overall strategy is developed, message and media strategies are determined, and steps are taken to implement them. While the marketer's advertising agencies may be used to perform some of the other IMC functions, they may also hire other communication specialists such as direct marketing and interactive and/or sales promotion agencies, as well as public relations firms.

Implement and Control the IMC Plan

It is important to determine how well the promotional program is meeting communications objectives and helping the firm accomplish its overall marketing goals and objectives. The promotional planner wants to know not only how well the promotional program is doing but also why. For example, problems with the advertising program may lie in the nature of the message or in a media plan that does not reach the target market effectively. The manager must know the reasons for the results in order to take the right steps to correct the program.

This final stage of the process is designed to provide managers with continual feedback concerning the effectiveness of the promotional program, which in turn can be used as input into the planning process. As Figure 1–4 shows, information on the results achieved by the promotional program is used in subsequent promotional planning and strategy development.

Perspective and Organization of This Text

Traditional approaches to teaching advertising, promotional strategy, or marketing communications courses have often treated the various elements of the promotional mix as separate functions. As a result, many people who work in advertising, sales promotion, direct marketing, or public relations tend to approach marketing communications problems from the perspective of their particular specialty. An advertising person may believe marketing communications objectives are best met through the use of media advertising; a promotional specialist argues for a sales promotion program to motivate consumer response; a public relations person advocates a PR campaign to tackle the problem. These orientations are not surprising, since each person has been trained to view marketing communications problems primarily from one perspective.

In the contemporary business world, however, individuals working in marketing, advertising, and other promotional areas are expected to understand and use a variety of marketing communications tools, not just the one in which they specialize. Ad agencies no longer confine their services to the advertising area. Many are involved in sales promotion, public relations, direct marketing, event sponsorship, and other marketing communications areas. Individuals working on the client or advertiser side of the business, such as brand, product, or promotional managers, are developing marketing programs that use a variety of marketing communications methods.

The purpose of this book is to provide you with a thorough understanding of the field of advertising and other elements of a firm's promotional mix and show how they are combined to form an integrated marketing communications program. The book is organized around six major parts to facilitate this goal.

Part I, "Understanding Integrated Marketing Communications," includes this chapter and Chapter 2. Its purpose is to familiarize you with the basic tools of IMC and how they relate to marketing. This chapter has given a brief description of IMC. Chapter 2 specifically explores the role of IMC tools in marketing and examines the process of market segmentation and positioning and considers their role in developing an IMC program.

To plan, develop, and implement an effective IMC program, those involved must understand consumer behaviour and the communications process. We focus on consumer behaviour theories and summarize various communication models in Chapters 3 and 4 respectively. Combined, these two chapters constitute Part II, "Connecting Consumers to IMC." Its purpose is to give you a conceptual foundation for developing the subsequent set of decisions of an IMC plan.

The heart of marketing communication lies in what we are trying to say. Part III, "Articulate the Message," concerns a number of decisions firms make to put together a persuasive message. Chapter 5 builds on the communication models of the previous chapter and explains how to set communication objectives to achieve the desired communication effects. Perhaps the most exciting aspects of IMC are discussed in Chapters 6 and 7 where we illustrate creative strategy and creative tactics decisions that result in vibrant and exciting ads.

Part IV, "Deliver the Message," explores the key media strategy and media tactics decisions in Chapter 8 and the six traditional media choices (i.e., television, radio, magazines, newspapers, out-of-home, and support) within Chapters 9, 10, and 11. Collectively, Parts III and IV provide a foundation for the advertising tool within the IMC program.

Our interest turns to the other areas of the promotional mix—sales promotion, public relations, direct marketing, and Internet marketing—in Part V, "Strengthen the Message." Each tool is explored in its own chapter and related to communication objectives as done in the advertising chapters.

The book concludes with Part VI, "Implement, Control, and Monitor the IMC Plan." We discuss how firms organize for IMC and make decisions regarding ad agencies and other firms that provide marketing and promotional services. Particular attention is given to measuring the effectiveness of advertising and other forms of promotion. Finally, the text concludes with an examination of regulatory, social, and economic factors that influence, and in turn are influenced by, an organization's advertising and promotional program.

Summary

Advertising and other forms of promotion are an integral part of the marketing process in most organizations. The elements of the marketing mix are the product or service, price, place (distribution), and promotion.

Promotion is the communication function of marketing. It is accomplished through a promotional mix that includes advertising, personal selling, public relations, sales promotion, direct marketing, and interactive/Internet marketing. The inherent advantages and disadvantages of each of these promotional mix elements influence the roles they play in the overall marketing program. In developing the promotional program, a marketer must decide which tools to use and how to combine them to achieve the organization's marketing and communication objectives.

For many years, the promotional function in most companies was dominated by mass-media advertising. However, more and more companies are recognizing the importance of integrated marketing communications, coordinating the various marketing and promotional elements to achieve more efficient and effective communication programs. A number of factors underlie the move toward IMC by marketers as well as ad agencies and other promotional facilitators. Reasons for the growing importance of the integrated marketing communications perspective include a rapidly changing environment with respect to consumers, technology, and media. The IMC movement is also being driven by changes in the ways companies market their products and services. A shift in marketing dollars from advertising to sales promotion, the rapid growth and development of database marketing, and the fragmentation of media markets are among the key changes taking place.

Promotional management involves coordinating the promotional mix elements to develop an integrated program of effective marketing communication. The model of the IMC planning process in Figure 1–4 contains a number of steps: review the marketing plan, assess the marketing communications situation, determine IMC plan objectives, develop IMC programs, and implement and control the IMC plan.

Key Terms

marketing, 4
marketing mix, 4
promotion, 4
promotional mix, 5
advertising, 5
sales promotion, 9
public relations, 11

publicity, 11
direct marketing, 11
direct-response
     advertising, 12
interactive media, 12
personal selling, 13

integrated marketing
     communications
     (IMC), 14
relationship
     marketing, 19
promotional
     management, 19

promotional plan, 20
marketing plan, 20
internal analysis, 22
external analysis, 23
marketing objectives, 24
communication
     objectives, 24

Discussion Questions

1. Consider all the marketing communication tools (i.e., advertising, sales promotions, public relations, direct marketing, Internet marketing, and personal selling) that are used to market a new car that a graduating student might be expected to buy. Explain why each tool would be effective or would not be effective to create awareness.

2. What is the most important communication tool for each of the following brands: Molson Canadian, Bell Mobility, Nortel Networks, Government of Canada? Give a good reason for each.

3. From your perspective as a consumer, what Canadian brand

(other than those discussed in the chapter) has had the most successful IMC plan during the past year or so?

4. Many sales promotions often look like ads these days. Why might this be occurring?

5. The various classifications of advertising to consumer and business-to-business markets are shown in Figure 1–3. Choose one category of advertising to consumer markets and one to the business-to-business market, and find an ad that is an example of each. Discuss the specific goals and objectives each company might have for the ads you have chosen.

6. Discuss the role of direct marketing as an IMC tool, giving attention to the various forms of direct marketing.

7. Analyze the role of the Internet in the integrated marketing communications program of a company. Discuss how the Internet can be used to execute the various elements of the promotional mix.

8. Why is it important for those who work in the field of advertising and promotion to understand and appreciate all various integrated marketing communications tools, not just the area in which they specialize?

Chapter Two
IMC Role in Marketing

Chapter Objectives

- To understand the marketing process and the role of advertising and promotion in an organization's integrated marketing program.

- To know how the various decisions of the marketing mix influence and interact with advertising and promotional strategy.

- To understand the target market process in an integrated marketing communications program.

- To recognize the role of market segmentation and its use in an integrated marketing communications program.

- To understand the concepts of market positioning and brand positioning.

Gaming Systems Jockey for a Market Position

Microsoft's foray into the competitive game-system market raises an exciting challenge of how to position Xbox through its marketing communications. Faced against the formidable Sony (i.e., Playstation 2) that commands 61 percent of the $700 million Canadian hardware market, Xbox would like to "change gaming forever."

To meet the challenge, Microsoft engaged a contingent of 14 Canadian marketing partners to develop a comprehensive and innovative IMC program. Rather than hiring one agency to run the global campaign, executives at Microsoft believed that they should work with the best agency for all the major advertising and promotional disciplines, from television creative to sales marketing.

The worldwide premiere of Xbox creative elements occurred at a special launch party in Toronto in September 2001. The three television commercials featured a "prophet-like" character who proclaimed that Xbox will change gaming forever. This central positioning message appears to have targeted Playstation 2 users and more importantly may resonate with the millions of consumers who have never purchased a gaming system previously or those with older existing technology. In either case, the $750 million North American budget makes the Xbox a significant attempt to rival Sony.

In addition to the TV ads, the Xbox launch included a CD retail promotion where users could download music from the Internet and alter the music originally associated with the games. The creative for the CD featured a man with many wires attached to his body. A tour bus with 15 game consoles trekked across Canada to allow for user demonstrations, and event marketing with game reps was also used to attract university students. In fact, special firms were hired to develop the interior and exterior of the bus! It sure looks like Microsoft wanted consumers to see Microsoft, Xbox, and game systems with a much different perspective. And if all these activities were not enough, Xbox delivered extensive media relations material in the hopes of generating publicity through the various news outlets.

Sources: "Prophet Heralds Xbox Campaign," *Marketing Magazine*, September 17, 2001; Chris Daniels, "Xbox's Inner Workings," *Marketing Magazine*, November 19, 2001; Chris Daniels, "The Xbox Players," *Marketing Magazine*, November 19, 2001.

The above example demonstrates a number of important marketing strategies that will be discussed in this chapter. These include market analysis, tarket market process, and marketing program development. In this chapter, we take a closer look at how marketing strategies influence the role of promotion and how promotional decisions must be coordinated with other areas of the marketing mix. In turn, all elements of the marketing mix must be consistent in a strategic plan that results in an integrated marketing communications program. We use the model in Figure 2–1 as a framework for analyzing how promotion fits into an organization's marketing strategy and programs.

This model consists of four major components: the organization's market analysis, the target market process, the marketing program development (which includes the promotional mix), and the target market. As the model shows, the marketing process begins with the development of a marketing strategy and analysis in which the company decides the product or service areas and particular markets where it wants to compete. The company must then coordinate the various elements of the marketing mix into a cohesive marketing program that will reach the target market effectively. Note that a firm's promotion program is directed not only to the final buyer but also to the channel or "trade" members that distribute its products to the ultimate consumer. These channel members must be convinced there is a demand for the company's products so they will carry them and will aggressively merchandise and promote them to consumers. Promotions play an important role in the marketing program for building and maintaining demand not only among final consumers but among the trade as well.

As noted in Chapter 1, all elements of the marketing mix—price, product, distribution, and promotions—must be integrated to provide consistency and maximum communications impact. Development of a marketing plan is instrumental in achieving this goal.

As Figure 2–1 shows, development of a marketing program requires an in-depth analysis of the market. This analysis may make extensive use of marketing research as an input into the planning process. This input, in turn, provides the basis for the development of marketing strategies in regard to product, pricing, distribution, and promotion decisions. Each of these steps requires a detailed analysis, since this plan serves as the road map to follow in achieving marketing goals. Once the detailed market analysis has been completed and marketing objectives have been estab-

Figure 2–1 Marketing and promotions process model

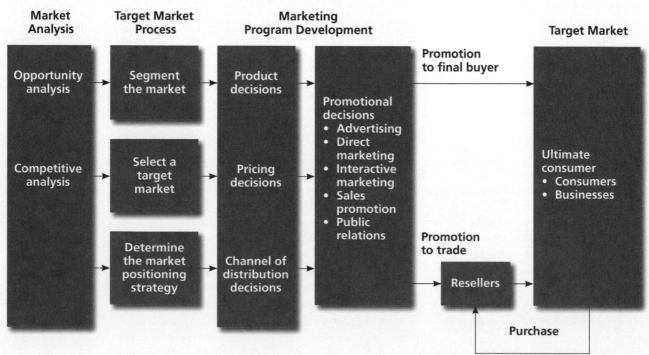

lished, each element in the marketing mix must contribute to a comprehensive integrated marketing program. Of course, the promotional program element (the focus of this text) must be combined with all other program elements in such a way as to achieve maximum impact.

Any organization that wants to exchange its products or services in the marketplace successfully should have a **strategic marketing plan** to guide the allocation of its resources. A strategic marketing plan usually evolves from an organization's overall corporate strategy and serves as a guide for specific marketing programs and policies. As we noted earlier, marketing strategy is based on a situation analysis—a detailed assessment of the current marketing conditions facing the company, its product lines, or its individual brands. From this situation analysis, a firm develops an understanding of the market and the various opportunities it offers, and the competition.

Market Analysis

Market Opportunity Analysis

A careful analysis of the marketplace should lead to alternative market opportunities for existing product lines in current or new markets, new products for current markets, or new products for new markets. **Market opportunities** are areas where there are favourable demand trends, where the company believes customer needs and opportunities are not being satisfied, and where it can compete effectively.

A company usually identifies market opportunities by carefully examining the marketplace and noting demand trends and competition in various market segments. A market can rarely be viewed as one large homogeneous group of customers; rather, it consists of many heterogeneous groups, or segments. In recent years, many companies have recognized the importance of tailoring their marketing to meet the needs and demand trends of different market segments.[1]

For example, different market segments in the personal computer (PC) industry include the home, education, science, and business markets. These segments can be even further divided. The business market consists of both small companies and large corporations; the education market can range from elementary schools to colleges and universities. A company that is marketing its products in the PC industry must decide in which particular market segment or segments it wishes to compete. This decision depends on the amount and nature of competition the brand will face in a particular market. For example, Apple Computer is firmly entrenched in the education market. Now it is also targeting the business segment, where IBM and Dell are strong competitors. IBM, in turn, has gained market share in the education segment. A competitive analysis is an important part of marketing strategy development and warrants further consideration.

Competitive Analysis

In developing the firm's marketing strategies and plans for its products and services, the manager must carefully analyze the competition to be faced in the marketplace. This may range from direct brand competition (which can also include its own brands) to more indirect forms of competition, such as product substitutes. For example, when Lay's introduced Baked Lay's low-fat chips, the product ended up taking away sales from the regular Lay's potato chip brand. At the same time, new consumers were gained from competing brands of potato chips.

In addition to having direct potato chip competitors, Lay's faces competition from other types of snack foods, such as pretzels and crackers. One might argue that other low-fat products also offer the consumer a choice and compete with Lay's as well (for example, fruits).

At a more general level, marketers must recognize they are competing for the consumer's discretionary income, so they must understand the various ways potential customers choose to spend their money. For example, sales of motorcycles in the United States had declined significantly in the late 1980s and early 1990s. This decline reflected shifting demographic patterns; aging baby boomers are less inclined to ride motorcycles, and the number of 18- to 34-year-old males has been declining. The drop in sales could also be attributed to the number of other options consumers could spend their discretionary income on, including Jet Skis, dirt bikes, home fitness equipment, spas, and home entertainment systems such as large-screen TVs and stereos. Thus, motorcycle marketers like Honda and Harley-Davidson had to convince potential buyers that a motorcycle was worth a sizable portion of their disposable income in comparison to other purchase options. Through successful marketing strategies, the industry was effective in reversing the downturn, increasing sales by over 25 percent by the late 1990s.[2]

A LOT OF TIRES COST LESS THAN A MICHELIN. THAT'S BECAUSE THEY SHOULD.

Exhibit 2–1 Michelin's campaign stresses safety and performance

An important aspect of marketing strategy development is the search for a **competitive advantage,** something special a firm does or has that gives it an edge over competitors. Ways to achieve a competitive advantage include having quality products that command a premium price, providing superior customer service, having the lowest production costs and lower prices, or dominating channels of distribution. Competitive advantage can also be achieved through advertising that creates and maintains product differentiation and brand equity, as shown by the long-running advertising campaign for Michelin tires, which stresses security as well as performance (Exhibit 2–1). For example, the strong brand images of Colgate toothpaste, Campbell's soup, Nike shoes, Kodak, and McDonald's give them a competitive advantage in their respective markets.

Recently, there has been concern that some marketers have not been spending enough money on advertising to allow leading brands to sustain their competitive edge.[3] Advertising proponents have been calling for companies to protect their brand equity and franchises by investing more money in advertising instead of costly trade promotions. Some companies, recognizing the important competitive advantage strong brands provide, have been increasing their advertising investment in them.

Companies must be concerned with the ever-changing competitive environment. Competitors' marketing programs have a major impact on the firm's marketing strategy, so they must be analyzed and monitored. The reactions of competitors to a company's marketing and promotional strategy are also very important. Competitors may cut price, increase promotional spending, develop new brands, or attack one another through comparative advertising. One of the more intense competitive rivalries is the battle between Coca-Cola and Pepsi. The latest round of the "cola wars" has gone international, as discussed in Global Perspective 2–1.

The Target Market Process

After evaluating the opportunities presented by various market segments, including a detailed competitive analysis, the company may select one, or more, as a target market. This target market becomes the focus of the firm's marketing effort, and specific sales, market share, and profitability objectives are set according to where the company wants to be and what it hopes to accomplish in this market. The method by which marketers do this (presented in Figure 2–2) is referred to as the **target market process** and

Figure 2–2 The target market process

| Segment the market | → | Select a target market | → | Determine the market positioning strategy |

Turning the World Coca-Cola Red

For more than two decades, The Coca-Cola Company and its archrival, PepsiCo, have been battling for control of the global soft-drink market. During the 1970s and 80s, most of the battles in the cola wars were fought in the U.S. market. In 1975 Pepsi launched its Pepsi Challenge, which showed consumers preferring the taste of Pepsi over Coke in blind taste tests, and by 1984 it had achieved a 2 percent market share lead over Coke in supermarket sales. Pepsi's success was a major factor in Coca-Cola's controversial decision to change the formula of its 99-year-old flagship brand and launch New Coke in 1985. Consumers loyal to the old formula protested, prompting the company to reintroduce the original Coke as Coca-Cola Classic.

Pepsi's success prompted its top executive, Roger Enrico, to write a book about the New Coke debacle titled *The Other Guy Blinked: How Pepsi Won the Cola Wars.* Pepsi continued to challenge Coke throughout the 1980s and into the 90s as the battle shifted to the fast-growing diet segment of the soft-drink market. Creative advertising such as the campaign for Diet Pepsi that featured Ray Charles singing "You've got the right one baby, uh-huh" seemed to give Pepsi the edge in advertising for a while. However, Enrico's proclamation of victory in the cola wars was premature. Coke has emerged the victor in both the U.S. and the worldwide markets in the most recent and fiercest battle yet of the cola titans.

Coca-Cola's assault on Pepsi actually began in 1993 when the company recognized that it needed to revitalize its advertising and overcome the perception that Pepsi is the hip soft drink for the youth market. The advertising for Coke Classic was turned over to the Hollywood talent firm Creative Artists Agency (CAA), which came up with the popular "Always Coca-Cola" campaign. Many analysts feel that commercials from the "Always" campaign, many of which were seen worldwide, were Coke's most successful advertising in over a decade. The new ad campaign helped The Coca-Cola Company expand its market share lead in the United States to 42 percent versus Pepsi's 31 percent, the largest in 20 years.

To go along with its gains in the United States, Coke also gained significant share in international markets. Coke overcame Pepsi's 10-year lead to become the market leader in Russia, and—through acquisitions—also became the leader in India and Venezuela (where it gained 80 percent market share overnight by convincing Pepsi's leading bottler to convert). Coke was also ahead of Pepsi in Mexico, Germany, Japan, and Brazil. But things do have a way of changing.

In Russia, sales of Coca-Cola quadrupled between 1991 and 1996, but by early 1999 that demand declined by one-third. Overall, in 1999 the bottling plants were operating at only 50 percent of capacity. Economic problems in Asia and South America also hurt the Atlanta-based company, to the point where net income dropped (by 14 percent) for the first time in a quarter of a century. Despite investing $1.4 billion in Brazil between 1995 and 1997, the company had lost 10 percent of the market by 1999. Demand was also declining in Venezuela, despite the billion-dollar acquisition, as Pepsi successfully fought back. A huge product recall in Europe in the spring of 1999 hurt Coke sales there and led to significant increases in marketing spending, though the company says that sales were just about at precrisis levels by the fall of 1999.

Things didn't go as well at home either. By the summer of 1999, according to *Beverage Digest,* Pepsi turned around a decade-long share loss to Coke, outperforming Coke in the first part of the year and gaining share. By midsummer, Pepsi had 31.4 percent of the market, while Coke held on to 44.5 percent.

In an attempt to turn around its slumping sales, Coca-Cola took on a new look in the late summer of 1999. While keeping the bottle to ensure its nostalgic image, a new label and presentation mode (cap off, soda fizzing out) were added to give the brand an "edgier" look. The "Always" slogan, adopted in 1993, was replaced in communications with "Enjoy." Bottle caps, stores signs, cans, bottles, and even the delivery trucks carried the new slogan. A new ad campaign was expected to follow.

Meanwhile, Pepsi was marketing a few changes of its own. The long-running "Generation Next"

campaign was replaced by the tagline "The Joy of Cola"—reflecting a more mainstream appeal. (Management and the bottlers came to believe the old campaign was too narrowly focused on teens and too off-the-wall.) Aretha Franklin, Isaac Hayes, and Marlon Brando provided voice-overs for the new spots—quite a change from the 80s look featuring Michael Jackson and Madonna.

Pepsi also spun off its restaurant business and placed more emphasis on bottlers to strengthen its distribution system. A new package design—solid blue to differentiate it from Coke's red—also attempted to bolster the new image.

It's been an interesting battle between Coca-Cola and Pepsi. Like a football game, the field position is constantly changing. New plays are constantly being sent in, as are new players—both companies had significant management changes in the late 1990s. Keep watching; the score seems to change as well!

Sources: Nikhil Deogun, "Pepsi Unveils New Advertising Effort, Scraps 'Generation Next' Campaign," *The Wall Street Journal,* March 5, 1999, p. B5; Betsy McKay, "New Look for the Top Pop Aims to Infuse Some Fizz into a Nostalgic Image," *The Wall Street Journal,* October 13, 1999, p. B1; Nikhil Deogun, "Aggressive Push Abroad Dilutes Coke's Strength as Big Markets Stumble," *The Wall Street Journal,* February 8, 1999, p. A1; Patricia Sellers, "How Coke Is Kicking Pepsi's Can," *Fortune,* October 28, 1996, pp. 70–84.

involves three basic steps: segment the market, select a target market, and determine the market positioning strategy of one's product or service. The selection of the target market (or markets) in which the firm will compete is an important part of its marketing strategy and has direct implications for its advertising and promotional efforts. Specific communication objectives are derived and the promotional mix strategies are developed to achieve these objectives. Thus, different objectives may be established, different budgets may be used, and the promotional mix strategies may vary, depending on the market approach used.

Exhibit 2–2 McDonald's offers a variety of products in different geographic markets

Segment the Market

When employing a target market strategy, the marketer identifies the specific needs of groups of people (or segments), selects one or more of these segments as a target, and develops marketing programs directed to each. This approach has found increased applicability in marketing for a number of reasons, including changes in the market (consumers are becoming much more diverse in their needs, attitudes, and lifestyles); increased use of segmentation by competitors; and the fact that more managers are trained in segmentation and realize the advantages associated with this strategy. Perhaps the best explanation, however, comes back to the basic premise that you must understand as much as possible about consumers to design marketing programs that meet their needs most effectively. Furthermore, as marketers establish a common ground with consumers, the more effective they will be in addressing these requirements in their communications programs and informing and/or persuading potential consumers that the product or service offering will meet their needs.

Marketers competing in nearly all product and service categories are constantly searching for ways to segment their markets in an attempt to better satisfy customers' needs (Exhibit 2–2). The remainder of this section discusses ways to approach this task and make the final segmentation decision.

Bases for Segmentation As shown in Figure 2–3, several methods are available for segmenting markets. Marketers may use one of the segmentation variables or a combination of approaches. Consider the market segmentation strategy

Figure 2–3 Some bases for market segmentation

Main Dimension	Segmentation Variables	Typical Breakdowns
A. Segmentation Variables and Breakdowns for Consumer Markets		
Customer Characteristics		
Geographic	Region	West, East
	City or metropolitan statistical area (MSA) size	Under 5,000; 5,000 to 19,999; 20,000 to 49,999; 50,000 to 99,999; 100,000 to 249,999; 250,000 to 499,999; 500,000 to 999,999; 1,000,000 or over
	Density	Urban; suburban; rural
Demographic	Age	Infant, under 6; 6 to 11; 12 to 17; 18 to 24; 25 to 34; 35 to 49; 50 to 64; 65 or over
	Sex	Male; female
	Family size	1 to 2; 3 to 4; 5 or over
	Stage of family life cycle	Young single; young married, no children; young married, youngest child under 6; young married, youngest child 6 or older; older married, with children; older married, no children under 18; older single; other older married, no children under 18
	Ages of children	No child under 18; youngest child 6 to 17; youngest child under 6
	Children under 18	0; 1; more than 1
	Income	Under $14,999; $15,000 to $24,999; $25,000 to $34,999; $35,000 to $49,999; $50,000 to $64,999; $65,000 or over
	Education	Grade school or less; some high school; high school graduate; some college or university; college or university graduate
	Race	Asian; black; white; other
	Homeownership	Own home; rent home
Psychographic	Personality	Gregarious; compulsive; extroverted; aggressive; ambitious
	Lifestyle	Use of one's time; values and importance; beliefs
Buying Situations		
Benefits sought	Product features	Situation specific; general
	Needs	Quality; service; economy
Usage	Rate of use	Light user; medium user; heavy user
	User states	Nonuser; ex-user; prospect; first-time user; regular user
Awareness and intentions	Readiness to buy	Unaware; aware; informed; interested; intending to buy
	Brand familiarity	Insistence; preference; recognition; nonrecognition; rejection
Buying condition	Type of buying activity	Minimum-effort buying; comparison buying; special-effort buying
	Kind of store	Convenience; wide breadth; specialty
B. Segmentation Variables and Breakdowns for Industrial Markets		
Customer Characteristics		
Geographic	Region	East, West
	Location	In MSA; not in MSA
Demographic	SIC code	2-digit; 3-digit; 4-digit categories
	Number of employees	1 to 19; 20 to 99; 100 to 249; 250 or over
	Number of production workers	1 to 19; 20 to 99; 100 to 249; 250 or over
	Annual sales volume	Less than $1 million; $1 million to $10 million; $10 million to $100 million; over $100 million
	Number of establishments	With 1 to 19 employees; with 20 or more employees
Buying Situations		
Nature of good	Kind	Product or service
	Where used	Installation; component of final product; supplies
	Application	Office use; limited production use; heavy production use
Buying condition	Purchase location	Centralized; decentralized
	Who buys	Individual buyer; group
	Type of buy	New buy; modified rebuy; straight rebuy

that might be employed to market snow skis. The consumer's lifestyle—active, fun-loving, enjoys outdoor sports—is certainly important. But so are other factors, such as age (participation in downhill skiing drops off significantly at about age 30) and income (Have you seen the price of a lift ticket lately?), as well as marital status. Let us review the bases for segmentation and examine some promotional strategies employed in each.

Geographic Segmentation   In the **geographic segmentation** approach, markets are divided into different geographic units. These units may include nations, states, counties, or even neighbourhoods. Consumers often have different buying habits depending on where they reside.

Demographic Segmentation   Dividing the market on the basis of demographic variables such as age, sex, family size, education, income, and social class is called **demographic segmentation.** Secret deodorant and the Lady Schick shaver are products that have met with a great deal of success by using the demographic variable of sex as a basis for segmentation.

Although market segmentation on the basis of demographics may seem obvious, companies sometimes discover that they need to focus more attention on a specific demographic group (Exhibit 2–3).

While demographics may still be the most common method of segmenting markets, it is important to recognize that other factors may be the underlying basis for homogeneity and/or consumer behaviour. The astute marketer will identify additional bases for segmenting and will recognize the limitations of demographics.

Psychographic Segmentation   Dividing the market on the basis of personality and/or lifestyles is referred to as **psychographic segmentation.** While there is some disagreement as to whether personality is a useful basis for segmentation, lifestyle factors have been used effectively. Many consider lifestyle the most effective criterion for segmentation.

Exhibit 2–3   Nail Fetish changed its image to appeal to Generation X

The determination of lifestyles is usually based on an analysis of the activities, interests, and opinions (AIOs) of consumers. These lifestyles are then correlated with the consumers' product, brand, and/or media usage. For many products and/or services, lifestyles may be the best discriminator between use and nonuse, accounting for differences in food, clothing, and car selections, among numerous other consumer behaviours.[4] (See IMC Perspective 2–2.)

Psychographic segmentation has been increasingly accepted with the advent of the values and lifestyles (VALS) program. Although marketers employed lifestyle segmentation long before VALS and although a number of alternatives—for example, PRIZM—are available, VALS remains one of the more popular options. Developed by the Stanford Research Institute (SRI), VALS has become a very popular method for applying lifestyle segmentation. VALS 2 divides Americans into eight lifestyle segments that exhibit distinctive attitudes, behaviours, and decision-making patterns.[5] SRI believes that when combined with an estimate of the resources the consumer can draw on (education, income, health, energy level, self-confidence, and degree of consumerism), the VALS 2 system is an excellent predictor of consumer behaviours. A variety of companies, including Mercedes and Eastman Kodak, have employed the VALS 2 program. Campbell's Soup embarked on a new campaign in 2000 to position the soup as a "lifestyle" choice.

Changing Images through Repositioning

There sometimes comes a point in a brand's life cycle where it is critical to decide between staying with an existing image or breathing life into the brand by changing its position. While most marketers would agree that it is easier to create an image than to change an existing one, a number of brands have been repositioned, some successfully, some not.

- When Oil of Olay was introduced in 1967, it was positioned as a brand for older women. More recently, Procter & Gamble has tried to reach a younger demographic to broaden the market,

successfully extending Oil of Olay beyond facial moisturizers into wash produces.

However, research has showed that "Oil" is unappealing to the younger generation. As a result, the word on its packaging has been getting progressively smaller, or disappearing altogether, while "Olay" has become the prominent brand name.

- Canadian menswear retailer Tip Top Tailors traditionally targeted consumers who were looking for low-priced clothing. In 1997, the company tried to change its image by focusing on higher-end merchandise. It was a strategy backed by advertising with a catchy new tag line: "We're changing our clothes." Less than a year later, Tip Top's sales dropped by 9.5 percent.

  Tip Top's repositioning turned off its traditional customer base who became upset with the higher prices. The upscale market, on the other hand, did not buy into the concept of Tip Top as an upscale clothing store. Tip Top was forced to reduce its prices slightly to deal with its positioning problem.

- High-end clothing retailer Holt Renfrew is attempting to update its dusty image as a retail haven for wealthy society matrons. It has launched an aggressive repositioning strategy to bring younger and more price-conscious shoppers into its stores.

  As part of its strategy, Holt Renfrew is expanding its selection of mid-priced clothing and increasing the focus on its private-label brands. This means less emphasis on power suits and evening gowns and more on casual clothing, particularly its Platinum private-label brand.

Sources: David Chilton, "Redefining Olay," *Marketing Magazine,* October 20, 1997; Erica Zlomislic, "What went wrong? Tip Top Repositions Too Far, Too Fast," *Strategy,* May 25, 1998, p.1; Craig Saunders, "Holt Renfrew Reaches out to New Shoppers," *Strategy,* September 27, 1999, p. 1.

Behaviouristic Segmentation   Dividing consumers into groups according to their usage, loyalties, or buying responses to a product is **behaviouristic segmentation**. For example, product or brand usage, degree of use (heavy versus light), and/or brand loyalty are combined with demographic and/or psychographic criteria to develop profiles of market segments. In the case of usage, the marketer assumes that nonpurchasers of a brand or product who have the same characteristics as purchasers hold greater potential for adoption than nonusers with different characteristics. A profile (demographic or psychographic) of the user is developed, which serves as the basis for promotional strategies designed to attract new users. For example, teenagers share certain similarities in their consumption behaviours. Those who do not currently own a Sony Discman are more likely to be potential buyers than people in other age groups.

Degree of use relates to the fact that a few consumers may buy a disproportionate amount of many products or brands. Industrial marketers refer to the **80–20 rule**, meaning 20 percent of their buyers account for 80 percent of their sales volume. Again, when the characteristics of these users are identified, targeting them allows for a much greater concentration of efforts and less wasted time and money. The same heavy-half strategy is possible in the consumer market as well. The majority of purchases of many products (for example, soaps and detergents, shampoos, cake mixes, beer, dog food, colas, bourbon, and toilet tissue—yes, toilet tissue!) are accounted for by a small proportion of the population. Perhaps you can think of some additional examples.

Exhibit 2–4 Rembrandt toothpaste stresses the benefit of its superior whitening ability

Benefit Segmentation   In purchasing products, consumers are generally trying to satisfy specific needs and/or wants. They are looking for products that provide specific benefits to satisfy these needs. The grouping of consumers on the basis of attributes sought in a product is known as **benefit segmentation** and is widely used.

Consider the purchase of a wristwatch. While you might buy a watch for particular benefits such as accuracy, water resistance, or stylishness, others may seek a different set of benefits. Watches are commonly given as gifts for birthdays, Christmas, and graduation. Certainly some of the same benefits are considered in the purchase of a gift, but the benefits the purchaser derives are different from those the user will obtain. Ads that portray watches as good gifts stress different criteria to consider in the purchase decision. The next time you see an ad or commercial for a watch, think about the basic appeal and the benefits it offers.

Another example of benefit segmentation can be seen in the toothpaste market. Some consumers want a product with fluoride (Crest, Colgate); others prefer one that freshens their breath (Close-Up, Aqua-Fresh). More recent benefit segments offer tartar control (Crest) and plaque reduction (Viadent). The Den-Mat Corp. introduced Rembrandt whitening toothpaste for consumers who want whiter teeth (Exhibit 2–4) and other brands followed with their own whitening attributes.

The Process of Segmenting a Market   The segmentation process develops over time and is an integral part of the situation analysis. It is in this stage that marketers attempt to determine as much as they can about the market: What needs are not being fulfilled? What benefits are being sought? What characteristics distinguish among the various groups seeking these products and services? A number of alternative segmentation strategies may be used. Each time a specific segment is identified, additional information is gathered to help the marketer understand this group.

For example, once a specific segment is identified on the basis of benefits sought, the marketer will examine lifestyle characteristics and demographics to help characterize this group and to further its understanding of this market. Behaviouristic segmentation criteria will also be examined. In the purchase of ski boots, for example, specific benefits may be sought—flexibility or stiffness—depending on the type of skiing the buyer does. All this information will be combined to provide a complete profile of the skier. The more marketers segment the market, the more precise is their understanding of it. But the more the market becomes divided, the fewer consumers are in each segment. Thus, a key decision is: How far should one go in the segmentation process?

In planning the promotional effort, managers consider whether the target segment is substantial enough to support individualized strategies. More specifically, they consider whether this group is accessible. Can it be reached with a communications program? For example, you will see in Chapter 8 that in some instances there are no media that can be used to reach some targeted groups. Or the promotions manager may identify a number of segments but be unable to develop the required programs to reach them. The firm may have insufficient funds to develop the required advertising campaign, inadequate sales staff to cover all areas, or other promotional deficiencies. A number of companies now offer research services to help marketing managers define their markets and develop strategies targeting them. The VALS and PRIZM systems discussed earlier are just a few of the services offered; others use demographic, socioeconomic, and geographic data to cluster consumer households into distinct "microgeographic" segments. Whether these microunits meet the criteria for useful segmentation is determined by the user of the system. A national company might not attempt to define such small segments, but it could be useful for companies operating within one city or geographic area.

After completing the segmentation analysis, the marketer moves to the second phase shown in Figure 2–2: targeting a specific market.

Select a Target Market

The outcome of the segmentation analysis will reveal the market opportunities available. The next phase in the target marketing process involves two steps: (1) determining how many segments to enter and (2) determining which segments offer the most potential.

Three market coverage alternatives are available. **Undifferentiated marketing** involves ignoring segment differences and offering just one product or service to the entire market. For many years, Coca-Cola offered only one product version. While this standardized strategy saves the company money, it does not allow the opportunity to offer different versions of the product to different markets.

Differentiated marketing involves marketing in a number of segments, developing separate marketing strategies for each. While an undifferentiated strategy offers reduced costs through increased production, it does not allow for variety or tailoring to specific needs. Through differentiation, products—or advertising appeals—may be developed for the various segments, increasing the opportunity to satisfy the needs and wants of various groups.

The third alternative, **concentrated marketing,** is used when the firm selects one segment and attempts to capture a large share of this market. Volkswagen used this strategy in the 1950s when it was the only major automobile company competing in the economy-car segment in the United States. While Volkswagen has now assumed a more differentiated strategy, other companies have found the concentrated strategy effective.

The second step in selecting a market involves determining the most attractive segment. The firm must examine the sales potential of the segment, the opportunities for growth, the competition, and its own ability to compete. Then it must decide whether it can market to this group. Stories abound of companies that have entered new markets only to find their lack of resources or expertise would not allow them to compete successfully. For example, Royal Crown (RC) Cola has often been quite successful in identifying new segment opportunities but because of limited resources has been less able to capitalize on them than Coke and Pepsi. RC was the first to bring to market diet colas and caffeine-free colas, but it has not been able to establish itself as a market leader in either market. After selecting the segments to target and determining that it can compete, the firm proceeds to the final step in Figure 2–2: the market positioning strategy phase.

Determine the Market Positioning Strategy

A **market positioning strategy** concerns the final decision of the market(s) in which firms wish to compete, combined with the specific elements of the marketing mix that are designed to fulfill the respective needs of the market(s). Typically, firms will write a market positioning statement in their marketing plan to accurately communicate this decision. This statement will be the guiding principle and direction for each of the four areas of decision within the marketing program development phase: product, price, distribution, and marketing communications.

As the firm develops its market positioning strategy, it may consider many combinations of product attributes with varying price levels across different retail outlets. Alternatively, it could evaluate narrow product choices with very wide distribution and a mass advertising appeal. A firm will consider as many feasible options as possible so that it does not miss an opportunity. At this stage, the firm uses its market research and experience wisely to put together a "package of benefits" that will be acceptable to the target market selected in the previous step.

The market naturally reacts to all the marketing programs after they are developed and implemented. It may be very close to what the firm intended or, for many reasons (i.e., competition, aspects of consumer acceptance), it could be quite different. We define this response to be the market position of a firm. This distinction signifies that it is not the current or past strategic plans of the marketing managers, but rather the intended or unintended consumer beliefs of the organization's efforts. For example, for a number of years Ford used the phrase "Quality is Job 1" to signal its organization-wide dedication to improving quality. Throughout many of its marketing efforts, Ford had a market positioning strategy of higher quality so that it could compete with Japanese imports that had gained substantial market share in North America. However, it took years before the majority of consumers truly believed that Ford could deliver a quality vehicle, indicating that there had been a tremendous lag between Ford's market positioning strategy and its actual market position.

To expand on these ideas, we will use the Canadian airline industry as an example. As of 2001, Air Canada represented essentially the only full-service national airline. While it has had various ad campaigns over the years, it has always attempted to maintain this full-service position, especially when it faced competition from Canadian Airlines. WestJet, previously a small regional discount carrier, purchased larger, newer jets so that it could offer services for cross-country routes.[6] Advertising now had to maintain its discount market position throughout the country.

We illustrate this situation with a simple market position diagram, recognizing that alternative interpretations may be feasible (Figure 2–4). We graph two axes, high and low service versus high and low price. WestJet and Air Canada are opposite ends of the service spectrum. It appears that both companies have followed some kind of target market process and are putting together the most appropriate marketing program to be successful. While these market positioning strategies appear suitable attempts to successfully deliver needed airline services, time will tell

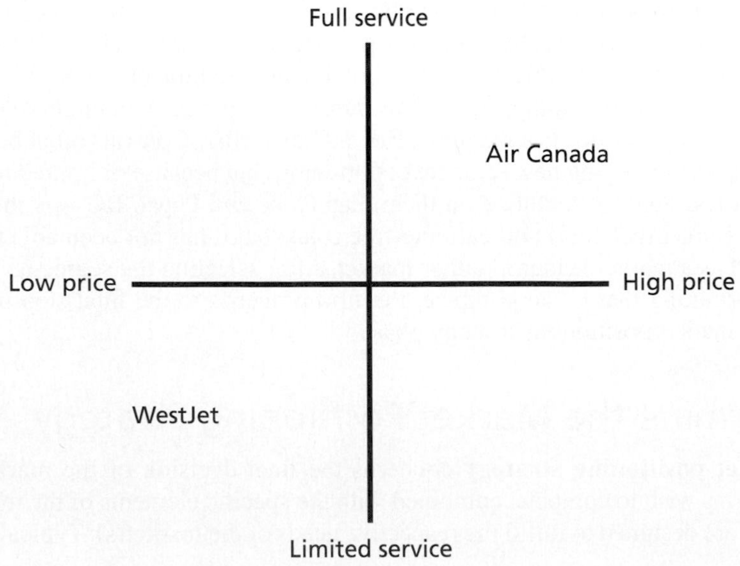

Figure 2–4 Hypothetical illustration of market positioning strategy

whether consumers truly believe that each occupies the intended market space and has the correct market position in the minds of consumers.

Marketing Program Development

The results of the target market process tell the marketing department which customers to focus on and what needs to attempt to satisfy. The next stage of the marketing and promotion process model involves combining the various elements of the marketing mix into a cohesive, effective marketing program. Each marketing mix element is multidimensional and includes a number of decision areas. Likewise, each must consider and contribute to the overall IMC program. We now examine how product, price, and distribution channel decisions influence and interact with the promotional program. Then, we discuss how the promotional mix supports and reinforces the marketing strategy. We focus on how advertising establishes a clear brand position for specific target audiences and plays a major role in enhancing the market position of the product.

Product Decisions and IMC

An organization exists because it has some product, service, or idea to offer consumers, generally in exchange for money. This offering may come in the form of a physical product (such as a soft drink, pair of jeans, or car), a service (banking, airlines, or legal assistance), a cause (United Way, March of Dimes), or even a person (a political candidate). The product is anything that can be marketed and that, when used or supported, gives satisfaction to the individual.

A *product* is not just a physical object; it is a bundle of benefits or values that satisfies the needs of consumers. The needs may be purely functional, or they may include social and psychological benefits. For example, the ad for Michelin tires shown earlier stresses the quality built into Michelin tires (value) as well as their performance and durability (function). The term **product symbolism** refers to what a product or brand means to consumers and what they experience in purchasing and using it.[7] For many products, strong symbolic features and social and psychological meaning may be more important than functional utility.[8] For example, designer clothing such as Versace, Gucci, and Ferragamo is often purchased on the basis of its symbolic meaning and image, particularly by teenagers and young adults. Advertising plays an important role in developing and maintaining the image of these brands (Exhibit 2–5).

Product planning involves decisions not only about the item itself, such as design and quality, but also about aspects such as service and warranties as well as brand

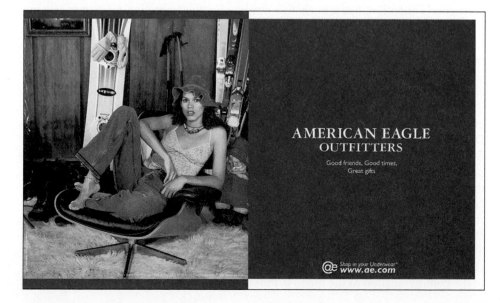

Exhibit 2–5 Advertising for designer clothing

name and package design. Consumers look beyond the reality of the product and its ingredients. The product's quality, branding, packaging, and even the company standing behind it all contribute to consumers' perceptions.[9] In an effective IMC program, advertising, branding, and packaging are all designed to portray the product as more than just a bundle of attributes. All are coordinated to present an image or positioning of the product that extends well beyond its physical attributes. Think for a minute about the ads for Nike; the product benefits and attributes are usually not even mentioned—yet information about the brand is communicated effectively.

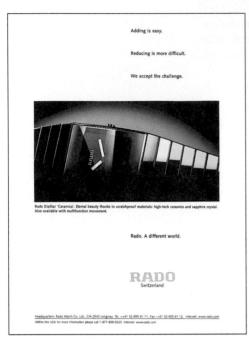

Exhibit 2–6 Rado creates strong brand equity through advertising

Branding   Choosing a brand name for a product is important from a promotional perspective because brand names communicate attributes and meaning. Marketers search for brand names that can communicate product concepts and help position the product in customers' minds. Names such as Safeguard (soap), I Can't Believe It's Not Butter! (margarine), Easy-Off (oven cleaner), Arrid (antiperspirant), and Spic and Span (floor cleaner) all clearly communicate the benefits of using these products and at the same time create images extending beyond the names themselves.

One important role of advertising in respect to branding strategies is creating and maintaining **brand equity,** which can be thought of as an intangible asset of added value or goodwill that results from the favourable image, impressions of differentiation, and/or the strength of consumer attachment to a company name, brand name, or trademark. Brand equity allows a brand to earn greater sales volume and/or higher margins than it could without the name, providing the company with a competitive advantage. The strong equity position a company and/or its brand enjoys is often reinforced through advertising. For example, Rado watches command a premium price because of their high quality as well as the strong brand equity they have developed through advertising (Exhibit 2–6).

Packaging   Packaging is another aspect of product strategy that has become increasingly important. Traditionally, the package provided functional benefits such as economy, protection, and storage. However, the role and function of the package have changed because of the self-service emphasis of many stores and the fact that more and more buying decisions are made at the point of purchase. One study estimated that as many as two-thirds of all purchases made in the supermarket are unplanned. The package is often the consumer's first exposure to the product, so it must make a favourable first impression. A typical supermarket has more than 20,000 items competing for attention. Not only must a package attract and hold the consumer's attention, but it must also communicate information on how to use the product, divulge its composition and content, and satisfy any legal requirements regarding disclosure. Moreover, many firms design the package to carry a sales promotion message such as a contest, sweepstakes, or premium offer.

Many companies view the package as an important way to communicate with consumers and create an impression of the brand in their minds. Notice the effective use of the battery tester on the Duracell package shown in Exhibit 2–7. Besides offering value-added attributes beyond the product itself, the packaging gives Duracell a unique way to convey the claim that its batteries last longer. Design factors such as size, shape, colour, and lettering all contribute to the appeal of a package and can be as important as a commercial in determining what goes from the store shelf to the consumer's shopping cart. Many products use packaging to create a distinctive brand image and identity. The next time you walk by a perfume counter, stop to look at the many unique package designs (see Exhibit 2–8). Packaging can also serve more functional purposes. For example, Tylenol's Safe-Ty-Lock bottle protects children from consuming the medicine when they shouldn't (Exhibit 2–9). One Canadian example of a package redesign playing a critical role in the communication of the brand is Polar Ice Vodka, which is trying to take on the

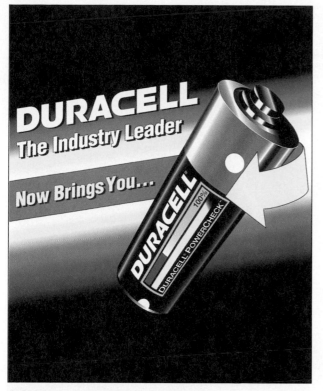

Exhibit 2–7 Duracell communicates through effective packaging

AT THE HEART OF A GREAT FRAGRANCE
is a scent that becomes yours alone.
It introduces you, compliments you, pleases you.
The classic fragrances of Tiffany.

VISIT TIFFANY & CO. DAYTON'S HUDSON'S AND MARSHALL FIELD'S TO SAMPLE THE FRAGRANCES OF TIFFANY.
FOR OTHER LOCATIONS AND INQUIRIES PLEASE CALL 800-526-0649.

Exhibit 2–8 The packaging creates product image

North American market with its market repositioning strategy. Previously, the bottle had sloping shoulders that did not contribute to the brand's character. Its replacement has an ovoid shape with sharp-edged shoulders. The front now has clear vinyl so that consumers can see the product, and the back has black vinyl to give the bottle a depth perspective.[10]

Price Decisions and IMC

The *price variable* refers to what the consumer must give up to purchase a product or service. While price is discussed in terms of the dollar amount exchanged for an item, the cost of a product to the consumer includes time, mental activity, and behavioural effort.[11] The marketing manager is usually concerned with establishing a price level, developing pricing policies, and monitoring competitors' and consumers' reactions to prices in the marketplace. A firm must consider a number of factors in determining the price it charges for its product or service, including costs, demand factors, competition, and perceived value (Exhibit 2–10). From an IMC perspective, the communications strategy must be consistent with the price of the product. Conversely, price communicates a significant product attribute that supports its market position.

Factors such as product quality, competition, and advertising all interact in determining what price a firm can and should charge. The relationship among price, product quality, and advertising was examined in one study using information on 227 consumer businesses from the PIMS (Profit Impact of Marketing Strategies) project of the Strategic Planning Institute.[12] The study concluded that pricing and advertising strategies go together. High relative ad expenditures should accompany premium

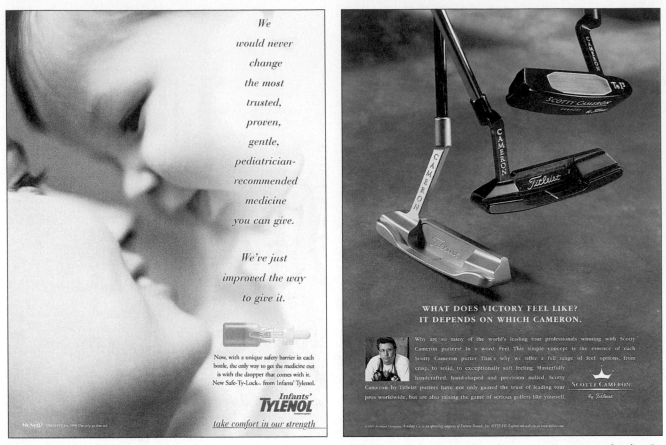

Exhibit 2–9 Packaging may also add product benefits

Exhibit 2–10 Some products compete on the basis of quality rather than price

prices, and low relative ad expenditures should be tailored to low prices. These results obviously support the IMC perspective that one voice must be conveyed.

Distribution Decisions and IMC

One of a marketer's most important marketing decisions involves the way it makes its products and services available for purchase. A firm can have an excellent product at a great price, but it will be of little value unless it is available where the customer wants it, when the customer wants it, and with the proper support and service. **Marketing channels,** the place element of the marketing mix, are "sets of interdependent organizations involved in the process of making a product or service available for use or consumption."[13] Channel decisions involve selecting, managing, and motivating intermediaries such as wholesalers, distributors, brokers, and retailers that help a firm make a product or service available to customers. These intermediaries, sometimes called **resellers,** are critical to the success of a company's marketing program.

The distribution strategy should also take into consideration the communication objectives and the impact that the channel strategy will have on the IMC program. Stewart and colleagues discuss the need for "integrated channel management," which "reflects the blurring of the boundaries of the communications and distribution functions."[14] Consistent with the product and pricing decisions, where the product is distributed will send a communications message. Does the fact that a product is sold at Holt Renfrew convey a different message regarding its image than if it were distributed at Wal-Mart? If you think about it for a moment, the mere fact that the product is distributed in these channels communicates an image about it in your mind. Stewart gives examples of how channel elements contribute to communications—for example, grocery store displays, point-of-purchase merchandising, and shelf footage. The distribution channel in a well-integrated marketing program serves as a form of reminder advertising as the consumer recognizes the brand based on previous advertising exposure.

There are a number of IMC decisions related to distribution. A company may have a program to motivate the channel members. Programs designed to persuade the trade to stock, merchandise, and promote a manufacturer's products are part of a **promotional push strategy**. The goal of this strategy is to push the product through the channels of distribution by aggressively selling and promoting the item to the resellers, or trade. Promotion to the trade includes all the elements of the promotional mix. Company sales representatives call on resellers to explain the product, discuss the firm's plans for building demand among ultimate consumers, and describe special programs being offered to the trade, such as introductory discounts, promotional allowances, and cooperative ad programs. The company may use **trade advertising** to interest wholesalers and retailers and motivate them to purchase its products for resale to their customers. Trade advertising usually appears in publications that serve the particular industry.

A push strategy tries to convince resellers they can make a profit on a manufacturer's product and to encourage them to order the merchandise and push it through to their customers. Sometimes manufacturers face resistance from channel members who do not want to take on an additional product line or brand. In these cases, companies may turn to a **promotional pull strategy,** spending money on advertising and sales promotion efforts directed toward the ultimate consumer. The goal of a pull strategy is to create demand among consumers and encourage them to request the product from the retailer. Seeing the consumer demand, retailers will order the product from wholesalers (if they are used), which in turn will request it from the manufacturer. Thus, stimulating demand at the end-user level pulls the product through the channels of distribution.

Whether to emphasize a push or a pull strategy depends on a number of factors, including the company's relations with the trade, its promotional budget, and demand for the firm's products. Companies that have favourable channel relationships may prefer to use a push strategy and work closely with channel members to encourage them to stock and promote their products. A firm with a limited promotional budget may not have the funds for advertising and sales promotion that a pull strategy requires and may find it more cost effective to build distribution and demand by working closely with resellers. When the demand outlook for a product is favourable because it has unique benefits, is superior to competing brands, or is very popular among consumers, a pull strategy may be appropriate. Companies often use a combination of push and pull strategies, with the emphasis changing as the product moves through its life cycle.

IMC Decisions Relating to Marketing Strategy

The previous section discussed the connection of the three other marketing mix variables to advertising and IMC. In this section, we seek to examine the role of the promotional mix within the marketing strategy. As one of the four programs of the marketing mix, an advertising or IMC campaign is intended to support or reinforce the market positioning strategy.

Since promotion is so visible, it is tempting to believe that it alone defines the market positioning strategy. While this may be true in some situations, in most cases, advertising and IMC campaigns typically focus on a particular message that helps the customer understand the product in comparison to other brands *within* a specific product market or category. Furthermore, most ads or other IMC tools speak to a very specific target audience. A bank can have a direct-mail piece to a current customer to obtain a mortgage renewal and focus the message on the ease of continuity and the good follow-up service. Or it may run a TV ad with a message of attractive interest rates and specialized options that may attract customers from competing banks. Since these are obviously different target audiences with different competitive reference points, we need to use the positioning concept appropriately in a communications context that is distinct from positioning in a marketing context.

This notion of positioning via marketing communication versus the overall marketing strategy is the topic to which we now turn. We distinguish between brand positioning strategy and market positioning strategy, provide options for brand positioning strategies, and summarize a framework for making this decision.

Brand Positioning Strategy   **Positioning** has been defined as "the art and science of fitting the product or service to one or more segments of the broad market in such a way as to set it meaningfully apart from competition."[15] Many advertising practitioners consider positioning the most important decision in establishing a brand in the marketplace. David Aaker and John Myers note that the term position has recently been used to indicate the brand's or product's image in the marketplace.[16] Jack Trout and Al Ries suggest that this brand image must contrast with competitors'. They say, "In today's marketplace, the competitors' image is just as important as your own. Sometimes more important."[17] Thus, a **brand positioning strategy,** as used in this text, relates to the image of the product or brand relative to a competing brand for a given competitive space as defined by certain product market or category characteristics. The brand positioning strategy is a key decision prior to determining the most effective selling message of the advertising or the IMC. For example, the two banking examples noted in Chapter 1 required a clear brand positioning strategy in terms of the target audience and competing banking services.

Now consider your reactions to having seen television commercials or any other communication for any type of product or service. What do you think about the brand, having experienced the message? Do you have positive or negative feelings for the brand? What unique attributes or benefits come to mind when considering the brand? All of these questions pertain to the reactions consumers have to promotions, and constitute what we will refer to as the **brand position.** We need to distinguish between what the firm plans to do with its image versus what the actual image of the brand is, since both occur at different points in time and reside in different locations. The brand positioning strategy is a part of the overall advertising or IMC plan while the brand position exists in the minds of consumers.

Let us return to our airline example. In the course of developing its discount market positioning strategy, WestJet has a number of options to communicate, of which we will highlight a couple. It could encourage those who never or rarely travel to consider flying since it is now so affordable. Or it may try to convince those who buy the cheapest economy-class tickets (i.e., red-eye flights back east) to buy a WestJet ticket and travel at a more civilized time of the day. In either case, there is a distinct brand positioning strategy decision made to reach each unique target audience. Accordingly, each target audience will have its own unique brand position based on its experiences with the ads and the service.

We continue this idea with a more competitive angle since Air Canada has entered the discount market with Tango. Both WestJet and Tango will compete to be the leader in the discount market, and WestJet may need some elements of their IMC plan to encourage WestJet customers not to switch to Tango or to switch Tango customers to WestJet. These are just a few example how WestJet could be using a brand positioning strategy to speak with unique target audiences who are a part of the overall target market and may be receptive to the overall market positioning strategy.

We now return to our brand position (i.e., consumer perceptions) diagram whereby WestJet and Tango are competing on certain salient attributes. Figure 2–5 shows two axes on which the companies *may* compete: frequency of flights and number of cities serviced. We hesitate to locate exactly where both of these firms are, since the discount market is starting to develop. We can also surmise that the airlines *may* be competing on certain salient benefits (Figure 2–6) of reliability (i.e., on-time departures, no mechanical delays) and convenience (i.e., check-in, ticket purchase).

We will examine how consumers arrive with a brand position in Chapter 4 when we discuss various models that explain how consumers react to communications.

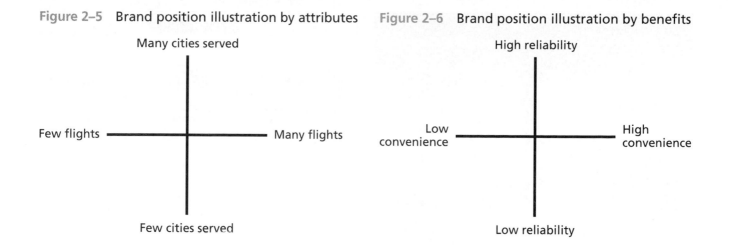

Figure 2–5 Brand position illustration by attributes

Figure 2–6 Brand position illustration by benefits

Further, we will discuss how the brand positioning strategy is put together throughout many of the chapters that describe the various decisions involved when determining an IMC plan. For now, we turn our attention to briefly describing various brand positioning strategy options.

Brand Positioning Strategy Options Positioning strategies generally focus on either the consumer or the competition. While both approaches involve the association of product benefits with consumer needs, the former does so by linking the product with the benefits the consumer will derive. The latter approach positions the product by comparing it and the benefit it offers with the competition, as shown in Exhibit 2–11. David Aaker and J. Gary Shansby discuss six brand positioning strategy options: positioning by product attributes, price/quality, use, product class, users, and competitor.[18]

Positioning by Product Attributes and Benefits A common approach to positioning is setting the brand apart from competitors on the basis of the specific characteristics or benefits offered. Sometimes a product may be positioned on more than one product benefit. Marketers attempt to identify **salient attributes** (those that are important to consumers and are the basis for making a purchase decision). For example, when Apple first introduced its computers, the key benefit stressed was ease of use—an effective strategy, given the complexity of computers in the market at that time.

Positioning by Price/Quality Marketers often use price/quality characteristics to position their brands. One way they do it is with ads that reflect the image of a high-quality brand where cost, while not irrelevant, is considered secondary to the quality benefits derived from using the brand. Premium brands positioned at the high end of the market use this approach to positioning.

Another way to use price/quality characteristics for positioning is to focus on the quality or value offered by the brand at a very competitive price. For example, the Oneida ad shown in Exhibit 2–12 uses this strategy by suggesting that quality need not be unaffordable. Remember that although price is an important consideration, the product quality must be comparable to, or even better than, competing brands for the positioning strategy to be effective.

Exhibit 2–11 Positioning that focuses on the competition

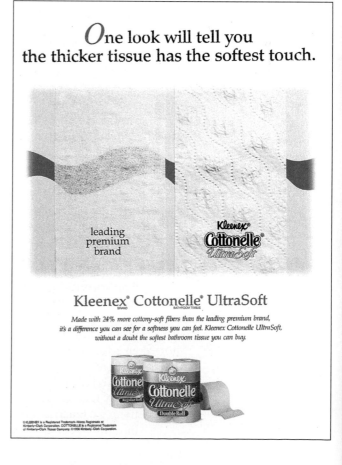

*O*ne look will tell you the thicker tissue has the softest touch.

leading premium brand

Kleenex® **Cottonelle®** *UltraSoft*

Kleenex® Cottonelle® UltraSoft

Made with 24% more cottony-soft fibers than the leading premium brand, it's a difference you can see for a softness you can feel. Kleenex Cottonelle UltraSoft, without a doubt the softest bathroom tissue you can buy.

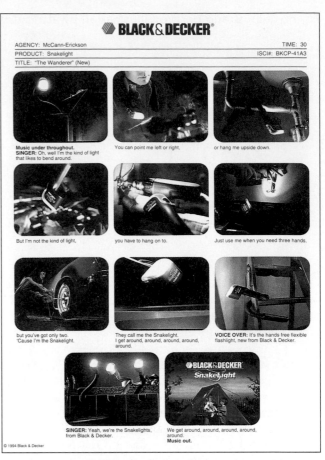

For those who thought they couldn't afford exquisite stainless on a shoestring.

ONEIDA

Shown: Anticipation in stainless.

BLACK & DECKER®

AGENCY: McCann-Erickson TIME: 30
PRODUCT: Snakelight ISCI#: BKCP-41A3
TITLE: "The Wanderer" (New)

Music under throughout.
SINGER: Oh, well I'm the kind of light that likes to bend around.

You can point me left or right,

or hang me upside down.

But I'm not the kind of light,

you have to hang on to.

Just use me when you need three hands,

but you've got only two. 'Cause I'm the Snakelight.

They call me the Snakelight. I get around, around, around, around, around.

VOICE OVER: It's the hands free flexible flashlight, new from Black & Decker.

SINGER: Yeah, we're the Snakelights, from Black & Decker.

We get around, around, around, around, around. Music out.

Exhibit 2–12 Oneida positions its brand as having high quality for the right price

Exhibit 2–13 Black & Decker shows the various uses of the SnakeLight

Positioning by Use or Application Another way to communicate a specific image or position for a brand is to associate it with a specific use or application. For example, Black & Decker introduced the SnakeLight as an innovative solution to the problem of trying to hold a flashlight while working. A TV commercial showed various uses for the product, while creative packaging and in-store displays were used to communicate the uses (Exhibit 2–13).

While this strategy is often used to enter a market based on a particular use or application, it is also an effective way to expand the usage of a product. For example, Arm & Hammer baking soda has been promoted for everything from baking to relieving heartburn to eliminating odors in carpets and refrigerators.

Positioning by Product User Positioning a product by associating it with a particular user or group of users is yet another approach. An example would be the Valvoline ad shown in Exhibit 2–14. This campaign emphasizes identification or association with a specific group, in this case, car hobbyists.

Positioning by Competitor Competitors may be as important to positioning strategy as a firm's own product or services. As Trout and Ries observe, the old strategy of ignoring one's competition no longer works.[19] (Advertisers used to think it was a cardinal sin to mention a competitor in their advertising.) In today's market, an effective positioning strategy for a product or brand may focus on specific competitors. Perhaps the best-known example of this strategy was Avis, which positioned itself against the car-rental leader, Hertz, by stating, "We're number two, so we try harder." The Kleenex ad shown earlier (Exhibit 2–11) is an example of positioning a brand against the competition. When positioning by competitor, a marketer must often employ another positioning strategy as well to differentiate the brand.

Repositioning   This positioning strategy involves altering or changing a product's or brand's position. **Repositioning** a product usually occurs because of declining or stagnant sales or because of anticipated opportunities in other market positions. Repositioning is often difficult to accomplish because of entrenched perceptions about and attitudes toward the product or brand. Many companies' attempts to change their positions have met with little or no success.

One extremely successful effort at repositioning was employed by *Rolling Stone* magazine. In an attempt to change advertisers' image of the type of person who reads *Rolling Stone*, the company embarked on an extensive advertising campaign directed at potential advertisers. The ad shown in Exhibit 2–15 is just one example of how this strategy was successfully implemented.

IMC Perspective 2–2 on page 37 describes how other companies have also been successful in their repositioning efforts.

Positioning by Product Class   Often the competition for a product comes from outside the product class. For example, airlines know that while they compete with other airlines, trains and buses are also viable alternatives. Amtrak has positioned itself as an alternative to airplanes, citing cost savings, enjoyment, and other advantages. Many margarines position themselves against butter. Rather than positioning against another brand, an alternative strategy is to position oneself against another product category, as shown in Exhibit 2–16.

Brand Positioning Strategy Process   Having explored the alternative brand positioning strategies available, the marketer must determine which strategy is best suited for the brand. Essentially, the development of a brand positioning strategy can be broken into a six-step process:[20]

1. *Identify competitors.*   The marketer must consider all likely competitors, as well as the various effects of use and situations on the consumer.

2. *Assess consumers' perceptions of competitors.*   Once we define the competition, we must determine how they are perceived by consumers. Which attributes are important to consumers in evaluating a product and/or brand? As you might expect, for many products, they consider a wide variety of attributes or product benefits—most if not all of which are important. Often, consumers are asked to take part in focus groups and/or complete surveys indicating which attributes are important in their purchase decisions.

3. *Determine competitors' positions.* After identifying the relevant attributes and their relative importance to consumers, we must determine how each competitor (including our own entry) is positioned with respect to each attribute. This will also show how the competitors are positioned relative to each other. Consumer research is required to make this assessment.

Some people have shrinks.
Some people have their garage.

Guys, take a road trip at www.valvoline.com.   **You can always tell the guys who use Valvoline.**

Exhibit 2–14   Valvoline positions by product user

Exhibit 2–15   This ad is one of a series used in the campaign to reposition *Rolling Stone* magazine

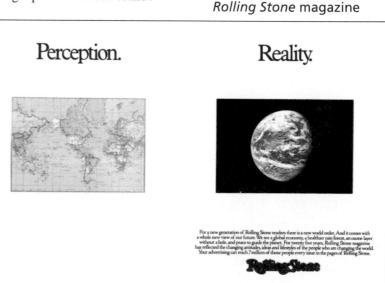

Perception.   Reality.

For a new generation of Rolling Stone readers there is a new world order. And it comes with a whole new view of our future. We see a global economy, a healthier rain forest, an ozone layer without a hole, and peace to guide the planet. For twenty-five years, Rolling Stone magazine has reflected the changing attitudes, ideas and lifestyles of the people who are changing the world. Your advertising can reach 7 million of those people every issue in the pages of Rolling Stone.

Rolling Stone

Surprise! A cup of yogurt
has more potassium than a banana.

One 8 oz. cup of non-fat yogurt has more potassium than a banana, along with
half your daily calcium requirement and many other essential nutrients.* So drink your
milk. Have some yogurt. Enjoy the natural goodness of dairy foods – for life. 🔵

Dairy Foods, Good For Life.

Exhibit 2–16 An example of positioning by product class

4. *Analyze the consumers' preferences.* Our discussion of segmentation noted various factors that may distinguish among groups of consumers, including lifestyles, purchase motivations, and demographic differences. Each of these segments may have different purchase motivations and different attribute importance ratings. One way to determine these differences is to consider the *ideal brand* or *product,* defined as the object the consumer would prefer over all others, including objects that can be imagined but do not exist.

5. *Make the brand positioning strategy decision.* Going through the first four steps should let us decide which position to assume in the marketplace. Such a decision is not always clear and well defined, however, and research may provide only limited input. In that case, the marketing manager or groups of managers must make some subjective judgments. These judgments raise a number of questions:

- *Is the segmentation approach appropriate?* Positioning entails a decision to segment the market. At this point, managers would re-evaluate or reconsider the previous segmentation decision.
- *Are there sufficient resources available to communicate the brand positioning strategy effectively?* It is very expensive to establish a position. One ad, or even a series of ads, is not likely to be enough. The marketer must commit to a long-range effort in all aspects of the marketing campaign to make sure the objectives sought are obtained. Too often, the firm abandons a position and/or advertising campaign long before it can establish a position successfully. Further, once a successful position is attained, it is likely to attract competitors. It may become expensive to ward off me-too brands and continue to hold on to the brand distinction.
- *How strong is the competition?* The marketing manager must ask whether a position sought is likely to be maintained, given the strengths of the competition.
- *Is the current brand positioning strategy working?* If current efforts are not working, it may be time to consider an alternative brand positioning strategy. But if they are working, a change is usually unwise. Sometimes executives become bored with a theme and decide it is time for a change, but this change causes confusion in the marketplace and weakens a brand's position.

6. *Monitor the position.* Once a brand position has been established, we want to monitor how well it is being maintained in the marketplace. Tracking studies measure the image of the product or firm over time. Changes in consumers' perceptions can be determined, with any slippage immediately noted and reacted to. At the same time, the impact of competitors can be determined.

Summary

Promotion plays an important role in an organization's efforts to market its product, service, or ideas to its customers. Figure 2–1 shows a model for analyzing how promotions fit into a company's marketing program. The model includes market analysis, target market process, program development, and the target market. The marketing process begins with a marketing strategy that is based on a detailed situation analysis and guides for target market selection and development of the firm's marketing program.

In the planning process, the situation analysis requires that the marketing strategy be assumed. The promotional program is developed with this strategy as a guide. One of the key decisions to be made pertains to the target market process, where we segment the market, select a target market, and determine the market positioning strategy.

Once the target market process has been completed, marketing program decisions regarding product, price, distribution, and promotions must be made. All of these must be coordinated to provide an integrated marketing communications perspective, in which the market positioning strategy is supported by one voice. Thus all product strategies, pricing strategies, and distribution choices must be made with the objective of contributing to the overall image of the product or brand. Advertising and promotion decisions, in turn, must be integrated with the other marketing mix decisions to accomplish this goal.

Key Terms

strategic marketing
  plan, 31
market opportunities, 31
competitive
  advantage, 32
target market process, 32
market segmentation, 34
geographic
  segmentation, 36
demographic
  segmentation, 36

psychographic
  segmentation, 36
behaviouristic
  segmentation, 37
80–20 rule, 38
benefit segmentation,
  38
undifferentiated
  marketing, 39
differentiated
  marketing, 39

concentrated
  marketing, 39
market positioning
  strategy, 39
product symbolism, 41
brand equity, 42
marketing channels, 44
resellers, 44
promotional push
  strategy, 45
trade advertising, 45

promotional pull
  strategy, 45
positioning, 46
brand positioning
  strategy, 46
brand position, 46
salient attributes, 47
repositioning, 49

Discussion Questions

1. Some marketers contend that demographics is not really a basis for segmentation, but a descriptor of the segment. Discuss examples to support both positions.

2. Establishing brand image is often difficult for new companies. Explain what these companies must do to establish a strong brand image.

3. More and more business-to-business companies have gone away from purely trade advertising to advertising on consumer media. Is this likely to be a successful strategy? Why or why not?

4. A number of approaches to segmentation have been cited in the text. Provide examples of companies and/or brands that employ each.

5. Discuss the concept of competitive advantage. Pick three brands or products and discuss the specific competitive advantage that each stresses.

6. Describe how the market positioning strategy adopted for a brand would need to be supported by all other elements of the marketing mix.

7. Discuss the target market process. Why is it so important to marketers?

8. What is meant by brand positioning strategy? Discuss the various approaches and give examples of companies or brands that use each approach.

9. What factors would lead a marketer to the use of a repositioning strategy? Find a product or service that has been repositioned recently and analyze the strategy.

Chapter Three

Consumer Behaviour Models

Chapter Objectives

- To understand the role consumer behaviour plays in the development and implementation of advertising and promotional programs.

- To understand the consumer decision-making process and how it varies for different types of purchases.

- To understand various internal psychological processes, their influence on consumer decision making, and implications for advertising and promotion.

- To recognize external factors such as culture, social class, group influences, and situational determinants and how they affect consumer behaviour.

Communicating to Kids

Communicating to kids is a fascinating part of some marketer's lives. There are 5.8 million Canadian children 14 years and under, according to Statistics Canada. And while it can be expected that many of these children "act their age," there is a growing trend of some kids getting older at a younger age. Some children are physically maturing at an earlier age, some pre-teens exhibit teenage-like behaviour, others have increased responsibility in their lives, and it seems all of them have increased disposable income. Consequently, children enter product categories at an earlier age than previously thought possible (i.e., cellphones), explore digital media, participate in complex purchase decisions, or make purchase decisions for their parents.

With increased involvement, marketers are using some interesting approaches to understand the consumer behaviour of children. Many marketers are using more direct and interactive marketing research techniques that have led to innovating communication practices. Levi's combined with MuchMusic on a contest micro website where consumers can make their own version of a song that is featured in TV ads. To follow up on the theme in an integrated manner, representatives organize spontaneous karaoke sessions and give participants free merchandise. Kellogg went a step further in 2000 and actually made the target audience the brand's managers, who had a say in how the brand would be communicated (i.e., ad, packaging) and other marketing decisions such as the product's colour. Examples of IMC tools that cosmetic firms use to reach teenage girls include samples, sponsorship, advertising with key spokespersons, websites with exclusive passwords, and interactive contests.

As marketers respond to this evolving consumer behaviour, the guidelines for communicating to children may be put to the test. Canada is a world leader in developing standards, policies, and educational initiatives for responsible advertising to children. In the 1970s, Canadian advertisers and broadcasters instituted the Broadcast Code for Advertising to Children, which ensured that all advertising directed to children would take into account the special needs and vulnerabilities of children. The Concerned Children's Advertisers is a non-profit association of Canadian companies and various partners who work together to deliver advertising messages and other communication devices to support children in their understanding of themselves and the role of media in their lives. Combined, these Canadian efforts are the envy of the rest of the world and many countries would like to see the Canadian standards become institutionalized globally.

Sources: Beth Hitchcock, "Thank Heaven for Little Girls," *Marketing Magazine*, January 1/8, 2001; Sunni Boot, "The Lolita Syndrome," *Marketing Magazine*, January 1/8, 2001; Cathy Loblaw, "The Whole World Is Watching," *Marketing Magazine*, August 6, 2001; Marlene Milczarek, "Voices Carry," *Marketing Magazine*, August 6, 2001.

The examples described above reveal that the development of effective marketing communication programs begins with understanding why consumers behave as they do. The motives for purchasing, attitudes, and lifestyles need to be understood before effective promotion strategies can be formulated. These are just a few of the aspects of consumer behaviour that promotional planners must consider in developing integrated marketing communication programs. As you will see, consumer choice is influenced by a variety of factors.

It is beyond the scope of this text to examine consumer behaviour in depth. However, promotional planners need a basic understanding of consumer decision making, factors that influence it, and how this knowledge can be used in developing promotional strategies and programs. We begin with an overview of consumer behaviour.

An Overview of Consumer Behaviour

A challenge faced by all marketers is how to influence the purchase behaviour of consumers in favour of the product or service they offer. For companies like American Express, this means getting consumers to charge more purchases on their AmEx cards. For BMW, it means getting them to purchase or lease a car; for business-to-business marketers like Canon or Ricoh, it means getting organizational buyers to purchase more of their copiers or fax machines. While their ultimate goal is to influence consumers' purchase behaviour, most marketers understand that the actual purchase is only part of an overall process.

Consumer behaviour can be defined as the process and activities people engage in when searching for, selecting, purchasing, using, evaluating, and disposing of products and services so as to satisfy their needs and desires. For many products and services, purchase decisions are the result of a long, detailed process that may include an extensive information search, brand comparisons and evaluations, and other activities. Other purchase decisions are more incidental and may result from little more than seeing a product prominently displayed at a discount price in a store. Think of how many times you have made impulse purchases in stores.

Marketers' success in influencing purchase behaviour depends in large part on how well they understand consumer behaviour. Marketers need to know the specific needs customers are attempting to satisfy and how they translate into purchase criteria. They need to understand how consumers gather information regarding various alternatives and use this information to select among competing brands. They need to understand how customers make purchase decisions. Where do they prefer to buy a product? How are they influenced by marketing stimuli at the point of purchase? Marketers also need to understand how the consumer decision process and reasons for purchase vary among different types of customers. For example, purchase decisions may be influenced by the personality or lifestyle of the consumer.[1] Notice how the ad shown in Exhibit 3–1 reflects the various roles in the life of the target audience member.

The conceptual model in Figure 3–1 will be used as a framework for analyzing the consumer decision process. We will discuss what occurs at the various stages of this model and how advertis-

Exhibit 3–1   New Balance appeals to the active lifestyle

Monday: Father. Husband. Banker. Friend. Runner.

Tuesday: Husband. Banker. Father. Runner. Friend.

Wednesday: Banker. Banker. Banker. Banker. Banker.

Thursday: Runner. Husband. Father. Friend. Banker.

Friday: ?

Achieve New Balance.

new balance

The M825, our newest and most advanced men's running shoe. For a dealer call 1-800-253-SHOE or visit http://www.newbalance.com

Figure 3–1   A basic model of consumer decision making

A. Stages in the Consumer Decision-Making Process

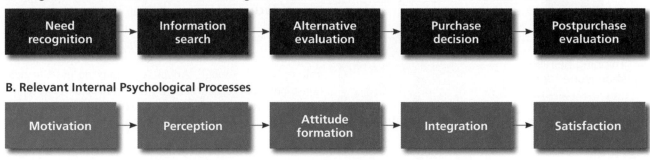

B. Relevant Internal Psychological Processes

ing and promotion can be used to influence decision making. We will also examine the influence of various psychological concepts, such as motivation, perception, attitudes, integration processes, and satisfaction. The five-stage decision process model of Figure 3–1 views the consumer as a problem solver and information processor who engages in a variety of mental processes to evaluate various alternatives and determine the degree to which they might satisfy needs or purchase motives. This model is a form of cognitive learning. Consumer learning has been defined as "the process by which individuals acquire the purchase and consumption knowledge and experience they apply to future related behaviour."[2] There are other perspectives regarding how consumers acquire the knowledge and experience they use in making purchase decisions. However, this model is the most widely accepted and managerially useful. Variations in the consumer decision-making process and environmental influences on the decision-making process will be explored.

As shown in Figure 3–1, the consumer's purchase decision process is generally viewed as consisting of stages through which the buyer passes in purchasing a product or service. This model shows that decision making involves a number of internal psychological processes. Motivation, perception, attitude formation, integration, and satisfaction are important to promotional planners, since they influence the general decision-making process of the consumer. We will examine each stage of the purchase decision model and discuss how the various subprocesses influence what occurs at this phase of the consumer behaviour process. We will also discuss how promotional planners can influence this process.

The Consumer Decision-Making Process

Need Recognition

Figure 3–1 shows that the first stage in the consumer decision-making process is **need recognition**, which occurs when the consumer perceives a need and becomes motivated to enter a decision-making process to resolve the felt need.

Need recognition is caused by a difference between the consumer's *ideal state* and *actual state*. A discrepancy exists between what the consumer wants the situation to be like and what the situation is really like. A goal exists for the consumer, and this goal may be the attainment of a more positive situation from a neutral state. Or, the goal could be a shift from a negative situation, and the consumer wishes to be at a neutral state.

Sources of Need Recognition   The causes of need recognition may be very simple or very complex and may result from changes in the consumer's current and/or desired state. These causes may be influenced by both internal and external factors.

Out of Stock   Need recognition occurs when consumers use their existing supply of a product and must replenish their stock. The purchase decision is usually simple

Exhibit 3–2 Rogaine helps women recognize hair loss problems

Exhibit 3–3 This ad for Baby Orajel shows that baby teeth have special needs

and routine and is often resolved by choosing a familiar brand or one to which the consumer feels loyal.

Dissatisfaction Need recognition is created by the consumer's dissatisfaction with the current state of affairs and/or the product or service being used. For example, a consumer may think her ski boots are no longer comfortable or stylish enough. Advertising may be used to help consumers recognize when they have a need to make a purchase. The Rogaine ad shown in Exhibit 3–2 helps women realize that hair thinning is not just a man's problem.

New Needs/Wants Changes in consumers' lives often result in new needs and wants. For example, changes in one's financial situation, employment status, or lifestyle may create new needs. As you will see, when you graduate from college and begin your professional career, your new job may necessitate a change in your wardrobe. (Good-bye blue jeans and T-shirts, hello suits and ties.)

Not all product purchases are based on needs. Some products or services sought by consumers are not essential but are nonetheless desired. A **want** has been defined as a felt need that is shaped by a person's knowledge, culture, and personality.[3] Many products sold to consumers satisfy their wants rather than their basic needs.

Related Products/Purchases Need recognition can also be stimulated by the purchase of a product. For example, the purchase of a new camera may lead to the recognition of a need for accessories, such as additional lenses or a carrying case. The purchase of a personal computer may prompt the need for software programs or upgrades.

Marketer-Induced Need Recognition Another source of need recognition is marketers' actions that encourage consumers not to be content with their current state or situation. Ads for personal hygiene products such as mouthwash, deodorant, and foot sprays may be designed to create insecurities that consumers can resolve through the use of these products. Marketers change fashions and clothing designs and create perceptions among consumers that their wardrobes are out of style. The Orajel ad in Exhibit 3–3 demonstrates the special needs of children's baby teeth to stimulate need recognition.

Marketers also take advantage of consumers' tendency toward *novelty-seeking behaviour,* which leads them to try different brands. Consumers often try new products or brands even when they are basically satisfied with their regular brand. Marketers encourage brand switching by introducing new brands into markets that are already saturated and by using advertising and sales promotion techniques such as free samples, introductory price offers, and coupons.

New Products Need recognition can also occur when innovative products are introduced. For example, the Ericsson ad shown in Exhibit 3–4 introduces a new mobile phone that allows the businessperson to have a virtually wireless office. Marketers' attempts to create need recognition among consumers are not always successful. Consumers may not see a need for the product the marketer is selling. A main reason many consumers were initially reluctant to purchase personal computers was that they failed to see how it fulfilled their needs. One way PC manufacturers successfully activated need recognition was by stressing how a computer helps children improve their academic skills and do better in school.

Examining Consumer Motivations

Marketers recognize that while need recognition is often a basic, simple process, the way a consumer perceives a purchase situation and becomes motivated to resolve it will influence the remainder of the decision process. For example, one consumer may perceive the need to purchase a new watch from a functional perspective and focus on reliable, low-priced alternatives. Another consumer may see the purchase of a watch as more of a fashion statement and focus on the design and image of various brands. To better understand the reasons underlying consumer purchases, marketers devote considerable attention to examining **motives**—that is, those factors that compel a consumer to take a particular action.

Hierarchy of Needs   One of the most popular approaches to understanding consumer motivations is based on the classic theory of human motivation popularized many years ago by psychologist Abraham Maslow.[4] His **hierarchy of needs** theory postulates five basic levels of human needs, arranged in a hierarchy based on their importance. As shown in Figure 3–2, the five needs are (1) *physiological*—the basic level of primary needs for things required to sustain life, such as food, shelter, clothing, and sex; (2) *safety*—the need for security and safety from physical harm; (3) *social/love and belonging*—the desire to have satisfying relationships with others and feel a sense of love, affection, belonging, and acceptance; (4) *esteem*—the need to feel a sense of accomplishment and gain recognition, status, and respect from others; and (5) *self-actualization*—the need for self-fulfillment and a desire to realize one's own potential.

According to Maslow's theory, the lower-level physiological and safety needs must be satisfied before the higher-order needs become meaningful. Once these

Exhibit 3–4   Ericsson introduces the wireless office

Figure 3–2   Maslow's hierarchy of needs

Self-actualization needs
(self-development and realization)

Esteem needs
(self-esteem, recognition, status)

Social needs
(sense of belonging, love)

Safety needs
(security, protection)

Physiological needs
(hunger, thirst)

Some things can be rough.

Her wipe shouldn't be one of them.
Do you think your wipe is gentle enough? Pampers is.
You can count on Pampers wipes to always be feathery soft.

Pamper the skin they're in.

Exhibit 3–5 Pampers appeals to needs for love and belonging in this ad

basic needs are satisfied, the individual moves on to attempting to satisfy higher-order needs such as self-esteem. In reality, it is unlikely that people move through the needs hierarchy in a stairstep manner. Lower-level needs are an ongoing source of motivation for consumer purchase behaviour. However, since basic physiological needs are met in most developed countries, marketers often sell products that fill basic physiological needs by appealing to consumers' higher-level needs. For example, in marketing its wipes, Pampers focuses on the love between parent and child (social needs) in addition to the gentleness of the product (Exhibit 3–5).

While Maslow's need hierarchy has flaws, it offers a framework for marketers to use in determining what needs they want their products and services to be shown satisfying. Advertising campaigns can then be designed to show how a brand can fulfill these needs. Marketers also recognize that different market segments emphasize different need levels. For example, a young single person may be attempting to satisfy social or self-esteem needs in purchasing a car, while a family with children will focus more on safety needs. Toyota used ads like the one in Exhibit 3–6 to position its cars as meeting the safety needs of consumers with children.

Motivation Research in Marketing Motivation researchers use a variety of qualitative methodologies to gain insight into the underlying causes of consumer behaviour. Methods employed include in-depth interviews, projective techniques, association tests, and focus groups in which consumers are encouraged to bring out associations related to products and brands (see Figure 3–3). As one might expect, such associations often lead to interesting insights as to why people purchase. For example:

- Consumers prefer large cars because they believe such cars protect them from the "jungle" of everyday driving.[5]
- A man buys a convertible as a substitute mistress.
- Women like to bake cakes because they feel like they are giving birth to a baby.
- Women wear perfume to "attract a man" and "glorify their existence."
- Men like frankfurters better than women do because cooking them (frankfurters, not men!) makes women feel guilty. It's an admission of laziness.
- When people shower, their sins go down the drain with the soap as they rinse.[6]

As you can see from these examples, motivation research has led to some very interesting, albeit controversial, findings and to much skepticism from marketing managers. Major corporations and advertising agencies continue to use motivation research to help them market their products. However, since motivation research studies typically use so few participants, there is also concern that it really discovers the idiosyncracies of a few individuals and its findings are not generalizable to the whole population. Still, it is difficult to ignore the motivation research in furthering our understanding of consumer behaviour. Its insights can often be used as a basis for advertising messages aimed at buyers' deeply rooted feelings, hopes, aspirations, and

Exhibit 3–6 Toyota uses an appeal to safety needs

IF IT WEREN'T FOR THE SAFETY RATING, YOU MIGHT NOT LET YOUR KIDS IN IT AT ALL.

SIENNA

Insurance Institute for Highway Safety "Best Pick."* A ★★★★★ rating in government crash tests.** And an immaculate, sumptuous, leather-trimmed interior! (For the first five minutes you own it, anyway.)
www.toyota.com ◆ 1·800·go·toyota ©1999 Toyota Motor Sales, U.S.A., Inc. Buckle Up! Do it for those who love you.

TOYOTA what matters. every day.

*Sienna test date: December 17, 1997. Vehicles evaluated to date, 122. (48-mph 40% frontal offset crash test.)
**NHTSA 2000 five-star ratings: Driver and passenger frontal crash tests. °Available on XLE model.

In-depth interviews
Face-to-face situations in which an interviewer asks a consumer to talk freely in an unstructured interview using specific questions designed to obtain insights into his or her motives, ideas, or opinions.

Projective techniques
Efforts designed to gain insights into consumers' values, motives, attitudes, or needs that are difficult to express or identify by having them project these internal states upon some external object.

Association tests
A technique in which an individual is asked to respond with the first thing that comes to mind when he or she is presented with a stimulus; the stimulus may be a word, picture, ad, and so on.

Focus groups
A small number of people with similar backgrounds and/or interests who are brought together to discuss a particular product, idea, or issue.

Figure 3–3 Some of the marketing research methods employed to probe the mind of the consumer

fears. Such strategies are often more effective than rationally based appeals. Examples include the following:[7]

- Chrysler had consumers sit on the floor, like children, and use scissors to cut words out of magazines to describe a car.[8]
- McCann-Erickson asked women to draw and describe how they felt about roaches. The agency concluded that many women associated roaches with men who had abandoned them and that this was why women preferred roach killers that let them see the roaches die.
- Saatchi & Saatchi used psychological probes to conclude that Ronald McDonald created a more nurturing mood than did the Burger King (who was perceived as more aggressive and distant).
- Foote, Cone & Belding gave consumers stacks of photographs of faces and asked them to associate the faces with the kinds of people who might use particular products.

While often criticized, motivation research has also contributed to the marketing discipline. The qualitative nature of the research is considered important in assessing how and why consumers buy. Focus groups and in-depth interviews are valuable methods for gaining insights into consumers' feelings, and projective techniques are often the only way to get around stereotypical or socially desirable responses. In addition, motivation research is the forerunner of psychographics (discussed in Chapter 2).

Information Search

The second stage in the consumer decision-making process is *information search.* Once consumers perceive a need that can be satisfied by the purchase of a product or service, they begin to search for information needed to make a purchase decision. The initial search effort often consists of an attempt to scan information stored in memory to recall past experiences and/or knowledge regarding various purchase alternatives.[9] This information retrieval is referred to as **internal search.** For many routine, repetitive purchases, previously acquired information that is stored in memory (such as past performance or outcomes from using a brand) is sufficient for comparing alternatives and making a choice.

If the internal search does not yield enough information, the consumer will seek additional information by engaging in **external search.** External sources of information include:

- *Personal sources,* such as friends, relatives, or co-workers.
- *Marketer-controlled (commercial) sources,* such as information from advertising, salespeople, or point-of-purchase displays and the Internet.
- *Public sources,* including articles in magazines or newspapers and reports on TV.
- *Personal experience,* such as actually handling, examining, or testing the product.

Determining how much and which sources of external information to use involves several factors, including the importance of the purchase decision, the effort needed to acquire information, the amount of past experience relevant, the degree of perceived risk associated with the purchase, and the time available. For example, the selection of a movie to see on a Friday night might entail simply talking to a friend or checking the movie guide in the daily newspaper. A more complex purchase such as a new car might use a number of information sources—perhaps a review of *Road & Track, Motor Trend,* or *Consumer Reports;* discussion with family members and friends; and test-driving of cars. At this point in the purchase decision, the information-providing aspects of advertising are extremely important.

Perception

Knowledge of how consumers acquire and use information from external sources is important to marketers in formulating communication strategies. Marketers are particularly interested in (1) how consumers sense external information, (2) how they attend to various sources of information, (3) how this information is interpreted and given meaning and (4) how the information is retained. These four processes are all part of **perception**, the process by which an individual receives, attends to, interprets, and stores information to create a meaningful picture of the world.[10] Perception is an individual process; it depends on internal factors such as a person's beliefs, experiences, needs, moods, and expectations. The perceptual process is also influenced by the characteristics of a stimulus (such as its size, colour, and intensity) and the context in which it is seen or heard. Selectivity occurs throughout the four stages of the consumer's perceptual process. Perception may be viewed as a filtering process in which internal and external factors influence what is received and how it is processed and interpreted. The sheer number and complexity of the marketing stimuli a person is exposed to in any given day require that this filtering occur. **Selective perception** may occur within all four stages of the perceptual process, as shown in Figure 3–4.

Sensation **Sensation** is the immediate, direct response of the senses (taste, smell, sight, touch, and hearing) to a stimulus such as an ad, package, brand name, or point-of-purchase display. Perception uses these senses to create a representation of the stimulus. Marketers recognize that it is important to understand consumers' physiological reactions to marketing stimuli. For example, the visual elements of an ad or package design must be designed so that consumers sense their existence. This is one reason why many TV ads start with a particular sound effect or noise.

Figure 3–4   The selective perception process

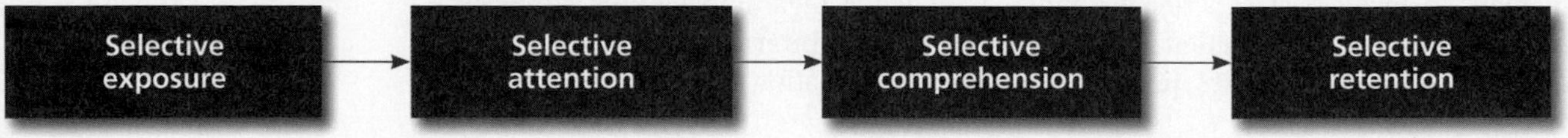

| Selective exposure | → | Selective attention | → | Selective comprehension | → | Selective retention |

Marketers sometimes try to increase the level of sensory input so that their advertising messages will get noticed. For example, marketers of colognes and perfumes often use strong visuals as well as scent strips to appeal to multiple senses and attract the attention of magazine readers. Some advertisers have even inserted microcomputer chips into their print ads to play a song or deliver a message. **Selective exposure** occurs as consumers choose whether or not to make themselves available to information. For example, a viewer of a television show may change channels or leave the room during commercial breaks.

Selecting Information   Sensory inputs are important but are only one part of the perceptual process. Other determinants of whether marketing stimuli will be attended to and how they will be interpreted include internal psychological factors such as the consumer's personality, needs, motives, expectations, and experiences. These psychological inputs explain why people focus attention on some things and ignore others. Two people may perceive the same stimuli in very different ways because they select and attend to messages differently. An individual's perceptual processes usually focus on elements of the environment that are relevant to his or her needs and tune out irrelevant stimuli. Think about how much more attentive you are to advertising for personal computers, tires, or stereos when you are in the market for one of these products. **Selective attention** occurs when the consumer chooses to focus attention on certain stimuli while excluding others. One study of selective attention estimates the typical consumer is exposed to nearly 1,500 ads per day yet perceives only 76 of these messages.[11] Other estimates range as high as 3,000 exposures per day. This means advertisers must make considerable effort to get their messages noticed. Advertisers often use the creative aspects of their ads to gain consumers' attention. For example, some advertisers set their ads off from others by showing their products in colour against a black-and-white background (Exhibit 3–7). This creative tactic has been used in advertising for many products, among them Cherry 7 UP, Nuprin, and Pepto-Bismol.[12]

Interpreting the Information   Once a consumer selects and attends to a stimulus, the perceptual process focuses on organizing, categorizing, and interpreting the incoming information. This stage of the perceptual process is very individualized and is influenced by internal psychological factors. The interpretation and meaning an individual assigns to an incoming stimulus also depend in part on the nature of the stimulus. For example, many ads are objective, and their message is clear and straightforward. Other ads are more ambiguous, and their meaning is strongly influenced by the consumer's individual interpretation.

Even if the consumer does notice the advertiser's message, there is no guarantee it will be interpreted in the intended manner. Consumers may engage in **selective comprehension**, interpreting information on the basis of their own attitudes, beliefs, motives, and experiences. They often interpret information in a manner that supports their own position. For example, an ad that disparages a consumer's favourite brand may be seen as biased or untruthful, and its claims may not be accepted.

Retaining the Information   The final stage of the perceptual process involves the storage of the information in short-term or long-term memory. Consumers may make mental notes or focus on some aspect of an advertising message to ensure that they will not forget, thus permitting easy retrieval during the information search stage. **Selective retention** means consumers do not remember all the information they see, hear, or read even after attending to and comprehending it. Advertisers attempt to make sure information will be retained in the consumer's memory so that it will be available when it is time to make a purchase. **Mnemonics** such as symbols, rhymes, associations, and images that assist in the learning and memory process are helpful. Many advertisers use telephone numbers that spell out the company name and are easy to remember. Eveready put pictures of its pink

Exhibit 3–7   Tropicana attempts to create attention with this ad

bunny on packages to remind consumers at the point of purchase of its creative advertising.

Subliminal Perception

Advertisers know consumers use selective perception to filter out irrelevant or unwanted advertising messages, so they employ various creative tactics to get their messages noticed. One controversial tactic advertisers have been accused of using is appealing to consumers' subconscious. **Subliminal perception** refers to the ability to perceive a stimulus that is below the level of consciousness. Psychologists generally agree it is possible to perceive something without any knowledge of having seen it. The possibility of using hidden persuaders such as subliminal audio messages or visual cues to influence consumers might be intriguing to advertisers but would not be welcomed by consumers. The idea of marketers influencing consumers at a subconscious level has strong ethical implications. The use of subliminal techniques is *not* a creative tactic we would recommend to advertisers.

Alternative Evaluation

After acquiring information during the information search stage of the decision process, the consumer moves to alternative evaluation. In this stage, the consumer compares the various brands or products and services he or she has identified as being capable of solving the consumption problem and satisfying the needs or motives that initiated the decision process. The various brands identified as purchase options to be considered during the alternative evaluation process are referred to as the consumer's *evoked set*.

The Evoked Set

The evoked set is generally only a subset of all the brands of which the consumer is aware. The consumer reduces the number of brands to be reviewed during the alternative evaluation stage to a manageable level. The exact size of the evoked set varies from one consumer to another and depends on such factors as the importance of the purchase and the amount of time and energy the consumer wants to spend comparing alternatives.

The goal of most advertising and promotional strategies is to increase the likelihood that a brand will be included in the consumer's evoked set and considered during alternative evaluation. Marketers use advertising to create *top-of-mind awareness* among consumers so that their brands are part of the evoked set of their target audiences. Popular brands with large advertising budgets use *reminder advertising* to maintain high awareness levels and increase the likelihood they will be considered by consumers in the market for the product. Marketers of new brands or those with a low market share need to gain awareness among consumers and break into their evoked sets. Advertising is a valuable promotional tool for making sure a brand is included in the evoked set. However, marketers also work to promote their brands in the actual environment where purchase decisions are made. Point-of-purchase materials and promotional techniques such as in-store sampling, end-aisle displays, or shelf tags touting special prices encourage consumers to consider brands that may not have initially been in their evoked set.

Evaluative Criteria and Consequences

Once consumers have identified an evoked set and have a list of alternatives, they must evaluate the various brands. This involves comparing the choice alternatives on specific criteria important to the consumer. **Evaluative criteria** are the dimensions or attributes of a product or service that are used to compare different alternatives. Evaluative criteria can be objective or subjective. For example, in buying an automobile, consumers use objective attributes such as price, warranty, and fuel economy as well as subjective factors such as image, styling, and performance.

Evaluative criteria are usually viewed as product or service attributes. Many marketers view their products or services as *bundles of attributes,* but consumers tend to think about products or services in terms of their *consequences* instead. J. Paul

Marketing Overseas? Keep It Canadian

If you're a homegrown Canadian corporation with a yen to expand to Japan, you might find that marketing overseas is easier then it's ever been. Sure you still need to hire local distributors and marketers with a feel for the local landscape, but when it comes to your overall positioning, branding, and even the ethnicity of your models, why translate when your Canadian-ness could add cachet?

Shin Kawai, president of Japan Communications, started his Toronto translating and consulting firm in 1984 in response to Canadian businesses' increased interest in Japan, the second most important foreign market after the U.S. But when it comes to translating brand messages, these days he will often advise clients, "Don't bother." Exact translations of slogans rarely work, he says, and it can be difficult to create a culturally sensitive interpretation.

Often involved in Team Canada junkets, Kawai cites the Ontario government's slogan, "Let's do business," as an example. He advised officials that it was "too direct" for Japanese sensibilities. Even the German translator found it too brash for Teutonic ears, he says. The solution? Leave it in English. It is the international language of commerce after all, says Kawai, and many Japanese businessmen will accept the message better in its Western cultural context.

And while cultural sensitivity is one reason to leave it in English, culture lust may be another. The reason? Asian societies are not only more open but also actively fascinated with the Western lifestyle. For instance, the Chinese distributors of Roots Canada apparel are using Caucasian models to market to fellow Chinese. And some English branding messages (or other foreign languages) are actually preferred by the Japanese.

It would be a letdown if Britain's Johnnie Walker or France's Chanel translated their brands into Japanese script or sayings, explains Kawai. "If it's produced in England, we want to feel that tradition. If it's a famous global logo, we want to see it."

Given their history of isolation, Kawai explains, "Japan is an island always interested in new things coming from outside.

"So, if Caucasian women are modelling European couture in a Japanese fashion magazine, or a natural outdoor type is wearing Roots, it is fitting. There's a reason that product line was born in Canada. Using Canadian models really tells Japanese consumers a story and depicts a different experience."

While Western branding can work for many products, Kawai says when it comes to detail information, of course, advertising must be translated. It's a matter of affecting a balance between bulldozing a foreign land with the Western way, and microtranslating everything for every region.

"It's not an either/or proposition," says Jeannette Hanna, director of strategic communications at Spencer Francey Peters, the Toronto branding and design firm responsible for the Four Seasons Hotels and Resorts brand since 1991. Another home-grown international success story, the Four Seasons now owns 53 properties in 23 countries around the globe, including hotels in Shanghai and Tokyo.

"It's not a matter of finding a creative way to be global and local at the same time," Hanna says. "Each of the Four Seasons properties is unique, from a 13th-century monastery in Milan to New York's 57th Street. It's not like the Holiday Inn where there are no surprises. At the same time, we want to showcase what is consistent—the level of service and reputation for luxury—and we created a design platform specifically to do that."

Within what she describes as the "overarching architecture," all collateral pieces have a similar high-end look, no matter what the local culture. Inside, specifics are elegantly written in both English and the local language, amidst photos emphasizing local scenic beauty. "It's a part of philosophy to build on the strength of diversity. One size does not fit all," she says.

Source: Adapted from Sharon Younger, "Marketing Overseas? Keep It Canadian," *Strategy*, February 11, 2002, p. 23. © Brunico Communications Inc. Reprinted with permission. STRATEGY and "The Canadian Marketing Report" are trademarks of Brunico Communications Inc.

Peter and Jerry Olson define consequences as specific events or outcomes that consumers experience when they purchase and/or consume a product or service.[13] They distinguish between two broad types of consequences. **Functional consequences** are concrete outcomes of product or service usage that are tangible and directly experienced by consumers. The taste of a soft drink or a potato chip, the acceleration of a car, and the clarity of a fax transmission are examples of functional consequences. **Psychosocial consequences** are abstract outcomes that are more intangible,

Exhibit 3–8 This ad emphasizes the positive consequences of using the Top-Flite XL golf ball

subjective, and personal, such as how a product makes you feel or how you think others will view you for purchasing or using it.

Marketers should distinguish between product/service attributes and consequences, because the importance and meaning consumers assign to an attribute are usually determined by its consequences for them. Moreover, advertisers must be sure consumers understand the link between a particular attribute and a consequence. For example, the Top-Flite ad in Exhibit 3–8 focuses on the consequences of using the new Top-Flite XL golf ball, such as more distance and lower scores. Note how the highlighted scorecard is used to reinforce the point that the Top-Flite XL can help golfers achieve better scores.

Product/service attributes and the consequences or outcomes consumers think they will experience from a particular brand are very important, for they are often the basis on which consumers form attitudes and purchase intentions and decide among various choice alternatives. Two subprocesses are very important during the alternative evaluation stage: (1) the process by which consumer attitudes are created, reinforced, and changed and (2) the decision rules or integration strategies consumers use to compare brands and make purchase decisions. We will examine each of these processes in more detail.

Attitudes

Attitudes are one of the most heavily studied concepts in consumer behaviour. According to Gordon Allport's classic definition, "attitudes are learned predispositions to respond to an object."[14] More recent perspectives view attitudes as a summary construct that represents an individual's overall feelings toward or evaluation of an object.[15] Consumers hold attitudes toward a variety of objects that are important to marketers, including individuals (celebrity endorsers such as Tiger Woods or Michael Jordan), brands (Cheerios), companies (Microsoft), product categories (beef, pork, tuna), retail stores (The Bay, Sears), or even advertisements (the Energizer bunny ads).

Attitudes are important to marketers because they theoretically summarize a consumer's evaluation of an object (or brand or company) and represent positive or negative feelings and behavioural tendencies. Marketers' keen interest in attitudes is based on the assumption that they are related to consumers' purchase behaviour. Considerable evidence supports the basic assumption of a relationship between attitudes and behaviour.[16] The attitude-behaviour link does not always hold; many other factors can affect behaviour.[17] But attitudes are very important to marketers. Advertising and promotion are used to create favourable attitudes toward new products/ services or brands, reinforce existing favourable attitudes, and/or change negative attitudes. An approach to studying and measuring attitudes that is particularly relevant to advertising is multiattribute attitude models.

Multiattribute Attitude Models Consumer researchers and marketing practitioners have been using multiattribute attitude models to study consumer attitudes for two decades.[18] A **multiattribute attitude model** views an attitude object, such as a product or brand, as possessing a number of attributes that provide the basis on which consumers form their attitudes. According to this model, consumers have beliefs about specific brand attributes and attach different levels of importance to these attributes. Using this approach, an attitude toward a particular brand can be represented as

$$A_B = \sum_{i=1}^{n} B_i \times E_i$$

where
A_B = attitude toward a brand
B_i = beliefs about the brand's performance on attribute i
E_i = importance attached to attribute i
n = number of attributes considered

For example, a consumer may have beliefs (B_i) about various brands of toothpaste on certain attributes. One brand may be perceived as having fluoride and thus preventing cavities, tasting good, and helping control tartar buildup. Another brand may not be perceived as having these attributes, but consumers may believe it performs well on other attributes such as freshening breath and whitening teeth.

To predict attitudes, one must know how much importance consumers attach to each of these attributes (E_i). For example, parents purchasing toothpaste for their children may prefer a brand that performs well on cavity prevention, a preference that leads to a more favourable attitude toward the first brand. Teenagers and young adults may prefer a brand that freshens their breath and makes their teeth white and thus prefer the second brand.

Consumers may hold a number of different beliefs about brands in any product or service category. However, not all of these beliefs are activated in forming an attitude. Beliefs concerning specific attributes or consequences that are activated and form the basis of an attitude are referred to as **salient beliefs.** Marketers should identify and understand these salient beliefs. They must also recognize that the saliency of beliefs varies among different market segments, over time, and across different consumption situations.

Attitude Change Strategies

Multiattribute models help marketers understand and diagnose the underlying basis of consumers' attitudes. By understanding the beliefs that underlie consumers' evaluations of a brand and the importance of various attributes or consequences, the marketer is better able to develop communication strategies for creating, changing, or reinforcing brand attitudes. The multiattribute model provides insight into several ways marketers can influence consumer attitudes, including:

- Increasing or changing the strength or belief rating of a brand on an important attribute.
- Changing consumers' perceptions of the importance or value of an attribute.
- Adding a new attribute to the attitude formation process.
- Changing perceptions of belief ratings for a competing brand.

The first strategy is commonly used by advertisers. They identify an attribute or consequence that is important and remind consumers how well their brand performs on this attribute. In situations where consumers do not perceive the marketer's brand as possessing an important attribute or the belief strength is low, advertising strategies may be targeted at changing the belief rating. Even when belief strength is high, advertising may be used to increase the rating of a brand on an important attribute. BMW's "The Ultimate Driving Machine" campaign is a good example of a strategy designed to create a belief and reinforce it through advertising.

Marketers often attempt to influence consumer attitudes by changing the relative importance of a particular attribute. This second strategy involves getting consumers to attach more importance to the attribute in forming their attitude toward the brand. Marketers using this strategy want to increase the importance of an attribute their particular brand has.

The third strategy for influencing consumer attitudes is to add or emphasize a new attribute that consumers can use in evaluating a brand. Marketers often do this by improving their products or focusing on additional benefits or consequences associated with using the brand. Exhibit 3–9 shows how Jeep is introducing Quadra-Drive in an attempt to influence consumers' attitudes.

A final strategy marketers use is to change consumer beliefs about the attributes of competing brands or product categories. This strategy has become much more common with the increase in comparative advertising, where marketers compare their brands to competitors' on specific product attributes. An example of this is the Progresso ad

Exhibit 3–9 Jeep adds a new attribute for consumers to consider

You don't sleep with a teddy bear.

Your favorite song isn't
Twinkle Twinkle Little Star.

So why are you eating the
Condensed Chicken Noodle Soup
you ate as a kid?

Isn't it time to go to a .... better tasting soup?

[Campbell's Condensed Chicken Noodle]   [Progresso White Meat Chicken Noodle]

Progresso Chicken Noodle has bigger pieces of tender white meat chicken and rich hearty noodles in a broth that's perfectly seasoned. It's not condensed. It's satisfying, so it leaves you feeling good to go.
It's time to go Progresso

Campbell's is a registered trademark of the Campbell Soup Company
Based on a national taste test comparing Progresso and Campbell's Condensed Chicken Noodle soups.   ©1999 TPC   Visit us at: www.progressosoup.com

Exhibit 3–10 Progresso compares its products to those offered by Campbell's

shown in Exhibit 3–10, where the company compares what it has to offer to what Campbell's offers.

Purchase Decision

At some point in the buying process, the consumer must stop searching for and evaluating information about alternative brands in the evoked set and make a *purchase decision*. As an outcome of the alternative evaluation stage, the consumer may develop a **purchase intention** or predisposition to buy a certain brand. Purchase intentions are generally based on a matching of purchase motives with attributes or characteristics of brands under consideration. Their formation involves many of the personal subprocesses discussed in this chapter, including motivation, perception, and attitude formation.

A purchase decision is not the same as an actual purchase. Once a consumer chooses which brand to buy, he or she must still implement the decision and make the actual purchase. Additional decisions may be needed, such as when to buy, where to buy, and how much money to spend. Often, there is a time delay between the formation of a purchase intention or decision and the actual purchase, particularly for highly involved and complex purchases such as automobiles, personal computers, and consumer durables.

For nondurable products, which include many low-involvement items such as consumer package goods, the time between the decision and the actual purchase may be short. Before leaving home, the consumer may make a shopping list that includes specific brand names because the consumer has developed **brand loyalty**—a preference for a particular brand that results in its repeated purchase. Marketers strive to develop and maintain brand loyalty among consumers. They use reminder advertising to keep their brand names in front of consumers, maintain prominent shelf positions and displays in stores, and run periodic promotions to deter consumers from switching brands. Maintaining consumers' brand loyalty is not easy. Competitors use many techniques to encourage consumers to try their brands, among them new product introductions and free samples. Marketers must continually battle to maintain their loyal consumers while replacing those who switch brands.

Purchase decisions for nondurable, convenience items sometimes take place in the store, almost simultaneous with the purchase. Marketers must ensure that consumers have top-of-mind awareness of their brands so that they are quickly recognized and considered. These types of decisions are influenced at the actual point of purchase. Packaging, shelf displays, point-of-purchase materials, and promotional tools such as on-package coupons or premium offers can influence decisions made through constructive processes at the time of purchase.

Integration Processes

A key part of the purchase decision stage is the way consumers combine information about the characteristics of brands. **Integration processes** are the way product knowledge, meanings, and beliefs are combined to evaluate two or more alternatives.[19] Analysis of the integration process focuses on the different types of *decision rules* or strategies consumers use to decide among purchase alternatives.

Consumers often make purchase selections by using formal integration strategies or decision rules that require examination and comparison of alternatives on specific attributes. This process involves a very deliberate evaluation of the alternatives, attribute by attribute. When consumers apply such formal decision rules, marketers need to know which attributes are being considered so as to provide the information the consumers require.

Sometimes consumers make their purchase decisions using more simplified decision rules known as **heuristics.** Peter and Olson note that heuristics are easy to use and are highly adaptive to specific environmental situations (such as a retail store).[20] For familiar products that are purchased frequently, consumers may use price-based heuristics (buy the least expensive brand) or promotion-based heuristics (choose the brand for which I can get a price reduction through a coupon, rebate, or special deal).

One type of heuristic is the **affect referral decision rule,**[21] in which consumers make a selection on the basis of an overall impression or summary evaluation of the various alternatives under consideration. This decision rule suggests that consumers have affective impressions of brands stored in memory that can be accessed at the time of purchase. How many times have you gone into a store and made purchases based on your overall impressions of the brands rather than going through detailed comparisons of the alternatives' specific attributes?

Marketers selling familiar and popular brands may appeal to an affect referral rule by stressing overall affective feelings or impressions about their products. Market leaders, whose products enjoy strong overall brand images, often use ads that promote the brand as the best overall. Coke's campaign "Enjoy Coke," Jeep's "There's only one," and Budweiser's "The king of beers" are all examples of this strategy (Exhibit 3–11).

Exhibit 3–11 Market leaders such as Labatt can appeal to consumer affect

Postpurchase Evaluation

The consumer decision process does not end with the purchase. After consumption, the consumer assesses the level of performance of the product or service. The postpurchase evaluation process is important because the feedback acquired from actual use of a product will influence the likelihood of future purchases. Positive performance means the brand is retained in the evoked set and increases the likelihood it will be purchased again. Unfavourable outcomes may lead the consumer to form negative attitudes toward the brand, lessening the likelihood it will be purchased again or even eliminating it from the consumer's evoked set.

Consumers engage in a number of activities during the postpurchase evaluation process. They may seek out reassurance and opinions from others to confirm the wisdom of their purchase decision, lower their attitudes or opinions of the unchosen alternative, deny or distort any information that does not support the choice they made, or look for information that does support their choice. An important source of supportive information is advertising; consumers tend to be more attentive to advertising for the brand they have chosen.[22] Thus, it may be important for companies to advertise to reinforce consumer decisions to purchase their brands.

Satisfaction

The most significant psychological concept during the post-purchase evaluation process is satisfaction. A leading expert in satisfaction research has recently defined **satisfaction** as a judgment that consumers make with respect to the pleasurable level of consumption-related fulfillment.[23] The notion of fulfillment implies that a consumer's goal has been achieved (i.e., needs met), and that the fulfillment is "judged with reference to a standard." Thus, consumers make a comparison between the consumption outcome and some other referent.

Consumers can make many comparisons. One is to compare the level of product performance to the expectations of the product that consumers had prior to purchase. Satisfaction can occur when the consumer's expectations are either met or exceeded whereas dissatisfaction results when performance is below expectations. Consumers can also compare the product performance to some absolute standard of quality to perceive satisfaction or dissatisfaction.

Another aspect of satisfaction is **cognitive dissonance,** a feeling of psychological tension or postpurchase doubt that a consumer experiences after making a difficult purchase choice. Dissonance is more likely to occur in important decisions where the consumer must choose among close alternatives (especially if the unchosen alternative has unique or desirable features that the selected alternative does not have).

Marketers must recognize the importance of the postpurchase evaluation stage. Dissatisfied consumers not only are unlikely to repurchase the marketer's product but may also spread negative word-of-mouth information that deters others from purchasing the product or service. The best guarantee of favourable postpurchase evaluations is to provide consumers with a quality product or service that always meets their expectations. Marketers must be sure their advertising and other forms of promotion do not create unreasonable expectations their products cannot meet.

Marketers have come to realize that postpurchase communication is also important. Some companies send follow-up letters and brochures to reassure buyers and reinforce the wisdom of their decision. Many companies have set up toll-free numbers for consumers to call if they need information or have a question or complaint regarding a product. Marketers also offer liberalized return and refund policies and extended warranties and guarantees to ensure customer satisfaction. Some have used customers' postpurchase dissatisfaction as an opportunity for gaining new business.

Variations in Consumer Decision Making

The preceding pages describe a general model of consumer decision making. But consumers do not always engage in all five steps of the purchase decision process or proceed in the sequence presented. They may minimize or even skip one or more stages if they have previous experience in purchasing the product or service or if the decision is of low personal, social, or economic significance. To develop effective promotional strategies and programs, marketers need some understanding of the problem-solving processes their target consumers use to make purchase decisions.[24]

Many of the purchase decisions we make as consumers are based on a habitual or routine choice process. For many low-priced, frequently purchased products, the decision process consists of little more than recognizing the need, engaging in a quick internal search, and making the purchase. The consumer spends little or no effort engaging in external search or alternative evaluation.

Marketers of products characterized by a routine response purchase process need to get and/or keep their brands in the consumer's evoked set and avoid anything that may result in their removal from consideration. Established brands that have strong market share position are likely to be in the evoked set of most consumers. Marketers of these brands want consumers to follow a routine choice process and continue to purchase their products. This means maintaining high levels of brand awareness through reminder advertising, periodic promotions, and prominent shelf positions in retail stores.

Marketers of new brands or those with a low market share face a different challenge. They must find ways to disrupt consumers' routine choice process and get them to consider different alternatives. High levels of advertising may be used to encourage trial or brand switching, along with sales promotion efforts in the form of free samples, special price offers, high-value coupons, and the like.

A more complicated decision-making process may occur when consumers have limited experience in purchasing a particular product or service and little or no knowledge of the brands available and/or the criteria to use in making a purchase decision. They may have to learn what attributes or criteria should be used in making a purchase decision and how the various alternatives perform on these dimensions. For products or services characterized by problem solving, whether limited or extensive, marketers should make information available that will help consumers

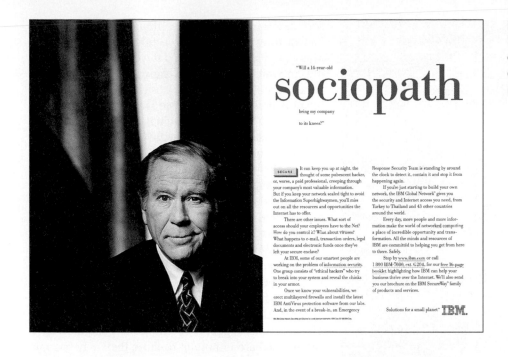

Exhibit 3–12 This ad for IBM shows how marketers can appeal to consumers engaging in extended problem solving

decide. Advertising that provides consumers with detailed information about a brand and how it can satisfy their purchase motives and goals is important. Marketers may also want to give consumers information at the point of purchase, through either displays or brochures. Distribution channels should have knowledgeable salespeople available to explain the features and benefits of the company's product or service and why it is superior to competing products.

The IBM ad in Exhibit 3–12 is a good example of how advertising can appeal to consumers who may be engaging in extended problem solving when considering corporate security. Notice how the ad communicates with consumers who know little about how to purchase this product. The ad also makes more detailed information available by offering a toll-free number and a website.

Behavioural Learning Theory

As noted, the main learning model discussed thus far is widely used, but we would be remiss if we did not briefly mention another perspective. Behavioural learning theories emphasize the role of external, environmental stimuli in causing behaviour; they minimize the significance of internal psychological processes. Behavioural learning theories are based on the *stimulus–response orientation* (S–R), the premise that learning occurs as the result of responses to external stimuli in the environment. Behavioural learning theorists believe learning occurs through the connection between a stimulus and a response. We will examine the basic principles of two behavioural learning theory approaches: classical conditioning and operant conditioning.

Classical Conditioning **Classical conditioning** assumes that learning is an *associative process* with an already existing relationship between a stimulus and a response. This process is transferred to a **conditioned stimulus** that elicits a **conditioned response** resembling the original unconditioned reaction. Two factors are important for learning to occur through the associative process. The first is contiguity, which means the unconditioned stimulus and conditioned stimulus must be close in time and space. The other important principle is *repetition,* or the frequency of the association. The more often the unconditioned and conditioned stimuli occur together, the stronger the association between them will be.

Learning through classical conditioning plays an important role in marketing. Buyers can be conditioned to form favourable impressions and images of various brands through the associative process. Advertisers strive to associate their products and

We can't bring you here.

But we can give you a taste.

How far do you have to go for clear, fresh, wonderful water? As far as your faucet. All you need is the Brita® Water Filtration Pitcher. Just fill with tap water. The remarkable filter does the rest, reducing chlorine taste, sediment, water hardness and copper. It even removes 93% of lead. You'll get some of the best tasting water in the world. And you don't have to go anywhere.

BRITA
Tap into great taste.

Exhibit 3–13 Brita associates itself with freshness

Exhibit 3–14 Energizer batteries shows how to avoid negative consequences

LO BATT

Yes, it is possible to lock yourself in your own trunk.

Should've used Energizer.

They last longer than ordinary Duracell® in cell phones.

services with perceptions, images, and emotions known to evoke positive reactions from consumers. Many products are promoted through image advertising, in which the brand is shown with an unconditioned stimulus that elicits pleasant feelings. When the brand is presented simultaneously with this unconditioned stimulus, the brand itself becomes a conditioned stimulus that elicits the same favourable response.

The ad for Brita in Exhibit 3–13 shows an application of this strategy. Notice how this ad associates Brita freshness with the freshness of a waterfall. The company's positioning plays off this association.

Classical conditioning can also associate a product or service with a favourable emotional state. A study by Gerald Gorn used this approach to examine how background music in ads influences product choice.[25] He found that subjects were more likely to choose a product when it was presented against a background of music they liked rather than music they disliked. These results suggest the emotions generated by a commercial are important because they may become associated with the advertised product through classical conditioning. Kellaris and colleagues also showed that music that was congruent with the message enhanced both ad recall and recognition.[26] Advertisers often attempt to pair a neutral product or service stimulus with an event or situation that arouses positive feelings, such as humour, an exciting sports event, or popular music.

Operant Conditioning Classical conditioning views the individual as a passive participant in the learning process who simply receives stimuli. Conditioning occurs as a result of exposure to a stimulus that occurs before the response. In the **operant conditioning** approach, the individual must actively *operate* or act on some aspect of the environment for learning to occur. Operant conditioning is sometimes referred to as *instrumental conditioning* because the individual's response is instrumental in getting a positive reinforcement (reward) or negative reinforcement (punishment).

Reinforcement, the reward or favourable consequence associated with a particular response, is an important element of instrumental conditioning. Behaviour that is reinforced strengthens the bond between a stimulus and a response. Thus, if a consumer buys a product in response to an ad and experiences a positive outcome, the likelihood that the consumer will use this product again increases. If the outcome is not favourable, the likelihood of buying the product again decreases.

The principles of operant conditioning can be applied to marketing. Companies attempt to provide their customers with products and services that satisfy their needs and reward them to reinforce the probability of repeat purchase. Reinforcement can also be implied in advertising; many ads emphasize the benefits or rewards a consumer will receive from using a product or service. Reinforcement also occurs when an ad encourages consumers to use a particular product or brand to avoid unpleasant consequences. For example, the ad for Energizer batteries in Exhibit 3–14 shows how using this product will help avoid negative consequences—that is, being without a working cellphone when you need it.

Two concepts that are particularly relevant to marketers in their use of reinforcement through promotional strategies are schedules of reinforcement and shaping. Different **schedules of reinforcement** result in varying patterns of learning and behaviour. Learning occurs most rapidly under a *continuous reinforcement schedule,* in which every response is rewarded—but the behaviour is likely to cease when the reinforcement stops. Marketers must provide continuous reinforcement to consumers or risk their switching to brands that do.

Learning occurs more slowly but lasts longer when a *partial* or *intermittent reinforcement schedule* is used and only some of the individual's responses are rewarded. Promotional programs have partial reinforcement schedules. A firm may offer consumers an incentive to use the company's product. The firm does not want to offer the incentive every time (continuous reinforcement), because consumers might become dependent on it and stop buying the brand when the incentive is withdrawn. A study that examined the effect of reinforcement on bus ridership found that discount coupons given as rewards for riding the bus were as effective when given on a partial schedule as when given on a continuous schedule.[27] The cost of giving the discount coupons under the partial schedule, however, was considerably less.

Reinforcement schedules can also be used to influence consumer learning and behaviour through a process known as **shaping,** the reinforcement of successive acts that lead to a desired behaviour pattern or response. Rothschild and Gaidis argue that shaping is a very useful concept for marketers:

> Shaping is an essential process in deriving new and complex behavior because a behavior cannot be rewarded unless it first occurs; a stimulus can only reinforce acts that already occur. New, complex behaviors rarely occur by chance in nature. If the only behavior to be rewarded were the final complex sought behavior, one would probably have to wait a long time for this to occur by chance. Instead, one can reward simpler existing behaviors; over time, more complex patterns evolve and these are rewarded. Thus the shaping process occurs by a method of successive approximations.[28]

In a promotional context, shaping procedures are used as part of the introductory program for new products. Samples and discount coupons can be used to introduce a new product and take a consumer from trial to repeat purchase. Marketers must be careful in their use of shaping procedures: If they drop the incentives too soon, the consumer may not establish the desired behaviour; but if they overuse them, the consumer's purchase may become contingent on the incentive rather than the product or service.

Environmental Influences on Consumer Behaviour

The consumer does not make purchase decisions in isolation. A number of external factors have been identified that may influence consumer decision making. They are shown in Figure 3–5 and examined in more detail in the next sections.

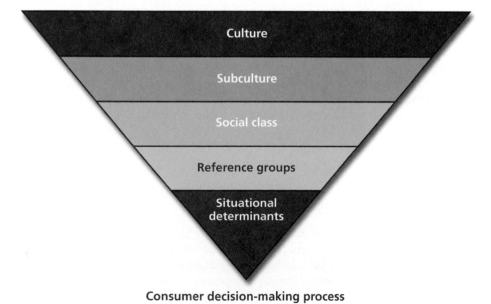

Figure 3–5 External influences on consumer behaviour

Culture

Subculture

Social class

Reference groups

Situational determinants

Consumer decision-making process

Culture

The broadest and most abstract of the external factors that influence consumer behaviour is **culture,** or the complexity of learned meanings, values, norms, and customs shared by members of a society. Cultural norms and values offer direction and guidance to members of a society in all aspects of their lives, including their consumption behaviour. It is becoming increasingly important to study the impact of culture on consumer behaviour as marketers expand their international marketing efforts. Each country has certain cultural traditions, customs, and values that marketers must understand as they develop marketing programs.

Marketers must also be aware of changes that may be occurring in a particular culture and the implications of these changes for their advertising and promotional strategies and programs. Canadian culture continually goes through many changes that have direct implications for advertising. Marketing researchers monitor these changes and their impact on the ways companies market their products and services.

While marketers recognize that culture exerts a demonstrable influence on consumers, they often find it difficult to respond to cultural differences in different markets. The subtleties of various cultures are often difficult to understand and appreciate, but marketers must understand the cultural context in which consumer purchase decisions are made and adapt their advertising and promotional programs accordingly.

Subcultures

Within a given culture are generally found smaller groups or segments whose beliefs, values, norms, and patterns of behaviour set them apart from the larger cultural mainstream. These **subcultures** may be based on age, geographic, religious, racial, and/or ethnic differences. A number of subcultures exist within Canada. These racial/ethnic subcultures are important to marketers because of their size, growth, purchasing power, and distinct purchasing patterns. Marketers develop specific marketing programs for various products and services for these target markets.

Social Class

Virtually all societies exhibit some form of stratification whereby individuals can be assigned to a specific social category on the basis of criteria important to members of that society. **Social class** refers to relatively homogeneous divisions in a society into which people sharing similar lifestyles, values, norms, interests, and behaviours can be grouped. While a number of methods for determining social class exist, class structures in Canada are usually based on occupational status, educational attainment, and income. For example, sociologists generally agree there are three broad levels of social classes in the United States: the upper (14 percent), middle (70 percent), and lower (16 percent) classes.[29]

Social class is an important concept to marketers, since consumers within each social stratum often have similar values, lifestyles, and buying behaviour. Thus, the various social class groups provide a natural basis for market segmentation. Consumers in the different social classes differ in the degree to which they use various products and services and in their leisure activities, shopping patterns, and media habits. Marketers respond to these differences through the positioning of their products and services, the media strategies they use to reach different social classes, and the types of advertising appeals they develop.

Reference Groups

Think about the last time you attended a party. As you dressed for the party, you probably asked yourself (or someone else) what others would be wearing. Your selection of attire may have been influenced by those likely to be present. This simple example reflects one form of impact that groups may exert on your behaviour.

Subliminal Perception: It Just Won't Go Away

One of the most controversial topics in all of advertising is subliminal advertising. Rooted in psychoanalytic theory, subliminal advertising supposedly influences consumer behaviours by subconsciously altering perceptions or attitudes toward products without the knowledge—or consent—of the consumer. Marketers have promoted subliminal self-help audiotapes, weight-loss videos, and golf game improvement tapes. Studies have shown that the majority of American consumers believe that advertisers sometimes use subliminal advertising and that it works.

The concept of subliminal advertising was introduced in 1957 when James Vicary, a motivational researcher, reported that he increased the sales of popcorn and Coke by subliminally flashing "Eat popcorn" and "Drink Coca-Cola" across the screen during a movie in New Jersey. Since then, numerous books and research studies have been published regarding the effectiveness of this advertising form. Some of these have reported on the use of this technique by advertisers to manipulate consumers.

Numerous articles have reviewed the research in this area. In 1982, Timothy Moore reported that the effects of subliminal advertising are so weak that they pose serious difficulties for any marketing applications. In 1988, after additional research in this area, Moore said, "There continues to be no evidence that subliminal messages can influence motivation or complex behaviour." Again in 1992, Moore concluded that "recent research in subliminal perception has provided very little evidence that stimuli below observers' subjective thresholds influence motives, attitudes, beliefs, or choices." Joel Saegart and Jack Haberstroh have supported Moore's conclusions in their studies. On the other hand, in 1994 Kathryn Theus concluded after an extensive review of the literature that "certain themes might be effectively applied by advertising or marketing specialists."

In more recent writings, opposite positions are again taken. In a study conducted in Australia by an ad agency and Mindtec (a consulting firm), 12 groups of television viewers were hypnotized and asked questions about specific commercials and programs. According to the study, 75 percent of the hypnotized subjects stated that sexy images were the main attraction for viewing, as opposed to only 22 percent of the nonhypnotized subjects. The researchers were surprised by the subliminal details that hypnotized participants were able to recall. In the ads, names and slogans that were visible only when the commercial was paused had high levels of recall, even when the brands recalled were not those being advertised. On the other hand, in his book, *Ice Cube Sex: The Truth about Subliminal Advertising*, Haberstroh reviews research and discussions with practitioners and concludes that subliminal advertising does not influence consumer behaviours, advertising recall, attitudes, or any other marketplace behaviour.

When Haberstroh asked ad agency executives in 1984 if they had ever deliberately used subliminal advertising, 96 percent said no, 94 percent said they had never supervised the use of implants, and 91 percent denied knowing anyone who had ever used this technique. A study by Rogers and Seiler in 1994 supported these results, with over 90 percent denying any use of this subliminal implant.

Going even further, Haberstroh contends that subliminal advertising does not even exist except for a few pranksters playing around with artwork for fun. But not so fast! Fashion retailer French Connection is not only employing subliminal advertising but incorporating it into a tagline. Using print and posters, the tagline "subliminal advertising experiment" is arranged in such a way as to spell out the word *sex* if one reads vertically. Likewise, Master Lock has become the first company to run a one-second national print commercial. The goal of the ad is to reinforce the brand name. And, in upstate New York, a personal-injury lawyer is paying $35 each for one-second spots in an attempt to gain new clients. At this time, no one knows if any of these efforts have been successful.

Thus, while most consumers believe subliminal techniques are used and effective, researchers are divided as to their effects. It seems few people in the advertising world think subliminal advertising works and even fewer claim to use it, but there are still those who feel they are wrong. Will there ever be an end to this controversy?

Sources: "Hypnosis Reveals Ad Effects," *Adweek Asia*, January 29, 1999, p. 4; "Breaking French Connection," *Ad Age*, March 22, 1999, p. 52; "Blink of an Ad," *Time*, August 3, 1998, p. 51; Jack Haberstroh, *Ice Cube Sex: The Truth about Subliminal Advertising*, New York Times Publishing, 1996; Kathryn Theus, "Subliminal Advertising and the Psychology of Processing Unconscious Stimuli: A Review of Research," *Psychology & Marketing* 11, no. 3, 1994, pp. 271–90; Timothy Moore, "Subliminal Advertising: What You See Is What You Get," *Journal of Marketing* 46, no. 2 (Spring 1982), pp. 38–47; Timothy Moore, "The Case against Subliminal Manipulation," *Psychology and Marketing* 5, no. 4 (Winter 1988), pp. 297–316.

Exhibit 3–15   These ads are examples of aspirational reference groups

Exhibit 3–16   This ad represents a disassociative reference group

A group has been defined as "two or more individuals who share a set of norms, values, or beliefs and have certain implicitly or explicitly defined relationships to one another such that their behavior is interdependent."[30] Groups are one of the primary factors influencing learning and socialization, and group situations constitute many of our purchase decisions.

A **reference group** is "a group whose presumed perspectives or values are being used by an individual as the basis for his or her judgments, opinions, and actions." Consumers use reference groups as a guide to specific behaviours, even when the groups are not present.[31] In the party example, your peers—although not present—provided a standard of dress that you referred to in your clothing selection. Likewise, your college classmates, family, and co-workers, or even a group to which you aspire, may serve as referents, and your consumption patterns will typically conform to the expectations of the groups that are most important to you.

Marketers use reference group influences in developing advertisements and promotional strategies. The ads in Exhibits 3–15 and 3–16 are examples of *aspirational* reference groups (to which we might like to belong) and *disassociative* groups (to which we do not wish to belong), respectively.

In some instances, the group may be involved more directly than just as a referent. Family members may serve as referents to each other, or they may actually be involved in the purchase decision process—acting as an individual buying unit. As shown in Figure 3–6, family members may assume a variety of roles in the decision-making process.[32] Each role has implications for marketers.

First, the advertiser must determine who is responsible for the various roles in the decision-making process so that messages can be targeted at that person (or those people). These roles will also dictate media strategies, since the appropriate magazines, newspapers, or TV or radio stations must be used. Second, understanding the decision-making process and the use of information by individual family members is critical to the design of messages and choice of promotional program elements. In sum, to create an effective promotional program, a marketer must have an overall understanding of how the decision process works and the role that each family member plays.

The initiator. The person responsible for initiating the purchase decision process; for example, the mother who determines she needs a new car.

The information provider. The individual responsible for gathering information to be used in making the decision; for example, the teenage car buff who knows where to find product information in specific magazines or collects it from dealers.

The influencer. The person who exerts influence as to what criteria will be used in the selection process. All members of the family may be involved. The mother may have her criteria, whereas others may each have their own input.

The decision maker(s). That person(s) who actually makes the decision. In our example, it may be the mother alone or in combination with another family member.

The purchasing agent. That individual who performs the physical act of making the purchase. In the case of a car, a husband and wife may decide to choose it together and sign the purchase agreement.

The consumer. The actual user of the product. In the case of a family car, all family members are consumers. For a private car, only the mother might be the consumer.

Figure 3–6 Roles in the family decision-making process

Situational Determinants

The final external factor is the purchase and usage situation. The specific situation in which consumers plan to use the product or brand directly affects their perceptions, preferences, and purchasing behaviours.[32] Three types of **situational determinants** may have an effect: the specific usage situation, the purchase situation, and the communications situation.

Usage refers to the circumstance in which the product will be used. For example, purchases made for private consumption may be thought of differently from those that will be obvious to the public. The *purchase* situation more directly involves the environment operating at the time of the purchase. Time constraints, store environments, and other factors may all have an impact. The *communications* situation is the condition in which an advertising exposure occurs (in a car listening to the radio, with friends, etc.). This may be most relevant to the development of promotional strategies, because the impact on the consumer will vary according to the particular situation. For example, a consumer may pay more attention to a commercial that is heard alone at home than to one heard in the presence of friends, at work, or anywhere distractions may be present. If advertisers can isolate a particular time when the listener is likely to be attentive, they will probably earn his or her undivided attention.

In sum, situational determinants may either enhance or detract from the potential success of a message. To the degree that advertisers can assess situational influences that may be operating, they will increase the likelihood of successfully communicating with their target audiences.

Summary

This chapter introduced you to the field of consumer behaviour and examined its relevance to promotional strategy. Consumer behaviour is best viewed as the process and activities that people engage in when searching for, selecting, purchasing, using, evaluating, and disposing of products and services to satisfy their needs and desires. A five-stage model of the consumer decision-making process consists of need recognition, information search, alternative evaluation, purchase, and post-purchase evaluation. Internal psychological processes that influence the consumer decision-making process include motivation, perception, attitude formation and change, and integration processes.

The decision process model views consumer behaviour primarily from a cognitive orientation.

The chapter considered other perspectives by examining various approaches to consumer learning and their implications for advertising and promotion. Behavioural learning theories such as classical conditioning and operant conditioning were discussed.

The chapter also examined relevant external factors that influence consumer decision making. Culture, subculture, social class, reference groups, and situational determinants were discussed, along with their implications for the development of promotional strategies and programs.

Key Terms

consumer behaviour, 54
need recognition, 55
want, 56
motives, 57
hierarchy of needs, 57
motivation research, 58
internal search, 59
external search, 60
perception, 60
selective perception, 60
sensation, 60
selective exposure, 61
selective attention, 61

selective comprehension, 61
selective retention, 61
mnemonics, 61
subliminal perception, 62
evaluative criteria, 62
functional consequences, 63
psychosocial consequences, 63
multiattribute attitude model, 64
salient beliefs, 65

purchase intention, 66
brand loyalty, 66
integration processes, 66
heuristics, 67
affect referral decision rule, 67
satisfaction, 67
cognitive dissonance, 68
classical conditioning, 69
conditioned stimulus, 69

conditioned response, 69
operant conditioning, 70
reinforcement, 70
schedules of reinforcement, 70
shaping, 71
culture, 72
subcultures, 72
social class, 72
reference group, 74
situational determinants, 75

Discussion Questions

1. Explain how consumers might engage in each of the processes of selective perception described in the chapter. Provide examples.

2. Focusing on the multiattribute attitude model discussed in the chapter, discuss how marketers might change consumers' beliefs about a product or service. Also explain how attitude change might be achieved through changing the importance of these beliefs. Cite current examples.

3. Describe how cultural differences might impact viewers' perceptions of advertisements. Provide examples.

4. In the text it was indicated that families may influence the consumer decision-making process. Describe how various family members may assume the different roles described in Figure 3–6. Also explain how these roles might change depending upon the product under consideration.

5. Explain how the screening processes involved in selective perception might impact a viewer of television commercials.

6. What is subliminal perception? Describe how marketers are attempting to use this concept in the marketing of goods and services.

7. Discuss the three variations of the consumer decision-making process. What is the importance of communications in each type?

Chapter Four

Communication Process Models

Chapter Objectives

- To understand the basic elements of the communication process and the role of communications in marketing.

- To examine various models of the communication process.

- To analyze the response processes of receivers of

marketing communications, including alternative response hierarchies and their implications for promotional planning and strategy.

- To examine the nature of consumers' cognitive processing of marketing communications.

Home Renovation Giants Vie for Customers

Establishing a presence in a new market against a significant competitor is daunting. Yet this is what two key competitors have been trying to do in each other's market lately. Home Depot has recently entered Quebec and now faces Reno-Depot and RONA, while Reno-Depot's brand, The Building Box, is trying to establish itself in Ontario and is up against, you guessed it, Home Depot. In each case, the marketer is faced with a similar problem of figuring out how the marketing communication efforts will affect consumers.

The growing $17 billion home improvement market is one in which the players appear to be competing on a similar set of features: low price, wide selection, and quality customer service. How will each company communicate with its potential customers, and what will be the customers' reactions?

After extensive customer research, Home Depot decided to focus on customer service. In a series of humourous TV ads, Home Depot depicted the poor service that customers may have experienced while shopping at their competitors. Of course, the message is to put Home Depot in a favourable light with respect to customer service. And the results indicate that maybe Home Depot got it right. Post-campaign surveys indicate strong awareness and effective understanding of the message. And executives report that the first Home Depot opening in Quebec was the most successful in Canada.

Reno-Depot is planning to open 15 Building Box stores in Ontario and claims it is trying to find the "best way to communicate to our customers that we offer them more than their current home improvement retailer." As a backdrop, Reno-Depot believes it has a wider selection of goods because of its European suppliers and strong customer service based on its experience in Quebec. Curiously, Reno-Depot decided to use "Hammer Head," a unique character or mascot that looks like a hammer to convey the "fun" of shopping at The Building Box instead of focusing on wide selection or customer service. The Building Box used a number of IMC tools (i.e., TV, radio, print, moving and regular billboards, direct mail, and public relations) and plans for this to result in customers completely understanding the brand and returning for many shopping visits.

Sources: Sylvain Toutant, "Make Room for The Building Box," *Marketing Magazine*, February 5, 2001; Nathalie Fortier, "Building Success," *Marketing Magazine*, September 24, 2001.

The function of all elements of the integrated marketing communications program is to communicate. An organization's IMC strategy is implemented through the various communications it sends to current or prospective customers as well as other relevant publics. Organizations send communications and messages in a variety of ways, such as through advertisements, brand names, logos and graphic systems, websites, press releases, package designs, promotions, and visual images. Thus, those involved in the planning and implementation of an IMC program need to understand the communications process and how it occurs. As you can see from the opening vignette, the way marketers communicate with their target audiences depends on many factors, including how much customers know and what they think about the company and the image it hopes to create. Developing an effective marketing communications program is far more complicated than just choosing a product feature or attribute to emphasize. Marketers must understand how consumers will perceive and interpret their messages and how these reactions will shape consumers' responses to the company and/or its product or service.

This chapter reviews the fundamentals of communication and examines various perspectives and models regarding how consumers respond to advertising and promotional messages. Our goal is to demonstrate how valuable an understanding of the communication process can be in planning, implementing, and evaluating the marketing communications program.

A Basic Model of Communication

Communication has been variously defined as the passing of information, the exchange of ideas, or the process of establishing a commonness or oneness of thought between a sender and a receiver.[1] These definitions suggest that for communication to occur, there must be some common thinking between two parties and information must be passed from one person to another (or from one group to another). As you will see in this chapter, establishing this commonality in thinking is not always as easy as it might seem; many attempts to communicate are unsuccessful.

The communication process is often very complex. Success depends on such factors as the nature of the message, the audience's interpretation of it, and the environment in which it is received. The receiver's perception of the source and the medium used to transmit the message may also affect the ability to communicate, as do many other factors. Words, pictures, sounds, and colours may have different meanings to different audiences, and people's perceptions and interpretations of them vary. Marketers must understand the meanings that words and symbols take on and how they influence consumers' interpretation of products and messages. This can be particularly challenging to companies marketing their products in foreign countries, as discussed in Global Perspective 4–1.

Over the years, a basic model of the various elements of the communication process has evolved, as shown in Figure 4–1.[2] Two elements represent the major participants in the communication process, the sender and the receiver. Another two are the major communication tools, message and channel. Four others are the major communication functions and processes: encoding, decoding, response, and feedback. The last element, noise, refers to any extraneous factors in the system that can interfere with the process and work against effective communication.

Source/Encoding

The sender, or **source**, of a communication is the person or organization that has information to share with another person or group of people. The source may be an individual (say, a salesperson or hired spokesperson, such as a celebrity, who appears in a company's advertisements) or a nonpersonal entity (such as the brand or organization itself). Because the receiver's perceptions of the source influence how the communication is received, marketers must be careful to select a communicator the receiver believes is knowledgeable and trustworthy or with whom the

Communication Problems in International Marketing

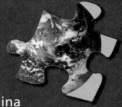

Communication is a major problem facing companies that market their products in foreign countries. Language is one of the main barriers to effective communication, as there are different languages in different countries, different languages or dialects within a single country, and more subtle problems of linguistic nuance and vernacular. International marketers must also be aware of the connotation of the words, signs, symbols, and expressions they use as brand names or logos or in various forms of promotion. Advertising copy, slogans, and symbols do not always transfer well into other languages. This not only impedes communication but also sometimes results in embarrassing blunders that can damage a company's or brand's credibility or image and cost it customers.

Mistranslations and faulty word choices have often created problems for firms engaging in international marketing. For example, the slogan "Come alive with Pepsi" translated too literally in some countries. The German translation was "Come out of the grave," while in Chinese it read, "Pepsi brings your ancestors back from the dead." A U.S. airline competing in Brazil advertised "rendezvous lounges" in its planes—until it discovered that in the Brazilian dialect of Portuguese this meant a place to make love. Budweiser's long-time slogan "The King of Beers" translates in Spanish as "Queen of Beers" because the noun *cerveza* (beer) has a feminine ending.

International marketers can also have linguistic problems with product and brand names and their meaning or pronunciation. China has many languages and dialects, with differences great enough that people from different regions of the country often cannot understand each other. Even among those who speak the same language, such as Mandarin, there often are substantial differences in the way the language is used. For example, *ji xuan ji* would be understood as "calculator" among Singaporean and Malaysian residents who speak Mandarin but as "computer" among many Chinese and Taiwanese Mandarin speakers. When Coca-Cola introduced its product to China, the Chinese characters sounded like *Coca-Cola* but meant "bite the wax tadpole." With the help of a language specialist, the company substituted four Mandarin characters that still sound like *Coca-Cola* but mean "can happy, mouth happy."

International marketers may also encounter problems with the way certain cultures interpret visual signs and symbols as well as nonverbal forms of communication. For example, signaling by making a circle with the thumb and forefinger has different meanings in various cultures. It means "OK" or "the best" to Americans and most Europeans, "money" to the Japanese, and "rudeness" to the Brazilians, while having a vulgar connotation in some Latin American countries. AT&T found that the thumbs-up in its "I plan" long-distance phone campaign presented a problem. Thumbs up signifies affirmation to most Americans, but to Russians and Poles, the fact that the person's palm was visible gave the ad an offensive meaning. AT&T hired a company that specializes in translations to reshoot the graphic element in the ad so that only the back of the hand showed, conveying the intended meaning.

Company and brand names can also get lost in translation. Before launching *Good Housekeeping* magazine in Japan, the Hearst Corporation experimented with a number of Japanese translations of the title. The closest word in Japanese, *kaji*, means "domestic duties," which can be interpreted as work performed by servants. Hearst decided to retain the American name for the magazine but the word *Good* appears in much larger type on the front cover than the word *Housekeeping*.

The fast-food chain Wienerschnitzel (which in Germany means "breaded veal cutlet" rather than "hot dog") had to deal with the fact that its name is a mouthful, particularly for Spanish-speaking consumers. When the chain expanded into Mexico, its franchise shortened the name to Wieners so that

сам**Я**-самая

СамаЯ высокая степень сервиса, предоставляемого сегодня, не предел для AT&T. Уже завтра, с помощью программы "Я План", я смогу получить большее.
Как только я позвоню в AT&T по номеру 1 800 542-2025.

people could pronounce it. Disc jockeys doing radio ads were told to read the name slowly and identify Wienerschnitzel as the place with the big red "W" on its sign.

Many multinational companies are trying to develop world brands that can be marketed internationally using the same brand name and advertising. However, they must be careful that brand names, advertising slogans, signs, symbols, and other forms of marketing communications don't lose something in the translation and are not misinterpreted by consumers in foreign countries.

Sources: Kevin Reagan, "In Asia, Think Globally, Communicate Locally," *Marketing News,* July 19, 1999, pp. 12, 14; Yumiko Ono, "Will *Good Housekeeping* Translate into Japanese?" *The Wall Street Journal,* December 30, 1997, p. B1; Greg Johnson, "Fast-Food Firms Learn Lessons of *El Mercado,*" *Los Angeles Times,* October 8, 1996, pp. A1, 16.

receiver can identify or relate in some manner. (How these characteristics influence the receiver's responses is discussed further in Chapter 6.)

The communication process begins when the source selects words, symbols, pictures, and the like, to represent the message that will be delivered to the receiver(s). This process, known as **encoding,** involves putting thoughts, ideas, or information into a symbolic form. The sender's goal is to encode the message in such a way that it will be understood by the receiver. This means using words, signs, or symbols that are familiar to the target audience. Many symbols have universal meaning, such as the familiar circle with a line through it to denote no parking, no smoking, and so forth. Many companies also have highly recognizable symbols—such as McDonald's golden arches, Nike's swoosh, or the Coca-Cola trademark—that are known to consumers around the world.

Message

The encoding process leads to development of a **message** that contains the information or meaning the source hopes to convey. The message may be verbal or nonverbal, oral or written, or symbolic. Messages must be put into a transmittable form that is appropriate for the channel of communication being used. In advertising, this

Figure 4–1 A model of the communication process

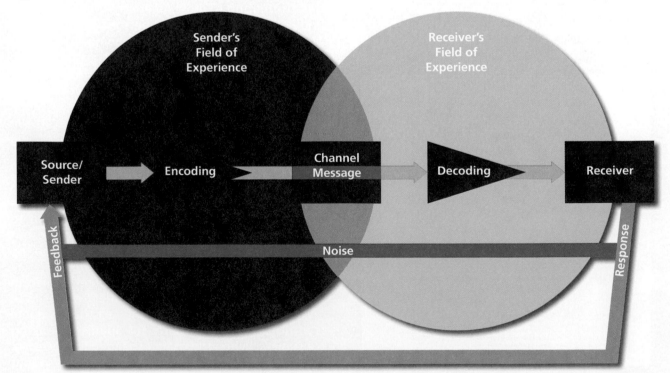

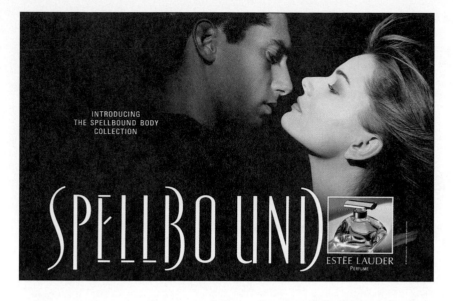

may range from simply writing some words or copy that will be read as a radio message to producing an expensive television commercial. For many products, it is not the actual words of the message that determine its communication effectiveness but rather the impression or image the ad creates. Notice how Spellbound perfume in Exhibit 4–1 uses only a picture to deliver its message. However, the product name and picture help communicate a feeling of attraction and fascination between the man and woman shown in the ad.

To better understand the symbolic meaning that might be conveyed in a communication, advertising and marketing researchers have begun focusing attention on **semiotics,** which studies the nature of meaning and asks how our reality—words, gestures, myths, signs, symbols, products/services, theories—acquire meaning.[3] Semiotics is important in marketing communications since products and brands acquire meaning through the way they are advertised and consumers use products and brands to express their social identities. Consumer researcher Michael Solomon notes: "From a semiotic perspective, every marketing message has three basic components: an object, a sign or symbol and an interpretant. The object is the product that is the focus of the message (e.g., Marlboro cigarettes). The sign is the sensory imagery that represents the intended meanings of the object (e.g., the Marlboro cowboy). The interpretant is the meaning derived (e.g., rugged, individualistic, American)."[4]

Marketers may use individuals trained in semiotics and related fields such as cultural anthropology to better understand the conscious and subconscious meanings the nonverbal signs and symbols in their ads transmit to consumers. For example, Levi Strauss & Co.'s agency, TBWA/Chiat/Day, hired a cultural anthropologist to help it better understand the image and meaning of clothing and fashion among young consumers. As part of the process, the agency research team recruited hip-looking young people in the streets of the East Village section of New York City, an area picked because they felt it is the best reflection of today's youth life. Those chosen were handed a piece of red cardboard and a white marker and asked to "write down something you believe in; something that's true about you or your world." The process provided the agency with insight into the teen market and was the impetus for an ad campaign featuring teenagers holding placards inscribed with their philosophical messages.[5] Exhibit 4–2 shows the thinking behind the various elements of one of the ads used in the campaign as explained by Sean Dee, the director of the Levi's brand.

Some advertising and marketing people are skeptical about the value of semiotics. They question whether social scientists read too much into advertising messages and are overly intellectual in interpreting them. However, the meaning of an advertising message or other form of marketing communication lies not in the message but with the people who see and interpret it. Moreover, consumers behave on the basis of meanings they ascribe to marketplace stimuli. Thus, marketers must

THE MODEL: A premed student at New York University
"We wanted people who are not defined by what they do but by what they are. We chose her because she looks like a Levi's type. She's young. She has her own point of view. She's sexy, but in an understated way. She's not trying too hard. She's definitely got something about her."

THE CLOTHES: Levi's cargo pants, her own T-shirt, zip-up sweatshirt, combat boots, and accessories
"It's important that she wore what she wanted. We're not trying to create a Levi's uniform; that wouldn't be very 'real.' We didn't use a professional stylist or a hairdresser; that wouldn't be real."

THE SETTING: Manhattan's East Village
"We picked New York City because it's the best reflection of today's youth life. We drove around the grittiest parts of the city. The people in the background [of this image] give it a street feel; it's obviously not staged in a studio."

THE STATEMENT: "Music is my female soul"
"It's hard for people to believe, but the [language] came totally from the kids; there was no prompting…. We liked the music theme [in this statement] because we do a lot to promote original music; we see music as being *the* voice of the young people."

THE TAG LINE: "What's true"
"The challenge with youth marketing these days is not to dictate to kids. This [line] is both a statement and a question. Is what we're saying true? Or is it a declaration? It works because it's provocative and ambiguous."

consider the meanings consumers attach to the various signs and symbols. Semiotics may be helpful in analyzing how various aspects of the marketing program—such as advertising messages, packaging, brand names, and even the nonverbal communications of salespeople (gestures, mode of dress)—are interpreted by receivers.[6]

Channel

The **channel** is the method by which the communication travels from the source or sender to the receiver. At the broadest level, channels of communication are of two types, personal and nonpersonal. *Personal channels* of communication are direct interpersonal (face-to-face) contact with target individuals or groups. Salespeople serve as personal channels of communication when they deliver their sales message to a buyer or potential customer. Social channels of communication such as friends, neighbours, associates, co-workers, or family members are also personal channels. They often represent *word-of-mouth communication,* a powerful source of information for consumers.[7]

Nonpersonal channels of communication are those that carry a message without interpersonal contact between sender and receiver. Nonpersonal channels are generally referred to as the **mass media** or mass communications, since the message is sent to many individuals at one time. For example, a TV commercial broadcast on a prime-time show may be seen by 20 million households in a given evening. Nonpersonal channels of communication consist of two major types, print and broadcast. Print media include newspapers, magazines, direct mail, and billboards; broadcast media include radio and television.

Receiver/Decoding

The **receiver** is the person(s) with whom the sender shares thoughts or information. Generally, receivers are the consumers in the target market or audience who read, hear, and/or see the marketer's message. The target audience may consist of individuals, groups, niche markets, market segments, or a general public or mass audience (Figure 4–2). Marketers approach each of these audiences differently.

The target market may consist of *individuals* who have specific needs and for whom the communication must be specifically tailored. This often requires person-to-person communication and is generally accomplished through personal selling. Other forms of communication, such as advertising, may be used to attract the audience's attention to the firm, but the detailed message is carried by a salesperson who can respond to the specific needs of the individual customer. Life insurance, financial services, and real estate are examples of products and services promoted this way.

A second level of audience aggregation is represented by the *group.* Marketers often must communicate with a group of people who make or influence the purchase decision. For example, marketers may have one message and medium directed towards parents who are the deciders and another towards children who are the influencers.

Marketers look for customers who have similar needs and wants and thus represent some type of market segment that can be reached with the same basic communication strategy. Very small, well-defined groups of customers are often referred to as *market niches.* They can usually be reached through personal selling efforts or highly targeted media such as direct mail. The next level of audience aggregation is *market segments,* broader classes of buyers who have similar needs and can be reached with similar messages using a variety of relevant media.

Marketers of most consumer products attempt to attract the attention of large numbers of present or potential customers (*mass markets*) through mass communication such as advertising or publicity. Mass communication is a one-way flow of information from the marketer to the consumer. Feedback on the audience's reactions to the message is generally indirect and difficult to measure. TV advertising, for example, lets the marketer send a message to millions of consumers at the same time. But this does not mean effective communication has occurred. This may be only one of several hundred messages the consumer is exposed to that day. There is no guarantee the information will be attended to, processed, comprehended, or stored in memory for later retrieval. Even if the advertising message is processed, it may not interest consumers or may be misinterpreted by them. Studies by Jacob Jacoby and Wayne D. Hoyer have shown that nearly 20 percent of all print ads and even more TV commercials are miscomprehended by readers.[8]

Decoding is the process of transforming the sender's message back into thought. This process is heavily influenced by the receiver's frame of reference or **field of experience,** which refers to the experiences, perceptions, attitudes, and values he or she brings to the communication situation. For effective communication to occur, the message decoding process of the receiver must match the encoding of the sender. Simply put, this means the receiver understands and correctly interprets what the source is trying to communicate. As Figure 4–1 showed, the source and the receiver each have a frame of reference (the circle around each) that they bring to

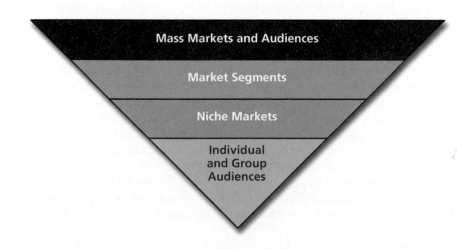

Figure 4–2   Levels of audience aggregation

the communication situation. Effective communication is more likely when there is some *common ground* between the two parties. (This is represented by the overlapping of the two circles.) The more knowledge the sender has about the receivers, the better the sender can understand their needs, empathize with them, and communicate effectively. Advertisers spend millions of dollars every year to understand the frames of reference of the target audiences who receive their messages. They also spend much time and money pretesting messages to make sure consumers understand and decode them in the manner the advertiser intended.

While this notion of common ground between sender and receiver may sound basic, it often causes great difficulty in the advertising communications process. Marketing and advertising people often have very different fields of experience from the consumers who constitute the mass markets with whom they must communicate. Most advertising and marketing people are university-educated and work and/or reside in large urban areas such as Toronto or Montreal. Yet they are attempting to develop commercials that will effectively communicate with millions of consumers who have never attended university, work in blue-collar occupations, and live in rural areas or small towns. Another factor that can lead to problems in establishing common ground between senders and receivers is age. IMC Perspective 4–2 discusses some interesting findings from a study that considered problems younger advertising professionals have in developing ads for older consumers.

Noise

Throughout the communication process, the message is subject to extraneous factors that can distort or interfere with its reception. This unplanned distortion or interference is known as **noise.** Errors or problems that occur in the encoding of the message, distortion in a radio or television signal, or distractions at the point of reception are examples of noise. Perhaps the foremost distraction is advertising clutter whereby the receiver is confronted with many competing messages.

Noise may also occur because the fields of experience of the sender and receiver don't overlap. Lack of common ground may result in improper encoding of the message—using a sign, symbol, or words that are unfamiliar or have different meaning to the receiver. The more common ground there is between the sender and the receiver, the less likely it is this type of noise will occur.

Response/Feedback

The receiver's set of reactions after seeing, hearing, or reading the message is known as a **response.** Receivers' responses can range from nonobservable actions such as storing information in memory to immediate action such as dialing a toll-free number to order a product advertised on television. Marketers are very interested in **feedback,** that part of the receiver's response that is communicated back to the sender. Feedback, which may take a variety of forms, closes the loop in the communications flow and lets the sender monitor how the intended message is being decoded and received.

Because advertisers are not in direct contact with the customers, they must use other means to determine how their messages have been received. While the ultimate form of feedback occurs through sales, it is often hard to show a direct relationship between advertising and purchase behaviour. So marketers use other methods to obtain feedback, among them customer inquiries, store visits, coupon redemptions, and reply cards. Research-based feedback analyzes readership and recall of ads, message comprehension, attitude change, and other forms of response. With this information, the advertiser can determine reasons for success or failure in the communication process and make adjustments.

Successful communication is accomplished when the marketer selects an appropriate source, develops an effective message or appeal that is encoded properly, and then selects the channels or media that will best reach the target audience so that

IMC Perspective 4–2
Marketing to Seniors Presents Challenges

There was a time when anyone over 50 was considered old. Want to reach 'em? Show some adorable grandchildren, and perhaps a kindly grandmother in a rocking chair, and that was that. Well, those days are gone. With the oldest of the baby boomers passing 50 and, according to some definitions, becoming seniors—but generally refusing to admit it—the old-fashioned way of reaching this market is gone.

Virtually everyone agrees that a monolithic 50-plus market no longer exists. Instead, there are all kinds of subgroups, each with its own preferences, disposable income, and inclination to buy. The problem is, the number and age range of these subgroups vary widely depending on who you talk to. At *Forever Young* magazine—formerly called *Today's Senior*, until the senior boomers' hostility to the word "senior" prompted a name change—they think in terms of "junior seniors" (50 to 70) and "senior seniors" (70 and up). "The junior seniors are people nearing retirement or newly retired," says Cathryn Oliver, *Forever Young*'s general manager. "In our minds as marketers, those people who are making crucial decisions in their lives," and thus are open to various sales pitches. Meanwhile, the "senior seniors" have largely made those decisions, which means they're of less interest.

However, David Tafler, editor/publisher of *CARP News* (which was reborn as *FiftyPlus* this month), sees three seniors' demographics. (CARP stands for the Canadian Association of Retired Persons. However, mindful of the fact that most boomers aren't retired, CARP now simply refers to itself as "Canada's Association for the Fifty-Plus.") According to Tafler, people 50 to 65 are "junior seniors," those 65 to 80 are "mid-seniors" and those over 80 are "senior seniors."

What are the implications for advertisers interested in targeting 50-plus? The first is to remember that boomers are boomers, whatever their age. (In Canada, the baby boom ran from 1947 to 1966, although most references to what "the boomers" are like tend to be about the older half of this group, who are now 43 to 52.) They like to think they're young, and likely always will. Hence much of the standard 25-to-54 advertising that's worked with them in the past will continue to do so in the future.

This said, even the boomers are looking towards their future. That's why certain product categories are heating up, like "active adult" communities (retirement subdivisions with an active slant), investments and products designed to enhance healthy living. Whatever their age, the boomers have money to spend and they like to spend it. That's why it makes good sense to advertise to them, period.

Source: Adapted from James Careless, "Re-evaluating the 50-Plus Sector," *Marketing Magazine,* October 18, 1999. Used with permission.

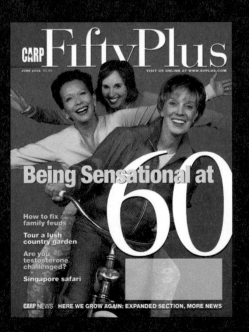

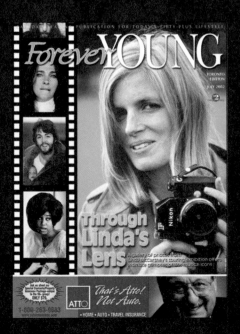

the message can be effectively decoded and delivered. Since these decisions must consider how the target audience will respond to the promotional message, the remainder of this chapter examines the process by which consumers respond to advertising and other forms of marketing communications.

The Response Process

Perhaps the most important aspect of developing effective communication programs involves understanding the *response process* the receiver may go through in moving toward a specific behaviour (like purchasing a product) and how the promotional efforts of the marketer influence consumer responses. In many instances, the marketer's only objective may be to create awareness of the company or brand name, which may trigger interest in the product. In other situations, the marketer may want to convey detailed information to change consumers' knowledge of and attitudes toward the brand and ultimately change their behaviour.

Traditional Response Hierarchy Models

A number of models have been developed to depict the stages a consumer may pass through in moving from a state of not being aware of a company, product, or brand to actual purchase behaviour. Figure 4–3 shows four of the best-known response hierarchy models. While these response models may appear similar, they were developed for different reasons.

The **AIDA model** was developed to represent the stages a salesperson must take a customer through in the personal selling process.[9] This model depicts the buyer as passing successively through attention, interest, desire, and action. The salesperson must first get the customer's attention and then arouse some interest in the company's product or service. Strong levels of interest should create desire to own or use the product. The action stage in the AIDA model involves getting the customer to make a purchase commitment and closing the sale. To the marketer, this is the most important stage in the selling process, but it can also be the most difficult. Companies train their sales reps in closing techniques to help them complete the selling process.

Figure 4–3   Models of the response process

Stages	Models			
	AIDA model[a]	Hierarchy of effects model[b]	Innovation adoption model[c]	Information processing model[d]
Cognitive stage	Attention	Awareness	Awareness	Presentation
				Attention
		Knowledge		Comprehension
Affective stage	Interest	Liking	Interest	Yielding
		Preference		
	Desire	Conviction	Evaluation	Retention
Behavioural stage			Trial	
	Action	Purchase	Adoption	Behaviour

Perhaps the best known of these response hierarchies is the model developed by Robert Lavidge and Gary Steiner as a paradigm for setting and measuring advertising objectives.[10] Their **hierarchy of effects model** shows the process by which advertising works; it assumes a consumer passes through a series of steps in sequential order from initial awareness of a product or service to actual purchase. A basic premise of this model is that advertising effects occur over a period of time. Advertising communication may not lead to immediate behavioural response or purchase; rather, a series of effects must occur, with each step fulfilled before the consumer can move to the next stage in the hierarchy. As we will see in Chapter 5, the hierarchy of effects model has become the foundation for objective setting and measurement of advertising effects in many companies.

The **innovation adoption model** evolved from work on the diffusion of innovations.[11] This model represents the stages a consumer passes through in adopting a new product or service. Like the other models, it says potential adopters must be moved through a series of steps before taking some action (in this case, deciding to adopt a new product). The steps preceding adoption are awareness, interest, evaluation, and trial. The challenge facing companies introducing new products is to create awareness and interest among consumers and then get them to evaluate the product favourably. The best way to evaluate a new product is through actual use so that performance can be judged. Marketers often encourage trial by using demonstration or sampling programs or allowing consumers to use a product with minimal commitment (Exhibit 4–3). After trial, consumers either adopt the product or reject it.

The final hierarchy model shown in Figure 4–3 is the **information processing model** of advertising effects, developed by William McGuire.[12] This model assumes the receiver in a persuasive communication situation like advertising is an information processor or problem solver. McGuire suggests the series of steps a receiver goes through in being persuaded constitutes a response hierarchy. The stages of this model are similar to the hierarchy of effects sequence; attention and comprehension are similar to awareness and knowledge, and yielding is synonymous with liking. McGuire's model includes a stage not found in the other models: retention, or the receiver's ability to retain that portion of the comprehended information that he or she accepts as valid or relevant. This stage is important since most promotional campaigns are designed not to motivate consumers to take immediate action but rather to provide information they will use later when making a purchase decision.

Each stage of the response hierarchy is a dependent variable that must be attained and that may serve as an objective of the communication process. As shown in Figure 4–4, each stage can be measured, providing the advertiser with feedback regarding the effectiveness of various strategies designed to move the consumer to purchase. The information processing model may be an effective framework for planning and evaluating the effects of a promotional campaign.

Implications of the Traditional Hierarchy Models   The hierarchy models of communication response are useful to promotional planners from several perspectives. First, they delineate the series of steps potential purchasers must be taken through to move them from unawareness of a product or service to readiness

Exhibit 4–3 Sampling or demonstration programs encourage trial of new products such as disposable contact lenses

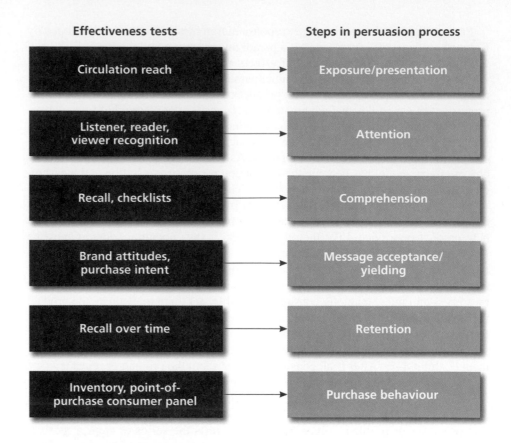

Figure 4–4   Methods of obtaining feedback in the response hierarchy

Effectiveness tests	Steps in persuasion process
Circulation reach	Exposure/presentation
Listener, reader, viewer recognition	Attention
Recall, checklists	Comprehension
Brand attitudes, purchase intent	Message acceptance/ yielding
Recall over time	Retention
Inventory, point-of-purchase consumer panel	Purchase behaviour

Exhibit 4–4   Advertising for innovative new products such as HDTV must make consumers aware of their features and benefits

Immaculate reception.

It's simply the most revolutionary idea in television broadcasting since color. It's called HDTV – high definition television. HDTV lets you experience a digital world of unprecedented picture clarity and detail. The most exciting colors ever seen. And the bone-jarring impact of Dolby Digital* surround sound. All in a captivating cinema-style, wide-screen format. At Panasonic, we're ready to launch you into the age of digital television now. With our HDTV-compatible, wide-screen projection television. And our remarkable digital set-top decoder box.** Panasonic HDTV. You've got to experience it for yourself. From now on, you'll never watch television the same way again.

16:9 wide screen

For information call 1-800-211-PANA or www.panasonic.com/tv

1.5 MILLION PIXEL CLARITY

Panasonic just slightly ahead of our time*

to purchase it. Second, potential buyers may be at different stages in the hierarchy, so the advertiser will face different sets of communication problems. For example, a company introducing an innovative product like Panasonic's high-definition television (HDTV) may need to devote considerable effort to making people aware of the product, how it works, and its benefits (Exhibit 4–4). Marketers of a mature brand that enjoys customer loyalty may need only supportive or reminder advertising to reinforce positive perceptions and maintain the awareness level for the brand.

The hierarchy models can also be useful as intermediate measures of communication effectiveness. The marketer needs to know where audience members are on the response hierarchy. For example, research may reveal that one target segment has low awareness of the advertiser's brand, whereas another is aware of the brand and its various attributes but has a low level of liking or brand preference.

For the first segment of the market, the communication task involves increasing the awareness level for the brand. The number of ads may be increased, or a product sampling program may be used. For the second segment, where awareness is already high but liking and preference are low, the advertiser must determine the reason for the negative feelings and then attempt to address this problem in future advertising.

When research or other evidence reveals a company is perceived favourably on a particular attribute or performance criterion, the company may want to take advantage of this in its advertising.

Evaluating Traditional Response Hierarchy Models   As you saw in Figure 4–3, the four models presented all view the response process as consisting of movement through a sequence of three basic stages. The *cognitive stage* represents what the receiver knows or perceives about the particular product or brand. This stage includes awareness that the brand exists and knowledge, information, or comprehension about its attributes, characteristics, or benefits. The *affective stage* refers to the receiver's feelings or affect level (like or dislike) for the particular brand. This stage also includes stronger levels of affect such as desire, preference, or conviction. The *conative* or *behavioural stage* refers to the consumer's action toward the brand: trial, purchase, adoption, or rejection.

All four models assume a similar ordering of these three stages. Cognitive development precedes affective reactions, which precede behaviour. One might assume that consumers become aware of and knowledgeable about a brand, develop feelings toward it, form a desire or preference, and then make a purchase. While this logical progression is often accurate, the response sequence does not always operate this way.

Over the past two decades, considerable research in marketing, social psychology, and communications has led to questioning of the traditional cognitive → affective → behavioural sequence of response. Several other configurations of the response hierarchy have been theorized.

Alternative Response Hierarchies

Michael Ray has developed a model of information processing that identifies three alternative orderings of the three stages based on perceived product differentiation and product involvement.[13] These alternative response hierarchies are the standard learning, dissonance/attribution, and low-involvement models (Figure 4–5).

The Standard Learning Hierarchy   In many purchase situations, the consumer will go through the response process in the sequence depicted by the traditional communication models. Ray terms this a **standard learning model,** which consists of a learn → feel → do sequence. Information and knowledge acquired or *learned* about the various brands are the basis for developing affect, or *feelings,* that guide what the consumer will *do* (e.g., actual trial or purchase). In this hierarchy, the consumer is viewed as an active participant in the communication process who gathers information through active learning.

Ray suggests the standard learning hierarchy is likely when the consumer is highly involved in the purchase process and there is much differentiation among competing brands. High-involvement purchase decisions such as those for industrial

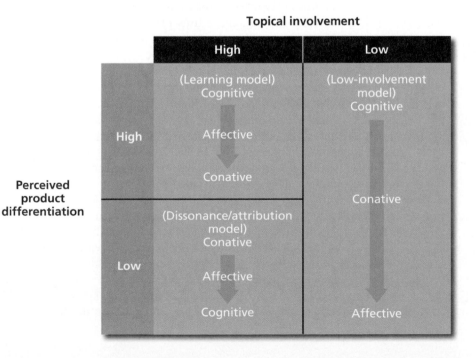

Figure 4–5   Alternative response hierarchies: the three-orders model of information processing

Exhibit 4–5 Ads for high-involvement products provide consumers with information to help them evaluate brands

Exhibit 4–6 This ad reinforces the wisdom of the decision to purchase Michelin tires

products and services and consumer durables like personal computers, printers, cameras, appliances, and cars are areas where a standard learning hierarchy response process is likely. Ads for products and services in these areas are usually very detailed and provide customers with information that can be used to evaluate brands and help them make a purchase decision (Exhibit 4–5).

The Dissonance/Attribution Hierarchy

A second response hierarchy proposed by Ray involves situations where consumers first behave, then develop attitudes or feelings as a result of that behaviour, and then learn or process information that supports the behaviour. This **dissonance/attribution model,** or do → feel → learn, occurs in situations where consumers must choose between two alternatives that are similar in quality but are complex and may have hidden or unknown attributes. The consumer may purchase the product on the basis of a recommendation by some nonmedia source and then attempt to support the decision by developing a positive attitude toward the brand and perhaps even developing negative feelings toward the rejected alternative(s). This reduces any *postpurchase dissonance* or anxiety the consumer may experience resulting from doubt over the purchase (as discussed in Chapter 3). Dissonance reduction involves *selective learning,* whereby the consumer seeks information that supports the choice made and avoids information that would raise doubts about the decision.

According to this model, marketers need to recognize that in some situations, attitudes develop *after* purchase, as does learning from the mass media. Ray suggests that in these situations the main effect of the mass media is not the promotion of original choice behaviour and attitude change but rather the reduction of dissonance by reinforcing the wisdom of the purchase or providing supportive information. For example, the ad shown in Exhibit 4–6 reinforces consumers' decisions to purchase Michelin tires by showing the number of awards the brand has received for customer satisfaction.

As with the standard learning model, this response hierarchy is likely to occur when the consumer is involved in the purchase situation; it is particularly relevant for postpurchase situations. For example, a consumer may purchase tires recommended by a friend and then develop a favourable attitude toward the company and pay close attention to its ads to reduce dissonance.

Some marketers resist this view of the response hierarchy because they can't accept the notion that the mass media have no effect on the consumer's initial purchase decision. But the model doesn't claim the mass media have no effect—just that their major impact occurs after the purchase has been made. Marketing communications planners must be aware of the need for advertising and promotion efforts not just to encourage brand selection but to reinforce choices and ensure that a purchase pattern will continue.

The Low-Involvement Hierarchy

Perhaps the most intriguing of the three response hierarchies proposed by Ray is the **low-involvement hierarchy,** in which the receiver is viewed as passing from cognition to behaviour to attitude change. This learn → do → feel sequence is thought to characterize situations of low consumer involvement in the purchase process. Ray suggests this hierarchy tends to occur when involvement in the purchase decision is low, there are minimal differences among brand alternatives, and mass-media (especially broadcast) advertising is important.

The notion of a low-involvement hierarchy is based in large part on Herbert Krugman's theory explaining the effects of television advertising.[14] Krugman wanted to find out why TV advertising produced a strong effect on brand awareness and recall but little change in consumers' attitudes toward the product. He hypothesized that TV is basically a low-involvement medium and the viewer's perceptual defenses are reduced or even absent during commercials. In a low-involvement situation, the consumer does not compare the message with previously acquired beliefs, needs, or past experiences. The commercial results in subtle changes in the consumer's knowledge structure, particularly with repeated exposure. This change in the consumer's knowledge does not result in attitude change but is related to learning something about the advertised brand, such as a brand name, ad theme, or slogan. According to Krugman, when the consumer enters a purchase situation, this information may be sufficient to trigger a purchase. The consumer will then form an attitude toward the purchased brand as a result of experience with it. Thus, in the low-involvement situation the response sequence is as follows:

Message exposure under low involvement →

Shift in cognitive structure → Purchase →

Positive or negative experience → Attitude formation

In the low-involvement hierarchy, the consumer engages in passive learning and random information catching rather than active information seeking. The advertiser must recognize that a passive, uninterested consumer may focus more on nonmessage elements such as music, characters, symbols, and slogans or jingles than actual message content. The advertiser might capitalize on this situation by developing a catchy jingle that is stored in the consumer's mind without any active cognitive processing and becomes salient when he or she enters the actual purchase situation.

Advertisers of low-involvement products also repeat simple product claims such as a key copy point or distinctive product benefit. A study by Scott Hawkins and Stephen Hoch found that under low-involvement conditions, repetition of simple product claims increased consumers' memory of and belief in those claims.[15] They concluded that advertisers of low-involvement products might find it more profitable to pursue a heavy repetition strategy than to reach larger audiences with lengthy, more detailed messages. For example, Heinz has dominated the ketchup market for over 20 years by repeatedly telling consumers that its brand is the thickest and richest. Heinz has used a variety of advertising campaigns over the years, but they all repeat the same basic theme and focus on the consistent quality of the brand (Exhibit 4–7).

Low-involvement advertising appeals prevail in much of the advertising we see for frequently purchased consumer products: For example, Tim Horton's doughnuts uses the catchy jingle, "You always have time for Tim Horton's." These appeals are designed to help consumers make an association without really attempting to formulate or change an attitude. Another popular creative strategy used by advertisers of low-involvement products is what advertising analyst Harry McMahan calls *VIP, or visual image personality*.[16] Advertisers often use symbols like the Pillsbury doughboy, Tony the tiger, and Mr. Clean to develop visual images that will lead consumers to identify and retain ads.

As the preceding discussion shows, consumer behaviour and advertising researchers have extensively studied the concept of involvement.[17] Involvement is viewed as a variable that can help explain how consumers process advertising information and how this information might affect message recipients. One problem that has plagued the study of involvement has been agreeing on how to define and measure it. Advertising managers must be able to determine targeted consumers' involvement levels with their products.

Exhibit 4–7 Advertising promoting consistent quality has helped Heinz dominate the ketchup market

Some of the problems in conceptualizing and measuring involvement have been addressed in extensive review by Judith Zaichkowsky. She has noted that although there is no single precise definition of involvement, there is an underlying theme focusing on *personal relevance*.[18] Zaichkowsky developed an involvement construct that includes three antecedents, or variables proposed to precede involvement (Figure 4–6). The first is traits of the person (value system, unique experiences, needs). The second factor is characteristics of the stimulus, or differences in type of media (TV, radio, or print), content of the communication, or product class variations. The third antecedent is situational factors, such as whether one is or is not in the market for a particular product.

The various antecedents can influence the consumer's level of involvement in several ways, including the way the consumer responds to the advertising, the products being advertised, and the actual purchase decision. This involvement theory shows that a variety of outcomes or behaviours can result from involvement with advertising, products, or purchase decisions.

The Integrated Information Response Model

Advertising and consumer researchers recognize that not all response sequences and behaviours are explained adequately by either the traditional or the alternative response hierarchies. Advertising is just one source of information consumers use in forming attitudes and/or making purchase decisions. Moreover, for many consumers, purchase does not reflect commitment to a brand but is merely a way to obtain firsthand information from trial use of a product.

Robert Smith and William Swinyard developed a revised interpretation of the advertising response sequence.[19] Their **integrated information response model,** shown in Figure 4–7, integrates concepts from both the traditional and the low-

Figure 4–6 Involvement construct

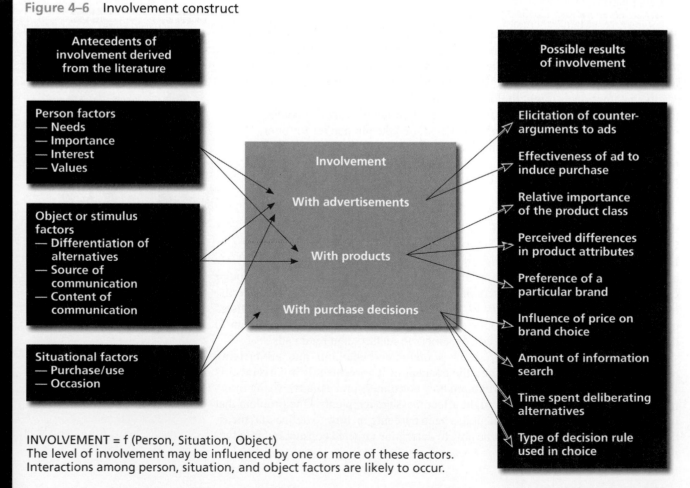

INVOLVEMENT = f (Person, Situation, Object)
The level of involvement may be influenced by one or more of these factors.
Interactions among person, situation, and object factors are likely to occur.

Figure 4–7   Integrated information response model

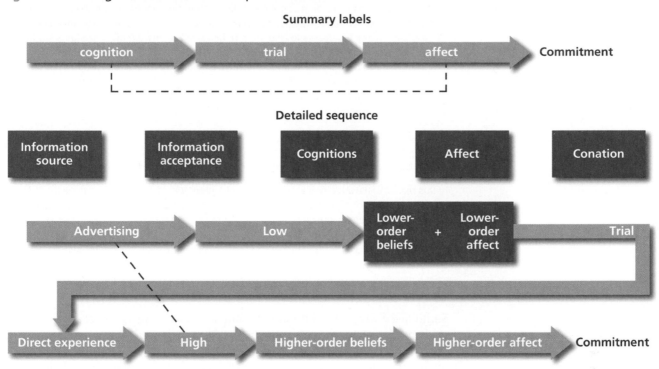

involvement response hierarchy perspectives. It also accounts for the effects of direct experience and recognizes that different levels of belief strength result from advertising versus personal experience with a product.

The integrated information response model suggests several different response patterns that can result from advertising. For low-involvement purchases, a cognition → trial → affect → commitment response sequence may be operating. This can be seen in the top line of Figure 4–7. According to this sequence, advertising generally leads to low information acceptance, lower-order beliefs, and low-order affect. However, as repetitive advertising builds awareness, consumers become more likely to engage in a trial purchase to gather information. The direct experience that results from trial purchase leads to high information acceptance and higher-order beliefs and affect, which can result in commitment or brand loyalty.

Advertising generally leads only to lower-order beliefs and affect because it is seen as a biased source of interest, subject to much source and message discounting and/or rejection. But in some situations, such as when perceived risk and involvement are low, advertising may move consumers directly to purchase.

If consumers are involved with the product, they may seek additional information from other external sources (for example, more advertising, word of mouth, salespeople) and/or from direct experience. This means the response sequence is similar to the traditional hierarchy of effects model (cognition → affect → commitment). The higher-order response path (bottom line of Figure 4–7) shows that direct experience, and in some cases advertising, is accepted at higher-order magnitudes, resulting in higher-order beliefs and affect. This strong affect is more likely to result in preferences and committed purchases.

Smith and Swinyard discuss the implications of the integrated response model regarding promotional strategy for low- versus high-involvement products. For example, they recommend less enthusiastic promotional goals for low-involvement products, because advertising has a limited ability to form or change higher-order beliefs and affect:

> Low-involvement products, for example, could benefit from advertisements oriented to inducing trial by creating generally favorable lower order beliefs. This could be accomplished with campaigns designed to reduce perceived risk through repetition and familiarity, or those directly advocating a trial purchase. In addition, the integrated response

model suggests that other marketing strategies designed to facilitate trial should be coupled with the advertising campaign. Free samples, coupons, price cuts, or effective point-of-purchase displays could all be integrated with media advertising to produce an environment highly conducive to trial. So too, because low-involvement products are frequently homogeneous, subsequent advertisements might be designed to reaffirm the positive aspects of trial. If successful, these efforts might generate brand loyalty based upon higher order beliefs and affect. This could be a major advantage for advertisers of low-involvement products where frequent brand switching may be based on the absence of antecedents for commitment (i.e., higher order beliefs and affect).[20]

For high-involvement products, more basic attitude change strategies are warranted. However, Smith and Swinyard note that the higher-order response sequence focuses attention on message acceptance as a prerequisite for affect development:

> In this instance, the advertising manager should attempt to isolate the conditions facilitating the formation of higher order beliefs. Factors influential in this process could include whether the message claims are easily verifiable (e.g., price) and/or demonstrable (e.g., styling), whether the individual knows the sponsoring company and its reputation/credibility, selection of a credible spokesperson to deliver the message, whether the message is consistent with already established beliefs, etc. It also is likely that interactions could exist between acceptance factors, and that certain message configurations would be much more successful than others.[21]

Smith and Swinyard point out that communication strategies for high-involvement products may be difficult to implement since media advertising often has little effect on higher-order attitude formation or change. Thus, they suggest that marketing communications focus on achieving a product demonstration rather than a direct urge to purchase. Product demonstrations and information received from compelling personal communication sources, such as knowledgeable and well-trained in-store sales personnel, are more likely to change higher-order beliefs and affect and lead to purchase.

An important implication of the integrated information response model is that consumers are likely to integrate information from advertising, other sources, and direct experience in forming judgments about a brand. For example, in a recent study Robert Smith found that advertising can lessen the negative effects of an unfavourable trial experience on brand evaluations when the ad is processed before the trial. However, when a negative trial experience precedes exposure to an ad, cognitive evaluations of the ad are more negative.[22] Thus it is important to consider how consumers integrate advertising with other brand information sources, both before and after trial or purchase.

Implications of the Alternative Response Models The various response models offer an interesting perspective on the ways consumers respond to advertising and other forms of marketing communications. They also provide insight into promotional strategies marketers might pursue in different situations. A review of these alternative models of the response process shows that the traditional standard learning model does not always apply. The notion of a highly involved consumer who engages in active information processing and learning and acts on the basis of higher-order beliefs and a well-formed attitude may be inappropriate for some types of purchases. Sometimes consumers make a purchase decision on the basis of general awareness resulting from repetitive exposure to advertising, and attitude development occurs after the purchase, if at all. The integrated information response model suggests that the role of advertising and other forms of promotion may be to induce trial, so consumers can develop brand preferences primarily on the basis of their direct experience with the product.

From a promotional planning perspective, it is important that marketers examine the communication situation for their product or service and determine which type of response process is most likely to occur. They should analyze involvement levels and product/service differentiation as well as consumers' use of various information sources and their levels of experience with the product or service. Once the manager has determined which response sequence is most likely to operate, the integrated marketing communications program can be designed to influence the response process in favour of the company's product or service.

The hierarchical response models were for many years the primary focus of approaches for studying the receivers' responses to marketing communications. Attention centred on identifying relationships between specific controllable variables (such as source and message factors) and outcome or response variables (such as attention, comprehension, attitudes, and purchase intentions). This approach has been criticized on a number of fronts, including its black-box nature, since it can't explain what is causing these reactions.[23] In response to these concerns, researchers began trying to understand the nature of cognitive reactions to persuasive messages. Several approaches have been developed to examine the nature of consumers' cognitive processing of advertising messages.

Cognitive Processing of Communications

The Cognitive Response Approach

One of the most widely used methods for examining consumers' cognitive processing of advertising messages is assessment of their **cognitive responses,** the thoughts that occur to them while reading, viewing, and/or hearing a communication.[24] These thoughts are generally measured by having consumers write down or verbally report their reactions to a message. The assumption is that these thoughts reflect the recipient's cognitive processes or reactions and help shape ultimate acceptance or rejection of the message.

The cognitive response approach has been widely used in research by both academicians and advertising practitioners. Its focus has been to determine the types of responses evoked by an advertising message and how these responses relate to attitudes toward the ad, brand attitudes, and purchase intentions. Figure 4–8 depicts the three basic categories of cognitive responses researchers have identified—product/message, source-oriented, and ad execution thoughts—and how they may relate to attitudes and intentions.

Product/Message Thoughts 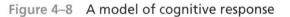 The first category of thoughts comprises those directed at the product or service and/or the claims being made in the communication. Much attention has focused on two particular types of responses, counterarguments and support arguments.

Figure 4–8   A model of cognitive response

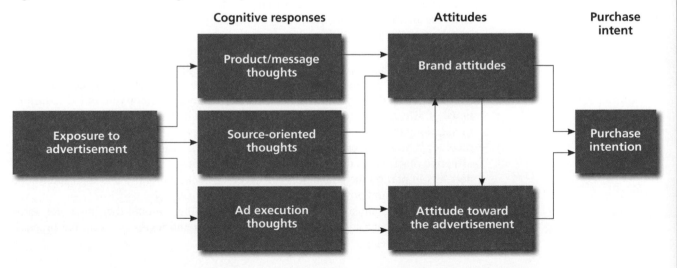

DEEP DISASTER:

Cherry Pie Packed Pleats.

DEEP CLEAN:

ULTRA Tide

WHEN STAINS GET DEEP IN ULTRA TIDE GETS THEM CLEAN OUT.

Exhibit 4–8 Consumers often generate support arguments in response to ads for quality products

Counterarguments are thoughts the recipient has that are opposed to the position taken in the message. For example, consider the ad for Ultra Tide shown in Exhibit 4–8. A consumer may express disbelief or disapproval of a claim made in an ad. ("I don't believe that any detergent could get that stain out!") Other consumers who see this ad may generate **support arguments,** or thoughts that affirm the claims made in the message. ("Ultra Tide looks like a really good product—I think I'll try it.")

The likelihood of counterarguing is greater when the message makes claims that oppose the receiver's beliefs. For example, a consumer viewing a commercial that attacks a favourite brand is likely to engage in counterarguing. Counterarguments relate negatively to message acceptance; the more the receiver counterargues, the less likely he or she is to accept the position advocated in the message.[25] Support arguments, on the other hand, relate positively to message acceptance. Thus, the marketer should develop ads or other promotional messages that minimize counterarguing and encourage support arguments.

Source-Oriented Thoughts   A second category of cognitive responses is directed at the source of the communication. One of the most important types of responses in this category is **source derogations,** or negative thoughts about the spokesperson or organization making the claims. Such thoughts generally lead to a reduction in message acceptance. If consumers find a particular spokesperson annoying or untrustworthy, they are less likely to accept what this source has to say.

Of course, source-related thoughts are not always negative. Receivers who react favourably to the source generate favourable thoughts, or **source bolsters.** As you would expect, most advertisers attempt to hire spokespeople their target audience likes so as to carry this effect over to the message. Considerations involved in choosing an appropriate source or spokesperson will be discussed in Chapter 6.

Ad Execution Thoughts   The third category of cognitive responses shown in Figure 4–8 consists of the individual's thoughts about the ad itself. Many of the thoughts receivers have when reading or viewing an ad do not concern the product and/or message claims directly. Rather, they are affective reactions representing the consumer's feelings toward the ad. These thoughts may include reactions to ad execution factors such as the creativity of the ad, the quality of the visual effects, colours, and voice tones. **Ad execution-related thoughts** can be either favourable or unfavourable. They are important because of their effect on attitudes toward the advertisement as well as the brand.

In recent years, much attention has focused on consumers' affective reactions to ads, especially TV commercials.[26] **Attitude toward the ad** (A → ad) represents the receivers' feelings of favourability or unfavourability toward the ad. Advertisers are interested in consumers' reactions to the ad because they know that affective reactions are an important determinant of advertising effectiveness, since these reactions may be transferred to the brand itself or directly influence purchase intentions. One study found that people who enjoy a commercial are twice as likely as those who are neutral toward it to be convinced that the brand is the best.[27]

Consumers' feelings about the ad may be just as important as their attitudes toward the brand (if not more so) in determining an ad's effectiveness.[28] The importance of affective reactions and feelings generated by the ad depend on several factors, among them the nature of the ad and the type of processing engaged in by the receiver.[29] Many advertisers now use emotional ads designed to evoke feelings and affective reactions as the basis of their creative strategy. The success of this strategy depends in part on the consumers' involvement with the brand and their likelihood of attending to and processing the message.

We end our analysis of the receiver by examining a model that integrates some of the factors that may account for different types and levels of cognitive processing of a message.

The Elaboration Likelihood Model

Differences in the ways consumers process and respond to persuasive messages are addressed in the **elaboration likelihood model (ELM)** of persuasion, shown in Figure 4–9.[30] The ELM was devised by Richard Petty and John Cacioppo to explain the process by which persuasive communications (such as ads) lead to persuasion by influencing *attitudes*. According to this model, the attitude formation or change process depends on the amount and nature of *elaboration,* or processing, of relevant information that occurs in response to a persuasive message. High elaboration means the receiver engages in careful consideration, thinking, and evaluation of the information or arguments contained in the message. Low elaboration occurs when the receiver does not engage in active information processing or thinking but rather makes inferences about the position being advocated in the message on the basis of simple positive or negative cues.

The ELM shows that elaboration likelihood is a function of two elements, motivation and ability to process the message. *Motivation* to process the message depends on such factors as involvement, personal relevance, and individuals' needs

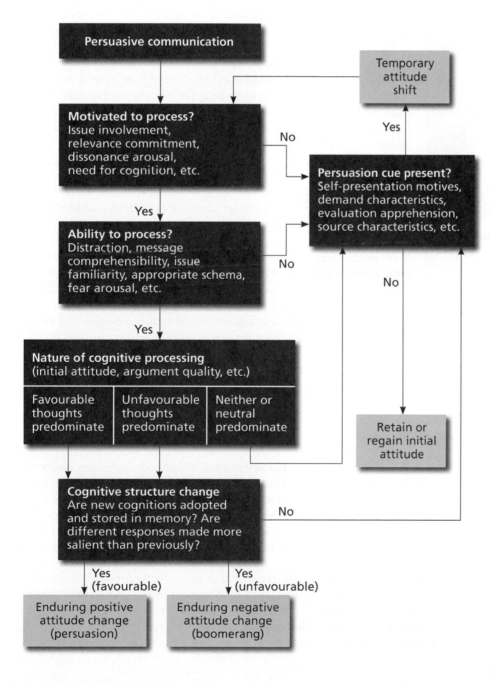

Figure 4–9 The elaboration likelihood model of persuasion

and arousal levels. *Ability* depends on the individual's knowledge, intellectual capacity, and opportunity to process the message. For example, an individual viewing a humourous commercial or one containing an attractive model may be distracted from processing the information about the product.

According to the ELM, there are two basic routes to persuasion or attitude change. Under the **central route to persuasion,** the receiver is viewed as a very active, involved participant in the communication process whose ability and motivation to attend, comprehend, and evaluate messages are high. When central processing of an advertising message occurs, the consumer pays close attention to message content and scrutinizes the message arguments. A high level of cognitive response activity or processing occurs, and the ad's ability to persuade the receiver depends primarily on the receiver's evaluation of the quality of the arguments presented. Predominantly favourable cognitive responses (support arguments and source bolsters) lead to favourable changes in cognitive structure, which lead to positive attitude change, or persuasion.

Conversely, if the cognitive processing is predominantly unfavourable and results in counterarguments and/or source derogations, the changes in cognitive structure are unfavourable and *boomerang,* or result in negative attitude change. Attitude change that occurs through central processing is relatively enduring and should resist subsequent efforts to change it.

Under the **peripheral route to persuasion,** shown on the right side of Figure 4–9, the receiver is viewed as lacking the motivation or ability to process information and is not likely to engage in detailed cognitive processing. Rather than evaluating the information presented in the message, the receiver relies on peripheral cues that may be incidental to the main arguments. The receiver's reaction to the message depends on how he or she evaluates these peripheral cues.

The consumer may use several types of peripheral cues or cognitive shortcuts rather than carefully evaluating the message arguments presented in an advertisement.[31] Favourable attitudes may be formed if the endorser in the ad is viewed as an expert or is attractive and/or likable or if the consumer likes certain executional aspects of the ad such as the way it is made, the music, or the imagery. Notice how the public relations photo in Exhibit 4–9 contains several positive peripheral cues, including popular celebrity endorsers and excellent visual imagery. These cues might help consumers form a positive attitude toward the brand even if they do not process the message portion of the ad.

Peripheral cues can also lead to rejection of a message. For example, ads that advocate extreme positions, use endorsers who are not well liked or have credibility problems, or are not executed well (such as low-budget ads for local retailers) may be rejected without any consideration of their information or message arguments. As shown in Figure 4–9, the ELM views attitudes resulting from peripheral processing as temporary. So favourable attitudes must be maintained by continual exposure to the peripheral cues, such as through repetitive advertising.

Exhibit 4–9 This public relations photo contains peripheral cues, most notably celebrity endorsers

Implications of the ELM   The elaboration likelihood model has important implications for marketing communications, particularly with respect to involvement. For example, if the involvement level of consumers in the target audience is high, an ad or sales presentation should contain strong arguments that are difficult for the message recipient to refute or counterargue. If the involvement level of the target audience is low, peripheral cues may be more important than detailed message arguments.

An interesting test of the ELM showed that the effectiveness of a celebrity endorser in an ad depends on the receiver's involvement level.[32] When involvement was low, a celebrity endorser had a significant effect on attitudes. When the receiver's involvement was high, however, the use of a celebrity had no effect on brand attitudes; the quality of the arguments used in the ad was more important.

The explanation given for these findings was that a celebrity may serve as a peripheral cue in the low-involvement situation, allowing the receiver to develop favourable attitudes based on feelings toward the source rather than engaging in extensive processing of the message. A highly involved consumer, however, engages in more detailed central processing of the message content. The quality of the message claims becomes more important than the identity of the endorser.

The ELM suggests that the most effective type of message depends on the route to persuasion the consumer follows. Many marketers recognize that involvement levels are low for their product categories and consumers are not motivated to process advertising messages in any detail. That's why marketers of low-involvement products often rely on creative tactics that emphasize peripheral cues and use repetitive advertising to create and maintain favourable attitudes toward their brand.

Summarizing the Response Process and the Effects of Advertising

As you have seen from our analysis of the receiver, the process consumers go through in responding to marketing communications can be viewed from a number of perspectives. Vakratsas and Ambler recently reviewed more than 250 journal articles and books in an effort to better understand how advertising works and affects the consumer.[33] On the basis of their review of these studies, they concluded that although effects hierarchies have been actively employed for nearly 100 years, there is little support for the concept of a hierarchy of effects in the sense of temporal sequence. They note that in trying to understand the response process and the manner in which advertising works, there are three critical intermediate effects between advertising and purchase (Figure 4–10). These include *cognition,* the "thinking" dimension of a person's response; *affect,* the "feeling" dimension; and *experience,* which is a feedback dimension based on the outcomes of product purchasing and usage. They conclude that individual responses to advertising are mediated or filtered by factors such as motivation and ability to process information, which can radically alter or change the individual's response to advertising. They suggest that the effects of advertising should be evaluated using these three dimensions, with some intermediate variables being more important than others, depending on factors such as the product category, stage of the product life cycle, target audience, competition, and impact of other marketing-mix components.

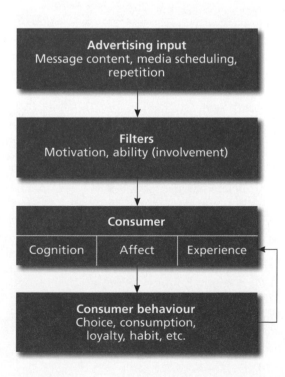

Figure 4–10   A framework for studying how advertising works

The implication is that marketers should focus on knowledge, liking, and trial as critical variables that advertising may affect. However, they should not assume a particular sequence of responses but rather engage in communications research and analysis to understand how advertising and other forms of promotion may affect these intermediate variables in various product/market situations. Those responsible for planning the IMC program need to learn as much as possible about their target market and how it may respond to advertising and other forms of marketing communications. The communication models presented in this chapter provide insight into how consumers may process and respond to persuasive messages and hopefully help marketers make better decisions in planning and implementing their promotional programs.

Summary

The function of all elements of the promotional mix is to communicate, so promotional planners must understand the communication process. This process can be very complex; successful marketing communications depend on a number of factors, including the nature of the message, the audience's interpretation of it, and the environment in which it is received. For effective communication to occur, the sender must encode a message in such a way that it will be decoded by the receiver in the intended manner. Feedback from the receiver helps the sender determine whether proper decoding has occurred or whether noise has interfered with the communication process.

Promotional planning begins with the receiver or target audience, as marketers must understand how the audience is likely to respond to various sources of communication or types of messages. Different orderings of the traditional response hierarchy include the standard learning, dissonance/attribution, and low-involvement models. The information response model integrates concepts from both the high- and low-involvement response hierarchy perspectives and recognizes the effects of direct experience with a product.

The cognitive response approach examines the thoughts evoked by a message and how they shape the receiver's ultimate acceptance or rejection of the communication. The elaboration likelihood model of attitude formation and change recognizes two forms of message processing, the central and peripheral routes to persuasion, which are a function of the receiver's motivation and ability to process a message. There are three critical intermediate effects between advertising and purchase including cognition, affect, and experience. Those responsible for planning the IMC program should learn as much as possible about their target audience and how it may respond to advertising and other forms of marketing communications.

Key Terms

Discussion Questions

1. Discuss the various elements of the communications process. Find an example of an advertising campaign being used by a company and analyze this campaign in terms of these elements of the communications model.

2. Discuss how semiotics can be of value to the field of integrated marketing communications. Select a marketing stimulus such as an advertisement, package, or other relevant marketing symbol and conduct a semiotic analysis of it such as the one shown in Exhibit 4–2.

3. Discuss the various forms feedback might take in the following situations:

- A consumer has just watched an infomercial for a revolutionary new exercise machine on late night television.
- An avid book reader has just logged onto the website of a company such as Amazon.com or Barnes & Noble.com.
- TV viewers watching the show "Friends" on a Thursday evening see a commercial for Calvin Klein jeans.

4. Explain how a company like Home Depot could use the four models of the response process shown in Figure 4–3 to develop IMC strategies for its various products.

5. An implication of the integrated information response model is that consumers are likely to take information from advertising and integrate it with direct experience to form judgments about a product. Explain how advertising could lessen the negative outcomes a consumer might experience when trying a brand.

6. What is meant by involvement in terms of advertising and consumer behaviour? How might marketers determine the degree of involvement consumers have with their products and services?

7. Select an ad you think would be processed by a central route to persuasion and one where you think peripheral processing would occur. Show the ads to several people and ask them to write down the thoughts they have about each ad. Analyze their thoughts using the cognitive response categories discussed in the chapter.

Chapter Five

Objectives for the IMC Plan

Chapter Objectives

- To recognize the value of setting specific objectives for advertising and promotion.

- To know the differences between marketing and communication objectives and the issues regarding the use of each.

- To know the historical approaches for setting communication objectives for advertising.

- To understand a comprehensive framework for setting communication and behavioural objectives for all aspects of the IMC plan.

Manitoba Telecom

Defining your communication objectives and finding the right campaign is an important step in IMC planning, and it looks like Manitoba Telecom Services (MTS) has hit a winner. A wise-talking bison has vaulted MTS to advertising recall of 80 percent and market shares of 98 percent for local access, 90 percent for long distance, 68 percent for cellular service (compared to 29 percent for the next competitor), and 62 percent for Internet access (compared to 23 percent for the next competitor).

Historically a provincial Crown corporation, MTS faced competition for the first time in the 1990s because of deregulation. With a conservative and stuffy image due to its monopoly situation for so many years, the now-public MTS needed to reposition itself in its marketing communications as new products and services emerged along with a growing, technologically oriented younger market. Clearly, MTS had to emphasize awareness as consumers evaluated the products and services of MTS and its competitors; but as importantly, MTS had to ensure that consumers perceived the need for new services and products, and believed that MTS was the firm to purchase from.

Enter Morty the talking bison. As the MTS executives noted, they are using a well-established strategy of having an animal to represent the brand. But in this case, it seems to resonate especially well with the people of Manitoba as the bison is the provincial symbol. In the first 16 months, MTS has run more than three dozen Morty commercials—that's about one new creative execution every two weeks! And just think, Morty the bison could have been Morty the prairie dog! It seems that the executives had already decided to use an animal to represent the brand, but a keen maintenance man overhearing the plan discreetly suggested that a bison might be more appropriate. Go figure; you never know when or where a creative idea will arise.

Initially, MTS restricted Morty across its IMC tools, but eventually, Morty was the "spokesperson" for all products and services and could be seen in all communications from advertising to direct mail and the company's website. Now when people see a bison, they naturally think MTS. And therein lies concern for the future. As one executive notes, "People are remembering the commercial but not the product." This suggests that the MTS company brand awareness is well entrenched but the awareness for individual products is weakening.

Sources: Judy Waytiuk, "Morty Mania," *Marketing Magazine,* March 5, 2001; "Manitoba Telecom Services," *Marketing Magazine,* November 19, 2001.

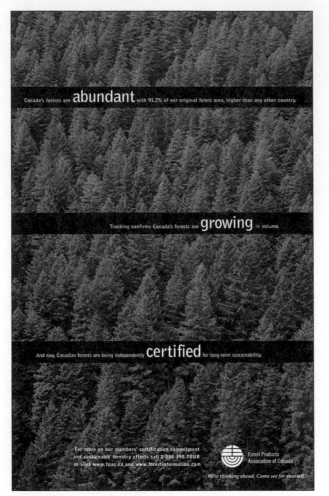

Exhibit 5–1 The objective of this ad is to promote the Canadian Pulp and Paper Association's concern for the environment

Many companies have difficulty with the most critical step in the promotional planning process—setting realistic objectives that will guide the development of the IMC program. Complex marketing situations, conflicting perspectives regarding what advertising and other promotional mix elements are expected to accomplish, and uncertainty over resources make the setting of marketing communication objectives "a job of creating order out of chaos."[1] While the task of setting objectives can be complex and difficult, it must be done properly, because specific goals and objectives are the foundation on which all other promotional decisions are made. Budgeting for advertising and other promotional areas, as well as creative and media strategies and tactics, evolve from these objectives. They also provide a standard against which performance can be measured.

Setting specific objectives should be an integral part of the planning process. However, many companies either fail to use specific marketing communication objectives or set ones that are inadequate for guiding the development of the promotional plan or measuring its effectiveness. Many marketers are uncertain as to what integrated marketing communications should be expected to contribute to the marketing program. Furthermore, with the selection of so many different integrated marketing communication tools and target audiences, it is difficult to know how each element of the IMC plan contributes to the complete IMC plan. And it is difficult to know what specific objectives each IMC tool should have to measure their effectiveness (Exhibit 5–1).

Often marketers mistakenly use only marketing objectives to assess whether their advertising and promotion plans were successful. As we know, advertising and promotion are not the only marketing activities involved in generating sales. Moreover, it is not always possible or necessary to measure the effects of advertising in terms of sales. Consider the Ford ad shown in Exhibit 5–2. What objectives (other than generating sales) might the company have for this ad? How might its effectiveness be measured?

This chapter examines the nature and purpose of objectives and the role they play in guiding the development, implementation, and evaluation of an IMC program. Attention is initially given to marketing and communication objectives. Then we consider the approaches of setting communication objectives for advertising based on the response models previously discussed in Chapter 4. We then turn our attention to new approaches for setting communication and behavioural objectives for each element of the IMC plan and for the overall IMC plan that will be consistently referred to in Parts Three, Four, and Five of the book.

Objective Setting

Value of Objectives

Perhaps one reason many companies fail to set specific objectives for their integrated marketing communications programs is that they don't recognize the value of doing so. Advertising and promotional objectives are needed for several reasons, including the functions they serve in communication, planning and decision-making, and measurement and evaluation.

Communications Specific objectives for the IMC program facilitate coordination of the various groups working on the campaign. Many people are involved in the planning and development of an integrated marketing communications program on the client side as well as in the various promotional agencies. The advertising and promotional program must be coordinated within the company, inside the ad agency, and between the two. Any other parties involved in the promotional campaign, such as public relations and/or sales promotion firms, research specialists, or media buying services, must also know what the company hopes to accomplish through its marketing communications program. Many problems can be avoided if all parties have written approved objectives to guide their actions and serve as a common base for discussing issues related to the promotional program.

Planning and Decision Making Specific promotional objectives also guide development of the integrated marketing communications plan. All phases of a firm's promotional strategy should be based on the established objectives, including budgeting, creative, and media decisions as well as supportive programs such as direct marketing, public relations/publicity, sales promotion, and/or reseller support.

Meaningful objectives can also be a useful guide for decision making. Promotional planners are often faced with a number of strategic and tactical options in terms of choosing creative options, selecting media, and allocating the budget among various elements of the promotional mix. Choices should be made based on how well a particular strategy matches the firm's promotional objectives.

Measurement and Evaluation of Results An important reason for setting specific objectives is that they provide a benchmark against which the success or failure of the promotional campaign can be measured. Without specific objectives, it is extremely difficult to determine what the firm's advertising and promotion efforts accomplished. One characteristic of good objectives is that they are measurable; they specify a method and criteria for determining how well the promotional program is working. By setting specific and meaningful objectives, the promotional planner provides measures that can be used to evaluate the effectiveness of the marketing communications program. Most organizations are concerned about the return on their promotional investment, and comparing actual performance against measurable objectives is the best way to determine if the return justifies the expense.

Exhibit 5–2 Ford's objectives for this ad may be other than sales

Types of Objectives

One difficulty in setting marketing and IMC programs is using the most appropriate objectives for the task at hand. While the IMC program supports the overall marketing program, each should have its own clear objective so that managers can assess where to make corrective decisions if some aspect of the brand's performance is not successful. We turn our attention to marketing and communication objectives and explain how they are related to one another.

Marketing Objectives **Marketing objectives** are generally stated in the firm's marketing plan and are statements of what is to be accomplished by the overall marketing program within a given time period. Marketing objectives are usually defined in terms of specific, measurable outcomes such as sales volume, market share, profits, or return on investment. Good marketing objectives are quantifiable; delineate the target market and note the time frame for accomplishing the goal (often one year). For example, a copy-machine company may have as its marketing objective "to increase sales by 10 percent in the small-business segment of the market during the next 12 months." To be effective, objectives must also be realistic and attainable.

The choice of the type of marketing objective is likely a function of market conditions. A company with a very high market share may seek to increase its sales volume by stimulating growth in the product category. It might accomplish this by increasing consumption by current users or encouraging nonusers to buy the product. A firm in a fast growing market may have market share as its marketing objective since this reflects that it is growing more quickly than its direct competitors. Alternatively, in mature markets with limited growth, firms tend to focus on profit as the key marketing objective. Finally, a firm that faces unique consumer preferences across various geographic markets (i.e., Ontario versus Quebec) may in fact have a separate marketing objective for each region.

Once the marketing communications manager has reviewed the marketing plan, he or she should understand the marketing objectives of the marketing program, how it intends to get there, and the role advertising and promotion will play. Marketing goals defined in terms of sales, profit, or market share increases are usually not appropriate promotional objectives. They are objectives for the entire marketing program, and achieving them depends on the proper coordination and execution of all the marketing mix elements, including not just promotion but also product planning and production, pricing, and distribution. In contrast, many promotional planners approach promotion from a communications perspective and believe the objective of advertising and other promotional mix elements is usually to communicate information or a selling message about a product or service.

Despite this prescription, some managers believe the only meaningful objective for their promotional program is sales. They take the position that the basic reason a firm spends money on advertising and promotion is to sell its product or service. Promotional spending represents an investment of a firm's scarce resources that requires an economic justification. Rational managers generally compare investment options on a common financial basis, such as return on investment (ROI). They believe that monies spent on advertising and other forms of promotion should produce measurable results, such as increasing sales volume by a certain percentage or dollar amount or increasing the brand's market share. These beliefs are partly a result of marketing and brand managers being under pressure to show sales results. They often take a short-term perspective in evaluating advertising and sales promotion programs and look for a quick fix for declining sales or loss of market share.

One problem with sales objectives for promotion is that poor sales results can be due to any of the other marketing mix variables, including product design or quality, packaging, distribution, or pricing. Advertising can make consumers aware of and interested in the brand, but it can't make them buy it, particularly if it is not readily available or is priced higher than a competing brand. As shown in Figure 5–1, sales are a function of many factors, not just advertising and promotion.

Figure 5–1   Factors influencing sales

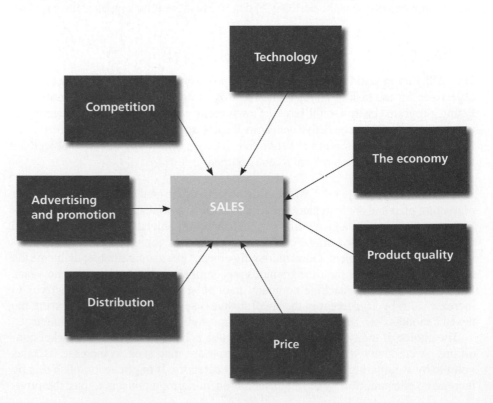

Reaching New L'Oréal Customers

A great product with a new technology targeted to young women ages 16 to 25 is what the managers at L'Oréal had on their hands when they introduced Open, Vibrantly Natural Colour gel. The key benefit of the technology is that it would offer "natural looking colour that is also visible, vibrant and translucent." Since the product was trying to attract first-time users of hair-colouring products, L'Oréal had the challenge of establishing many objectives for the campaign, including category need, awareness, brand attitude, trial, and a key purchase-related action objective of word-of-mouth communication.

L'Oréal used traditional advertising media to build awareness. The use of three different media —television ads, cinema ads, and transit ads— helped to ensure a certain amount or reach and frequency. It might be expected that this contributed to awareness at the critical need-arousal stage.

It appears that the Internet played a key role in establishing communication objectives at the important information search and evaluation stage. A "mini" website contributed to the target's understanding of the benefits of "freshest colour and light," "vibrant and natural," and "soft and luminous" (i.e. brand-attitude objective), as well as a desire for this type of product by stating that "It is a technological innovation that brightens your natural hair colour" (i.e., establish category need). L'Oreal used the advertising media and other Internet tools (i.e., e-banners, e-newsletter, and virtual postcards). The website also facilitated delivery samples to spur trial usage and future trial purchases.

To generate additional trial and, more importantly, word-of-mouth communication at the product usage stage, L'Oréal used two key IMC tools. A contest was run in *Verve* magazine in which the target audience voted for their choice of the "Open Girl," who was later featured on the cover of the magazine. L'Oréal created events such as *Open Tour, Open Lounge,* and *Open Happenings* where consumers could interact together and sample the product.

Sources: Ron Szekely, "L'Oréal Generates Buzz," *Marketing Magazine*, January 7, 2002; www.lorealparis.ca/en/home.asp.

Another problem with sales objectives is that the effects of advertising often occur over an extended period. Many experts recognize that advertising has a lagged or **carryover effect**; monies spent on advertising do not necessarily have an immediate impact on sales.[2] Advertising may create awareness, interest, and/or favourable attitudes toward a brand, but these feelings will not result in an actual purchase until the consumer enters the market for the product, which may occur later. A review of econometric studies that examined the duration of cumulative advertising effects found that for mature, frequently purchased, low-priced products, advertising's effect on sales lasts up to nine months.[3] Models have been developed to account for the carryover effect of advertising and to help determine the long-term effect of advertising on sales.[4] The carryover effect adds to the difficulty of determining the precise relationship between advertising and sales.

A third problem with sales objectives is that they offer little guidance to those responsible for planning and developing the promotional program. The creative and media people working on the account need some direction as to the nature of the advertising message the company hopes to communicate, the intended audience, and the particular effect or response sought. As you will see shortly, communication objectives are recommended because they provide operational guidelines for those involved in planning, developing, and executing the advertising and promotional program.

The counter argument to these three points is that sales objectives are appropriate when the above three factors are not relevant. If a marketer is certain that other marketing or environmental factors were not influencing sales, that the carryover effect was not occurring, or that the managers involved did not require guidance, then a sales objective could be plausible. In general, the likelihood of such conditions arising appears quite remote, which necessitates the use of communication objectives as the primary approach for promotional planning purposes. To illustrate this point we will discuss two examples: direct response advertising and the marketing practices of packaged-goods firms.

Direct-response advertising is one type of advertising that typically evaluates its effectiveness on the basis of sales. Merchandise is advertised in material mailed to customers, in newspapers and magazines, or on television. The consumer purchases the merchandise by mail or by calling a toll-free number. The direct-response advertiser generally sets objectives and measures success in terms of the sales response generated by the ad. For example, objectives for and the evaluation of a direct-response ad on TV are based on the number of orders received each time a station broadcasts the commercial. Because advertising is really the only form of communication and promotion used in this situation and response is generally immediate, setting objectives in terms of sales appear appropriate.

However, this is an example where a carryover effect may be working. Consumers receive the ad many times during the campaign and decide not to purchase. During subsequent campaigns during the year, these consumers have the communication effect of the previous campaign combined with word-of-mouth communication and evaluation considerations. The cumulative impact of all communications can influence the consumer as he or she proceeds through the usual decision-making process. Establishing communication objectives is still a critical step in understanding the effectiveness of the ads once again indicating that sales objectives alone are not sufficient.

We now turn to our second example. Many package-goods companies compete in mature markets with established channels of distribution, stable competitive prices and promotional budgets, and products of similar quality. They view advertising and sales promotion as the key determinants of a brand's sales or market share, so it may be possible to isolate the effects of these promotional mix variables.[5] Many companies have accumulated enough market knowledge with their advertising, sales promotion, and direct-marketing programs to have considerable insight into the sales levels that should result from their promotional efforts. Thus, they believe it is reasonable to set objectives and evaluate the success of their promotional efforts in terms of sales results (Exhibit 5–3).

Again, this appears to be a plausible explanation; however, we can surmise a few factors that make the setting of communication objectives an important step for predicting the sales results. Even mature categories have new customers entering the market to which communication effects are important considerations for seeing if these customers are gravitating to one's own or a competing brand. Consumer perceptions of campaign-message changes and promotional-mix alterations may have a delayed effect on sales, and an understanding of consumer psychological reactions (i.e., attitude) may be more immediately forthcoming.

Exhibit 5–3 Sales objectives for new products are difficult to determine

Communication Objectives   Communication objectives are statements of what the communications will accomplish. In general, objectives are based on one or more consumer response models discussed in Chapter 4. We can speak of communication objectives on three levels depending upon the decision at hand. There are communication objectives for the overall IMC plan. We can also speak of communication objectives for individual IMC tools (i.e., advertising). Often, as was shown in Chapter 1, these communication objectives are referred to as objectives for the particular tool (i.e., advertising objectives). When working in this field, marketers may use either of these terms depending upon their background or company practices. Finally, we can also use the concept of communication objectives for individual elements of a communication tool. For example, when we design an individual print ad, we want to make sure it achieves the communication objectives we set for it.

Irrespective of whether we are speaking of communication objectives for the IMC plan, a particular tool, or a specific ad, **the communication objectives should be based on the particular communication tasks required to deliver the appropriate messages to the specific target audience at a relevant point within the target audience's purchase decision-making process and consumption experience.**

Managers must be able to translate general marketing goals into communication goals and specific promotional objectives. Some guidance in doing this may be available from the situation analysis of the marketing plan, which includes the following:

- The market segments the firm wants to target and the target audiences (customer status, demographics, psychographics, and purchase motives) that the firm wishes to communicate with.
- The product's main features, attributes, benefits, uses, and applications.
- The company's and competitors' brands (sales and market share in various segments, market positioning, competitive strategies, promotional expenditures, creative and media strategies, and tactics).

After reviewing all the information, the promotional planner should see how integrated marketing communications fit into the marketing program and what the firm hopes to achieve through advertising and other promotional elements. The importance of setting communication objectives of a promotional plan that contributes to sales is seen in the Del Monte example. The ads for Del Monte stewed tomatoes and snack cups in Exhibit 5–4 were part of the company's marketing strategy to increase sales and market share for its various food products by targeting existing or lapsed users as well as new, younger customers. The 12-month, $20 million advertising

Exhibit 5–4   These ads for Del Monte food products were part of a marketing strategy designed to increase sales and market share

campaign used a series of four-colour ads featuring new recipe ideas and serving suggestions. All of the ads used the same graphic format to help build the Del Monte brand through improved recognition and stronger attitudes while promoting individual products. The campaign resulted in increased market share for all four of the advertised categories.

In some situations, promotional planners may gain insight into the relationship between communication objectives and sales from industry research. Evalucom, Inc., conducted a study of commercials for new products. Some succeeded in stimulating anticipated levels of sales; others did not. Figure 5–2 shows four factors the study identified that affect whether a commercial for a new product is successful in generating sales. For each of these factors, we can see the importance of setting clear communication objectives.

When setting specific communication objectives, promotional planners often are not sure what constitutes adequate levels of awareness, knowledge, liking, preference, or conviction. No formulas provide this information. The promotional manager will have to use his or her personal experience and that of the brand or product managers, as well as the marketing history of this and similar brands. Average scores on various communication measures for this and similar products should be considered, along with the levels achieved by competitors' products. We now turn to various approaches for setting communication objectives that provide guidelines for some of these concerns.

From Communication Models to Communication Objectives

Over the years, a number of methods have been developed for deciding upon communication objectives for advertising, related tools, and complete IMC plans. We review three approaches from a historical perspective in this section: the DAGMAR model, an application of more comprehensive response hierarchies, and new IMC approaches. We begin with the DAGMAR model that provided guidance for setting advertising objectives. Next we consider an application of the Lavidge and Steiner model discussed in Chapter 4. Then we investigate new IMC approaches that attempt to go beyond the limitations of the traditional response hierarchies.

Defining Advertising Goals for Measured Results

In 1961, Russell Colley prepared a report for the Association of National Advertisers titled **Defining Advertising Goals for Measured Advertising Results (DAGMAR)**.[6] In it, Colley developed a model for setting advertising objectives and measuring the results of an ad campaign. The major contribution of the DAGMAR model is its recognition that communication effects are the logical basis for adver-

Figure 5–2 Factors related to success of advertising for new products

- **Communicating that something is different about the product.** Successful introductory commercials communicated some point of difference for the new product.
- **Positioning the brand difference in relation to the product category.** Successful commercials positioned their brand's difference within a specific product category. For example, a new breakfast product was positioned as the "crispiest cereal" and a new beverage as the "smoothest soft drink."
- **Communicating that the product difference is beneficial to consumers.** Nearly all of the successful commercials linked a benefit directly to the new product's difference.
- **Supporting the idea that something about the product is different and/or beneficial to consumers.** All the successful commercials communicated support for the product's difference claim or its relevance to consumers. Support took the form of demonstrations of performance, information supporting a uniqueness claim, endorsements, or testimonials.

tising goals and objectives against which success or failure should be measured. Colley's rationale for communication-based objectives was as follows:

> Advertising's job, purely and simply, is to communicate to a defined audience information and a frame of mind that stimulates action. Advertising succeeds or fails depending on how well it communicates the desired information and attitudes to the right people at the right time and at the right cost.[7]

Under the DAGMAR approach, an advertising goal involves a communication task that is specific and measurable. A **communication task**, as opposed to a marketing task, can be performed by, and attributed to, advertising rather than to a combination of several marketing factors. Colley proposed that the communication task be based on a hierarchical model of the communication process with four stages:

- Awareness—making the consumer aware of the existence of the brand or company.
- Comprehension—developing an understanding of what the product is and what it will do for the consumer.
- Conviction—developing a mental disposition in the consumer to buy the product.
- Action—getting the consumer to purchase the product.

While the hierarchical model of advertising effects was the basic model of the communication response process used in DAGMAR, Colley also studied other specific tasks that advertising might be expected to perform in leading to the ultimate objective of a sale. He developed a checklist of 52 advertising tasks to characterize the contribution of advertising and serve as a starting point for establishing objectives.

Characteristics of Objectives

A second major contribution of DAGMAR to the advertising planning process was its definition of what constitutes a good objective. Colley argued that advertising objectives should specify a target audience, be stated in terms of concrete and measurable communication tasks, indicate a benchmark starting point and the degree of change sought, and specify a time period for accomplishing the objective(s).

Target Audience An important characteristic of good objectives is a well-defined target audience. The primary target audience for a company's product or service is described in the situation analysis. It may be based on descriptive variables such as geography, demographics, and psychographics (on which advertising media selection decisions are based) as well as on behavioural variables such as customer status (i.e. brand loyal users), usage rate, or benefits sought. This step is critical since the communication effect has to be interpreted from the perspective of the intended receiver.

Concrete, Measurable Tasks The communication task specified in the objective should be a precise statement of what appeal or message the advertiser wants to communicate to the target audience. Advertisers generally use a copy platform to describe their basic message. The objective or copy platform statement should be specific and clear enough to guide the creative specialists who develop the advertising message. According to DAGMAR, the objective must also be measurable. There must be a way to determine whether the intended message has been communicated properly.

Benchmark and Degree of Change Sought To set objectives, one must know the target audience's present status concerning response hierarchy variables (e.g., awareness) and then determine the degree to which consumers must be changed by the advertising campaign. Determining the target audience's present position regarding the various response stages requires **benchmark measures**. Often a marketing research study must be conducted to determine prevailing levels of the response hierarchy. In the case of a new product or service, the starting conditions are generally at or near zero for all the variables, so no initial research is needed.

Establishing benchmark measures gives the promotional planner a basis for determining what communication tasks need to be accomplished and for specifying particular objectives. For example, a preliminary study for a brand may reveal that awareness is high but consumer perceptions and attitudes are negative. The objective for the advertising campaign must then be to change the target audience's perceptions of and attitudes toward the brand.

Quantitative benchmarks are not only valuable in establishing communications goals and objectives but essential for determining whether the campaign was successful. Objectives provide the standard against which the success or failure of a campaign is measured. An ad campaign that results in a 90 percent awareness level for a brand among its target audience cannot really be judged effective unless one knows what percentage of the consumers were aware of the brand before the campaign began. A 70 percent pre-campaign awareness level would lead to a different interpretation of the campaign's success than would a 30 percent level.

Specified Time Period   A final consideration in setting advertising objectives is specifying the time period in which they must be accomplished. Appropriate time periods can range from a few days to a year or more. Most ad campaigns specify time periods from a few months to a year, depending on the situation facing the advertiser and the type of response being sought. For example, awareness levels for a brand can be created or increased fairly quickly through an intensive media schedule of widespread, repetitive advertising to the target audience. Repositioning of a product requires a change in consumers' perceptions and takes much more time.

Assessment of DAGMAR

The DAGMAR approach to setting objectives has had considerable influence on the advertising planning process. Many promotional planners use this model as a basis for setting objectives and assessing the effectiveness of their promotional campaigns. DAGMAR also focused advertisers' attention on the value of using communications-based rather than sales-based objectives to measure advertising effectiveness and encouraged the measurement of stages in the response hierarchy to assess a campaign's impact. Colley's work has led to improvements in the advertising and promotional planning process by providing a better understanding of the goals and objectives toward which planners' efforts should be directed. This usually results in less subjectivity and also leads to better communication and relationships between the client and its agency.

While DAGMAR has contributed to the advertising planning process, it has not been totally accepted by everyone in the advertising field. A number of problems have led to questions regarding its value as an advertising planning tool:[8]

- *Problems with the response hierarchy.* A major criticism of the DAGMAR approach is its reliance on the hierarchy of effects model. The fact that consumers do not always go through this sequence of communication effects before making a purchase has been recognized, and alternative response models have been developed.[9]

- *Practicality and costs.* Another criticism of DAGMAR concerns the difficulties involved in implementing it. Money must be spent on research to establish quantitative benchmarks and measure changes in the response hierarchy. This is costly and time-consuming and can lead to considerable disagreement over method, criteria, measures, and so forth. Many critics argue that DAGMAR is practical only for large companies with big advertising and research budgets. Many firms do not want to spend the money needed to use DAGMAR effectively.

- *Inhibition of creativity.* A final criticism of DAGMAR is that it inhibits advertising creativity by imposing too much structure on the people responsible for developing the advertising. Many creative personnel think the DAGMAR approach is too concerned with quantitative assessment of a campaign's impact on awareness, brand name recall, or specific persuasion measures. The emphasis is on passing the numbers test rather than developing a message that is truly creative and contributes to brand equity.

Comprehensive Response Model Applications

The DAGMAR model was the impetus for the application of more involved or comprehensive response models for setting communication objectives. Over time, advertising theorists prefer the Lavidge and Steiner hierarchy of effects model, as it is more specific and provides a better way to establish and measure results.[10] Thus, this particular hierarchical model has been used as a basis for analyzing the communication response processes of consumers and has been the foremost application for setting communication objectives.

Figure 5–3 shows the various steps in the Lavidge and Steiner hierarchy of effects model as the consumer moves from awareness to purchase, along with examples of types of promotion or advertising relevant to each step. Recall from Chapter 4 that consumers pass through three successive stages: cognitive, affective, and behavioural. As consumers proceed through the three stages, they move closer to making a purchase. Consumers are not expected to respond immediately; rather, advertisers realize they must provide relevant information and create favourable predispositions toward the brand before purchase behaviour will occur. For example, the ad for Waterford crystal in Exhibit 5–5 is designed to inform consumers of

Related behavioural dimensions	Movement toward purchase	Example of types of promotion or advertising relevant to various steps
Conative The realm of motives. Ads stimulate or direct desires.	Purchase	Point-of-purchase Retail store ads Deals "Last-chance" offers Price appeals Testimonials
	Conviction	
Affective The realm of emotions. Ads change attitudes and feelings.	Preference	Competitive ads Argumentative copy
	Liking	"Image" copy Status, glamour appeals
Cognitive The realm of thoughts. Ads provide information and facts.	Knowledge	Announcements Descriptive copy Classified ads Slogans Jingles Skywriting
	Awareness	Teaser campaigns

Figure 5–3 Effects of advertising on consumers: movement from awareness to action

Exhibit 5–5 Waterford creates an image of quality products

the product's tradition and craftsmanship. While it has no call for immediate action, the ad creates favourable impressions about the product so that consumers will consider it when they enter the market for crystal.

Setting communication objectives with a model like this is the same way that a pyramid is built, by first accomplishing lower-level objectives such as awareness and knowledge or comprehension.[11] Subsequent tasks involve moving consumers who are aware of or knowledgeable about the product or service to higher levels in the pyramid (Figure 5–4). The initial stages, at the base of the pyramid, are easier to accomplish than those toward the top, such as trial and repurchase or regular use. Thus, the percentage of prospective customers will decline as they move up the pyramid. Figure 5–5 shows how a company introducing a new brand of shampoo targeted at 18- to 34-year-old females might set its IMC objectives using the communications effects pyramid.

The communication effects pyramid can also be used to determine promotional objectives for an established brand. The promotional planner must determine where the target audience lies with respect to the various blocks in the pyramid. If awareness levels for a brand and knowledge of its features and benefits are low, the communication objective should be to increase them. If these blocks of the pyramid are already in place, but liking or preference is low, the advertising goal may be to change the target markets' image of the brand and move consumers through to purchase.

Even though comprehensive response models have been used to set communication objectives for many years, research shows that its acceptance has been limited over time. A 1969 study showed that most advertising agencies did not state appropriate objectives for determining advertising success.[12] Another more recent study found that most of advertisers of their sample did not set concrete advertising objectives, specify objective tasks, measure results in terms of stages of a hierarchy of effects, or match objectives to evaluation measures.[13] The authors concluded: "Advertising practitioners have only partially adopted the con-

Figure 5–4
Communication effects pyramid

Product: Backstage Shampoo

Time period: Six months

Objective 1: Create awareness among 90 percent of target audience. Use repetitive advertising in newspapers, magazines, TV and radio programs. Simple message.

Objective 2: Create interest in the brand among 70 percent of target audience. Communicate information about the features and benefits of the brand—i.e., that it contains no soap and improves the texture of the hair

Objective 3: Create positive feelings about the brand among 40 percent and preference among 25 percent of the target audience. Create favourable attitudes by conveying information, promotions, sampling, etc.

Objective 4: Obtain trial among 20 percent of the target audience. Use sampling and cents-off coupons along with advertising and promotions.

Objective 5: Develop and maintain regular use of Backstage Shampoo among 5 percent of the target audience. Use continued reinforcement advertising, fewer coupons and promotions

Figure 5–5 Setting objectives using the communications effects pyramid

cepts and standards of objective setting and evaluation set forth 25 years ago."[14] Finally, another recent study measured the attitudes of chairs, presidents, and other senior managers of business-to-business advertising companies, more than half of the 427 respondents said they did not know whether their advertising was working and less than 10 percent thought it was working well.[15]

A New IMC Approach

One reason so much attention is given to advertising objectives is that, for many companies, advertising has traditionally been the major way of communicating with target audiences. Other promotional mix elements such as sales promotion, direct marketing, and publicity are used intermittently to support and complement the advertising program.

Another reason is that traditional advertising-based views of marketing communications planning have dominated the field for so long. These approaches are based on a hierarchical response model and consider how marketers can develop and disseminate advertising messages to move consumers along an effects path. This approach, shown in Figure 5–6, is what professor Don Schultz calls inside-out planning. He says, "It focuses on what the marketer wants to say, when the marketer wants to say it, about things the marketer believes are important about his or her brand, and in the media forms the marketer wants to use."[16]

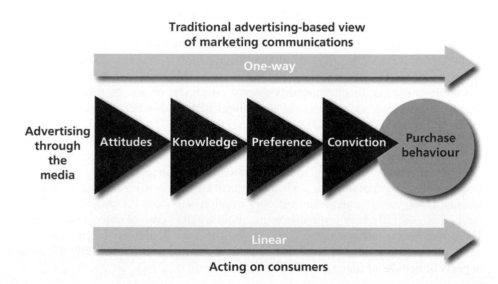

Traditional advertising-based view
of marketing communications

One-way

Advertising through the media — Attitudes — Knowledge — Preference — Conviction — Purchase behaviour

Linear

Acting on consumers

Figure 5–6 Traditional advertising-based view of marketing communications

Schultz advocates an outside-in planning process for IMC that starts with the customer and builds backward to the brand. This means that promotional planners study the various media that customers and prospects use, when the marketer's messages might be most relevant to customers, and when they are likely to be most receptive to the message.

A similar approach is suggested by Professor Tom Duncan, who argues that IMC should use **zero-based communications planning**, which involves determining what tasks need to be done and which marketing communications functions should be used and to what extent.[17] This approach focuses on the task to be done and searches for the best ideas and media to accomplish it. Duncan notes that as with a traditional advertising campaign, the basis of an IMC campaign is a big idea. However, in IMC the big idea can be public relations, direct response, packaging, or sales promotion. Duncan suggests that an effective IMC program should lead with the marketing communications function that most effectively addresses the company's main problem or opportunity and should use a promotional mix that draws on the strengths of whichever communications functions relate best to the particular situation.

Both of these views represent how communication objectives should be set within the emerging field of IMC. The next section presents a comprehensive framework for making IMC decisions at all three levels: IMC plan, IMC tool, and an individual element (i.e., print ad). It builds on this IMC vision, retains the key strengths of DAGMAR, and accounts for the limitations of response hierarchies.

Setting IMC Objectives

We now turn our attention to the Rossiter and Percy (R&P) perspective of communication objectives.[18] Compared to the other methods for setting objectives, this perspective has three main characteristics. It provides unique guidelines for target audience identification and selection and is consistent with the original DAGMAR model. Secondly, it provides guidelines for behavioural or action objectives that are not specified completely in the previous approaches. This step is critical for linking communication objectives and marketing objectives (i.e., sales). Finally, it provides guidelines for communication objectives that are more managerially useful and do not completely rely on a set hierarchy of effects.

This section will review each of these topics and also connect the communication objectives to the various stages of the buyer decision model described in Chapter 3. We include the R&P perspective since it attempts to resolve the limitations of other communication models and approaches for objective setting. Furthermore, their perspective provides guidelines for creative tactics as will be seen in Chapter 7.

Target Audience

R&P state that the primary and most logical factor for initially defining a target audience is the current behaviour of consumers. The importance of this factor is critical since it is the individual decision of each customer to purchase a brand that dictates a firm's total sales. Thus, in setting the direction for any IMC plan or component of an IMC plan (i.e., advertising), the manager must have a clear idea of the customer status of the target audience. Essentially, this decision hinges on a key question. Is the communication directed towards current customers or non-customers? As we discuss these ideas, we will use the term **focal brand** to indicate the brand that a manager is responsible for.

For customer groups, the manager has the opportunity to direct communications to **brand loyal customers** who regularly buy their firm's products. Recent marketing strategies (i.e., relationship marketing discussed in Chapter 1) and communication strategies regularly focus on a firm's current customers to ensure that customers maintain their current purchasing and consumption behaviour. As we noted in Chapter 1, it is generally very profitable to maintain a stable core of current customers. From a communication standpoint, it suggests that we do not have to advertise as often or we do not have to have as many sales promotions. We will discuss more aspects of behaviour in the next section.

Favourable brand switchers are a second customer group highlighted by R&P. These customers buy the focal brand but also buy other brands within a given relevant time period for the product category. For some product categories, consumers habitually purchase from a few favourites or those brands within their evoked set. As discussed in Chapter 3, these types of purchases may occur for many reasons. Consumers often face different purchase situations (e.g., own purchase versus gift). Sometimes certain moods influence brand choice. Whatever the motivation or external influencing factor, consumers adjust their purchases accordingly. While a manager would dearly love to have all customers be truly loyal, favourable brand switchers are an important source of purchases and are loyal to a degree. For these reasons, marketers would like to communicate directly with these consumers so that the focal brand remains in the evoked set (Exhibit 5–6). Alternatively, continued communication may influence stronger loyalty in the future.

Communication directed to non-customers are the focus of much advertising and promotion. R&P identify three key groups: **new category users, other brand switchers,** and **other brand loyals.** New category users, as the name implies, are those customers that are not purchasing within a product category. For example, after graduating from college or university many young adults begin to enter numerous categories partly because they have the income but also because they are at a stage of their life when new or latent needs emerge. Many advertisers attempt to court this target audience since many of these consumers are potentially ready to make a purchase. Marketers believe that steady communication may entice these customers to their brand when the time comes for these consumers to actually purchase.

Other brand switchers are like the previous group in that they purchase a few different brands within a category. However from a manager's perspective, they are fundamentally different, as they are not purchasing the focal brand. This is a challenging target audience, as the focal brand needs to break into consumer's evoked set and within the brands that these consumers are currently purchasing. This is a formidable task but still the focus of a considerable amount of advertising and promotion.

R&P's final group for target audience selection concerns other brand loyals. As this implies, these consumers purchase only one other brand and are completely loyal. It is difficult to say how much advertising and promotion expenditures are directed to these types of consumer across many industries. Logically, it would be very difficult to break the strongly held behaviour in which these consumers currently engage. Nevertheless, this is still a potential target that a firm may wish to establish communication objectives with and deliver some form of advertising and promotion.

After prioritizing the target audience in terms of customer status, R&P argue that other factors such as lifestyle or demographics are added on. For example, one clever ad by Tide detergent shows a child, sitting in a highchair, who has just finished eating a bowl of spaghetti. The child is naturally very messy, and the headline reads, "The day I switched to Tide." It appears that this message is targeted towards other brand switchers or other brand loyals who have a particular family-centred lifestyle. Thus, in order to truly define a target audience, the behavioural variable needs to be combined with other variables.

Another example from a broader perspective is warranted. Many companies target a younger demographic. We may read in the press that they are targeting an 18- to 24-year-old demographic. While this may be true, often an inherent behavioural variable is implied. Sometimes it is more like a new category user because young adults start to consume new categories of products as they mature. Other times, it is

Exhibit 5–6 A strong basis for differentiation could show a noticeable effect of advertising on sales (Courtesy Palm, Inc. Photography by Timothy Greenfield-Sanders.)

more like favourable brand switchers in an attempt to make these consumers exhibit stronger loyalty. The underlying point is that a communication message has to resonate with the target audience based on their current behaviour, whether they buy the brand or not, and some other key variable.

Thus far we have spoken of the target audience, which is the group an ad or a promotional campaign is directed towards, versus the target market, which is the segment the entire marketing mix is directed towards. The difference between target audience and target market can be seen in a recent campaign for Imodium Quick Dissolve tablets, a diarrhea remedy. The campaign tried to reach Canadian vacationers to foreign countries who do not want to be inconvenienced with this unfortunate gastronomic ailment. The secondary target audience was frequent business travelers who may have overlooked being prepared for their discomfort and who could not afford to miss important meetings. Combined together, it appears that Imodium is trying to reach new category users. Imodium used humour to cleverly point out the need for the product with a message, "Visit the country, not just its restrooms," and visuals of various facilities used throughout the world. Naturally, the product has other consumers, and how this product is positioned in the marketplace versus competing products is relevant, but clearly, Imodium has selected a certain part of the market to speak within this campaign that is a sub-set of the overall target market.[18]

Behavioural Objectives

A second part of R&P's approach is to have a clear behavioural objective for each target audience since summating the individual purchasing behaviour of many customers leads to a firm's overall sales. From another perspective, the link between marketing objectives (i.e., sales) and communication objectives (i.e., attitude towards the brands) is behavioural objectives. Advertising and promotion can focus on influencing a particular form of behaviour based on the nature of the advertising message or IMC tool used. We now discuss various types of behavioural objectives.

Trial   A **brand trial purchase** is defined as a consumer's first purchase of a focal brand. For many everyday products, this purchase occurred many years ago; it is probably difficult for you to remember when you purchased your first soft drink or snack food. However, these firms continue to have a **brand trial objective** to some degree as consumers naturally enter the market when they attain a certain age or have income (i.e., allowance from parents). In fact, a brand trial objective is a behavioural objective for almost all firms, but it is not necessarily the primary behavioural objective for all campaigns or all communication tools.

Let's return to the soft drink scenario. It is quite unlikely that you have continued to purchase the same brand of soft drink as the first trial purchase all these years. In fact, many people consume more than one brand of soft drink. Many brand managers are faced with this dilemma. For whatever reason, it is possible that consumers have not purchased a focal brand for a period of time (i.e., perhaps a year). Thus, firms would like consumers to have a new trial experience of the brand. A **brand re-trial purchase** is defined as a consumer's first purchase of a focal brand after some time delay. The length of the delay to focus on when setting a **brand re-trial objective** is a decision the promotion manager makes. It depends upon the purchase frequency of the product, among other factors observed from the situation analysis.

A manager may plan for a brand trial or brand re-trial objective when consumers are purchasing another brand. A **brand-switching purchase** is defined as a consumer's purchase towards a focal brand from some other competing brand. A brand-switching purchase occurs whereby the consumer makes a re-trial purchase of a focal brand and leaves the new favourite. A brand-switching purchase also occurs when the consumer makes a trial purchase of a focal brand from a competing brand. Thus, brand trial or brand re-trial objectives are also known as **brand-switching objectives.**

Now let's put the trial purchase in another perspective, consider the purchase of a cellphone that many young adults presently own. If you have one, what brand did you select and why? How did the advertising and promotion influence this purchase? The cellphone is a different kind of product and likely a somewhat involved purchase for many consumers. Despite this, cellphone companies and service providers had trial objectives as they attempted to attract consumers who did not own such technology. While this is obviously a brand trial purchase, it is also something broader. A **category trial purchase** is defined as a consumer's first purchase in a product category that the consumer has not purchased previously. Marketers of new products, like the cellphone, have a dual challenge of attaining both **category trial objectives** and **brand trial objectives.**

Repeat Purchase   In the age of relationship marketing and a focus on customer retention, this form of purchase behaviour is most critical. A **repeat-purchase** is defined as a consumer's continued purchase of a focal brand within a specified time period. Again, the time factor is at the discretion of the marketer, and once again it is contingent upon purchase frequency of the product or other factors derived from the situation analysis.

Firms can have a **repeat-purchase objective** in many situations. As noted above, marketers desire to have a stable core of customers that remain loyal to the brand. Many firms communicate with these consumers to maintain their positive attitude towards the focal brand. For example, some argue that most of Coca-Cola's advertising and promotions are directed towards its repeat customers. In many product categories, a group of consumers habitually consume two or three brands continuously. For instance, of fifteen purchases, over ten consecutive purchases might be of the focal brand with the remaining five purchases spread across two other brands. This is another situation where a marketer may emphasize a repeat-purchase objective in their communications plan. While this type of consumer does not purchase the focal brand for every single occasion, the consumer is a consistent contributor to the firm's sales and a marketer would want to communicate appropriately to ensure future sales.

The repeat-purchase objective is so pervasive for most organizations. Thus, we identify three alternatives to guide managers in setting their behavioural objectives for IMC: how often to purchase, how much to purchase, and when to purchase.

The first alternative concerns the rate or how often to purchase the brand. This implies that a marketer may set an objective pertaining to consumers purchasing their brand every week instead of every two weeks. This example shows an option where a manager may want to increase the rate of purchase from a "half" product per week to "one" product per week. A second managerial option is to maintain the rate of purchase. While this is a more conservative objective, it is still a viable option in very competitive environments. Finally, a manager may want to decrease the rate of purchase. This option may be viable in unique situations of high demand or with products that have potentially negative consequences (i.e., alcohol).

The amount or how much to purchase each occasion is the second alternative. As this alternative implies, a marketer may set an objective where consumers purchase two products per occasion versus one per occasion. As above, this option is to increase the amount per occasion, but a marketer could still evaluate whether to maintain or decrease the amount per occasion.

The final alternative is the timing or when to purchase. Certain products are seasonal, have a peak in their sales, or can be easily stored. Marketers may have a behavioural objective to influence when consumers will make the purchase. For example, Wendy's restaurant advertises on television in the evening and communicates the fact that its drive-through service stays open late, thus prompting consumers to purchase at a certain time of day. Consistent with the other two alternatives, we can conceive three options: maintain, accelerate, and delay.

Purchase-Related Behaviour   Often, communication is designed to encourage a consumer to progress through the decision-making process more smoothly. Or, communication is deemed a necessary part of the process. For example, most people find it imperative to visit a car dealership prior to buying a car. So the focus of some parts of an IMC plan is to have consumers take action that will lead them one step closer to the final destination of a purchase. **Purchase-related behaviour** is an action that consumers take that will lead to a higher probability of purchasing the brand. Many types of purchase-related action exist, but in general, most concern the consumer seeking some amount of information (e.g., visiting a website) about the brand or some kind of experience with the brand (e.g., demonstration, sample). Accordingly, marketers can have many purchase-related behaviour objectives to know whether enough of the target audience is involved with the brand during the decision-making process. For example, the firm can track the number of sales inquiries or requests for samples, or demonstrations to gauge how well it is performing for the objective.

Repeat Consumption   Thus far we have considered repeat purchase as a behavioural objective. Related to this is repeat consumption as a behavioural objective. **Repeat consumption** is defined as the continued consumption of the brand once purchased. Marketers may have a **repeat-consumption objective** when communicating with their current customers who have previously purchased the brand and have the product at their home or work. Some communications have an objective of modifying how often to consume the brand, how much to consume each occasion, and when to consume.

To give an idea of a repeat-consumption objective in action, we will cite two common approaches. Often, food and drink products advertise certain television commercials that show consumption visuals that may prompt consumers to snack or have another beverage. Another approach is to show consumers how to enjoy the product for other uses, or in new or alternative situations.

As you can see, the type of purchase and consumption behaviour that firms may try to influence is quite varied. If a firm has multiple target audiences to reach, quite likely it will have to carefully specify the type of behaviour associated with each target audience so that it can develop the most appropriate message and select the most relevant IMC tool. To assist a manager in making these subsequent decisions, it is important to set clear communication objectives.

Application   By the end of 2001, approximately one-third of the Canadian population, or 10 million consumers, had a wireless phone, with 2 million of those signing up during 2001. Some sales for companies come from new users, and some sales naturally come from customers who decide to switch for one reason or another. The end of 2001 was a watershed moment as all brands were available across the entire country. Telus had moved east with its purchase of Clearnet, while Fido, Rogers, and Bell Mobility marketed their services in the west. Bell faced the unusual situation of having to operate as a new brand in the west because it was a mature company with a previous monopoly status in the east. The national campaign, "GO," certainly helped the transition when combined with the regional message.

This situation shows many of the above concepts. It shows the importance of defining the target audience initially with a behavioural perspective for marketing communications. It is easier for Bell to move into the new market and attract new users with a trial purchase by establishing an initial brand position with this target audience as opposed to trying to switch consumers from competing brands. In contrast, the "GO" campaign in the east represents a brand re-position as it attempts to switch consumers. Overall, this example shows how an IMC approach is critical as Bell has the challenge of managing at least two target audiences with multiple message and IMC tools.[19]

Communication Objectives

Previously we saw how the past response hierarchy models were used to formulate communication objectives. The R&P approach is similar in that it subscribes to a hierarchy; however, it has an application that overcomes the limitations of other models. R&P summarize five **communication effects** that an ad, advertising campaign, or IMC plan may have on consumers.

Enticing Loyal Playland Customers

Playland and Rethink get results! In January of 2000, Playland, a Vancouver amusement park, selected the freshly established Rethink as its new ad agency for their upcoming summer campaign. Rethink's principal, Chris Staples, has held on to the Playland account for seven years despite Playland having four reviews for other agencies during that time. Rethink was so confident in its ability to deliver results that in the recent review it guaranteed to meet Playland's attendance goals or waive its fees! While some agencies grumbled that the guarantee was a stunt or that Rethink had an inside connection to the account, the fact remains that Playland previously used and continues to use outstanding, and sometimes controversial, creative advertising to help achieve its communication and behavioural objectives without spending a lot of money.

It seems that the ads aren't the only IMC tool having an effect. In 2000, Playland used a religious theme. For example, in one TV ad, the turnstile stayed at 666 after each person entered the park. The campaign ran without any problems initially but considerable complaints ensued after the *Vancouver Sun* ran the front-page headline, "Playland is making fun of God." The saying "Any publicity is good publicity" comes to mind. While this is not a universal truth, it certainly seems to work with a product like an amusement park.

Interestingly, the target audience of this recent campaign appears to be directed to the loyal riders of Playland because the focus of the campaign was on three new rides. What better way to market a new ride than to attract previously satisfied customers and show them entering the park.

Sources: Eve Lazarus, "Not Playing Around," *Marketing Magazine,* March 5, 2001; Eve Lazarus, "What a long, strange ride it's been," *Marketing Magazine,* March 5, 2001.

- *Category need:* Target audience perception of requiring a product to satisfy a need.
- *Brand awareness:* Target audience ability to recognize and/or recall the brand within the category in sufficient detail to make a purchase.
- *Brand attitude:* Target audience overall evaluation of the brand in relation to its ability to satisfy the reason they want it.
- *Brand purchase intention:* Target audience self-instruction to respond (purchase, purchase-related action) to the brand.
- *Purchase facilitation:* Target audience perception that a marketing factor could affect their purchase or use of the brand.

Communication effect refers to the lasting brand impression that remains with the target audience after the target audience processes the message. The R&P model has a few noteworthy features compared with the previous hierarchy models. First, there is an obvious and clear connection to the purchase of a particular brand. This is apparent with its reference to the brand in three communication effects. It is also seen in the connection to category need, which speaks to the underlying reason why the consumer is motivated to buy the brand and the consumer's understanding of where the brand fits in the market in relation to other brand. Finally, it is observed with the link to purchase facilitation, which highlights the importance of marketers communicating information to make sure the purchase occurs.

The second feature is that the R&P model recognizes brand attitude as a central communication effect. Recall that the other models described in Chapter 4 viewed the entire process (i.e., cognition, affect, behaviour) as reflecting an attitude, and that some models argued that consumers experienced various steps in various orders depending upon the purchase situation. Brand attitude evaluation includes both cognitive and affective components recognizing that each aspect is relevant no matter what the purchase situation.

The third feature of the R&P model is that it views the communication effect with respect to the brand as being distinct from other aspects of the overall response to advertising. It views communication effects as the step between processing (i.e., consumer's responses to the immediate exposure of a message) and behaviour (e.g., trial).

Finally, this model translates these consumer communication effects into clear options for managers to set communication objectives. It offers a number of options for each of the five communication objectives that can be applied to one target audience or multiple target audiences. Further, these communication objectives can be a universal framework for (1) a specific communication, such as one print ad or television commercial; (2) a specific campaign, such as advertising or sponsorship; and (3) a complete IMC program that includes all promotional tools. It should be noted that the characteristics of good objectives still retain the characteristics set forth earlier (i.e., specific benchmark with the degree of change sought within a specified time period). We now turn to summarizing the various options for each communication objective.

Category Need

As noted above, category need pertains to whether the target audience feels the need to purchase within the actual product category. Before describing the three options available for managers, it is useful to understand what we mean by category. Cellphones are a clear product for which some people are consumers and some are not. A cellphone company may try to build demand by convincing new users of the benefits of owning a cellphone versus not owning one. This type of message is likely to be different than the type of message used to convince a current user to switch to another brand when the technology improves with new features. In this example, it is a question of whether the target audience feels their life would be more fulfilled with the product or without it.

Another example of category need occurs with transportation. If you were thinking about buying a "car" upon graduation, your choice may in fact be a truck or a sports utility vehicle. In a broad sense, all vehicles can be used for transportation, but consumers have particular needs that are satisfied more easily with some types or categories of vehicles versus others. A marketer for SUVs may try to communicate in a way so that a target audience will feel the need for an SUV more strongly than the need for a sporty sub-compact, which might be the initial category of product that young consumers would gravitate towards. In this example, it is a question of which distinct yet related category fulfills the target audience's need more completely.

In either of these situations or others, a manager has three options with respect to the category need objective:

- *Category need is omitted.* If the need is quite apparent, then it does not need to be the focus of a particular message or campaign.
- *Category need is reminded.* One obvious example of this is reminder advertising (discussed in Chapter 7), where the brand is communicated and the need for the product is communicated clearly. Often, the reminder option of category need is the focus of campaigns for lapsed users.
- *Category need is emphasized* (that is, "sold"). The above two examples (that is, cellphone and vehicle) show two situations where we actively attempt to persuade the target audience to feel the need for the product.

Brand Awareness

Brand awareness is a universal communication objective. This means that every single point of communication should contribute to a target audience's understanding and knowledge of the brand name. This understanding and knowledge should go even further such that the target audience knows the category that the brand typically competes in when the consumer is in position to make a purchase or some other related action. This stronger interpretation of awareness is important for the brand to be considered in the decision-making process.

Essentially, there are two types of brand awareness:

- *Brand awareness is through recognition.* If the target audience makes a choice at the point of purchase, then simple recognition of past brand messages can be sufficient for brand consideration or purchase.

- *Brand awareness is through recall.* If the target audience feels the need for a product but needs to remember what brands to consider away from the point of purchase, then recall becomes the focus of the campaign.

Naturally, if both forms of brand awareness are relevant, then a manager may have both as awareness objectives.

Brand recall is often referred to as unaided brand awareness when measuring. After its launch in western Canada in 2001, Bell had achieved only 10 percent unaided brand recall. What this means is that when people are thinking about buying a cellphone service, only one in ten will think of Bell. Obviously, this reduces Bell's chances of having many consumers enter Bell's stores or call to enquire about its services.

Brand Attitude

Brand attitude is another universal communication objective. Like brand awareness, every aspect of a firm's IMC program or any particular element, such as a television commercial, should contribute to some aspect of the overall evaluation of the brand from the perspective of the target audience. A logical conclusion to this point is that there should be no such thing as an "awareness campaign," as the campaign should surely influence brand awareness and some aspect of brand attitude.

Since brand attitude is such an important communication objective, prior understanding of the existing brand attitude is a critical guide for each option:

- *Brand attitude is established.* A new target audience that has no awareness and therefore no prior attitude towards the brand generally requires extensive communication so that an attitude is created or established.
- *Brand attitude is maintained.* Often, advertising is performed so that existing attitude levels will remain constant in order to ensure future sales. Stopping communication is one reason for declining sales that have been seen in many examples over time. In contrast, many major advertisers (e.g., Coca-Cola) consistently follow this approach to maintain sales.
- *Brand attitude is increased.* Target audiences who are familiar with the brand and moderately favourable towards the brand can be influenced. For example, we can increase their brand attitude by getting the target audience to believe that the brand delivers better performance on a particular attribute or benefit.
- *Brand attitude is modified.* Similar to the previous option, if the target audience is moderately favourable, we still seek to improve their attitude. However, we modify the brand attitude if no increase is possible. In this option, marketers use a different point of reference in communicating the benefits. Typically, marketers focus on a new consumer motive for purchasing the brand that the target audience will be receptive towards.
- *Brand attitude is changed.* Negative attitudes are difficult to influence, but in some communication situations, the marketer is faced with the challenge of changing the brand attitude for a target audience.

Brand Purchase Intention

There are two fairly simple options here:

- *Brand purchase intention is assumed.* In situations (i.e., low involvement) where the strength of an intention to purchase is consistent (i.e., highly correlated) with brand attitude, a marketer is not required to include this objective.
- *Brand purchase intention is generated.* In contrast, managers need the target audience to have a plan to purchase a brand in situations of high involvement.

Purchase Facilitation

A proactive interpretation of marketing communication pervades this option in these two options:

- *Purchase facilitation is included.* If the target audience believes that some aspect of the marketing mix is weak or problematic (i.e., availability at certain types of stores), then the marketer should take this into account when designing ads, and offer reassurance, explanation, or information.

- *Purchase facilitation is omitted.* Naturally, this is not a focus of the ad if there are no perceived problems.

Application   Communication objectives seem quite obvious and easy to do sometimes; however, without careful planning, firms can run into difficulties. ITI, a firm that offers private training in information technology, had difficulties with its marketing communications as it grew from a $2 million company in 1995 to a $50 million company in 2000. Because its ten locations often did their own advertising, ITI claimed that, "The brand was all over the map." Essentially, consumers had difficulty knowing what ITI was or where it fit compared to other training and educational institutions (i.e., connection of brand to category). Consumers were confused as to who the program was for (i.e., connection of brand to the user) and what the program offered (i.e., connection of brand to benefits). Despite success so far, ITI was having trouble achieving key category need, brand awareness, and brand attitude communication objectives.

After research, a carefully constructed IMC campaign that had a clear message, and included TV, radio, print, and the Web, resulted in 35,000 calls in 2000 versus 12,000 in 1999. ITI has successfully positioned itself at the high end of private training services of information technology for consumers who have completed university or college. Not only that, it has set the standard for the industry in terms of communication and branding.[20]

Communication Objectives for Buyer Decision Stages

In Chapter 3, we presented a model of consumer decision making that showed the stages typically experienced when making a purchase. We outlined several steps: need recognition, information search, alternative evaluation, purchase decision, and post-purchase evaluation. One important role of marketing communications is to help the target audience move through theses stages. Marketers require specific communication tools and messages that will resonate with each target audience as they proceed through these stages. We assess this decision-making process for each target audience and make a conclusion as to which communication objectives are most relevant for each stage. Figure 5–7 illustrates how this works.

The analysis occurs in the first six rows where the marketer includes the target audience information and makes a conclusion on the key communication objectives that need to be attained so that the target audience will continue to the next stage. We have addressed some of these ideas already. The first question (Who?) looks at the key participants in the decision. We highlighted these roles in Chapter 3. The next three questions are descriptors of where, when, and how the shopping behaviour will occur. This is based on market research, managerial experience, flashes of inspiration, and assumptions. The key point is that we need to make clear the behaviour that we are trying to influence.

After summarizing these questions, we determine which communication objectives are necessary to ensure that the consumer continues through all stages. For example, what aspect of brand attitude needs to be addressed at the need-recognition stage versus the alternative-evaluation stage? Is recall an awareness objective at the need-recognition stage and recognition an awareness objective at the purchase-decision stage?

Once this assessment has been done, then the marketer can outline preliminary options concerning the types of messages and communication tools that would be most useful. Returning to the first question above, a marketer may decide to have a fun television commercial (e.g., communication tool option) that emphasizes the emotional attachment (e.g., brand attitude) to the product. It should be noted that when identifying some options, the marketer has not fully committed or recommended that this is exactly the plan, but rather that this is the template of analysis for making the final decision.

Figure 5–7   Assessing the consumer decision-making process

Analysis & Conclusions	Need Recognition	Information Search	Alternative Evaluation	Purchase Decision	Post-Purchase Evaluation
Who? (Roles)					
Where? (Location)					
When? (Time, Timing)					
How? (Shopping Behaviour)					
Why? (Key motivator)					
Communication Objectives					
Message Options					
Communication Tool Options					

The Rogers@Home "Download Rigor Mortis" IMC campaign is an excellent example of these concepts. In the spring and fall of 2000, Rogers put together a campaign to attract new users for its high-speed cable Internet service. It featured the humourous result of consumers requiring medical attention after experiencing rigor mortis when they waited for Internet downloads to occur through regular phone lines. The campaign included TV, print, radio, billboards, Web, and direct mail, and resulted in 100,000 new subscribers. As one Rogers executive noted, "I don't think any one piece works entirely on its own. That's what is nice about integrated campaigns; each piece layered on helps build it."

We can now surmise how each IMC tool played a key role in achieving key communication objectives at each stage of the decision-making process. TV worked well at the need-arousal stage, as it generated initial awareness and allowed consumers to easily see the benefit of a new type of Internet service for them (i.e., category need) and understand that Rogers could deliver the key attribute of speed (i.e., brand attitude). Print and Web enhanced the belief that Rogers could deliver the complete service package, as they contained more information (i.e., brand attitude) that consumers would be seeking at the information-search stage. Radio and poster likely reminded consumers to seek additional information (i.e., purchase facilitation) by phoning the company or visiting the website, if the consumer had not done so previously when they were in the purchase-intention stage. Direct mail encouraged consumers to act (i.e., purchase decision).[21]

The rest of this book focuses on how to make IMC plan decisions that are based on the target audience, behaviour objectives, and communication objectives established at the start of the plan. Chapters 6 and 7 focus on the message, while Chapters 8–15 focus on the communication tools. As we noted at the start of this chapter, content of this framework becomes the key criteria for making all promotional decisions and the criteria by which the results are measured. While all firms may not be able to afford comprehensive studies to assess communication effects, they would benefit from the use of the framework because it provides disciplined thinking before investing in promotion.

Summary

This chapter has examined the role of objectives in the planning and evaluation of the IMC. Specific objectives are needed to guide the development of the promotional program, as well as to provide a benchmark against which performance can be measured and evaluated. Objectives serve important functions as communications devices, as a guide to planning the IMC program and deciding on various alternatives, and for measurement and evaluation.

Objectives for IMC evolve from the organization's overall marketing plan and are based on the roles various promotional mix elements play in the marketing program. Many managers use sales or a related measure such as market share as the basis for setting objectives. However, many promotional planners believe the role of advertising and other promotional mix elements is to communicate because of the various problems associated with sales-based objectives. They use communications-based objectives like those in the response hierarchy as the basis for setting goals. The first approach for this was DAGMAR, which outlined four principles for setting communication objectives for advertising: well-defined target audience, concrete measurable tasks, benchmark with degree of change sought, and a specified time period.

Much of the emphasis in setting objectives has been on traditional advertising-based views of marketing communications. However, many companies are moving toward zero-based communications planning, which focuses on what tasks need to be done, which marketing communication functions should be used, and to what extent. Many of the principles used in setting advertising objectives can be applied to other elements in the promotional mix.

We presented a comprehensive framework for setting communication objectives and communication-objective options for all levels: IMC plans, individual IMC tools (i.e., advertising) and specific elements (i.e., print ad). This approach was consistent with DAGMAR in that it outlines a model for specifying a specific target audience. This model was based on an attitude-behaviour perspective combined with other variables such as demographics and lifestyle. The model went a step further by suggesting key behavioural objectives to guide the formation of communication objectives. The framework was then linked to the buyer decision-making model to see the connection between a consumer's behaviour and a particular brand's objectives.

Key Terms

marketing objectives, 107
carryover effect, 109
DAGMAR, 112
communication task, 113
benchmark measures, 113
zero-based communications planning, 118
focal brand, 118

brand loyal customers, 118
favourable brand switchers, 119
new category users, 119
other brand switchers, 119
other brand loyals, 119
brand trial purchase, 120
brand trial objective, 120
brand re-trial purchase, 120

brand re-trial objective, 120
brand-switching objective, 120
category trial objective, 121
repeat-purchase objective, 121
purchase-related behaviour objective, 122

repeat-consumption objective, 122
communication effects, 122
category need, 123
brand awareness, 123
brand attitude, 123
brand purchase intention, 123
brand purchase facilitation, 123

Discussion Questions

1. Discuss the value of setting objectives for the integrated marketing communications program. What important functions do objectives serve?

2. In meeting with your new boss, he informs you that the only goal of advertising and promotion is to generate sales. Present your argument as to why communications objectives must also be considered.

3. What are some of the problems associated with using sales objectives as the only measure of advertising performance? Can you think of any situation where it may be the best and only measure?

4. What are the strengths and weaknesses of using traditional hierarchy models for setting communication objectives?

5. In what situations is the target audience and the target market the same? In what situations is the size of the target audience larger or smaller than the target market?

6. When defining a target audience for communications, why is it a good idea to use consumer behaviour with respect to your brand as the primary variable before using other variables such as demographics or lifestyle?

7. Some claim that promotion is all about communication, so we should only focus on communication objectives and not worry about behavioural objectives. Convince them otherwise.

8. If a firm cannot afford large market research studies to quantitatively assess whether communication objectives have been achieved, why should the firm bother setting communication objectives?

9. How is the framework discussed in the last section similar to and different from setting communications objectives based on the traditional hierarchy models?

10. In what situations would brand awareness be the only communication objective for an advertising campaign?

11. A firm is running a campaign with advertising, sales promotion, and public relations. Why might it have different communication objectives for each IMC tool?

12. Find a print ad and explain what its communication objectives are. Look at the company's website and determine whether the communication objectives are similar or different.

Chapter Six
Creative Strategy Decisions

Chapter Objectives

- To discuss the importance and definition of advertising creativity.

- To examine the creative strategy planning process.

- To identify three key decisions that comprise a creative strategy: creative theme/idea, message appeal, and message source.

- To explore various approaches used for determining the creative theme/idea that forms the basis of an advertising campaign.

- To summarize the different types of message appeals that advertisers use to persuade their target audience.

- To highlight the source or communicator options a marketer has for a promotional message.

Telus Can See the Future Clearly

With the takeover of Clearnet Communications in the summer of 2000, Telus had a significant creative decision. What should Telus do with Clearnet's creative use of animals, insects, and flowers in all its marketing communications in Clearnet's famous "The Future Is Friendly" slogan?

Clearnet was an upstart firm offering digital PCS service in the Windsor–Quebec corridor. It had successfully launched its services in the 1990s with an innovative creative that featured various scenes from nature that were associated with the brand's benefits. In one memorable campaign, a frog was seen leaping from a glass jar to freedom. This creative cleverly conveyed the experience of a person who goes completely wireless at home! Clearnet attempted to persuade consumers with a phone line to their house to give it up and move to a completely wireless communication with its PCS product.

The creative concept has been hailed as a simple way to communicate the features and benefits of Clearnet's technology that may appear complex or difficult for new users of advanced technology products and services. Many also believed that the creative offered a unique visual that clearly identified Clearnet and helped it achieve significant brand awareness.

Almost from the start it was obvious that the Clearnet brand name would be discontinued, but many wondered how a recognizable creative that had put Clearnet on the map could possibly whither away. Complicating the issue was the fact that Telus was originally a Western Canada firm whose customers had no direct experience with Clearnet's creative. Likewise, most of Clearnet's customers would be mostly unfamiliar with the new Telus name.

The answer came quickly as Telus used Clearnet's "Disco Duck" for a national ad in January 2001. It was launched during the Super Bowl and an episode of *Survivor*, and the full campaign of TV, print, and billboard started a short time later with a direct-mail follow-up to existing customers. The ad showed two ducks playing catch with an egg to the music of "Sweet Georgia Brown," made famous by the Harlem Globetrotters. When the ducks inevitably drop the egg, it breaks open and the old Clearnet frog quacks. The key message is that two-way wireless e-mail messaging is available to all customers. Clearnet's signature leaf closes the ad, as done previously, but it changes into the new Telus Mobility logo. In an egg shell, we have an established creative attempting to generate key communication effects for a new brand—quite a significant marketing challenge, to say the least.

To complete the transformation, Telus adopted the recognizable purple and green colours and the "The Future Is Friendly" slogan from Clearnet for all six of its business units at the end of 2001. All Telus products and services have the same distinctive and consistent colours and visuals for all its marketing communications. And the website (Telus.com) uses this consistent strategy with the same colours and many of the same characters that have been featured in the advertising messages over the past five years.

Sources: Eve Lazarus, "One Voice," *Marketing Magazine*, December 17, 2001; Lesley Young, "Turning Over a New Leaf," *Marketing Magazine*, February 26, 2001; Lesley Young, "Telus Mobility Spares Dancing Duck," *Marketing Magazine*, February 5, 2001; Lesley Young, "Merger Means End of Clearnet Name," *Marketing Magazine*, August 28, 2000.

One of the most important components of an integrated marketing communications program is the advertising message. While the fundamental role of an advertising message is to communicate information, it does much more. The commercials we watch on TV or hear on radio and the print ads we see in magazines and newspapers are a source of entertainment, motivation, fascination, fantasy, and sometimes irritation as well as information. Ads and commercials appeal to, and often create or shape, consumers' problems, desires, and goals. From the marketer's perspective, the advertising message is a way to tell consumers how the product or service can solve a problem or help satisfy desires or achieve goals. Advertising can also be used to create images or associations and position a brand in the consumer's mind as well as transform the experience of buying and/or using a product or service. Many consumers who have never driven or even ridden in a BMW perceive it as "the ultimate driving machine" (Exhibit 6–1). Many people feel good about sending Hallmark greeting cards because they have internalized the company's advertising theme, "when you care enough to send the very best."

One need only watch an evening of commercials or peruse a few magazines to realize there are a myriad of ways to convey an advertising message. Underlying all of these messages, however, is a **creative strategy** that determines what the advertising message will say or communicate and **creative tactics** for how the message strategy will be executed. In this chapter, we focus on advertising creative strategy. In the next chapter, we will focus on advertising creative tactics.

In this chapter, we consider what is meant by advertising creativity by looking at its importance and providing a definition. Next we examine key aspects of planning creative strategy in terms of the challenges and process. We then turn to three creative strategy decisions. First, we describe various approaches to determining the big idea that will be used as the central theme of the advertising campaign and translated into attention-getting, distinctive, and memorable messages. Second, we

Exhibit 6–1 Excellent advertising helps create an image for BMW automobiles as "the ultimate driving machine"

132

review the many appeals that advertisers use to develop messages designed to persuade consumers. Third, we focus on the key source characteristics that advertisers typically use to gain attention and alter consumers' attitudes.

Many of you may not be directly involved in the design and creation of ads. However, because creative strategy is often so crucial to the success of the firm's promotional effort, everyone involved in the promotional process should understand the creative strategy and tactics that underlie the development of advertising campaigns and messages, as well as the creative options available to the advertiser. Also, individuals on the client side as well as agency people outside the creative department must work with the creative specialists in developing the advertising campaign, implementing it, and evaluating its effectiveness. Thus, marketing and product managers, account representatives, researchers, and media personnel must appreciate the creative process and develop a productive relationship with creative personnel.

Advertising Creativity

Importance of Advertising Creativity

For many students, as well as many advertising and marketing practitioners, the most interesting aspect of advertising is the creative side. We have all at one time or another been intrigued by an ad and admired the creative insight that went into it. A great ad is a joy to behold and often an epic to create, as the cost of producing a TV commercial can exceed $1 million. Many companies see this as money well spent. They realize that the manner in which the advertising message is developed and executed is often critical to the success of the promotional program, which in turn can influence the effectiveness of the entire marketing program. Procter & Gamble, Levi Strauss, Nissan, Coke, Pepsi, Nike, McDonald's, and many other companies spend a lot of money each year to produce advertising messages and a lot more to purchase media time and space to run them. While these companies make excellent products, they realize creative advertising is also an important part of their marketing success.

Good creative strategy and tactics can often be central to determining the success of a product or service or reversing the fortunes of a struggling brand. Consistency in the creative theme/idea is generally regarded as a key success factor. Pepsi-Cola's campaign in Quebec has starred comedian Claude Meunier for 16 years. The campaign is a unique creative strategy for Pepsi from a worldwide perspective, and it is the longest running campaign and celebrity endorsement in the history of the brand. In fact, the relationship is so established that Meunier writes many of the spots and creates the characters he portrays. A consistent campaign also gets rewarded in a sense. By 2000, Kraft Canada's six-year-old theme of an angel consuming Philadelphia cream cheese in the clouds was picked up by its U.S. and European counterparts.[1]

The Dairy Farmers of Canada took creative consistency of their "spokesperson" to a new level during the past three Olympic Games. For the 1998 Winter Olympics, the cows were in the barn watching the Games. For the 2002 Winter Games, they were seen on their way to the Olympics. They finally made it by attending events in Salt Lake City. In fact, they surprised a pair of figure skaters with a bale of hay as a reward at the end of one spot.[2]

Conversely, an advertising campaign that is poorly conceived or executed can be a liability. Many companies have solid marketing and promotional plans and spend substantial amounts of money on advertising, yet have difficulty coming up with a creative campaign that will differentiate them from their competitors. For example, Burger King changed its advertising theme 19 times in the past 25 years and changed agencies 7 times in search of a campaign that would give the chain a strong identity in the fast-food market. During many of these campaigns, market share dropped and franchisees were unhappy with the company's inability to come up with an effective campaign.[3] Recently, Burger King returned to its original theme of "Have it your way" but is seeking to extend beyond the simple customization of toppings and into the customer service dimension with a new campaign theme, "Going the distance," which began running in late 1999[4] (Figure 6–1).

Figure 6–1 Burger King advertising campaign themes

- Burger King dismisses BBDO, creator of its most famous slogan, "Have it your way," and hires J. Walter Thompson, New York (Aug. 1976)
- "America loves burgers, and we're America's Burger King" (Nov. 1977–Feb. 1978)
- "Who's got the best darn burger?" (Feb. 1978–Jan. 1980)
- "Make it special. Make it Burger King" (Jan. 1980–Jan. 1982)
- "Aren't you hungry for Burger King now?" (Jan. 1982–Sept. 1982)
- "Battle of the burgers" (Sept. 1982–Mar. 1983)
- "Broiling vs. frying" campaign tied to "Aren't you hungry?" (Mar. 1983–Sept. 1983)
- "The big switch" campaign (Sept. 1983–Nov. 1985)
- "Search for Herb" campaign (Nov. 1985–June 1986)
- "This is a Burger King town" (June 1986–Jan. 1987)
- "The best food for fast times" (Jan. 1987–Oct. 1987)
- BK hires NW Ayer, New York, and fires JWT (Oct. 1987)
- "We do it like you'd do it" (Apr. 1988–May 1989)
- BK hires D'Arcy Masius Benton & Bowles, and Saatchi & Saatchi, New York, firing Ayer (May 1989)
- "Sometimes you gotta break the rules" (Oct. 1989–Apr. 1991)
- "Your way. Right away" (April 1991–Oct. 1992)
- "BK Tee Vee: I love this place!" (Oct. 1992–1994)
- "Get your burger's worth" (1994–1998)
- "It just tastes better" (1998–1999)
- "Go the distance" (1999–)

Just because an ad or commercial is creative does not mean it will effectively communicate the intended message. Many ads have won awards for creativity but failed to increase sales. And sometimes this failure has cost the agency the account. For example, many advertising people believe some of the best ads of all time were those done for Alka-Seltzer years ago, including the classic "Mama Mia! That's a spicy meatball!" and "I can't believe I ate the whole thing." While the commercials won numerous creative awards, Alka-Seltzer sales still declined and the agencies lost the account.[5] When its sales declined, Nissan asked its agency to replace the popular and amusing "Enjoy the ride" campaign with ads featuring the cars and, in some cases, comparisons with the competition[6] (Exhibit 6–2).

Exhibit 6–2 In Nissan's new ads, the cars are once again the stars

IMC Perspective 6–1
Canada Goes for the Gold at Cannes

On a global level, the Cannes International Advertising Film Festival is now widely considered the most prestigious advertising award competition. The Cannes competition receives entries from agencies around the world hoping to win Lions (the name of the award) in each of the major categories: television, print and poster, online (cyber) advertising, media buying and planning, and direct. Canada has done fabulously at recent Cannes competitions with a total of 27 Lions over the past 4 years. The number of entries has increased from 352 in 2000 to 491 for 2002. And the Canadian entries are up against a lot of worldwide competition, with a total of over 17,000 entries.

The number of Lions per year received by Canadian firms has been a bit of a roller coaster. Canada received eleven Lions in 1998 and eight Lions in 2000 but only three and five Lions respectively for 1999 and 2001. Not to be dismayed, however, even winning a few Lions is quite an achievement. For example, three of the five Lions in 2001 were in the film category (i.e., TV ads, cinema ads) and that placed Canada in a tie for fifth with Australia. Not too bad when the film category alone had over 6,000 entries.

Just winning a Lion is quite an achievement as only about 100 Lions are handed out in any given year. Canada ended a dry spell for a Gold Lion in the film category only a couple of years ago, but at the same time, things look pretty good for creative advertising in Canada as Critical Mass of Calgary won our first Grand Prix ever last year!

Despite the recent success, some question the overall effectiveness of Canadian creativity due to the nature of our culture to not take risks and the fact that many of the brands advertised are part of American or other global brands. However, others contend the increased presence of Canadians in attendance and on the juries of all five categories bodes well for future Canadian creative advertising and their recognition on the international stage. In fact, some argue that countries that have emerged recently with stronger advertising is a result of their advertisers taking the competition more seriously by sending a large contingent of committed agency and client personnel who learn considerably from international counterparts.

Sources: "Cannes-ada," *Marketing Magazine,* July 3, 2000; "Cannes 2001," *Marketing Magazine,* July 2, 2001; "Cannes Ad Festival can be a real eye-opener for marketers," *Marketing Magazine,* July 2, 2001; "The Bashful Beaver," *Marketing Magazine,* November 26, 2001; "More Canuck work entered at Cannes," *Marketing Magazine,* May 29, 2002.

Many advertising and marketing people have become ambivalent toward, and in some cases even critical of, advertising awards.[7] They argue that agency creative people are often more concerned with creating ads that win awards than ones that sell their clients' products. Other advertising people believe awards are a good way to recognize creativity that often does result in effective advertising. IMC Perspective 6–1 discusses how the emphasis on creative awards has shifted to the international arena with awards like the Cannes Gold Lion trophies. Finding a balance between creative advertising and effective advertising is difficult. To better understand this dilemma, we turn to the issue of creativity and its role in advertising.

Definition of Advertising Creativity

Creativity is probably one of the most commonly used terms in advertising. Ads are often called creative. The people who develop ads and commercials are known as creative specialists. These specialists work for ad agencies that develop ad campaigns or for markets that handle their own advertising without the help of an agency. Perhaps so much attention is focused on the concept of creativity because many people view the specific challenge given to those who develop an advertising message as being creative. It is their job to turn all of the information regarding product features and benefits, marketing plans, consumer research, and communication objectives into a creative concept that will bring the advertising message to life. This begs the question: What is meant by *creativity* in advertising?

Perspectives on what constitutes creativity in advertising differ. At one extreme are people who argue that advertising is creative only if it sells the product. An advertising message's or campaign's impact on sales counts more than whether it is innovative or wins awards. At the other end of the continuum are those who judge the creativity of an ad in terms of its artistic or aesthetic value and originality. They contend creative ads can break through the competitive clutter, grab the consumer's attention, and have some impact.

As you might expect, perspectives on advertising creativity often depend on one's role. A study by Elizabeth Hirschman examined the perceptions of various individuals involved in the creation and production of TV commercials, including management types (brand managers and account executives) and creatives (art director, copywriter, commercial director, and producer).[8] She found that product managers and account executives view ads as promotional tools whose primary purpose is to communicate favourable impressions to the marketplace. They believe a commercial should be evaluated in terms of whether it fulfills the client's marketing and communicative objectives. The perspective of those on the creative side was much more self-serving, as Hirschman noted:

> In direct contrast to this client orientation, the art director, copywriter, and commercial director viewed the advertisement as a communication vehicle for promoting their own aesthetic viewpoints and personal career objectives. Both the copywriter and art director made this point explicitly, noting that a desirable commercial from their standpoint was one which communicated their unique creative talents and thereby permitted them to obtain "better" jobs at an increased salary.[9]

In her interviews, Hirschman also found that brand managers were much more risk-averse and wanted a more conservative commercial than the creative people, who wanted to maximize the impact of the message.

What constitutes creativity in advertising is probably somewhere between the two extremes. To break through the clutter and make an impression on the target audience, an ad often must be unique and entertaining. Research has shown that a major determinant of whether a commercial will be successful in changing brand preferences is its "likability," or the viewer's overall reaction.[10] TV commercials and print ads that are well designed and executed and generate emotional responses can create positive feelings that are transferred to the product or service being advertised. Many creative specialists believe this type of advertising can come about only if they are given considerable latitude in developing advertising messages. But ads that are creative only for the sake of being creative often fail to communicate a relevant or meaningful message that will lead consumers to purchase the product or service.

Everyone involved in planning and developing an advertising campaign must understand the importance of balancing the "it's not creative unless it sells" perspective with the novelty/uniqueness and impact position. Marketing and brand managers or account executives must recognize that imposing too many sales- and marketing-oriented communications objectives on the creative team can result in mediocre advertising, which is often ineffective in today's competitive, cluttered media environment. At the same time, the creative specialists must recognize that the goal of advertising is to assist in selling the product or service and good advertising must communicate in a manner that helps the client achieve this goal.

Advertising creativity is the ability to generate fresh, unique, and appropriate ideas that can be used as solutions to communications problems. To be *appropriate* and *effective*, a creative idea must be relevant to the target audience. Many ad agencies recognize the importance of developing advertising that is creative and different yet communicates relevant information to the target audience. Figure 6–2 shows the perspective on creativity that the D'Arcy, Masius Benton & Bowles agency developed to guide its creative efforts and help achieve superior creativity consistently. The agency views a creative advertising message as one that is built around a creative core or power idea and uses excellent design and execution to communicate information that interests the target audience.

Advertising creativity is not the exclusive domain of creative specialists. The nature of the business requires creative thinking from everyone involved in the

Figure 6–2 D'Arcy, Masius Benton & Bowles's universal advertising standards

1. *Does this advertising position the product simply and with unmistakable clarity?*

   The target audience for the advertised product or service must be able to see and sense in a flash *what* the product is for, *whom* it is for, and *why* they should be interested in it.

   Creating this clear vision of how the product or service fits into their lives is the first job of advertising. Without a simple, clear, focused positioning, no creative work can begin.

2. *Does this advertising bolt the brand to a clinching benefit?*

   Our advertising should be built on the most compelling and persuasive consumer benefit—not some unique-but-insignificant peripheral feature.

   Before you worry about how to say it, you must be sure you are saying *the right thing.* If you don't know what the most compelling benefit is, you've got to find out before you do anything else.

3. *Does this advertising contain a Power Idea?*

   The Power Idea is the vehicle that transforms the strategy into a dynamic, creative communications concept. It is the core creative idea that sets the stage for brilliant executions to come. The ideal Power Idea should:

   • Be describable in a simple word, phrase, or sentence without reference to any final execution.

   • Be likely to attract the prospect's attention.

   • Revolve around the clinching benefit.

   • Allow you to brand the advertising.

   • Make it easy for the prospect to vividly experience our client's product or service.

4. *Does this advertising design in Brand Personality?*

   The great brands tend to have something in common: the extra edge of having a Brand Personality. This is something beyond merely identifying what the brand does for the consumer; all brands *do* something, but the great brands also *are* something.

   A brand can be whatever its designers want it to be—and it can be so from day one.

5. *Is this advertising unexpected?*

   Why should our clients pay good money to wind up with advertising that looks and sounds like everybody else's in the category? They shouldn't.

   We must dare to be different, because sameness is suicide. We can't be outstanding unless we first stand out.

   The thing is not to *emulate* the competition but to *annihilate* them.

6. *Is this advertising single-minded?*

   If you have determined the right thing to say and have created a way to say it uncommonly well, why waste time saying anything else?

   If we want people to remember one big thing from a given piece of advertising, let's not make it more difficult than it already is in an overcommunicated world.

   The advertising should be all about that one big thing.

7. *Does this advertising reward the prospect?*

   Let's give our audience something that makes it easy—even pleasurable—for our message to penetrate: a tear, a smile, a laugh. An emotional stimulus is that special something that makes them want to see the advertising again and again.

8. *Is this advertising visually arresting?*

   Great advertising you remember—and can play back in your mind—is unusual to look at: compelling, riveting, a nourishing feast for the eyes. If you need a reason to strive for arresting work, go no further than Webster: "Catching or holding the attention, thought, or feelings. Gripping. Striking. Interesting."

9. *Does this advertising exhibit painstaking craftsmanship?*

   You want writing that is really written. Visuals that are designed. Music that is composed.

   Lighting, casting, wardrobe, direction—all the components of the art of advertising are every bit as important as the science of it. It is a sin to nickel-and-dime a great advertising idea to death.

   Why settle for good, when there's great? We should go for the absolute best in concept, design, and execution.

   This is our craft—the work should sparkle.

   "Our creative standards are not a gimmick," the agency emphasizes. "They're not even revolutionary. Instead, they are an explicit articulation of a fundamental refocusing on our company's only reason for being.

   "D'Arcy's universal advertising standards are the operating link between our vision today—and its coming reality."

promotional planning process. Agency people, such as account executives, media planners, researchers, and attorneys, as well as those on the client side, such as marketing and brand managers, must all seek creative solutions to problems encountered in planning, developing, and executing an advertising campaign. An excellent example of creative synergy between the media and creative departments of an agency, as well as with the client, is seen in the TBWA/Chiat/Day agency and its relationship with Absolut vodka. As discussed in Chapter 1, the creative strategy for the brand plays off the distinctive shape of its bottle and depicts it with visual puns and witty headlines that play off the Absolut name. The agency and client recognized they could carry the advertising campaign further by tailoring the print ads for the magazines or regions where they appear. Absolut's media schedule includes over 100 magazines, among them various consumer and business publications. The creative and media departments work together selecting magazines and deciding on the ads that will appeal to the readers of each publication. The creative department is often asked to create media-specific ads to run in a particular publication.

Planning Creative Strategy

Creative Challenges

Creative specialists face a real challenge. They must take all the research, creative briefs, strategy statements, communications objectives, and other input and transform them into an advertising message. Their job is to write copy, design layouts and illustrations, or produce commercials that effectively communicate the central theme on which the campaign is based. Rather than simply stating the features or benefits of a product or service, they must put the advertising message into a form that will engage the audience's interest and make the ads memorable.[11]

The job of the creative team is challenging because every marketing situation is different and each campaign or advertisement may require a different creative approach. Numerous guidelines have been developed for creating effective advertising,[12] but there is no magic formula. As copywriter Hank Sneiden notes in his book *Advertising Pure and Simple:*

> Rules lead to dull stereotyped advertising, and they stifle creativity, inspiration, initiative, and progress. The only hard and fast rule that I know of in advertising is that there are no rules. No formulas. No right way. Given the same problem, a dozen creative talents would solve it a dozen different ways. If there were a sure-fire formula for successful advertising, everyone would use it. Then there'd be no need for creative people. We would simply program robots to create our ads and commercials and they'd sell loads of product—to other robots.[13]

Many creative people follow proven formulas when creating ads because they are safe. Clients often feel uncomfortable with advertising that is too different. Bill Tragos, former chair of TBWA, the advertising agency noted for its excellent creative work for Absolut vodka, Evian, and many other clients, says, "Very few clients realize that the reason that their work is so bad is that they are the ones who commandeered it and directed it to be that way. I think that at least 50 percent of an agency's successful work resides in the client."[14] Many creative people say it is important for markets to take some risks if they want breakthrough advertising that gets noticed. One agency that has been successful in getting its clients to take risks is Rethink, the agency responsible for the very creative campaigns for Playland. Moreover, Taxi has won agency of the year in Canada because of their willingness to take risks.

Not all agree that advertising has to be risky to be effective, however. Many marketing managers are more comfortable with advertising that simply communicates product or service features and benefits and gives the consumer a reason to buy. They see their ad campaigns as multimillion-dollar investments whose goal is to sell the product rather than finance the whims of their agency's creative staff. They argue that some creative people have lost sight of advertising's bottom line: Does it sell?

Creative Personnel

If a marketer is using an agency, planning for creative strategy often involves two groups of individuals who have their unique specializations. Creative personnel use their artistic talents to translate communication objectives into an exciting advertising campaign. Client service personnel use account planning (and their marketing skills) to deliver the right communication solution for the client's opportunity. The interaction between these two groups and the client results in a balance between creative risk and sound marketing management for the brand.

The issue of how much latitude creative specialists should be given and how much risk the marketer should be willing to take is open to considerable debate. However, both generally agree that the ability to develop novel yet appropriate approaches to communicating with the customer makes the creative specialist valuable—and often hard to find.

Most agencies thrive on creativity, for it is the major component in the product they produce. Thus, they must create an environment that fosters the development of creative thinking and creative advertising. Clients must also understand the differences between the perspectives of the creative personnel and marketing and product managers. While the client has ultimate approval of the advertising, the opinions of creative specialists must be respected when advertising ideas and content are evaluated.

Many agencies have account reps of client service personnel who manage the relationship between the creative specialists and the client's marketing managers. Jon Steel, vice president and director of account planning at the agency's San Francisco office, has written an excellent book on the process titled *Truth, Lies & Advertising: The Art of Account Planning.*[15] He notes that the account planner's job is to provide the key decision makers with all the information they require to make an intelligent decision. According to Steel, "Planners may have to work very hard to influence the way that the advertising turns out, carefully laying out a strategic foundation with the client, handing over tidbits of information to creative people when, in their judgment, that information will have the greatest impact, giving feedback on ideas, and hopefully adding some ideas of their own."

Account planning plays an important role during creative strategy development by driving the process from the customers' point of view. Planners will work with the client as well as other agency personnel, such as the creative team and media specialists. They discuss how the knowledge and information they have gathered can be used in the development of the creative strategy as well as other aspects of the advertising campaign. Account planners are usually responsible for all the research (both qualitative and quantitative) conducted during the creative strategy development process.

Creative Process

Some advertising people say creativity in advertising is best viewed as a process and creative success is most likely when some organized approach is followed. This does not mean there is an infallible blueprint to follow to create effective advertising; as we saw earlier, many advertising people reject attempts to standardize creativity or develop rules. However, most do follow a process when developing an ad.

One of the most popular approaches to creativity in advertising was developed by James Webb Young, a former creative vice president at the J. Walter Thompson agency. Young said, "The production of ideas is just as definite a process as the production of Fords; the production of ideas, too, runs an assembly line; in this production the mind follows an operative technique which can be learned and controlled; and that its effective use is just as much a matter of practice in the technique as in the effective use of any tool."[16]

Young's process of creativity is similar to a four-step approach outlined much earlier by English sociologist Graham Wallas:

1. *Preparation.* Gathering background information needed to solve the problem through research and study.
2. *Incubation.* Getting away and letting ideas develop.

3. *Illumination.* Seeing the light or solution.

4. *Verification.* Refining and polishing the idea and seeing if it is an appropriate solution.

Models of the creative process are valuable to those working in the creative area of advertising, since they offer an organized way to approach an advertising problem. These models do not say much about how this information will be synthesized and used by the creative specialist because this part of the process is unique to the individual. Despite this limitation, the models offer a useful way of describing the creative process.

Preparation, Incubation, Illumination

Only the most foolish creative person or team would approach an assignment without first learning as much as possible about the product or service, the target audience, the competition, and any other relevant **research**. Much of this information would come from the client (i.e., marketing plan, advertising plan), which would give the creative specialist an idea as to the direction of the brand's strategy. The creative specialist can acquire background information in numerous ways. Some informal fact-finding techniques have been noted by Sandra Moriarty:

- Reading anything related to the product or market.
- Talking to many people (i.e., marketers, designers, engineers, salespeople, consumers).
- Visits to stores, malls.
- Using the product or service and becoming familiar with it.
- Working in and learning about the business.[17]

Humpty Dumpty saw the importance of research for making advertising and promotion decisions. A brand of potato chips that had seen little change in its communications for some time undertook a comprehensive review of its identity with a market research firm and its advertising agency. The results indicated that while the brand was outdated, old-fashioned, and tired, the teenage target audience would still be receptive to the brand. A key challenge was to find the right creative message that would modify the target's attitude. TV ads led this IMC campaign and the initial two spots communicated taste and flavour attributes while "re-inventing" the Humpty Dumpty character as strong and confident. It appears that consumer were connecting with the brand with shelf space and sales starting to grow.[18]

Creative people use both general and product-specific preplanning input. **General preplanning input** can include books, periodicals, trade publications, scholarly journals, pictures, and clipping services, which gather and organize magazine and newspaper articles on the product, the market, and the competition, including the latter's ads. Another useful general preplanning input concerns trends, developments, and happenings in the marketplace. Information is available from a variety of sources, including local, state, and federal governments, secondary research suppliers, and various industry trade associations, as well as advertising and media organizations that publish research reports and newsletters that provide information on market trends and developments and how they might affect consumers. Those involved in developing creative strategy can also gather relevant and timely information by reading Canadian publications like *Marketing* or *Strategy*, and American publications like *Adweek*, *Advertising Age*, and *Brand Week*.

In addition to getting general background research and preplanning input, creative people receive **product/service-specific preplanning input.** This information generally comes in the form of specific studies conducted on the product or service, the target audience, or a combination of the two. Quantitative and qualitative consumer research such as attitude studies, market structure and positioning studies such as perceptual mapping and lifestyle research, focus group interviews, and demographic and psychographic profiles of users of a particular product, service, or brand are examples of product-specific preplanning input.

IMC Perspective 6–2
The Power of Humour in Getting Ads Noticed

The hands-down most effective advertising technique in Canada is humour, according to Leger Marketing's latest poll on advertising effectiveness. One-third of Canadians said that a sense of humour in a commercial is the one thing that can make it more appealing than another commercial.

Television advertisers have only a few key seconds to grab the viewer's attention before the target audience flips channels, leaves the room, or picks up a book or newspaper. They also have to compete with hundreds of other commercials just to hold the consumer's attention for a mere 30 seconds. A variety of difference techniques and tools have been implemented in an attempt to do just that. While humour is the most important tool, other techniques can also be used effectively in certain market segments.

Leger Marketing asked 1,514 people across Canada about what works for them in terms of television advertising techniques. No other technique even comes close to the level of appeal that humour has. Whereas a third of Canadians find humour appealing, the next best tool is the product itself, at a 12 percent response rate. Another element in TV advertising that ranked high was music. Ten percent of all Canadians find commercials with music more appealing than commercials without, especially among women (14 percent) and younger people (16 percent of 18- to 34-year-olds).

It's pretty amazing to find that less than 1 percent of Canadians think that truth and honesty in advertising is appealing. In fact, it's a little bit funny, which ties in with the whole humour theme. It would be amiss not to mention that humour has many faces, and what may be funny to those in Quebec, for example, will not necessarily be funny to those in Alberta. Now, it's okay to say that in the abstract world of ad philosophizing, Canadians prefer humour to honesty. But a closer look is needed to see if this is really what makes a TV commercial attractive to the viewer. So Leger Marketing decided to scrutinize the matter.

They asked Canadians to compare the commercials in different product categories and tell which tend to have the most appealing advertising. This was a two-horse race between cars and beer, with 33 percent saying that car ads are the most appealing and 31 percent saying that beer ads are the most appealing.

There's a definite difference between the people who like car ads and those who like beer ads. Car spots appeal to basically everybody, but beer spots appeal most to a specific segment of 18- to 34-year-old (43 percent) English-speaking (34 percent) males (38 percent) who make more than $60,000 per year (39 percent). These ads are often rich with humour and almost always accompanied by music. Honesty is seldom of great consequence. In fact, many of these commercials simply present the product without many claims of quality. When a commercial does make a claim towards quality, it's often understated and a third-party endorsement.

Source: Adapted from Jean-Marc Leger and Dave Scholz, "The Last Laugh," *Marketing Magazine*, April 15, 2002. Used with permission.

It is beyond the scope of this chapter to explore all forms of market research. Some key tools are highlighted in Chapter 17, which examines the topic of measuring the effectiveness of IMC. We will however explain the role of focus groups and profiles since they are so prevalent in the creative process.

Focus groups can provide the creative team with valuable insight at the early stages of the creative process. **Focus groups** are a research method whereby consumers (usually 10 to 12 people) from the target audience are led through a discussion regarding a particular topic. Focus groups give insight as to why and how consumers use a product or service, what is important to them in choosing a particular brand, what they like and don't like about various products or services, and any special needs they might have that aren't being satisfied. A focus group session might also include a discussion of types of ad appeals to use or evaluate the advertising of various companies.

Focus group interviews bring the creative people and others involved in creative strategy development into contact with the customers. Listening to a focus group gives copywriters, art directors, and other creative specialists a better sense of who the target audience is, what the audience is like, and who the creatives need to write,

Westin Hotels & Resorts
"Male/No Jeans" :30TV ZDNE 6103

(MUSIC: UNDER THROUGHOUT)

(AVO): Broke his neck to get this job...

(MUSIC)

(AVO): ...then broke the corporate sales record.

Even broke the corporate "No Jeans" rule.

Who's he sleeping with?

(MUSIC)

(MUSIC)

Westin.

Choose...

your travel partner wisely.

(MUSIC)

(MUSIC)

(MUSIC)

(MUSIC)

Exhibit 6–3 DDB Needham's Life Style Study provided valuable input in the development of this campaign for Westin

design, or direct to in creating an advertising message. Focus groups can also be used to evaluate the viability of different creative approaches under consideration and suggest the best direction to pursue.[19]

Some agencies conduct psychographic studies annually and construct detailed psychographic or lifestyle profiles of product or service users. DDB Needham conducts a large-scale psychographic study each year using a sample of 4,000 U.S. adults. The agency's Life Style Study provides its creative teams with a better understanding of the target audience for whom they are developing ads.

For example, information from its Life Style Study was used by DDB Needham's creative department in developing a recent advertising campaign for Westin. The agency's Life Style Study showed that the younger business travelers the luxury hotel chain was targeting are highly confident, intelligent, assertive, and classy and considered themselves to be a "winner." Rather than using the traditional images that feature buildings and golf courses, the creative team decided to "brand the user" by playing to their ego and reinforcing their strong self-image. The ad campaign used the tagline "Who is he/she sleeping with? Westin. Choose your travel partner wisely" (Exhibit 6–3).

Verification and Revision

The verification and revision stage of the creative process evaluates ideas generated during the illumination stage, rejects inappropriate ones, refines and polishes those that remain, and gives them final expression. Techniques used at this stage include directed focus groups to evaluate creative ideas/themes; message communication studies; portfolio tests; and evaluation measures such as viewer reaction profiles.

At this stage of the creative process, members of the target audience may be asked to evaluate rough creative layouts and to indicate what meaning they get from the ad, what they think of its execution, or how they react to a slogan or theme. The creative team can gain insight into how a TV commercial might communicate its message by having members of the target audience evaluate the ad in storyboard form. A **storyboard** is a series of drawings used to present the visual plan or layout of a proposed commercial. It contains a series of sketches of key frames or scenes along with the copy or audio portion for each scene.

Testing a commercial in storyboard form can be difficult because storyboards are too abstract for many consumers to understand. To make the creative layout more realistic and easier to evaluate, the agency may produce an **animatic,** a videotape of the storyboard along with an audio soundtrack. Storyboards and animatics are useful for research purposes as well as for presenting the creative idea to other agency personnel or to the client for discussion and approval. At this stage of the process, the creative team is attempting to find the best creative strategy before moving ahead with the actual production of the ad. The verification/revision process may include more formal, extensive pretesting of the ad before a final decision is made. Pretesting and related procedures are examined in detail in Chapter 17.

Copy Platform

The end result of the creative process is the written document referred to as copy platform. It specifies the basic elements of the creative strategy and other relevant information that the creative team used. The **copy platform** may have other names (i.e., creative work plan, creative brief, creative blueprint) depending upon the firm. Essentially, it is plan that summarizes the entire creative approach that is agreed upon by the creative team and the marketing managers.

Matching the Celebrity to the Product

Canadian jazz singer Diana Krall is front and centre in a national Daimler Chrysler Canada campaign. Krall is featured in a campaign that includes print, TV, and cinema components for Chrysler's Sebring Convertible, Sebring Sedan, and Chrysler 300M Special. The ads, which feature Krall and music from her latest album, "The Look of Love," represent the second phase of Chrysler's "This is my car" campaign.

According to Pearl Davies, Chrysler brand manager, Krall epitomizes the core essence of the Chrysler brand. Davies says: "We talk about four things: expressive, refined, athletic, and romantic. When we talk about expressive, we mean the self-evident beauty of the vehicles. You could call them drop-dead gorgeous. When you look at Diana, you don't have to say another thing about that. Then we talk about the refinement of the vehicles, the quality of the craftsmanship, and we can draw a parallel between her art and our vehicles. When we talk about athleticism, we mean performance and grace. When Diana performs, and everything else about her, it suggests graceful poise. And this year we've added the concept of romantic. That's about passion, building cars people fall in love with. What better way to express it than with Diana Krall, who sings about love, the look of love, let's fall in love…"

Sources: David Hayes, "The Boys in the Band," *National Post Business Magazine,* March, 2002, p. 46; "The Artist as a Young Brand," *Marketing Magazine,* March 4, 2002; "Krall Has the Look of Love," *Marketing Magazine,* February 25, 2002.

If an agency is used, the account representative or manager assigned to the account usually prepares the copy platform. In larger agencies, an individual from research or the strategic account planning department may write it. People from the agency team or group assigned to the account, including creative personnel as well as representatives from media and research, have input. The advertising manager and/or the marketing and brand managers from the client side ultimately approve the copy platform.

Figure 6–3 shows a sample copy-platform outline that can be used to guide the creative process. Just as there are different names for the copy platform, there are variations in the outline and format used and in the level of detail included. Copy platforms also include supporting information and requirements (i.e., brand identifications, disclaimers) that should appear in any advertising message to ensure uniformity across various executions of the ads used in a campaign or in meeting any legal requirements.

The first three sections are derived from the client's marketing plan and prior communications between the agency and client. These sections may be revised slightly as the agency experiences the creative process. The content of these sections were discussed in previous chapters. For example, Chapter 5 showed how the

1. Basic problem or opportunity the advertising must address
2. Target audience and behaviour objective
3. Communication objectives
4. Brand positioning statement
5. Creative strategy (creative theme/idea, message appeal, source characteristics)
6. Supporting information and requirements

Figure 6–3 Copy-platform outline

143

setting of communication objectives requires specifying a well-defined target audience and developing a communication task statement that spells out what message must be communicated to this audience. Determining what problem the product or service will solve or what issue must be addressed in the ad helps in establishing communication objectives for the campaign to accomplish.

We can see these first few steps in campaign developed for Polaroid a few years ago. Goodby, Silverstein & Partners was faced with the challenge of redefining the relevancy of instant photography and bringing Polaroid cameras out of the closet and back into everyday use. This suggests that the target audience was lapsed users of existing Polaroid instant cameras (and potentially new users of instant cameras) with the intention of generating greater awareness and modifying their attitude. Working with Polaroid's marketing personnel, the agency came up with the idea of focusing on an instant picture as a solution to a problem, an instant tool or "catalyst" to make something happen. The advertising message is designed to give people ideas about how to use their forgotten Polaroid cameras. Thus, a clear brand positioning statement with a specific motive identified.

The three key decisions of the creative strategy are usually included in the copy platform: creative theme/idea, message appeal, and source characteristics. These are often the responsibility of the creative team or specialist and form the basis of the advertising campaign theme. For Polaroid, the creative idea was "the picture is only the beginning," and the resulting campaign theme built around this idea was "See what develops." The creative strategy was to have each ad in the campaign tell a story in which a Polaroid camera sets off a chain reaction. For example, one of the TV commercials featured a harried architect in a meeting telling his wife on the phone that he can't possibly come home for lunch. But in a sultry voice she tells him to look in his briefcase, saying "I left you something this morning." He pulls out a Polaroid photo, his eyes widen, and he says, "I'll be there in 10 minutes." Another humourous spot from the campaign shows a dog, wrongfully being scolded for upsetting the trash while an evil-looking cat sneers from the other side of the kitchen. The owner leaves, and the cat goes for the trash once again. However, this time the dog takes a Polaroid snapshot of the cat, astride the trash with a chicken bone in its mouth, and then patiently waits, incriminating photo in mouth, as the door opens and the owner returns. "Oh dear," we hear as the picture fades (Exhibit 6–4). As suggested, these creative examples use a humour appeal with ordinary consumers from the target audience as the source of the message.

Exhibit 6–4   The major selling idea behind this Polaroid commercial is that the picture is only the beginning of the story

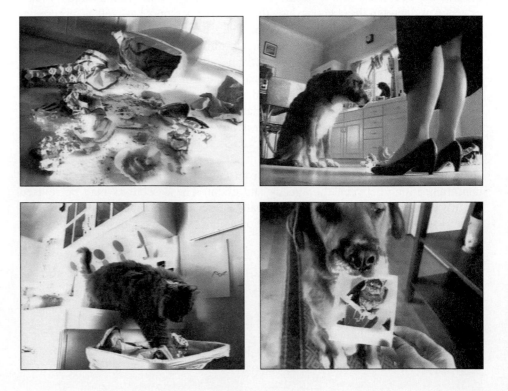

Firms sometimes use a different creative strategy to reach a new target audience. Sleeman Brewery has maintained an authentic quality position as a microbrewer that makes craft beer (its market position). Much of Sleeman's recent success can be attributed to reaching a core of loyal drinkers in the 35+ age demographic who value its ingredients and brewing methods (brand position). Seeking to grow, Sleeman naturally tried to attract a group of drinkers who were looking to switch as they matured (i.e., aged 25-35). So the issue focused on the appropriate brand positioning strategy to encourage these potential customers to believe that they would now value some of the attributes and benefits of this kind of beer, Sleeman beer in particular. Naturally, the brand positioning strategy that Sleeman used for its new target audience should not alienate the brand position of its loyal drinkers while at the same time maintaining its clear market position. This is quite the challenge and the creative strategy used seems to work.

Sleeman's decided to minimize the use of their long-time spokesperson John Sleeman for their English ads in 2001 while connecting consumption experiences with an attribute of the bottle. The clear glass shows the product clearly such that there is "nothing to hide." Picking up on this idea, the ads symbolically conveyed this with social situations where consumers had "nothing to hide." For example, we do not conceal our true thoughts and feelings when meeting someone. Sleeman continued the theme in 2002 and focused on the fact that the beer does not have a label. It played on the meaning of the word "label" and featured new music groups that had not been signed by a "record label." In both cases, these messages resonate more with a new younger audience.[20]

Creative Theme/Idea

Thus far we have discussed advertising creativity in general and the planning activities that occur as a campaign is developed. We now turn our attention to examining the content of the creative strategy in greater detail. This section and the next two sections explore the three primary decisions that are required for a complete creative strategy: creative theme/idea, message appeal, and source. Within each section we identify the key options for each decision.

Most ads are part of a series of messages that make up an IMC or **advertising campaign**, which is a set of interrelated and coordinated marketing communication activities that centre on a single theme or idea that appears in different media across a specified time period. Determining the unifying theme around which the campaign will be built is a critical part of the creative process, as it sets the tone for the individual ads and other forms of marketing communications that will be used. A **campaign theme** should be a strong idea, as it is the central message that will be communicated in all the advertising and other promotional activities. Advertising creative theme/idea is short-term in nature and, like marketing and IMC plans, done on an annual basis. However, the creative themes are usually developed with the intention of being used for a longer time period. While some marketers change their campaign themes often, a successful creative theme may last for years. Figure 6–4 lists the slogans of some enduring ad campaign themes.

There have been two interesting decisions for slogans in Canada. With a mandate to generate re-trial from lapsed users or increased frequency of repurchase from current customers, KFC Canada (that's Kentucky Fried Chicken) went back to their famous "Finger lickin' good" slogan. Sometimes firms have trouble working with new slogans and have to revert to previous ones.[21] In 2001, for the first time ever, McDonald's Canada used its own slogan ("There's a little McDonald's in every one") instead of using the one in the United States ("We'd love to see you smile"). Did you notice this difference recently? While Molson Canadian has used two slogans simultaneously ("I am Canadian" and "It's a Canadian game"), you might have concluded that McDonald's was doing the same. To signal the difference, McDonald's shows a small red maple leaf to let you know that it is the Canadian version.

Putting together a creative for Canada can be met with some obstacles. Canadian managers who market U.S. brands in Canada often feel the pressure to run the same

Figure 6–4 Examples of
successful long-running
advertising campaigns

Company or Brand	Slogan
Nike	"Just do it."
Allstate Insurance	"You're in good hands with Allstate."
Hallmark cards	"When you care enough to send the very best."
De Beers	"A diamond is forever."
Intel	"Intel inside."
State Farm Insurance	"Like a good neighbour, State Farm is there."
Timex watches	"It takes a licking and keeps on ticking."
Dial soap	"Aren't you glad you use Dial? Don't you wish everyone did?"

campaign in Canada that is being run in the U.S. While this obviously saves on production costs of new ads, it can be more than offset with lower sales due to messages not resonating with Canadian culture. Sometimes firms need to perform specific market research to demonstrate that a unique creative is warranted for the Canadian market. For example, Lever Pond's of Canada felt the U.S. creative for Degree deodorant featuring CEOs and race car drivers would not be acceptable to Canadian consumers. Research was done, a discussion ensued with U.S. managers, and finally a humourous campaign that looked at stressful situations where the dryness benefit of product could be understood. Ironically, the ads in the U.S. barely registered with consumers in follow-up research while the Canadian campaign tested above average.[22]

We've seen creative ideas based on many things such as consumption habits, people, invented characters, and animals. An unlikely one is found in the campaign for the Canadian Tourism Commission, which recently used a map to encourage Canadians to travel within their own country. In the TV ad, a map folded like an orgami decoration unfolds to show that within Canada there is so much to do. The map appears in other IMC tools like the quarterly tourism magazine to give it a consistent look.[23]

Some advertising experts argue that for an ad campaign to be effective it must contain a big idea that attracts the consumer's attention, gets a reaction, and sets the advertiser's product or service apart from the competition's. Well-known adman John O'Toole describes the *big idea* as "that flash of insight that synthesizes the purpose of the strategy, joins the product benefit with consumer desire in a fresh, involving way, brings the subject to life, and makes the reader or audience stop, look, and listen."[24]

Of course, the real challenge to the creative team is coming up with the big idea to use in the ad. Many products and services offer virtually nothing unique, and it can be difficult to find something interesting to say about them. David Ogilvy, generally considered one of the most creative advertising copywriters ever to work in the business, has stated:

> I doubt if more than one campaign in a hundred contains a big idea. I am supposed to be one of the more fertile inventors of big ideas, but in my long career as a copywriter I have not had more than 20, if that.[25]

While really great ideas in advertising are difficult to come by, there are many big ideas that became the basis of very creative, successful advertising campaigns. A classic example is the "Pepsi generation" theme and subsequent variations like "the taste of a new generation" and "GenerationNext." More recent big ideas that have resulted in effective advertising campaigns include the "Intel inside" campaign for Intel microprocessors that go in personal computers; Nike's "Just do it"; the "It keeps going and going" theme for Energizer batteries, featuring the pink bunny; and the "Like a rock" theme for Chevrolet trucks.

It is difficult to pinpoint the inspiration for a big idea or to teach advertising people how to find one. However, several approaches can guide the creative team's search for a creative theme/idea and offer solutions for developing effective advertising. Some of the best-known approaches follow:

- Using a unique selling proposition.
- Creating a brand image.
- Finding the inherent drama.
- Positioning.

Unique Selling Proposition

The concept of the **unique selling proposition (USP)** was developed by Rosser Reeves, former chair of the Ted Bates agency, and is described in his influential book *Reality in Advertising*. Reeves noted three characteristics of unique selling propositions:

1. Each advertisement must make a proposition to the consumer. Not just words, not just product puffery, not just show-window advertising. Each advertisement must say to each reader: "Buy this product and you will get this benefit."

2. The proposition must be one that the competition either cannot or does not offer. It must be unique either in the brand or in the claim.

3. The proposition must be strong enough to move the mass millions, that is, pull over new customers to your brand.[26]

Reeves said the attribute claim or benefit that forms the basis of the USP should dominate the ad and be emphasized through repetitive advertising. An example of advertising based on a USP is the campaign for Trident gum (Exhibit 6–5).The brand's unique attributes make it the only chewing gum with the seal of approval from the Canadian Dental Association.

For Reeves's approach to work, there must be a truly unique product or service attribute, benefit, or inherent advantage that can be used in the claim. The approach may require considerable research on the product and consumers, not only to determine the USP but also to document the claim.

Creating a Brand Image

In many product and service categories, competing brands are so similar that it is very difficult to communicate a unique attribute or benefit. Many of the package-goods products that account for most of the advertising dollars spent are difficult to differentiate on a functional or performance basis. The creative strategy used to sell these products is based on the development of a strong, memorable identity for the brand through **image advertising.**

David Ogilvy popularized the idea of brand image in his famous book *Confessions of an Advertising Man*. Ogilvy said that with image advertising, "every advertisement should be thought of as a contribution to the complex symbol which is the brand image." He argued that the image or personality of the brand is particularly important when brands are similar:

> The greater the similarity between brands, the less part reason plays in brand selection. There isn't any significant difference between the various brands of whiskey, or cigarettes, or beer. They are all about the same. And so are the cake mixes and the detergents and the

Exhibit 6–5 This ad uses a unique selling proposition

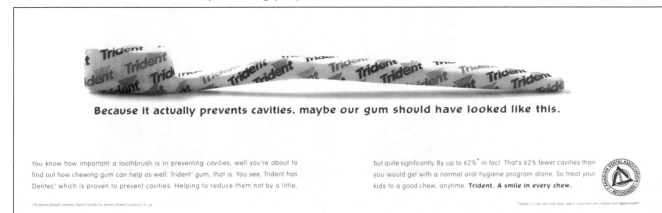

Because it actually prevents cavities, maybe our gum should have looked like this.

You know how important a toothbrush is in preventing cavities, well you're about to find out how chewing gum can help as well. Trident gum, that is. You see, Trident has Dentec, which is proven to prevent cavities. Helping to reduce them not by a little, but quite significantly. By up to 62%* in fact. That's 62% fewer cavities than you would get with a normal oral hygiene program alone. So treat your kids to a good chew, anytime. **Trident. A smile in every chew.**

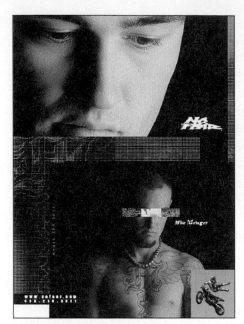

Exhibit 6–6 Advertising for No Fear creates a unique image for the brand as representing the outer limits of human performance

margarines. The manufacturer who dedicates his advertising to building the most sharply defined personality for his brand will get the largest share of the market at the highest profit. By the same token, the manufacturers who will find themselves up the creek are those shortsighted opportunists who siphon off their advertising funds for promotions.[27]

Image advertising has become increasingly popular and is used as the creative theme/idea for a variety of products and services, including soft drinks, liquor, cigarettes, cars, airlines, financial services, perfume/colognes, and clothing. Many people consume certain brands of these products because of image. The key to successful image advertising is developing an image that will appeal to product users. For example, the sports apparel company No Fear uses this type of advertising to create a unique image for the brand as representing the outer limits of human performance. Ads like the one in Exhibit 6–6 have helped create this image for No Fear.

Finding the Inherent Drama   Another approach to determining the creative theme/idea is finding the **inherent drama** or characteristic of the product that makes the consumer purchase it. The inherent drama approach expresses the advertising philosophy of Leo Burnett, founder of the Leo Burnett agency in Chicago. Burnett said inherent drama "is often hard to find but it is always there, and once found it is the most interesting and believable of all advertising appeals."[28] He believed advertising should be based on

Exhibit 6–7 This Hallmark commercial uses an inherent drama approach

a foundation of consumer benefits with an emphasis on the dramatic element in expressing those benefits.

Burnett advocated a down-home type of advertising that presents the message in a warm and realistic way. Some of the more famous ads developed by his agency using the inherent drama approach are for McDonald's, Maytag appliances, Kellogg's cereals, and Hallmark cards. Notice how the Hallmark commercial shown in Exhibit 6–7 uses this approach to deliver a poignant message.

Positioning   Since advertising is used to establish the brand position in consumers' minds, it can also be the source of the creative theme/idea. Positioning is done for companies as well as for brands. For example, the ad shown in Exhibit 6–8 is part of a campaign designed to reinforce 3M's position as an innovative company. Positioning is often the basis of a firm's creative strategy when it has multiple brands competing in the same market. For example, Procter & Gamble markets many brands of laundry detergent—and positions each one differently.

Trout and Ries originally described positioning as the image consumers had of the brand in relation to competing brands in the product or service category, but the concept has been expanded beyond direct competitive positioning.[29] As discussed in Chapter 2, products can be positioned on the basis of product attributes, price/quality, usage or application, product users, or product class. Any of these can spark a creative theme/idea that becomes the

Exhibit 6–8 This ad positions 3M as an innovative company

basis of the creative strategy and results in the brand's occupying a particular place in the minds of the target audience. Since brand positioning can be done on the basis of a distinctive attribute, the positioning and unique selling proposition approaches can overlap.

Molson Export returned to a brand positioning strategy of heritage; original or authentic in Quebec was the source of an interesting creative idea. Research indicated that consumers young and old alike still perceived Export as having a strong 100-year history and associated it with classic beer-drinking moments, even though the brand had inconsistent advertising and weak marketing support in recent years. The slogan captured the essence of the repositioning, "Molson Ex. Today's beer since 1903." The first few executions of the creative strategy showed the progression and similarity of Export consumption since its inception. For example, the first spot, "Evolution," says it all as a number of scenes depicted people bringing cases of Export to various parties over the course of time. Using the computer morphing techniques, the images also showed how the labels of the brand had changed.[30]

Message Appeals

The message or **advertising appeal** refers to the approach used to attract the attention of consumers and/or to influence their attitude toward the product, service, or cause. A message appeal can also be viewed as "something that moves people, speaks to their wants or needs, and excites their interest."[31] The **creative execution** style is the way a particular appeal is turned into an advertising message presented to the consumer. According to William Weilbacher:

> The appeal can be said to form the underlying content of the advertisement, and the execution the way in which that content is presented. Advertising appeals and executions are usually independent of each other; that is, a particular appeal can be executed in a variety of ways and a particular means of execution can be applied to a variety of advertising appeals. Advertising appeals tend to adapt themselves to all media, whereas some kinds of executional devices are more adaptable to some media than others.[32]

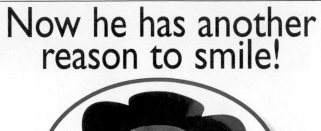

Now he has another reason to smile!

Heart healthy news announced by the FDA.

Soluble fiber from oatmeal, as part of a low saturated fat, low cholesterol diet, may reduce the risk of heart disease.

Quaker Oatmeal. Oh, what those Oats can do.™

©1997 QOC.   http://www.quakeroatmeal.com

Exhibit 6–9 Quaker Oatmeal uses a rational appeal to promote the health benefits of oatmeal

Exhibit 6–10 Singapore Airlines uses a feature appeal ad to promote its new Raffles class

As this implies, the message appeal is a creative strategy decision whereas the execution style is more of a creative tactic decision. (We will discuss the tactics in more detail in the next chapter.) One of the advertiser's most important creative strategy decisions involves the choice of an appropriate appeal. Hundreds of different appeals can be used as the basis for advertising messages. We concentrate on four broad appeals: rational appeals, emotional appeals, fear appeals, and humour appeals. In this section, we focus on ways to use these appeals as part of a creative strategy and consider how they can be combined in developing the advertising message.

Rational Appeals

Rational appeals focus on the consumer's practical, functional, or utilitarian need for the product or service and emphasize features of a product or service and/or the benefits or reasons for owning or using a particular brand. The content of these messages emphasizes facts, learning, and the logic of persuasion.[33] Rational-based appeals tend to be informative, and advertisers using them generally attempt to convince consumers that their product or service has a particular attribute(s) or provides a specific benefit that satisfies their needs. Their objective is to persuade the target audience to buy the brand because it is the best available or does a better job of meeting consumers' needs. For example, the Quaker Oats company uses a rational appeal in noting how fibre from oatmeal may help reduce the risk of heart disease (Exhibit 6–9).

Many rational motives can be used as the basis for advertising appeals, including comfort, convenience, economy, health, and sensory benefits such as touch, taste, and smell. Other rational motives or purchase criteria commonly used in advertising include quality, dependability, durability, efficiency, efficacy, and performance. The particular features, benefits, or evaluative criteria that are important to consumers and can serve as the basis of a rational appeal vary from one product or service category to another as well as among various market segments.

Weilbacher identified several types of advertising appeals that fall under the category of rational approaches, among them feature, comparative, favourable price, news, and product/service popularity appeals. We also include reminder appeals in this list.

Ads that use a *feature appeal* focus on the dominant traits of the product or service. These ads tend to be highly informative and present the customer with a number of important product attributes or features that will lead to favourable attitudes and can be used as the basis for a rational purchase decision. Technical and high-involvement products often use this advertising approach. This type of appeal can also be used for a service. Notice how the Singapore Airlines ad in Exhibit 6–10 focuses on the various features of its new Raffles class of service.

A *comparative appeal* is the practice of either directly or indirectly naming competitors in an ad and comparing one or more specific attributes.[34] A comparative appeal can also be made for different product formats, as shown in Exhibit 6–11. Some studies show that recall is higher for comparative than noncomparative messages, but comparative ads are generally not more effective for other response variables, such as brand attitudes or purchase intentions.[35] Advertisers must also consider how comparative messages affect credibility. Users of the brand being attacked in a comparative message may be especially skeptical about the advertiser's claims.

Exhibit 6–11 A comparative appeal across product formats

Comparative appeals may be particularly useful for new brands, since it allows a new market entrant to position itself directly against the more established brands and to promote its distinctive advantages. Direct comparisons can help position a new brand in the evoked, or choice, set of brands the customer may be considering.

Comparative appeals are often used for brands with a small market share. They compare themselves to an established market leader in hopes of creating an association and tapping into the leader's market. Market leaders, on the other hand, often hesitate to use comparison ads, as most believe they have little to gain by featuring competitors' products in their ads.

A *favourable price appeal* makes the price offer the dominant point of the message. Price appeal advertising is used most often by retailers to announce sales, special offers, or low everyday prices. Price appeal ads are often used by national advertisers during recessionary times. Many fast-food chains have made price an important part of their marketing strategy through promotional deals and "value menus" or lower overall prices, and their advertising strategy is designed to communicate this. Many other types of advertisers use price appeals as well.

News appeals are those in which some type of news or announcement about the product, service, or company dominates the ad. This type of appeal can be used for a new product or service or to inform consumers of significant modifications or improvements. This appeal works best when a company has important news it wants to communicate to its target audience. The Quaker Oatmeal ad shown in Exhibit 6–9, which announced the news from the U.S. Food and Drug Administration regarding the health benefits of eating oatmeal, is an example of a news appeal.

Product/service popularity appeals stress the popularity of a product or service by pointing out the number of consumers who use the brand, the number who have switched to it, the number of experts who recommend it, or its leadership position in the market. The main point of this advertising appeal is that the wide use of the brand proves its quality or value and other customers should consider using it. The Excedrin ad in Exhibit 6–12 uses this type of advertising appeal.

A *reminder appeal* has the objective of building brand awareness and/or keeping the brand name in front of consumers. Well-known brands and market leaders often use a reminder appeal which is often referred to as reminder advertising. Products and services that have a seasonal pattern to their consumption also use reminder advertising, particularly around the appropriate period. For example, marketers of candy products often increase their media budgets and run reminder advertising around Halloween, Valentine's Day, Christmas, and Easter.

Emotional Appeals

Emotional appeals relate to the customers' social and/or psychological needs for purchasing a product or service. Many of consumers' motives for their purchase decisions are emotional, and their feelings about a brand can be more important than knowledge of its features or attributes. Advertisers for many products and services view rational, information-based appeals as dull. Many advertisers believe appeals to con-

Exhibit 6–12 This ad promotes the popularity of Excedrin among doctors

Figure 6–5 Bases for emotional appeals

Personal States or Feelings	Social-Based Feelings
Safety	Recognition
Security	Status
Fear	Respect
Love	Involvement
Affection	Embarrassment
Happiness	Affiliation/belonging
Joy	Rejection
Nostalgia	Acceptance
Sentiment	Approval
Excitement	
Arousal/stimulation	
Sorrow/grief	
Pride	
Achievement/accomplishment	
Self-esteem	
Actualization	
Pleasure	
Ambition	
Comfort	

sumers' emotions work better at selling brands that do not differ markedly from competing brands, since rational differentiation of them is difficult.[36]

Many feelings or needs can serve as the basis for advertising appeals designed to influence consumers on an emotional level, as shown in Figure 6–5. These appeals are based on the psychological states or feelings directed to the self (such as pleasure or excitement), as well as those with a more social orientation (such as status or recognition).

Advertisers can use emotional appeals in many ways in their creative strategy. Kamp and Macinnis note that commercials often rely on the concept of *emotional integration,* whereby they portray the characters in the ad as experiencing an emotional benefit or outcome from using a product or service.[37] Ads using humour, sex, and other appeals that are very entertaining, arousing, upbeat, and/or exciting can affect the emotions of consumers and put them in a favourable frame of mind. Many TV advertisers use poignant ads that bring a lump to viewers' throats. Hallmark, AT&T, and Kodak often create commercials that evoke feelings of warmth, nostalgia, and/or sentiment.

Marketers use emotional appeals in hopes that the positive feeling they evoke will transfer to the brand and/or company. Research shows that positive mood states and feelings created by advertising can have a favourable effect on consumers' evaluations of a brand.[38] Studies also show that emotional advertising is better remembered than nonemotional messages.[39]

McDonald's changed its advertising strategy recently and is putting more emotion in its commercials to evoke a feel-good connection with consumers. The company's senior vice president of marketing explained the change by stating, "Over the last couple of years, we had been very good on the humour side but we really hadn't done a lot to reach and touch people with heart-warming or wholesome or romantic or heart-tugging emotions."[40] One of the heart-tugging commercials, called "New Math," shows a big sister teaching her brother how to count as only an older sibling can. Using McDonald's french fries as an aid, while her mother isn't watching, she methodically counts out a big pile for herself and a small one for her increasingly distressed brother. McDonald's and its agencies feel the new ads take advantage of the chain's unique bond with consumers, which is a significant point of differentiation in the highly competitive fast-food business.

Fear Appeals Fear is an emotional response to a threat that expresses, or at least implies, some sort of danger. Ads sometimes use **fear appeals** to evoke this emotional response and arouse individuals to take steps to remove the threat. Some, like anti-smoking ads, stress physical danger that can occur if behaviours are not altered. Others—like those for deodorant, mouthwash, or dandruff shampoos—threaten disapproval or social rejection.

How Fear Operates Before deciding to use a fear appeal–based message strategy, the advertiser should consider how fear operates, what level to use, and how different target audiences may respond. One theory suggests that the relationship between the level of fear in a message and acceptance or persuasion is curvilinear, as shown in Figure 6–6.[41] This means that message acceptance increases as the amount of fear used rises—to a point. Beyond that point, acceptance decreases as the level of fear rises.

This relationship between fear and persuasion can be explained by the fact that fear appeals have both facilitating and inhibiting effects.[42] A low level of fear can have facilitating effects; it attracts attention and interest in the message and may motivate the receiver to act to resolve the threat. Thus, increasing the level of fear in a message from low to moderate can result in increased persuasion. High levels of fear, however, can produce inhibiting effects; the receiver may emotionally block the message by tuning it out, perceiving it selectively, or denying its arguments outright. Figure 6–6 illustrates how these two countereffects operate to produce the curvilinear relationship between fear and persuasion.

A recent study by Anand-Keller and Block provides support for this perspective on how fear operates.[43] Their study indicated that a communication using a low level of fear may be ineffective because it results in insufficient motivation to elaborate on the harmful consequences of engaging in the destructive behaviour (smoking). However, an appeal arousing high levels of fear was ineffective because it resulted in too much elaboration on the harmful consequences. This led to defensive tendencies such as message avoidance and interfered with processing of recommended solutions to the problem.

Another approach to the curvilinear explanation of fear is the protection motivation model.[44] According to this theory, four cognitive appraisal processes mediate the individual's response to the threat: appraising (1) the information available regarding the severity of the perceived threat, (2) the perceived probability that the threat will occur, (3) the perceived ability of a coping behaviour to remove the threat, and (4) the individual's perceived ability to carry out the coping behaviour.

This model suggests that both the cognitive appraisal of the information in a fear appeal message and the emotional response mediate persuasion. An audience is more likely to continue processing threat-related information, thereby increasing the likelihood that a coping behaviour will occur. The protection motivation model suggests that ads using fear appeals should give the target audience information about the severity of the threat, the probability of its occurrence, the effectiveness of a

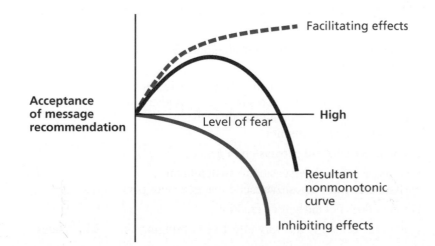

Acceptance of message recommendation

Level of fear — High

Facilitating effects

Resultant nonmonotonic curve

Inhibiting effects

Figure 6–6 Relationship between fear levels and message acceptance

Exhibit 6–13 This ad uses a mild fear appeal but reduces anxiety by offering a solution to a problem

Exhibit 6–14 This clever ad is an example of how humour can be executed in print media

coping response, and the ease with which the response can be implemented (Exhibit 6–13).[45]

It is also important to consider how the target audience may respond. Fear appeals are more effective when the message recipient is self-confident and prefers to cope with dangers rather than avoid them.[46] They are also more effective among nonusers of a product than among users. Thus, a fear appeal may be better at keeping nonsmokers from starting than persuading smokers to stop.

In reviewing research on fear appeals, Herbert Rotfeld has argued that some of the studies may be confusing different types of threats and the level of potential harm portrayed in the message with fear, which is an emotional response.[47] He concludes that the relationship between the emotional responses of fear or arousal and persuasion is not curvilinear but rather is monotonic and positive, meaning that higher levels of fear do result in greater persuasion. However, Rotfeld notes that not all fear messages are equally effective, because different people fear different things. Thus they will respond differently to the same threat, so the strongest threats are not always the most persuasive. This suggests that marketers using fear appeals must consider the emotional responses generated by the message and how they will affect reactions to the message.

Humour Appeals   Humourous ads are often the best known and best remembered of all advertising messages. Humour is usually presented through radio and TV commercials as these media lend themselves to the execution of humourous messages. However, humour is occasionally used in print ads as well (Exhibit 6–14).

Advertisers use humour for many reasons. Humourous messages attract and hold consumers' attention. They enhance effectiveness by putting consumers in a positive mood, increasing their liking of the ad itself and their feeling toward the product or service. And humour can distract the receiver from counterarguing against the message.[48]

Critics argue that funny ads draw people to the humourous situation but distract them from the brand and its attributes. Also, effective humour can be difficult to produce and some attempts are too subtle for mass audiences.

Clearly, there are valid reasons both for and against the use of humour in advertising. Not every product or service lends itself to a humourous approach. A number of studies have found that the effectiveness of humour depends on several factors, including the type of product and audience characteristics.[49] For example, humour has been more prevalent and more effective with low-involvement, feeling products than high-involvement, thinking products.[50] An interesting study surveyed the research and creative directors of the top 150 advertising agencies.[51] They were asked to name which communications objectives are facilitated through the appropriate situational use of humour in terms of media, product, and audience factors. The general conclusions of this study are as follows:

- Humour does aid awareness and attention, which are the objectives best achieved by its use.
  - Humour may harm recall and comprehension in general.
  - Humour may aid name and simple copy registration.
  - Humour may harm complex copy registration.
  - Humour may aid retention.
- Humour does not aid persuasion in general.
  - Humour may aid persuasion to switch brands.
  - Humour creates a positive mood that enhances persuasion.
- Humour does not aid source credibility.
- Humour is generally not very effective in bringing about action/sales.

- Creatives are more positive on the use of humour to fulfill all the above objectives than research directors are.
- Radio and TV are the best media in which to use humour; direct mail and newspapers are least suited.
- Consumer nondurables and business services are best suited to humour; corporate advertising and industrial products are least suited.
- Humour should be related to the product.
- Humour should not be used with sensitive goods or services.
- Audiences that are younger, better educated, upscale, male, and professional are best suited to humour; older, less educated, and downscale groups are least suited to humour appeals.

Combining Rational and Emotional Appeals In many advertising situations, the decision facing the creative specialist is not whether to choose an emotional or a rational appeal but rather determining how to combine the two approaches. As noted copywriters David Ogilvy and Joel Raphaelson have stated:

> Few purchases of any kind are made for entirely rational reasons. Even a purely functional product such as laundry detergent may offer what is now called an emotional benefit—say, the satisfaction of seeing one's children in bright clean clothes. In some product categories the rational element is small. These include soft drinks, beer, cosmetics, certain personal care products, and most old-fashioned products. And who hasn't experienced the surge of joy that accompanies the purchase of a new car?[52]

Consumer purchase decisions are often made on the basis of both emotional and rational motives, and attention must be given to both elements in developing effective advertising. Exhibit 6–15 shows a very clever ad that uses the Freudian concepts of id and superego to suggest that there are both emotional and rational reasons for purchasing the Lexus SC 400 coupe.

Advertising researchers and agencies have given considerable thought to the relationship between rational and emotional motives in consumer decision making and how advertising influences both. McCann-Erickson Worldwide, in conjunction with advertising professor Michael Ray, developed a proprietary research technique known as *emotional bonding*. This technique evaluates how consumers feel about brands and the nature of any emotional rapport they have with a brand compared to the ideal emotional state they associate with the product category.[53]

The basic concept of emotional bonding is that consumers develop three levels of relationships with brands, as shown in Figure 6–7. The most basic relationship indicates how consumers *think* about brands in respect to product benefits. This

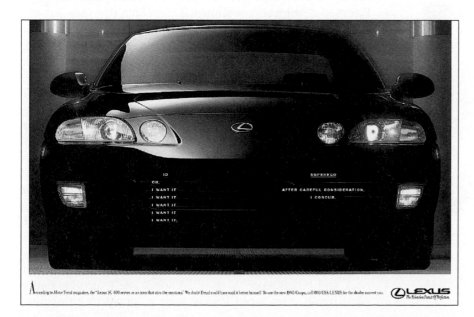

Exhibit 6–15 Lexus addresses both rational and emotional appeals in this clever ad

Figure 6–7 Levels of relationships with brands

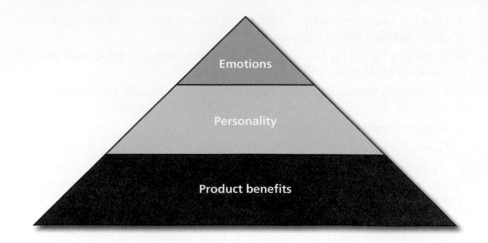

occurs, for the most part, through a rational learning process and can be measured by how well advertising communicates product information. Consumers at this stage are not very brand loyal, and brand switching is common.

At the next stage, the consumer assigns a *personality* to a brand. For example, a brand may be thought of as self-assured, aggressive, and adventurous, as opposed to compliant and timid. The consumer's judgment of the brand has moved beyond its attributes or delivery of product/service benefits. In most instances, consumers judge the personality of a brand on the basis of an assessment of overt or covert cues found in its advertising.

McCann-Erickson researchers believe the strongest relationship that develops between a brand and the consumer is based on feelings or emotional attachments to the brand. Consumers develop *emotional bonds* with certain brands, which result in positive psychological movement toward them. The marketer's goal is to develop the greatest emotional linkage between its brand and the consumer. McCann-Erickson believes advertising can develop and enrich emotional bonding between consumers and brands. McCann and its subsidiary agencies use emotional bonding research to provide strategic input into the creative process and determine how well advertising is communicating with consumers. McCann-Erickson used emotional

Exhibit 6–16 MasterCard's "Priceless" campaign creates an emotional bond with consumers

18 speed bike: $525

portable pup tent: $90

the longest paperback you could find: $9.99

seven days without email:

priceless

there are some things money can't buy.
for everything else there's MasterCard.®

MasterCard

©2006 MasterCard International Incorporated

www.mastercard.com

bonding research as the basis for its award-winning "Priceless" campaign for MasterCard International. When the agency took over the account a few years ago, MasterCard was perceived as an ordinary credit card you keep in your wallet. The challenge was to create an emotional bond between consumers and MasterCard without losing the brand's functional appeal. McCann-Erickson developed a sentimental campaign that uses ads that take the sum total of an experience and declare that it has no price tag. Each commercial and print ad ends with the theme "There are some things money can't buy. For everything else there's MasterCard" (Exhibit 6–16).

A unique example of combining rational and emotional appeals is the use of teaser advertising. Advertisers introducing a new product often use **teaser advertising,** which is designed to build curiosity, interest, and/or excitement about a product or brand by talking about it but not actually showing it. Teasers, or *mystery ads* as they are sometimes called, are also used by marketers to draw attention to upcoming advertising campaigns and generate interest and publicity for them. For example, Lee Jeans used teaser ads as part of its successful "Can't bust 'em" campaign for its new Dungarees line that features the Buddy Lee doll. The denim-dressed doll, which was used in Lee's promotional displays from the 1920s through the 50s, was brought back and billed as a "Man of Action." Lee's agency, Fallon McElligott, introduced Buddy with a "phantom campaign" designed to intrigue influential trendsetters among the 17- to 22-year-old target market. Posters of Buddy Lee, unidentified and unbranded, were wild-posted in "cool" areas of 15 markets to generate curiosity. The agency then produced a six-minute film, *The Buddy Lee Story,* that was run on "graveyard cable," 2 A.M. slots on Comedy Central and other cable channels. Again, the product was never mentioned, but the film did associate Buddy with the Lee Company and its "Can't bust 'em" spirit.

The goal of the teaser campaign was to let the trendsetters discover Buddy and spread the news about him. The teaser campaign was successful in generating word of mouth and helped accelerate the popularity of the brand as subsequent advertising featuring Buddy hawking the Dungarees line was introduced. The campaign helped make initial sales of the Dungaree's line four times higher than anticipated and resulted in a 3 percent increase in market share for Lee even though overall denim sales were flat.[54]

Teaser ads are especially popular among automotive advertisers for introducing a new model or announcing significant changes in a vehicle. For example, Chrysler has used teaser ads to introduce its Neon subcompact and new models of the Jeep Grand Cherokee. Teaser campaigns can generate interest in a new product, but advertisers must be careful not to extend them too long or they will lose their effectiveness.[55] Many advertising experts thought the teaser campaign used by Infiniti to introduce its cars in 1989 ran too long and created confusion among consumers.[56] As one advertising executive says, "Contrary to what we think, consumers don't hold seminars about advertising. You have to give consumers enough information about the product in teaser ads to make them feel they're in on the joke."[57]

Source Characteristics

The third creative strategy decision is the source of the message appeal. We use the term **source** to mean the person involved in communicating a marketing message, either directly or indirectly. A *direct source* is a spokesperson who delivers a message and/or demonstrates a product or service, like tennis star Andre Agassi who endorses Head tennis rackets in Exhibit 6–17. An *indirect source,* say, a model, doesn't actually deliver a message but draws attention to and/or enhances the appearance of the ad. Some ads use neither a direct nor an indirect source; the source is the organization with the message to communicate. Since most research focuses on individuals as a message source, our examination of source factors follows this approach.

Companies are very careful when selecting individuals to deliver their selling messages. Many firms spend huge sums of money for a specific person to endorse their product or company. They recognize that the characteristics of the source affect the sales and advertising message. Marketers try to select individuals whose traits will maximize message influence. The source may be knowledgeable, popular, and/or physically attractive; typify the target audience; or have the power to reward or punish the receiver in some manner. Herbert Kelman developed three basic categories of source attributes: credibility, attractiveness, and power.[58] Each influences the recipient's attitude or behaviour through a different process (see Figure 6–8).

Source Credibility

Credibility is the extent to which the recipient sees the source as having relevant knowledge, skill, or experience and trusts the source to give unbiased, objective information. There are two important dimensions to credibility, expertise and trustworthiness.

A communicator seen as knowledgeable—someone with expertise—is more persuasive than one with less expertise. But the source also has to be trustworthy—honest, ethical, and believable. The influence of a knowledgeable source will be lessened if audience members think he or she is biased or has underlying personal motives for advocating a position (such as being paid to endorse a product).

Exhibit 6–17 Tennis star Andre Agassi serves as a spokesperson for Head

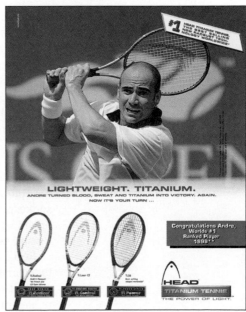

Figure 6–8 Source attributes and receiver processing modes

Source attribute	Process
Credibility	Internalization
Attractiveness	Identification
Power	Compliance

One of the most reliable effects found in communications research is that expert and/or trustworthy sources are more persuasive than sources who are less expert or trustworthy.[59] Information from a credible source influences beliefs, opinions, attitudes, and/or behaviour through a process known as **internalization,** which occurs when the receiver adopts the opinion of the credible communicator since he or she believes information from this source is accurate. Once the receiver internalizes an opinion or attitude, it becomes integrated into his or her belief system and may be maintained even after the source of the message is forgotten.

A highly credible communicator is particularly important when message recipients have a negative position toward the product, service, company, or issue being promoted, because the credible source is likely to inhibit counterarguments. As discussed in Chapter 4, reduced counterarguing should result in greater message acceptance and persuasion.

Applying Expertise   Because attitudes and opinions developed through an internalization process become part of the individual's belief system, marketers want to use communicators with high credibility. Spokespeople are often chosen because of their knowledge, experience, and expertise in a particular product or service area. Endorsements from individuals or groups recognized as experts, such as doctors or dentists, are also common in advertising (Exhibit 6–18). The importance of using expert sources was shown in a study by Roobina Ohanian, who found that the perceived expertise of celebrity endorsers was more important in explaining purchase intentions than their attractiveness or trustworthiness. She suggests that celebrity spokespeople are most effective when they are knowledgeable, experienced, and qualified to talk about the product they are endorsing.[60]

Dermatologists have put something unusually strong in this skin cleanser.

Their trust.

Exhibit 6–18 Dove promotes the fact that it is recommended by experts in skin care

Applying Trustworthiness   While expertise is important, the target audience must also find the source believable. Finding celebrities or other figures with a trustworthy image is often difficult. Many trustworthy public figures hesitate to endorse products because of the potential impact on their reputation and image. Advertisers use various techniques to increase the perception that their sources are trustworthy. Hidden cameras are used to show that the consumer is not a paid spokesperson and is making an objective evaluation of the product. Disguised brands are compared. (Of course, the sponsor's brand always performs better than the consumer's regular brand, and he or she is always surprised.) Most consumers are skeptical of these techniques, so they may have limited value in enhancing perceptions of credibility.

Using Corporate Leaders as Spokespeople   Another way of enhancing source credibility is to use the company president or chief executive officer as a spokesperson in the firm's advertising. Many companies believe the use of their president or CEO is the ultimate expression of the company's commitment to quality and customer service.

Some research suggests the use of a company president or CEO can improve attitudes and increase the likelihood that consumers will inquire about the company's product or service.[61] It is becoming common for local retailers to use the owner or president in their ads. Companies are likely to continue using their top executives in their advertising, particularly when they have celebrity value that helps enhance the firms' image. However, there can be problems with this strategy. CEO spokespeople who become very popular may get more attention than their company's product/service or advertising message. And if a firm's image becomes too closely tied to a popular leader, there can be problems if that person leaves the company.

Limitations of Credible Sources   Several studies have shown that a high-credibility source is not always an asset, nor is a low-credibility source always a liability. High- and low-credibility sources are equally effective when they are arguing for a position opposing their own best interest.[62] A very credible source is more effective when message recipients are not in favour of the position advocated in the message.[63] However, a very credible source is less important when the audience has a neutral position, and such a source may even be less effective than a moderately credible source when the receiver's initial attitude is favourable.[64]

Another reason a low-credibility source may be as effective as a high-credibility source is the **sleeper effect,** whereby the persuasiveness of a message increases with the passage of time. The immediate impact of a persuasive message may be inhibited because of its association with a low-credibility source. But with time, the association of the message with the source diminishes and the receiver's attention focuses more on favourable information in the message, resulting in more support arguing. However, many studies have failed to demonstrate the presence of a sleeper effect.[65] Many advertisers hesitate to count on the sleeper effect, since exposure to a credible source is a more reliable strategy.[66]

Source Attractiveness

A source characteristic frequently used by advertisers is **attractiveness,** which encompasses similarity, familiarity, and likability.[67] *Similarity* is a supposed resemblance between the source and the receiver of the message, while *familiarity* refers to knowledge of the source through exposure. *Likability* is an affection for the source as a result of physical appearance, behaviour, or other personal traits. Even when the sources are not famous, consumers often admire their physical appearance, talent, and/or personality.

Source attractiveness leads to persuasion through a process of **identification,** whereby the receiver is motivated to seek some type of relationship with the source and thus adopts similar beliefs, attitudes, preferences, or behaviour. Maintaining this position depends on the source's continued support for the position as well as the receiver's continued identification with the source. If the source changes position, the receiver may also change. Unlike internalization, identification does not usually integrate information from an attractive source into the receiver's belief system. The receiver may maintain the attitudinal position or behaviour only as long as it is supported by the source or the source remains attractive.

One requirement for a national campaign with an identifiable and likeable spokesperson who actually speaks in the ads is the fact that the person has to be fluent in both official languages. Danone did this with actress Sophie Lorain, who convincingly played a strong central character in all of their commercials. She demonstrated that Danone was for women who wanted yoghurt as a healthy part of their busy everyday lives. Lorain had previously been the spokesperson in the Quebec ads for two years when Danone tested her in an English ad. The results were encouraging and the rest is history. While the language was a necessary requirement for success, Danone executives believed that Lorain's character (i.e., likability, similarity) communicated the benefits of the brand effectively, which was the primary concern.[68]

Applying Similarity   Marketers recognize that people are more likely to be influenced by a message coming from someone with whom they feel a sense of similarity.[69] If the communicator and receiver have similar needs, goals, interests, and lifestyles, the position advocated by the source is better understood and received.

Exhibit 6–19 Chris Dollard appears in many commercials because he looks like an everyday guy

Similarity can be used to create a situation where the consumer feels empathy for the person shown in the commercial. In a slice-of-life commercial, the advertiser usually starts by presenting a predicament with the hope of getting the consumer to think, "I can see myself in that situation." This can help establish a bond of similarity between the communicator and the receiver, increasing the source's level of persuasiveness. Many companies feel that the best way to connect with consumers is by using regular-looking, everyday people with whom the average person can easily identify (Exhibit 6–19).

Applying Likability: Using Celebrities

Advertisers recognize the value of using spokespeople who are admired: TV and movie stars, athletes, musicians, and other popular public figures. The top celebrity endorser is basketball superstar Michael Jordan. Jordan has an estimated $40 million a year in endorsement deals with companies such as Nike, Bijan Fragrances, Rayovac, Oakley, General Mills, and Quaker Oats (makers of Gatorade).[70] One of the hottest new celebrity endorsers is golf phenom Tiger Woods, who has signed endorsement contracts worth more than $100 million with Nike, American Express, General Mills, and Buick (Exhibit 6–20). Most people would probably agree that P&G scored a winner when they signed Jamie Sale and David Pelletier to an endorsement contract for Crest Whitestrips right after the pair won the gold medal at the 2002 Olympic Games for figure-skating. Both have a natural and bright smile that reinforces the key brand benefit. And their victory and the excellent handling of the judging controversy will certainly add to the brand experience for consumers.[71]

Why do companies spend huge sums to have celebrities appear in their ads and endorse their products? They think celebrities have stopping power. That is, they draw attention to advertising messages in a very cluttered media environment. Marketers think a popular celebrity will favourably influence consumers' feelings, attitudes, and purchase behaviour. And they believe celebrities can enhance the target audience's perceptions of the product in terms of image and/or performance. For example, a well-known athlete may convince potential buyers that the product will enhance their own performance.

A number of factors must be considered when a company decides to use a celebrity spokesperson, including the dangers of overshadowing the product and being overexposed, and the target audience's receptivity.

Overshadowing the Product How will the celebrity affect the target audience's processing of the advertising message? Consumers may focus their attention on the celebrity and fail to notice the brand. Advertisers should select a celebrity spokesperson who will attract attention and enhance the sales message, yet not overshadow the brand.

Overexposure Consumers are often skeptical of endorsements because they know the celebrities are being paid.[72] This problem is particularly pronounced when a celebrity endorses too many products or companies and becomes overexposed. Advertisers can protect themselves against overexposure with an exclusivity clause limiting the number of products a celebrity can endorse. However, such clauses are usually expensive, and most celebrities agree not to endorse similar products anyway. Many celebrities try to earn as much endorsement money as pos-

Exhibit 6–20 Tiger Woods has endorsement contracts with a number of companies including Buick

sible, yet they must be careful not to damage their credibility by endorsing too many products. For example, Wayne Gretzky received some criticism while he was a spokesperson for many brands shortly after he retired from the NHL.

Target Audiences' Receptivity   Consumers who are particularly knowledgeable about a product or service or have strongly established attitudes may be less influenced by a celebrity than those with little knowledge or neutral attitudes. One study found that college-age students were more likely to have a positive attitude toward a product endorsed by a celebrity than were older consumers.[73] The teenage market has generally been very receptive to celebrity endorsers, as evidenced by the frequent use of entertainers and athletes in ads targeted to this group for products such as apparel, cosmetics, and beverages. However, many marketers are finding that teenage consumers are more skeptical and cynical toward the use of celebrity endorsers and respond better to ads using humour, irony, and unvarnished truth (Exhibit 6–21).[74]

Some studies suggest that celebrity endorsements are becoming less important in influencing purchase decisions for a broad range of consumers.[75] In a survey of 30,000 consumers age 13 to 75 conducted by the Athletic Footwear Association, celebrity endorsements were the least important factor for buying a particular brand of shoe. One company that believes celebrity endorsements are not worthwhile is New Balance, which has an across-the-board policy against them. The president of the company notes, "If you want the best shoe for yourself, you don't generally give a hoot if Michael Jordan wears it. We'd rather put the money into our factories than into the hands of celebrities."[76]

CUT OUT AND PLACE OVER A 🖘 PICTURE OF ANY MEDIOCRE ATHLETE HOLDING OUT FOR A $100 MILLION CONTRACT. SPRITE WON'T BE MORE REFRESHING, BUT IT'S CHEAPER THAN ACTUALLY PAYING THE BUM. IMAGE IS NOTHING. THIRST IS EVERYTHING. **OBEY YOUR THIRST.**

"**Does Sprite really refresh me? I don't know. Ask my agent.**"

©1999 The Coca-Cola Company. "Sprite" and "Obey Your Thirst" are registered trademarks of The Coca-Cola Company.

Exhibit 6–21   Sprite parodies the use of celebrity endorsers in this ad

Understanding the Meaning of Celebrity Endorsers

Advertisers must try to match the product or company's image, the characteristics of the target audience, and the personality of the celebrity.[77] The image that celebrities project to consumers can be just as important as their ability to attract attention. An interesting perspective on celebrity endorsement was developed by Grant McCracken.[78] He argues that credibility and attractiveness don't sufficiently explain how and why celebrity endorsements work and offers a model based on meaning transfer (Figure 6–9).

According to this model, a celebrity's effectiveness as an endorser depends on the culturally acquired meanings he or she brings to the endorsement process. Each celebrity contains many meanings, including status, class, gender, and age as well as personality and lifestyle. In explaining stage 1 of the meaning transfer process, McCracken notes:

> Celebrities draw these powerful meanings from the roles they assume in their television, movie, military, athletic, and other careers. Each new dramatic role brings the celebrity into contact with a range of objects, persons, and contexts. Out of these objects, persons, and contexts are transferred meanings that then reside in the celebrity.[79]

Examples of celebrities who have acquired meanings include tennis star Andre Agassi as the defiant tennis star (from his antics and performance on and off the court) and actor Jerry Seinfeld as the quirky comedian (from his role on the sitcom "Seinfeld").

McCracken suggests celebrity endorsers bring their meanings into the ad and transfer them to the product they are endorsing (stage 2 of the model in Figure 6–3). For example, Subaru's use of actor Paul Hogan as its spokesperson takes advantage of Hogan's image as a rugged, tough guy from the Australian outback, which he developed from his roles in the *Crocodile Dundee* movies and other films. Subaru

Figure 6–9 Meaning movement and the endorsement process

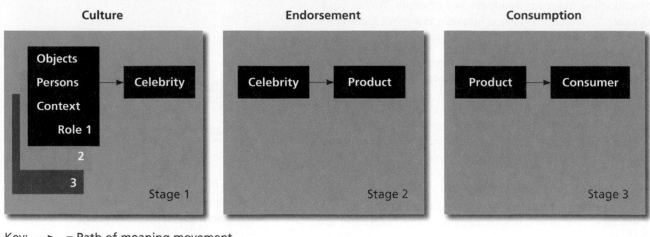

Key: → = Path of meaning movement

□ = Stage of meaning movement

Exhibit 6–22 Australian actor Paul Hogan helps position the Subaru Outback as a rugged, go-anywhere vehicle

has done an excellent job of using Hogan in its ads for its Outback—a vehicle the company positions as the first sport utility wagon (Exhibit 6–22).

In the final stage of McCracken's model, the meanings the celebrity has given to the product are transferred to the consumer. Subaru touts the Outback as a vehicle that combines rough-terrain driving capability with the ride and comfort of a passenger car, and the use of Paul Hogan helps in creating this image. Subaru's vice president of marketing says, "A lot of sport utility shoppers are buying the rugged, go-anywhere image. Paul Hogan not only gives us a nice play on the Outback name but also a chance to help rugged-ize the Outback image."[80] McCracken notes that this final stage is complicated and difficult to achieve. The way consumers take possession of the meaning the celebrity has transferred to a product is probably the least understood part of the process.

The meaning transfer model has some important implications for companies using celebrity endorsers. Marketers must first decide on the image or symbolic meanings important to the target audience for the particular product, service, or company. They must then determine which celebrity best represents the meaning or image to be projected. An advertising campaign must be designed that captures that meaning in the product and moves it to the consumer. Marketing and advertising personnel often rely on intuition in choosing celebrity endorsers for their companies or products, but some companies conduct research studies to determine consumers' perceptions of celebrities' meaning.

Marketers may also pretest ads to determine whether they transfer the proper meaning to the product. When celebrity endorsers are used, the marketer should track the campaign's effectiveness. Does the celebrity continue to be effective in communicating the proper meaning to the target audience? Celebrities who are no longer in the limelight may lose their ability to transfer any significant meanings to the product.

Applying Likability: Decorative Models

Advertisers often draw attention to their ads by featuring a physically attractive person who serves as a passive or decorative model rather than as an active communicator. Research suggests that physically attractive communicators generally have a positive impact and generate more favourable evaluations of both ads and products than less attractive models.[81] The gender appropriateness of the model for the product being advertised and his or her relevance to the product are also important considerations.[82] Products such as cosmetics or fashionable clothing are likely to benefit from the use of an attractive model, since physical appearance is very relevant in marketing these items. For example, Revlon uses supermodel Cindy Crawford in advertising for various cosmetics products such as its Fire & Ice fragrance (Exhibit 6–23).

Some models draw attention to the ad but not to the product or message. Studies show that an attractive model facilitates recognition of the ad but does not enhance copy readership or message recall.[83] Thus, advertisers must ensure that the consumer's attention will go beyond the model to the product and advertising message.

Source Power

The final characteristic in Kelman's classification scheme is **source power.** A source has power when he or she can actually administer rewards and punishments to the receiver. As a result of this power, the source may be able to induce another person(s) to respond to the request or position he or she is advocating. The power of the source depends on several factors. The source must be perceived as being able to administer positive or negative sanctions to the receiver *(perceived control)* and the receiver must think the source cares about whether or not the receiver conforms *(perceived concern).* The receiver's estimate of the source's ability to observe conformity is also important *(perceived scrutiny).*

When a receiver perceives a source as having power, the influence process occurs through a process known as **compliance.** The receiver accepts the persuasive influence of the source and acquiesces to his or her position in hopes of obtaining a favourable reaction or avoiding punishment. The receiver may show public agreement with the source's position but not have an internal or private commitment to this position. Persuasion induced through compliance may be superficial and last only as long as the receiver perceives that the source can administer some reward or punishment.

Power as a source characteristic is very difficult to apply in a nonpersonal influence situation such as advertising. A communicator in an ad generally cannot apply any sanctions to the receiver or determine whether compliance actually occurs. An indirect way of using power is by using an individual with an authoritative personality as a spokesperson.

PLAY WITH FIRE.
SKATE ON THIN ICE.

REVLON
FIRE & ICE

Exhibit 6–23 Revlon makes effective use of supermodel Cindy Crawford in this ad

Summary

The creative development and execution of the advertising message are a crucial part of a firm's integrated marketing communications program. The creative specialist or team is responsible for developing an effective way to communicate the marketer's message to the customer. Marketers often turn to ad agencies to develop, prepare, and implement their creative strategy since these agencies are specialists in the creative function of advertising.

The challenge facing the writers, artists, and others who develop ads is to be creative and come up with fresh, unique, and appropriate ideas that can be used as solutions to communications problems. Creativity in advertising is a process of several stages, including preparation, incubation, illumination, verification, and revision. Various sources of information are available to help the creative specialists determine the best creative strategy.

Creative strategy is guided by marketing goals and objectives and is based on a number of factors, including the basic problem the advertising must address, the target audience, behavioural and communication objectives the message seeks to accomplish, and key benefits the advertiser wants to communicate as reflected in the brand positioning strategy. These factors and the creative strategy decisions are generally stated in a copy platform or creative brief which is a work plan used to guide development of the ad campaign.

The creative strategy often contains three key decisions. An important part of creative strategy is determining the creative theme/idea of the campaign. There are several approaches to doing this, including using a unique selling proposition, creating a brand image, looking for inherent drama in the brand, and positioning. In general, the creative theme/idea guides much of the advertising campaign or IMC program. Consistency and originality and its ability to effectively communicate are three key strengths of good creative.

A message appeal, the second decision of the creative strategy is the central message used in the ad to elicit cognitive and emotional processing responses and communication effects from the target audience. Appeals can be broken into two broad categories, rational and emotional. Rational appeals focus on consumers' practical, functional, or utilitarian need for the product or service; emotional appeals relate to social and/or psychological reasons for purchasing a product or service. Numerous types of appeals are available to advertisers within each category.

Selection of the appropriate source or communicator to deliver a message is the third creative strategy decision. Three important attributes are source credibility, attractiveness, and power. Marketers enhance message effectiveness by hiring communicators who are experts in a particular area and/or have a trustworthy image. The use of celebrities to deliver advertising messages has become very popular; advertisers hope they will catch the receivers' attention and influence their attitudes or behaviour through an identification process. The chapter discusses the meaning a celebrity brings to the endorsement process and the importance of matching the image of the celebrity with that of the company or brand.

Key Terms

creative strategy, 132
creative tactics, 132
advertising creativity, 136
account planning, 139
research, 140
general preplanning
   input, 140
product/service-specific
   preplanning input, 140
focus groups, 141

storyboard, 142
animatic, 142
copy platform, 142
advertising campaign,
   145
campaign theme, 145
creative theme/idea,
   145
unique selling
   proposition (USP), 147

image advertising, 147
inherent drama, 148
advertising appeal, 149
creative execution, 149
rational appeal, 150
emotional appeal, 151
fear appeal, 153
humour appeal, 154
teaser advertising, 156
source, 157

credibility, 157
internalization, 158
sleeper effect, 159
attractiveness, 159
identification, 159
source power, 163
compliance, 163

Discussion Questions

1. How important was creativity for the Telus (previously Clearnet) campaign?

2. What are the differences between creative strategy and creative tactics? Why is it important to make a distinction between these two concepts?

3. Review the various advertising campaign themes used by Burger King that are shown in Figure 6–1. Why do you think Burger King has had such a difficult time finding an effective campaign theme?

4. What is your opinion of advertising awards, such as the Cannes Lions, that are based solely on creativity? If you were a marketer looking for an agency, would you take these creative awards into consideration in your agency evaluation process? Why or why not?

5. Find an example of a print ad that you think is very creative and an ad you feel is dull and boring.

Evaluate each ad from a creative perspective. What makes one ad creative and the other bland?

6. Assume you have been assigned to work on the advertising campaign for a new soft drink. Describe the various types of general and product-specific preplanning input you might provide to the creative team.

7. Canadian Tire maintained similar creative themes for many years. Why do you think they did this for so long? Canadian Tire started a new theme in 2002. Can you describe it? Why did they change it?

8. Find an example of an ad or campaign that you think reflects one of the approaches used to develop a creative theme/idea such as unique selling proposition, brand image, inherent drama, or positioning. Discuss how the creative theme/idea is used in this ad or campaign.

9. Discuss the pros and cons of using a comparative advertising appeal for the following products: beer, cellphones, furniture, airlines.

10. Assume that you have been asked to consult for a government agency that wants to use a fear appeal message to encourage college students not to drink and drive. Explain how fear appeals might affect persuasion and what factors should be considered in developing the ads.

11. It has been observed that Canadian advertisers use fewer celebrity endorsers compared to American advertisers. Do you agree with this? If it is true, what is the explanation?

12. Find a celebrity who is currently appearing in ads for a particular company or brand and analyze and use McCracken's meaning transfer model (shown in Figure 6–9) to analyze the use of the celebrity as a spokesperson.

Chapter Seven

Creative Tactics Decisions

Chapter Objectives

- To identify three key decisions for creative tactics: execution style, message structure, and design elements.

- To analyze the various creative execution styles that advertisers can use and the advertising situations where they are most appropriate.

- To examine different types of message structures that can be used to develop a promotional message.

- To analyze various design elements involved in the creation of print advertising and TV commercials.

- To understand a planning model for making creative tactics decisions.

- To consider how clients evaluate the creative work of their agencies and discuss guidelines for the evaluation and approval process.

Sleeman Speaks His Mind in Quebec

Parlez-vous Français, John? In an interesting turn of events, John Sleeman, chair and CEO of Sleeman Breweries, took to the radio airwaves speaking French in ads running in Quebec. John has been a spokesperson for the brewery in its home Ontario market, and when Sleeman entered the Quebec market, they continued with him. But in this case, French was not exactly his mother tongue. However, Sleeman speaking to French consumers in their language has won over their hearts!

John speaking in a relaxed manner on the radio to consumers who appreciate a craft beer from a micro-brewery was the strategy in Ontario for a few years. The plan was to use the same idea in Quebec for some of the same reasons. It was affordable for a low advertising budget, and the larger brewers were not in this media. However, as in Ontario, it meant that consumers would have to learn about the beer without seeing. Imagine, consumers having to purchase a beer by remembering the brand name and not recognizing its label or bottle on the shelves!

The Quebec agency recognized that they would have to use slightly different tactics since Quebecers might not be too receptive to a beer from Ontario in 1996, less than a year after the 1995 referendum. Furthermore, Quebec beer drinkers were accustomed to European craft beers that had relied on public relations and very little advertising. So an interesting radio tactic of not speaking the language perfectly correct was born and voilà, the Sleeman beer tactic is "a typical case of turning a liability into an asset." The other key tactic was to use wittier dialogue so that consumers would overlook the language "liability." In fact, some of the early versions of the campaign poked fun at some cultural differences between French and English Canadians. Part of the success of the campaign can be seen by the fact that there have been over 30 creative executions, and one recent spot simply played the brand's jingle!

More recently, John Sleeman appeared on TV ads in Quebec after many radio ads, like he did in Ontario. Well, he sort of appeared on TV. Viewers heard his voice, like in the radio ads, but only saw his hands! Score another for Sleeman's using a unique tactic to effectively communicate. These ads continued a similar approach as the radio ads with witty dialogue, but each of three initial spots were curious comparisons to mainstream beers. One Sleeman executive attributes these new ads as a way of obtaining new customers from mainstream beers who are age 20 to 30 versus the usual target of age 30 to 40.

Sleeman used billboards as part of this campaign, just like in Ontario. The ads had a picture of the bottle with the signature and a short copy that makes mainstream beer comparisons once again. Recent ones include, "Labels are there to hide the beer," "Nothing to win under the cap," "No gadget to be won in our case," "No dry extra-strong or kiwi-pineapple version," and "No need for bikinis in our ads." So far so good for Sleeman; it reached 25 percent of the premium beer market in Quebec and 2 percent of the overall market.

Sources: Danny Kucharsky, "Sex doesn't sell Sleeman in Quebec," *Marketing Magazine*, July 23, 2001; Eric Vincent, "Simplicity, honesty, authenticity . . . and no BS!" *Marketing Magazine*, December 17, 2001; Bertrand Cesvet, "The Universal Language of Beer," *Marketing Magazine*, October 23, 2000.

In Chapter 6, we discussed advertising creativity, examining the various steps in the creative process and the three creative strategy decisions. This chapter focuses on the key creative tactics decisions. It examines various execution styles that can be used to develop the ad, the important message structure choices available, and the tactical issues involved in the design and production of effective advertising messages. We also present a framework for guiding the creative tactics decisions. We conclude by presenting some guidelines clients can use to evaluate the creative work of their agencies.

Creative Tactics

Creative Execution Style

Once the specific advertising appeal that will be used as the basis for the advertising message has been determined, the creative specialist or team decides the creative tactics. One critical creative tactic is the *creative execution style*, which is the way an advertising appeal is presented. While it is obviously important for an ad to have a meaningful appeal or message to communicate to the consumer, the manner in which the ad is executed is also important.

One of the best-known advocates of the importance of creative tactics in advertising was William Bernbach, founder of the Doyle Dane Bernbach agency. In his famous book on the advertising industry, *Madison Avenue*, Martin Mayer notes Bernbach's reply to David Ogilvy's rule for copywriters that "what you say in advertising is more important than how you say it." Bernbach replied, "Execution can become content, it can be just as important as what you say. A sick guy can utter some words and nothing happens; a healthy vital guy says them and they rock the world."[1] Bernbach was one of the revolutionaries of his time who changed advertising creativity on a fundamental level by redefining how headlines and visuals were used, how art directors and copywriters worked together, and how advertising could be used to arouse feelings and emotions.

An advertising message can be presented or executed in numerous ways:

- Straight sell or factual message
- Scientific/technical evidence
- Demonstration
- Comparison
- Testimonial
- Slice of life
- Animation
- Personality symbol
- Fantasy
- Dramatization
- Humour
- Combinations

We now examine these formats and considerations involved in their use. Many of these techniques can be combined to present the advertising message.

Clorox Company of Canada had two things going for it when it decided to revisit its Man from Glad character: The icon has instant recognition among consumers, but it had been so underused in recent years that the company was able to update his look and give him a sense of humour without making it look like his entire personality had been re-engineered.

"He was a little stiff and people would describe him as not the funniest guy at the party," explains Melanie Johnston, group accountant director at Palmer Jarvis DDB in Toronto, the brand's ad agency. "We wanted to make him a little more friendly and loosen him up a bit."

Although the Man from Glad is an American invention, he can be claimed as a Canadian phenomenon since the icon hasn't been used in U.S. advertising for about 20 years. He has consistently appeared in Canada since the 1960s—and his role and look hasn't changed much in over 30 years—although recently he had been relegated to the end of TV spots, almost as a throwaway, says Johnston. "He wasn't integral to the commercials anymore."

Clorox and its agency mulled whether it would be wiser just to dump the Man From Glad. "That was the debate: Is this guy old-fashioned; is he totally passé?" Johnston says. But after talking to consumers, the company discovered that the Man from Glad still embodies Glad's values of dependability and cleanliness. Consumers also consider the character to be a friend and a helper, sort of an educator about Glad products. They wanted to see more of him, so Clorox kept the impeccably dressed Man—same antiseptic white hair and suit—but added a tongue-in-cheek element. TV ads, launched in December 1999, depict the Man from Glad in a secret underground laboratory where Glad products are put through a series of extreme and ridiculous tests including mechanical raccoons trying to tear bags apart. Besides TV commercials, the icon also appears on in-store and promotional materials for both Glad garbage bags and Glad-Ware food protection products.

Source: Adapted from Angela Kryhul, "The Great Canadian Icon," *Marketing Magazine,* June 26, 2000, pp. 11–15. Used with permission.

Straight Sell or Factual Message   One of the most basic types of creative executions is the straight sell or factual message. This type of ad relies on a straightforward presentation of information concerning the product or service. This execution is often used with rational appeals, where the focus of the message is the product or service and its specific attributes and/or benefits.

Straight-sell executions are commonly used in print ads. A picture of the product or service occupies part of the ad, and the factual copy takes up the rest of the space. (See the ad for Castrol Syntec motor oil in Exhibit 7–1.) They are also used in TV advertising, with an announcer generally delivering the sales message while the product/service is shown on the screen. Ads for high-involvement consumer products as well as industrial and other business-to-business products generally use this format.

Scientific/Technical Evidence   In a variation of the straight sell, scientific or technical evidence is presented in the ad. Advertisers often cite technical information, results of scientific or laboratory studies, or endorsements by scientific bodies or agencies to support their advertising claims. The ad for Dermasil Pharmaceutical Dry Skin Treatment shown in Exhibit 7–2 uses this execution style to emphasize the breakthrough from Vaseline Research.

Demonstration   Demonstration advertising is designed to illustrate the key advantages of the product/service by showing it in actual use or in some staged situation. Demonstration executions can be very effective in convincing consumers of a product's utility or quality and of the benefits of owning or using the brand. TV is particularly well suited for demonstration

Exhibit 7–1   Castrol uses a straight-sell execution style in this ad

executions, since the benefits or advantages of the product can be shown right on the screen. Although perhaps a little less dramatic than TV, demonstration ads can also work in print, as shown in the ad for DuPont's Teflon® Bakeware Liners (Exhibit 7–3). Dove soap provides a neat example of demonstration presentation tactic. The magazines ads, TV ad, direct mail, and in-store demonstrations encouraged consumers to use litmus paper to test the alkalinity of various soaps. The key attribute of mildness of Dove was naturally communicated, albeit in a subtle manner, and the brand name was not highlighted in an obvious manner in the print and TV ads.[2]

Comparison   Brand comparisons can also be the basis for the advertising execution. The comparison execution approach is increasingly popular among advertisers, since it offers a direct way of communicating a brand's particular advantage over its competitors or positioning a new or lesser-known brand with industry leaders. Comparison executions are often used to execute comparative appeals, as discussed earlier.

Testimonial   Many advertisers prefer to have their messages presented by way of a testimonial, where a person praises the product or service on the basis of his or her personal experience with it (Exhibit 7–4). Testimonial executions can have ordinary satisfied customers discuss their own experiences with the brand and the benefits of using it. This approach can be very effective when the person delivering the testimonial is someone with whom the target audience can identify or who has an interesting story to tell. The testimonial must be based on

Exhibit 7–2   This Dermasil ad cites a scientific study

Exhibit 7–3   This ad demonstrates the benefits of Du Pont's Teflon® Bakeware Liners

Exhibit 7–4   This ad uses a testimonial execution effectively

actual use of the product or service to avoid legal problems, and the spokesperson must be credible. Testimonials can be particularly effective when they come from a recognizable or popular source.

A related execution technique is the endorsement, where a well-known or respected individual such as a celebrity or expert in the product or service area speaks on behalf of the company or the brand. When endorsers promote a company or its products or services, the message is not necessarily based on their personal experiences. Endorsements can also be from professional associations. For example, an endorsement from the American Council on Dental Therapeutics on how fluoride helps prevent cavities was the basis of the campaign that made Crest the leading brand on the market.

Slice of Life   A widely used advertising format, particularly for package-goods products, is the slice-of-life execution, which is generally based on a problem/solution approach. This type of ad portrays a problem or conflict that consumers might face in their daily lives. The ad then shows how the advertiser's product or service can resolve the problem.

Slice-of-life executions are often criticized for being unrealistic and irritating to watch because they are often used to remind consumers of problems of a personal nature, such as dandruff, bad breath, body odour, and laundry problems. Often these ads come across as contrived, silly, phony, or even offensive to consumers. However, many advertisers still prefer this style because they believe it is effective at presenting a situation to which most consumers can relate and at registering the product feature or benefit that helps sell the brand.

For many years, Procter & Gamble was known for its reliance on slice-of-life advertising executions. In 1980, two-thirds of the company's commercials used either the slice-of-life or testimonial format. However, P&G has begun using humour, animation, and other less traditional execution styles. Now only one in four of the company's ads relies on slice-of-life or testimonials.[3]

Some business-to-business marketers use a variation of this execution that is sometimes referred to as *slice-of-death advertising*.[4] This execution style is used in conjunction with a fear appeal, as the focus is on the negative consequences that result when businesspeople make the wrong decision in choosing a supplier or service provider. For example, FedEx has used this type of advertising for nearly three decades through humourous, but to-the-point, commercials that show what might happen when important packages and documents aren't received on time.

Animation   An advertising execution approach that has become popular in recent years is animation. With this technique, animated scenes are drawn by artists or created on the computer, and cartoons, puppets, or other types of fictional characters may be used. Cartoon animation is especially popular for commercials targeted at children. Animated cartoon characters have also been used successfully by the Leo Burnett agency in campaigns for Green Giant vegetables (the Jolly Green Giant). Another successful example of animation execution was the ad campaign developed for the California Raisin Advisory Board. A technique called Claymation was used to create the dancing raisin characters used in these ads. The use of animation as an execution style may increase as creative specialists discover the possibilities of computer-generated graphics and other technological innovations.[5]

Personality Symbol   Another type of advertising execution involves developing a central character or personality symbol that can deliver the advertising message and with which the product or service can be identified. This character can be a person, like Scrooge, who reflects the money consumers can save while shopping at Canadian Tire, or the Maytag repairman, who sits anxiously by the phone but is never needed because the company's appliances are so reliable (Exhibit 7–5).

Anheuser-Busch has created popular personality symbols in the talking lizards, Frank and Louie, who have been appearing in ads for Budweiser beer for the past five years. However, the company has had to deal with complaints from some con-

Exhibit 7–5 The Maytag repairman is an example of an advertising personality symbol

sumer groups who argue that the animated characters are popular among children and might encourage underage drinking. The company strongly denies that it is using the characters to target minors and argues that the ads do not have any effect on children or encourage underage drinking.[6]

Fantasy An execution technique that is popular for emotional types of appeals such as image advertising is fantasy. Fantasy executions are particularly well suited for television, as the commercial can become a 30-second escape for the viewer into another lifestyle. The product or service becomes a central part of the situation created by the advertiser. Cosmetics ads often use fantasy appeals to create images and symbols that become associated with the brand.

Dramatization Another execution technique particularly well suited to television is dramatization, where the focus is on telling a short story with the product or service as the star. Dramatization is somewhat akin to slice-of-life execution in that it often relies on the problem/solution approach, but it uses more excitement and suspense in telling the story. The purpose of using drama is to draw the viewer into the action it portrays. Advocates of drama note that when it is successful, the audience becomes lost in the story and experiences the concerns and feelings of the characters.[7] According to Sandra Moriarty, there are five basic steps in a dramatic commercial:

> First is exposition, where the stage is set for the upcoming action. Next comes conflict, which is a technique for identifying the problem. The middle of the dramatic form is a period of rising action where the story builds, the conflict intensifies, the suspense thickens. The fourth step is the climax, where the problem is solved. The last part of a drama is the resolution, where the wrap-up is presented. In advertising that includes product identification and call to action.[8]

Humour Like comparisons, humour was discussed in Chapter 6 as a type of advertising appeal, but this technique can also be used as a way of presenting other advertising appeals. Humourous executions are particularly well suited to television or radio, although some print ads attempt to use this style. The pros and cons of using humour as an executional technique are similar to those associated with its use as an advertising appeal.

Message Structure

The way marketing communications are presented is very important in determining their effectiveness. Promotional managers must consider not only the content of their persuasive messages but also how this information will be structured for presentation. Advertising, in all media except radio, relies heavily on visual as well as verbal information. Many options are available with respect to the design and presentation of a message. This section examines the structure of messages, which is the second key creative tactic decision.

Marketing communications usually consist of a number of message points that the communicator wants to get across. It is important to communicate these points to overcome any opposing viewpoints audience members may hold. Extensive research has been conducted on how the structure of a persuasive message can influence its effectiveness, including order of presentation, conclusion drawing, message sidedness, refutation, and verbal versus visual message characteristics.

Order of Presentation

A basic consideration in the design of a persuasive message is the arguments' order of presentation. Should the most important message points be placed at the beginning of the message, in the middle, or at the end? Research on learning and memory generally indicates that items presented first and last are remembered better than those presented in the middle (see Figure 7–1).[9] This suggests that a communicator's

IMC Perspective 7–2
How Do Our Eyes Perceive Print Ads?

The purpose of many advertising creative tactics is to facilitate the processing of the ads in terms of attention, cognitive responses, or emotional responses. An important step here is our perceptual system with respect to how our eyes scan or receive the incoming stimuli. Interesting research at The National Gallery in London, England, has "opened our eyes" to long-standing assumptions on how people perceive art work, and these findings may have important implications for how consumers react to print ads.

Established beliefs on this topic in the arts and design suggest that humans perceive the whole object of a picture and then follow certain cues to fully understand the perspective. However, using infra-red laser technology, the gallery's preliminary evidence suggests that people's eyes look at the cues first until they arrive at an understanding of the complete picture.

Some in the advertising world are skeptical and still believe in the traditional view. A quote from the creative director of The Watt Design Group, Hans Kleefeld, says it all, "Human brains are structured and programmed to process visual infor-mation by proceeding from dominant to secondary to minor elements—from a whole to its details. Information organized to assist this process tends to be rapidly absorbed and well remembered." Essentially, this point of view comes from da Vinci, the master of design who estab-lished the basic elements as darkness, light, body, colour, shape, location, distance, nearness, motion, and rest.

One example of the traditional view working is the visually oriented campaign originally used by Clearnet and now taken over by Telus. It has a white background with clear and colourful images of an appropriate size to encourage effective per-ception in the "correct order" of colour, then form, and then the advertising message. Subsequent research will likely continue, and if it confirms this new theory to be a "clear picture," can you "visual-ize" the effect it will have on advertisers?

Source: Anita Lahey, "What the Eye Sees," *Marketing Magazine*, March 12, 2001.

strongest arguments should be presented early or late in the message but never in the middle.

Presenting the strongest arguments at the beginning of the message assumes a **primacy effect** is operating, whereby information presented first is most effective. Putting the strong points at the end assumes a **recency effect,** whereby the last argu-ments presented are most persuasive.

Whether to place the strongest selling points at the beginning or the end of the message depends on several factors. If the target audience is opposed to the com-municator's position, presenting strong points first can reduce the level of counter-arguing. Putting weak arguments first might lead to such a high level of counterarguing that strong arguments that followed would not be believed. Strong

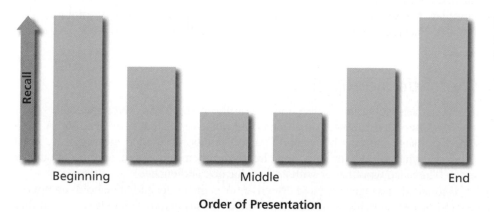

Figure 7–1 Ad message recall as a function of order of presentation

173

arguments work best at the beginning of the message if the audience is not interested in the topic, so they can arouse interest in the message. When the target audience is predisposed toward the communicator's position or is highly interested in the issue or product, strong arguments can be saved for the end of the message. This may result in a more favourable opinion as well as better retention of the information.

The order of presentation can be critical when a long, detailed message with many arguments is being presented. For short communications, such as a 15- or 30-second TV or radio commercial, the order may be less critical. However, many product and service messages are received by consumers with low involvement and minimal interest. Thus, an advertiser may want to present the brand name and key selling points early in the message and repeat them at the end to enhance recall and retention.

Conclusion Drawing

Marketing communicators must decide whether their messages should explicitly draw a firm conclusion or allow receivers to draw their own conclusions. Research suggests that, in general, messages with explicit conclusions are more easily understood and effective in influencing attitudes. However, other studies have shown that the effectiveness of conclusion drawing may depend on the target audience, the type of issue or topic, and the nature of the situation.[10]

More highly educated people prefer to draw their own conclusions and may be annoyed at an attempt to explain the obvious or to draw an inference for them. But stating the conclusion may be necessary for a less educated audience, who may not draw any conclusion or may make an incorrect inference from the message. Marketers must also consider the audience's level of involvement in the topic. For highly personal or ego-involving issues, message recipients may want to make up their own minds and resent any attempts by the communicator to draw a conclusion. One study found that open-ended ads (without explicit conclusions) were more effective than closed-ended arguments that did include a specific conclusion—but only for involved audiences.[11]

Whether to draw a conclusion for the audience also depends on the complexity of the topic. Even a highly educated audience may need assistance if its knowledge level in a particular area is low. Does the marketer want the message to trigger immediate action or a more long-term effect? If immediate action is an objective, the message should draw a definite conclusion. This is a common strategy in political advertising, particularly for ads run close to election day. When immediate impact is not the objective and repeated exposure will give the audience members opportunities to draw their own conclusions, an open-ended message may be used.

Drawing a conclusion in a message may make sure the target audience gets the point the marketer intended. But many advertisers believe that letting customers draw their own conclusions reinforces the points being made in the message. The ad for Hewlett-Packard personal computers in Exhibit 7–6 is a very good example of an open-ended ad. The questions encourage individuals choosing a PC for their company to consider the benefits of purchasing from a well-known corporation like Hewlett-Packard rather than from a smaller, less reliable company.

Message Sidedness

Another message structure decision facing the marketer involves message sidedness. A **one-sided message** mentions only positive attributes or benefits. A **two-sided message** presents both good and bad points. One-sided messages are most effective when the target audience already holds a favourable opinion about the topic. They also work better with a less educated audience.[12]

Two-sided messages are more effective when the target audience holds an opposing opinion or is highly educated. Two-sided messages may enhance the credibility

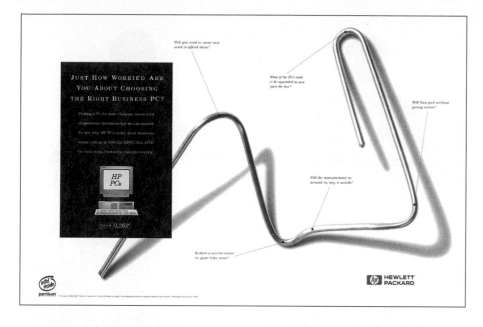

of the source.[13] A better-educated audience usually knows there are opposing arguments, so a communicator who presents both sides of an issue is likely to be seen as less biased and more objective.

Most advertisers use one-sided messages. They are concerned about the negative effects of acknowledging a weakness in their brand or don't want to say anything positive about their competitors. There are exceptions, however. Sometimes advertisers compare brands on several attributes and do not show their product as being the best on every one.

In some situations, marketers may focus on a negative attribute as a way of enhancing overall perceptions of the product. For example, W. K. Buckley Limited has become one of the leading brands of cough syrup by using a blunt two-sided slogan, "Buckley's Mixture. It tastes awful. And it works." Ads for the brand poke fun at the cough syrup's terrible taste but also suggest that the taste is a reason why the product is effective (Exhibit 7–7). They have used this slogan for 16 years and have built the brand from 2 percent to now 16 percent market share. It helps that this slogan is a bit of truth in advertising that consumers certainly appreciate.[14]

A special type of two-sided message is known as a **refutation**. The communicator presents both sides of an issue and then refutes the opposing viewpoint. Since this tends to "inoculate" the target audience against a competitor's counterclaims, they are more effective than one-sided messages in making consumers resistant to an opposing message.[15] Refutational messages may be useful when marketers wish to build attitudes that resist change and must defend against attacks or criticism of their products or the company. Market leaders, who are often the target of comparative messages, may find that acknowledging competitors' claims and then refuting them can help build resistant attitudes and customer loyalty.

Verbal versus Visual Messages

Thus far our discussion has focused on the information, or verbal, portion of the message. However, the nonverbal, visual elements of an ad are also very important. Many ads provide minimal amounts of information and rely on visual elements to communicate. Pictures are commonly used in advertising to convey information or reinforce copy or message claims.

Both the verbal and visual portions of an ad influence the way the advertising message is processed.[16] Consumers may develop images or impressions based on visual elements such as an illustration in an ad or the scenes in a TV commercial. In

Exhibit 7–7 Buckley's Cough Syrup uses a two-sided message to promote the product's effectiveness

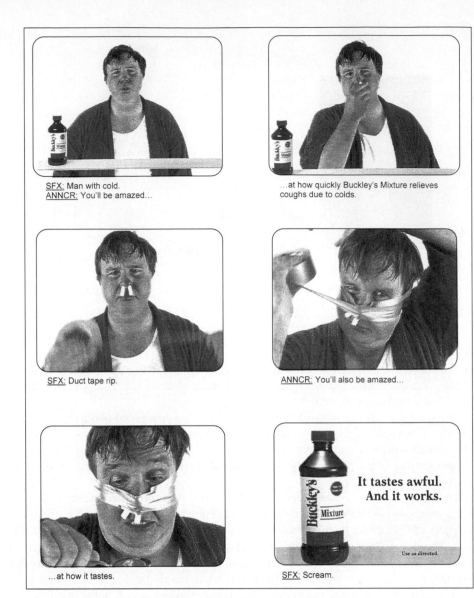

SFX: Man with cold.
ANNCR: You'll be amazed...

...at how quickly Buckley's Mixture relieves coughs due to colds.

SFX: Duct tape rip.

ANNCR: You'll also be amazed...

...at how it tastes.

It tastes awful.
And it works.

Use as directed.

SFX: Scream.

Exhibit 7–8 Visual images are often designed to support verbal appeals

BY 2 PM YOUR BODY IS THIS PARCHED.
(YOUR PERFORMANCE IS DRYING UP, TOO.)

You've been on the slopes all morning. The last thing you remember is to drink H₂O. Sure you get thirsty. But by then, it's too late. Your performance is sliding, a headache is coming on and you're feeling the altitude. And you're not skiing at your peak. Dehydration occurs quickly out there. The cold, high-altitude air is dry. You lose a lot of water just breathing. And since you're working hard and wearing lots of layers,

you sweat a ton. We know that skiers who don't drink lose 1.5 liters of water in one morning. That's where CamelBak® comes in. Convenient, Hands-Free Hydration™ provides enough water to keep your turns as sharp at 2 PM as they were at 9 AM.
For the scoop on all our products, call 800-767-8725 or hit our website at www.camelbak.com

CAMELBAK

some cases, the visual portion of an ad may reduce its persuasiveness, since the processing stimulated by the picture may be less controlled and consequently less favourable than that stimulated by words.[17]

Pictures affect the way consumers process accompanying copy. A recent study showed that when verbal information was low in imagery value, the use of pictures providing examples increased both immediate and delayed recall of product attributes.[18] However, when the verbal information was already high in imagery value, the addition of pictures did not increase recall. Advertisers often design ads where the visual image supports the verbal appeal to create a compelling impression in the consumer's mind. Notice how the ad for the CamelBak SnoBowl uses visual elements to support the claims made in the copy regarding the importance of being hydrated when skiing (Exhibit 7–8).

Sometimes advertisers use a different strategy; they design ads in which the visual portion is incongruent with or contradicts the verbal information presented. The logic behind this strategy is that the use of an unexpected picture or visual image will grab consumers' attention and get them to engage in more effortful or elaborative processing.[19] A number of studies have shown that the use of a visual that is inconsistent with the verbal content leads to more recall and greater processing of the information presented.[20]

Once the creative strategy and initial two tactics decisions have been determined, attention turns to creating the actual advertisement. The design and production of advertising messages involve a number of activities, among them writing copy, developing illustrations and other visual elements of the ad, and bringing all of the pieces together to create an effective message. In this section, we examine the verbal and visual elements of an ad and discuss tactical considerations in creating print ads and TV commercials. Most of the points here can be applied to out-of-home print ads and radio ads.

Creative Tactics for Print Advertising

The basic components of a print ad are the headline, the body copy, the visual or illustrations, and the layout (the way they all fit together). The headline and body copy portions of the ad are the responsibility of the copywriters; artists, often working under the direction of an art director, are responsible for the visual presentation. Art directors also work with the copywriters to develop a layout, or arrangement of the various components of the ad: headlines, subheads, body copy, illustrations, captions, logos, and the like. We briefly examine the three components of a print ad and how they are coordinated.

Headlines   The **headline** is the words in the leading position of the ad—the words that will be read first or are positioned to draw the most attention.[21] Headlines are usually set in larger, darker type and are often set apart from the body copy or text portion of the ad to give them prominence. Most advertising people consider the headline the most important part of a print ad.

The most important function of a headline is attracting readers' attention and interesting them in the rest of the message. While the visual portion of an ad is obviously important, the headline often shoulders most of the responsibility of attracting readers' attention. Research has shown the headline is generally the first thing people look at in a print ad, followed by the illustration. Only 20 percent of readers go beyond the headline and read the body copy.[22] So in addition to attracting attention, the headline must give the reader good reason to read the copy portion of the ad, which contains more detailed and persuasive information about the product or service. To do this, the headline must put forth the main theme, appeal, or proposition of the ad in a few words. Some print ads contain little if any body copy, so the headline must work with the illustration to communicate the entire advertising message.

Headlines also perform a segmentation function by engaging the attention and interest of consumers who are most likely to buy a particular product or service. Advertisers begin the segmentation process by choosing to advertise in certain types of publications (e.g., a travel, general interest, or fashion magazine). An effective headline goes even further in selecting good prospects for the product by addressing their specific needs, wants, or interests. For example, the headline in the ad for RCA's LYRA personal digital player shown in Exhibit 7–9 catches the attention of consumers who want the latest technology in audio products.

Types of Headlines   There are numerous headline possibilities. The type used depends on several factors, including the creative strategy, the particular advertising situation (e.g., product type, media vehicle(s) being used, timeliness), and its relationship to other components of the ad, such as the illustration or body copy. Headlines can be categorized as direct and indirect. **Direct headlines** are straightforward and informative in terms of the message they are presenting and the target audience they are directed toward. Common types of direct headlines include those offering a specific benefit, making a promise, or announcing a reason the reader should be interested in the product or service.

Exhibit 7–9   The headline of this ad catches the attention of young consumers

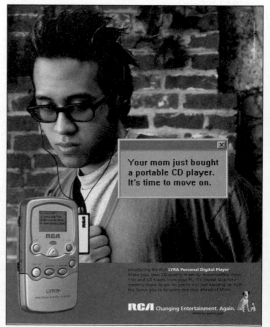

Indirect headlines are not straightforward about identifying the product or service or getting to the point. But they are often more effective at attracting readers' attention and interest because they provoke curiosity and lure readers into the body copy to learn an answer or get an explanation. Techniques for writing indirect headlines include using questions, provocations, how-to statements, and challenges.

Indirect headlines rely on their ability to generate curiosity or intrigue so as to motivate readers to become involved with the ad and read the body copy to find out the point of the message. This can be risky if the headline is not provocative enough to get the readers' interest. Advertisers deal with this problem by using a visual appeal that helps attract attention and offers another reason for reading more of the message.

Subheads   While many ads have only one headline, it is also common to see print ads containing the main head and one or more secondary heads, or **subheads.** Subheads are usually smaller than the main headline but larger than the body copy. They may appear above or below the main headline or within the body copy. The AT&T ad shown in Exhibit 7–10 uses subheads within the body copy.

Subheads are often used to enhance the readability of the message by breaking up large amounts of body copy and highlighting key sales points. Their content reinforces the headline and advertising slogan or theme.

Exhibit 7–10   This ad uses subheads to make the copy easier to read

Body Copy   The main text portion of a print ad is referred to as the **body copy** (or sometimes just *copy*). While the body copy is usually the heart of the advertising message, getting the target audience to read it is often difficult. The copywriter faces a dilemma: The body copy must be long enough to communicate the advertiser's message yet short enough to hold readers' interest.

Body copy content often flows from the points made in the headline or various subheads, but the specific content depends on the type of advertising appeal and/or execution style being used. For example, straight-sell copy that presents relevant information, product features and benefits, or competitive advantages is often used with the various types of rational appeals discussed earlier in the chapter. Emotional appeals often use narrative copy that tells a story or provides an interesting account of a problem or situation involving the product.

Advertising body copy can be written to go along with various types of creative appeals and executions—comparisons, price appeals, demonstrations, humour, dramatizations, and the like. Copywriters choose a copy style that is appropriate for the type of appeal being used and effective for executing the creative strategy and communicating the advertiser's message to the target audience.

Visual Elements   The third major component of a print ad is the visual element. The illustration is often a dominant part of a print ad and plays an important role in determining its effectiveness. The visual portion of an ad must attract attention, communicate an idea or image, and work in a synergistic fashion with the headline and body copy to produce an effective message. In some print ads, the visual portion of the ad is essentially the message and thus must convey a strong and meaningful image. For example, the award-winning ad for Sims Snowboards shown in Exhibit 7–11 uses a powerful visual image. In a scene reminiscent of the protestor blocking military vehicles in Beijing's Tiananmen Square during the 1989 student uprising, a snowboarder stands in the path of snow-grooming machines (which pack the snow, to the distress of snowboarders). The single line of copy, "In a courageous act of solidarity, a lone snowboarder stands up for freedom," reinforces the message presented by the visual image.

Many decisions have to be made regarding the visual portion of the ad: what identification marks should be included (brand name, company or trade name, trademarks, logos); whether to use photos or hand-drawn or painted illustrations; what colours to use (or even perhaps black and white or just a splash of colour); and what the focus of the visual should be.

Layout While each individual component of a print ad is important, the key factor is how these elements are blended into a finished advertisement. A **layout** is the physical arrangement of the various parts of the ad, including the headline, subheads, body copy, illustrations, and any identifying marks. The layout shows where each part of the ad will be placed and gives guidelines to the people working on the ad. For example, the layout helps the copywriter determine how much space he or she has to work with and how much copy should be written. The layout can also guide the art director in determining the size and type of photos. In the ad for Sims Snowboards shown in Exhibit 7–12, the layout is designed to make the ad look like it was reprinted from a newspaper page. Notice how this theme is carried through in the copy, which reads like a newspaper photo caption and ends with "Story on 2C." Layouts are often done in rough form and presented to the client so that the advertiser can visualize what the ad will look like before giving preliminary approval. The agency should get client approval of the layout before moving on to the more costly stages of print production.

Exhibit 7–11 This ad for Sims Snowboards uses a strong visual image and a layout that resembles a newspaper page

Creative Tactics for Television

As consumers, we see so many TV commercials that it's easy to take for granted the time, effort, and money that go into making them. Creating and producing commercials that break through the clutter on TV and communicate effectively is a detailed, expensive process. On a cost-per-minute basis, commercials are the most expensive productions seen on television.

TV is a unique and powerful advertising medium because it contains the elements of sight, sound, and motion, which can be combined to create a variety of advertising appeals and executions. Unlike print, the viewer does not control the rate at which the message is presented, so there is no opportunity to review points of interest or reread things that are not communicated clearly. As with any form of advertising, one of the first goals in creating TV commercials is to get the viewers' attention and then maintain it. This can be particularly challenging because of the clutter and because people often view TV commercials while doing other things (reading a book or magazine, talking).

Like print ads, TV commercials have several components. The video and audio must work together to create the right impact and communicate the advertiser's message.

Video The video elements of a commercial are what the consumer sees on the TV screen. The visual portion generally dominates the commercial, so it must attract viewers' attention and communicate an idea, message, and/or image. A number of visual elements may have to be coordinated to produce a successful ad. Decisions have to be made regarding the product, the presenter, action sequences, demonstrations, and the like, as well as the setting(s), the talent or characters who will appear in the commercial, and such other factors as lighting, graphics, colour, and identifying symbols. Many TV commercials cost a small fortune in production costs to get the product and actors looking just right. In attempting to attract new users who were of a younger demographic, Becel margarine used a new filming technique called Dogme that is very inexpensive but highly interesting, and as it turns out, highly effective. The filming is predicated on 35-mm film, no lighting, no sets, all shooting on location, natural sounds, and natural actors (no wardrobe or make-up). Becel was placed in several places to remind customers of the alternative, which was both a healthier way to live and a key reinforcement of Becel's positioning. For example, Becel was placed between elevator doors so that consumers would use the stairs. Executives at the head office in Amsterdam took notice of the technique and message to new younger consumers and considered running the ads internationally.[23]

Audio The audio portion of a commercial includes voices, music, and sound effects. Voices are used in different ways in commercials. They may be heard through the direct presentation of a spokesperson or as a conversation among various people appearing in the commercial. A common method for presenting the audio portion of a commercial is through a **voiceover,** where the message is delivered or action on the screen is narrated or described by an announcer who is not visible. A trend among major advertisers is to have celebrities with distinctive voices do the voiceovers for their commercials.[24]

Music is also an important part of many TV commercials and can play a variety of roles.[25] In many commercials, the music provides a pleasant background or helps create the appropriate mood. Advertisers often use **needledrop,** which Linda Scott describes as follows:

> Needledrop is an occupational term common to advertising agencies and the music industry. It refers to music that is prefabricated, multipurpose, and highly conventional. It is, in that sense, the musical equivalent of stock photos, clip art, or canned copy. Needledrop is an inexpensive substitute for original music; paid for on a one-time basis, it is dropped into a commercial or film when a particular normative effect is desired.[26]

In some commercials, music is much more central to the advertising message. It can be used to get attention, break through the advertising clutter, communicate a key selling point, help establish an image or position, or add feeling.[27] For example, music can work through a classical conditioning process to create positive emotions that become associated with the advertised product or service. Music can also create a positive mood that makes the consumer more receptive toward the advertising message.[28]

Because music can play such an important role in the creative strategy, many companies have paid large sums for the rights to use popular songs in their commercials. For example, Microsoft paid a reported $4 million to use the Rolling Stones' classic "Start Me Up" to introduce the advertising campaign for Windows 95.[29] Nortel Networks licensed the rights to use the classic Beatles' song "Come Together" (although it is performed by a different group) as the central theme in the company's new global advertising campaign.[30] Bud Light spoofed love songs of the 1970s for its Bud Light Institute campaign. One infamous title is "I Love You Dearly Because You Let Me Go Out With My Friends On A Weekly Basis." Unexpectedly, people requested the songs, and the company responded by selling a complete CD entitled "Ulterior Emotions." Consumers can download the music featured in recent commercials from Coca-Cola and Bell Canada's websites. The widespread diffusion of technology has clearly created opportunities for marketers to enhance awareness.[31]

Another important musical element in both TV and radio commercials is **jingles,** catchy songs about a product or service that usually carry the advertising theme and a simple message. For example, Doublemint gum has used the well-known "Double your pleasure, double your fun with Doublemint, Doublemint gum" for years. The jingle is very memorable and serves as a good reminder of the product's minty flavour.

Jingles can be used by themselves as the basis for a musical commercial. Diet Coke brought back its old slogan "Just for the taste of it," set it to a luxurious musical score, and made it the basis of a multimillion-dollar ad campaign. In some commercials, jingles are used more as a form of product identification and appear at the end of the message. Jingles are often composed by companies that specialize in writing commercial music for advertising. These jingle houses work with the creative team to determine the role music will play in the commercial and the message that needs to be communicated.

Planning and Production of TV Commercials Advertisers recognize that they need to do more than talk about, demonstrate, or compare their products or services. Their commercials have to break through the clutter and grab viewers' attention; they must often appeal to emotional, as well as rational, buying motives. Television is essentially an entertainment medium, and many advertisers recognize that their commercials are most successful when they entertain as well as inform. Many of the most popular advertising campaigns are characterized by commercials with strong entertainment value, like the Budweiser spots featuring the talking lizards, the humourous "Got milk?" ads, and the musical spots for the Gap. Some of the most popular commercials recently have been those created for Volkswagen's "Drivers wanted" campaign, which explores drivers' life experiences with their VWs[32] (Exhibit 7–12). Given the inherent entertainment value of television ads, it is no surprise that the planning and production resembles the making of a movie!

Planning the Commercial   The various elements of a TV commercial are brought together in a **script,** a written version of a commercial that provides a detailed description of its video and audio content. The script shows the various audio components of the commercial—the copy to be spoken by voices, the music, and sound effects. The video portion of the script provides the visual plan of the commercial—camera actions and angles, scenes, transitions, and other important descriptions. The script also shows how the video corresponds to the audio portion of the commercial.

Once the basic script has been conceived, the writer and art director get together to produce a storyboard, a series of drawings used to present the visual plan or layout of a proposed commercial. The storyboard contains still drawings of the video scenes and descriptions of the audio that accompanies each scene. Like layouts for print ads, storyboards provide those involved in the production and approval of the commercial with a good approximation of what the final commercial will look like. In some cases an aniamatic (a videotape of the storyboard along with the soundtrack) may be produced if a more finished form of the commercial is needed for client presentations or pretesting.

Production   Once the storyboard or aniamatic of the commercial is approved, it is ready to move to the production phase, which involves three stages:

1. *Preproduction*—all the work and activities that occur before the actual shooting/recording of the commercial.
2. *Production*—the period during which the commercial is filmed or videotaped and recorded.
3. *Postproduction*—activities and work that occur after the commercial has been filmed and recorded.

The various activities of each phase are shown in Figure 7–2. Before the final production process begins, the client must usually review and approve the creative strategy and the various tactics that will be used in creating the advertising message.

Exhibit 7–12   Volkswagen's award-winning commercials are some of the most popular in recent years

Figure 7–2   The three phases of production for commercials

Preproduction
- Selecting a director
- Choosing a production company
- Bidding
- Cost estimation and timing
- Production timetable
  - Set construction
  - Location
  - Agency and client approvals
  - Casting
  - Wardrobes
- Preproduction meeting

Production
- Location versus set shoots
- Night/weekend shoots
- Talent arrangements

Postproduction
- Editing
- Processing
- Recording sound effects
- Audio/video mixing
- Opticals
- Client/agency approval
- Duplicating
- Release/shipping

In this section, we present two models that guide the decision for selecting the most appropriate creative tactics. Each model builds on a perspective of the consumer response processes that we describe in Chapter 4. We discuss the models from a historical perspective to explain how the more recent model is an improvement over the initial model.

The FCB Planning Model

An interesting approach to analyzing the communication situation comes from the work of Richard Vaughn of the Foote, Cone & Belding advertising agency. Vaughn and his associates developed an advertising planning model by building on traditional response theories such as the hierarchy of effects model and its variants and research on high and low involvement.[35] They added the dimension of thinking versus feeling processing at each involvement level by bringing in theories regarding brain specialization. The right/left brain theory suggests the left side of the brain is more capable of rational, cognitive thinking, while the right side is more visual and emotional and engages more in the affective (feeling) functions. Their model, which became known as the FCB grid, delineates four primary advertising planning strategies—informative, affective, habit formation, and satisfaction—along with the most appropriate variant of the alternative response hierarchies (Figure 7–3).

Vaughn suggests that the *informative strategy* is for highly involving products and services where rational thinking and economic considerations prevail and the standard learning hierarchy is the appropriate response model. The *affective strategy* is for highly involving/feeling purchases. For these types of products, advertising should stress psychological and emotional motives such as building self-esteem or enhancing one's ego or self-image.

The *habit formation strategy* is for low-involvement/thinking products with such routinized behaviour patterns that learning occurs most often after a trial purchase. The response process for these products is consistent with a behaviouristic learning-by-doing model (remember our discussion of operant conditioning in Chapter 3?). The *self-satisfaction strategy* is for low-involvement/feeling products where appeals

Figure 7–3 The Foote, Cone & Belding (FCB) grid

	Thinking	Feeling
High involvement	**1. Informative (thinker)** Car–house–furnishings– new products model: Learn–feel–do (economic?) **Possible implications** Test: Recall Diagnostics Media: Long copy format Reflective vehicles Creative: Specific information Demonstration	**2. Affective (feeler)** Jewelry–cosmetics– fashion apparel– motorcycles model: Feel–learn–do (psychological?) **Possible implications** Test: Attitude change Emotional arousal Media: Large space Image specials Creative: Executional Impact
Low involvement	**3. Habit formation (doer)** Food–household items model: Do–learn–feel (responsive?) **Possible implications** Test: Sales Media: Small space ads 10-second I.D.s Radio; POS Creative: Reminder	**4. Self-satisfaction (reactor)** Cigarettes–liquor–candy model: Do–feel–learn (social?) **Possible implications** Test: Sales Media: Billboards Newspapers POS Creative: Attention

to sensory pleasures and social motives are important. Again, the do →
feel or do → learn hierarchy is operating, since product experience is an
important part of the learning process. Vaughn acknowledges that some
minimal level of awareness (passive learning) may precede purchase of
both types of low-involvement products, but deeper, active learning is
not necessary. This is consistent with the low-involvement hierarchy
discussed earlier (learn → do → feel).

The FCB grid provides a useful way for those involved in the advertising planning process, such as creative specialists, to analyze consumer–product relationships and develop appropriate promotional
strategies. Consumer research can be used to determine how consumers
perceive products or brands on the involvement and thinking/feeling
dimensions.[36] This information can then be used to develop effective
creative options such as using rational versus emotional appeals,
increasing involvement levels, or even getting consumers to evaluate a
think-type product on the basis of feelings. The ad for the Kenmore Elite
refrigerator in Exhibit 7–13 is an example of the latter strategy. Notice
how it uses beautiful imagery to appeal to emotional concerns such as
style and appearance. Appliances have traditionally been sold on the
basis of more rational, functional motives.

Exhibit 7–13 A think-type
product is advertised by an
appeal to feelings

The R&P Planning Model

We highlighted the R&P perspective in Chapter 5 when discussing objectives for the
IMC plan. Another part of their framework concerns recommendations for creative
tactics so that the appropriate communication effects will occur with the target audience while they are processing the message. On the surface, their planning model
appears similar to the FCB planning model as both represent consumer attitudes and
explain how marketers use creative tactics to influence attitudes. However, we will
discuss four improvements as we explain the R&P model.

Brand Awareness Tactics   The first consideration is that the R&P model
argues that brand awareness is a necessary precursor to brand attitude. According to
R&P, both brand awareness and brand attitude are universal communication objectives for all circumstances (i.e., one ad, ad campaign, IMC plan). In this view, all
communications should strive to achieve awareness to make brand attitude operational. R&P have three suggestions for awareness:

- Match the brand stimuli and the type of response behaviour of the target
  audience so that understanding of the brand in a category is unambiguous.
- Use a unique brand execution style to connect the brand to the category.
- Maximize brand contact time in the exposure to reinforce name and category
  connection.

In order for awareness to be fully established, the target audience needs to understand the context (brand, behaviour, category) as this is a clue as to how or why the
brand exists. If the context is not clear, then the target audience has trouble remembering when it comes time to purchase. A unique execution style helps cut through
the clutter. The connection to the category and sufficient enough exposure is
required to make sure that the message is retained. For example, TV ads can sometimes show the package or brand name for too short a time for target audiences to
fully grasp where the brand competes in the market.

We also noted that R&P suggest that awareness can be achieved via recognition
and/or recall. R&P have two suggestions for recognition that require less media frequency as consumers need only to be familiar with the brand stimuli at the point of
purchase:

- The brand package and name should have sufficient exposure in terms of
  time or size depending on the media.
- Category need should be mentioned or identified.

Since recall is a more difficult mental task, R&P have six suggestions for this aspect of awareness. Recall also requires high levels of frequency since the brand has to be remembered prior to being at the point of purchase:

- The brand and the category need should be connected in the primary benefit claim.
- The primary benefit claim should be short to be easily understood.
- Within an exposure, the primary benefit claim should be repeated often.
- The message should have or imply a clear personal reference.
- A bizarre or unusual execution style can be used if it is consistent with the brand attitude objective.
- A jingle or similar "memory" tactics should be included.

We have many more specific recommendations for recall since it is a much more difficult mental task for consumers. Advertisers have to help their target audience know their brand prior to purchasing. Thus, careful attention has to be put on all three creative tactics decisions to ensure the target audience can retrieve the brand name from long-term memory when the need to purchase a product category arises.

Brand Attitude Grid Tactics

The R&P view of consumer attitudes is also framed as a matrix with the dimensions of involvement and motivation. For each of these dimensions, R&P argue that their view is a more accurate representation of attitude for planning purposes than the FCB model, and the use of these two concepts represent the second and third improvements.

Low-involvement decision Informational motivation	Low-involvement decision Transformational motivation
High-involvement decision Informational motivation	High-involvement decision Transformational motivation

The involvement dimension is similar to the FCB model, from low involvement to high involvement. However, R&P argue that theirs is specific to the brand as the target audience makes a purchase decision. This point is consistent with an emerging view of involvement that we discussed in Chapter 4 where involvement was influenced by the target audience or the decision situation. Further, the high- and low-involvement levels are also consistent with the central and peripheral routes to persuasion. More precisely, R&P interpret involvement as the degree of risk perceived by the target audience (i.e., new category user or loyal customer) in choosing a particular brand for the next purchase occasion. One extension of this idea, not fully developed by R&P, is that the concept can extend to purchase-related behaviour that we discussed in Chapter 5. For example, how much risk does a person buying a car for the first time take in deciding to visit a particular dealer for a test drive?

The motivation dimension is a continuum from negative motive, or informational-based attitude, to positive motive, or transformational-based attitude. The historic interpretation of an informational-based attitude implies that it is based on careful reasoning that results from the cognitive responses that the target audience has while experiencing advertising messages. This purely cognitive orientation is also the foundation of the "think" dimension of the FCB model. However, R&P argue that this is too limiting as attitude is based on both cognition and affect. Accordingly, they suggest that creative tactics for this side of the matrix should account for the benefit claims (i.e., cognition) and the emotional portrayal of the motive (i.e., affect). The emphasis of the benefit claim is stronger than the emotional portrayal for informational-based attitudes to make it an informational-based attitude. While this cognition and affect issue has been researched for many years, it is often the simplest observation that rings true as some very basic factual ads leave us with a smile on our faces.

The notion of transformational-based attitude is partly based on a recent idea. A transformational ad is defined as "one which associates the experience of using (consuming) the advertised brand with a unique set of psychological characteristics which would not typically be associated with the brand experience to the same degree without exposure to the advertisement."[33] Transformational ads create feelings, images, meanings, and beliefs about the product or service that may be activated when consumers use it, transforming their interpretation of the usage experience.

Just like informational-based attitude is not purely cognitive, the transformational-based attitude is not purely based on emotion but includes some cognitive elements. Intuitively, this makes a lot of sense as some ads with a very strong fear appeal often leave us thinking. Overall, the emphasis of the emotional portrayal is stronger than the benefit claim for transformational-based attitude. Providing information in transformational ads is at the heart of two recent Saturn car ads. From a transformational perspective, both ads showed emotional elements of the purchase-and-consumption experience of owning a Saturn by demonstrating situations where the salesperson goes above and beyond "normal" service-level expectations to deliver a new Saturn. In both cases, however, key attribute information was conveyed. In one, online purchasing and its simplicity were communicated, while in the other, Saturn's 30-day/2,500-kilometre guarantee was explained. [34]

The fourth improvement of the R&P model is that its guidelines for creative tactics balance elements in the ad for both cognitive and emotional responses that contribute to both aspects of brand attitude. On the emotional side, we are concerned with how the motive is portrayed or conveyed in the ad. To consider this, we have three characteristics: its authenticity, or how real it appears to the target audience; whether the target audience likes the ad; and finally, the target audience's reaction to the execution style. On the informational side, we are concerned with the brand's message with respect to the benefit claims. We also have three characteristics to consider: the number, the intensity, and the repetition of the claims.

While the guidelines for all six characteristics may be a function of all three creative tactics decisions, we can make a stronger connection for some. The authenticity and whether the target audience likes the ad are typically associated with the design elements of the ad. Quite obviously, there is a direct connection between the execution style of the framework and that particular creative tactic decision discussed in this chapter. The benefit claims are mostly a function of the message structure since the latter concerns the details of explaining the product's benefits. We now turn our attention to creative tactics recommendations for the four brand attitude cells.

Low Involvement—Informational Creative Tactics   Ads designed to influence target audiences' attitude based on low involvement—informational persuasion should have a very obvious benefit claim with an unusual execution style. Since the intention is to persuade the target audience so that they automatically learn the connection between the brand, its category, and the benefit, consumer acceptance or rejection of the message is not a factor. Further, the emotion demonstrated in the ad and whether the target audience likes the ad are not necessary as the message is intended to make a creative link among the brand, category, and benefit.

Low Involvement—Informational

Emotional portrayal of motive

Authenticity	Not necessary.
Like ad	Not necessary.
Execution style	Unusual, problem-solution format.

Benefit claim of brand message

Number of benefits	One or two, or one clear group.
Intensity of benefit claim	State extremely.
Repetition of benefit claim	Few required for reminder.

Low Involvement—Transformational Creative Tactics   Three emotional portrayal guidelines are critical for this type of attitude. These points are consistent with transformational ads described above. For example, the representation of the consumption of the brand in the drama or story of the ad must "ring true" with the target audience such that it is perceived as a very enjoyable ad. In a low-involvement situation, some benefit claims are still included but may be indirectly communicated through the story or emotion surrounding the story. Actual acceptance of the benefit claim is not a requirement; however, rejection of the overall message can lead to a reduction in the attitude of the target audience.

Low Involvement—Transformational

Emotional portrayal of motive

Authenticity	Key element and is the single benefit.
Like ad	Necessary.
Execution style	Unique to the brand.

Benefit claim of brand message

Number of benefits	One or two, or one clear group.
Intensity of benefit claim	Imply extremely by association.
Repetition of benefit claim	Many exposures to build-up before trial purchase and reinforce attitude after trial

High Involvement—Informational Creative Tactics   This side of the model illustrates the importance of information as high involvement implies the requirement of considerable and accurate benefit claims. Many benefits can be claimed here but they must be organized and presented in a manner that respects the current attitude of the target audience. Since this is an informational-based attitude, the emotional portrayal is important but not the primary consideration. Furthermore, the high-involvement characteristic means that the target audience has to accept the benefit claims. Rejection of the benefit claims may not result in any negative change in attitude if the copy respected the prior attitude of the target audience.

High Involvement—Informational

Emotional portrayal of motive

Authenticity	Key element early in product life cycle and declines as product reaches later stages.
Like ad	Not necessary.
Execution style	Unusual.

Benefit claim of brand message

Number of benefits	Overall claim to summarize multiple (no more than seven) benefits.
Intensity of benefit claim	Initial attitude is key reference point. Very accurate claim; cannot over-claim or under-claim. Comparative or refutation messages are strong options.
Repetition of benefit claim	Many claims within an exposure.

High Involvement—Transformational Creative Tactics   Persuasion through this type of attitude formation requires strong emphasis of the emotion. A positive attitude towards the ad leads to a positive brand attitude. Likewise, the target audience must truly relate to the execution style and feel like the ad supports their lifestyle. The end result is that if the target audience rejects the message because the emotion is not accurate, then the persuasion will not work and may even cause significant attitude reduction. The remaining guidelines illustrate that considerable information is required similar to what is seen for the high involvement—informational attitude. Once again this implies that acceptance of the benefit claims are critical for the attitude to take hold with the target audience.

High Involvement—Transformational

Emotional portrayal of motive

Authenticity	Paramount; must reflect lifestyle of target audience.
Like ad	Necessary.
Execution style	Unique; target audience must identify with product, people, or consumption situation shown.

Benefit claim of brand message

Number of benefits	Acceptable number to provide key information.
Intensity of benefit claim	Very accurate claim; may over-claim but do not under-claim
Repetition of benefit claim	Many are required to support informational message.

Process of Evaluation

While the creative specialists have much responsibility for determining the advertising appeal and execution style to be used in a campaign, the client must evaluate and approve the creative approach before any ads are produced. A number of people on the client side may be involved in evaluating the creative work of the agency, including the advertising or communications manager, product or brand managers, marketing director or vice president, representatives from the legal department, and sometimes even the president or chief executive officer (CEO) of the company or the board of directors.

The amount of input each of these individuals has in the creative evaluation and approval process varies depending on the company's policies, the importance of the product to the company, the role of advertising in the marketing program, and the advertising approach being recommended.

Earlier in this chapter, we noted that Procter & Gamble has been moving away from testimonials and slice-of-life advertising executions to somewhat riskier and more lively forms of advertising. But the company remains conservative and has been slow to adopt the avant-garde ads used by many of its competitors. Agencies that do the advertising for various P&G brands recognize that quirky executions that challenge the company's subdued corporate culture are not likely to be approved.[37]

In many cases, top management is involved in selecting an ad agency and must approve the theme and creative strategy for the campaign. Evaluation and approval of the individual ads proposed by the agency often rest with the advertising and product managers who are primarily responsible for the brand. The account executive and a member of the creative team present the creative concept to the client's advertising and product and/or marketing managers for their approval before beginning production. A careful evaluation should be made before the ad actually enters production, since this stage requires considerable time and money as suppliers are hired to perform the various functions required to produce the actual ad.

The client's evaluation of the print layout or commercial storyboard can be difficult, since the advertising or brand manager is generally not a creative expert and must be careful not to reject viable creative approaches or accept ideas that will result in inferior advertising. However, personnel on the client side can use the

Evaluating Creative Designs

guidelines discussed next to judge the efficacy of creative approaches suggested by the agency.

Guidelines for Evaluation

Advertisers use numerous criteria to evaluate the creative approach suggested by the ad agency. In some instances, the client may want to have the rough layout or storyboard pretested to get quantitative information to assist in the evaluation. However, the evaluation process is usually more subjective; the advertising or brand manager relies on qualitative considerations. Basic criteria for evaluating creative approaches are discussed next:

- *Is the creative approach consistent with the brand's marketing and advertising objectives?* One of the most important factors the client must consider is whether the creative strategy and tactics recommended by the agency are consistent with the marketing strategy for the brand and the role advertising and promotion have been assigned in the overall marketing program. This means the creative approach must be compatible with the image of the brand and the way it is positioned in the marketplace.

- *Is the creative approach consistent with the communication objectives?* The creative strategy and tactics must meet the established communication objectives. Creative specialists can lose sight of what the advertising message is supposed to be and come up with an approach that fails to execute the advertising strategy. Individuals responsible for approving the ad should ask the creative specialists to explain how the creative strategy and tactics achieve the creative and communications objectives.

- *Is the creative approach appropriate for the target audience?* Generally, much time has been spent defining, locating, and attempting to understand the target audience for the advertiser's product or service. Careful consideration should be given to whether the creative strategy and tactics recommended will appeal to, be understood by, and communicate effectively with the target audience. This involves studying all elements of the ad and how the audience will respond to them. Advertisers do not want to approve advertising that they believe will receive a negative reaction from the target audience.

- *Does the creative approach communicate a clear and convincing message to the customer?* Most ads are supposed to communicate a message that will help sell the brand. Many ads fail to communicate a clear and convincing message that motivates consumers to use a brand. While creativity is important in advertising, it is also important that the advertising communicate information attributes, features and benefits, and/or images that give consumers a reason to buy the brand.

- *Does the creative approach keep from overwhelming the message?* A common criticism of advertising, and TV commercials in particular, is that so much emphasis is placed on creative approach that the advertiser's message gets overshadowed. Many creative, entertaining commercials have failed to register the brand name and/or selling points effectively.

  With the increasing amount of clutter in most advertising media, it may be necessary to use a novel creative approach to gain the viewer's or reader's attention. However, the creative approach cannot overwhelm the message. Clients must walk a fine line: Make sure the sales message is not lost, but be careful not to stifle the efforts of the creative specialists and force them into producing dull, boring advertising.

- *Is the creative approach appropriate for the media environment in which it is likely to be seen?* Each media vehicle has its own specific climate that results from the nature of its editorial content, the type of reader or viewer it attracts, and the nature of the ads it contains. Consideration should be given to how well the ad fits into the media environment in which it will be shown.

- *Is the ad truthful and tasteful?* Marketers also have to consider whether an ad is truthful, as well as whether it might offend consumers. The ultimate responsibility for determining whether an ad deceives or offends the target audience lies with the client. It is the job of the advertising or brand manager to evaluate the approach suggested by the creative specialists against company standards. The firm's legal department may be asked to review the ad to determine whether the creative appeal, message content, or execution could cause any problems for the company. It is much better to catch any potential legal problems before the ad is shown to the public.

The advertising manager, brand manager, or other personnel on the client side can use these basic guidelines in reviewing, evaluating, and approving the ideas offered by the creative specialists. There may be other factors specific to the firm's advertising and marketing situation. Also, there may be situations where it is acceptable to deviate from the standards the firm usually uses in judging creative output. As we shall see in Chapter 17, the client may want to move beyond these subjective criteria and use more sophisticated pretesting methods to determine the effectiveness of a particular approach suggested by the creative specialist or team.

Summary

In this chapter, we examined how the advertising message is implemented and executed. Once the creative strategy that will guide the ad campaign has been determined, attention turns to the specific creative tactics that will enhance the cognitive and emotional processing of the message. This chapter summarizes three decisions that are critical when developing creative tactics: execution style, message structure, and design elements.

The creative execution style is the way the advertising appeal is presented in the message. A number of common execution techniques were examined in the chapter, along with considerations for their use. The most appropriate style is a matter of balancing uniqueness in the market versus effective communication to achieve the stated objectives.

The design of the advertising message is a critical part of the communication process and is the second creative tactic discussed. There are various options regarding the message structure, including order of presentation of message arguments, conclusion drawing, message sidedness, refutation, and verbal versus visual traits.

Attention was also given to tactical issues involved in creating print and TV advertising. The components of a print ad include headlines, body copy, illustrations, and layout. We also examined the video and audio components of TV commercials and various considerations involved in the planning and production of commercials. Together, these showed some of the important design decisions that have to be made to complete the creative approach.

We presented a framework for creative specialists and marketers to help them make the appropriate decisions for the creative tactics. The framework uses the target audience's attitude as the key factor when deciding upon the correct execution style, message structure, and design.

Creative specialists are responsible for determining the creative strategy and tactics from the marketer's input. However, the client must review, evaluate, and approve the creative approach before any ads are produced or run. A number of criteria can be used by advertising, product or brand managers, and others involved in the promotional process to evaluate the advertising messages before approving final production.

Key Terms

creative execution
   style, 168
primacy effect, 173
recency effect, 173
one-sided message, 174
two-sided message,
   174

refutation, 175
headline, 177
direct headlines, 177
indirect headlines, 178
subheads, 178
body copy, 178
layout, 179

voiceover, 180
needledrop, 180
jingles, 180
script, 181
informational
   motive, 184

transformational
   motive, 184
low-involvement
   decision, 184
high-involvement
   decision, 184

Discussion Questions

1. Discuss the difference between an advertising appeal and a creative execution style. Why is it important to make this distinction?

2. Explain how the dramatization advertising execution technique could be used for the following products: beer, cellphones, furniture, airlines.

3. Why do consumer packaged-goods advertisers such as Procter & Gamble often use slice-of-life executions? Can this advertising technique be used for business-to-business products?

4. Identify the various motives that can be used as the basis of rational advertising appeals and emotional advertising appeals. Are there any motives that can be addressed with both rational and emotional advertising appeals?

5. What emotions did "The Rant" commercial evoke from Canadian consumers? How did these emotional responses result in greater sales for Molson Canadian?

6. What is meant by one-sided versus two-sided message? Discuss some ofthe reasons marketers may or may not want to use a two-sided message.

7. Discuss the role of headlines and subheads in print advertisements. Would you say that headlines are more important for processing (i.e., gaining attention) or establishing a communication effect (i.e., awareness).

8. Discuss the role of music in advertising. Why might companies such as Microsoft and Nortel Networks pay large sums of money for the rights to use popular songs in their commercials?

9. What are the similarities and differences of creative tactics across the four cells of the planning matrix?

Chapter Eight

Media Strategy and Tactics Decisions

Chapter Objectives

- To understand the key terminology used in media planning.

- To know how a media plan is developed.

- To know the process of deciding and implementing media strategies and tactics.

- To understand the theoretical and managerial approaches for media budget setting.

I Am Canadian!

"My name is Joe, and I am Canadian!" So ends one of the most successful Canadian commercials of all time for Molson Breweries' brand Canadian. In March 2000, unsuspecting viewers in movie theatres were surprised with "The Rant," a tribute to Canadian culture and nationalistic pride. Later, the ad received extensive air time on television that has been the forefront of a successful IMC campaign.

Shortly before and during the campaign, Molson had been regaining its corporate focus on beer with divestment of non-related businesses and purchases of other beer brands internationally. Despite this, Molson needed a winner in 2000 as it had experienced weak sales in its traditionally strong brands of Canadian and Export and a roughly $100 million gap in profitability compared to its rival Labatt Breweries.

Molson began by replacing its agency of 42 years and hiring new agencies for key brands including Canadian. Curiously, the new agency found success with the already established theme "I AM," created in 1994 but since dropped. The link of "I AM" to Canadian was indirect in the initial campaign as the focus was more on an individual identity or independent attitude.

Does the message of nationalism play? Some argued that globalization of the past ten years has given rise to a new view of Canada that is reflected in everyday life rather than our institutions or moral principles, which can now be leveraged in marketing programs. In contrast, others were concerned that the meaning of a brand gets lost with such extreme emotions. Luckily for Molson Canadian, the pride and brand go hand-in-hand, which makes it a powerful combination.

The campaign has garnered extensive publicity. The front page of the *National Post* reproduced a large and colourful image from the ad on April 12, 2000. The campaign was featured in many Canadian and American news publications and news shows. And to top it off, Jeff Douglas, The Rant's actor, re-enacted his performance prior to NHL games and other venues that tied in with Canadian's rock concert promotions. Perhaps the most flattering example of the campaign's success is that it was adapted for Foster's Beer in Australia with the theme "I Believe."

Sales promotions were a key part of the mix. In the spring of 2001, Canadian was inserting caps and T-shirts in its cases, and offering its "Best Seats in the House" contest and a ticket giveaway contest for the hockey playoffs. It was also the closed captioning sponsor on *Survivor*. The website www.iam.ca carried the promotions and featured other elements to support the nationalistic theme. And the ultimate sponsorship program emerged as Canadian organized a swearing-in ceremony of new Canadians prior to the hockey playoffs in Toronto and Ottawa.

A number of spots added momentum to the campaign. One included scenes that poked fun at many Canadian attributes (e.g., polite, nice, humble, passive). For Canada Day, we received birthday wishes from Joe and other friendly Molson Canadian beer drinkers. Molson also tweaked and ran a spot that followed a red maple leaf gliding along a small river. In 2001, Canada received a "toast" from a half-Scottish, half-Irish beer drinker who poetically describes many unique Canadian attributes (i.e., hockey hair, long underwear, and multi-coloured money), sang a new "anthem" that highlighted many historical Canadian images, and watched a Myles walk "500 miles" for a case of Canadian.

The campaign is a success based on a couple of factors. Unaided brand awareness rose from 55 percent to 61 percent among English Canadians for those in the legal drinking age (LDA) to 55 years category. The number of English Canadians claiming the brand as their regular beer rose from 16 to 17 percent in the same age bracket. Market share for Canadian increased by 1.8 percent in 2000 and 2.5 percent in 2001. Labatt's Blue market share experienced a similar decline each year. "The Rant" won a bronze at the Cannes festival and a Gold in two categories for the Cassies. The entire campaign also earned Molson the Grand Prix at the Cassies.

Sources: "*Post* goes big with Molson image," *Marketing Magazine*, April 12, 2000; Chris Daniels, "Cashing in on the new nationalism," *Marketing Magazine*, May 22, 2000; Astrid Van Den Broek, "Molson pours on more stereotypes," *Marketing Magazine*, June 26, 2000; "A Down Under twist on Molson's *Rant*," *Marketing Magazine*, September 18, 2000; Astrid Van Den Broek, "I AM Marketer of the Year," *Marketing Magazine*, December 18/25, 2000; "Molson readies Canadian hockey promos," *Marketing Magazine*, March 15, 2001; Astrid Van Den Broek, "Molson Canadian toasts Canadiana," *Marketing Magazine*, April 9, 2001; "Molson 'sponsors' new citizens," *Marketing Magazine*, April 23, 2001; "Molson's 'Anthem' tugs at history," *Marketing Magazine*, June 18, 2001; "Myles the latest Molson Canadian spot," *Marketing Magazine*, October 22, 2001; "Molson Canadian," *Marketing Magazine*, November 19, 2001; Lesley Young, "The Rant dominates the Cassie awards," *Marketing Magazine*, November 19, 2001; "Molson Canadian—Cassies Grand Prix Winner," *Marketing Magazine*, November 19, 2001.

The marketer has many media opportunities available that require in-depth knowledge of all the alternatives, since integrated marketing communications programs are a necessity. Media planners must now consider new options as well as recognize the changes that are occurring in traditional sources. New and evolving media contribute to the already difficult task of media planning. Planning when, where, and how the advertising message will be delivered is a complex and involved process. The primary objective of the media plan is to develop a framework that will deliver the message to the target audience in the most efficient, cost-effective manner possible—that will communicate what the product, brand, and/or service can do.

This chapter illustrates the media planning process, presents issues related to setting a media budget, and discusses the development of decisions for media strategy and tactics. Later chapters will explore the relative strengths and limitations of the various media and examine each in more detail.

Media Planning

The media planning process is not an easy one. Options include mass media such as television, newspapers, radio, and magazines (and the choices available within each of these categories) as well as out-of-the-home media such as outdoor advertising, transit advertising, and electronic billboards (Figure 8–1). A variety of support media such as direct marketing, interactive media, promotional products advertising, and in-store point-of-purchase options must also be considered.

While at first glance the choices among these alternatives might seem relatively straightforward, this is rarely the case. Part of the reason media selection becomes so involved is the nature of the media themselves. TV combines both sight and sound, an advantage not offered by other media. Magazines can convey more information and may keep the message available to the potential buyer for a much longer time. Newspapers also offer their own advantages, as do outdoor, direct media, and each of the others. The Internet offers many of the advantages of other media but is also limited in its capabilities. The characteristics of each alternative must be considered, along with many other factors. This process becomes even more complicated when the manager has to choose between alternatives within the same medium.

Figure 8–1   Canadian market data: net advertising revenues

Medium		Components of Net Advertising Revenues by Medium (in millions of dollars)											
		1994	%	1995	%	1996	%	1997	%	1998	%	1999	%
Television	Total	$1,772	25%	$1,850	26%	$1,982	26%	$2,101	26%	$2,312	26%	$2,377	27%
	Network	$388	6%	$370	5%	$440	6%	$406	5%	$452	5%	$449	5%
	Selective	$1,275	18%	$1,348	19%	$1,373	18%	$1,499	19%	$1,607	18%	$1,609	18%
	Specialty	$109	2%	$122	2%	$155	2%	$184	2%	$241	3%	$304	3%
	Infomercial	—	—	$10	0%	$14	0%	$12	0%	$12	0%	$15	0%
Radio	Total	$741	11%	$758	11%	$792	11%	$849	11%	$921	11%	$952	11%
Daily Newspapers (ex. classified)	Total	$1,319	19%	$1,368	19%	$1,315	18%	$1,545	19%	$1,596	18%	$1,630	18%
Weeklies/ Community Newspapers	Total	$562	8%	$579	8%	$597	8%	$634	8%	$765	9%	$788	9%
Trade Publications	Total	$235	3%	$229	3%	$233	3%	$252	3%	$277	3%	$283	3%
Consumer Magazines	Total	$327	5%	$316	4%	$318	4%	$347	4%	$381	4%	$389	4%
Outdoor	Total	$132	2%	$167	2%	$200	3%	$220	3%	$250	3%	$270	3%
Internet	Total	$0	—	$0	—	$0	—	$10	0%	$25	0%	$56	1%
Other	Total	$1,966	28%	$1,902	27%	$2,050	27%	$2,115	26%	$2,235	26%	$2,214	25%
Yellow Pages		$847	12%	$864	12%	$892	12%	$899	11%	$935	11%	$975	11%
Direct Mail		$1,071	15%	$991	14%	$1,110	15%	$1,168	14%	$1,251	14%	$1,190	13%
Other Print (religious, school, farm, weekend)		$48	1%	$47	1%	$48	1%	$48	1%	$49	1%	$49	1%
Total, All Media		$7,054		$7,169		$7,487		$8,073		$8,762		$8,959	

As compiled by the TVB from Statistics Canada, CRTC, CNA, CCNA/Les Hebdos du Québec, Magazines Canada/LNA, CARD, Mediacom/ACN, TeleDirect, Canada Post, IAB/Ernst & Young and industry estimates

Media planning is the series of decisions involved in delivering the promotional message to the prospective purchasers and/or users of the product or brand. Media planning is a process, which means a number of decisions are made, each of which may be altered or abandoned as the plan develops. The media plan is the guide for media selection. It requires development of specific **media objectives** and a specific **media strategy** (plan of action) designed to attain these objectives. Once the decisions have been made and the objectives, strategies and tactics formulated, this information is organized into the media plan.

The **medium** is the general category of available delivery systems, which includes broadcast media (like TV and radio), print media (like newspapers and magazines), direct mail, outdoor advertising, and other support media. The **media vehicle** is the specific carrier within a medium category. For example, *Maclean's* is a print vehicle; *Hockey Night in Canada* is a broadcast vehicle. As you will see in later chapters, each vehicle has its own characteristics as well as its own relative strengths and limitations. Specific decisions must be made as to the value of each in delivering the message.

As we discuss media, we will work with three key concepts. **Reach** is a measure of the number of different audience members exposed at least once to a media vehicle in a given period of time. **Coverage** refers to the potential audience that might receive the message through a vehicle. Coverage relates to potential audience; reach refers to the actual audience delivered. (The importance of this distinction will become clearer later in this chapter.) Finally, **frequency** refers to the number of times the receiver is exposed to the media vehicle in a specified period.

Media Plan

The media plan determines the best way to get the advertiser's message to the market. In a basic sense, the goal of the media plan is to find that combination of media that enables the marketer to communicate the message in the most effective manner to the largest number of potential customers at the lowest cost. The activities involved in developing the media plan and the purposes of each are presented in Figure 8–2.

As you can see, a number of decisions must be made throughout this process. The promotional planning model in Chapter 1 discussed the process of identifying target markets, establishing objectives, and formulating strategies for attaining them. The development of the media plan and strategies follows a similar path, except that the focus is to determine the best way to deliver the message. Thus, the media plan is generally comprised of a short section containing media objectives, an explanation of the media strategy decisions, and fine-tuning details that are known as media execution or media tactics.

While most media plans are written annually, advertisers find it necessary to alter their objectives and strategies because of the rapidly changing marketing environment. An effective media plan requires a degree of flexibility. If the plan has not built in some flexibility, opportunities may be lost and/or the company may not be able to address new threats. Flexibility may be needed to address the following:

1. *Market opportunities.* Sometimes a market opportunity arises that the advertiser wishes to take advantage of. For example, a special television show may prompt an advertiser to shift their expenditures from another media.

2. *Market threats.* External factors may pose a threat to the firm, and a change in media strategy is dictated. For example, a competitor may alter its media strategy to gain an edge. Failure to respond to this challenge could create problems for the firm.

3. *Availability of media.* Sometimes a desired medium (or vehicle) is not available to the marketer. Perhaps the medium does not reach a particular target audience or has no time or space available. There are still some geographic areas that certain media do not reach. Alternative vehicles or media must then be considered.

4. *Changes in media vehicles.* A change in a particular media vehicle may require a change in the media strategy. A drop in ratings or a change in editorial format may lead the advertiser to use different programs or print alternatives.

Media Objectives

Just as the situation analysis leads to establishment of marketing and communications objectives, it should also lead to specific media objectives. The media objectives are not ends in themselves. Rather, they are derived from and are designed to lead to the attainment of communication and marketing objectives. Media objectives are the goals for the media program and should be limited to those that can be accomplished through media strategies, as in the following example:

Create awareness in the target audience through the following:

- Use broadcast media to provide coverage of 80 percent of the target audience over a six-month period.
- Reach 60 percent of the target audience at least three times over the same six-month period.
- Concentrate heaviest advertising in winter and spring, with lighter emphasis in summer and fall.

The media objectives give direction for the media strategy and tactics decisions. Upon implementation, marketers need to know whether or not they were successful. Measures of effectiveness must consider two factors: (1) How well did these strategies achieve the media objectives? (2) How well did this media plan contribute to attaining the overall marketing and communications objectives? If the strategies were successful, they should be used in future plans. If not, their flaws should be analyzed.

Figure 8–2 Activities involved in developing the media plan

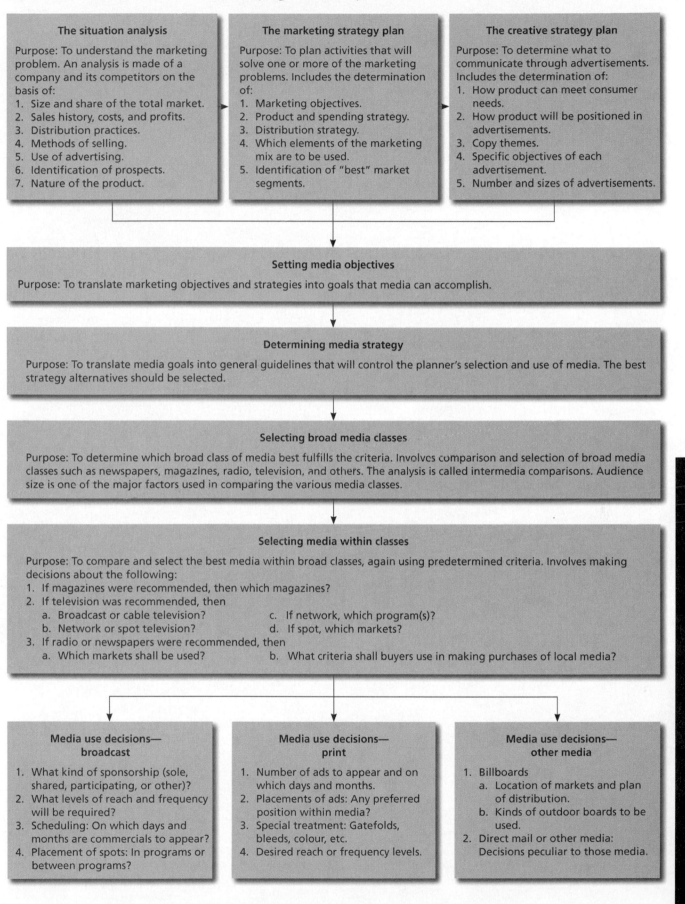

The situation analysis

Purpose: To understand the marketing problem. An analysis is made of a company and its competitors on the basis of:
1. Size and share of the total market.
2. Sales history, costs, and profits.
3. Distribution practices.
4. Methods of selling.
5. Use of advertising.
6. Identification of prospects.
7. Nature of the product.

The marketing strategy plan

Purpose: To plan activities that will solve one or more of the marketing problems. Includes the determination of:
1. Marketing objectives.
2. Product and spending strategy.
3. Distribution strategy.
4. Which elements of the marketing mix are to be used.
5. Identification of "best" market segments.

The creative strategy plan

Purpose: To determine what to communicate through advertisements. Includes the determination of:
1. How product can meet consumer needs.
2. How product will be positioned in advertisements.
3. Copy themes.
4. Specific objectives of each advertisement.
5. Number and sizes of advertisements.

Setting media objectives

Purpose: To translate marketing objectives and strategies into goals that media can accomplish.

Determining media strategy

Purpose: To translate media goals into general guidelines that will control the planner's selection and use of media. The best strategy alternatives should be selected.

Selecting broad media classes

Purpose: To determine which broad class of media best fulfills the criteria. Involves comparison and selection of broad media classes such as newspapers, magazines, radio, television, and others. The analysis is called intermedia comparisons. Audience size is one of the major factors used in comparing the various media classes.

Selecting media within classes

Purpose: To compare and select the best media within broad classes, again using predetermined criteria. Involves making decisions about the following:
1. If magazines were recommended, then which magazines?
2. If television was recommended, then
   a. Broadcast or cable television?
   b. Network or spot television?
   c. If network, which program(s)?
   d. If spot, which markets?
3. If radio or newspapers were recommended, then
   a. Which markets shall be used?
   b. What criteria shall buyers use in making purchases of local media?

Media use decisions— broadcast

1. What kind of sponsorship (sole, shared, participating, or other)?
2. What levels of reach and frequency will be required?
3. Scheduling: On which days and months are commercials to appear?
4. Placement of spots: In programs or between programs?

Media use decisions— print

1. Number of ads to appear and on which days and months.
2. Placements of ads: Any preferred position within media?
3. Special treatment: Gatefolds, bleeds, colour, etc.
4. Desired reach or frequency levels.

Media use decisions— other media

1. Billboards
   a. Location of markets and plan of distribution.
   b. Kinds of outdoor boards to be used.
2. Direct mail or other media: Decisions peculiar to those media.

Visible Minorities Are Still Sparse in Media Advertising

The statistics speak for themselves. **Visible minorities** represent 80 percent of newcomers to Canada, 14 percent of the entire Canadian population, and nearly 20 percent of Canadians under 45. Not only are these groups a major force in the Canadian population, but they also have education levels about the Canadian average and represent over $76 billion in buying power.

A number of companies are reflecting Canada's diversity in their advertising campaigns and they're reaping the rewards. Why, then, are many Canadian advertisers still failing to portray the "real" Canada?

Three basic reasons or misconceptions are reinforcing this trend:

- *Marketers and agencies worry that including visible minorities in advertising will alienate white Canadians.* According to recent research, this is far from reality. A recent omnibus survey revealed that 45 percent of Canadians believe current advertising is too geared to whites, and 48 percent feel visible minorities are under-represented. This means that nearly half of all Canadians recognize that Canadian advertising doesn't accurately reflect today's population.

- *Decision makers think the changing face of Canada is limited to Toronto.* This, too, is untrue. In fact, in the ten largest Canadian cities, the proportion of visible minorities is over 20 percent of the population.

- *Open casting calls do not always specify that visible minorities are welcome.* As a result, some actors who are visible minorities don't bother to audition.

The failure to represent Canadians of diverse racial and multicultural backgrounds is not just a television issue. Visible minorities are often not given fair play in other marketing communications, including print, Internet, and direct mail.

The beer industry is doing its share to showcase minorities in its ad campaigns. It realizes that its audience is made up of more than just white people. Some say the real change for the beer category came with Budweiser's award-winning "Whassup" campaign from DDB Chicago in early 2000. The well-known ads featured four African-American men hanging out, asking each other "Whassup?" The much-imitated campaign has since evolved to include Italian men (in a *Friends'* Joey-esque "How you doin'?" tone), as well as other groups.

On the Canadian front, the first beer ad that many remember that featured an actor of colour was a late 1990s Carlsberg spot in which a black man takes various beloved items to the curb. Ethnicity was an underlying theme when Molson Canadian relaunched its brand featuring "The Rant." In the spot, "Joe" talks about appreciating Canada for qualities such as diversity, not assimilation, while pictures of people from different ethnic groups flash by in the background. With this year's "Toast" campaign, Molson adapted the theme into a salute with a "Scirish" (part Scottish, part Irish) narrator doing a tribute to what he likes about Canada. And, one step further to connecting drinkers to the campaign, Molson (with the help of Citizenship and Immigration Canada) sponsored the swearing in of new Canadians during several games in the NHL playoffs.

Sources: Astrid Van Den Broek, "A Toast to More Colour in Beer Ads," *Marketing Magazine,* June 4, 2001; Tony Pigott and Michael Sullivan, "Including Visible Minorities," *Marketing Magazine,* June 4, 2001; Astrid Van Den Broek, "Canada's Advertising Still Too White," *Marketing Magazine,* June 5, 2000.

Media Strategy Challenges

Unfortunately, the media strategy decision has not become a standardized task. A number of problems contribute to the difficulty of establishing the plan and reduce its effectiveness. These problems include insufficient information, inconsistent terminologies, and difficulty measuring effectiveness.

Insufficient Information   While a great deal of information about markets and the media exists, media planners often require more than is available. Some data are just not measured, either because they cannot be or because measuring them would be too expensive. For example, continuous measures of radio listenership exist, but only periodic listenership studies are reported due to sample size and cost constraints.

The timing of measurements is also a problem; some audience measures are taken only at specific times of the year. (For example, **sweeps periods** in February, May, July, and November are used for measuring TV audiences and setting advertising rates.) This information is then generalized to succeeding months, so future planning decisions must be made on past data that may not reflect current behaviours. Think about planning for TV advertising for the fall season. There are no data on the audiences of new shows, and audience information taken on existing programs during the summer may not indicate how these programs will do in the fall because summer viewership is generally much lower. While the advertisers can review these programs before they air, they do not have actual audience figures.

The lack of information is even more of a problem for small advertisers, who may not be able to afford to purchase the information they require. As a result, their decisions are based on limited or out-of-date data that was provided by the media themselves, or no data at all.

Inconsistent Terminologies   Problems arise because the cost bases used by different media often vary and the standards of measurement used to establish these costs are not always consistent. For example, print media may present cost efficiency data in terms of the cost to reach a thousand people (cost per thousand, or CPM), while broadcast and outdoor media use the cost per ratings point (CPRP). Audience information that is used as a basis for these costs has also been collected by different methods. Finally, terms that actually mean something different (such as *reach* and *coverage*) may be used synonymously, adding to the confusion.

Difficulty Measuring Effectiveness   Because it is so hard to measure the effectiveness of advertising and promotions in general, it is also difficult to determine the relative effectiveness of various media or media vehicles. While progress is being made in this regard (particularly in the area of direct-response advertising), the media planner must usually guess at the impact of these alternatives.

Because of these problems, not all media decisions are quantitatively determined. Sometimes managers have to assume the image of a medium in a market with which they are not familiar, anticipate the impact of recent events, or make judgments without full knowledge of all the available alternatives.

While these problems complicate the media decision process, they do not render it an entirely subjective exercise. The remainder of this chapter explores in more detail how media strategies are developed and ways to increase their effectiveness.

Media Budget

We noted above that the media plan has to contribute its part in achieving communication objectives such as brand awareness and brand attitude. While establishing media and communication objectives are an important part of the planning process, the degree to which these objectives can be obtained is a function of the media budget or how much the firm wishes to invest in advertising. No organization has an unlimited budget, so objectives must be set with the budget in mind and the budget has to be realistic to achieve any media and communication objectives.

We include the media budget issues in this chapter because of this inherent trade-off between objectives and financial resources. We do not discuss budget issues for other IMC tools extensively in this book for two reasons. First, the remaining IMC tools are often dependent on media expenditures. For example, aspects of public relations campaigns use media. Advertisers use media advertising to direct visitors to their websites. Second, as we noted earlier in this book, the planning process for all marketing communications follows established planning processes of advertising. Thus, the budgeting concepts here directly transfer to other IMC tools.

The size of a firm's advertising and promotions budget can vary from a few thousand dollars to millions. When companies such as Procter & Gamble and General Motors spend millions of dollars per year to promote their products, they expect such expenditures to accomplish their stated objectives. The budget decision is no less critical to a firm spending only a few thousand dollars; its ultimate success or failure may depend on the monies spent. One of the most critical decisions facing the marketing manager is how much to spend on the promotional effort.

Unfortunately, many managers fail to realize the value of advertising and promotion. They treat the communications budget as an expense rather than an investment. Instead of viewing the dollars spent as contributing to additional sales and market share, they see budget expenses as cutting into profits. As a result, when times get tough, the advertising and promotional budget is the first to be cut—even though there is strong evidence that exactly the opposite should occur. Moreover, the decision is not a one-time responsibility. A new budget is formulated every year, each time a new product is introduced, or when either internal or external factors necessitate a change to maintain competitiveness.

The remainder of this section provides insight into some underlying theory with respect to budget setting, discusses how companies budget for promotional efforts, and demonstrates the inherent strengths and weaknesses associated with these theoretical and managerial approaches.

Theoretical Approaches in Budget Setting

Most of the approaches used to establish advertising budgets are based on marginal analysis or sales response models.

Marginal Analysis   Figure 8–3 graphically represents the concept of **marginal analysis.** As advertising/promotional expenditures increase, sales and gross margins also increase to a point, but then they level off. Profits are shown to be a result of the gross margin minus advertising expenditures. Using this theory to establish its budget, a firm would continue to spend advertising/promotional dollars as long as the marginal revenues created by these expenditures exceeded the incremental advertising/promotional costs. As shown on the graph, the optimal expenditure level is the point where marginal costs equal the marginal revenues they generate (point A). If the sum of the advertising/promotional expenditures exceeded the revenues they generated, one would conclude the appropriations were too high and scale down the budget. If revenues were higher, a higher budget might be in order.

While marginal analysis seems logical intuitively, certain weaknesses limit its usefulness. These weaknesses include the assumptions that (1) sales are a direct result of advertising and promotional expenditures and this effect can be measured and (2) advertising and promotion are solely responsible for sales. Let us examine each of these assumptions in more detail.

1. *Assumption that sales are a direct measure of advertising and promotions efforts.* Previously, we discussed the fact that the advertiser needs to set communications objectives that contribute to accomplishing overall marketing objectives but at the same time are separate. One reason for this strategy is that it is often difficult, if not impossible, to demonstrate the effects of advertising and promotions on sales. In studies using sales as a direct measure, it has been almost impossible

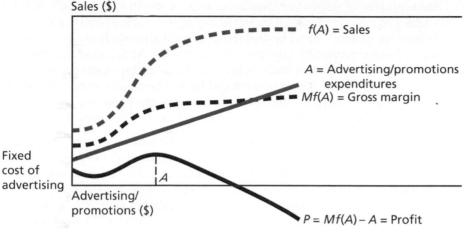

Figure 8–3   Marginal analysis

to establish the contribution of advertising and promotion.[1] Thus, to try to show that the size of the budget will directly affect sales of the product is misleading. A more logical approach would be to examine the impact of specific budgets for each communication tool on the attainment of specific communications objectives for each tool.

2. *Assumption that sales are determined solely by advertising and promotion.* This assumption ignores the remaining elements of the marketing mix—price, product, and distribution—which do contribute to a company's success. Environmental factors may also affect the promotional program, leading the marketing manager to assume the advertising was or was not effective when some other factor may have helped or hindered the accomplishment of the desired objectives.

Sales Response Models   You may have wondered why the sales curve in Figure 8–3 shows sales levelling off even though advertising and promotions efforts continue to increase. The relationship between advertising and sales has been the topic of much research and discussion designed to determine the shape of the response curve.

Almost all advertisers subscribe to one of two models of the advertising/sales response function: the concave-downward function or the S-shaped response curve.

• *The concave-downward function.* After reviewing more than 100 studies of the effects of advertising on sales, Julian Simon and Johan Arndt concluded that the effects of advertising budgets follow the microeconomic law of diminishing returns.[2] That is, as the amount of advertising increases, its incremental value decreases. The logic is that those with the greatest potential to buy will likely act on the first (or earliest) exposures, while those less likely to buy are not likely to change as a result of the advertising. For those who may be potential buyers, each additional ad will supply little or no new information that will affect their decision. Thus, according to the **concave-downward function model,** the effects of advertising quickly begin to diminish, as shown in Figure 8–4A. Budgeting under this model suggests that fewer advertising dollars may be needed to create the optimal influence on sales.

• *The S-shaped response function.* Many advertising managers assume the **S-shaped response curve** (Figure 8–4B), which projects an S-shaped response function to the budget outlay (again measured in sales). Initial outlays of the advertising budget have little impact (as indicated by the essentially flat sales curve in range A). After a certain budget level has been reached (the beginning of range B), advertising and promotional efforts begin to have an effect, as additional increments of expenditures result in increased sales. This incremental gain continues only to a point, however, because at the beginning of range C additional expenditures begin to return little or nothing in the way of sales. This model suggests a small advertising budget is likely to have no impact beyond the sales that may have been generated through other means (for example, word of mouth). At the other extreme, more does not necessarily mean better: Additional dollars spent beyond range B have no additional impact on sales and for the most part can be considered wasted. As with marginal analysis, one would attempt to operate at that point on the curve in area B where the maximum return for the money is attained.

Even though marginal analysis and the sales response curves may not apply directly, they give managers some insight into a theoretical basis of how the budgeting process should work. Some empirical evidence indicates the models may have validity. One study, based on industry experience, has provided support for the S-shaped response curve; the results indicate that a minimum amount of advertising dollars must be spent before there is a noticeable effect on sales.[3] Despite this, it is important to consider other issues.

A weakness in attempting to use sales as a *direct* measure of response to advertising is that various situational factors may have an effect. In one comprehensive study, 20 variables were shown to affect the advertising/sales ratio. Figure 8–5 lists these factors and their relationships.[4] For a product characterized by emotional buying motives, hidden product qualities, and/or a strong basis for differentiation, advertising would have a noticeable impact on sales. Products characterized as large dollar purchases and those in the maturity or decline stages of the product would be less likely to benefit. The study showed that other factors involving the market, customer, costs, and strategies employed have different effects.

The results of this study are interesting but limited, since they relate primarily to the percentage of sales dollars allocated to advertising and the factors influencing these ratios. As we will see later in this chapter, the percentage-of-sales method of budgeting has inherent weaknesses in that the advertising and sales effects may be reversed. So we cannot be sure whether the situation actually led to the advertising/sales relationship or vice versa. Thus, while these factors should be considered in the budget appropriation decision, they should not be the sole determinants of where and when to increase or decrease expenditures.

Managerial Approaches in Budget Setting

The theoretical approaches to establishing the promotional budget are seldom employed. In smaller firms, they may never be used. Instead, a number of methods developed through practice and experience are implemented. This section reviews some of the more traditional methods of setting budgets and the relative advantages

Figure 8–4 Advertising sales/response functions

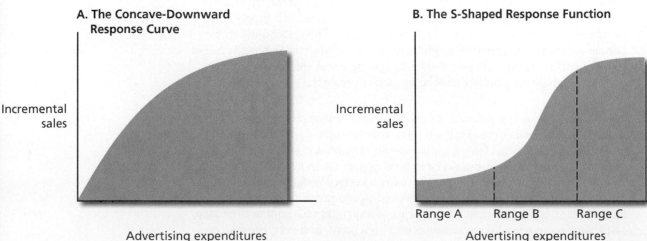

Figure 8–5 Factors influencing advertising budgets

Factor	Relationship of Advertising/Sales	Factor	Relationship of Advertising/Sales
Product Factors		**Customer Factors**	
Basis for differentiation	+	Industrial products users	—
Hidden product qualities	+	Concentration of users	+
Emotional buying motives	+	**Strategy Factors**	
Durability	—	Regional markets	—
Large dollar purchase	—	Early stage of brand life cycle	+
Purchase frequency	Curvilinear	High margins in channels	—
Market Factors		Long channels of distribution	+
Stage of product life cycle		High prices	+
Introductory	+	High quality	+
Growth	+	**Cost Factors**	
Maturity	—	High profit margins	+
Decline	—		
Inelastic demand	+		
Market share	—		
Competition			
Active	+		
Concentrated	+		
Pioneer in market	—		

Note: + relationship means the factor leads to a positive effect of advertising on sales; — relationship indicates little or no effect of advertising on sales.

and disadvantages of each. First, you must understand two things: (1) Many firms employ more than one method, and (2) budgeting approaches vary according to the size and sophistication of the firm. Prior to discussing these approaches, we review a few factors that managers consider as they set the budget.

Factors Influencing the Budget Decision

Market Size The size of the market affects the amount of money invested in promotion. In smaller markets, it is often easier and less expensive to reach the target audience. Too much of an expenditure in these markets will lead to saturation and a lack of effective spending. In larger markets, the target audience may be more dispersed and thus more expensive to reach. These cost issues are explored further in the media tactics section.

Market Potential For a variety of reasons, some markets hold more potential than others. When particular markets hold higher potential, the marketing manager may decide to allocate additional monies to them. Keep in mind that just because a market does not have high sales does not mean it should be ignored. The key is potential—and a market with low sales but high potential may be a candidate for additional appropriations.

Market Share Goals Two recent studies in the *Harvard Business Review* discussed advertising spending with the goal of maintaining and increasing market share.[5] John Jones compared the brand's share of market with its share of advertising voice (the total value of the main media exposure in the product category). Jones classified the brands as "profit taking brands, or underspenders" and "investment brands, those whose share of voice is clearly above their share of market." His study indicated that for those brands with small market shares, profit takers are in the minority; however, as the brands increase their market share, nearly three out of five have a proportionately smaller share of voice.

Jones noted that three factors can be cited to explain this change. First, new brands generally receive higher-than-average advertising support. Second, older, more mature brands are often "milked"—that is, when they reach the maturity stage, advertising support is reduced. Third, there's an advertising economy of scale whereby advertising works harder for well-established brands, so a lower expenditure is required. Jones concluded that for larger brands, it may be possible to reduce advertising expenditures and still maintain market share. Smaller brands, on the other hand, have to continue to maintain a large share of voice.

James Schroer addressed the advertising budget in a situation where the marketer wishes to increase market share. His analysis suggests that marketers should:

- Segment markets, focusing on those markets where competition is weak and/or underspending instead of on a national advertising effort.
- Determine their competitors' cost positions (how long the competition can continue to spend at the current or increased rate).
- Resist the lure of short-term profits that result from ad budget cuts.
- Consider niching strategies as opposed to long-term wars.

Figure 8–6 shows Schroer's suggestions for spending priorities in various markets.

Economies of Scale in Advertising   Some studies have presented evidence that firms and/or brands maintaining a large share of the market have an advantage over smaller competitors and thus can spend less money on advertising and realize a better return.[6] Larger advertisers can maintain advertising shares that are smaller than their market shares because they get better advertising rates, have declining average costs of production, and accrue the advantages of advertising several products jointly. In addition, they are likely to enjoy more favourable time and space positions, cooperation of middlepeople, and favourable publicity. These advantages are known as **economies of scale**.

Reviewing the studies in support of this position and then conducting research over a variety of small package products, Kent Lancaster found that this situation did not hold true and that in fact larger brand share products might actually be at a disadvantage.[7] His results indicated that leading brands spend an average of 2.5 percentage points more than their brand share on advertising. The results of this and other studies suggest there really are no economies of scale to be accrued from the size of the firm or the market share of the brand.[8]

IMC Tools   Direct marketing, the Internet, and other promotional tools are also receiving increased attention and requiring additional budget for marketing communications. The degree to which a firm engages in more tools to achieve its communication objectives also has an impact on a firm's investment in marketing communications. This strategic decision among IMC tools has organization implications that guide the marketing communications investment.

In a review of the literature on how allocation decisions are made between advertising and sales promotion, George Low and Jakki Mohr concluded that organizational factors play an important role in determining how communications dollars are

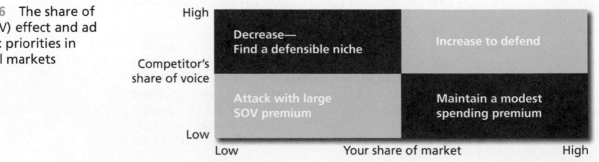

Figure 8–6   The share of voice (SOV) effect and ad spending: priorities in individual markets

spent.[9] The authors note that the following factors influence the allocation decision. These factors vary from one organization to another, and each influences the relative amounts assigned to advertising and promotion:

- The organization's structure—centralized versus decentralized, formalization, and complexity.
- Power and politics in the organizational hierarchy.
- The use of expert opinions (e.g., consultants).
- Characteristics of the decision maker (preferences and experience).
- Approval and negotiation channels.
- Pressure on senior managers to arrive at the optimal budget.

One example of how these factors might influence allocations relates to the level of interaction between marketing and other functional departments, such as accounting and operations. The authors note that the relative importance of advertising versus sales promotion might vary from department to department. Accountants, being dollars-and-cents minded, would argue for the sales impact of promotions, while operations would argue against sales promotions because the sudden surges in demand that might result would throw off production schedules. The marketing department might be influenced by the thinking of either of these groups in making its decision.

Top-Down Approaches   The approaches discussed in this section may be referred to as **top-down approaches** because a budgetary amount is established (usually at an executive level) and then the monies are passed down to the various departments (as shown in Figure 8–7). These budgets are essentially predetermined and have no true theoretical basis. Top-down methods include the affordable method, arbitrary allocation, percentage of sales, competitive parity, and return on investment (ROI).

The Affordable Method   In the **affordable method** (often referred to as the "all-you-can-afford method"), the firm determines the amount to be spent in various areas such as production and operations. Then it allocates what's left to advertising and promotion, considering this to be the amount it can afford. The task to be performed by the advertising/promotions function is not considered, and the likelihood of under- or overspending is high, as no guidelines for measuring the effects of various budgets are established.

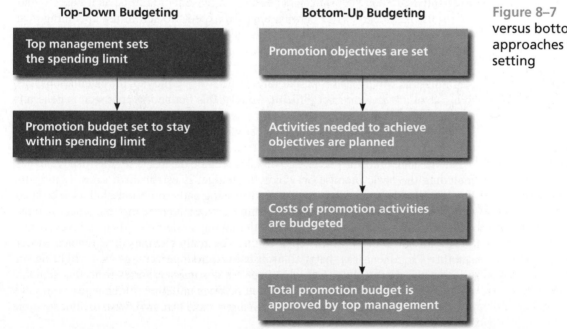

Top-Down Budgeting

- Top management sets the spending limit
- Promotion budget set to stay within spending limit

Bottom-Up Budgeting

- Promotion objectives are set
- Activities needed to achieve objectives are planned
- Costs of promotion activities are budgeted
- Total promotion budget is approved by top management

Figure 8–7   Top-down versus bottom-up approaches to budget setting

Strange as it may seem, this approach is common among small firms. Unfortunately, it is also used in large firms, particularly those that are not marketing-driven and do not understand the role of advertising and promotion. For example, many high-tech firms focus on new product development and engineering and assume that the product, if good enough, will sell itself. In these companies, little money may be left for performing the advertising and promotions tasks.

The logic for this approach stems from "We can't be hurt with this method" thinking. That is, if we know what we can afford and we do not exceed it, we will not get into financial problems. While this may be true in a strictly accounting sense, it does not reflect sound managerial decision making from a marketing perspective. Often this method does not allocate enough money to get the product off the ground and into the market. In terms of the S-shaped sales response model, the firm is operating in range A. Or the firm may be spending more than necessary, operating in range C. When the market gets tough and sales and/or profits begin to fall, this method is likely to lead to budget cuts at a time when the budget should be increased.

Arbitrary Allocation   Perhaps an even weaker method than the affordable method for establishing a budget is **arbitrary allocation,** in which virtually no theoretical basis is considered and the budgetary amount is often set by fiat. That is, the budget is determined by management solely on the basis of what is felt to be necessary. In a discussion of how managers set advertising budgets, Melvin Salveson reported that these decisions may reflect "as much upon the managers' psychological profile as they do economic criteria."[10] While Salveson was referring to larger corporations, the approach is no less common in small firms and nonprofit organizations.

The arbitrary allocation approach has no obvious advantages. No systematic thinking has occurred, no objectives have been budgeted for, and the concept and purpose of advertising and promotion have been largely ignored. Other than the fact that the manager believes some monies must be spent on advertising and promotion and then picks a number, there is no good explanation why this approach continues to be used. Yet budgets continue to be set this way, and our purpose in discussing this method is to point out only that it is used—not recommended.

Percentage of Sales   Perhaps the most commonly used method for budget setting (particularly in large firms) is the **percentage-of-sales method,** in which the advertising and promotions budget is based on sales of the product. Management determines the amount by either (1) taking a percentage of the sales dollars or (2) assigning a fixed amount of the unit product cost to promotion and multiplying this amount by the number of units sold. These two methods are shown in Figure 8–8.

Proponents of the percentage-of-sales method cite a number of advantages. It is financially safe and keeps ad spending within reasonable limits, as it bases spending on the past year's sales or what the firm expects to sell in the upcoming year. Thus, there will be sufficient monies to cover this budget, with increases in sales leading to budget increases and sales decreases resulting in advertising decreases. The percentage-of-sales method is simple, straightforward, and easy to implement. Regardless of which basis—past or future sales—is employed, the calculations used to arrive at a budget are not difficult. Finally, this budgeting approach is generally stable. While the budget may vary with increases and decreases in sales, as long as these changes are not drastic the manager will have a reasonable idea of the parameters of the budget.

At the same time, the percentage-of-sales method has some serious disadvantages, including the basic premise on which the budget is established: sales. Letting the level of sales determine the amount of advertising and promotions dollars to be spent reverses the cause-and-effect relationship between advertising and sales. It treats advertising as an expense associated with making a sale rather than an investment.

Another problem with this approach was actually cited as an advantage earlier: stability. Proponents say that if all firms use a similar percentage, that will bring stability to the marketplace. But what happens if someone varies from this standard percentage? The problem is that this method does not allow for changes in strategy either internally or from competitors. An aggressive firm may wish to allocate more

Method 1: Straight Percentage of Sales		
2000	Total dollar sales	$1,000,000
	Straight % of sales at 10%	$100,000
2001	Advertising budget	$100,000

Method 2: Percentage of Unit Cost		
2000	Cost per bottle to manufacturer	$4.00
	Unit cost allocated to advertising	1.00
2001	Forecasted sales, 100,000 units	
2001	Advertising budget (100,000 × $1)	$100,000

Figure 8–8 Alternative methods for computing percentage of sales for Eve Cologne

monies to the advertising and promotions budget, a strategy that is not possible with a percentage-of-sales method unless the manager is willing to deviate from industry standards.

The percentage-of-sales method of budgeting may result in severe misappropriation of funds. If advertising and promotion have a role to perform in marketing a product, then allocating more monies to advertising will, as shown in the S-shaped curve, generate incremental sales (to a point). If products with low sales have smaller promotion budgets, this will hinder sales progress. At the other extreme, very successful products may have excess budgets, some of which may be better appropriated elsewhere.

The percentage-of-sales method is also difficult to employ for new product introductions. If no sales histories are available, there is no basis for establishing the budget. Projections of future sales may be difficult, particularly if the product is highly innovative and/or has fluctuating sales patterns.

Finally, if the budget is contingent on sales, decreases in sales will lead to decreases in budgets when they most need to be increased. Continuing to cut the advertising and promotion budgets may just add impetus to the downward sales trend (Figure 8–9). On the other hand, some of the more successful companies have allocated additional funds during hard times or downturns in the cycle of sales. Companies that maintain or increase their ad expenditures during recessions achieve increased visibility and higher growth in both sales and market share (compared to those that reduce advertising outlays). For example, Sunkist can attribute at least some of its success in maintaining its strong image to the fact that it has maintained consistent levels of advertising expenditures over 80 years, despite recessions.[11]

A variation on the percentage-of-sales method uses a percentage of projected future sales as a base. This method also uses either a straight percentage of projected sales or a unit cost projection. One advantage of using future sales as a base is that the budget is not based on last year's sales. As the market changes, management must factor the effect of these changes on sales into next year's forecast rather than relying on past data. The resulting budget is more likely to reflect current conditions and be more appropriate. While this appears to be a remedy for some of the problems discussed here, the reality is that problems with forecasting, cyclical growth, and uncontrollable factors limit its effectiveness.

Figure 8–9 Investments pay off in later years

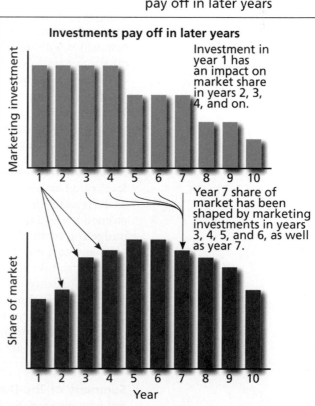

Investments pay off in later years

Investment in year 1 has an impact on market share in years 2, 3, 4, and on.

Year 7 share of market has been shaped by marketing investments in years 3, 4, 5, and 6, as well as year 7.

Competitive Parity   If you asked marketing managers if they ever set their advertising and promotions budgets on the basis of what their competitors allocate, they would probably deny it. Yet if you examined the advertising expenditures of these companies, both as a percentage of sales and in respect to the media where they are allocated, you would see little variation in the percentage-of-sales figures for firms within a given industry. Such results do not happen by chance alone. Companies that provide competitive advertising information, trade associations, and other advertising industry periodicals are sources for competitors' expenditures. Larger corporations often subscribe to services that track media and other communication expenditures. For example, videotape services provide competitors with information, and Nielsen's new technology (discussed in Chapter 9) allows full reporting of all commercials. Smaller companies often use a **clipping service,** which clips competitors' ads from local print media, allowing the company to work backward to determine the cumulative costs of the ads placed.

In the **competitive parity method,** managers establish budget amounts by matching the competition's percentage-of-sales expenditures. The argument is that setting budgets in this fashion takes advantage of the collective wisdom of the industry. It also takes the competition into consideration, which leads to stability in the marketplace by minimizing marketing warfare. If companies know that competitors are unlikely to match their increases in promotional spending, they are less likely to take an aggressive posture to attempt to gain market share. This minimizes unusual or unrealistic ad expenditures.

The competitive parity method has a number of disadvantages, however. For one, it ignores the fact that advertising and promotions are designed to accomplish specific objectives by addressing certain problems and opportunities. Second, it assumes that because firms have similar expenditures, their programs will be equally effective. This assumption ignores the contributions of creative executions and/or media allocations, as well as the success or failure of various promotions. Further, it ignores possible advantages of the firm itself; some companies simply make better products than others.

Also, there is no guarantee that competitors will continue to pursue their existing strategies. Since competitive parity figures are determined by examination of competitors' previous years' promotional expenditures (short of corporate espionage), changes in market emphasis and/or spending may not be recognized until the competition has already established an advantage. Further, there is no guarantee that a competitor will not increase or decrease its own expenditures, regardless of what other companies do. Finally, competitive parity may not avoid promotional wars.

In summary, few firms employ the competitive parity method as a sole means of establishing the promotional budget. This method is typically used in conjunction with the percentage-of-sales or other methods. It is never wise to ignore the competition; managers must always be aware of what competitors are doing. But they should not just emulate them in setting goals and developing strategies.

Return on Investment (ROI)   In the percentage-of-sales method, sales dictate the level of advertising appropriations. But advertising causes sales. In the marginal analysis and S-shaped curve approaches, incremental investments in advertising and promotions lead to increases in sales. The key word here is *investment.* In the **ROI budgeting method,** advertising and promotions are considered investments, like plant and equipment. Thus, the budgetary appropriation (investment) leads to certain returns. Like other aspects of the firm's efforts, advertising and promotion are expected to earn a certain return.

While the ROI method looks good on paper, the reality is that it is rarely possible to assess the returns provided by the promotional effort—at least as long as sales continue to be the basis for evaluation. Thus, while managers are certain to ask how much return they are getting for such expenditures, the question remains unanswered, and ROI remains a virtually unused method of budgeting.

Summary of Top-Down Budgeting Methods   You are probably asking yourself why we even discussed these budgeting methods if they are not recommended for use or have severe disadvantages that limit their effectiveness. But you must understand the various methods used in order to recognize their limitations, especially since these flawed methods are commonly employed by marketers throughout the United States, Europe, and Canada, as demonstrated in the results of a number of research studies shown in Figure 8–10. Tradition and top management's desire for control are probably the major reasons why top-down methods continue to be popular. As shown in Figure 8–10, the use of percentage-of-sales methods and competitive parity remains high. Unfortunately, the affordable method appears to be on the increase. We now turn our attention to two methods in the figure that are considered to be bottom-up approaches.

Bottom-Up Approaches   The major flaw associated with the top-down methods is that these judgmental approaches lead to predetermined budget appropriations often not linked to objectives and the strategies designed to accomplish them. A more effective budgeting strategy would be to consider the firm's communications objectives and budget what is deemed necessary to attain these goals. As noted earlier, the promotional planning model shows the budget decision as an interactive process, with the communications objectives on one hand and the promotional mix alternatives on the other. The idea is to budget so these promotional mix strategies can be implemented to achieve the stated objectives.

Objective and Task Method   It is important that objective setting and budgeting go hand in hand rather than sequentially. It is difficult to establish a budget without specific objectives in mind, and setting objectives without regard to how much money is available makes no sense. For example, a company may wish to create awareness among X percent of its target market. A minimal budget amount will be required to accomplish this goal, and the firm must be willing to spend this amount.

Figure 8–10   Comparison of methods for budgeting

Study	San Augustine and Foley (1975)	Patti and Blasko (1981)	Lancaster and Stern (1983)	Blasko and Patti (1984)	Hung and West (1991)
Population	Large Consumer/ Industrial Advertisers	Large Consumer/ Services Advertisers	Large Consumer Advertisers	Large Industrial Advertisers	Large & Medium Advertisers in U.K., U.S., & Canada
Sample	50/50	54	60	64	100
Methods					
Quantitative models	2/4	51	20	3	NA
Objective and task	6/10	63	80	74	61
Percent anticipated sales	50/28	53	53	16	32
Unit anticipated sales	8/10	22	28	NA	9
Percent past year's sales	14/16	20	20	23	10
Unit past year's sales	6/4	NA	15	2	NA
Affordable	30/26	20	13	33	41
Arbitrary	12/34	4	NA	13	NA
Competitive parity	NA	24	33	21	25
Previous budget	NA	NA	3	NA	NA
Share of voice	NA	NA	5	NA	NA
Others	26/10	NA	12	NA	NA

Note: Figures exceed 100% due to multiple responses. NA = No answer.

The **objective and task method** of budget setting consists of three steps: (1) defining the communications objectives to be accomplished, (2) determining the specific strategies and tasks needed to attain them, and (3) estimating the costs associated with performance of these strategies and tasks. The total budget is based on the accumulation of these costs.

Implementing the objective and task approach is somewhat more involved. The manager must monitor this process throughout and change strategies depending on how well objectives are attained. As shown in Figure 8–11, this process involves several steps:

1. *Isolate objectives.* When the promotional planning model is presented, a company will have two sets of objectives to accomplish—the marketing objectives for the product and the communications objectives. After the former are established, the task involves determining what specific communications objectives will be designed to accomplish these goals. Communications objectives must be specific, attainable, and measurable, as well as time limited.

2. *Determine tasks required.* A number of elements are involved in the strategic plan designed to attain the objectives established. (These strategies constitute the remaining chapters in this text.) These tasks may include advertising in various media, sales promotions, and/or other elements of the promotional mix, each with its own role to perform.

3. *Estimate required expenditures.* Buildup analysis requires determining the estimated costs associated with the tasks developed in the previous step. For example, it involves costs for developing awareness through advertising, trial through sampling, and so forth.

4. *Monitor.* As you will see in Chapter 17 on measuring effectiveness, there are ways to determine how well one is attaining established objectives. Performance should be monitored and evaluated in light of the budget appropriated.

5. *Reevaluate objectives.* Once specific objectives have been attained, monies may be better spent on new goals. Thus, if one has achieved the level of consumer awareness sought, the budget should be altered to stress a higher-order objective such as evaluation or trial.

The major advantage of the objective and task method is that the budget is driven by the objectives to be attained. The managers closest to the marketing effort will have specific strategies and input into the budget-setting process.

The major disadvantage of this method is the difficulty of determining which tasks will be required and the costs associated with each. For example, specifically what tasks are needed to attain awareness among 50 percent of the target market? How much will it cost to perform these tasks? While these decisions are easier to determine for certain objectives—for example, estimating the costs of sampling required to stimulate trial in a defined market area—it is not always possible to

Figure 8–11 The objective and task method

Establish objectives (create awareness of new product among 20 percent of target market)

Determine specific tasks (advertise on market area television and radio stations and in major newspapers)

Estimate costs associated with tasks (television advertising, $575,000; radio advertising, $225,000; newspaper advertising, $175,000)

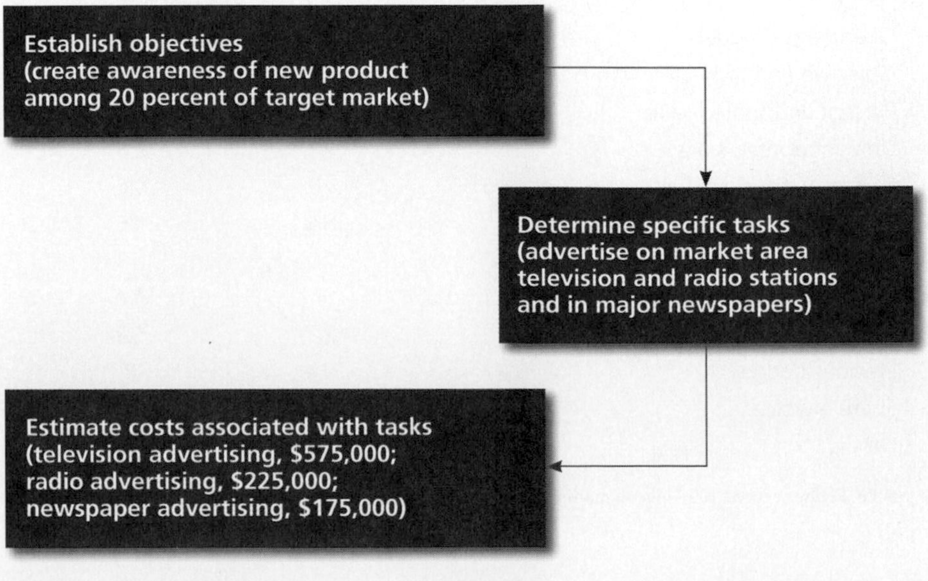

know exactly what is required and/or how much it will cost to complete the job. This process is easier if there is past experience to use as a guide, with either the existing product or a similar one in the same product category. But it is especially difficult for new product introductions. As a result, budget setting using this method is not as easy to perform or as stable as some of the methods discussed earlier. Given this disadvantage, many marketing managers have stayed with those top-down approaches for setting the total expenditure amount.

The objective and task method offers advantages over methods discussed earlier but is more difficult to implement when there is no track record for the product. The following section addresses the problem of budgeting for new product introductions.

Payout Planning The first months of a new product's introduction typically require heavier-than-normal advertising and promotion appropriations to stimulate higher levels of awareness and subsequent trial. After studying more than 40 years of Nielsen figures, James O. Peckham estimated that the average share of advertising to sales ratio necessary to launch a new product successfully is approximately 1.5:2.0.[12] This means that a new entry should be spending at approximately twice the desired market share, as shown in the two examples in Figure 8–12. For example, in the food industry, brand 101 gained a 12.6 percent market share by spending 34 percent of the total advertising dollars in this category. Likewise, brand 401 in the toiletry industry had a 30 percent share of advertising dollars to gain 19.5 percent of sales.

To determine how much to spend, marketers often develop a **payout plan** that determines the investment value of the advertising and promotion appropriation. The

A. New Brands of Food Products

Brand	Average share of advertising	Attained share of sales	Ratio of share of advertising to share of sales
101	34%	12.6%	2.7
102	16	10.0	1.6
103	8	7.6	1.1
104	4	2.6	1.5
105	3	2.1	1.4

B. New Brands of Toiletry Products

Brand	Average share of advertising	Attained share of sales	Ratio of share of advertising to share of sales
401	30%	19.5%	1.5
402	25	16.5	1.5
403	20	16.2	1.2
404	12	9.4	1.3
405	16	8.7	1.8
406	19	7.3	2.6
407	14	7.2	1.9
408	10	6.0	1.7
409	7	6.0	1.2
410	6	5.9	1.0
411	10	5.9	1.7
412	6	5.2	1.2

Figure 8–12 Share of advertising/sales relationship (two-year summary)

Figure 8–13 Example of
three-year payout plan
($ millions)

	Year 1	Year 2	Year 3
Product sales	15.0	35.50	60.75
Profit contribution (@ $0.50/case)	7.5	17.75	30.38
Advertising/promotions	15.0	10.50	8.50
Profit (loss)	(7.5)	7.25	21.88
Cumulative profit (loss)	(7.5)	(0.25)	21.63

basic idea is to project the revenues the product will generate, as well as the costs it will incur, over two to three years. Based on an expected rate of return, the payout plan will assist in determining how much advertising and promotions expenditure will be necessary when the return might be expected. A three-year payout plan is shown in Figure 8–13. The product would lose money in year 1, almost break even in year 2, and finally begin to show substantial profits by the end of year 3.

The advertising and promotion figures are highest in year 1 and decline in years 2 and 3. This appropriation is consistent with Peckham's findings and reflects the additional outlays needed to make as rapid an impact as possible. (Keep in mind that shelf space is limited, and store owners are not likely to wait around for a product to become successful.) The budget also reflects the firm's guidelines for new product expenditures, since companies generally have established deadlines by which the product must begin to show a profit. Finally, keep in mind that building market share may be more difficult than maintaining it—thus the substantial dropoff in expenditures in later years.

While the payout plan is not always perfect, it does guide the manager in establishing the budget. When used in conjunction with the objective and task method, it provides a much more logical approach to budget setting than the top-down approaches previously discussed. Yet on the basis of the studies reported on in Figure 8–10, payout planning does not seem to be a widely employed method.

Summary of Budgeting Methods   There is no universally accepted method of setting a budget figure. Weaknesses in each method may make it unfeasible or inappropriate. As Figure 8–10 shows, the use of the objective and task method continues to increase, whereas less sophisticated methods are declining in favour. More advertisers are also employing the payout planning approach.

In a more recent study of how managers make decisions regarding advertising and promotion budgeting decisions, George Low and Jakki Mohr interviewed 21 managers in eight consumer-product firms. Their research focused on the decision processes and procedures used to set spending levels on the factors that influence the allocation of advertising and promotion dollars.

On the basis of their results, the authors concluded that the budget-setting process is still a perplexing issue to many managers and that institutional pressures led to a greater proportion of dollars being spent on sales promotions than managers would have preferred. In addition, the authors concluded that to successfully develop and implement the budget, managers must (1) employ a comprehensive strategy to guide the process, avoiding the piecemeal approach often employed, (2) develop a strategic planning framework that employs an integrated marketing communications philosophy, (3) build in contingency plans, (4) focus on long-term objectives, and (5) consistently evaluate the effectiveness of programs.[13]

Media Strategy Decisions

Having determined what is to be accomplished, media planners consider how to achieve the media objectives based on the budget. They develop and implement media strategies that consist of five main topics for decision: target audience coverage, media mix, geographic coverage, scheduling, and reach and frequency.

Target Audience Coverage

The media planner determines which target audiences should receive the most media emphasis. Developing media strategies involves matching the most appropriate media to this audience by asking, "Through which media and media vehicles can I best get my message to prospective buyers?" The issue here is to get coverage of the audience, as shown in Figure 8–14. The optimal goal is full audience coverage, shown in the second pie chart. But this is a very optimistic scenario. More realistically, conditions shown in the third and fourth charts are most likely to occur. In the third chart, the coverage of the media does not allow for coverage of the entire audience, leaving some potential customers without exposure to the message. In the fourth chart, the marketer is faced with a problem of overexposure (also called **waste coverage**), in which the media coverage exceeds the targeted audience. If media coverage reaches people who are not sought as buyers and are not potential users, then it is wasted. (This term is used for coverage that reaches people who are not potential buyers and/or users. Consumers may not be part of the intended target audience but may still be considered as potential—for example, those who buy the product as a gift for someone else.)

The goal of the media planner is to extend media coverage to as many of the members of the target audience as possible while minimizing the amount of waste coverage. The situation usually involves trade-offs. Sometimes one has to live with less coverage than desired; other times, the most effective media expose people not sought. In this instance, waste coverage is justified because the media employed are likely to be the most effective means of delivery available and the cost of the waste coverage is exceeded by the value gained from their use.

A variety of factors can assist media planners in making the target audience coverage decision. Some will require primary research, whereas others will be available from published (secondary) sources. This research can show the number of consumers for a particular product category across many demographic variables. We review audience information in Chapters 9, 10, and 11 as each media has its own method.

When examining this data, media planners are often more concerned with the percentage figures and index numbers than with the raw numbers. This is largely due to the fact that the numbers provided may not be specific enough for their needs, or they question the numbers provided because of the methods by which they were collected. Another key reason is that index numbers and percentages provide a comparative view of the market.

Overall, the **index number** is considered a good indicator of the potential of the market. This number is derived from the formula

$$\text{Index} = \frac{\text{Percentage of users in a demographic segment}}{\text{Percentage of population in the same segment}} \times 100$$

An index number over 100 means use of the product is proportionately greater in that segment than in one that is average (100) or less than 100. Depending on their

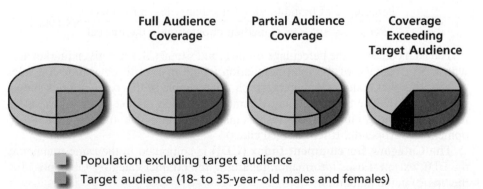

| Full Audience Coverage | Partial Audience Coverage | Coverage Exceeding Target Audience |

Figure 8–14 Marketing coverage possibilities

- Population excluding target audience
- Target audience (18- to 35-year-old males and females)
- Media coverage
- Media overexposure

overall strategy, marketers may wish to use this information to determine which groups are now using the product and target them or to identify a group that is currently using the product less and attempt to develop that segment. While the index is helpful, it should not be used alone. Percentages and product usage figures are also needed to get an accurate picture of the market. Just because the index for a particular segment of the population is very high, that doesn't always mean it is the only attractive segment to target. The high index may be a result of a low denominator (a very small proportion of the population in this segment).

The Media Mix

A wide variety of media and media vehicles are available to advertisers. While it is possible that only one medium and/or vehicle might be employed, it is much more likely that a number of alternatives will be used. The objectives sought, the characteristics of the product or service, the size of the budget, and individual preferences are just some of the factors that determine what combination of media will be used.

As an example, consider a promotional situation in which a product requires a visual demonstration to be communicated effectively. In this case, TV may be the most effective medium. If the promotional strategy calls for coupons to stimulate trial, print media may be necessary. For in-depth information, the Internet may be best.

By employing a media mix, advertisers can add more versatility to their media strategies, since each medium contributes its own distinct advantages. By combining media, marketers can increase coverage, reach, and frequency levels while improving the likelihood of achieving overall communications and marketing goals. In Chapters 9, 10, and 11, you will see that each medium has its own characteristics that make it better or worse for attaining specific communication objectives. Figure 8–15 provides an overall comparison of media and some of the characteristics by which they are evaluated. This is a very general comparison, and the various media options must be analyzed for each situation.

Geographic Coverage

The question of where to promote relates to geographic considerations. The question is, where will the ad dollars be more wisely spent? Should we allocate additional promotional monies to those markets where the brand is already the leader to maintain market share, or does more potential exist in those markets where the firm is not doing as well and there is more room to grow? Perhaps the best answer is that the firm should spend advertising and promotion dollars where they will be the most effective—that is, in those markets where they will achieve the desired objectives. Two useful calculations that markets examine to make this decision are the Brand Development Index and the Category Development Index.

The Brand Development Index (BDI) helps marketers factor the rate of product usage by geographic area into the decision process.

$$\text{BDI} = \frac{\text{Percentage of brand to total Canadian sales in the market}}{\text{Percentage of total Canadian population in the market}} \times 100$$

The BDI compares the percentage of the brand's total sales in a given market area with the percentage of the total population in the market to determine the sales potential for that brand in that market area. An example of this calculation is shown in Figure 8–16. The higher the index number, the more market potential exists. In this case, the index number indicates this market has high potential for brand development (see Appendix B for targeted cities).

The Category Development Index (CDI) is computed in the same manner as the BDI, except it uses information regarding the product category (as opposed to the brand) in the numerator:

$$\text{CDI} = \frac{\text{Percentage of product category total sales in market}}{\text{Percentage of total Canadian population in market}} \times 100$$

Figure 8–15 Media characteristics

Media	Advantages	Disadvantages
Television	Mass coverage High reach Impact of sight, sound, and motion High prestige Low cost per exposure Attention getting Favourable image	Low selectivity Short message life High absolute cost High production costs Clutter
Radio	Local coverage Low cost High frequency Flexible Low production costs Well-segmented audiences	Audio only Clutter Low attention getting Fleeting message
Magazines	Segmentation potential Quality reproduction High information content Longevity Multiple readers	Long lead time for ad placement Visual only Lack of flexibility
Newspapers	High coverage Low cost Short lead time for placing ads Ads can be placed in interest sections Timely (current ads) Reader controls exposure Can be used for coupons	Short life Clutter Low attention-getting capabilities Poor reproduction quality Selective reader exposure
Outdoor	Location specific High repetition Easily noticed	Short exposure time requires short ad Poor image Local restrictions
Direct mail	High selectivity Reader controls exposure High information content Opportunities for repeat exposures	High cost/contact Poor image (junk mail) Clutter
Internet and interactive media	User selects product information User attention and involvement Interactive relationship Direct selling potential Flexible message platform	Limited creative capabilities Websnarl (crowded access) Technology limitations Few valid measurement techniques Limited reach

The CDI provides information on the potential for development of the total product category rather than specific brands. When this information is combined with the BDI, a much more insightful promotional strategy may be developed. One might first look at how well the product category does in a specific market area. In Alberta, for example, the category potential is low (see Figure 8–17). The marketer analyzes the BDI to find how the brand is doing relative to other brands in this area. This

Figure 8–16 Calculating BDI

$$BDI = \frac{\text{Percentage of brand sales in Ontario}}{\text{Percentage of Canadian population in Ontario}} \times 100$$

$$= \frac{50\%}{16\%} \times 100$$

$$= 312$$

Figure 8–17 Using CDI and BDI to determine market potential

$$CDI = \frac{\text{Percentage of product category sales in Alberta}}{\text{Percentage of total Canadian population in Alberta}} \times 100$$

$$= \frac{10\%}{10\%} \times 100$$

$$= 100$$

$$BDI = \frac{\text{Percentage of total brand sales in Alberta}}{\text{Percentage of total Canadian population in Alberta}} \times 100$$

$$= \frac{20\%}{10\%} \times 100$$

$$= 200$$

information can then be used in determining how well a particular product category and a particular brand are performing and figuring what media weight (or quantity of advertising) would be required to gain additional market share, as shown in Figure 8–18.

Scheduling

Obviously, companies would like to keep their advertising in front of consumers at all times as a constant reminder of the product and/or brand name. In reality, this is not possible for a variety of reasons (not the least of which is the budget). Nor is it necessary. The primary objective of *scheduling* is to time promotional efforts so that they will coincide with the highest potential buying times. For some products these times are not easy to identify; for others they are very obvious. Three scheduling methods available to the media planner—continuity, flighting, and pulsing—are shown in Figure 8–19.

Continuity refers to a continuous pattern of advertising, which may mean every day, every week, or every month. The key is that a regular (continuous) pattern is developed without gaps or nonadvertising periods. Such strategies might be used for advertising for food products, laundry detergents, or other products consumed on an ongoing basis without regard for seasonality.

A second method, **flighting,** employs a less regular schedule, with intermittent periods of advertising and nonadvertising. At some time periods there are heavier

Figure 8–18 Using BDI and CDI indexes

	High BDI	Low BDI
High CDI	High market share Good market potential	Low market share Good market potential
Low CDI	High market share Monitor for sales decline	Low market share Poor market potential

High BDI and high CDI	This market usually represents good sales potential for both the product category and the brand.
High BDI and low CDI	The category is not selling well, but the brand is; probably a good market to advertise in but should be monitored for declining sales.
Low BDI and high CDI	The product category shows high potential but the brand is not doing well; the reasons should be determined.
Low BDI and low CDI	Both the product category and the brand are doing poorly; not likely to be a good place for advertising.

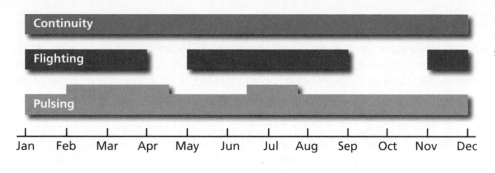

Figure 8–19 Three methods of promotional scheduling

promotional expenditures, and at others there may be no advertising. Many banks, for example, spend no money on advertising in the summer but maintain advertising throughout the rest of the year. Snow skis are advertised heavily between October and April; less in May, August, and September; and not at all in June and July.

Pulsing is actually a combination of the first two methods. In a pulsing strategy, continuity is maintained, but at certain times promotional efforts are stepped up. In the automobile industry, advertising continues throughout the year but may increase in April (income-tax refund time), September (when new models are brought out), and the end of the model year. The scheduling strategy depends on the objectives, buying cycles, and the budget, among other factors. There are certain advantages and disadvantages to each scheduling method, as shown in Figure 8–20. One very recent and comprehensive study (acclaimed by many in the TV research community as "the most comprehensive study ever to shed light on scheduling") indicates that continuity is more effective than flighting. On the basis of the idea that it is important to get exposure to the message as close as possible to when the consumer is going to make the purchase, the study concludes that advertisers should continue weekly schedules as long as possible.[14] The key here may be the "as long as possible" qualification. Given a significant budget, continuity may be more of an option than it is for those with more limited budgets.

Figure 8–20 Characteristics of scheduling methods

Continuity	
Advantages	Serves as a constant reminder to the consumer
	Covers the entire buying cycle
	Allows for media priorities (quantity discounts, preferred locations, etc.)
Disadvantages	Higher costs
	Potential for overexposure
	Limited media allocation possible

Flighting	
Advantages	Cost efficiency of advertising only during purchase cycles
	May allow for inclusion of more than one medium or vehicle with limited budgets
Disadvantages	Weighting may offer more exposure and advantage over competitors
	Increased likelihood of wearout
	Lack of awareness, interest, retention of promotional message during nonscheduled times
	Vulnerability to competitive efforts during nonscheduled periods

Pulsing	
Advantages	All of the same as the previous two methods
Disadvantages	Not required for seasonal products (or other cyclical products)

Reach versus Frequency

Since advertisers have a variety of objectives and face budget constraints, they usually must trade off reach and frequency. They must decide whether to have the message be seen or heard by more people (reach) or by fewer people more often (frequency).

How Much Reach Is Necessary? A universal communication objective is awareness of the product and/or brand. The more consumers are aware, the more they are likely to consider the brand throughout the decision-making process. Achieving awareness requires reach—that is, exposing potential buyers to the message. New brands or products need a very high level of reach, since the objective is to make all potential buyers aware of the new entry. High reach is also desired at later purchase-decision stages. For example, a promotional strategy might use cents-off coupons or free samples to encourage brand trial. An objective of the marketer is to reach a larger number of people with these samples, in an attempt to make them learn of the product, try it, and develop favourable attitudes toward it. (In turn, these attitudes may lead to purchase.)

The problem arises because there is no known way of determining how much reach is required to achieve levels of awareness, attitude change, or buying intentions, nor can we be sure an ad placed in a vehicle will actually reach the intended audience. (There has been some research on the first problem, which will be discussed in the section below on effective reach.)

If you buy advertising time on a popular news program, will everyone who is tuned to the program see the ad? No. Many viewers will leave the room, be distracted during the commercial, and so on, as shown in Figure 8–21 (which also provides a good example of the difference between reach and coverage). If I expose everyone in my target audience to the message once, will this be sufficient to create a 100 percent level of awareness? The answer again is no. This leads to the next question: What frequency of exposure is necessary for the ad to be seen and to have a communication effect?

What Frequency Level Is Needed? With respect to media planning, *frequency* carries a slightly different meaning. (Remember when we said one of the problems in media planning is that terms often take on different meanings?) Here frequency is the number of times one is exposed to the media vehicle, not necessar-

Figure 8–21 Who's still there to watch the ads?

How many viewers actually watch a commercial? R. D. Percy & Co. reports that its advanced people meters, equipped with heat sensors that detect viewers present, indicate that spots retain, on average, 82 percent of the average-minute ratings for the quarter hour. During early morning news programs, "commercial efficiency" (as Percy calls it) is lower because so many people are bustling about, out of the room (blue), but the rate rises at night.

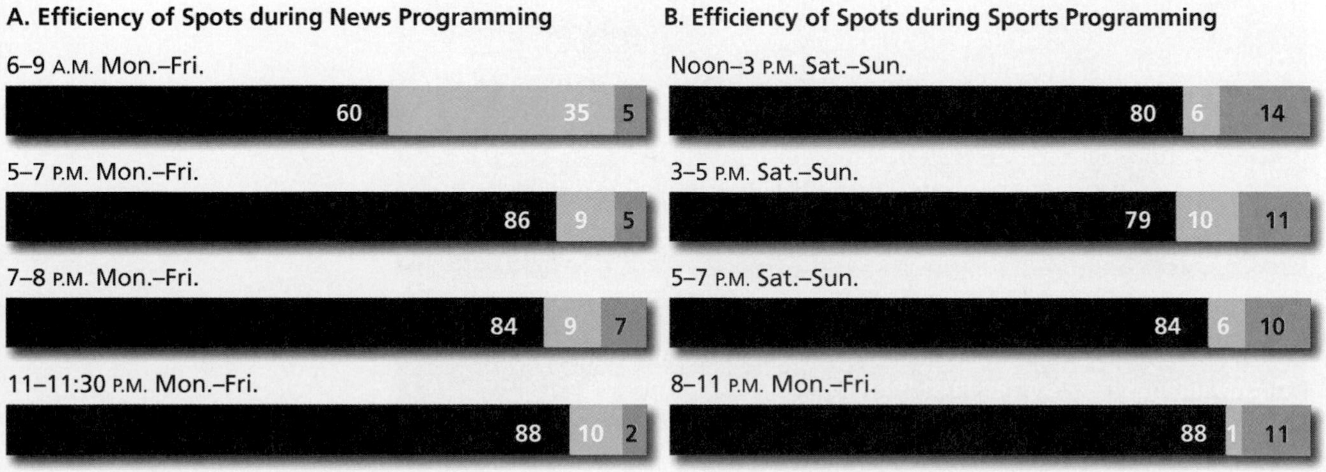

A. Efficiency of Spots during News Programming

6–9 A.M. Mon.–Fri. — 60 | 35 | 5

5–7 P.M. Mon.–Fri. — 86 | 9 | 5

7–8 P.M. Mon.–Fri. — 84 | 9 | 7

11–11:30 P.M. Mon.–Fri. — 88 | 10 | 2

B. Efficiency of Spots during Sports Programming

Noon–3 P.M. Sat.–Sun. — 80 | 6 | 14

3–5 P.M. Sat.–Sun. — 79 | 10 | 11

5–7 P.M. Sat.–Sun. — 84 | 6 | 10

8–11 P.M. Mon.–Fri. — 88 | 1 | 11

ily to the ad itself. While one study has estimated the actual audience for a commercial may be as much as 30 percent lower than that for the program, not all researchers agree.[15] Figure 8–21 demonstrates that depending on the program, this number may range from 12 percent to 40 percent.

Most advertisers do agree that a 1:1 exposure ratio does not exist. So while your ad may be placed in a certain vehicle, the fact that a consumer has been exposed to that vehicle does not ensure that your ad has been seen. As a result, the frequency level expressed in the media plan overstates the actual level of exposure to the ad. This overstatement has led some media buyers to refer to the reach of the media vehicle as "opportunities to see" an ad rather than actual exposure to it.

Because the advertiser has no sure way of knowing whether exposure to a vehicle results in exposure to the ad, the media and advertisers have adopted a compromise: One exposure to the vehicle constitutes reach, given that this exposure must occur for the viewer even to have an opportunity to see the ad. Thus, the exposure figure is used to calculate reach and frequency levels. But this compromise does not help determine the frequency required to make an impact. The creativity of the ad, the involvement of the receiver, noise, and many other intervening factors confound any attempts to make a precise determination.

At this point, you may be thinking, "If nobody knows this stuff, how do they make these decisions?" That's a good question, and the truth is that the decisions are not always made on hard data. Says Joseph Ostrow, executive vice president/director of communications services with Young and Rubicam, "Establishing frequency goals for an advertising campaign is a mix of art and science but with a definite bias toward art."[16] Let us first examine the process involved in setting reach and frequency objectives and then discuss the logic of each.

Establishing Reach and Frequency Levels   It is possible to be exposed to more than one media vehicle with an ad, resulting in repetition (frequency). If one ad is placed on one TV show one time, the number of people exposed is the reach. If the ad is placed on two shows, the total number exposed once is **unduplicated reach.** Some people will see the ad twice. The reach of the two shows, as depicted in Figure 8–22, includes a number of people who were reached by both shows (C). This overlap is referred to as **duplicated reach.**

Both unduplicated and duplicated reach figures are important. Unduplicated reach indicates potential new exposures, while duplicated reach provides an estimate of frequency. Most media buys include both forms of reach. Let us consider an example.

A. Reach of One TV Program

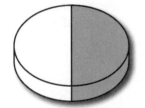

Total market audience reached

B. Reach of Two Programs

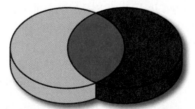

Total market audience reached

C. Duplicated Reach

Total market reached
with both shows

D. Unduplicated Reach

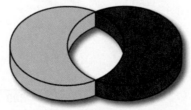

Total reach less
duplicated reach

Figure 8–22   Representation of reach and frequency

A measure of potential reach in the broadcast industry is the TV (or radio) **program rating.** This number is expressed as a percentage. For an estimate of the total number of homes reached, multiply this percentage times the number of homes with TV sets. For example, if there are 12 million homes with TV sets in Canada and the program has a rating of 30, then the calculation is 0.30 times 12, or 3.6 million homes. (We go into much more detail on ratings and other broadcast terms in Chapter 9.)

Using Gross Ratings Points   The media buyer typically uses a numerical indicator to know how many potential audience members may be exposed to a series of commercials. A summary measure that combines the program rating and the average number of times the home is reached during this period (frequency of exposure) is a commonly used reference point known as **gross ratings points (GRP):**

$$GRP = Reach \times Frequency$$

GRPs are based on the total audience the media schedule may reach; they use a duplicated reach estimate. GRPs can be calculated for the total population aged 2+, Adults 18+, Adults 18–34, Adults 18–49, or several other measured demographic groups.

The advertiser must ask: How many GRPs are needed to attain a certain reach? How do these GRPs translate into effective reach? For example, how many GRPs must one purchase to attain an unduplicated reach of 50 percent, and what frequency of exposure will this schedule deliver? The following example may help you to understand how this process works.

First you must know what these ratings points represent. A purchase of 100 GRPs could mean 100 percent of the market is exposed once or 50 percent of the market is exposed twice or 25 percent of the market is exposed four times, and so on. As you can see, this information must be more specific for the marketer to use it effectively. To know how many GRPs are necessary, the manager needs to know how many members of the intended audience the schedule actually reaches. The chart in Figure 8–23 helps make this determination.

In Figure 8–23, a purchase of 100 GRPs on one network would yield an estimated reach of 32 percent of the total households in the target audience. This figure would climb to 37.2 percent if two networks were used and 44.5 percent with three. Working backward through the formula for GRPs, the estimate of frequency of exposure— 3.125, 2.688, and 2.247, respectively—demonstrates the trade-off between reach and frequency. This naturally leads to the question of how much frequency is required.

Figure 8–24 summarizes the effects that can be expected at different levels of exposure, on the basis of research in this area. A number of factors may be operating, and direct relationships may be difficult to establish.[17] In addition to the results shown in Figure 8–24, Joseph Ostrow has shown that while the number of repetitions increases awareness rapidly, it has much less impact on attitudinal and behavioural responses.[18]

Figure 8–23 Estimates of reach for network GRPs

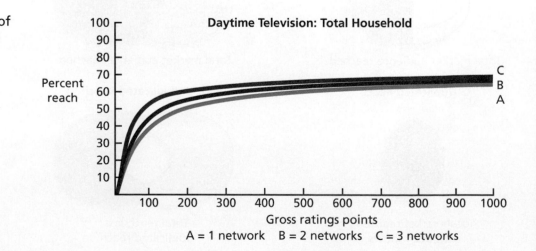

Figure 8–24   The effects of reach and frequency

1. One exposure of an ad to a target group within a purchase cycle has little or no effect in most circumstances.

2. Since one exposure is usually ineffective, the central goal of productive media planning should be to enhance frequency rather than reach.

3. The evidence suggests strongly that an exposure frequency of two within a purchase cycle is an effective level.

4. Beyond three exposures within a brand purchase cycle or over a period of four or even eight weeks, increasing frequency continues to build advertising effectiveness at a decreasing rate but with no evidence of decline.

5. Although there are general principles with respect to frequency of exposure and its relationship to advertising effectiveness, differential effects by brand are equally important.

6. Nothing we have seen suggests that frequency response principles or generalizations vary by medium.

7. The data strongly suggest that wearout is not a function of too much frequency; it is more of a creative or copy problem.

Determining Effective Reach   Since marketers have budget constraints, they must decide whether to increase reach at the expense of frequency or increase the frequency of exposure but to a smaller audience. A number of factors influence this decision. For example, a new product or brand introduction will attempt to maximize reach, particularly unduplicated reach, to create awareness in as many people as possible as quickly as possible. At the same time, for a high-involvement product or one whose benefits are not obvious, a certain level of frequency is needed to achieve effective reach.

Effective reach represents the percentage of a vehicle's audience reached at each effective frequency increment. This concept is based on the assumption that one exposure to an ad may not be enough to convey the desired message. As we saw earlier, no one knows the exact number of exposures necessary for an ad to make an impact, although advertisers have settled on three as the minimum. Effective reach (exposure) is shown in the shaded area in Figure 8–25 in the range of 3 to 10 exposures. Fewer than 3 exposures is considered insufficient reach, while more than 10 is considered overexposure and thus ineffective reach. This exposure level is no guarantee of effective communication; different messages may require more or fewer exposures. For example, Jack Myers, president of Myers Reports, argues that the three-exposure theory was valid in the 1970s when consumers were exposed to approximately 1,000 ads per day. Now that they are exposed to 3,000 to 5,000 per day, three exposures may not be enough. Adding in the fragmentation of television,

Figure 8–25   Graph of effective reach

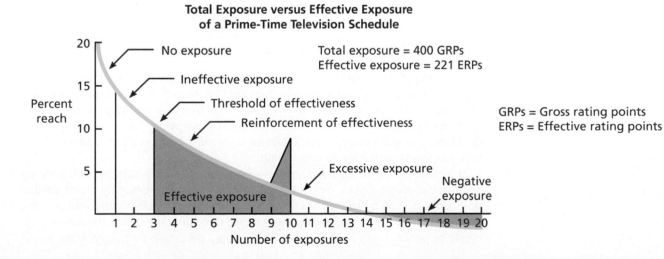

Total Exposure versus Effective Exposure of a Prime-Time Television Schedule

Total exposure = 400 GRPs
Effective exposure = 221 ERPs

GRPs = Gross rating points
ERPs = Effective rating points

the proliferation of magazines, and the advent of a variety of alternative media leads Myers to believe that 12 exposures may be the *minimum* level of frequency required. Also, Jim Surmanek, vice president of International Communications Group, contends that the complexity of the message, message length, and recency of exposure also impact this figure.[19]

Since they do not know how many times the viewer will actually be exposed, advertisers typically purchase GRPs that lead to more than three exposures to increase the likelihood of effective reach and frequency.

Determining effective reach is further complicated by the fact that when calculating GRPs, advertisers use a figure that they call **average frequency,** or the average number of times the target audience reached by a media schedule is exposed to the vehicle over a specified period. The problem with this figure is revealed in the following scenario:

Consider a media buy in which:

50 percent of audience is reached 1 time.

30 percent of audience is reached 5 times.

20 percent of audience is reached 10 times.

Average frequency = 4

In this media buy, the average frequency is 4, which is slightly more than the number established as effective. Yet a full 50 percent of the audience receives only one exposure. Thus, the average frequency number can be misleading, and using it to calculate GRPs might result in underexposing the audience.

Although GRPs have their problems, they can provide useful information to the marketer. A certain level of GRPs is necessary to achieve awareness, and increases in GRPs are likely to lead to more exposures and/or more repetitions—both of which are necessary to have an effect on higher-order objectives. Perhaps the best advice for purchasing GRPs is offered by Ostrow, who recommends the following strategies:[20]

1. Instead of using average frequency, the marketer should decide what minimum frequency goal is needed to reach the advertising objectives effectively and then maximize reach at that frequency level.

2. To determine effective frequency, one must consider marketing factors, message factors, and media factors. (See Figure 8–26.)

In summary, the reach-versus-frequency decision, while critical, is very difficult to make. A number of factors must be considered, and concrete rules do not always apply. The decision is often more of an art than a science.

Media Tactics Decisions

Once the initial media strategy has been determined, the marketer addresses three media tactics decisions: media class and vehicle, budget adjustments, and blocking chart.

Media Class and Vehicle

The context of the medium in which the ad is placed may also affect viewers' perceptions. A specific creative strategy may require certain media. Because TV provides both sight and sound, it may be more effective in generating emotions than other media; magazines may create different perceptions from newspapers. In developing a media strategy, marketers must consider both creativity and mood factors. Let us examine each in more detail.

It is possible to increase the success of a product significantly through a strong creative campaign. But to implement this creativity, you must employ a medium that will support such a strategy. Kodak and McDonald's, among many others, have effectively used TV to create emotional appeals. In some situations, the media strategy to be pursued may be the driving force behind the creative strategy, as the media

Figure 8–26 Factors important in determining frequency levels

Marketing Factors

- *Brand history.* Is the brand new or established? New brands generally require higher frequency levels.
- *Brand share.* An inverse relationship exists between brand share and frequency. The higher the brand share, the lower the frequency level required.
- *Brand loyalty.* An inverse relationship exists between loyalty and frequency. The higher the loyalty, the lower the frequency level required.
- *Purchase cycles.* Shorter purchasing cycles require higher frequency levels to maintain top-of-mind awareness.
- *Usage cycle.* Products used daily or more often need to be replaced quickly, so a higher level of frequency is desired.
- *Competitive share of voice.* Higher frequency levels are required when a lot of competitive noise exists and when the goal is to meet or beat competitors.
- *Target group.* The ability of the target group to learn and to retain messages has a direct effect on frequency.

Message or Creative Factors

- *Message complexity.* The simpler the message, the less frequency required.
- *Message uniqueness.* The more unique the message, the lower the frequency level required.
- *New versus continuing campaigns.* New campaigns require higher levels of frequency to register the message.
- *Image versus product sell.* Creating an image requires higher levels of frequency than does a specific product sell.
- *Message variation.* A single message requires less frequency; a variety of messages requires more.
- *Wearout.* Higher frequency may lead to wearout. This effect must be tracked and used to evaluate frequency levels.
- *Advertising units.* Larger units of advertising require less frequency than smaller ones to get the message across.

Media Factors

- *Clutter.* The more advertising that appears in the media used, the more frequency is needed to break through the clutter.
- *Editorial environment.* The more consistent the ad is with the editorial environment, the less frequency is needed.
- *Attentiveness.* The higher the level of attention achieved by the media vehicle, the less frequency is required. Low-attention-getting media require more repetitions.
- *Scheduling.* Continuous scheduling requires less frequency than does flighting or pulsing.
- *Number of media used.* The fewer media used, the lower the level of frequency required.
- *Repeat exposures.* Media that allow for more repeat exposures (for example, monthly magazines) require less frequency.

and creative departments work closely together to achieve the greatest impact with the audience of the specific media.

Certain media enhance the creativity of a message because they create a mood that carries over to the communication. For example, think about the moods created by the following magazines: *Gourmet, Skiing, Travel,* and *House Beautiful.* Each of these special-interest vehicles puts the reader in a particular mood. The promotion of fine wines, ski boots, luggage, and home products is enhanced by this mood. What different images might be created for your product if you advertised it in the following media?

The New York Times versus the *National Enquirer*

Architectural Digest versus *Reader's Digest*

A highly rated prime-time TV show versus an old rerun

The message may require a specific medium and a certain media vehicle to achieve its objectives. Likewise, certain media and vehicles have images that may carry over to the perceptions of messages placed within them.

Budget Adjustments

One of the more important decisions in the development of media strategy is cost estimating. The value of any strategy can be determined by how well it delivers the message to the audience with the lowest cost and the least waste. We have already explored a number of factors, such as reach, frequency, and availability, that affect this decision. The marketer tries to arrive at the optimal delivery by balancing cost with each of these. As the following discussion shows, understanding cost figures may not be as easy as it seems.

Advertising and promotional costs can be categorized in two ways. The **absolute cost** of the medium or vehicle is the actual total cost required to place the message. For example, a full-page four-colour ad in *Chatelaine* magazine costs about $42,000. **Relative cost** refers to the relationship between the price paid for advertising time or space and the size of the audience delivered; it is used to compare media vehicles. Relative costs are important because the manager must try to optimize audience delivery within budget constraints. Since a number of alternatives are available for delivering the message, the advertiser must evaluate the relative costs associated with these choices. The way media costs are provided and problems in comparing these costs across media often make such evaluations difficult.

Determining Relative Costs of Media   To evaluate alternatives, advertisers must compare the relative costs of media as well as vehicles within these media. Unfortunately, the broadcast, print, and out-of-home media do not always provide the same cost breakdowns, nor necessarily do vehicles within the print media. Following are the cost bases used:

1. **Cost per thousand (CPM).** For years the magazine industry has provided cost breakdowns on the basis of cost per thousand people reached. The formula for this computation is

$$\text{CPM} = \frac{\text{Cost of ad space (absolute cost)}}{\text{Circulation}} \times 1,000$$

Figure 8–27 provides an example of this computation for two vehicles in the same medium—*Canadian Living* and *Chatelaine*—and shows that (all other things being equal) *Canadian Living* is a more cost-effective buy. (We will come back to "all other things being equal" in a moment.)

2. **Cost per ratings point (CPRP).** The broadcast media provide a different comparative cost figure, referred to as cost per ratings point or *cost per point (CPP)*, based on the following formula:

$$\text{CPRP} = \frac{\text{Cost of commercial time}}{\text{Program rating}}$$

An example of this calculation for a spot ad in a local TV market is shown in Figure 8–28. It indicates that *ER* would be more cost-effective than *Who Wants to be a Millionaire*.

3. **Daily inch rate.** Like magazines, newspapers now use the cost-per-thousand formula discussed earlier to determine relative costs. As shown in Figure 8–29, the

	Canadian Living	Chatelaine
Per-page cost	$30,935	$41,750
Circulation	542,815	717,249
Calculation of CPM	$\dfrac{\$30,935 \times 1,000}{542,815}$	$\dfrac{\$41,750 \times 1,000}{717,249}$
CPM	$56.99	$58.21

Figure 8–27 Cost per thousand computations: *Canadian Living* versus *Chatelaine*

	Who Wants to Be a Millionaire	ER
Cost per spot ad	$3,500	$4,000
Rating	11	15
Reach (households)	109,000	135,000
Calculation	$3,500/11	$4,000/15
CPRP (CPP)	$318.18	$266.67

Figure 8–28 Comparison of cost per ratings point: *Who Wants to Be a Millionaire* versus *ER* in a local TV market

National Post costs significantly more to advertise in than does the *Globe and Mail* (again, all other things being equal).

As you can see, it is difficult to make comparisons across various media. What is the broadcast equivalent of cost per thousand? In an attempt to standardize relative costing procedures, the broadcast and newspaper media have begun to provide costs per thousand, using the following formulas:

Television: $\dfrac{\text{Cost of 1 unit of time} \times 1,000}{\text{Program rating}}$ Newspapers: $\dfrac{\text{Cost of ad space} \times 1,000}{\text{Circulation}}$

While the comparison of media on a cost-per-thousand basis is important, inter-media comparisons can be misleading. The ability of TV to provide both sight and sound, the longevity of magazines, and other characteristics of each medium make direct comparisons difficult. The media planner should use the cost-per-thousand numbers but must also consider the specific characteristics of each medium and each media vehicle in the decision.

The cost per thousand may overestimate or underestimate the actual cost effectiveness. Consider a situation where some waste coverage is inevitable because the circulation exceeds the target audience. If the people reached by this message are not potential buyers of the product, then having to pay to reach them results in too low a cost per thousand, as shown in scenario A of Figure 8–30. We must use the potential reach to the target audience—the destination sought—rather than the over-all circulation figure. A medium with a much higher cost per thousand may be a wiser buy if it is reaching more potential receivers. (Most media buyers rely on

	Globe and Mail	National Post
Cost per page	$50,850	$45,993
Circulation	363,058	311,343
Calculation	$CPM = \dfrac{\text{Page cost} \times 1,000}{\text{Circulation}}$	
	$= \dfrac{\$50,850 \times 1,000}{363,058}$	$\dfrac{\$45,993 \times 1,000}{311,343}$
	$140.06	$147.72

Figure 8–29 Comparative costs in newspaper advertising

Figure 8–30 Cost per thousand estimates

Scenario A: Overestimation of Efficiency

Target audience	18–49
Magazine circulation	400,000
Circulation to target audience	65% (260,000)
Cost per page	$15,600

$$\text{CPM} = \frac{\$15,600 \times 1,000}{400,000} = \$39$$

$$\text{CPM (actual target audience)} = \frac{\$15,600 \times 1,000}{260,000} = \$60$$

Scenario B: Underestimation of Efficiency

Target audience	All age groups, male and female
Magazine circulation	400,000
Cost per page	$15,600
Pass-along rate	3

$$\text{CPM (based on readers per copy)} = \frac{\text{Page cost} \times 1,000}{260,000 + 3(260,000)} = \frac{\$15,600 \times 1,000}{1,040,000}$$

$$= \$15.00$$

*Assuming pass-along was valid.

target CPM (TCPM), which calculates CPMs based on the target audience, not the overall audience.)

CPM may also underestimate cost efficiency. Magazine advertising space sellers have argued for years that because more than one person may read an issue, the actual reach is underestimated. They want to use the number of **readers per copy** as the true circulation. This would include a **pass-along rate,** estimating the number of people who read the magazine without buying it. Scenario B in Figure 8–30 shows how this underestimates cost efficiency. Consider a family in which a father, mother, and two teenagers read each issue of *Maclean's*. While the circulation figure includes only one magazine, in reality there are four potential exposures in these households, increasing the total reach.

While the number of readers per copy makes intuitive sense, it has the potential to be extremely inaccurate. The actual number of times the magazine changes hands is difficult to determine. While research is conducted, pass-along estimates are very subjective and using them to estimate reach is speculative. These figures are regularly provided by the media, but managers are selective about using them. At the same time, the art of media buying enters, for many magazines' managers have a good idea how much greater the reach is than their circulation figures provided.

In addition to the potential for over- or underestimation of cost efficiencies, CPMs are limited in that they make only *quantitative* estimates of the value of media. While they may be good for comparing very similar vehicles, they are less valuable in making intermedia comparisons. We have already noted some differences among media that preclude direct comparisons.

Blocking Chart

The media planning process typically concludes with a blocking chart. The **blocking chart** summarizes many of the media strategy and media tactics decisions made thus far, and includes extensive implementation details that guide the media buyers as they attempt to achieve the media objectives.

Cereal Makers Change Objectives and Slash Budgets—without Much Success

A variety of factors can account for changes in the advertising and promotional budgets companies establish. One of the most common of these is a drop in sales. Take the cereal industry for example. In 1996, when Post Cereal found itself losing market share to the number 1 and 2 companies—Kellogg and General Mills, respectively—it tried to bring consumers back by slashing prices on its 22 cereal brands by an average of 20 percent (about a dollar). Kellogg immediately followed suit, as did General Mills (which had already announced a smaller price cut two years earlier).

How did these companies finance the lower prices? One way was by reducing advertising and promotional spending. As cereal prices continued to climb faster than the grocery price index in almost every year since 1983, much of the revenue was used to fund the advertising and promotions campaigns. (One estimate was that $1.02 of a $3.39 box of Kellogg's Corn Flakes went to advertising.) Once the revenues were reduced, the expenditures were reduced. Judann Pollack noted that if the cereal manufacturers maintained their price cuts for a year, advertising and promotional spending would decrease by $70 million (from $353 million) at Kellogg and $40 million (from $203 million) at Post.

But isn't it counterintuitive to decrease advertising and promotional spending when sales go down? Post didn't think so. The cuts were an attempt to make the name brands more price-competitive with store brands, which had experienced a 7 percent gain in market share from 1990 to 1997, due in part to the fact that they cost about a third as much as the Post and Kellogg offerings. Post attempted to follow the success its parent brand, Philip Morris, had when it employed the same strategy with Marlboro cigarettes. Brand managers considered the cuts a "return to rational marketing,"

noting that in the past price increases were often offset by heavy couponing and promotional incentives offered to dealers. These programs would be the first to feel the impact. Advertising would also feel it. Media spending on Kellogg's Frosted Flakes (over $51 million) and Frosted Mini-Wheats (approximately $49 million) also saw reductions.

Thomas Knowlton, Kellogg's North America president, claimed that the advertising and promotional spending cuts would be a short-term strategy. He said that with the price cuts, "we can't afford advertising that isn't working. We are going to be more demanding with our brands, and only proven ad campaigns will get full funding." More testing of ads and media would take place to help determine what was and was not working, said Knowlton.

So now, with the vision of hindsight, how did the strategy work? In the fall of 1998, Kellogg's announced a major layoff, and the chiefs of the North American and European Divisions quit. Earnings missed their targets in the previous two quarters of that year, and stock was down 30 percent for the year. Kellogg's share continued to fall, experiencing an 11 percent drop in the first half of the year and falling below General Mills in 1999. The cereal price cuts not only cut profits but, over recent years, resulted in $1.5 billion less in advertising outlays. A change in advertising agencies was initiated in the early fall, with six additional agencies asked to compete.

Information Resources, Inc., a research company that tracks sales using scanner data, announced that in the six-month period following the price cuts, Post's volume also fell, by 2.1 percent. Tim Callahan, general manager of cereals at Kraft (the parent company of Post Cereals), disagreed with these numbers, arguing that the strategy was a success and noting that other "intangibles" were not taken into consideration. Looking at these numbers he might have problems finding someone to agree with him.

Sources: "General Mills Outsells Kellogg's Cereals," *TulsaWorld*, Tulsa, OK, December 30, 1999, p. 2; Judann Pollack, "Price Cuts Unsettling to Cereal Business," *Advertising Age*, September 28, 1998, p. 510; "Kellogg Marketing Strategies under Revision," *PR Newswire*, September 4, 1998, p. 1087; John Greenwald, "Cereal Showdown," *Time*, April 29, 1996, pp. 60–61; Judann Pollack, "Cereals to Pare Ad Plans," *Advertising Age*, June 24, 1996, p. 1; Rance Crain, "Cereals Shouldn't Squeeze Ad Bucks," *Advertising Age*, July 1, 1996, p. 15.

A blocking chart is typically formatted according to some type of calendar. While it is often done on a weekly basis, a firm with limited communications may organize it monthly. On the other hand, a firm with extensive communications may produce a blocking chart on a daily basis for all or critical parts of its annual media plan. For example, if a firm launches a new product, daily communications during the first few weeks can be critical and specific media exposure is planned in minute detail.

A synopsis of the media choice decisions with respect to television, print, and out-of-home media may also be contained in the blocking chart. In this age of IMC, the blocking chart can also contain elements of other communication tools such as marketing events, public relations, or direct response tools. In all likelihood, the blocking chart will break these media choices down by different vehicles and different geographic markets.

Another key detail of the blocking chart is showing the relative weight of media expenditures. For example, it could illustrate the number of GRPs per week for each city. Related to this is a clear indication of the reach and frequency of each media decision.

Because the blocking chart concludes the media planning process, the media expenditures have to be included either in summary form or accompanying the blocking chart. This information allows managers to assess the quality of the media plan and to determine if any adjustments need to be made during the planning time frame.

While we have briefly highlighted the nature of a blocking chart, it may in fact be more than one chart. If a firm is using multiple media across many months and geographic markets, it may have one summary chart and other supporting charts that break the information down into more readable and action-oriented subsections. Remember that a blocking chart is also a communication tool that has to be organized and presented so that all participants are familiar with all decisions.

Summary

The media strategy must be designed to supplement and support the overall marketing and communications objectives. The objectives of this plan are designed to deliver the message the program has developed. Theoretical methods for determining the media budget have some major problems. Economic models are limited, often try to demonstrate the effects on sales directly, and ignore other elements of the marketing mix. Some of the methods discussed have no theoretical basis and ignore the roles advertising and promotion are meant to perform.

One possible way to improve the budget appropriation is to tie the measures of effectiveness to communications objectives rather than to the broader-based marketing objectives. Using the objective and task approach with communications objectives may not be the ultimate solution to the budgeting problem, but it is an improvement over the top-down methods. Marketers often find it advantageous to employ a combination of methods.

The basic task involved in the development of media strategy is to determine the best matching of media to the target audience, given the constraints of the budget. The media planner attempts to balance reach and frequency and to deliver the message to the intended audience with a minimum of waste coverage. At the same time, a number of additional factors affect the media decision. Media strategy development has been called more of an art than a science because while many quantitative data are available, the planner also relies on creativity and nonquantifiable factors.

This chapter discussed many media strategy decisions, including developing a proper media mix, determining target audience, geographic coverage, scheduling, and balancing reach and frequency. A summary chart of advantages and disadvantages of various media was provided. The chapter also looked at key media tactics decisions that fine-tune the media strategy.

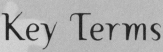

Key Terms

Discussion Questions

1. Using the BDI and CDI indices, explain the least desirable market situation for marketers. Provide an example. Then do the same for the most desirable situation.

2. Media planning involves a tradeoff between reach and frequency. Explain what this means and give examples of when reach should be emphasized over frequency and vice versa.

3. What is meant by readers per copy? Explain the advantages and disadvantages associated with the use of this figure.

4. One long-time advertising agency executive noted that buying media is both an art and a science, with a leaning toward art.

Explain what this means and provide examples.

5. Discuss some of the factors that are important in determining frequency levels. Give examples of each factor.

6. What are the advantages and disadvantages of CPM?

7. Critics of the percentage-of-sales method of budget setting contend that this method "reverses the advertising and sales relationship," and that it "treats advertising as an expense rather than an investment." Explain what these arguments mean and discuss their merits.

8. Discuss some of the reasons managers continue to set budgets

using "top-down" budgeting methods.

9. Explain the difference between investing in advertising and spending. Cite examples of companies that have successfully invested.

10. Discuss how you would explain to a small-business owner why he or she needs to budget a larger amount to advertising and promotion. Base your argument on the S-shaped response function.

11. Some advertisers believe economies of scale are accrued in the advertising process. Discuss their reasons for taking this position. Does research evidence support it?

Chapter Nine
Television and Radio Media

Chapter Objectives

- To examine the structure of the television and radio industries and the role of each medium in the advertising program.

- To consider the strengths and limitations of TV and radio as advertising media.

- To explain how advertising time is purchased for television and radio media, how audiences are measured, and how rates are determined.

Tracking Your Competitors

You're ready to launch a huge multi-million dollar advertising campaign with the majority of your budget dedicated to television spots on numerous networks. You've analyzed everything, from your target audience and their viewing patterns to which local TV stations are best suited to run your commercials. You're now ready to execute the planning and strategy of your media plan. But there is one important factor you overlooked, one that could either increase or reduce the effectiveness of your entire television campaign. That factor is the past and present success of your competitor's media strategies.

In the past, big marketing players in Canada's television world had a tough time reading what their competitors were doing in their media plans. The only way one could get a sense of their competitor's media plans was by wading through loads of numbers or watching a heck of a lot of TV!

Enter SpotWatch, a new service available through Nielsen Media Research of Markham, Ont. Nielsen bills SpotWatch as "the highest-quality competitive advertising intelligence and spot verification service available for television in Canada." The system automatically identifies when programs and commercials are aired through "passive pattern recognition" technology. Each ad has a video and audio signature that signals to the system so that key information is stored (i.e., when and where it has aired). This data is also linked to Nielsen's TV viewing data to determine who has received the messages.

The most obvious benefit is that the service offers accuracy in determining audience delivery for particular commercials and campaigns. But more importantly, the reports are especially detailed since SpotWatch can provide charts for each brand's TV spot, or for a whole category, that include the distributor, creative theme, day of the week and time it aired, position of the ad in a pod (commercial break), length, flighting patterns (periods of activity and inactivity for a campaign), and share of voice (the percentage of a brand's advertising in relation to the total advertising in its category). Another key benefit is the fact that Nielsen is providing the reports in 15 days so that planners have the opportunity to make quick appropriate changes depending upon what the data indicates. And finally, there is a user-friendly decision support system to let planners work with the data.

It all sounds pretty good but there are a few potential drawbacks. The cost ranges from $200 to $1,500 per month, depending on the category. And while the service boasts a correct identification for commercials about 95 percent of the time, which many people are happy with, it is still not 100 percent accurate. Finally, the distribution was still limited to Toronto and Vancouver in 2001. In all, however, you can be sure that Nielsen's SpotWatch service will level the competitive media planning and strategy playing field.

Source: Sarah Smith, "The Spying Game," *Marketing Magazine*, May 7, 2001.

TV has virtually saturated households throughout Canada and most other countries and has become a mainstay in the lives of most people. The average Canadian household watches almost six hours of TV a day, and the average person (age 2+) watches about 3.5 hours of TV per day.[1] The large numbers of people who watch television are important to the TV networks and stations because they can sell time on these programs to marketers who want to reach that audience with their advertising messages. Moreover, the qualities that make TV a great medium for news and entertainment also encourage creative ads that can have a strong impact on customers.

Radio is also an integral part of our lives. Many of us wake up to clock radios in the morning and rely on radio to inform and/or entertain us while we drive to work or school. For many people, radio is a constant companion in their cars, at home, even at work. The average Canadian listens to the radio about three hours each day.[2] Like TV viewers, radio listeners are an important audience for marketers.

In this chapter, we examine TV and radio media, including the general characteristics of each as well as their specific strengths and limitations. We examine how advertisers use TV and radio as part of their advertising and media strategies, how they buy TV and radio time, and how audiences are measured and evaluated for each medium. We also examine the factors that are changing the role of TV and radio as advertising media.

Television

It has often been said that television is the ideal advertising medium. Its ability to combine visual images, sound, motion, and colour presents the advertiser with the opportunity to develop the most creative and imaginative appeals of any medium. However, TV does have certain characteristics that limit or even prevent its use by many advertisers.

Strengths of Television

TV has numerous strengths compared to other media, including creativity and impact, coverage and cost effectiveness, captivity and attention, and selectivity and flexibility.

Creativity and Impact   Perhaps the greatest advantage of TV is the opportunity it provides for presenting the advertising message. The interaction of sight and sound offers tremendous creative flexibility and makes possible dramatic, lifelike representations of products and services. TV commercials can be used to convey a mood or image for a brand as well as to develop emotional or entertaining appeals that help make a dull product appear interesting.

Television is also an excellent medium for demonstrating a product or service. For example, print ads are effective for showing a car and communicating information regarding its features, but only a TV commercial can put you in the driver's seat and give you the sense of actually driving, as shown by the Porsche commercial in Exhibit 9–1.

Coverage and Cost Effectiveness   Television advertising makes it possible to reach large audiences. Nearly everyone, regardless of age, sex, income, or

VO: It's the car you own before you've ever really been inside one...

The car you feel, before you've ever even driven one.

For all of you who think that maybe you've been able to put this youthful desire behind you...

we've got some bad news.

S-PW 632

(MUSIC UP)

(MUSIC OUT)
VO: There's a new 911.

(MUSIC UP)

(MUSIC OUT)
VO: We'll be expecting your call.

educational level, watches at least some TV. During prime time (7:00 P.M. to 11:00 P.M.), an average of 40 percent of adults will tune in. Most people do so on a regular basis since 99 percent of all Canadian households own a TV, and 57 percent have more than one. Marketers selling products and services that appeal to broad target audiences find that TV lets them reach mass markets, often very cost efficiently. For example, one estimate is that the average cost per thousand (cpm) to reach English-speaking women 18 to 49 is about $18.[3] Because of its ability to reach large audiences in a cost-efficient manner, TV is a popular medium among companies selling mass-consumption products. Companies with widespread distribution and availability of their products and services use TV to reach the mass market and deliver their advertising messages at a very low cost per thousand. Television has become indispensable to large consumer package-goods companies, carmakers, and major retailers. Companies like Procter & Gamble and Coca-Cola spend more than 80 percent of their media advertising budget on television. Figure 9–1 shows the top 25 network TV advertisers and their expenditures.

Captivity and Attention Television is basically intrusive in that commercials impose themselves on viewers as they watch their favourite programs. Unless we make a special effort to avoid commercials, most of us are exposed to thousands of them each year. The increase in viewing options and the penetration of VCRs, remote controls, and other automatic devices have made it easier for TV viewers to avoid commercial messages. Studies of consumers' viewing habits found that as much as a third of program audiences may be lost during commercial breaks.[4] However, the remaining viewers are likely to devote some attention to many advertising messages. As discussed in Chapter 4, the low-involvement nature of consumer learning and response processes may mean TV ads have an effect on consumers simply through heavy repetition and exposure to catchy slogans and jingles.

Figure 9–1   Top 25 network
TV advertisers, 1999*

Rank	Company	Measured Advertising ($ millions)
1	General Motors Corp.	$887.7
2	Procter & Gamble Co.	621.5
3	Johnson & Johnson	438.4
4	Philip Morris Cos.	383.2
5	Ford Motor Co.	359.2
6	McDonald's Corp.	296.8
7	Tricon Global Restaurants	287.9
8	DaimlerChrysler	286.5
9	MCI WorldCom	274.4
10	Diageo	270.0
11	AT&T Corp.	259.2
12	Warner-Lambert Co.	245.0
13	Walt Disney Co.	228.0
14	Toyota Motor Sales USA	227.5
15	Unilever	223.4
16	Anheuser-Busch	210.6
17	L'Oréal	209.9
18	Sprint Corp.	205.2
19	Time Warner	189.9
20	PepsiCo	189.0
21	Sears, Roebuck & Co.	186.9
22	US Government	180.1
23	Visa USA	168.8
24	American Home Products Corp.	166.0
25	Nissan Motor Corp. USA	163.9

*No Canadian data is publicly available

Selectivity and Flexibility   Television has often been criticized for being a nonselective medium, since it is difficult to reach a precisely defined target audience through the use of TV advertising. But some selectivity is possible due to variations in the composition of audiences as a result of program content, broadcast time, and geographic coverage. For example, Saturday morning TV caters to children; Saturday and Sunday afternoon programs are geared to the sports-oriented male; and weekday daytime shows appeal heavily to homemakers.

With the growth of cable TV, advertisers refine their coverage further by appealing to groups with specific interests such as sports, news, history, the arts, or music. Exhibit 9–2 shows an ad promoting Animal Planet, a new cable network launched by the Discovery Channel, that focuses solely on animals. Advertisers can also adjust their media strategies to take advantage of different geographic markets through spot ads in specific market areas. Ads can be scheduled to run repeatedly or to take advantage of special occasions.

Limitations of Television

Although television is unsurpassed from a creative perspective, the medium has several disadvantages that limit or preclude its use by many advertisers. These problems include high costs, the lack of selectivity, the fleeting nature of a television message, commercial clutter, limited viewer attention, and distrust of TV ads.

Costs   Despite the efficiency of TV in reaching large audiences, it is an expensive medium in which to advertise. The high cost of TV stems not only from the expense of buying airtime but also from the costs of producing a quality commercial. Production costs for a national brand 30-second spot average nearly $300,000 and can reach over a million for more elaborate commercials.[5] More advertisers are using media-driven creative strategies that require production of a variety of commercials, which drive up their costs. Even local ads can be expensive to produce and often are not of high quality. The high costs of producing and airing commercials often price small- and medium-size advertisers out of the market.

Lack of Selectivity   Some selectivity is available in television through variations in programs and cable TV. But advertisers who are seeking a very specific, often small, target audience find the coverage of TV often extends beyond their market, reducing its cost effectiveness (as discussed in Chapter 8). Geographic selectivity can be a problem for local advertisers such as retailers, since a station bases its rates on the total market area it reaches. For example, stations in Ottawa reach viewers in western Quebec and eastern Ontario. The small company whose market is limited to the immediate Ottawa area may find TV an inefficient media buy, since the stations cover a larger geographic area than the merchant's trade area.

Audience selectivity is improving as advertisers target certain groups of consumers through the type of program or day and/or time when they choose to advertise. However, TV still does not offer as much audience selectivity as radio, magazines, newspapers, or direct mail for reaching precise segments of the market.

Fleeting Message   TV commercials usually last only 30 or 15 seconds and leave nothing tangible for the viewer to examine or consider. Commercials have become shorter and shorter as the demand for a limited amount of broadcast time has intensified and advertisers try to get more impressions from their media budgets.

An important factor in the decline in commercial length has been the spiraling inflation in media costs over the past two decades. Many advertisers see shorter commercials as the only way to keep their media costs in line. A 15-second spot typically sells for about ⅔ the price of a 30-second spot. By using 15-second commercials, advertisers think they can run additional spots to reinforce the message or reach a larger audience. Some advertisers believe shorter commercials can deliver a message just as effectively as longer spots for much less money.

Clutter   The problems of fleeting messages and shorter commercials are compounded by the fact that the advertiser's message is only one of many spots and other nonprogramming material seen during a commercial break, so it may have trouble being noticed. One of advertisers' greatest concerns with TV advertising is the potential decline in effectiveness because of such *clutter.*

The next time you watch TV, count the number of commercials, promotions for the news or upcoming programs, or public service announcements that appear during a station break and you will appreciate why clutter is a major concern. In the USA, a recent study sponsored by the advertising industry found a record level of clutter during prime-time television broadcasts on the major networks. The study analyzed one week of broadcasts during May and November of 1999 and found that

Exhibit 9–2   Animal Planet is a new cable network that focuses entirely on animals

IMC Perspective 9–1
New Digital Channels off to Rough Start

During 2001, broadcasters worked furiously to inform agencies and clients about the more than 50 **digital channels** that launched in September of that year. But months later, the excitement and fear have waned.

Digital's share of total national TV viewing is less than 2 percent, and that's the aggregate number for dozens of stations. The challenge is that the only digital stations any agency can legitimately recommend in these early days (outside of direct response) are the ones that are truly niche and deliver against an advertiser's core target group. While broadcasters have not publicized the revenue numbers of individual digital channels, they do indicate that the revenue, such as it is, supports this strategy. It's not the numbers; it's the niche!

Some years ago the Federal Communications Commission, the U.S. broadcast regulator, decided that the consumer wanted and needed digital television and the enhanced viewing experience that the technology allows. Canada followed suit. Unfortunately, the price of digital TV sets and the lukewarm support of the cable companies in marketing of the stations have limited the success of the digital launch. The question remains: Can these stations, in a softened television market, survive the slow-growth period necessary as the consumer interest in digital expands? If one accepts the logic that target group is king when it comes to the value of the digitals, let's consider the winners.

One is MTV Canada. The strength of the brand and its target group make it a "must buy" for teens and young adults. Brands that want to be associated with a young, fun, hip environment will find it easy to justify including MTV on the buy. Advertisers attempting to reach this elusive group can only win by extending their campaign beyond the traditional purchases on MuchMusic. Direct-response advertisers will tell you that MTV can sell. Of course, the beauty of digital specialty is that it doesn't take a huge investment to establish a clear association with the station.

The ability to reach males outside of the traditional sports environment has always posed a challenge for Canadian buyers. Today we have several options that deliver that group. Lonestar is the clear leader in the digital sweepstakes, if the numbers are to be believed. CanWest Global has taken the formula that made Prime the success it is today and applied it to Lonestar. And Showcase Action, backed by the Alliance Atlantis movie list, can also deliver that elusive male.

Surprisingly, most of the sports channels have delivered well below expectations. Could it be that we finally have enough sports inventory with the three established sports specialty stations? Or do we consider them a success because of their narrow appeal? Depending on the product positioning, sports fanatics may remain key, but why not extend the campaign reach and go elsewhere? MenTV and SexTV: These channels are certainly options worth considering, although conservative advertisers may choose to stay away.

Why haven't the diginets done better? First, there are only 2.5 million Canadian cable and satellite TV households who have a digital set-top box required to get the diginet signals. The boxes add a cost of $199 to own or an extra rental fee charged by the cable operators. Second, the attacks on the World Trade Center and Pentagon stole the thunder from the diginet's September 7 launch.

To win over media buyers, the diginets either have to boost their audience shares, or prove that the few who are watching belong to the high-spending demographics that advertisers lust over.

Sources: Sherry O'Neil, "Digital TV Winners," *Marketing Magazine*, May 6, 2002; James Careless, "A Rough Start for the Diginets," *Marketing Magazine*, December 10, 2001.

---

the four major networks averaged 16 minutes and 43 seconds of nonprogramming content. The hour-long police drama "NYPD Blue" had the most clutter of any prime-time show with one episode having nearly 18 minutes of clutter.[6] With all of these messages competing for our attention, it is easy to understand why the viewer comes away confused or even annoyed and unable to remember or properly identify the product or service advertised.

One cause of clutter is the use of shorter commercials and **split-30s,** 30-second spots in which the advertiser promotes two different products with separate messages. Clutter also results when the networks and individual stations run promotional announcements for their shows, make more time available for commercials, and redistribute time to popular programs. The Canadian Radio-television and

Telecommunications Commission (CRTC), which regulates television only permits 12 minutes of commercials per hour. However, when simulcast Canadian commercials are run, there is extra "time" since U.S. TV stations often show more than 12 minutes of commercials. To fill this "time," Canadian stations run "ads" for other shows, public service announcements, or news/entertainment vignettes. Thus, Canadian viewers experience a different kind of clutter than their American counterparts.

Limited Viewer Attention   When advertisers buy time on a TV program, they are not purchasing guaranteed exposure but rather the opportunity to communicate a message to large numbers of consumers. But there is increasing evidence that the size of the viewing audience shrinks during a commercial break. People leave the room to go to the bathroom or to get something to eat or drink, or they are distracted in some other way during commercials.

Getting consumers to pay attention to commercials has become an even greater challenge in recent years. The increased presence of VCRs and remote controls has led to the problems of zipping and zapping. **Zipping** occurs when customers fast-forward through commercials as they play back a previously recorded program. A study by Nielsen Media Research found that while 80 percent of recorded shows are actually played back, viewers zip past more than half of the commercials.[7] Another study found that most viewers fully or partially zipped commercials when watching a prerecorded program.[8]

Zapping refers to changing channels to avoid commercials. An observational study conducted by John Cronin found as much as a third of program audiences may be lost to electronic zapping when commercials appear.[9] The Nielsen study found that most commercial zapping occurs at the beginning and, to a lesser extent, the end of a program. Zapping at these points is likely to occur because commercial breaks are so long and predictable. Zapping has also been fueled by the emergence of 24-hour continuous-format programming on cable channels. Viewers can switch over for a few news headlines, sports scores, or a music video and then switch back to the program. Research shows that young adults zap more than older adults, and men are more likely to zap than women.[10]

How to inhibit zapping? The networks use certain tactics to hold viewers' attention, such as previews of the next week's show or short closing scenes at the end of a program. Some programs start with action sequences before the opening credits and commercials. Some advertisers believe that producing different executions of a campaign theme is one way to maintain viewers' attention. Others think the ultimate way to zap-proof commercials is to produce creative advertising messages that will attract and hold viewers' attention. However, this is easier said than done, as many consumers just do not want to watch commercials. As more viewers gain access to remote controls and the number of channels increases, the zapping problem is likely to continue.

A recent study on zapping among viewers of the five major commercial channels in the Netherlands was conducted by Lex van Meurs.[11] He found that during commercial breaks, 29 percent of the audience stopped watching television or switched away to another channel. This loss of viewers was partially compensated for by an average increase of 7 percent of new viewers who zapped in from another channel. The study also found that people stop viewing TV during a commercial break because they have a reason to stop watching television altogether or they want to find out what is being shown on other channels. The number of people zapping in and out during breaks was not caused by the type of products being advertised or by specific characteristics of the commercials.

Distrust and Negative Evaluation   To many critics of advertising, TV commercials personify everything that is wrong with the industry. Critics often single out TV commercials because of their pervasiveness and the intrusive nature of the medium. Consumers are seen as defenseless against the barrage of TV ads, since they cannot control the transmission of the message and what appears on their

Is Television Advertising Doomed?

How much would you be willing to pay to never have to watch another TV commercial, be able to automatically record shows with your favourite actor, or record more than one show at a time? How about being able to leave the room in the middle of an exciting football game to answer the door or go to the bathroom and, when you return, being able to resume watching the game from the point where you left? These capabilities are no longer the dreams of TV viewers. They are now realities thanks to new consumer electronic devices called *personal video recorders,* or *PVRs* (also called digital video recorders) that have recently hit the market.

Two companies, Replay Networks and TiVo, have developed the new digital TV-recording devices, which save programs to a massive multigigabyte internal hard drive that can hold 10 to 30 hours of programming. Using a phone line, the PVRs download program schedules that pop up on the screen, and with some simple programming through a remote control, consumers can click on shows they want to watch rather than punching in times and channels. The devices also allow users to create "channels" based on their own search criteria, such as types of shows or names of entertainers. The TiVo device even makes recommendations on the basis of how users have rated other programs.

PVRs also allow users to rewind or pause in the middle of a live broadcast while the device keeps recording, resume watching from the point where they stopped, and then skip ahead to catch up to the live broadcast. And among the player's most anticipated, and controversial, features are buttons that allow users to skip past commercials at superhigh speeds. Replay Networks and TiVo hope that these features, along with the ease of using their devices, will win over consumers, many of whom have given up trying to master their VCRs. And if consumers do embrace the new technology, the result will be TV on demand, which will have a dramatic impact on television advertising.

Television shows have always belonged in time slots, and viewers watch whatever is on at that particular time. Moreover, advertisers are used to this world of synchronous viewing and buy ad time based on Nielsen ratings, which measure how many people are watching a show at a given moment. However, the digital PVRs make it very easy for TV viewers to watch shows on their own time. Watching TV will be more like surfing the Web than viewing a movie. This may reduce the influence of the Nielsen ratings and bring the one-to-one world of the Internet to television. PVRs will also make it much easier for content providers to push programming directly to end-users, potentially on a pay-per-view, commercial-free basis.

The PVR companies note that rather than fearing their new technology, advertisers should be embracing it, since the marriage of TV and online will make possible interactive advertising and the ability to purchase products right off of the television screen. PVR companies could take certain commercials out of a program and replace them with ads that are of more interest to specific types of TV viewers or ads that include contests or other incentives that will encourage consumers not to skip them. Moreover, the CEO of Replay Networks notes that the company is not out to kill the television networks, because its business relies on the programming they provide. Without commercials, there would be no money to pay for new programming, which would mean the supply of new shows could end unless other means of funding were found.

Both Replay Networks and TiVo have begun marketing their new PVRs and personal television service. However, experts predict that it will take at least a few years before the new PVR technology reaches enough homes to become a major threat to TV advertising's traditional business model. Television will remain a passive medium, and network TV will thrive for years to come as companies continue to pay millions of dollars to hawk their products and services on the air. However, it appears that changes are under way that may revolutionize the way we watch television and make the traditional TV advertising business model obsolete. In the future, TV viewers may not have to sit through all those ads for paper towels, toothpaste, and automobiles. On the other hand, would TV really be as much fun without the commercials?

Sources: Thomas Kupper, "TV Ads May Be Doomed, Expert Says," *San Diego Union-Tribune,* November 3, 1999, pp. C1, 4; James Poniewozik, "Here Come PVRs, Is Network TV Doomed?" *Time,* September 27, 1999, pp. 62–63; J. William Gurley, "How the Web Will Warp Advertising," *Fortune,* November 9, 1998, pp. 119–120.

screens. Viewers dislike TV advertising when they believe it is offensive, uninformative, or shown too frequently or when they do not like its content.[12] Studies have shown that of the various forms of advertising, distrust is generally the highest for TV commercials.[13] Also, concern has been raised about the effects of TV advertising on specific groups, such as children or the elderly.[14]

A number of options are available to advertisers that choose to use TV as part of their media mix. They can purchase ads on shows that are shown across the national or regional network versus a local spot announcement in a few cities. They can sponsor an entire program.

Buying Television Advertising Time

They can purchase time in a variety of program formats that appeal to various types and sizes of audiences. With the growth of new television services, advertisers decide the degree to which they want to advertise on specialty channels. We explore these four decisions in this section.

The purchase of TV advertising time is a highly specialized phase of the advertising business, particularly for large companies spending huge sums of money. Large advertisers that do a lot of TV advertising generally use agency media specialists or specialized media buying services to arrange the media schedule and purchase TV time. Consequently, we conclude this section with a discussion on measuring TV audiences since it is a critical input for TV decisions.

Network, Spot, Sponsorship

A basic decision for all advertisers is allocating their TV media budget to network versus local or spot announcements. Most national advertisers use network schedules to provide national coverage and supplement this with regional or local spot purchases to reach markets where additional coverage is desired.

Network Advertising   A common way advertisers disseminate their messages is by purchasing airtime from a **television network.** A network assembles a series of affiliated local TV stations, or **affiliates,** to which it supplies programming and services. These affiliates, most of which are independently owned, contractually agree to preempt time during specified hours for programming provided by the networks and to carry the national advertising within the program. The networks share the advertising revenue they receive during these time periods with the affiliates. The affiliates are also free to sell commercial time in nonnetwork periods and during station breaks in the preempted periods to both national and local advertisers.

Canada's television industry features three national networks. The Canadian Broadcasting Corporation (CBC) is a Crown Corporation of the Federal Government of Canada. Its full network includes 36 stations, including 19 private affiliates that reach 99 percent of English-language homes. Radio-Canada is the CBC cousin for the French-language network consisting of 13 stations (7 in Quebec, 6 outside of Quebec). The Canadian Television Network (CTV) operates as a national English-language service and owns 25 stations in most Canadian provinces.

Canada has a number of regional networks. The CBC also consists of five regional networks; Atlantic, Central (Ontario and English Montreal), Pacific (B.C.), Western, and North (NWT). CTV has three regional networks: Ontario, Atlantic, and Saskatchewan. Global Television Network sends its signal from Toronto to 14 transmitters to reach 97 percent of the Ontario population. Global Atlantic operates in similar manner to reach the majority of people in New Brunswick, PEI, and Nova Scotia. NewNet is an amalgamation of five Ontario stations reaching over 4 million people. Citytv, based in Toronto, reaches an audience of 4 million households from Windsor to Ottawa. CHTV operates similarly out of Toronto/Hamilton and covers 90 percent of Ontario through its seven transmitters. There are three regional networks in Quebec. TVA has 10 stations and reaches 99 percent of the province. Television Quatre Saisons has nine stations and reaches 94 percent of the province.

Finally, sports programming has reached the regional network status as Sportsnet operates in four regions: Pacific, West, Ontario, and East.

The networks have affiliates throughout the nation for almost complete national coverage. When an advertiser purchases airtime from one of these four national networks, the commercial is transmitted across the nation through the affiliate station network. Network advertising truly represents a mass medium, as the advertiser can broadcast its message simultaneously throughout the country.

A major advantage of network advertising is the simplification of the purchase process. The advertiser has to deal with only one party or media representative to air a commercial nationwide. The networks also offer the most popular programs and generally control prime-time programming. Advertisers interested in reaching huge nationwide audiences generally buy network time during the prime viewing hours of 8 to 11 P.M. eastern time.

The major drawback is the high cost of network time. Figure 9–2 shows cost estimates for a 30-second spot on many national and regional networks for the 2000–2001 television season. The cost for a most watched show or special on the CTV network would be $55,000. As an absolute cost, this is quite prohibitive for many marketers.

Availability of time can also be a problem as more advertisers turn to network advertising to reach mass markets. Traditionally, most prime-time commercial spots, particularly on the popular shows, are sold during the buying period in May/June/July that occurs before the TV season begins. Advertisers hoping to use prime-time network advertising must plan their media schedules and often purchase TV time as much as a year in advance. Demands from large clients who are heavy TV advertisers force the biggest agencies to participate in the up-front market. However, TV time is also purchased during the **scatter market** that runs through the TV season. Some key incentives for buying up front, such as cancellation options and lower prices, are becoming more available in the quarterly scatter market. Network TV can also be purchased on a regional basis, so an advertiser's message can be aired in certain sections of the country with one media purchase.

Spot Advertising   **Spot advertising** refers to commercials shown on local TV stations, with time negotiated and purchased directly from the individual stations or their national station representatives. **Station reps** act as sales agents for a number of local stations in dealing with national advertisers.

Spot advertising offers the national advertiser flexibility in adjusting to local market conditions. The advertiser can concentrate commercials in areas where market potential is greatest or where additional support is needed. This appeals to advertisers with uneven distribution or limited advertising budgets, as well as those interested in test marketing or introducing a product in limited market areas. National advertisers sometimes use spot television advertising through local retailers or dealers as part of their cooperative advertising programs and to provide local dealer support.

Sponsorship Advertising   Under a **sponsorship** arrangement, an advertiser assumes responsibility for the production and usually the content of the program as well as the advertising that appears within it. In the early days of TV, most programs were produced and sponsored by corporations and were identified by their name, for example, "Texaco Star Theater" and "The Colgate Comedy Hour." Today most shows are produced by either the networks or independent production companies that sell them to a network.

Several major companies have been sponsoring special programs for many years, such as the Kraft Masterpiece Theater and Hallmark Hall of Fame dramatic series. In 1994 Hallmark acquired RHI Entertainment Inc., the company that produces its wholesome Hall of Fame productions as well as TV miniseries and movies. Sole sponsorship of programs is usually limited to specials and has been declining. However, some companies, including Ford, AT&T, General Electric, IBM, and Chrysler, do still use program sponsorships occasionally.

A company might choose to sponsor a program for several reasons. Sponsorship allows the firm to capitalize on the prestige of a high-quality program, enhancing the

Figure 9–2 Estimated cost of network commercials 2000–2001 (30-second rates)

Network	# of Stations	Basic Range $	Network	# of Stations	Basic Range $
National			**Specialty**		
CBC full	36	100 – 46,000	Bravo!	1	200 – 1,500
CBC National	17	100 – 25,000	CBC Newsworld	1	10 – 800
CTV	21	730 – 54,600	CMT	1	50 – 500
Radio-Canada	15	250 – 18,530	Comedy	1	450 – 600
TVA	10	1,500 – 23,000	Discovery	1	100 – 2,400
Regional			Fairchild (Chinese)	3	240 – 690
ASN	1	10 – 380	Food Network	1	48 – 1,485
ATV	3	50 – 2,100	Headline Sports	1	30 – 250
CBC Regional			HGTV Canada	1	54 – 2,755
Atlantic	6	100 – 2,800	History	1	55 – 2,200
Central	12	100 – 21,000	LCN	1	20 – 225
Western	12	100 – 7,500	Life Network	1	30 – 4,235
Pacific	6	100 – 4,200	Météomédia	1	50 – 100
Global	1	150 – 48,000	MuchMoreMusic	1	100 – 5,000
MITV	2	55 – 3,400	MuchMusic	1	1,000 – 7,500
CTV Ontario	8	100 – 36,200	MusiquePlus	1	480 – 5,000
Quatre Saisons (TQS)	10	350 – 15,000	OLN	1	25 – 1,500
Télé-Québec	10	175 – 3,500	Prime	1	20 – 1,200
CTV Saskatchewan	6	40 – 3,170	RDS	1	25 – 13,200
			ROB TV	1	35 – 105
			Showcase	1	45 – 3,670
			Space	1	300 – 5,000
			Sportsnet (national)	1	300 5,300
			Telelatino	1	100 – 500
			Teletoon (English)	1	75 – 1,400
			Télétoon (French)	1	70 – 250
			Toronto Star TV	1	275 – 4,374
			TSN	1	100 – 20,000
			Vision TV	1	100 – 800
			WTN	1	25 – 15,000
			Weather Network	1	75 – 350
			YTV	1	125 – 5,000

Source: *Media Digest*, September 24, 2001.

image of the company and its products. For example, the Ford Motor Company received a great deal of favourable publicity when it sponsored the commercial-free television debut of the Holocaust movie *Schindler's List*. Companies also sponsor programs to gain more control over the shows carrying their commercials. For example, Wendy's International has been involved in sponsorship of family-oriented programs.

Another reason is that the sponsor has control over the number, placement, and content of its commercials. Commercials can be of any length as long as the total amount of commercial time does not exceed network or station regulations. Advertisers introducing a new product line often sponsor a program and run commercials that are several minutes long to introduce and explain the product. Eaton's used this approach when it tried to re-brand itself in 2000. It sponsored the premiere of a

James Bond movie and ran very lengthy commercials that continued across advertising segments. IBM used this strategy to introduce new generations of products. While these factors make sponsorship attractive to some companies, the high costs of sole sponsorship limit this option to large firms.

Time Periods and Programs

Another decision in buying TV time is selecting the right period and program for the advertiser's commercial messages. The cost of TV advertising time varies depending on the time of day and the particular program, since audience size varies as a function of these two factors. TV time periods are divided into **dayparts,** which are specific segments of a broadcast day.

The time segments that make up the programming day vary from station to station. However, a typical classification of dayparts for a weekday is shown in Figure 9–3. The various daypart segments attract different audiences in both size and nature, so advertising rates vary accordingly. Prime-time draws the largest audiences, with 8:30 to 9 P.M. being the most watched half-hour time period and Sunday the most popular night for television. Since firms that advertise during prime time must pay premium rates, this daypart is dominated by the large national advertisers.

The various dayparts are important to advertisers since they attract different demographic groups. For example, daytime TV generally attracts women; early morning attracts women and children. The late-fringe (late-night) daypart period has become popular among advertisers trying to reach young adults. Audience size and demographic composition also vary depending on the type of program. Situation comedies attract the largest prime-time audiences, with women 18 to 34 comprising the greatest segment of the audience. Feature films rank second, followed by general drama shows. Women 55 and older are the largest audience segment for these programs. Another factor to consider is the time of year. Figure 9–4 shows that TV viewership drops significantly in the summer.

Specialty Television Advertising

Canada has an extensive variety of specialty television networks that advertisers run commercials on to reach specific target audiences. These specialty networks require either cable or satellite technology on the part of consumers to access this entertainment. We will briefly review these two technologies and then discuss the advertising on these specialty channels.

Cable and Satellite Technology   Perhaps the most significant development in the broadcast media has been the expansion of **cable television**. Cable, or CATV (community antenna television), which delivers TV signals through fibre or coaxial wire rather than the airways, was developed to provide reception to remote areas that couldn't receive broadcast signals. Canadians readily accepted cable in the 1970s since it was the easiest or only method of receiving the feed of American channels. Today, cable penetration stands at about 73 percent.

Figure 9–3   Common television dayparts

Morning	7:00 A.M.–9:00 A.M., Monday through Friday
Daytime	9:00 A.M.–4:30 P.M., Monday through Friday
Early fringe	4:30 P.M.–7:30 P.M., Monday through Friday
Prime-time access	7:30 P.M.–8:00 P.M., Sunday through Saturday
Prime time	8:00 P.M.–11:00 P.M., Monday through Saturday, and 7:00 P.M.–11 P.M., Sunday
Late news	11:00–11:30 P.M., Monday through Friday
Late fringe	11:30–1:00 A.M., Monday through Friday

Figure 9–4   Television summer drop-off

	Total hours tuned: % difference					
	Daytime: M–F 6 A.M.–4:30 P.M.	Fringe: M–F 4:30 P.M.–7 P.M.	Prime time: M–Sun 7 P.M.–11 P.M.	Late night: M–Sun 11 P.M.–2 A.M.	Weekend: Sat/Sun 6 A.M.–7 P.M.	Total
All Persons 2+	–12	–23	–25	– 2	–23	–20
Children 2–11	+ 4	–30	–19	+14	–23	–14
Teens 12–17	+73	–18	–22	+49	–27	– 5
Women 18+	–18	–22	–26	– 5	–22	–22
Men 18+	–18	–23	–26	– 4	–24	–22

Total = % drop-off from fall and spring averages for 10 EM's (Halifax, Quebec City, Montreal, Ottawa–Hull, Kitchener–Waterloo, London, Winnipeg, Calgary, Edmonton, Vancouver)

Source: 2000–2001 BBM Television Data Book

Direct broadcast satellite (DBS) services emerged in the 1990s. TV and radio programs are sent digitally from a satellite to homes equipped with a small dish. DBS penetration reached 11 percent in 2001, mostly at the expense of cable companies. DBS companies have been aggressively marketing their service, superior picture quality, and greater channel choice as subscribers receive as many as 200 channels that include news, music, and sports in crisp, digital video and CD-quality sound. However, the pendulum can swing back the other way as more cable operators offer digital cable that allows them to match the number of channels received on satellites. Note that the combined penetration of these technologies is 84 percent indicating that a sizable number of Canadians cannot be reached through specialty television advertising.

Cable and satellite subscribers pay a monthly fee for which they receive many channels, including the local Canadian and American network affiliates and independent stations, various specialty networks, American superstations, and local cable system channels. Both operators also offer programming that is not supported by commercial sponsorship and is available only to households willing to pay a fee beyond the monthly subscription charge (i.e., The Movie Channel). Cable and satellite broadens the program options available to the viewer as well as the advertiser by offering specialty channels, including all-news, pop music, country music, sports, weather, educational, and cultural channels as well as children's programming. Many cable systems also carry American **superstations**, independent local stations that send their signals via satellite to operators to make their programs available to subscribers. Programming on superstations such as TBS and WGN generally consists of sports, movies, and reruns of network shows.

Specialty Networks   The proliferation of channels in both technologies has influenced the nature of television as an advertising medium. Expanded viewing options have led to considerable audience fragmentation. Much of the audience growth of specialty networks has come at the expense of national and regional networks. Specialty networks now have about 28 percent of the viewing audience. Many specialty networks have become very popular among consumers, leading advertisers to re-evaluate their media plans and the prices they are willing to pay for network and spot commercials on network affiliate stations. Advertising on specialty networks reached $381 million in 2000 up from $109 million in 1994. In comparison, all other television ad revenue increased from $1.663 billion in 1994 to $2.075 billion.

This change in advertising revenue indicates that advertisers are using specialty networks to reach specific target audiences (Exhibit 9–3).

Exhibit 9–3   CNBC has become the leader in business news and has a very affluent viewing audience

THE WORLD'S MOST TRUSTED NEWS SOURCE CAPTURES ALL THE WORLD'S STORIES.

And all of the world's attention.

Each week, over 11.4 million business professionals who reside in Europe, Asia and Latin America watch CNN International. The fact is, more people in more places tune in to the world's most trusted news network. No one reaches an international audience like CNN International.

For more information on advertising opportunities, contact David Levy in New York at 212-852-6791 or Nan Richards in London at 0171-307-6100.

CNN INTERNATIONAL...

THE WORLD'S NEWS LEADER

▶

Access CNN on the World Wide Web at CNN.com

Sources: EMS, 1995 (Europe), LMML, 1995 (Latin America), ACE, 1996 and Turner Projections (Asia) Within CNNI universe.
©1996 Turner Broadcasting System, Inc.

Exhibit 9–4 CNN International is the authoritative source for news throughout the world

Advertisers are also interested in specialty networks because of their low cost and flexibility. Advertising rates on cable programs are much lower than those for the shows on the major networks (see Figure 9–2). This makes TV a much more viable media option for smaller advertisers with limited budgets and those interested in targeting their commercials to a well-defined target audience. Also, specialty network advertisers generally do not have to make the large up-front commitments, which may be as much as a year in advance, the networks require.

In addition to costing less, specialty networks give advertisers much greater flexibility in the type of commercials that can be used. While most network commercials are 30- or 15-second spots, commercials on specialty networks can be longer (i.e., **infomercials** ranging from 3 to 30 minutes in length). Direct-response advertisers often use these longer ads to describe their products or services and encourage consumers to call in their orders during the commercial. The use of infomercials by direct-response advertisers is discussed in Chapter 14. Finally, specialty network advertising can be purchased on a national or a regional basis. Many large marketers advertise on specialty networks to reach large numbers of viewers across the country with a single media buy. Regional advertising on specialty networks is available but limited.

While specialty networks have become increasingly popular among national, regional, and local advertisers, they still have limitations. One concern is that specialty networks are overshadowed by the networks. The average person will watch more hours per week of a CBC or CTV affiliate than a single specialty network, although this is changing. The average Canadian watches TSN an average of 1.8 hours per week while the average person in Ottawa watches the CBC affiliate 3.1 hours per week. Although specialty networks' share of the TV viewing audience has increased significantly, the viewers are spread out among the large number of channels available. Collectively, the specialty channels contribute to greater audience fragmentation as the number of viewers who watch any one cable channel is generally quite low (Exhibit 9–4).

Measuring the TV Audience

One of the most important considerations in TV advertising is the size and composition of the viewing audience. Audience measurement is critical to advertisers as well as to the networks and stations. Advertisers want to know the size and characteristics of the audience they are reaching when they purchase time on a particular program. And since the rates they pay are a function of audience size, advertisers want to be sure audience measurements are accurate.

Audience size and composition are also important to the network or station, since they determine the amount it can charge for commercial time. Shows are frequently cancelled because they fail to attract enough viewers to make their commercial time attractive to potential advertisers. Determining audience size is not an exact science and has been the subject of considerable controversy through the years. In this section, we examine how audiences are measured and how advertisers use this information in planning their media schedules.

Audience Measurement Resources The size and composition of television audiences are important to media planners as they weigh the value of buying commercial time on a program. In Canada, television audiences are measured and communicated by BBM Bureau of Measurement of Canada (BBM Canada) and Nielsen Media Research. A third organization, the Television Bureau of Canada, offers additional information related to television audiences.

BBM Canada   BBM Canada is a not-for-profit broadcast research company based on cooperative between the Canadian Association of Broadcasters, the Association of Canadian Advertisers, and Canadian advertising agencies. BBM Canada produces audience measurement data for its TV and radio members. This member relationship gives BBM Canada the reputation as the industry's rating service.

BBM Canada uses the diary research method for collecting television audience information in 35 smaller local markets during the fall and spring, and 12 larger local markets during the fall, spring, and summer. A booklet for each television owned in the household is sent to a representative sample of households. BBM gathers viewership information from this sample and then projects this information to the total viewing area.

The diary method work as follows. Each person aged two years or older records his or her viewing for one week in the booklet. The recordings are based on 15-minute increments from 6:00 A.M. until 2:00 A.M. Viewers write down station call letters, channel numbers, programs, and who is watching. The booklet also contains a number of based demographic questions to be completed by each individual. All participants receive a small incentive to encourage their responses. BBM receives completed diaries from about 40 percent of those that are mailed, although the rates vary by region and other factors. These and other aspects of the research process are done according to standard market research practices to ensure valid and reliable information; however, one drawback is that some diaries are not filled out correctly.

Due to this methodological concern and the pace of technology, BBM Canada is currently implementing the people-meter technology for local audience measurement. BBM Canada has begun to use meters to continuously record television audiences for local and regional markets. It started with Vancouver in 1998 and has now reached the Toronto local market and the Ontario and Quebec regional markets. As of June 2002, BBM Canada had tested preliminary data from a national panel of 2,100 households and plans a commercial launch of the service in the near future.

To help its customers understand the data, BBM Canada provides an extensive array of products. Market reports are a summary of the audience sizes across all markets by time block, program listings, and time period. Their reach book summarizes the demographic information across each province, data area, and station. BBM Canada also offers guidelines on population estimates and booklets that assist its members in understanding the geographic boundaries studied and the research methodology. BBM Canada's television data book breaks down the viewing habits across different markets with user-friendly graphs and charts. The EM Stats Card provides detailed information for each extended market in terms of cable, satellite, and VCR penetration in addition to other similar macro-level data. Finally, two different documents tabulate the audiences for the different televisions shows. As a complement, BBM Canada also offers four different software packages that allow its members to analyze the data in a variety of ways.

Nielsen Media Research   Nielsen is a Canadian subsidiary of an American firm with the same name. Nielsen gathers viewership information from a panel of TV homes that is a representative sample. It then projects this information to the total viewing area. The resulting data is presented as the Nielsen Television Index (NTI). In Canada, the only technique used to gather audience measurement information is the electronic meter. Nielsen had previously used both the diary and electronic meter in Canada, like the practice done in the United States. In 2002, Nielsen's had the technology to measure audiences for the national market and for the Vancouver, Calgary, Toronto/Hamilton, and Montreal (French only) markets. Nielsen has recently launched a similar service to measure the audiences for the new digital channels offered on both cable and satellite.

Nielsen provides audience viewing information by household across a number of variables including income, language, cable status, pay TV, children residing, household size, age of head of household, number of TVs, rent or own home, kind of dwelling, ownership of VCRs and other durables, principal shopper, and restaurant and movie usage. The data is also presented by age, gender, education, and occupation. Like BBM Canada, Nielsen also provides various data management tools and services to help its clients understand the data.

With BBM Canada and Nielsen offering very similar services, Canada is in a unique position of being the only country in the world that has two firms measuring TV audiences. The U.S. has only Nielsen; historically, there has been significant concern as to whether the advertisers are getting their money's worth and whether the data is sufficiently accurate as Nielsen uses two different methods (i.e., diary and meter). In Canada, the debate has centred on a couple of other facets. Some argue that Canada should return to a single firm measuring TV audiences as this would reduce overall costs; however, others contend that a dual system gives advertisers and agencies greater choice in making their TV media purchases.[15]

Television Bureau of Canada (TVB)   The TVB is an industry association for television networks, television stations, and sales firms that sell television advertising time. It offers resources to those in the television industry to demonstrate the value and importance of television as a media versus competing media (i.e., magazines). It publishes basic facts garnered from various sources and conducts primary research through independent market research firms.

Most of the information is from BBM Canada or Nielsen Media Research. Based on this research, television consistently outperforms the other media on a number of variables. Television reaches 85 percent of the country on a daily basis, with the average Canadian watching about 3.5 hours per day. Furthermore, television is perceived as being the most authoritative (43 percent) and most influential (71 percent) compared to radio, the Internet, daily newspapers, and magazines.

Audience Measures   We now review some of the concepts associated with television audience measurement that are the basis for the reports published by these three organizations.

Television Households   The number of households in the market that own a TV is sometimes referred to as the *universe estimate* (UE). Since over 98 percent of Canadian households own a TV set, **television households** generally correspond to the number of households in a given market.

Program Rating   Probably the best known of all audience measurement figures is the **program rating,** the percentage of TV households in an area that are tuned to a specific program during a specific time period. The program rating is calculated by dividing the number of households tuned to a particular show by the total number of households in the area. For example, if 1.2 million households (HH) watched a show, the national rating would be 10.9, calculated as follows:

$$\text{Rating} = \frac{\text{HH tuned to show}}{\text{Total HH}} = \frac{1,200,000}{11,000,000} = 10.9$$

A **ratings point** represents 1 percent of all the television households in a particular area tuned to a specific program. On a national level, 1 ratings point represents 110,000 households. Thus, a top-rated program with an average rating of 19 reaches 2.1 million households each week ($19 \times 110,000$).

The program rating is the key number to the stations, since the amount of money they can charge for commercial time is based on it. Ratings points are very important to the networks as well as to individual stations. A 1 percent change in a program's ratings over the course of a viewing season can gain or lose millions of dollars in advertising revenue. Advertisers also follow ratings closely, since they are the key measure for audience size and commercial rates.

Households Using Television   The percentage of homes in a given area where TV is being watched during a specific time period is called **households using tele-**

vision (HUT). This figure, sometimes referred to as sets in use, is always expressed as a percentage. For example, if 5.5 million of Canadian TV households have their sets turned on at 10 P.M. on a Thursday night, the HUT figure is 50 percent (5.5 million out of 11 million). Television usage varies widely depending on the time of day and season of the year.

Share of Audience   Another important audience measurement figure is the **share of audience,** which is the percentage of households using TV in a specified time period that are tuned to a specific program. This figure considers variations in the number of sets in use and the total size of the potential audience, since it is based only on those households that have their sets turned on. Audience share is calculated by dividing the number of households (HH) tuned to a show by the number of households using television (HUT). Thus, if 5.5 million Canadian households had their sets turned on during the 10 P.M. time slot, the share of audience would be 20, calculated as follows:

$$\text{Share} = \frac{\text{HH tuned to show}}{\text{Households using TV}} = \frac{1.1}{5.5} = 20$$

Audience share is always higher than the program rating unless all the households have their sets turned on (in which case they would be equal). Share figures are important since they reveal how well a program does with the available viewing audience. For example, late at night the size of the viewing audience drops substantially, so the best way to assess the popularity of a late-night program is to examine the share of the available audience it attracts relative to competing programs.

Ratings services also provide an audience statistic known as **total audience,** the total number of homes viewing any five-minute part of a telecast. This number can be broken down to provide audience composition figures that are based on the distribution of the audience into demographic categories.

Audience Measurement Technology

Nielsen Television Index   The source of national and network TV audience information is the Nielsen Television Index (NTI), which provides daily and weekly estimates of TV viewing and national sponsored network and major cable program audiences. Currently, BBM Canada is planning a national service to be launched in the spring of 2002. Historically, Nielsen provided this information using a two-pronged system consisting of a national sample of metered households along with a separate sample of diary households. In the metered households, an electronic measurement device known as the **audimeter** (audience meter) was hooked up to the TV set to continuously measure the channels to which the set was tuned. Network viewing for the country (the famous Nielsen ratings) was based on the results provided by audimeters placed in a national sample of homes carefully selected to represent the population of households. The metered households were supported by a separate panel of households that recorded viewing information in diaries. Since the audimeter could measure only the channel to which the set was tuned, the diary panel was used to gather demographic data on the viewing audience.

For many years, the television and advertising industries expressed concern over the audimeter/diary system. The information from diaries was not available to the network and advertising analysts for several weeks, and studies indicated the method was overstating the size of some key demographic audiences. Cooperation rates among diary keepers declined, and often the person who kept a household's diary did not note what other family members watched when he or she wasn't home. The complex new video environment and explosion in viewing options also made it difficult for diary keepers to maintain accurate viewing records.

As a result of these problems, and in response to competitive pressure from an audience measurement company from England, AGB, in 1987 Nielsen made the people meter the sole basis of its national rating system and eliminated the use of the diary panel.

Exhibit 9–5 Nielsen Media Research uses the people meter to measure national TV audiences

The People Meter The **People Meter** is an electronic measuring device that incorporates the technology of the audimeter in a system that records not only what is being watched but also by whom in 3350 homes. The actual device is a small box with eight buttons—seven for the family and one for visitors—that can be placed on the top of the TV set (Exhibit 9–5). A remote control unit permits electronic entries from anywhere in the room. Each member of the sample household is assigned a button that indicates his or her presence as a viewer. The People Meter collects what station is being tuned and, through interaction with the meter, who is sitting down and watching the programs.

The viewership information the People Meter collects from the household is stored in the Home Unit which in turn reports television use over a telephone line to a central computer at Nielsen Media Research head office. Data collected include when the set is turned on, which channel is viewed, when the channel is changed, and when the set is off, in addition to who is viewing. The demographic characteristics of the viewers are also in the system, and viewership can be matched to these traits. Nielsen's operation centre processes all this information each night for release to the TV and advertising industries. Nielsen uses a sample of metered households to provide overnight viewing results.

Many people believe People Meters are only the first step in improving the way audiences are measured. While the People Meter is seen as an improvement over the diary method, it still requires cooperation on an ongoing basis from people in the metered homes. Viewers in the Nielsen households, including young children, must punch a preassigned number on the remote control device each time they start or stop watching.

We now summarize a few basic facts of television viewership as you now understand how these numbers are compiled. Figures 9–5 and 9–6 summarize the relative viewership data from three perspectives. Figure 9–5 compares viewership of all station groups, while Figure 9–6 shows viewership for conventional Canadian networks. Earlier we mentioned that television viewing is organized by dayparts. Figure 9–7 shows the viewing of different age demographics across these dayparts. Figure 9–8 shows the viewership of pay-TV and specialty networks.

Figure 9–5   Viewership by station groups

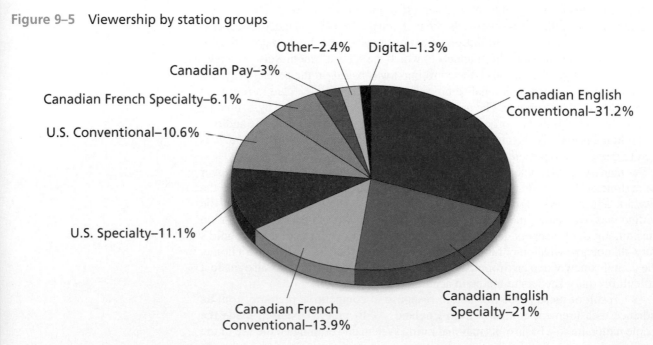

Other–2.4%   Digital–1.3%
Canadian Pay–3%
Canadian French Specialty–6.1%
U.S. Conventional–10.6%
Canadian English Conventional–31.2%
U.S. Specialty–11.1%
Canadian French Conventional–13.9%
Canadian English Specialty–21%

Figure 9–6   Viewership for Canadian networks

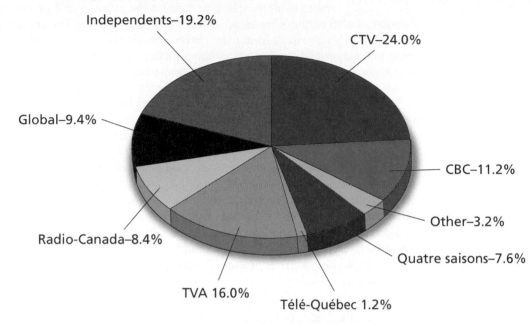

Independents–19.2%

CTV–24.0%

Global–9.4%

CBC–11.2%

Other–3.2%

Radio-Canada–8.4%

Quatre saisons–7.6%

TVA 16.0%

Télé-Québec 1.2%

Source: Based on Media Digest 2001–2002, BBM Fall '00, CRTC, Telecaster Committee of Canada.

Figure 9–7   Average weekly hours viewed per capita by dayparts

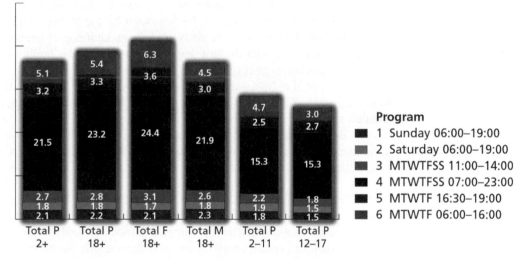

Program

1 Sunday 06:00–19:00
2 Saturday 06:00–19:00
3 MTWTFSS 11:00–14:00
4 MTWTFSS 07:00–23:00
5 MTWTF 16:30–19:00
6 MTWTF 06:00–16:00

Copyright Nielsen Media Research Limited, 2002.

Figure 9–8   Average weekly hours tuned per capita, specialty vs. pay

	Total P 2+	Total P 18+	Total F 18+	Total M 18+	Total P 2–11	Total P 12–17
Cdn Eng Spec	5.0	4.9	4.4	5.4	6.2	4.3
Cdn Pay	0.7	0.8	0.6	0.9	0.4	0.7

Copyright Nielsen Media Research Limited, 2002.

Radio

Television has often been referred to as the ideal advertising medium, and to many people it personifies the glamour and excitement of the industry. Radio, on the other hand, has been called the Rodney Dangerfield of media because it gets no respect from many advertisers. Dominated by network programming and national advertisers before the growth of TV, radio has evolved into a primarily local advertising medium. Radio has also become a medium characterized by highly specialized programming appealing to very narrow segments of the population.

The importance of radio is best demonstrated by the numbers. There are 867 radio stations in Canada, including 308 AM stations and 559 FM stations. Radio reaches 93 percent of all Canadians over the age of 12 each week and has grown into a ubiquitous background to many activities, among them reading, driving, running, working, and socializing. The average Canadian listens to radio 3 hours and 6 minutes every weekday. The pervasiveness of this medium has not gone unnoticed by advertisers; radio advertising revenue grew from $741 million in 1994 to over $1 billion in 2000.

Radio has survived and flourished as an advertising medium because it offers advertisers certain strengths for communicating messages to their potential customers. However, radio has inherent limitations that affect its role in the advertiser's media strategy.

Strengths of Radio

Radio has many strengths compared to other media, including cost and efficiency, selectivity, flexibility, mental imagery, and integrated marketing opportunities.

Cost and Efficiency   One of the main strengths of radio as an advertising medium is its low cost. Radio commercials are very inexpensive to produce. They require only a script of the commercial to be read by the radio announcer or a copy of a prerecorded message that can be broadcast by the station. The cost for radio time is also low. The low relative costs of radio make it one of the most efficient of all advertising media, and the low absolute cost means the budget needed for an effective radio campaign is often lower than that for other media.

The low cost of radio means advertisers can build more reach and frequency into their media schedule within a certain budget. They can use different stations to broaden the reach of their messages and multiple spots to ensure adequate frequency. Radio commercials can be produced more quickly than TV spots, and the companies can afford to run them more often.[16] Many national advertisers also recognize the cost efficiency of radio and use it as part of their media strategy.

Selectivity   Another major advantage of radio is the high degree of audience selectivity available through the various program formats and geographic coverage of the numerous stations. Radio lets companies focus their advertising on specialized audiences such as certain demographic and lifestyle groups. Most areas have radio stations with formats such as adult contemporary, easy listening, classical music, country, news/talk shows, jazz, and all news, to name a few. For example, among 18- to 24-year olds, the most popular radio format is top 40, while those between the ages of 45 and 54 prefer news/talk. Elusive consumers like teenagers, college students, and working adults can be reached more easily through radio than most other media.

Radio can reach consumers other media can't. Light television viewers spend considerably more time with radio than with TV and are generally an upscale market in terms of income and education level. Light readers of magazines and newspapers also spend more time listening to radio. As mass marketing gives way to market segmentation and regional marketing, radio will continue to grow in importance.

Flexibility   Radio is probably the most flexible of all the advertising media because it has a very short closing period, which means advertisers can change their message almost up to the time it goes on the air. Radio commercials can usually be produced and scheduled on very short notice. Radio advertisers can easily adjust their messages to local market conditions and marketing situations.

Mental Imagery A potential advantage of radio that is often overlooked is that it encourages listeners to use their imagination when processing a commercial message. While the creative options of radio are limited, many advertisers take advantage of the absence of a visual element to let consumers create their own picture of what is happening in a radio message.

Radio may also reinforce television messages through a technique called **image transfer,** where the images of a TV commercial are implanted into a radio spot.[17] First the marketer establishes the video image of a TV commercial. Then it uses a similar, or even the same, audio portion (spoken words and/or jingle) as the basis for the radio counterpart. The idea is that when consumers hear the radio message, they will make the connection to the TV commercial, reinforcing its video images. Image transfer offers advertisers a way to make radio and TV ads work together synergistically. This promotional piece put out by the Radio Advertising Bureau of the U.S. shows how the image transfer process works (Exhibit 9–6).

Integrated Marketing Opportunities Radio provides marketers with a variety of integrated marketing opportunities. Radio stations become an integral part of many communities, and the deejays and program hosts may become popular figures. Advertisers often use radio stations and personalities to enhance their involvement with a local market and to gain influence with local retailers. Radio also works very effectively in conjunction with place-based/point-of-purchase promotions. Retailers often use on-site radio broadcasts combined with special sales or promotions to attract consumers to their stores and get them to make a purchase (Exhibit 9–7). Live radio broadcasts are also used in conjunction with event marketing.

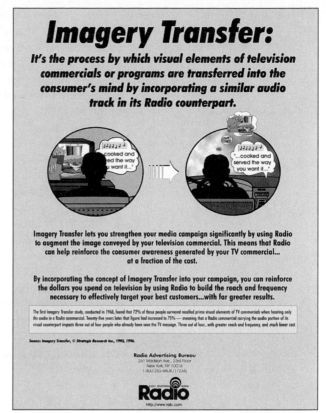

Exhibit 9–6 The Radio Advertising Bureau promotes the concept of imagery transfer

Limitations of Radio

Several factors limit the effectiveness of radio as an advertising medium, among them creative limitations, fragmentation, limited research data, limited listener attention, and clutter. The media planner must consider them in determining the role the medium will play in the advertising program.

Exhibit 9–7 Banana Boat uses live radio broadcasts to promote its sun-care products

Creative Limitations
A major drawback of radio as an advertising medium is the absence of a visual image. The radio advertiser cannot show the product, demonstrate it, or use any type of visual appeal or information. A radio commercial is, like a TV ad, a short-lived and fleeting message that is externally paced and does not allow the receiver to control the rate at which it is processed. Because of these creative limitations many companies tend to ignore radio, and agencies often assign junior people to the development of radio commercials.

Fragmentation
Another problem with radio is the high level of audience fragmentation due to the large number of stations. The percentage of the market tuned to any particular station is usually very small. The top-rated radio station in many major metropolitan areas with a number of AM and FM stations may attract less than 10 percent of the total listening audience. Advertisers that want a broad reach in their radio advertising media schedule have to buy time on a number of stations to cover even a local market.

Limited Research Data
Audience research data on radio are often limited, particularly compared with TV, magazines, or newspapers. The BBM audience research measurement mostly focuses on demographics and a handful of lifestyle factors. Most users of radio are local companies that cannot support research on radio listenership in their markets. Thus, media planners do not have as much audience information available to guide them in their purchase of radio time as they do with other media.

Limited Listener Attention
Another problem that plagues radio is that it is difficult to retain listener attention to commercials. Radio programming, particularly music, is often the background to some other activity and may not receive the listeners' full attention. Thus they may miss all or some of the commercials. One environment where radio has a more captive audience is in cars. But getting listeners to pay attention to commercials can still be difficult. Most people preprogram their car radio and change stations during commercial breaks. A study by Avery Abernethy found large differences between exposure to radio programs versus advertising for listeners in cars. They were exposed to only half of the advertising broadcast and changed stations frequently to avoid commercials.[18] Another factor that is detracting from radio listening in motor vehicles is the rapid growth of cellular phones. A recent study found that half of commuters surveyed who own a cellphone reported listening to less radio than they did a year earlier.[19]

Clutter
Clutter is just as much a problem with radio as with other advertising media. Radio stations can play as many minutes of advertising as they like. Most radio stations carry an average of nearly 10 minutes of commercials every hour. During the popular morning and evening rush hours, the amount of commercial time may exceed 12 minutes. Advertisers must create commercials that break through the clutter or use heavy repetition to make sure their messages reach consumers. In a study of radio listeners conducted by Edison Research, perceptions of increased ad clutter were cited by participants as a reason for spending less time listening to radio.[20]

Buying Radio Time

The purchase of radio time is similar to that of television, as advertisers can make either network, or spot buys. Since these options were reviewed in the section on buying TV time, they are discussed here only briefly.

Network Radio
Advertising time on radio can be purchased on a network basis. This is a relatively new option for advertisers who can now run ads on the CHUM radio network, The Team Sports Radio Network, and a few others. Using networks minimizes the amount of negotiation and administrative work needed to get national or regional coverage, and the costs are lower than those for individual

stations. However, the number of affiliated stations on the network roster and the types of audiences they reach may vary, so the use of network radio reduces advertisers' flexibility in selecting stations.

Spot Radio   National advertisers can also use spot radio to purchase airtime on individual stations in various markets. The purchase of spot radio provides greater flexibility in selecting markets, individual stations, and airtime and adjusting the message for local market conditions. By far the heaviest users of radio are local advertisers; the majority of radio advertising time is purchased from individual stations by local companies. Auto dealers, retailers, restaurants, and financial institutions are among the heaviest users of local radio advertising.

Time Classifications

As with television, the broadcast day for radio is divided into various time periods or dayparts, as shown in Figure 9–9. The size of the radio listening audience varies widely across the dayparts, and advertising rates follow accordingly. The largest radio audiences (and thus the highest rates) occur during the early morning and late afternoon drive times. Radio rates also vary according to the number of spots or type of audience plan purchased, the supply and demand of time available in the local market, and the ratings of the individual station. Rate information is available directly from the stations and is summarized in CARD. Some stations issue grid rate cards. But many stations do not adhere strictly to rate cards. Their rates are negotiable and depend on factors such as availability, time period, and number of spots purcahsed.

Measuring the Radio Audience

As noted earlier, BBM Canada also provides information on radio listenership using a diary method similar to television. Surveys are done up to three times per year in over 130 radio markets. BBM Canada publishes many reports associated with these surveys. Market reports summarize each radio station's audience by occupation, language, and other important characteristics. Other similar reports with greater aggregation across regions are also published. As for television, BBM Canada provides its members with many supporting documents to understand how to use radio as a communication tool. It also offers many software applications so that advertisers can purchase radio media effectively and efficiently. The three basic elements in the BBM Canada reports are:

- Person estimates—the estimated number of people listening.
- Rating—the percentage of listeners in the survey area population.
- Share—the percentage of the total estimated listening audience.

These three estimates are further defined by using quarter-hour and cume figures. The **average quarter-hour (AQH) figure** expresses the average number of people estimated to have listened to a station for a minimum of five minutes during any quarter-hour in a time period. This figure helps to determine the audience and cost of a spot schedule within a particular time period.

Cume stands for cumulative audience, the estimated total number of different people who listened to a station for at least five minutes in a quarter-hour period within a reported daypart. Cume estimates the reach potential of a radio station.

Morning drive time	6:00–10:00 A.M.
Daytime	10:00 A.M.–3:00 P.M.
Afternoon/evening drive time	3:00–7:00 P.M.
Nighttime	7:00 P.M.–12:00 A.M.
All night	12:00–6:00 A.M.

Figure 9–9 Dayparts for radio

The **average quarter-hour rating (AQH RTG)** expresses the estimated number of listeners as a percentage of the survey area population. The **average quarter-hour share (AQH SHR)** is the percentage of the total listening audience tuned to each station. It shows the share of listeners each station captures out of the total listening audience in the survey area. Figures 9–10 to 9–14 provide a summary of Canadian radio listening habits.

The Radio Marketing Bureau is an organization that plays a similar role for radio as the Television Bureau of Canada, discussed earlier in this chapter. It acts as a resource for radio stations and those involved with selling airtime for radios. Its mission is to educate advertisers on the effective use of the radio medium and to assist advertisers in meeting their communication objectives. The Radio Marketing Bureau offers professional services to advertisers if needed. It also offers a training and certificate program for those working in the radio industry. Finally, this organization does some research to help support radio as a viable communication medium.

Figure 9–10 Weekly reach and share of total hours tuned by demographic

Canada		Reach		Share	
		AM (%)	FM (%)	AM (%)	FM (%)
12+		40	79	28	72
Women 18+		42	78	29	71
Men 18+		44	78	29	71
Teens 12–17		17	84	8	92

Source: BBM, Fall '00

Quebec		Reach		Share	
		AM (%)	FM (%)	AM (%)	FM (%)
12+	(Fr.)	13	87	15	85
	(Eng.)	17	83	30	70
Women 18+	(Fr.)	13	87	16	84
	(Eng.)	21	79	32	68
Men 18+	(Fr.)	13	87	15	85
	(Eng.)	19	81	30	70
Teens 12–17	(Fr.)	16	84	3	97
	(Eng.)	17	83	8	92

Source: BBM, Fall '00

Figure 9–11 Audience composition by time block

Time block			Women 18+ %	Men 18+ %	Teens 12–17 %
Breakfast	Mon.–Fri.	6 A.M.–10 A.M.	47	45	8
Midday	Mon.–Fri.	10 A.M.–4 P.M.	50	44	6
Drive	Mon.–Fri.	4 P.M.–7 P.M.	47	45	8
Evening	Mon.–Fri.	7 P.M.–Midnight	46	43	11

Source: BBM, Fall '00

Note: Various dayparts may be combined to reach the largest possible audiences

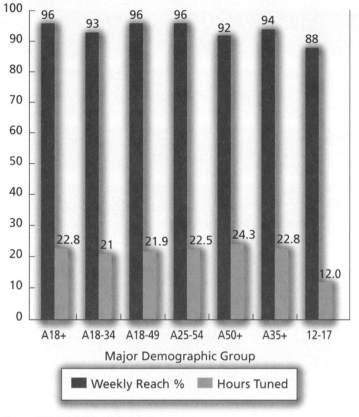

Figure 9–12 Percentage weekly reach and hours tuned by major demographic

Source: BBM, Fall '00, All Canada

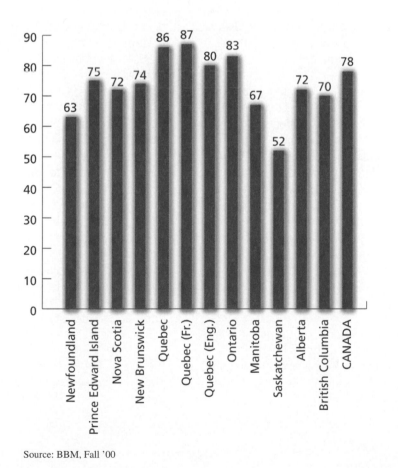

Figure 9–13 Weekly radio FM listening—percentage reach (12+)

Source: BBM, Fall '00

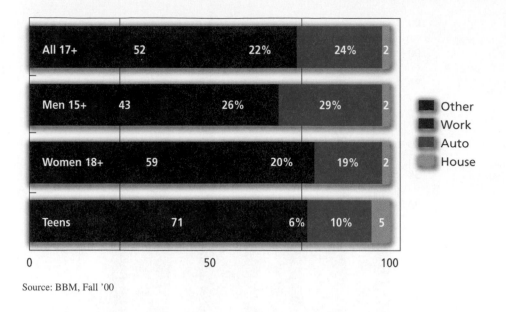

Figure 9–14 Radio listening by location—all persons (12+)

	House	Auto	Work	Other
All 17+	52	22%	24%	2
Men 15+	43	26%	29%	2
Women 18+	59	20%	19%	2
Teens	71	6%	10%	5

Source: BBM, Fall '00

Summary

Television and radio media are the most pervasive media in most consumers' daily lives and offer advertisers the opportunity to reach vast audiences. Both media are time rather than space oriented and organized similarly in that they use a system of affiliated stations belonging to a network, as well as individual stations, to broadcast their programs and commercial messages. Advertising on radio or TV can be done on national or regional network programs or purchased in spots from local stations.

TV has grown faster than any other advertising medium in history and has become the leading medium for national advertisers. No other medium offers its creative capabilities; the combination of sight, sound, and movement give the advertiser a vast number of options for presenting a commercial message with high impact. Television also offers advertisers mass coverage at a low relative cost. Variations in programming and audience composition, along with the growth of cable, are helping TV offer more audience selectivity to advertisers. While television is often viewed as the ultimate advertising medium, it has several limitations, including the high cost of producing and airing commercials, a lack of selectivity relative to other media, the fleeting nature of the message, and the problem of commercial clutter.

Information regarding the size and composition of national and local TV audiences is provided by BBM Canada and Nielsen. The amount of money networks or stations can charge for commercial time on their programs is based on its audience measurement figures. This information is also important to media planners, as it is used to determine the combination of shows needed to attain specific levels of reach and frequency with the advertiser's target audience.

The role of radio as an entertainment and advertising medium has changed with the rapid growth of television. Radio has evolved into a primarily local advertising medium that offers highly specialized programming appealing to narrow segments of the market. Radio offers advertisers the opportunity to build high reach and frequency into their media schedules and to reach selective audiences at a very efficient cost. It also offers opportunities for integrated marketing programs such as place-based promotions and event sponsorships.

The major drawback of radio is its creative limitations owing to the absence of a visual image. The short and fleeting nature of the radio commercial, the highly fragmented nature of the radio audience, and clutter are also problems.

As with TV, the rate structure for radio advertising time varies with the size of the audience delivered. The primary sources of listener information are BBM and RMB.

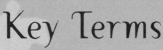

Key Terms

Discussion Questions

1. Discuss the advantages of television as an advertising medium and the importance of these factors to major advertisers such as automobile companies or packaged goods marketers.

2. Television is often described as a mass medium that offers little selectivity to advertisers. Do you agree with this statement? What are some of the ways selectivity can be achieved through TV advertising?

3. Choose a particular television daypart other than prime time and analyze the products and services advertised during this period. Why do you think these companies have chosen to advertise during this daypart?

4. Discuss how technological developments are likely to affect the way viewers watch television in the near future. What are the implications for TV advertising?

5. Discuss the advantages and limitation of advertising on cable TV. Discuss how both large national advertisers and small local companies might use cable TV effectively in their media plans.

6. Discuss the methods used to measure network and local TV viewing audiences. Do you think the measurement methods used for each are producing reliable and valid estimates of the viewing audiences? How might they be improved?

7. What are the advantages and disadvantages of advertising on radio? What types of advertisers are most likely to use radio?

8. What is meant by imagery transfer in radio advertising? Find an example of a radio campaign that is using this concept and evaluate it.

9. Discuss some of the factors that media buyers should take into consideration when buying advertising time on radio.

Chapter Ten
Print Media

Chapter Objectives

- To examine the structure of the magazine and newspaper industries and the role of each medium in the advertising program.

- To analyze the strengths and limitations of magazines and newspapers as advertising media.

- To examine the various types of magazines and newspapers and the value of each as an advertising medium.

- To discuss how advertising space is purchased in magazines and newspapers, how readership is measured, and how rates are determined.

- To consider future developments in magazines and newspapers and how these trends will influence their use as advertising media.

Luxury Car Companies Use Similar Media Strategy

A car purchase is typically a drawn-out affair where consumers will engage in all steps of the buyer decision process and take up to six months to make a new car purchase (or lease). Print ads are an option for creating awareness and highlighting key attributes and benefits to consumers as they proceed through the information search and evaluation stages. In fact, newspaper print ads played a key role in the recent launch of two luxury cars, the Infiniti G35 by Nissan and the Lexus ES 300 by Toyota.

As a new high-performance luxury sedan, the G35 was targeting European sports-sedan consumers, or those who were intending to purchase one. The plan was to develop a specific G35 brand image instead of riding on the coattails of Infiniti advertising and branding. Media research indicated that the luxury automotive buyer was a heavy newspaper reader. In fact, about a half a billion dollars is spent on newspaper ads in Canada per year, and new car launches for the luxury market typically spend 71 percent of their budget in newspaper ads.

To attract the attention of consumers in the market for a European sports sedan, while they were reading the news, the G35 used compelling, full-page, four-colour ads in newspaper "A" sections. Supporting this initial exposure were black-and-white ads in automotive sections. The clear intention of the ad was to put the G35 in the target audience's evoked set such that they would visit the Infiniti dealer. And the message was clear at promising a key attribute of power via the 260-horsepower engine, something that would definitely get the target audience to give it serious consideration. The result? Sales exceeded the target of 57 percent, and dealership traffic was very high.

The decision by Lexus to use newspaper print media as a key part of their media strategy had different reasons, but the end result of its usage was similar to Infiniti's. The agency for Lexus considered many innovative media alternatives to reach current Lexus buyers who would be interested in the new ES 300 model. However, it decided that while the Lexus brand was somewhat young, it still had a well-defined brand image with its current users who preferred to receive factual messages of the automobile's benefits.

Naturally, newspaper was a useful vehicle to communicate the comfort and tranquility of driving the new Lexus. And since the target audience of Lexus was known to routinely read certain parts of identifiable newspapers, it was a logical choice to show the creative with full-page ads that would truly capture their attention and achieve the intended communications objectives. In the end, the agency says that the plan is living up to expectations.

Sources: "How to get noticed ... fast," *Marketing Magazine*, May 6, 2002; "Driving the Message Home," *Marketing Magazine*, February 4, 2002.

Magazines and newspapers have been advertising media for more than two centuries; for many years, they were the only major media available to advertisers. With the growth of the broadcast media, particularly television, reading habits declined. More consumers turned to TV viewing not only as their primary source of entertainment but also for news and information. But despite the competition from the broadcast media, newspapers and magazines have remained important media vehicles to both consumers and advertisers.

Thousands of magazines are published in Canada and throughout the world. They appeal to nearly every specific consumer interest and lifestyle, as well as to thousands of businesses and occupations. By becoming a highly specialized medium that reaches specific target audiences, the magazine industry has prospered. Newspapers are still the primary advertising medium in terms of both ad revenue and number of advertisers. Newspapers are particularly important as a local advertising medium for hundreds of thousands of retail businesses and are often used by large national advertisers as well.

Magazines and newspapers are an important part of our lives. For many consumers, newspapers are their primary source of product information. They would not think of going shopping without checking to see who is having a sale or clipping coupons from the weekly food section or Saturday inserts. Many people read a number of different magazines each week or month to become better informed or simply entertained. Individuals employed in various occupations rely on business magazines to keep them current about trends and developments in their industries as well as in business in general.

The role of magazines and newspapers in the advertiser's media plan differs from that of the broadcast media because they allow the presentation of detailed information that can be processed at the reader's own pace. The print media are not intrusive like radio and TV, and they generally require some effort on the part of the reader for the advertising message to have an impact. For this reason, newspapers and magazines are often referred to as *high-involvement media.*[1] While both magazines and newspapers are print media, the advantages and disadvantages of the two are quite different, as are the types of advertising each attracts. This chapter focuses on these two major forms of print media. It examines the specific strengths and limitations of each, along with factors that are important in determining when and how to use newspapers and magazines in the media plan.

Evaluation of Magazines

Over the past several decades, magazines have grown rapidly to serve the educational, informational, and entertainment needs of a wide range of readers in both the consumer and business markets. Magazines are the most specialized of all advertising media. While some magazines—such as *Reader's Digest, Time,* and *TV Guide*—are general mass-appeal publications, most are targeted to a very specific audience. There is a magazine designed to appeal to nearly every type of consumer in terms of demographics, lifestyle, activities, interests, or fascination. Numerous magazines are targeted toward specific businesses and industries as well as toward individuals engaged in various professions.

The wide variety makes magazines an appealing medium to a vast number of advertisers. Users of magazines range from large consumer products companies such as Procter & Gamble and General Motors to a small company advertising gardening equipment in *Canadian Gardening* magazine.

Classifications of Magazines

To gain some perspective on the various types of magazines available and the advertisers that use them, consider the way magazines are generally classified. Canadian Advertising Rates and Data (CARD), the primary reference source on periodicals for media planners, divides magazines into three broad categories based on the audience to which they are directed: consumer, farm, and business publications. Each category is then further classified according to the magazine's editorial content and audience appeal.

Consumer Magazines Consumer magazines are bought by the general public for information and/or entertainment. CARD divides 550 domestic consumer magazines into 44 classifications, among them general interest, sports, travel and tourism, and women's. Another way of classifying consumer magazines is by distribution: They can be sold through subscription, store distribution, or controlled distribution (free) to selected individuals. Figures 10–1 and 10–2 show the top Canadian magazines in terms of circulation. Magazines can also be classified by frequency; weekly, monthly, and bimonthly are the most common. Figure 10–3 shows the top U.S. magazines with paid Canadian circulation.

Consumer magazines represent the major portion of the magazine industry, accounting for nearly two-thirds of all advertising dollars spent in magazines. The distribution of advertising revenue in consumer magazines is highly concentrated; the top 10 magazines receive more than 60 percent of total consumer magazine advertising. Consumer magazines are best suited to marketers interested in reaching general consumers of products and services as well as to companies trying to reach a specific target market. The most frequently advertised categories in consumer magazines are automotive, direct response, toiletries and cosmetics, computers, office equipment and stationery, and business and consumer services.

Figure 10–1 Top English-language magazines by circulation and readership

Publication	Average Total Circulation	IP 4CB Rate ($)	Readers Per Copy	(000s) Total
Westworld/Going Places	1,063,786	25,695	1.3	1,322
Reader's Digest	1,025,256	31,870	7.2	7,117
Chatelaine	737,984	39,765	6.3	4,292
LeisureWays/Journal	694,907	14,950	N/A	1,039
Starweek Magazine (Stock)	693,038	13,430	2.6	1,626
Elm Street	642,578	25,910	1.5	918
Feature	578,912	11,950	1.4	666
Homemaker's Magazine	561,947	21,260	4.2	2,162
Canadian Living	547,793	30,035	8.0	4,219
Food & Drink	518,760	13,309	3.3	1,592
Maclean's	502,750	31,960	6.1	2,844
Touring (bilingual)	501,403	10,485	N/A	N/A
TV Guide	561,107	19,775	7.2	3,579
Tribute	501,028	16,475	3.7	1,290

Source: PMB 2001 rates and circulation as of April 2001 CARD

Figure 10-2 Top French-language magazines by circulation and readership

Publication	Average Total Circulation	IP 4CB Rate ($)	Readers Per Copy	(000s) Total
Touring	501,403	10,845	1.3	644
Télé Horaire-Montréal	321,659	5,250	N/A	N/A
Primeurs	307,849	7,125	1.8	471
Télé Plus	275,116	8,750	1.3	453
Selection du Reader's Digest	230,054	10,650	4.8	1,055
Virage	215,646	4,300	N/A	N/A
TV 7 Jours/TV Hebo	189,716	9,575	4.4	1,239
L'actualité	187,694	14,880	5.2	914
Chatelaine	186,987	13,245	5.4	896
Coup de Pouce	172,413	2,395	6.2	963
Le Coureur des Neiges	159,082	5,600	N/A	N/A
Le Bel Age	149,754	6,255	5.2	765
Madame	129,340	6,520	3.6	415
Télé Horaire-Québec City	128,073	2,400	N/A	N/A
Info Plein Air	125,000	4,995	N/A	N/A
7 Jours	121,546	11,090	9.7	1,040
Voir (Montréal)	114,011	7,610	2.8	255

Source: PMB 2001 rates and circulation as of April 2001 CARD

While large national advertisers tend to dominate consumer magazine advertising in terms of expenditures, consumer magazines are also important to smaller companies selling products that appeal to specialized markets. Special-interest magazines assemble consumers with similar lifestyles or interests and offer marketers an efficient way to reach these people with little wasted coverage or circulation. For example, a manufacturer of ski equipment such as Nordica, Rossignol, or Salomon might find *Ski Canada* magazine the best vehicle for advertising to serious skiers. Not only are these specialty magazines of value to firms interested in reaching a specific market segment, but their editorial content often creates a very favourable advertising environment for relevant products and services (see Exhibit 10–1).

Farm Publications The second major CARD category consists of all the magazines directed to farmers and their families. About 86 publications are tailored to nearly every possible type of farming or agricultural interest (e.g., *Ontario Milk Producer*, *Ontario Produce Farmer*). A number of farm publications are directed at farmers in specific provinces or regions, such as *Alberta Beef* (see Exhibit 10–2). Farm publications are not classified with business publications because historically farms were not perceived as businesses.

Business Publications Business publications are those magazines or trade journals published for specific businesses, industries, or occupations. CARD breaks down magazines and trade journals into 109 categories. The major categories include

1. Magazines directed at specific professional groups, such as *Canadian Lawyer* for lawyers and *Canadian Architect* for architects.

Figure 10-3 Top U.S. magazines with paid Canadian circulation

Publication	Circulation
National Geographic	510,781
Maxim	239,055
Cosmopolitan	219,117
People	196,961
Woman's World	191,825
National Enquirer	186,784
YM	161,279
Prevention	154,796
Teen People	151,129
Star	149,856
Good Housekeeping	133,360
Seventeen	124,271
Playboy	119,089
Martha Stewart Living	118,750
Sports Illustrated	118,017
In Style	109,066
First For Women	101,352

Source: MediaDigest, September 24, 2001

Exhibit 10–1 *Outpost* magazine is an excellent vehicle for reaching adventure travel tourists

Exhibit 10–2 *Alberta Beef* is read by many cattle ranchers

2. Industrial magazines directed at businesspeople in various manufacturing and production industries—for example, *Process Equipment and Control News* and *Heavy Construction.*

3. Trade magazines targeted to wholesalers, dealers, distributors, and retailers, among them *Canadian Grocer.*

4. General business magazines aimed at executives in all areas of business, such as *Canadian Grocer.*

The numerous business publications reach specific types of professional people with particular interests and give them important information relevant to their industry, occupation, and/or careers. Business publications are important to advertisers because they provide an efficient way of reaching the specific types of individuals who constitute their target market. Much marketing occurs at the trade and business-to-business level, where one company sells its products or services directly to another.

Strengths of Magazines

Magazines have a number of characteristics that make them attractive as an advertising medium. Strengths of magazines include their selectivity, excellent reproduction quality, creative flexibility, permanence, prestige, and readers' high receptivity and involvement.

Selectivity   One of the main advantages of using magazines as an advertising medium is their **selectivity,** or ability to reach a specific target audience. Magazines are the most selective of all media except direct mail. Most magazines are published for special-interest groups. The thousands of magazines published in Canada reach all types of consumers and businesses and allow advertisers to target their advertising to segments of the population who buy their products. For example, *PhotoLife* is targeted toward camera buffs, *Exclaim!* reaches those with an avid interest in music, and *What!* claims to be "the voice and choice of Canadian youth." Many new magazines are introduced each year targeting new interests and trends.

In addition to providing selectivity based on interests, magazines can provide advertisers with high demographic and geographic selectivity. *Demographic selectivity,* or the ability to reach specific demographic groups, is available in two ways. First, most magazines are, as a result of editorial content, aimed at fairly well-defined demographic segments. *Canadian Living* and *Chatelaine* are read predominantly by women; *The Hockey News* is read mostly by men. Older consumers can be reached through publications like *FiftyPlus.*

Exhibit 10–3 City magazines such as *Toronto Life* offer advertisers high geographic selectivity

Geographic selectivity lets an advertiser focus ads in certain cities or regions. One way to achieve geographic selectivity is by using a magazine that is targeted toward a particular area. One of the more successful media developments of recent years has been the growth of city magazines in some Canadian cities. *Toronto Life, Vancouver Magazine,* and *Montréal Scope,* to name a few, provide residents of these areas with articles concerning lifestyle, events, and the like, in these cities and their surrounding metropolitan areas (Exhibit 10–3).

Another way to achieve geographic selectivity in magazines is through purchasing ad space in specific geographic editions of national or regional magazines. A number of publications (e.g., *Maclean's, Chatelaine*) divide their circulation into groupings based on regions or major metropolitan areas and offer advertisers the option of concentrating their ads in these editions.

CARD lists the consumer magazines offering geographic and/or demographic editions. Regional advertisers can purchase space in editions that reach only areas where they have distribution, yet still enjoy the prestige of advertising in a major national magazine. National advertisers can use the geographic editions to focus their advertising on areas with the greatest potential or those needing more promotional support. They can also use regional editions to test-market products or alternative promotional campaigns in various regions of the country.

Ads in regional editions can also list the names of retailers or distributors in various markets, thus encouraging greater local support from the trade. The trend toward regional marketing is increasing the importance of having regional media available to marketers. The availability of regional and demographic editions can also reduce the cost per thousand for reaching desired audiences.

Reproduction Quality One of the most valued attributes of magazine advertising is the reproduction quality of the ads. Magazines are generally printed on high-quality paper stock and use printing processes that provide excellent reproduction in black and white or colour. Since magazines are a visual medium where illustrations are often a dominant part of an ad, this is a very important property. The reproduction quality of most magazines is far superior to that offered by the other major print medium of newspapers, particularly when colour is needed. The use of colour has become a virtual necessity in most product categories, and more than two-thirds of all magazine ads now use colour.

Creative Flexibility In addition to their excellent reproduction capabilities, magazines also offer advertisers a great deal of flexibility in terms of the type, size,

Lack of Targeted Canadian Magazines Is a Problem

When Deborah Coyne was buying advertising for Club Monaco, she remembers that the Toronto–based fashion retailer was frustrated by the lack of Canadian magazines. In the U.S., Club Monaco was buying advertising in magazines such as *Jane* and *Vogue,* but the retailer found the Canadian market lacked suitable equivalents.

Instead, she says that the portion of the budget for the Canadian market that had been intended to be used for magazines went almost entirely to outdoor. "From a production standpoint, it would have been much easier to use the magazine ads that we were using in the U.S. here in Canada," says Coyne, who worked for Club Monaco while an account manager at Harrison Young Pesonen & Newell before leaving last year to become group client services director at Genesis Media, also in Toronto. "There is not much choice in Canada. It is very frustrating for both the buyer and the client. It's a challenge."

Indeed, media buyers and planners in Canada say that the magazine industry here offers so little selection relative to the U.S. as to be almost non-existent. "We need and want more successful magazines," says Ann Boden, president of media-buying giant OMD Canada in Toronto. "We want more advertising vehicles." Media buyers say that because the Canadian population is smaller than that of the U.S., magazines here try to target everyone and, in effect, become, well, boring. "Magazines have always been perceived as a specialty medium—but I question that in Canada," says Evelyn Ewert, director of planning at Carat Cairns in Toronto. "I find a lot of Canadian magazines are very broad and try to be all things to all people and end up being watery versions of what they started out to be."

As the media audience becomes more fragmented than ever, media planners and buyers say they wish Canadian magazine publishers would take a cue from their U.S. cousins by being more targeted. They'd like to see new titles in categories where no Canadian magazines now exist, or in some cases to see existing Canadian titles sharpen their focus to deliver more attitude. Planners and buyers say that titles with a better-defined niche often have more bite. That, in turn, attracts a well-defined target audience. And *that* is the best assurance that advertisers will come running.

In the case of Club Monaco, Coyne admits that "the Canadian market has a ton of women's magazines," ranging from *Chatelaine* to *Canadian Living* to *Elm Street.* But she says none has a distinctive, edgy, young women's voice like that of *Jane* in the U.S., which mixes fun features such as "Hot Beefcake Special" and "Who's Scuzzier, Men or Women?" with more hard-hitting fare like "I'm Too Young to Get My Breasts Removed." Coyne says the closest equivalent to *Jane* in Canada is *Flare.* But the latter, with stories such as "Relax, New Ways to Restore and Renew," she considers "way too conservative. Is an 18- to 24-year-old going to pick up *Flare* or *Jane*? I think they are going to pick up the U.S. magazine." Coyne says that a Canadian equivalent of *Jane* "would do well because there are a lot of fashion retailers who want to reach that younger age group and have very limited choices in print." She says it would also prove to be good vehicle for cosmetic companies.

Source: Adapted from Chris Daniels, "Missing the Target," *Marketing Magazine,* September 18, 2000. Reprinted with permission of Marketing Magazine.

and placement of the advertising material. Some magazines offer (often at extra charge) a variety of special options that can enhance the creative appeal of the ad and increase attention and readership. Examples include gatefolds, bleed pages, inserts, and creative space buys.

Gatefolds enable an advertiser to make a striking presentation by using a third page that folds out and gives the ad an extra-large spread. Gatefolds are often found at the inside cover of large consumer magazines or on some inside pages. Advertisers use gatefolds to make a very strong impression, especially on special occasions such as the introduction of a new product or brand. For example, automobile advertisers often use gatefolds to introduce new versions of their cars each model year. Not all magazines offer gatefolds, however, and they must be reserved well in advance and are sold at a premium.

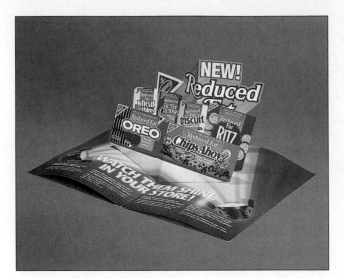

Exhibit 10–4 Nabisco used a pop-up ad to get the attention of trade magazine readers

Bleed pages are those where the advertisement extends all the way to the end of the page, with no margin of white space around the ad. Bleeds give the ad an impression of being larger and make a more dramatic impact. Many magazines charge an extra 10 to 20 percent for bleeds.

In addition to gatefolds and bleed pages, creative options available through magazines include unusual page sizes and shapes. Some advertisers have grabbed readers' attention by developing three-dimensional pop-up ads that jump off the page. Exhibit 10–4 shows a pop-up ad that Nabisco used in several trade magazines to promote its Reduced Fat cracker and cookie products.

Various other *inserts* are used in many magazines. These include return cards, recipe booklets, coupons, and even product samples. Cosmetic companies use scratch-and-sniff inserts to introduce new fragrances, and some companies use them to promote deodorants, laundry detergents, or other products whose scent is important. Inserts are also used in conjunction with direct-response ads and as part of sales promotion strategies.

Scented ads, pop-ups, singing ads, and other techniques are ways to break through the clutter in magazines and capture consumers' attention. However, there recently has been some backlash against various types of *printaculars*. Critics argue that they alter the appearance and feel of a magazine and the reader's relationship to it. Advertisers do not want to run regular ads that have to compete against heavy inserts, pop-ups, talking ads, or other distractions. Some advertisers and agencies are even asking publishers to notify them when they plan to run any spectacular inserts so that they can decide whether to pull their regular ads from the issue.[2]

Creative space buys are another option of magazines. Some magazines let advertisers purchase space units in certain combinations to increase the impact of their media budget. For example, WD-40, an all-purpose lubrication product, uses half- or quarter-page ads on consecutive pages of several magazines, mentioning a different use for the product on each page, as shown in Exhibit 10–5. This strategy gives the company greater impact for its media dollars and is helpful in promoting the product's variety of uses.

Permanence   A distinctive strength offered by magazines is their long life span. TV and radio are characterized by fleeting messages that have a very short life span; newspapers are generally discarded soon after being read. Magazines, however, are generally read over several days and are often kept for reference. They are retained in the home longer than any other medium and are generally referred to on several occasions. A study of magazine audiences found that readers devote nearly an hour over a period of two or three days to reading an average magazine.[3] Studies have also found that nearly 75 percent of consumers retain magazines for future reference.[4] One benefit of the longer life of magazines is that reading occurs at a less hurried pace and there is more opportunity to examine ads in considerable detail. This means ads can use longer and more detailed copy, which can be very important for high-involvement and complex products or services. The permanence of magazines also means readers can be exposed to ads on multiple occasions and can pass magazines along to other readers.

Prestige   Another positive feature of magazine advertising is the prestige the product or service may gain from advertising in publications with a favourable image. Companies whose products rely heavily on perceived quality, reputation, and/or image often buy space in prestigious publications with high-quality editorial content whose consumers have a high level of interest in the advertising pages. For example, *Flare* covers young women's fashions in a very favourable environment, and a clothing manufacturer may advertise its products in these magazines to enhance the prestige of its lines. *Canadian Geographic* provides an impressive editorial environment that includes high-quality photography. The magazine's upscale

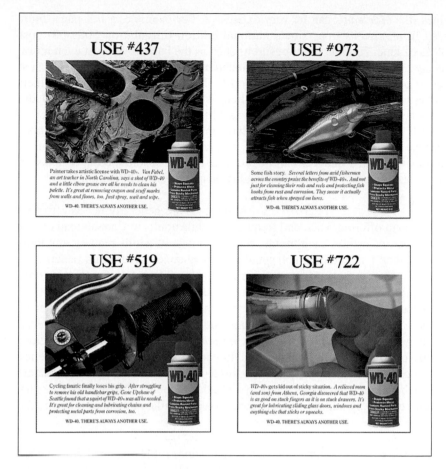

readers are likely to have a favourable image of the publication that may transfer to the products advertised on its pages.

While most media planners recognize that the environment created by a publication is important, it can be difficult to determine the image a magazine provides. Subjective estimates based on media planners' experience are often used to assess a magazine's prestige, as are objective measures such as reader opinion surveys.

Consumer Receptivity and Involvement   With the exception of newspapers, consumers are more receptive to advertising in magazines than in any other medium. Magazines are generally purchased because the information they contain interests the reader, and ads provide additional information that may be of value in making a purchase decision.

In addition to their relevance, magazine ads are likely to be received favourably by consumers because, unlike broadcast ads, they are nonintrusive and can easily be ignored. Studies show that the majority of magazine readers welcome ads; only a small percentage have negative attitudes toward magazine advertising.[5] Some magazines, such as bridal or fashion publications, are purchased as much for their advertising as for their editorial content. Some studies have shown that magazine readers are more likely to attend to and recall ads than are TV viewers.

Limitations of Magazines

Although the strengths offered by magazines are considerable, they have certain drawbacks too. These include the costs of advertising, their limited reach and frequency, the long lead time required in placing an ad, and the problem of clutter and heavy advertising competition.

Costs   The costs of advertising in magazines vary according to the size of the audience they reach and their selectivity. Advertising in large mass-circulation magazines like *Maclean's* can be very expensive. For example, a full-page, four-colour ad in *Maclean's* magazine's national edition (circulation 500,000) cost $25,000 as of June, 2000. Popular positions such as the back cover cost even more.

Like any medium, magazines must be considered not only from an absolute cost perspective but also in terms of relative costs. Most magazines emphasize their effectiveness in reaching specific target audiences at a low cost per thousand. Media planners generally focus on the relative costs of a publication in reaching their target audience. However, they may recommend a magazine with a high cost per thousand because of its ability to reach a small, specialized market segment. Of course, advertisers with limited budgets will be interested in the absolute costs of space in a magazine and the costs of producing quality ads for these publications.

Limited Reach and Frequency

Magazines are generally not as effective as other media in offering reach and frequency. While adults in Canada read one or more consumer magazines each month, the percentage of adults reading any individual publication tends to be much smaller, so magazines have a thin penetration of households. For example, *Maclean's* has a high circulation, but it represents only 4 percent of the 11.6 million households in Canada.

Thus, advertisers seeking broad reach must make media buys in a number of magazines, which means more negotiations and transactions. For a broad reach strategy, magazines are used in conjunction with other media. Since most magazines are monthly or at best weekly publications, the opportunity for building frequency through the use of the same publication is limited. Using multiple ads in the same issue of a publication is an inefficient way to build frequency. Most advertisers try to achieve frequency by adding other magazines with similar audiences to the media schedule.

Long Lead Time

Another drawback of magazines is the long lead time needed to place an ad. Most major publications have a 30- to 90-day lead time, which means space must be purchased and the ad must be prepared well in advance of the actual publication date. No changes in the art or copy of the ad can be made after the closing date. This long lead time means magazine ads cannot be as timely as other media, such as radio or newspapers, in responding to current events or changing market conditions.

Clutter and Competition

While the problem of advertising clutter is generally discussed in reference to the broadcast media, magazines also have this drawback. Clutter is not as serious an issue for the print media as for radio or TV, since consumers tend to be more receptive and tolerant of print advertising. They can also control their exposure to a magazine ad simply by turning the page. The clutter problem for magazines is something of a paradox: The more successful a magazine becomes, the more advertising pages it attracts, and this leads to greater clutter. In fact, magazines generally gauge their success in terms of the number of advertising pages they sell.

Magazine publishers do attempt to control the clutter problem by maintaining a reasonable balance of editorial pages to advertising. However, many magazines contain ads on more than half of their pages. This clutter makes it difficult for an advertiser to gain readers' attention and draw them into the ad. Thus, many print ads use strong visual images, catchy headlines, or some of the creative techniques discussed earlier to grab the interest of magazine readers. Some advertisers create their own custom magazines to sidestep the advertising clutter problem as well as to have control over editorial content. A number of companies have also been publishing their own magazines to build relationships with their customers. Federal Express publishes *Via FedEx,* a free magazine full of career and office management tips for some of its most important customers, professional secretaries.

A recent trend among some companies is to enter into joint agreement with traditional publishers to produce custom magazines that they sell to their customers. For example, Swedish retailer IKEA has partnered with

Exhibit 10–6 *Sun* is a magazine custom-published for Ray-Ban

John Brown Contract Publishing to custom-publish a magazine titled *space*.[6] *space* is both a showcase for IKEA merchandise and a magazine that contains informative articles about home furnishings, modern design, and lifestyle trends. *space* is sold at IKEA stores, and on newsstands, throughout North America. The custom-publishing division of Hachette Filapacchi publishes a magazine for Ray-Ban Sunglasses called *Sun* (Exhibit 10–6) and one for Sony that doubles as a catalogue called *Sony Style*. Custom-published magazines have also become very popular among tobacco companies, such as Philip Morris, which direct-mail them to their customer base.[7]

The strengths and limitations of magazines are part of the decision to use this media. Another key factor is a complete understanding of the readers of magazines to assess whether there is a fit between them and the target audience of the promotion plan. In this section, we review a few issues related to this part of the decision: circulation and readership, audience measurement, and magazine advertising rates.

Buying Magazine Advertising Space

Magazine Circulation and Readership

Two of the most important considerations in deciding whether to use a magazine in the advertising media plan are the size and characteristics of the audience it reaches. Media buyers evaluate magazines on the basis of their ability to deliver the advertiser's message to as many people as possible in the target audience. To do this, they must consider the circulation of the publication as well as its total readership and match these figures against the audience they are attempting to reach.

Circulation   Circulation figures represent the number of individuals who receive a publication through either subscription or store purchase, or through controlled distribution (free). Given that circulation figures are the basis for a magazine's advertising rates and one of the primary considerations in selecting a publication for placement, the credibility of circulation figures is important. Most major publications are audited by the Audit Bureau of Circulations (ABC), which was organized in 1914 and is sponsored by advertisers, agencies, and publishers. The Canadian division of this U.S.-based organization is known as the Canadian Circulations Audit Board. ABC collects and evaluates information regarding the subscriptions and sales of magazines and newspapers to verify their circulation figures. Only publications with 70 percent or more paid circulation (which means the purchaser paid at least half the magazine's established base price) are eligible for verification audits by ABC. Certain business publications are audited by the Business Publications Audit (BPA) of Circulation. Many of these are published on a **controlled-circulation basis**, meaning copies are sent (usually free) to individuals who the publisher believes can influence the company's purchases.

ABC provides media planners with reliable figures regarding the size and distribution of a magazine's circulation, which helps them evaluate its worth as a media vehicle. The ABC statement also provides detailed circulation information that gives a media planner an indication of the quality of the target audience. For example, it shows how the subscription was sold, the percentage of circulation sold at less than full value, the percentage of circulation sold with some kind of incentive, and the percentage of subscriptions given away. Many advertisers believe that subscribers who pay for a magazine are more likely to read it than are those who get it at a discount or for free. Media buyers are generally skeptical about publications whose circulation figures are not audited and will not advertise in unaudited publications. Circulation data, along with the auditing source, are available from CARD or from the publication itself.

Readership   Advertisers are often interested in the number of people a publication reaches as a result of secondary, or pass-along, readership. **Pass-along readership** can occur when the primary subscriber or purchaser gives a magazine to another person or when the publication is read in doctors' waiting rooms or beauty salons, on airplanes, and so forth.

Advertisers generally attach greater value to the primary in-home reader than the pass-along reader or out-of-home reader, as the former generally spends more time with the publication, picks it up more often, and receives greater satisfaction from it. Thus, this reader is more likely to be attentive and responsive to ads. However, the value of pass-along readers should not be discounted. They can greatly expand a magazine's readership.

You can calculate the **total audience,** or **readership,** of a magazine by multiplying the readers per copy (the total number of primary and pass-along readers) by the circulation of an average issue. For example, a magazine that has a circulation of 1 million and 3.5 readers per copy has a total audience of 3.5 million. However, rate structures are generally based on the more verifiable primary circulation figures, and many media planners devalue pass-along readers by as much as 50 percent. Total readership estimates are reported by the Print Measurement Bureau (PMB), to which we now turn our attention.

Magazine Audience Measurement—PMB

Print Measurement Bureau (PMB) is a non-profit Canadian industry association of nearly 500 members drawn from advertisers, print magazine publishers, and advertising agencies. Its primary mandate is to collect readership information for print magazines, which allows all three constituents to make more effective advertising decisions. Its foremost research is known simply as the **PMB study.**

The first national PMB study was conducted in 1973 and originally concerned print magazines only. It has grown since then and is now Canada's primary syndicated source for print and non-print media exposure, as well as responses to survey questions. The current study has resulted in a 2-year database of 30,000 respondents, over 2,500 products, and over 3,500 brands.

The research method is an in-home interview conducted throughout the year. Respondents are screened by asking whether they have read any of the listed publications within the past 12 months; they are subsequently qualified if they have read the publications recently enough, depending upon the frequency of publication (e.g., weekly, monthly). A number of reading-related questions are asked, including frequency of reading, number of reading occasions, time spent reading, source of copy, where read, and interest.

Respondents are then asked many demographic, lifestyle, media consumption, product usage, retail shopping, and psychographic questions. The demographic questions are quite exhaustive and total over 20 in number. The lifestyle questions include life events, leisure activities, education, sporting activities, and attendance of sporting events. Media consumption questions are very extensive and include TV viewing, radio listening, community and daily newspaper reading, transit usage, distance traveled, shopping mall trips, and Yellow Pages usage. Product usage data is recorded for 17 broad product categories (e.g., personal care, groceries, financial, business, and so on). Questions pertaining to shopping at approximately 30 different retail environments are also asked. And finally, many questions are asked to determine psychographic clusters for nine broad product categories and one general societal category.

As you may imagine, the data available for analysis is a virtual gold mine of information for media planners. They can relate many of the variables together to accurately reach a specific target audience in terms of their behaviour (i.e., the primary target variable), demographics, lifestyle, and psychographics. And, as you also may expect, the database works with specialized software to allow media planners to make their effective decisions efficiently.

One final useful feature of the PMB study is "return to sample." Individual firms can confidentially re-contact respondents to ask them proprietary questions with respect to specific brand attitudes, purchase intentions, or purchase influences. An advertiser would then have the broad data tied in with some specific measures of their own brand.

Magazine Advertising Rates

Magazine rates are primarily a function of circulation: the greater the circulation, the higher cost of the ad. Other variables include the size of the ad, its position in the publication, the particular editions (geographic, demographic) chosen, any special mechanical or production requirements, the number and frequency of insertions, and whether the circulation is controlled (free) or paid.

Advertising space is generally sold on the basis of space units such as full page, half page, and quarter page, although some publications quote rates on the basis of column inches. The larger the ad, the greater the cost. However, many advertisers use full-page ads since they result in more attention and readership. Studies have found that full-page ads generated 36 percent more readership than half-page ads.[8]

Ads can be produced or run using black and white, black and white plus one colour, or four colours. The more colour used in the ad, the greater the expense because of the increased printing costs. On average, a four-colour ad costs 30 percent more than a black-and-white ad. Advertisers generally prefer colour ads because they have greater visual impact and are superior for attracting and holding attention.[9] Starch INRA Hooper, Inc., analyzed the effect of various factors on the readership of magazine ads. The "noted" scores (the percentage of readers who remember seeing the ad in a publication they read) are 45 percent higher for a four-colour full-page ad than for a black-and-white ad. A four-colour spread (two facing pages) outperforms a black-and-white spread by 53 percent.[10] Ads requiring special mechanical production such as bleed pages or inserts may also cost extra.

Rates for magazine ad space can also vary according to the number of times an ad runs and the amount of money spent during a specific period. The more often an advertiser contracts to run an ad, the lower are the space charges. Volume discounts are based on the total space purchased within a contract year, measured in dollars or number of insertions.

The Future for Magazines

Magazine advertising revenue totaled $779 million in 2000, up from $700 million in 1994. This represents about a 2 percent growth per year and equals the inflation rate for this time period. Beyond this stable period, publishers are looking at a number of ways to improve their position—including stronger editorial platforms, better circulation management, niche marketing, technological advances, and electronic delivery methods—to make advertising in magazines more appealing to marketers.

Stronger Editorial Platforms Magazines with strong editorial platforms that appeal to the interests, lifestyles, and changing demographics of consumers as well as business and market trends in the new millennium are in the best position to attract readers and advertisers.

Circulation Management Circulation is the second major source of revenue for most publications, and publishers must carefully manage the costs of attracting and maintaining additional readers or subscribers.

Niche Marketing Many advertisers are increasingly turning to magazines as a cost-efficient way of reaching specialized audiences. As marketers continue to move toward greater market segmentation, market niche strategies, and regional marketing, they are making greater use of magazines because of their high selectivity and ability to avoid wasted coverage or circulation.

Exhibit 10–7 *Newsweek* promotes the value of ink-jet imaging

Advances in Technology Two important technological developments are making it possible for advertisers to deliver personalized messages to tightly targeted audiences: selective binding technology and ink-jet imaging. **Selective binding** is a computerized production process that allows the creation of hundreds of copies of a magazine in one continuous sequence. Selective binding enables magazines to target and address specific groups within a magazine's circulation base. They can then send different editorial or advertising messages to various groups of subscribers within the same issue of a publication. **Ink-jet imaging** reproduces a message by projecting ink onto paper rather than using mechanical plates. This process makes it possible to personalize an advertising message. Many publishers believe selective binding and ink-jet imaging will let advertisers target their messages more finely and let magazines compete more effectively with direct mail and other direct-marketing vehicles. Exhibit 10–7 shows how *Newsweek* promotes the capabilities of ink-jet imaging for targeting advertising messages.

Publishers are also developing new technologies that will enhance the creative opportunities available to magazine advertisers. Advertisers use a variety of techniques in print ads to capture readers' attention, including sound, scents, moving images, and pop-up ads. Current technologies are being refined and made more cost effective, and a number of new technologies will be incorporated into print ads soon. These include anaglyphic images (three-dimensional materials that are viewed with coloured glasses); lenticular (colour) images printed on finely corrugated plastic that seem to move when tilted; and pressure- or heat-sensitive inks that change colour on contact. These new technologies will give advertisers ways to break through the advertising clutter. However, these new print technologies can be very costly. Moreover, many advertisers and agencies are concerned that ads that use these new technologies may do so at the expense of other ads in the magazine, so they may pressure publishers to control their use. Some creative people have also expressed concern that these new technologies are gimmicks being substituted for creative advertising ideas.[11]

Online Delivery Methods Many magazines are keeping pace with the digital revolution and the continuing consumer interest in technology by making their publications available online (Exhibit 10–8). They provide advertisers with

Exhibit 10–8 Magazines such as *Business Week* are now available online

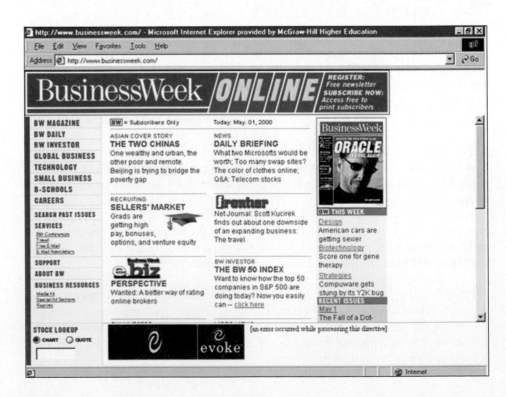

Proving That Magazine Ads Work

For years magazine publishers focused most of their attention on selling ads in their magazines and devoted less attention to proving the ads were effective. At many magazines, efforts at measuring effectiveness were often limited to tracking consumer response to 800 numbers that appeared in print ads. However, the carefree days are over as many new advertising media have emerged, such as niche-oriented cable TV networks, narrowly targeted radio stations, and the Internet. Moreover, there are more than twice as many magazines competing for media dollars as there were a decade ago. With so many media options available, marketers now want tangible proof that magazine advertising is effective and can build brand awareness, help position a brand, or actually deliver sales.

Magazines have typically promised advertisers *exposure* or access to a well-defined audience such as fashion-conscious young women, sports-obsessed men, or automotive buffs. However, advertisers want evidence of more than exposure. They want proof that seeing an ad for Calvin Klein jeans in *Cosmo* makes readers more likely to spend $80 to buy them or that placing an ad for a Volkswagen Jetta in *Rolling Stone* helps the brand stick in consumers' minds long enough to influence their next auto purchase. The executive vice president of Condé Nast Publications, Inc., which publishes popular titles such as *Vogue, GQ, Glamour,* and *Vanity Fair,* says: "Twenty years ago, our only obligation to advertisers was to gather people who would see the ad. Now we must prove the ad actually does something. Sometimes, that's possible; sometimes it's not."

Magazines increasingly have to compete against media that can provide evidence that their ads do indeed do something. For example, the Internet can show accountability instantly because consumers' movements and purchases can be tracked through their mouse clicks. And with new digital technology, television sets will soon become transactional tools, allowing consumers to order information and goods right from their sofas with a remote control. Magazines can ill afford to wait any longer to prove that they work. For example, General Motors, the nation's largest advertiser, spent only 21 percent of its advertising budget on consumer magazines in 1998, down from 27 percent just four years earlier. GM's top marketing executive argues that magazines spend too much time in a self-congratulatory mode. He notes: "The only thing we've learned at GM about magazines is through our own proprietary research. There's so much upside potential, but they need to reposi-

tion themselves in the new world."

The magazine industry is taking steps to address the accountability issue. The industry's lead trade group, Magazine Publishers of America (MPA), recently spent half a million dollars investigating ways to prove magazine effectiveness. One of the group's studies found that boosting ad spending in magazines increased short-term sales of products and also generated more sales over time. Sales increased among magazine-exposed households for 8 of the 10 brands measured. Individual magazines are also trying to prove how advertising in their pages can help build a brand or move the sales needle. Some magazines are finding ways to mesh the print side of their business with the e-commerce potential of the Internet. For example, print ads in Meredith Corp.'s *Wood* magazine will direct readers to Wood's website, where they will be able to buy wood tools and equipment in a virtual mall. The magazine's publisher feels that the print ads will drive traffic to the website that it would not normally get. In turn, the magazine expects to attract more print advertising because it will offer the additional e-commerce component.

Magazines are taking other steps to demonstrate the efficacy of print ads. Some are forging closer alliances with advertising agencies, which are also under strong pressure to exhibit accountability to their clients. Other publishers are opening up their subscriber databases to advertisers. For example, at the American Express Co. publishing division, which prints upscale titles such as *Travel & Leisure* and *Food & Wine,* the magazines often make use of the database the parent company gleans from its 19 million credit-card holders. For some advertisers, American Express magazines track credit-card activity to help determine whether sales of a specific product increased during a particular magazine promotion.

Consumers' loyalty to magazines and their willingness to spend uninterrupted, focused time with them has always been a powerful selling point for the medium. Now, however, magazines must prove that their connection with readers will generate sales for the companies that advertise in them. As Chris Miller, the MPA's head of marketing, notes: "One of the most important questions for this industry is the bottom-line question—does it drive sales?"

Source: Wendy Bounds, "Magazines Seek to Demonstrate Efficacy of Ads," *The Wall Street Journal,* April 12, 1999, pp. B1, 3.

the opportunity for sponsorships as well as banner ads and promotions on the online versions of the magazines. However, it remains to be seen whether people will want their magazines delivered online or prefer to read them in more traditional form. As the presence of magazines online grows, the industry will also have to address important issues regarding audience measurement and how to determine consumers' exposure to and interactions with online advertising. Advertising on the Internet is discussed in Chapter 15.

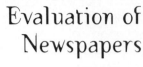

Evaluation of Newspapers

Newspapers, the second major form of print media, are the largest of all advertising media in terms of total dollar volume. In 1999 more than $1.6 billion was spent on daily newspaper advertising, or about 18 percent of the total advertising expenditures in Canada. Community newspapers accounted for almost $800 million, or 9 percent. Newspapers are an especially important advertising medium to local advertisers, particularly retailers. However, newspapers are also valuable to national advertisers. Many of the advertising dollars spent by local retailers are actually provided by national advertisers through cooperative advertising programs (discussed in Chapter 12). Newspapers vary in terms of their characteristics and their role as an advertising medium.

Types of Newspapers

The traditional role of newspapers has been to deliver prompt, detailed coverage of news as well as to supply other information and features that appeal to readers. The vast majority of newspapers are daily publications serving a local community. However, weekly, national, and special-audience newspapers have special characteristics that can be valuable to advertisers.

Daily Newspapers Daily newspapers, which are published each weekday, are found in cities and larger towns across the country. Many areas have more than one daily paper. Daily newspapers are read by nearly 60 percent of adults each weekday. They provide detailed coverage of news, events, and issues concerning the local area as well as business, sports, and other relevant information and entertainment. Daily newspapers can further be classified as morning, evening, or Sunday publications. In 2000, there were 108 daily newspapers in Canada; of these, 47 were evening papers and 61 morning. There were also 29 Sunday newspapers, most of which were published by daily newspapers.

Community Newspapers Most community newspapers publish weekly and originate in small towns or suburbs where the volume of news and advertising cannot support a daily newspaper. These papers focus primarily on news, sports, and events relevant to the local area and usually ignore national and world news, sports, and financial and business news. Community newspapers appeal primarily to local advertisers because of their geographic focus and lower absolute cost. Most national advertisers avoid community newspapers because of their duplicate circulation with daily papers in the large metropolitan areas.

National Newspapers Newspapers in Canada with national circulation include *The National Post* and *The Globe and Mail*. Both are daily publications and have editorial content with a national appeal. *The National Post* has a weekday circulation of about 330,000 and a Saturday circulation of almost 400,000. *The Globe and Mail* has a weekday circulation of about 354,000 and a Saturday circulation of approximately 416,000. National newspapers appeal primarily to large national advertisers and to regional advertisers that use specific geographic editions of these publications. Exhibit 10–9 shows an ad run by *The New York Times* informing advertisers of its classification as a national newspaper.

Special-Audience Newspapers A variety of papers offer specialized editorial content and are published for particular groups, including labour unions, professional organizations, industries, and hobbyists. Many people working in advertising and marketing read *Marketing Magazine*. Specialized newspapers are also published in areas with large foreign-language-speaking ethnic groups, among them Chinese. Newspapers targeted at various religious groups compose another large class of special-interest papers. Another type of special-audience newspaper is one most of you probably read regularly during the school year, the university newspaper.

Newspaper Supplements Although not a category of newspapers per se, some papers include magazine-type supplements. For example, the *Globe and Mail* publishes a glossy *Report on Business* magazine at the end of each month.

Types of Newspaper Advertising

The ads appearing in newspapers can also be divided into different categories. The major types of newspaper advertising are display and classified. Other special types of ads and preprinted inserts also appear in newspapers.

Display Advertising **Display advertising** is found throughout the newspaper and generally uses illustrations, headlines, white space, and other visual devices in addition to the copy text. Display ads account for approximately 70 percent of the advertising revenue of the average newspaper. The two types of display advertising in newspapers are local and national (general).

Local advertising refers to ads placed by local organizations, businesses, and individuals who want to communicate with consumers in the market area served by the newspaper. Supermarkets and department stores are among the leading local display advertisers, along with numerous other retailers and service operations such as banks and travel agents. Local advertising is sometimes referred to as retail advertising because retailers account for 85 percent of local display ads.

National or *general advertising* refers to newspaper display advertising done by marketers of branded products or services that are sold on a national or regional level. These ads are designed to create and maintain demand for a company's product or service and to complement the efforts of local retailers that stock and promote the advertiser's products. Major retail chains, automakers, and airlines are heavy users of newspaper advertising.

Classified Advertising **Classified advertising** also provides newspapers with a substantial amount of revenue. These ads are arranged under subheads according to the product, service, or offering being advertised. Employment, real estate, and automotive are the three major categories of classified advertising. While most classified ads are just text set in small type, some newspapers also accept classified display advertising. These ads are run in the classified section of the paper but use illustrations, larger type sizes, white space, borders, and even colour to stand out.

Special Ads and Inserts Special advertisements in newspapers include a variety of government and financial reports and notices and public notices of changes in business and personal relationships. Other types of advertising in newspapers include political or special-interest ads promoting a particular candidate, issue, or cause. **Preprinted inserts** are another type of advertising distributed

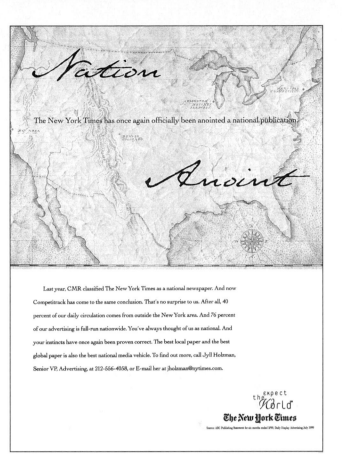

The New York Times has once again officially been anointed a national publication.

Last year, CMR classified The New York Times as a national newspaper. And now Competitrack has come to the same conclusion. That's no surprise to us. After all, 40 percent of our daily circulation comes from outside the New York area. And 76 percent of our advertising is full-run nationwide. You've always thought of us as national. And your instincts have once again been proven correct. The best local paper and the best global paper is also the best national media vehicle. To find out more, call Jyll Holzman, Senior VP, Advertising, at 212-556-4058, or E-mail her at jholzman@nytimes.com.

the expect World
The New York Times
Source: ABC Publishing Statement for six months ended 3/99, Daily Display Advertising July 1999

Exhibit 10–9 *The New York Times* promotes its classification as a national newspaper

through newspapers. These ads do not appear in the paper itself; they are printed by the advertiser and then taken to the newspaper to be inserted before delivery. Many retailers use inserts such as circulars, catalogues, or brochures in specific circulation zones to reach shoppers in their particular trade areas.

Strengths of Newspapers

Newspapers have a number of characteristics that make them popular among both local and national advertisers. These include their extensive penetration of local markets, flexibility, geographic selectivity, reader involvement, and special services.

Extensive Penetration   One of the primary advantages of newspapers is the high degree of market coverage, or penetration, they offer an advertiser. In most areas, 60 percent or more of households read a daily newspaper, and the reach figure may exceed 70 percent among households with higher incomes and education levels. Most areas are served by one or two daily newspapers.

The extensive penetration of newspapers makes them a truly mass medium and provides advertisers with an excellent opportunity for reaching all segments of the population with their message. Also, since many newspapers are published and read daily, the advertiser can build a high level of frequency into the media schedule.

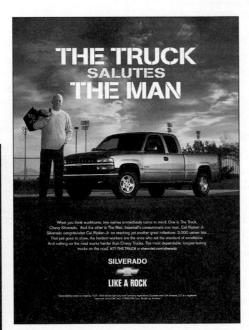

Exhibit 10–10   Chevy Trucks used a newspaper ad for a timely salute to Cal Ripken

Flexibility   Another advantage of newspapers is the flexibility they offer advertisers. First, they are flexible in terms of requirements for producing and running the ads. Newspaper ads can be written, laid out, and prepared in a matter of hours. For most dailies, the closing time by which the ad must be received is usually only 48 hours before publication (although closing dates for special ads, such as those using colour, and supplements are longer). The short production time and closing dates make newspapers an excellent medium for responding to current events or presenting timely information to consumers. For example, Chevrolet Trucks ran a newspaper ad congratulating major league baseball star Cal Ripken, Jr. the day after he got his 3,000 career hit (see Exhibit 10–10).

A second dimension of newspapers' flexibility stems from the creative options they make available to advertisers. Newspaper ads can be produced and run in various sizes, shapes, and formats; they can use colour or special inserts to gain the interest of readers. A variety of scheduling options are possible, depending on the advertiser's purpose.

Geographic Selectivity   Newspapers generally offer advertisers more geographic or territorial selectivity than any other medium except direct mail. Advertisers can vary their coverage by choosing a paper—or combination of papers—that reaches the areas with the greatest sales potential. National advertisers take advantage of the geographic selectivity of newspapers to concentrate their advertising in specific areas they can't reach with other media or to take advantage of strong sales potential in a particular area. For example, more expensive automobile manufacturers advertise in Toronto newspapers that reach the greater Toronto area and beyond with their wide distribution.

A number of companies use newspapers in their regional marketing strategies. Newspaper advertising lets them feature products on a market-by-market basis, respond and adapt campaigns to local market conditions, and tie into more retailer promotions, fostering more support from the trade.

Local advertisers like retailers are interested in geographic selectivity or flexibility within a specific market or trade area. Their media goal is to concentrate their advertising on the areas where most of their customers are. Many newspapers now offer advertisers various geographic areas or zones for this purpose.

Reader Involvement and Acceptance   Another important feature of newspapers is consumers' level of acceptance and involvement with papers and the ads they contain. The typical newspaper reader spends considerable time each day reading. Most consumers rely heavily on newspapers not only for news, information, and entertainment but also for assistance with consumption decisions.

Many consumers actually purchase a newspaper *because* of the advertising it contains. Consumers use retail ads to determine product prices and availability and to see who is having a sale. One aspect of newspapers that is helpful to advertisers is readers' knowledge about particular sections of the paper. Most of us know that ads for automotive products and sporting goods are generally found in the sports section, while ads for financial services are found in the business section. The weekly food section in many newspapers is popular for recipe and menu ideas as well as for the grocery store ads and coupons offered by many stores and companies.

The value of newspaper advertising as a source of information has been shown in several studies. One study found that consumers look forward to ads in newspapers more than in other media. In another study, 80 percent of consumers said newspaper ads were most helpful to them in doing their weekly shopping. Newspaper advertising has also been rated the most believable form of advertising in numerous studies.

Services Offered The special services newspapers offer can be valuable to advertisers. For example, many newspapers offer merchandising services and programs to manufacturers that make the trade aware of ads being run for the company's product and help convince local retailers they should stock, display, and promote the item. Newspapers can also assist small companies through free copywriting and art services. Small advertisers without an agency or advertising department often rely on the newspaper to help them write and produce their ads.

Limitations of Newspapers

While newspapers have many strengths, like all media they also have limitations that media planners must consider. The limitations of newspapers include their reproduction problems, short life span, lack of selectivity, and clutter.

Poor Reproduction One of the greatest limitations of newspapers as an advertising medium is their poor reproduction quality. The coarse paper stock used for newspapers and the absence of extensive colour limits the quality of most newspaper ads. Newspapers have improved their reproduction quality in recent years, and colour reproduction has become more available. Also, advertisers desiring high-quality colour in newspaper ads can turn to such alternatives as freestanding inserts or supplements. However, these are more costly and may not be desirable to many advertisers. As a general rule, if the visual appearance of the product is important, the advertiser will not rely on newspaper ads. Ads for food products and fashions generally use magazines to capitalize on their superior reproduction quality and colour.

Short Life Span Unlike magazines, which may be retained around the house for several weeks, a daily newspaper is generally kept less than a day. So an ad is unlikely to have any impact beyond the day of publication, and repeat exposure is very unlikely. Compounding this problem are the short amount of time many consumers spend with the newspaper and the possibility they may not even open certain sections of the paper. Media planners can offset these problems somewhat by using high frequency in the newspaper schedule and advertising in a section where consumers who are in the market for a particular product or service are likely to look.

Lack of Selectivity While newspapers can offer advertisers geographic selectivity, they are not a selective medium in terms of demographics or lifestyle characteristics. Most newspapers reach broad and very diverse groups of consumers,

Exhibit 10–11 Island ads are a way to break through the clutter in newspaper advertising

which makes it difficult for marketers to focus on narrowly defined market segments. For example, manufacturers of fishing rods and reels will find newspapers very inefficient because of the wasted circulation that results from reaching all the newspaper readers who don't fish. Thus, they are more likely to use special-interest magazines. Any newspaper ads for their products will be done through cooperative plans whereby retailers share the costs or spread them over a number of sporting goods featured in the ad.

Clutter   Newspapers, like most other advertising media, suffer from clutter. Because a substantial amount of the average daily newspaper in Canada is devoted to advertising, the advertiser's message must compete with numerous other ads for consumers' attention and interest. Moreover, the creative options in newspapers are limited by the fact that most ads are black and white. Thus, it can be difficult for a newspaper advertiser to break through the clutter without using costly measures such as large space buys or colour. Some advertisers use creative techniques like *island ads*—ads surrounded by editorial material. Island ads are found in the middle of the stock market quotes on the financial pages of many newspapers. Exhibit 10–11 shows an island ad for Cathay Pacific Airways that targets business travelers to Hong Kong and other Asian destinations.

Buying Newspaper Advertising Space

The strengths and limitations of newspapers are part of the decision to use this media. Another key factor is a complete understanding of the readers of newspapers to assess whether there is a fit between them and the target audience of the promotion plan. In this section, we review a few issues related to this part of the decision: circulation and readership, audience measurement, and newspaper advertising rates.

Newspaper Circulation and Readership

As with any medium, the media planner must understand the nature and size of the audience reached by a newspaper in considering its value in the media plan. Since newspapers as a class of media do an excellent job of penetrating their market, the typical daily newspaper gives advertisers the opportunity to reach most of the households in a market. But, while local advertisers aim to cover a particular market or trade area, national advertisers want to reach broad regions or even the entire country. They must purchase space in a number of papers to achieve the desired level of coverage.

Circulation   The basic source of information concerning the audience size of newspapers comes from circulation figures available through CARD, discussed earlier in this chapter. The Audit Bureau of Circulation (ABC) verifies circulation figures for many newspapers, as illustrated in the media section. Advertisers using a number of papers in their media plan generally find CARD to be the most convenient source. The Canadian Community Newspapers Association (CCNA) verifies the circulation if an advertiser decides to use this vehicle.

The CCNA is a network of seven regional newspaper associations: Atlantic Community Newspapers Association, the Quebec Community Newspapers Association, the Ontario Community Newspapers Association, the Manitoba Community Newspapers Association, the Saskatchewan Weekly Newspapers Association, the Alberta Weekly Newspapers Association and the British Columbia & Yukon Community Newspapers Association. Membership of an individual community newspaper in a regional association includes membership in the national association. CCNA currently represents more than 670 English-language community newspapers with a total first-edition circulation of more than 6.8 million copies per week.

The CCNA gives an individual community newspaper a national voice in working with the public, business, and government, and its mission is to ensure a strong community newspaper industry. For advertisers, the CCNA plays a strong role in coordinating the placement of ads throughout the network. Its services include a one-order–one-bill system, ROP ads and pre-printed inserts, digital transmission of ads, Geographic Information System (GIS), and national or regional classified advertising. Presently, CCNA does not have audience information like NADbank; however, in June 2002, CCNA announced the implementation of a readership study. Despite this limitation, the CCNA claims community newspapers offer key benefits: precise coverage of specific markets with no wasted circulation, strong household penetration, state-of-the-art newspaper reproduction, and audited circulation figures.

CCNA has a self-administered audit program for all its members. The program includes a manual with detailed instructions and necessary forms. The member newspaper collects its own circulation data according to the VC rules and regulations. These data are reported to the CCNA and the CCNA Circulation Auditor or a Public (Chartered) Accountant audits the data thoroughly and a circulation report is published.

Newspaper circulation figures are generally broken down into three categories: the city zone, the retail trading zone, and all other areas. The **city zone** is a market area composed of the city where the paper is published and contiguous areas similar in character to the city. The **retail trading zone** is the market outside the city zone whose residents regularly trade with merchants within the city zone. The "all other" category covers all circulation not included in the city or retail trade zone.

Sometimes circulation figures are provided only for the primary market, which is the city and retail trade zones combined, and the other area. Both local and national advertisers consider the circulation patterns across the various categories in evaluating and selecting newspapers.

Readership   Circulation figures provide the media planner with the basic data for assessing the value of newspapers and their ability to cover various market areas. However, the media planner also wants to match the characteristics of a newspaper's readers with those of the advertiser's target audience. Data on newspaper audience size and characteristics are available from NADbank.

Newspaper Audience Measurement—NADbank

Newspaper Audience Databank Inc. (NADbank) is an organization comprised of newspaper, advertising agency, and advertiser members. Its primary mandate is to publish audience research information of Canadian daily newspapers. The purpose of this research is to provide its members with valid readership information to facilitate the buying and selling of newspaper advertising space.

NADbank uses a phone interview of respondents that takes approximately 15 minutes. The interview asks questions pertaining to readership of local and non-local newspapers, time spent reading, frequency of reading, method of receipt of newspapers into the home or outside the home, readership of TV magazine publications, radio listening, TV viewing and magazine readership, Internet readership of on-line newspapers, demographics, and media reliance. Product usage data is collected by a self-completion questionnaire that is sent to respondents after the telephone interview. These questions focus on 28 product categories and 18 retail shopping categories.

The study is conducted in 46 Canadian urban markets covering 76 newspapers. Sixteen markets annually receive both the media and product usage surveys while ten markets annually receive the media survey only. Another 20 smaller markets receive the media survey once every 3 years. NADbank recently updated the data collection process to minimize any seasonal effects. For 2002, data was collected for 17 weeks during January to June and 16 weeks during September to December. The schedule called for publication of results in the spring of 2003 when media planners need data updated to finalize their decisions for the fall.

The readership study indicates that adults read the newspaper an average of 48 minutes per weekday and over 90 minutes on the weekend. The reach of newspaper is quite pervasive even though there are many media choices and reading is more time-consuming and involving than other media. For example, 57 percent of adults 18 and older across all markets read a newspaper yesterday, 64 percent read a newspaper last weekend, and 83 percent have read a newspaper in the past week. Figures 10-4 through 10-6 give you an overview of the Canadian newspaper reader.

As we have seen in the audience measurement for other media, the NADbank data is available to use with specialized software that is available through two authorized suppliers (IMS, Harris/Telmar). It provides consultation services to assist its members who use the information. Proprietary questions may also be added to the survey if an advertiser or marketer wants to link brand specific data with the media and product usage data.

Newspaper Advertising Rates

Advertisers are faced with a number of options and pricing structures when purchasing newspaper space. The cost of advertising space depends on the circulation, and whether the circulation is controlled (free) or paid. It also depends on factors such as premium charges for colour in a special section, as well as discounts available. National rates can be about 15 percent higher than local rates, to account for agency commission.

Figure 10–4 Readership in all markets—adults (18+)

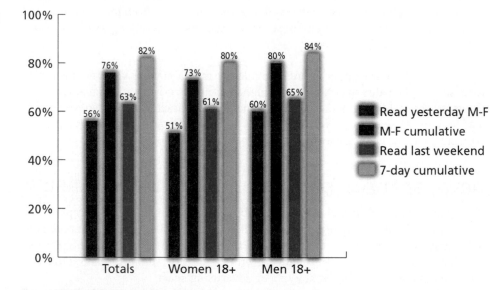

Source: NADbank 2002 Interim Report

Figure 10–5 Readership by region—adults (18+)

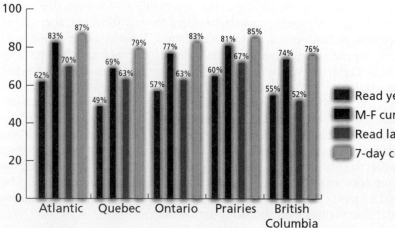

Source: NADbank 2002 Interim Report

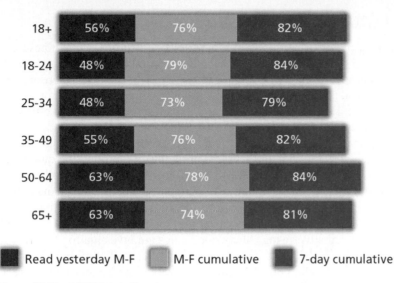

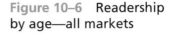
Figure 10–6 Readership by age—all markets

Source: NADbank 2002 Interim Report

Newspaper is sold by the **agate line** and **column width.** A line (or agate line) is a unit of space measuring one column wide and $\frac{1}{14}$-inch deep. One problem with this unit is that newspapers use columns of varying width, from 6 columns per page to 10 columns per page, which affects the size, shape, and costs of an ad. This results in a complicated production and buying process for national advertisers that purchase space in a number of newspapers.

Advertisers need to know the number of lines and number of columns on a newspaper page in order to calculate the cost of an ad. For example, the following calculation is for the weekday cost of a full-page ad in the national edition of *The National Post.* The paper has 301 lines and 10 columns per page, and the open cost per line is $15.28.

$$10 \text{ columns} \times 301 \text{ lines} \times \$15.28/\text{line per column} = \$45,993$$

This calculation could be done differently with the same result when you know the entire length of the paper (301 lines/14 agate lines per column inch).

$$10 \text{ columns} \times 21.5 \text{ inches} \times 14 \text{ agate lines per column inch} \times \$15.28 = \$45,993$$

You can use this principle to calculate the cost of ads of various sizes once you know the size of the ad in terms of columns and inches deep. For example, for an ad that is 5 columns wide and 6 inches deep, the calculation would then be the following:

$$5 \text{ columns} \times 6 \text{ inches} \times 14 \text{ agate lines per column inch}$$
$$\times \$15.28 \text{ per column inch} = \$6,418$$

Newspaper rates for local advertisers continue to be based on the column inch, which is 1 inch deep by 1 column wide. Advertising rates for local advertisers are quoted per column inch, and media planners calculate total space costs by multiplying the ad's number of column inches by the cost per inch.

Most newspapers have an **open-rate structure,** which means various discounts are available. These discounts are generally based on frequency or bulk purchases of space and depend on the number of column inches purchased in a year.

Newspaper space rates also vary with an advertiser's special requests, such as preferred position or colour. The basic rates quoted by a newspaper are **run of paper (ROP),** which means the paper can place the ad on any page or in any position it desires. While most newspapers try to place an ad in a requested position, the advertiser can ensure a specific section and/or position on a page by paying a higher **preferred position rate.** Colour advertising is also available in many newspapers on an ROP basis or through preprinted inserts or supplements.

The Future for Newspapers

Newspapers' major strength lies in their role as a medium that can be used effectively by local advertisers on a continual basis. It is unlikely that newspapers' importance to local advertisers will change in the near future. However, there are a number of problems and issues newspapers must address to maintain their strong position as a dominant local advertising medium and to gain more national advertising. These include competition from other advertising media and declining readership.

The newspaper industry's battle to increase its share of national advertising volume has been difficult. In addition to the problems of reproduction quality and rate differentials, newspapers face competition from other media for both national and local advertisers' budgets. The newspaper industry is particularly concerned about the *bypass*, or loss of advertisers to direct marketing and telemarketing.

The intermedia battle that newspapers find themselves involved in is no longer limited to national advertising. Many companies are investigating the Internet as a marketing tool and a place to invest advertising dollars that might otherwise go to newspapers. Local radio and TV stations, as well as the Yellow Pages, are aggressively pursuing local advertisers. Newspapers will have to fight harder to retain those advertisers. Many newspapers have expanded their marketing capabilities and are making efforts to develop and sustain relationships with their advertisers.

The growth of the Internet and online services is another factor that may erode newspaper readership. As penetration of the Internet into households increases, newspapers and magazines are among the most threatened of the major media. A survey conducted for *Advertising Age* found that consumers with home Internet access are less likely to use magazines or newspapers as a primary information source when shopping for a car, financial services, travel, or fashion. The study also found that consumers from teens to seniors are comfortable with the idea of using the Internet in the future to read books, magazines, and newspapers.[12] Newspaper publishers are addressing this threat by making their papers available online. Nearly every major newspaper has established a website, and many publishers now make their papers available online.

Summary

Magazines and newspapers, the two major forms of print media, play an important role in the media plans and strategy of many advertisers. Magazines are a very selective medium and are very valuable for reaching specific types of customers and market segments. The three broad categories of magazines are consumer, farm, and business publications. Each of these categories can be further classified according to the publication's editorial content and audience appeal.

In addition to their selectivity, the strengths of magazines include their excellent reproduction quality, creative flexibility, long life, prestige, and readers' high receptivity to magazine advertising, as well as the services they offer to advertisers. Limitations of magazines include their high cost, limited reach and frequency, long lead time, and the advertising clutter in most publications.

Advertising space rates in magazines vary according to a number of factors, among them the size of the ad, position in the publication, particular editions purchased, use of colour, and number and frequency of insertions. Rates for magazines are compared on the basis of the cost per thousand, although other factors such as the editorial content of the publication and its ability to reach specific target audiences must also be considered.

Newspapers represent the largest advertising medium in terms of total volume, receiving about a fourth of all advertising dollars. Newspapers are a very important medium to local advertisers, especially retailers. Newspapers are a broad-based medium that reaches a large percentage of households in a particular area. Newspapers' other advantages include flexibility, geographic selectivity, reader involvement, and special services. Drawbacks of newspapers include their lack of high-quality ad reproduction, short life span, lack of audience selectivity, and clutter.

Trends toward market segmentation and regional marketing are prompting many advertisers to make more use of newspapers and magazines. However, both magazines and newspapers face increasing competition from such other media as direct marketing and the Internet, and both are working to improve the quality of their circulation bases.

Key Terms

selectivity, 263
gatefolds, 265
bleed pages, 266
controlled-circulation basis, 269

pass-along readership, 269
total audience/readership, 270
selective binding, 272
ink-jet imaging, 272

display advertising, 275
classified advertising, 275
preprinted inserts, 276
city zone, 279
retail trading zone, 279
agate line, 280

column width, 280
open-rate structure, 282
run of paper (ROP), 282
preferred position rate, 282

Discussion Questions

1. Discuss the strengths and limitations of magazines as an advertising medium. How do magazines differ from television and radio as advertising media?

2. Describe what is meant by selectivity with regard to the purchase of advertising media and discuss some of the ways magazines provide selectivity to advertisers.

3. Explain why advertisers of products such as cosmetics or women's clothing would choose to advertise in magazines such as *Flare, Elm Street,* or *Chatelaine.*

4. Discuss how circulation figures are used in evaluating magazines and newspapers as part of a media plan and setting advertising rates.

5. If you were purchasing magazine ad space for a manufacturer of snowboarding equipment, what factors would you consider? Would your selection of magazines be limited to snowboarding publications? Why or why not?

6. Discuss the strengths and limitations of newspapers as an advertising medium. How might the decision to use newspapers in a media plan differ for national versus local advertisers?

7. Discuss the challenges and opportunities magazines and newspapers are facing from the growth of the Internet.

8. Cereal advertizers would typically use magazines for advertising, but some have recently used newspapers. Why would they select this new option? Your answer should address how the media would help achieve the advertizer's communication objectives.

Chapter Eleven

Out-of-Home and Support Media

Chapter Objectives

- To recognize the various out-of-home and support media available to the marketer in developing an IMC program.

- To develop an understanding of the strengths and limitations of out-of-home and support media.

- To know how audiences for out-of-home and support media are measured.

New Options in Out-of-Home Media

The only entertaining thing to do when waiting for a bus in a bus shelter is probably to meticulously stare at the bus shelter advertisement in all its glory from multiple perspectives. However, after the 15th day of staring at the same creative, the ad loses its punch, and can even become annoying. Thankfully for daily commuters, transit advertising is becoming almost as instantaneous as radio, as visual as television, and as responsive as newspapers. One-week shelter campaigns, scrolling ads, and redesigned, glass transit shelters that allow ads to be seen clearly by both pedestrians and passing motorists are coming to a bus stop near you.

Viacom Outdoor Canada, previously known as Mediacom, is now selling seven-day transit-shelter campaigns in Toronto and Montreal that are targeted to advertisers like retailers and car dealerships who have short-term promotions. Furthermore, the idea is "good for someone who wants to change their creative a lot, for those who want to say more in a short period of time," says Viacom marketing director Kim Warburton. Alternatively, it is a wonderful tool to reach consumers as they near their purchase decision. Toronto–based Labatt Breweries of Canada, for example, used outdoor advertising to promote the Carlsberg brand in specific locations, close to beer stores or clubs, for example. To facilitate this, Viacom guarantees one-day posting and takedown for up to 250 transit shelters and two-day postings/takedown for anything above 250 shelters.

Another development in transit-shelter advertising is the scrolling units that Viacom is placing in some downtown Toronto locations. The units allow the company to increase the number of ad faces it offers per location and allows advertisers to change their creative in as little as three seconds. The ads in the units are regular posters that scroll from one creative to the next. As Viacom suggests, this could be ideal for businesses such as restaurants. One could promote its breakfast menu until noon, then promote its lunch menu, and end the day with a dinner menu offer.

Viacom's final innovation is new transit shelters that have a clear view of the ads, to be installed in Toronto and Mississauga over the next seven years. The roof of the shelter is slightly curved glass, giving the creative a more distinct look. "The new bus shelters are great. That'll be the bus shelter of the future," predicts Glenn McConnell, president of Viacom's main rival, Pattison Outdoor. It sure sounds like waiting for the bus won't be quite the same anymore!

Source: "Short and Sweet," *Marketing Magazine*, November 19, 2001.

Every time we step out of the house, we encounter media directing an advertising message to us. Often we see ads while travelling. Most places we go have some form of advertising. And when we shop, we continue to see more ads! **Out-of-home media** is quite pervasive, and it delivers the advertising messages that we encounter while moving throughout our town or city, accomplishing our day-to-day activities. Some are new to the marketplace, and others have been around a while. In this chapter, we review four broad categories of out-of-home media: outdoor, transit, place-based, and point-of-purchase. We discuss the relative strengths and limitations, cost information, and audience measurement of each.

We use the term out-of-home media because it is a general term that encompasses all media that goes beyond the traditional media—television, print, or radio—that we consume typically at home. Often it is referred to as outdoor media; however, as we shall see, some of the media is, in fact, not outdoor. An example of this confusion is the fact that all of these media represent $269 million in advertising revenue that is often labelled outdoor media, but may never see the sun!

A major reason for the continued success of out-of-home media is its ability to remain innovative. As Exhibit 11–1 shows, billboards are no longer limited to standard sizes and two dimensions; 3-D forms and extensions are now used to attract attention. You probably have been exposed to either signboards or electronic billboards at sports stadiums, in supermarkets, in the campus bookstore and dining halls, in shopping malls, or on the freeways, or from neon signs on the sides of buildings in major Canadian cities.

We also encounter ads from non-traditional media. **Support media** are used to reach those people in the target audience that the primary media may not have reached or to reinforce the message contained in primary media. We conclude this chapter by summarizing three broad categories of support media: promotional products, Yellow Pages, and product placement.

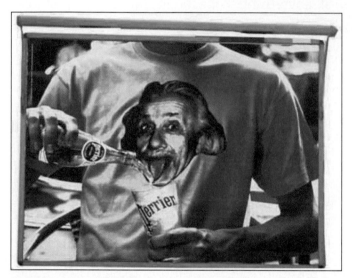

Exhibit 11–1 Outdoor advertising goes beyond two dimensions

Outdoor Media

Outdoor media is pervasive, and if you really tried to pay attention to the many exposures possible, you would find that we appear to be surrounded. However, the amount spent on this media is about $200 million, which is about 10 percent of TV or newspaper advertising revenue. (Figure 11–1 shows the outdoor media category breakdown for the U.S. market.) Despite this, outdoor media have just about doubled over the past 6 years, compared to the 25- to 35-percent growth for TV and newspaper media. We now turn our attention to the many outdoor media options available for an advertiser.

Outdoor Media Options

Posters describe the typical billboard, which can be horizontal (e.g., 10 feet by 20 feet) or vertical (e.g., 12 feet by 16 feet). These displays are front lit for visibility at night and are located in high vehicle-traffic areas. They may be purchased on an individual basis or for a certain level of GRPs in cities such as Toronto or in smaller markets such as Timmins, Ontario. As the name implies, **backlit posters** are posters of generally the same size that have a light behind them so that they are more clearly illuminated. These units are located at major intersections or high traffic-volume areas in or near major cities in Canada.

Larger billboards, known as **bulletins, superboards,** or **spectaculars,** are larger displays (two to three times more square footage) that have a variety of sizes depending upon the media company. These displays are sold on a per location basis due to their size and the low number of options available in major Canadian mar-

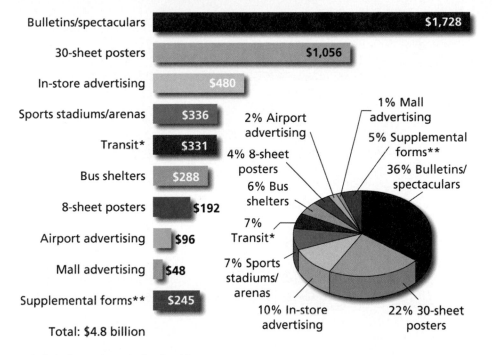

Bulletins Post the Best Numbers
Estimated gross billings by out-of-home media category (in millions) and percentage of market.

Bulletins/spectaculars $1,728
30-sheet posters $1,056
In-store advertising $480
Sports stadiums/arenas $336
Transit* $331
Bus shelters $288
8-sheet posters $192
Airport advertising $96
Mall advertising $48
Supplemental forms** $245

Total: $4.8 billion

1% Mall advertising
2% Airport advertising
5% Supplemental forms**
4% 8-sheet posters
36% Bulletins/spectaculars
6% Bus shelters
7% Transit*
7% Sports stadiums/arenas
10% In-store advertising
22% 30-sheet posters

Figure 11–1 Estimated gross billings by media category show that outdoor ads are still the most popular

* Includes bus, train, and cab advertising.
** Includes painted walls, mobile truck advertising, catering trucks, displays on college campuses, displays on military bases, air banner towing, airplane advertising, movie theatre advertising, doctor's offices waiting rooms, health clubs, JumboTrons, golf course signage, ski resort signage, phone kiosks, truck stop advertising.

kets. Smaller backlit displays, known as **street-level posters** or **transit-shelter posters** and measuring about 6 feet by 4 feet, are available across the country.

The aforementioned outdoor options are typically purchased for 4 weeks and provide anywhere from 25 GRPs to 150 GRPs per day, depending upon the number of displays or showings chosen within a local market. Recall from Chapter 8 that one GRP represents 1 percent of the market seeing the ad once. Thus, buying 50 GRPs implies that the marketer is reaching 50 percent of the market every day. (Figure 11-2 shows some outdoor rates broken down by three GRP levels.)

Audience Measurement for Outdoor Media

Audience measurement to determine the amount of reach and frequency is done by the Canadian Outdoor Measurement Bureau (COMB), an independent organization comprised of members from advertisers, advertising agencies, and media firms known as outdoor operators. COMB maintains a national database of all products for outdoor operators in order to calculate daily or weekly audience averages for each media in all markets. COMB acts as an auditor to ensure an authentic media purchase and produces specific reports as documentation. COMB conducts 6,000 randomly selected field audits per year, calculates performance statistics for all operators, and disseminates these findings to all members.

You may wonder whether the GRPs are accurate. COMB's methodology to determine the reach and frequency is comprehensive. COMB obtains traffic circulation numbers from municipalities. This data is then analysed with respect to three key questions:

- What is the average number of people in the vehicle?
- What is the vehicle's origin within the CMA?
- Is the sign illuminated? If so, for how long?

Figure 11–2   Outdoor: Rates—by weekly GRP delivery

	25 GRPs weekly		50 GRPs weekly		75 GRPs weekly	
	# of panels	4-week rate Cost ($000s)	# of panels	4-week rate Cost ($000s)	# of panels	4-week rate Cost ($000s)
Horizontal Posters						
Top 3 markets (Tor./Osh./Ham., Mtl., Van.)	80–147	139–196	170–292	306–371	250–444	399–550
Top 10 Markets	111–263	176–283	205–522	378–514	508–734	508–852
Vertical Posters						
Top 3 markets (Tor./Osh./Ham., Mtl., Van.)	78–136	125–179	155–219	238–266	224–357	280–357
Top 10 Markets	96–193	161–244	170–294	271–345	256–314	373–406
Street Level						
Top 3 markets (Tor./Osh./Ham., Mtl., Van.)	139–188	46–125	277–375	144–240	415–563	131–314
Top 10 Markets	188–217	155–180	431–592	144–301	597–647	149–450
Mall						
Top 3 markets (Tor./Osh./Ham., Mtl., Van.)	62	26	115	44	164	55
Top 10 Markets	82	34	149	56	210	69
Backlit						
Top 3 markets (Tor./Osh./Ham., Mtl., Van.)	12	23	29–32	53–76	44–47	81–111
Top 10 Markets	21	40	44–52	78–114	65–72	115–159
Superboards*						
Top 3 markets Series 10		12				
Top 3 markets Series 14		15				
Top 10 markets Series 10		23				
Top 10 markets Series 14		35				

Note: Data range reflects the expected minimum and maximum number of panels and cost generically by product, taking into account all major suppliers. Buyer should check with sales reps for correct inventory and pricing.

Source: 2001 rate cards

This analysis is known as the total number of circulations. These circulations are applied to each poster along a certain part of the road that is known as a link. The numbers are adjusted to account for time-of-day variations throughout the week to arrive at an adjusted circulation, which is then divided by the target population so that the reach is expressed as 1 percent of the population.

Most outdoor operators can present examples of past outdoor campaigns producing awareness and other communication effects. The examples can be for a product category or for individual campaigns. The operators can also provide maps to illustrate the posters' locations and other relevant data (e.g., demographics).

A number of innovative outdoor tools have emerged in Canada. Some firms are setting up large video-display units that have full animation and colour. Electronic message signs offer short ads (e.g., 10 seconds) on 2- or 3-minute rotation. As expected, both of these displays are located in high-traffic locations in a few large urban markets, with various sizes and packages available depending on the media firm. Murals and wall banners are sold in a few major markets in Canada (e.g., Toronto, Vancouver) with varying sizes. A number of firms offer **mobile signage** by placing displays on trucks or vehicles (see Exhibit 11-2). These are sold by the number of vehicles and the number of months.

Finally, we find outdoor media in some unusual outdoor locations. Signage can be purchased in parking lots, garbage receptacles, and in the air through aerial advertising on airplanes or hot-air balloons. It seems that no matter where we turn outside, there will be some form of advertising message directed towards us.

Despite the pervasiveness of outdoor advertising, there is some concern. In a Maritz AmeriPoll asking consumers about their opinions of billboards, 62 percent of the respondents said that they thought billboards should not be banned, while 52 percent said that they should be strictly regulated. When asked if billboards were entertaining, 80 percent of those surveyed said no; when asked if billboards could be beautiful, only 27 percent said yes.[1] Media buyers have not completely adopted outdoor media, partially because of image problems and the limited message that can be communicated. Let us examine some of the strengths and limitations of the medium in more detail.

Strengths of Outdoor Media

1. *Wide coverage of local markets.* With proper placement, a broad base of exposure is possible in local markets, with both day and night presence. A 100 GRP **showing** (the percentage of duplicated audience exposed to an outdoor poster daily) could yield exposure to an equivalent of 100 percent of the marketplace daily, or 3,000 GRPs over a month. This level of coverage is likely to yield high levels of reach.

2. *Frequency.* Because purchase cycles are typically for 4-week periods, consumers are usually exposed a number of times, resulting in high levels of frequency.

3. *Geographic flexibility.* Outdoor can be placed along highways, near stores, or on mobile billboards, almost anywhere that laws permit. Local, regional, or even national markets may be covered.

4. *Creativity.* As shown in Exhibit 11–1, outdoor ads can be very creative. Large print, colours, and other elements attract attention.

5. *Ability to create awareness.* Because of its impact (and the need for a simple message), outdoor can lead to a high level of awareness.

6. *Efficiency.* Outdoor usually has a very competitive CPM when compared to other media. The average CPM of outdoor is less than that of radio, TV, magazines, and newspapers.

7. *Effectiveness.* Outdoor advertising can often lead to sales. In a study reported by BBDO advertising, 35 percent of consumers surveyed said they had called a phone number they saw on an out-of-home ad.[2] A study reported by Mukesh Bhargava and Naveen Donthu showed that outdoor advertising can have a significant effect on sales, particularly when combined with a promotion.[3]

Exhibit 11–2 An interesting and unusual example of a mobile billboard

Trucks often serve as mobile billboards

8. *Production capabilities.* Modern technologies have reduced production times for outdoor advertising to allow for rapid turnaround time.

Limitations of Outdoor Media

1. *Waste coverage.* While it is possible to reach very specific audiences, in many cases the purchase of outdoor results in a high degree of waste coverage. It is not likely that everyone driving past a billboard is part of the target audience.

2. *Limited message capabilities.* Because of the speed with which most people pass by outdoor ads, exposure time is short, so messages are limited to a few words and/or an illustration. Lengthy appeals are not likely to be effective.

3. *Wearout.* Because of the high frequency of exposures, outdoor may lead to a quick wearout. People are likely to get tired of seeing the same ad every day.

4. *Cost.* Because of the need for high weight levels to achieve impact, outdoor media can be expensive in absolute terms. The higher costs of spectaculars makes outdoor costly in a relative CPM sense.

5. *Image problems.* Outdoor advertising has suffered some image problems as well as some disregard among consumers.

Transit Media

Another form of out-of-home advertising is **transit advertising.** While similar to outdoor in the sense that it uses billboards and electronic messages, transit is targeted at the millions of people who are exposed to commercial transportation facilities, including buses, subways, light-rail trains, and airplanes. The first three we cover in the form of local transit options, and then we consider the airplane option. Transit advertising has been around for a long time, but recent years have seen a renewed interest in this medium due in part to the increased number of women in the work force (they can be reached on their way to work more easily than at home), audience segmentation, and the rising cost of TV advertising.

Exhibit 11–3 Outside posters often appear on buses

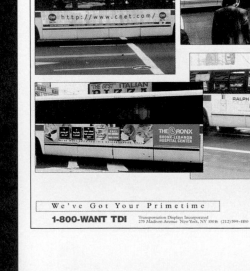

Commuter Transit Options

If you have ever ridden a bus, you have probably noticed the **interior transit cards** placed above the seating area that advertises restaurants, TV or radio stations, or a myriad of other products and services. Ads are positioned in backlit units above windows and along both sides of the bus, streetcar, subway, or light-rail transit cars. **Interior door cards** are available in major markets where there is subway-like transit. These cards are placed on both sides of the doors and are about 50 percent larger than the aforementioned cards.

While waiting for your bus, you cannot help notice the ads on the side or back of the bus going in the opposite direction or on another route (see Exhibit 11-3). These **exterior posters** can be purchased in three sizes: exterior 70s for the side or tail, measuring 70 inches by 21 inches, and exterior kings that come in 139 inches by 30 inches or 190 inches by 30 inches. Clearly it is difficult not to notice these ads when you just miss your bus! The increased sophistication of this medium was demonstrated in a test market in Barcelona, Spain, during the 1992 Summer Olympics. Viatex—a joint venture among Atlanta-based

Bevilaqua International (a sports marketing company), Saatchi & Saatchi Lifestyle Group, and Warrec Co., a Connecticut–based international business firm—mounted electronic billboards on the sides of buses. These monitors flashed Olympic news and ads that could change at scheduled times. Electronic beacons located throughout the city were activated as the buses drove by to change the message for the various locations.

Station posters are of varying sizes and forms that attempt to attract the attention of those waiting for a subway-like ride or bus. The most common size is 4 feet by 6 feet, which is also found in bus shelters. As Exhibit 11–4 shows, station posters can be very attractive and attention-getting. Bus shelters often provide the advertiser with expanded coverage where other outdoor boards may be restricted.

Transit media is sold in select markets on a 4-week basis with a certain desired level of GRPs. The range of GRPs is quite varied, going from a low of 5 GRPs to a high of 100 GRPs. Other purchases of transit media are based on the number of showings. For example, if an operator has the rights to 400 buses or subway cars, then an advertiser could typically buy displays in varying numbers (i.e., 25 percent, 50 percent, 75 percent, 100 percent) over a 4-week time period. (Figure 11-3 shows some transit rates broken down by a number of GRP levels.)

Recent innovations in transit media include the super-bus where an advertiser "owns the bus" and places a vinyl ad on the entire surface of the bus. This is often done for a longer-term contract of a half- or full-year because of the application on the bus. On a less grand scale in a few select markets, smaller bus murals can be applied to the side or tail for a shorter period of time. Recently, the Toronto and Montreal subway systems have featured station domination where a single advertiser can

Exhibit 11–4 Station posters can be used to attract attention

Figure 11–3 Transit advertising: Rates for selected buys

Markets*	Fleet Size	Exterior 70s				Exterior Kings			
		25 Daily GRPs		50 Daily GRPs		25 Daily GRPs		50 Daily GRPs	
		Cost/ 4 wks.	# Units	Cost/ 4 wks.	# Units	Cost/ 4 wks.	# Units	Cost/ 4 wks.	# Units
Top 3 Total	5,026	$ 91.7	349	$181.8	711	$109.7	283	$208.7	596
Top 10 Total	8,710	$135.1	554	$266.0	1,121	$162.0	461	$308.1	948
Top 25 Total	9,998	$261.3	1,046	$517.1	2,125	$311.4	874	$592.1	1,799

Markets*	Fleet Size	Interior Transit Cards-Singles				Interior Transit Cards-Doubles			
		25 Daily GRPs		50 Daily GRPs		25 Daily GRPs		50 Daily GRPs	
		Cost/ 4 wks.	# Units	Cost/ 4 wks.	# Units	Cost/ 4 wks.	# Units	Cost/ 4 wks.	# Units
Top 3 Total	5,744	$ 29.2	1,544	$ 57.0	3,177	$ 51.0	1,544	$100.0	3,177
Top 10 Total	9,428	$ 53.6	3,684	$ 92.7	6,539	$ 89.9	3,629	$158.1	6,429
Top 25 Total	10,706	$ 89.5	5,705	$163.6	10,735	$152.7	5,693	$281.7	10,668

*Top 3, 10 & 25: Based upon Top 25 markets by population. Top 10: Interior Calgary rates and units represents 30 Daily GRPs and 50 Daily GRPs. Top 25: Certain Interior market rates and units represent only 10–20 Daily GRPs; check CARD for details. Other Available Markets: Check other available suppliers in CARD.

Source: March 2001, CARD

be the sole sponsor of all points of communication within that station. **Subway on-line** is located in the 10 busiest subway stations in Toronto. It features digital news centres with video capabilities that delivers news, sports, and weather highlights with 20-second ads.

Strengths of Commuter Transit Media

1. *Exposure.* Long length of exposure to an ad is one major strength of indoor forms. The average ride on mass transit is 30 to 44 minutes, allowing for plenty of exposure time.[4] The audience is essentially a captive one, with nowhere else to go and nothing much to do. As a result, riders are likely to read the ads—more than once. A second form of exposure transit advertising provides is the absolute number of people exposed. Millions of people ride mass transit every week, providing a substantial number of potential viewers.

2. *Frequency.* Because our daily routines are standard, those who ride buses, subways, and the like are exposed to the ads repeatedly. If you rode the same subway to work and back every day, in one month you would have the opportunity to see the ad 20 to 40 times. The locations of station and shelter signs also afford high frequency of exposure.

3. *Timeliness.* Many shoppers get to stores on mass transit. An ad promoting a product or service at a particular shopping area could be a very timely communication.

4. *Geographic selectivity.* For local advertisers in particular, transit advertising provides an opportunity to reach a very select segment of the population. A purchase of a location in a certain neighbourhood will lead to exposure to people of specific ethnic backgrounds, demographic characteristics, and so on.

5. *Cost.* Transit advertising tends to be one of the least expensive media in terms of both absolute and relative costs. An ad on the side of a bus can be purchased for a very reasonable CPM.

Limitations of Commuter Transit Media

1. *Image factors.* To many advertisers, transit advertising does not carry the image they would like to represent their products or services. Some advertisers may think having their name on the side of a bus or on a bus stop bench does not reflect well on the firm.

2. *Reach.* While an advantage of transit advertising is the ability to provide exposure to a large number of people, this audience may have certain lifestyles and/or behavioural characteristics that are not true of the target market as a whole. For example, in rural or suburban areas, mass transit is limited or nonexistent, so the medium is not very effective for reaching these people.

3. *Waste coverage.* While geographic selectivity may be an advantage, not everyone who rides a transportation vehicle or is exposed to transit advertising is a potential customer. For products that do not have specific geographic segments, this form of advertising incurs a good deal of waste coverage.

Another problem is that the same bus may not run the same route every day. To save wear and tear on the vehicles, some companies alternate city routes (with much stop and go) with longer suburban routes. Thus, a bus may go downtown one day and reach the desired target group but spend the next day in the suburbs, where there may be little market potential.

4. *Copy and creative limitations.* It may be very difficult to place colourful, attractive ads on cards or benches. And while much copy can be provided on inside cards, on the outside of buses and taxis the message is fleeting and short copy points are necessary.

Airline Transit Options

Related to transit media while traveling *within* cities and towns is media while traveling *between* cities and towns. As the number of flying passengers increases so too does the attractiveness of three **in-flight advertising** options and many airport terminal options. In-flight magazines are free magazines published by the airlines and are offered on almost every plane in the air (see Exhibit 11–5). In-flight videos have been common on international flights for some time and are now being used on domestic flights. Commercials were not originally included in these videos. Now, Air Canada sells different packages depending on the type of show (e.g., news, movie). Some of these commercial messages are as long as 3 minutes. In-flight radio is a pleasant way to pass the time while flying, and it offers another opportunity for advertisers to deliver an audio message beyond standard radio. Finally, similar to transit and outdoor, most airports have various displays available ranging from smaller backlit posters in the terminal to superboards near the terminal and various other types of displays depending upon the media company and airport terminal.

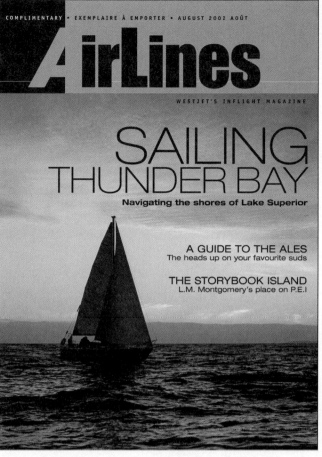

Exhibit 11–5 In-flight magazines are available on most carriers

Strengths of In-Flight Advertising

1. *A desirable audience.* The average traveler is 45 years old and has a household income over $83,700. Both business and tourist travelers tend to be upscale, an attractive audience to companies targeting these groups. Many of these passengers hold top management positions in their firms. *Hemispheres* reaches over 4 percent of business professionals and estimates that almost 71 percent of the magazine's readership are professionals. Other demographics are favourable as well.[5]

2. *A captive audience.* As noted in the discussion about ticket covers, the audience in an airplane cannot leave the room. Particularly on long flights, many passengers are willing (and even happy) to have in-flight magazines to read, news to listen to, and even commercials to watch.

3. *Cost.* The cost of in-flight commercials is lower than that of business print media. A 30-second commercial on United Airlines that offers exposure to 3,500,000 passengers costs approximately $27,500. A four-colour spread in *Forbes* and *Fortune* would cost double that amount. The in-flight videos mentioned earlier cost less than a half-page ad in *The Wall Street Journal.*

4. *Segmentation capabilities.* In-flight allows the advertiser to reach specific demographic groups, as well as travelers to a specific destination.

Limitations of In-Flight Advertising

1. *Irritation.* Many consumers are not pleased with the idea of ads in general and believe they are already too intrusive. In-flight commercials are just one more place, they think, where advertisers are intruding.

2. *Limited availability.* Many airlines limit the amount of time they allow for in-flight commercials. Japan Air Lines, for example, allows a mere 220 seconds per flight.

3. *Lack of attention.* Many passengers may decide to tune out the ads, not purchase the headsets required to get the volume, or simply ignore the commercials.

4. *Wearout.* Given projections for significant increases in the number of in-flight ads being shown, airline passengers may soon be inundated by these commercials.

Advertisers promote their products in supermarkets and other stores with a number of different "media" options. In the preceding sentence, we put media in quotation marks because often the tools used

Point-of-Purchase Media

Fake Transit Ads Draw Anger

In 2000, Transportation Displays Inc. created a buzz with a Toronto bus ad for "client" Shades For Men lipstick. The poster showed a close-up of a man's stubbled face framing bright purple lips, above the now-defunct Web address, www.shadesformen.com.

Anyone curious enough to visit the site was asked the burning question of whether men should wear lipstick. They were also asked their sex and age, where they live or work, if they had seen the ad on buses, and whether they would buy the "product" as a gift or for personal use. A note at the bottom of the page reveals that Shades for Men is actually fictitious and that the real intent of the campaign isn't to sell a legitimate product but "to gauge interest in such a product and to test bus advertising as a vehicle for launching new products."

Some people call these kinds of ads hoaxes or fakes. They use words such as frustrated and cheated to describe their feelings once they realize they've been manipulated into participating in an elaborate research scheme designed to put more advertising in public spaces. Advocates, on the other hand, use words such as intriguing, brilliant, and breakthrough.

Once the jig is up and people clue in to the fakery, the measure of success is almost always the number of consumers who can be herded toward a website or other media, or the number of people gullible enough to demand to buy a bogus product at retail.

There's been a recent wave of fake ads. In January, transit shelters across the country featured an ongoing mid-life "spat" between the fictional Harry and Doris (Pierre and Marie in the Quebec version). "Harry, this mid-life thing has gone too far. Make a choice. Doris." "Doris baby, I was born to be w-w-wild. Harry." The goal was to entice people to www.harrydoris.com (since expired), where the pitch was for Mediacom of Toronto. Mediacom's assertion that transit-shelter advertising is an effective mass-market medium for Web advertisers echoed a campaign it ran 10 years ago in which Harry and Doris squabbled over their dog, Rover.

Most people realize that advertising is a form of fiction. We don't actually believe a real Maxwell House couple exists, but we do believe Maxwell House coffee does. You have to wonder whether fake ads are effective if consumers come away feeling jerked around. Especially when the originator of a campaign boasts about the volume of people who can be led by the nose from traditional media to the Internet, and once there, give up valuable personal information.

Source: Adapted from Angela Kryhul, "When Faking It Doesn't Work," *Marketing Magazine*, July 31, 2000. Used with permission.

---

do not appear to be typical media. However, we use media as a general term to describe a method of transmitting an advertising message. It should be noted that some of these media are also thought of as sales promotions because some messages include a sales promotion (e.g., discount). Furthermore, some require the participation of retailers, which necessitates a payment that is often recorded as a trade promotion expense in the budget.

Much of the attraction of point-of-purchase media is based on figures from Point of Purchase Advertising International (POPAI), which state that approximately two-thirds of consumers' purchase decisions are made in the store; some impulse categories demonstrate an 80-percent rate.[6] Many advertisers are spending more of their dollars where decisions are made now that they can reach consumers at the point of purchase, providing additional product information while reducing their own efforts

Point-of-purchase media includes tools such as wall signs, displays, banners, shelf signs, video displays on shopping carts, kiosks that provide recipes and beauty tips, coupons at counters and cash registers, LED (light-emitting diode) boards, and ads that broadcast over in-house screens.

Strengths of Point-of-Purchase Media

1. *Target audience.* The main purpose of point-of-purchase media is to reach the target audience while making the purchase decision.

2. *Cost.* The absolute cost and CPM are generally reasonable compared to other media options.

3. *Message.* Key or deterministic benefits can be communicated just prior to purchase. These benefits may only become salient during the final choice decision.

Limitations of Point-of-Purchase Media

1. *Shopping experience.* One source of discontent for a consumer may be that the shopping experience is hindered in some manner with too many commercial messages.

2. *Implementation.* A marketer may be reliant on a third-party service provider who may not install or set up the tool correctly.

3. *Clutter.* If you want to be there, so does the competition. The clutter that consumers feel while watching television or reading a magazine may also be felt in the purchase environment.

4. *Audience measurement.* Point-of-purchase media lack objective audience measurement.

Place-Based Media

As noted earlier in this chapter, the variety of out-of-home media continues to increase, and discussing or even mentioning all of it is beyond the scope of this text. The idea of bringing the advertising medium to consumers wherever they may be underlies the strategy behind place-based media. However, the following are provided to illustrate a few of the many options.

Place-Based Media Options

An original example of place-based media is signage and displays in malls. The popular mall poster is often backlit like the transit shelter or transit-station poster and is located throughout a shopping mall. The key feature of the mall poster is that it is in the shopping environment and therefore one step closer to the actual purchase. These posters are sold in most markets across the country similarly to outdoor posters with individual spot buys and varying levels of GRPs. Firms also sell various sizes of mall banners for branding purposes.

A number of place-based media are outdoor media brought into a particular environment. Backlit posters, superboards, electronic message signs, and video displays are used in many other locations such as convention centres, movie theatres, hotels, sports stadiums or arenas, or wherever there is a sufficient number of people. The method of selling the time or space is similar to what was described above.

Continuing this idea of bringing a message to a target audience based on where they are illustrates two emerging place-based media outlets. Firms attempt to reach younger consumers on the campuses of many universities with various sizes of indoor posters that are standard and non-standard. Furthermore, with closed-circuit television, firms attempt to reach travellers or patients in designated hotel rooms or hospital or doctor waiting rooms, respectively. And to reach virtually anyone and everyone, it is possible to place small print ads inside elevators and washrooms!

Strengths of Place-Based Media

1. *Target audience.* The main purpose of place-based media is to reach a specific target audience or to reach the target audience while closer to the purchase decision.

2. *Cost.* The absolute cost and CPM are generally reasonable compared to other media options.

3. *Processing.* Because the target and place are intertwined, the message may generate more in-depth cognitive responses or stronger emotional responses.

1. *Experience.* Often, place-based media are exposed to consumers when they do not expect a selling message to occur, which may cause some amount of resentment.

2. *Clutter.* The clutter that consumers feel while watching television or reading a magazine may also be felt.

Place-Based Media at the Movies

We now turn our attention to a specific form of place-based media: movie theatres. One of the first advertisers at the movies was Coca-Cola, which advertised Coke Classic and Fruitopia. Some of the original advertisers faced hostile crowds who would boo and throw popcorn at the screen. It is estimated that about $25 to $30 million in advertising is spent in theatres on commercials, slides, posters, and sales promotions, with about $15 million of that for the commercials. And with the commercials lasting 60 to 90 seconds, advertisers have a unique opportunity to communicate for a longer period of time than with a TV ad, which typically runs 30 seconds. In fact, 95 percent of the theatre ads are also shown on television, albeit in a shortened format. A wide variety of products have been advertised using the medium including cars, government, telcos, food, video games, and health and beauty products, representing main brand names such as Toyota, Nissan, Telus, Bell Mobility, Health Canada, Department of National Defence, and Pepsi-Cola.

As a media grows, so does its sophistication, and theatre media is no exception; it now reports audience measurement information. One study estimated that total recall (aided plus unaided) reached 74 percent compared to 37 percent for radio and 32 percent for television. Yet while there appears to be good communication effect, and the cost is reasonable, the overall revenue is still only 1 percent of the TV advertising revenue per year. Part of the problem is that the reach is still limited, only 3.6 million per month for Cineplex Odeon, for example.[7]

Strengths of Movie Theatres as a Media

1. *Exposure.* The viewers constitute a captive audience who are also known to watch less television than the average.[8]

2. *Mood.* If viewers like the movie, the mood can carry over to the product advertised.

3. *Cost.* The cost of advertising in a theatre varies from one setting to the next. However, it is low in terms of both absolute and relative costs per exposure.

4. *Recall.* Research indicates that on the day following the viewing, about 74 percent of viewers can recall the ads they saw in a movie theatre. This compares with a 32-percent recall rate for television.[9]

5. *Clutter.* Lack of clutter is another advantage offered by advertising in movie theatres. Most theatres limit the number of ads.

6. *Proximity.* Because many theatres are located in or adjacent to shopping malls, potential customers are "right next door."

Limitations of Movie Theatres as a Media

1. *Irritation.* Perhaps the major disadvantage is that many people do not wish to see advertising in this media. A number of studies suggest that these ads may create a high degree of annoyance.[10] This dissatisfaction may carry over to the product itself, to the movies, or to the theatres. Mike Stimler, president of the specialty video label Water Bearer Films, says, "People boo in movie theatres when they see product advertising."[11] Anne-Marie Marcus, vice president of sales for Screenvision, contends that the furor has died down.[12]

2. *Cost.* While the cost of advertising in local theatres has been cited as a strength because of the low rates charged, ads exposed nationally can be expensive, with a corresponding high CPM compared to other media.

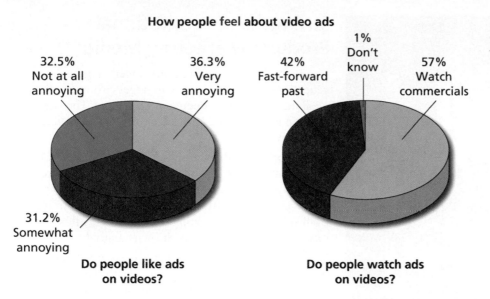

How people feel about video ads

32.5%
Not at all
annoying

36.3%
Very
annoying

31.2%
Somewhat
annoying

**Do people like ads
on videos?**

1%
Don't
know

42%
Fast-forward
past

57%
Watch
commercials

**Do people watch ads
on videos?**

Figure 11–4 Consumer opinions about ads on video

While only two limitations of theatre advertising have been mentioned, the first is a strong one. Many people who have paid to see a movie (or rent a video—see Figure 11-4) perceive advertising as an intrusion. In a study by Michael Belch and Don Sciglimpaglia, many moviegoers stated that not only would they not buy the product advertised, but also they would consider boycotting it. So advertisers should be cautious in their use of this medium. If they want to use movies, they may want to consider an alternative—placing products in the movies.

Promotional Products Marketing Media

According to the Promotional Products Association International (PPA), **promotional products marketing** is "the advertising or promotional medium or method that uses promotional products, such as ad specialties, premiums, business gifts, awards, prizes, or commemoratives." Promotional products marketing is the more up-to-date name for what used to be called specialty advertising. **Specialty advertising** has now been provided with a new definition:

> A medium of advertising, sales promotion, and motivational communication employing imprinted, useful, or decorative products called advertising specialties, a subset of promotional products.
>
> Unlike premiums, with which they are sometimes confused (called advertising specialties), these articles are always distributed free—recipients don't have to earn the specialty by making a purchase or contribution.[13]

As you can see from these descriptions, specialty advertising is often considered both an advertising and a sales promotion medium. In our discussion, we treat it as a supportive advertising medium in the IMC program (Exhibit 11–6).

There are over 15,000 *advertising specialty* items, including ballpoint pens, coffee mugs, key rings, calendars, T-shirts, and matchbooks. Unconventional specialties such as plant holders, wall plaques, and gloves with the advertiser's name printed on them are also used to promote a company or its product; so are glassware, trophies, awards, and vinyl products. In fact, advertisers spend over $13.1 billion per year on specialty advertising items. The increased use of this medium makes it the fastest-growing of all advertising or sales promotion media.[14]

If you stop reading for a moment and look around your desk (or bed or beach blanket), you'll probably find some specialty advertising item nearby. It may be the pen you are using, a matchbook, or even a book cover with the campus bookstore name on it. (Figure 11–5 shows the percentage of sales by product category.) Specialty items are used for many promotional purposes: to thank a customer for patronage, keep the name of the company in front of consumers, introduce new products, or reinforce the name of an existing company, product, or service. Advertising specialties are often used to support other forms of product promotions.

Exhibit 11–6 Promotional products can be a valuable contributor to the IMC program

Strengths of Promotional Products Marketing Media

1. *Selectivity.* Because specialty advertising items are generally distributed directly to target customers, the medium offers a high degree of selectivity. The communication is distributed to the desired recipient, reducing waste coverage.

2. *Flexibility.* As the variety of specialty items in Figure 11–5 demonstrates, this medium offers a high degree of flexibility. A message as simple as a logo or as long as is necessary can be distributed through a number of means. Both small and large companies can employ this medium, limited only by their own creativity.

3. *Frequency.* Most forms of specialty advertising are designed for retention. Key chains, calendars, and pens remain with the potential customer for a long time, providing repeat exposures to the advertising message at no additional cost.

4. *Cost.* Some specialty items are rather expensive (for example, leather goods), but most are affordable to almost any size organization. While they are costly on a CPM basis when compared with other media, the high number of repeat exposures drives down the relative cost per exposure of this advertising medium

5. *Goodwill.* Promotional products are perhaps the only medium that generates goodwill in the receiver. Because people like to receive gifts and many of the products are functional (key chains, calendars, etc.), consumers are grateful to receive them. In a recent study of users of promotional products, goodwill was cited as the number 1 reason for use.

6. *Supplementing other media.* A major advantage of promotional products marketing is its ability to supplement other media. Because of its low cost and repeat exposures, the simplest message can reinforce the appeal or information provided through other forms. For example, the Cartoon Network, which includes two of the world's largest animated film libraries, used specialty products to target 500 cable TV stations featuring "Wile E. Coyote and the Roadrunner." It delivered a crowbar and a brown box whose lid read "One ACME Launch Assistance Tool" to each station. The crates contained promotional launch items such as ad slicks, literature, videos, and audiotapes describing the new network. Of the 500 networks, 480 signed up for the new program.

Limitations of Promotional Products Marketing Media

1. *Image.* While most forms of specialty advertising are received as friendly reminders of the store or company name, the firm must be careful choosing the specialty item. The company image may be cheapened by a chintzy or poorly designed advertising form.

2. *Saturation.* With so many organizations now using this advertising medium, the marketplace may become saturated. While you can always use another ballpoint pen or book of matches, the value to the receiver declines if replacement is too easy, and the likelihood that you will retain the item or even notice the message is reduced. The more unusual the specialty, the more value it is likely to have to the receiver.

3. *Lead time.* The lead time required to put together a promotional products message is significantly longer than that for most other media.

Figure 11–5 Sales of promotional products by category (numbers in parentheses indicate sales by product category)

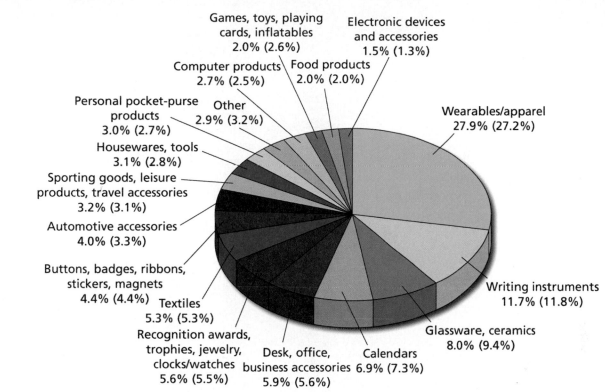

Product Category	Items Included
Wearables/apparel	Aprons, uniforms, blazers, caps, headbands, jackets, neckwear, footwear, etc.
Writing instruments	Pens, pencils, markets, highlighters, etc.
Glassware/ceramics	China, crystal, mugs, figurines, etc.
Calendars	Wall and wallet calendars, desk diaries, pocket secretaries, etc.
Desk/office/business accessories	Briefcases, folders, desk pen sets, calculators, cubed paper, etc.
Recognition awards/trophies/ emblematic jewelry/clocks and watches	Plaques, certificates, etc.
Textiles	Totebags, flags, towels, umbrellas, pennants, throws, blankets, etc.
Buttons/badges/ribbons/ stickers/magnets	Decals, transfers, signs, banners, etc.
Automotive accessories	Key tags, bumper strips, road maps, floormats, window shades, etc.
Sporting goods/leisure products/ travel accessories	Picnic/party products, camping equipment, barbecue items, bar products, plastic cups, binoculars, luggage, passport cases, etc.
Houseware/tools	Measuring devices, kitchen products, picture frames, household decorations, ornaments, tool kits, first aid kits, furniture, flashlights, cutlery, weather instruments, etc.
Personal/pocket-purse products	Pocket knives, grooming aids, lighters, matches, sunglasses, wallets, etc.
Computer products	Mouse pads, monitor frames, disk carriers, wrist pads, software, etc.
Games/toys/playing cards/ inflatables	Kites, balls, puzzles, stuffed animals, etc.
Food gifts	Candy, nuts, gourmet meat, spices, etc.
Electronic devices and accessories	Radios, TVs, videotapes, music CDs, phone cards, etc.

Product Placements Go International

By now you are certainly aware of product placements in movies and on television. (If you are not, you haven't been paying attention!) While product placements have been around in movies for quite some time, their popularity and growth really started with the movie *E.T.*, in which the space creature who visits earth eats Reese's Pieces. Subsequent successes led to significant growth in the industry and eventually the move to television programming. Now it is quite common to see product placements in almost every movie and numerous television shows.

If you are a Warren Miller ski fan, you may have noticed the product placements in many of the company's adventure ski films. These 90-minute films feature skiers and snowboarders navigating the steepest terrain in the world while performing unbelievable stunts. The films, which attract about a half-million enthusiasts per release, follow a simple formula: some of the world's best skiers and riders challenging the most dangerous and beautiful mountains on virtually every continent, with numerous and humourous scenes and product placements for companies like Salomon, Burton, Rossignol, and nonendemic companies like Nissan, Motorola, and Ocean Spray interspersed. The films have a strong U.S. and international following.

While Salomon and Ocean Spray go skiing, Pedigree dog food and McDonald's (among others) reach the "stay at home" crowd through product placements on a Spanish-language television show known as "Sabado Gigante" (Gigantic Saturday) aired by Univision. Originating in Chile, the takeoff on the U.S.'s "Newlywed Game" not only shows products but actively engages the audience in promoting them. For example, on one show, the host had the audience sing the jingle for sponsor Payless Shoe Source to thank the company for providing money for the contestants. The sponsors couldn't be more pleased.

But the product-placement nirvana may have recently been uncovered in yet another foreign market—China. The world's most populated country has recently opened up its doors to foreign companies, which are enamored by the sales potential. However, the government-controlled television stations keep a close watch on what is allowed to be shown, as well as on who will be permitted to advertise. Because advertisements are in 10-minute blocks, it is usually difficult for the advertiser to attract attention—thus the popularity of product placements for getting one's products noticed. For example, in the popular show "Love Talks," star Q Ying (a young business professional) rushes to work and then realizes that she has left an important folder at home. The camera zeros in on the folder, which just happens to be next to a tube of Pond's Vaseline Intensive Care lotion. In another scene she borrows a Motorola cell phone from a stranger. The show, also seen throughout Asia, is sold on video in Canada and the United States, and is being followed by a sequel called "Home"—another young-professional-themed program.

The cost to sponsor a product on "Love Talks" ranges from $240,000 to $360,000, reaping quite a profit for the show's producer United Media—a Hong Kong–based company. Those placing the products love the show as well, as the plugs are quite obvious and just about any product can be scripted into the show—with little or no concern for pretext. In addition, exposure is not limited to television. United Media manages and promotes the show's stars and features them in promotions on its website. Just about anything (and any product) goes, except for Viagra, cigarettes, and condoms.

The companies mentioned above are just a few of the many taking their product placements international. Giant advertising agencies like Saatchi & Saatchi and McCann-Erikson are increasing their efforts in this area, primarily because of the ability to get products noticed. While traditional advertising methods are certainly still used, many viewers are tuning them out. But when you have to sing along with the sponsor's commercial jingle—well, that makes the sponsor a little harder to ignore!

Sources: Peter Wonacott, "Chinese TV Is an Eager Medium for (Lots of) Product Placement," *The Wall Street Journal*, January 26, 2000, p. B12; Bob Ortega, "Extreme Skiing Meets Extreme Product Placement," *The Wall Street Journal*, December 28, 1998, p. B1.

Audience Measurement in Promotional Products Marketing

Owing to the nature of the industry, specialty advertising has no established ongoing audience measurement system. Research has been conducted in an attempt to determine the impact of this medium, however, including the following reports.

A study by Schreiber and Associates indicated 39 percent of people receiving advertising specialties could recall the name of the company as long as six months later, and a study conducted by A. C. Nielsen found that 31 percent of respondents were still using at least one specialty they had received a year or more earlier.[15]

A study by Gould/Pace University found the inclusion of a specialty item in a direct-mail piece generated a greater response rate and 321 percent greater dollar purchases per sale than mail pieces without such items.[16] Studies at Baylor University showed that including an ad specialty item in a thank-you letter can improve customers' attitudes toward a company's sales reps by as much as 34 percent and toward the company itself by as much as 52 percent.[17] Finally, Richard Manville Research reported the average household had almost four calendars; if they had not been given such items free, two-thirds of the respondents said they would purchase one, an indication of the desirability of this particular specialty item.[18] Figure 11–6 demonstrates how promotional products can be used effectively in an IMC program.

The Promotional Products Association International (www.ppai.org) is the trade organization of the field. The PPAI helps marketers develop and use specialty advertising forms. It also provides promotional and public relations support for specialty advertising and disseminates statistical and educational information.

Yellow Pages Media

When we think of advertising media, many of us overlook one of the most popular forms in existence—the **Yellow Pages.** While most of us use the Yellow Pages frequently, we tend to forget they are advertising. The Yellow Pages are often referred to as a **directional medium** because the ads do not create awareness or demand for products or services; rather, once consumers have decided to buy, the Yellow Pages point them in the direction where their purchases can be made.[19] The Yellow Pages are thus considered the final link in the buying cycle.

Strengths of Yellow Pages Media

1. *Wide availability.* Directories are usually delivered to every home and business within a given geographic area, ensuring wide availability.

Figure 11–6   The impact of promotional products in an IMC program

Combining Promotional Products with:	Effect
Advertising	Including direct mail with a promotional product increased response to a print ad to 4.2%, versus 2.3% with direct mail only and .7% with an ad only.
Personal selling	Customers receiving a promotional product expressed more goodwill toward the company than did those receiving a letter. They rated the company more positively in 52% of the cases and rated the salespeople more proficient (34%) and more capable (16%). Business-to-business customers receiving a promotional product were 14% more likely to provide leads, while salespersons who gave gifts to customers received 22% more leads than those who did not.
Trade shows	Responses to invitations to visit a booth were higher when a promotional product was enclosed.
Direct	Responses to direct-mail sales pieces were 1.9% with only a letter but 3.3% with a promotional product (75% higher). Other studies have shown increases of 50 to 66%.

2. *Action orientation.* Consumers use the Yellow Pages when they are considering, or have decided to take, action.

3. *Costs.* Ad space and production costs are relatively low compared to other media.

4. *Frequency.* Because of their longevity (Yellow Pages are published yearly), consumers return to the directories time and again. The average adult refers to the Yellow Pages about twice a week.[20]

5. *Nonintrusiveness.* Because consumers choose to use the Yellow Pages, they are not considered an intrusion. Studies show that most consumers rate the Yellow Pages very favourably.[21]

Limitations of Yellow Pages Media

1. *Market fragmentation.* Since Yellow Pages are essentially local media, they tend to be very localized. Add to this the increasing number of specialized directories, and the net result is a very specific offering.

2. *Timeliness.* Because Yellow Pages are printed only once a year, they become outdated. Companies may relocate, go out of business, or change phone numbers in the period between editions.

3. *Lack of creativity.* While the Yellow Pages are somewhat flexible, their creative aspects are limited.

4. *Lead times.* Printing schedules require that ads be placed a long time before the publications appear. It is impossible to get an ad in after the deadline, and advertisers need to wait a long time before the next edition.

5. *Clutter.* A recent study by Avery Abernethy indicates that the Yellow Pages (like other media) experience problems with clutter.

Product Placements in Movies

An increasingly common way to promote a product is by showing the actual product or an ad for it as part of a movie or TV show. While such **product placement** does not constitute a major segment of the advertising and promotions business, it has proved effective for some companies. (Note: Like specialty advertising, product placement is sometimes considered a promotion rather than an advertising form. This distinction is not a critical one, and we have decided to treat product placement as a form of advertising.)

A number of companies pay to have their products used in movies and music videos. Exhibit 11–7 shows how BMW was able to get its product featured in the movie *The World Is Not Enough.* Avis, Ericcson, and BMW were all in the James Bond movie *Tomorrow Never Dies.* The movie had its own website with links to the companies with placements, and the companies, in turn, had links on their websites to the movie site. Essentially, this form is advertising without an advertising medium. The impact of product placement can be significant. Sales of Ray-Ban Wayfarer sunglasses tripled after Tom Cruise wore them in the movie *Risky Business,* and Ray-Ban Aviator sales increased 40 percent after he wore them in *Top Gun.*[22]

Exhibit 11–7 Many companies use movies to promote their products

Strengths of Product Placements

1. *Exposure.* A large number of people see movies each year. The average film is estimated to have a life span of three and one-half years, and most of these moviegoers are very attentive audience members. When this is combined with the increasing home video rental market and network and specialty channels, the potential expo-

sure for a product placed in a movie is enormous. And this form of exposure is not subject to zapping, at least not in the theatre.

2. *Frequency.* Depending on how the product is used in the movie (or program), there may be ample opportunity for repeated exposures (many, for those who like to watch a program or movie more than once).

3. *Support for other media.* Ad placements may support other promotional tools. For example, Mirage Resorts ran four minutes of commercials promoting its Treasure Island Resort on an NBC special titled "Treasure Island: The Adventure Begins," a story about a boy's adventures at the Treasure Island Resort. Kimberly-Clark Corp. created a sweepstakes, coupon offer, and TV-based ad around its Huggies diapers, featured in the movie *Baby Boom.*

4. *Source association.* We previously discussed the advantages of source identification. When consumers see their favourite movie star wearing Keds, drinking Gatorade, or driving a Mercedes, this association may lead to a favourable product image.

5. *Cost.* While the cost of placing a product may range from free samples to $1 million, these are extremes. The CPM for this form of advertising can be very low, owing to the high volume of exposures it generates.

6. *Recall.* A study provided by Pola Gupta and Kenneth Lord showed that prominently displayed placements led to strong recall.[23]

7. *Bypassing regulations.* Some products are not permitted to advertise on television or to specific market segments. Product placements have allowed the cigarette and liquor industries to have their products exposed, circumventing these restrictions.

8. *Acceptance.* A study by Pola Gupta and Stephen Gould indicated that viewers are accepting of promotional products and in general evaluate them positively, though some products (alcohol, guns, cigarettes) are perceived as less acceptable.[24]

Limitations of Product Placements

1. *High absolute cost.* While the CPM may be very low for product placement in movies, the absolute cost of placing the product may be very high, pricing some advertisers out of the market. For example in the Disney film *Mr. Destiny,* it cost $20,000 to have a product seen in the film, $40,000 for an actor to mention the product, and $60,000 for the actor to actually use it.[25]

2. *Time of exposure.* While the way some products are exposed to the audience has an impact, there is no guarantee viewers will notice the product. Some product placements are more conspicuous than others. When the product is not featured prominently, the advertiser runs the risk of not being seen (although, of course, the same risk is present in all forms of media advertising).

3. *Limited appeal.* The appeal that can be made in this media form is limited. There is no potential for discussing product benefits or providing detailed information. Rather, appeals are limited to source association, use, and enjoyment. The endorsement of the product is indirect, and the flexibility for product demonstration is subject to its use in the film.

4. *Lack of control.* In many movies, the advertiser has no say over when and how often the product will be shown. Sony, as noted, found its placement in the movie *Last Action Hero* did not work as well as expected. Fabergé developed an entire Christmas campaign around its Brut cologne and its movie placement, only to find the movie was delayed until February.

5. *Public reaction.* Many TV viewers and moviegoers are incensed at the idea of placing ads in programs or movies. These viewers want to maintain the barrier between program content and commercials. If the placement is too intrusive, they may develop negative attitudes toward the brand.

Exhibit 11–8 Ads often appear in the strangest places

6. *Competition.* The appeal of product placements has led to increased competition to get one's product placed. BMW was originally placed in the movie *The Firm*—only to be ousted when Mercedes offered a higher bid. In *Wall Street*, Michael Douglas refers to *Fortune* magazine as the financial bible rather than *Forbes* because the former offered more money.[26] The result of this competition is higher prices and no guarantee that one's product will be placed.

7. *Negative placements.* Some products may appear in movie scenes that are disliked by the audience or create a less than favourable mood. For example, in the movie *Missing,* a very good, loyal father takes comfort in a bottle of Coke, while a Pepsi machine appears in a stadium where torturing and murders take place—not a good placement for Pepsi.

Audience Measurement for Product Placements

To date, no audience measurement is available except from the providers. Potential advertisers often have to make decisions based on their own creative insights (see Exhibit 11–8) or rely on the credibility of the source. However, at least two studies have demonstrated the potential effectiveness of product placements. Research by Eva Steortz showed that viewers had an average recall for placements of 38 percent.[27] And Damon Darlin has provided evidence that an aura of glamour is added to products associated with celebrities.[28]

Summary

This chapter introduced you to the vast number of out-of-home and support media available to marketers. Out-of-home media include outdoor, transit, place-based, and point-of-purchase. Support media include promotional products, Yellow Pages, and product placement. While these constitute many examples and options for a marketer, it seems the choices are quite endless at times.

Collectively, these media offer a variety of strengths. Cost, ability to reach the target audience, and flexibility are just a few of those cited in this chapter. In addition, many of the media discussed here have effectively demonstrated the power of their specific medium to get results.

But each of these media has limitations. Perhaps the major weakness with most is the lack of audience measurement and verification. The advertiser is forced to make decisions without hard data or based on information provided by the media. As the number and variety of media continue to grow, it is likely the major weaknesses will be overcome.

Key Terms

Discussion Questions

1. What are promotional products? List some of the advantages and disadvantages of this medium. Provide examples where the use of this medium would be appropriate.

2. Discuss some of the merits of in-flight advertising. What types of products might most effectively use this medium?

3. Explain how various support media might be used as part of an IMC program. Take any three of the media discussed in the chapter and explain how they might be used in an IMC program for automobiles, cellular telephones, and Internet services.

4. A prevalent strategy among advertisers is to get themselves into television shows and movies. Discuss the possible advantages and disadvantages that might result from such exposures.

5. The Yellow Pages has been proven to be an extremely effective advertising medium for some firms. Explain why the Yellow Pages are so effective. Are there any limitations associated with this medium? If so, what are they?

6. Discuss advantages and disadvantages associated with advertising in movie theatres. For what types of products and/or services might these media be most effective?

7. What are place-based media? Explain what type of advertisers would most benefit from their use.

Chapter Twelve

Sales Promotion

Chapter Objectives

- To understand the role of sales promotion in a company's integrated marketing communications program and to examine why it is increasingly important.

- To examine the objectives, strategy, and tactical components of a sales promotion plan.

- To examine the consumer and trade sales promotion strategy options and the factors to consider in using them.

- To understand key IMC issues related to sales-promotion decisions.

A New Twist on an Established Sales Promotion

Look into any Canadian's wallet, or glove compartment, and you're sure to find a wad of Canadian Tire "money" stashed away somewhere. That same promotional tool, which was introduced in 1958 to launch Canadian Tire's entry into the retail gasoline industry, provided the needed inspiration to launch their "Big Spender" ad campaign, and also their first-ever integrated in-store and online national "Big Spender Giveaway" contest in late 2001.

Canadian Tire is a brand icon these days, with a number of things going well for them. About 90 percent of Canadians have shopped at their locations. It equally attracts men and women, and it has loyal following from young to retired people. Ninety-nine percent of Canadians recognize the Canadian Tire name, one of the five most-recognized brands in Canada. And a Canadian Tire "money" is in fact one of the country's most successful and popular customer rewards program, boasting a 90 percent redemption and participation level.

The "Big Spender" campaign marked the first time that Canadian Tire "money" was communicated in a broadcast ad that featured the song, "Big Spender," and showed many people buying various items at Canadian Tire with the Canadian Tire "money" that they had won. "We knew that putting Canadian Tire 'money' front and centre in our advertising and promotional programs would hold tremendous appeal for customers because it is such an important part of the Canadian Tire shopping experience today," writes Eymbert Vaandering, vice president of marketing at Canadian Tire in Toronto. "Customers love Canadian Tire 'money' because it's simple to use, it's earned in dollars and cents, it can be used anytime, in any quantity and to buy any item."

From an IMC perspective, the "Big Spender" contest was cutting edge, using a multi-channel media campaign that included TV and radio, an in-store contest supported by flyers, card-member statement inserts, POP at stores and in gas bars, and an online contest featuring a total of $350,000 in Canadian Tire "money" and merchandising prizes. The online part of the contest included a scavenger hunt to create greater excitement for consumers. Overall, the IMC approach drove traffic to the store, gas bars, and the website and strongly increased sales.

Source: "Hey, Big Spender," *Marketing Magazine*, January 14, 2002.

As discussed in the opening vignette, marketers have come to recognize that advertising alone is not always enough to move their products off store shelves and into the hands of consumers. Companies also use sales promotion methods targeted at both consumers and the wholesalers and retailers that distribute their products to stimulate demand. Most companies' integrated marketing communications programs include consumer and trade promotions that are coordinated with advertising, direct marketing, and publicity/public relations campaigns as well as sales force efforts.

This chapter focuses on the role of sales promotion in a firm's IMC program. We examine how marketers use both consumer- and trade-oriented promotions to influence the purchase behaviour of consumers as well as wholesalers and retailers. We explore the objectives of sales promotion programs and the various types of sales promotion tools that can be used at both the consumer and trade level. We also consider how sales promotion can be integrated with other elements of the promotional mix and look at problems that can arise when marketers become overly dependent on consumer and trade promotions, especially the latter.

Sales Promotion Planning

Characteristics and Types of Sales Promotion

Sales promotion has been defined as "a direct inducement that offers an extra value or incentive for the product to the sales force, distributors, or the ultimate consumer with the primary objective of creating an immediate sale."[1] Keep in mind several important aspects of sales promotion as you read this chapter.

First, sales promotion involves some type of inducement that provides an *extra incentive* to buy. This incentive is usually the key element in a promotional program; it may be a coupon or price reduction, the opportunity to enter a contest or sweepstakes, a money-back refund or rebate, or an extra amount of a product. The incentive may also be a free sample of the product, given in hopes of generating a future purchase, or a premium that serves as a reminder of the brand and reinforces its image, such as the miniature race car premium offer that ties into Tide's NASCAR sponsorship (Exhibit 12–1). Most sales promotion offers attempt to add some value to the product or service. While advertising appeals to the mind and emotions to give the consumer a reason to buy, sales promotion appeals more to the pocketbook and provides an incentive for purchasing a brand.

Sales promotion can also provide an inducement to marketing intermediaries such as wholesalers and retailers. A trade allowance or discount gives retailers a financial incentive to stock and promote a manufacturer's products. A trade contest directed toward wholesalers or retail personnel gives them extra incentive to perform certain tasks or meet sales goals.

A second point is that sales promotion is essentially an *acceleration tool,* designed to speed up the selling process and maximize sales volume.[2] By providing an extra incentive, sales promotion techniques can motivate consumers to purchase a larger quantity of a brand or shorten the purchase cycle of the trade or consumers by encouraging them to take more immediate action.

Companies also use limited-time offers such as price-off deals to retailers or a coupon with an expiration date to accelerate the purchase process.[3] Sales promotion attempts to maximize sales volume by motivating customers who have not responded to advertising. The ideal sales promotion program generates sales that would not be achieved by other

Exhibit 12–1 Procter & Gamble offers a premium offer to provide extra incentive to purchase Tide and Downy

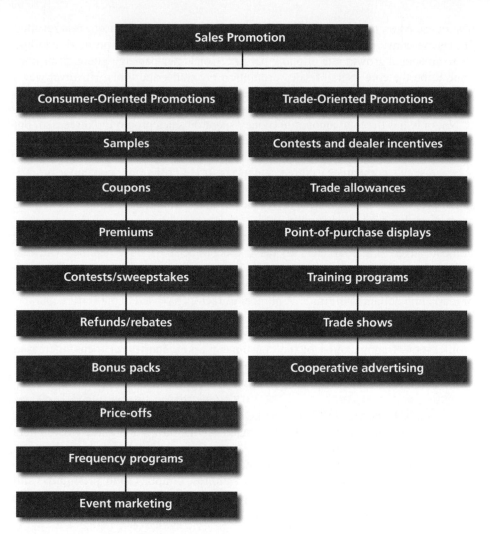

Figure 12–1 Types of sales promotion activities

means. However, as we shall see later, many sales promotion offers end up being used by current users of a brand rather than attracting new users.

A final point regarding sales promotion activities is that they can be *targeted to different parties* in the marketing channel. As shown in Figure 12–1, sales promotion can be broken into two major categories: consumer-oriented and trade-oriented promotions. Activities involved in **consumer sales promotion** include sampling, couponing, premiums, contests and sweepstakes, refunds and rebates, bonus packs, price-offs, and event marketing. These promotions are directed at consumers, the end purchasers of goods and services, and are designed to induce them to purchase the marketer's brand.

As discussed in Chapter 2, consumer-oriented promotions are part of a promotional pull strategy; they work along with advertising to encourage consumers to purchase a particular brand and thus create demand for it. Consumer promotions are also used by retailers to encourage consumers to shop in their particular stores. Many grocery stores use their own coupons or sponsor contests and other promotions to increase store patronage.

Trade sales promotion includes dealer contests and incentives, trade allowances, point-of-purchase displays, sales training programs, trade shows, cooperative advertising, and other programs designed to motivate distributors and retailers to carry a product and make an extra effort to push it to their customers. Many marketing programs include both trade- and consumer-oriented promotions, since motivating both groups maximizes the effectiveness of the promotional program.

Growth of Sales Promotion

While sales promotion has been part of the marketing process for a long time, its role and importance in a company's integrated marketing communications programs has increased dramatically over the past decade. The strong economy has resulted in massive consumer spending which has helped propel the sales promotion industry to an annual growth rate of 5 to 7 percent. Consumer-package-goods firms continue to be the core users of sales promotion programs and tools. However, sales promotion activity is also increasing in new categories, including health care, computer hardware and software, electronics, and deregulated utilities.[4]

Not only has the total amount of money spent on sales promotion increased, but the percentage of marketers' budgets allocated to promotion has skyrocketed. Annual studies by Carol Wright Promotions track the marketing spending of major package-goods companies in three categories: trade promotion, consumer promotion, and media advertising. The percentage of the marketing budget spent on consumer promotions has held steady over the past decade, while the allocation to trade promotions has risen dramatically.

This increase in trade promotion spending has come almost totally at the expense of media advertising. Marketers say they expect trade spending to decline somewhat in the future, with corresponding increases in consumer promotions and media advertising. However, many marketing people believe it will be difficult to reverse the flow of marketing dollars to the trade. A number of factors have led to the shift in marketing dollars to sales promotion from media advertising. Among them are the growing power of retailers, declining brand loyalty, increased promotional sensitivity, brand proliferation, fragmentation of the consumer market, short-term focus, increased accountability, competition, clutter, and reaching a specific target audience.

The Growing Power of Retailers

One reason for the increase in sales promotion is the power shift in the marketplace from manufacturers to retailers. For many years, manufacturers of national brands had the power and influence; retailers were just passive distributors of their products. Consumer products manufacturers created consumer demand for their brands by using heavy advertising and some consumer-oriented promotions, such as samples, coupons, and premiums, and exerted pressure on retailers to carry the products. Retailers did very little research and sales analysis; they relied on manufacturers for information regarding the sales performance of individual brands.

In recent years, however, several developments have helped to transfer power from the manufacturers to the retailers. With the advent of optical checkout scanners and sophisticated in-store computer systems, retailers gained access to data concerning how quickly products turn over, which sales promotions are working, and which products make money.[5] Retailers use this information to analyze sales of manufacturers' products and then demand discounts and other promotional support from manufacturers of lagging brands. Companies that fail to comply with retailers' demands for more trade support often have their shelf space reduced or even their product dropped.

Another factor that has increased the power of retailers is the consolidation of the grocery store industry, which has resulted in larger chains with greater buying power and clout. These large chains have become accustomed to trade promotions and can pressure manufacturers to provide deals, discounts, and allowances. Consolidation has also given large retailers more money for advancing already strong private label initiatives, and sales promotion is the next step in the marketing evolution of private label brands. Private label brands in various package-good categories such as foods, drugs, and health and beauty care products are giving national brands more competition for retail shelf space and increasing their own marketing, including the use of traditional sales promotion tools. Well-marketed private label products are forcing national brand leaders, as well as second-tier brands, to develop more innovative promotional programs and to be more price-competitive.[6]

Declining Brand Loyalty

Another major reason for the increase in sales promotion is that consumers have become less brand loyal to one brand. Some consumers are always willing to buy their preferred brand at full price without any type of promotional offer. However, many consumers are loyal coupon users and/or are conditioned to look for deals when they shop. They may switch back and forth among a set of brands they view as essentially equal. These brands are all perceived as being satisfactory and interchangeable, and favourable brand switches (discussed in Chapter 5) purchase whatever brand is on special or for which they have a coupon.

Increased Promotional Sensitivity

Marketers are making greater use of sales promotion in their marketing programs because consumers respond favourably to the incentives it provides. A major research project completed by Promotion Decisions, Inc., in 1999 tracked the purchase behaviour of over 33,000 consumers and their response to both consumer and trade promotions. The results showed that 42 percent of the total unit volume of the 12 package-good products analyzed was purchased with some type of incentive while 58 percent was purchased at full price. Coupons were particularly popular among consumers, as 24 percent of the sales volume involved the use of a coupon.[7]

An obvious reason for consumers' increased sensitivity to sales promotion offers is that they save money. Another reason is that many purchase decisions are made at the point of purchase by consumers who are increasingly time-sensitive and facing too many choices. Some studies have found that up to 70 percent of purchase decisions are made in the store, where people are very likely to respond to promotional deals.[8] Buying a brand that is on special or being displayed can simplify the decision-making process and solve the problem of overchoice. Professor Leigh McAlister has described this process:

> As consumers go down the supermarket aisle they spend 3 to 10 seconds in each product category. They often don't know the regular price of the chosen product. However, they do have a sense of whether or not that product is on promotion. As they go down the aisle, they are trying to pensively fill their baskets with good products without tiresome calculations. They see a "good deal" and it goes in the cart.[9]

Brand Proliferation

A major aspect of many firms' marketing strategies over the past decade has been the development of new products. Consumer-product companies are launching more new products each year. The market has become saturated with new brands, which often lack any significant advantages that can be used as the basis of an advertising campaign. Thus, companies increasingly depend on sales promotion to encourage consumers to try these brands. Marketers are relying more on samples, coupons, rebates, premiums, and other innovative promotional tools to achieve trial usage of their new brands and encourage repeat purchase (Exhibit 12–2).

Promotions are also important in getting retailers to allocate some of their precious shelf space to new brands. The competition for shelf space for new products in stores is enormous. Supermarkets carry an average of 30,000 products (compared with 13,067 in 1982). Retailers favour new brands with strong sales promotion support that will bring in more customers and boost their sales and profits. Many retailers require special discounts or allowances from manufacturers just to handle a new product. These slotting fees or allowances, which are discussed later in the chapter, can make it expensive for a manufacturer to introduce a new product.

Exhibit 12–2 Sales promotion tools such as coupons are often used to encourage trial of a new brand

Fragmentation of the Consumer Market

As the consumer market becomes more fragmented and traditional mass-media–based advertising less effective, marketers are turning to more segmented, highly targeted approaches. Many companies are tailoring their promotional efforts to specific regional markets. Sales promotion tools have become one of the primary vehicles for doing this, through programs tied into local flavour, themes, or events. For example, fast-food restaurants and take-out pizza chains such as Domino's spent a high percentage of their marketing budget on local tie-ins and promotions designed to build traffic and generate sales from their trade areas.[10]

Marketers are also shifting more of their promotional efforts to direct marketing, which often includes some form of sales promotion incentive. Many marketers use information they get from premium offers, trackable coupons, rebates, and sweepstakes to build databases for future direct-marketing efforts. As marketers continue to shift from media advertising to direct marketing, promotional offers will probably be used even more to help build databases. The technology is already in place to enable marketers to communicate individually with target consumers and transform mass promotional tools into ways of doing one-to-one marketing.[11]

Short-Term Focus   Many businesspeople believe the increase in sales promotion is motivated by marketing plans and reward systems geared to short-term performance and the immediate generation of sales volume. Some think the package-goods brand management system has contributed to marketers' increased dependence on sales promotion. Brand managers use sales promotions routinely, not only to introduce new products or defend against the competition but also to meet quarterly or yearly sales and market share goals. The sales force, too, may have short-term quotas or goals to meet and may also receive requests from retailers and wholesalers for promotions. Thus, reps may pressure marketing or brand managers to use promotions to help them move the products into the retailers' stores.

Many managers view consumer and trade promotions as the most dependable way to generate short-term sales, particularly when they are price related. The reliance on sales promotion is particularly high in mature and slow-growth markets, where it is difficult to stimulate consumer demand through advertising. This has led to concern that managers have become too dependent on the quick sales fix that can result from a promotion and that the brand franchise may be eroded by too many deals.

Increased Accountability   In addition to pressuring their marketing or brand managers and sales force to produce short-term results, many companies are demanding to know what they are getting for their promotional expenditures. Sales promotion is more economically accountable than advertising. In companies struggling to meet their sales and financial goals, top management is demanding measurable, accountable ways to relate promotional expenditures to sales and profitability.

Managers who are being held accountable to produce results often use price discounts or coupons, since they produce a quick and easily measured jump in sales. It takes longer for an ad campaign to show some impact and the effects are more difficult to measure. Marketers are also feeling pressure from the trade as powerful retailers demand sales performance from their brands. Real-time data available from computerized checkout scanners make it possible for retailers to monitor promotions and track the results they generate on a daily basis.

Competition   Another factor that led to the increase in sales promotion is manufacturers' reliance on trade and consumer promotions to gain or maintain competitive advantage. The markets for many products are mature and stagnant, and it is increasingly difficult to boost sales through advertising. Exciting, breakthrough creative ideas are difficult to come by, and consumers' attention to mass media advertising continues to decline. Rather than allocating large amounts of money to run dull ads, many marketers have turned to sales promotion.

Many companies are tailoring their trade promotions to key retail accounts and developing strategic alliances with retailers that include both trade and consumer promotional programs. A major development in recent years is **account-specific marketing** (also referred to as *comarketing*), whereby a manufacturer collaborates with an individual retailer to create a customized promotion that accomplishes mutual objectives (see Exhibit 12–3).

Retailers may use a promotional deal with one company as leverage to seek an equal or better deal with its competitors. Consumer and trade promotions are easily

Exhibit 12–3   Cox Target Media promotes its Carol Wright Account Specific marketing program

IMC Perspective 12-1
Are Loyalty Programs Living Up to Their Hype?

As a vice president of marketing at the Wine Council of Ontario, and the operator of his own marketing consultancy, Kevin Nullmeyer has done a lot of thinking about the logic of loyalty programs. His conclusion: Most aren't living up to their hype.

"Loyalty programs are sexy and fun and the latest thing," he says, "But not nearly enough marketers sit back and ask themselves 'what's our strategy here?'" In fact, according to Nullmeyer, the vast majority have no real grasp of whether their programs are working. Too many, he suggests, fail to address the fundamentals before they begin: Is the initiative simply to pull in more customers, or is it intended to provide data about these consumers? If so, and most importantly, what's to be done with this data?

Most marketers will argue that data collection and loyalty incentives work symbiotically, and that it only makes sense to collect one while pursuing the other. But so far, says Nullmeyer, he sees little evidence that data collected part and parcel with loyalty programs is being put to much use.

For instance, as a member of Air Miles, which is run by Toronto-based The Loyalty Group, Nullmeyer is professionally aware that he's among that program's higher-spending category. "But do they target me? No. All I get is a fat envelope every quarter filled with crap: vouchers for women's shoes—I don't buy women's shoes—and vouchers for cat food—I don't buy cat food. It's like, guys, can't you read what I'm spending on and target something?"

As a matter of fact, replies Air Miles president Bryan Pearson, the guys at Air Miles *don't* know exactly what Nullmeyer is buying. "We know where he shopped. We know when he shopped. We know roughly how much he spent by comparing how many miles he earned." But no, acknowledged Pearson, "We don't actually understand that you are not buying in the cat-food category. The ability to merge that data with the SKU-level data (down to the individual stock-keeping units, or SKU) is something that we're not engaged in."

But there are others out there who are. When the Hudson Bay Company created HBC Rewards, scrapping Zeller's iconic Club Z and incorporating its data with that of its sister retailer, The Bay, it created the most comprehensive and potentially far-reaching customer database in Canada. David Strickland, senior vice president of marketing at Zellers, feels that the information is being used to get a better profile of its customers.

"I know the new moms who are coming into our store. And I don't know them on only one dimension. I know them because of the baby food they're buying, the new crib they bought, the stroller they bought, the sizes of the kids' clothing they're buying, and the diapers they're buying and the size of those diapers."

Then, says Strickland, he takes it to the next step. "I know how often those groups of customers use our pharmacy and how many of them do or don't use our pharmacy," he says. "I know what the customers look like that do use the pharmacy, and therefore I'll be able to project a picture of those who don't use the pharmacy." This understanding, he says, gives him the capability to develop a program to try to get more moms to use the pharmacy at Zellers, as well as buy clothing for their kids.

It's the sort of deduction that Sherlock Holmes would have found familiar. One piece of information provides a probability; the next reinforces it. With the sheer volume of information at its disposal, HBC can march from clue to clue to clue, refining knowledge as it goes.

Source: Adapted from Scott Gardiner, "A Truly Awesome Database," *Marketing Magazine,* April 29, 2002. Used with permission.

---

matched by competitors, and many marketers find themselves in a promotional trap where they must continue using promotions or be at a competitive disadvantage. (We discuss this problem in more detail later in the chapter.)

Clutter   A promotional offer in an ad can break through the clutter that is prevalent in most media today. A premium offer may help attract consumers' attention to an ad, as will a contest or sweepstakes. Some studies have shown that readership scores are higher for print ads with coupons than for ads without them.[12] However, more recent studies by Starch INRA Hooper suggest that magazine ads with coupons do not generate higher readership.[13]

Reaching a Specific Target Audience   Most companies focus their marketing efforts on specific market segments and are always looking for ways to reach their target audiences. Many marketers are finding that sales promotion tools such as contests and sweepstakes, events, coupons, and samplings are very effective ways to reach specific geographic, demographic, psychographic, and ethnic markets. Sales promotion programs can also be targeted to specific user-status groups such as nonusers or light versus heavy users.

Sales Promotion versus Advertising

Many factors have contributed to the increased use of sales promotion by consumer product manufacturers. Marketing and advertising executives are concerned about how this shift in the allocation of the promotional budget affects brand equity. As noted in Chapter 2, *brand equity* is an intangible asset of added value or goodwill that results from consumers' favourable image, impressions of differentiation, and/or strength of attachment to a brand.

Some critics argue that sales promotion increases come at the expense of brand equity and every dollar that goes into promotion rather than advertising devalues the brand.[14] They say trade promotions in particular contribute to the destruction of brand franchises and equity as they encourage consumers to purchase primarily on the basis of price.

Proponents of advertising argue that marketers must maintain strong equity if they want to differentiate their brands and charge a premium price for them. They say advertising is still the most effective way to build the long-term value of a brand: it informs consumers of a brand's features and benefits, creates an image, and helps build and maintain brand loyalty. However, many marketers are not investing in their brands as they take monies away from media advertising to fund short-term promotions. For example, H. J. Heinz Co., whose major products include ketchup and condiments, allocated nearly all its marketing budget to trade promotions in the early to mid-'90s while cutting back substantially on advertising.[15] In 1996, Heinz had $9 billion in sales but spent only $90 million advertising its brands in the United States. Some analysts argued that the lack of ad spending was turning some Heinz brands into commodities, making it difficult for them to maintain prices. By the end of the decade, Heinz had announced plans to increase advertising spending for its core business categories. Brands such as Heinz ketchup are being advertised more in an effort to rebuild their brand equity and make them less dependent on trade promotions.[16]

Marketing experts generally agree that advertising plays an important role in building and maintaining a brand's image and position, which are core components of its equity. Many are concerned that if the trend toward spending more on sales promotion at the expense of media advertising continues, brands may lose the equity that advertising helped create and be forced to compete primarily on the basis of price. Many of these concerns are justified, but not all sales promotion activities detract from the value of a brand.

For example, Coors Canada has used sales promotion to build its brand equity in the face of stiff sales promotion competition from other brands. Just a few years ago, Coors was offering only one sales promotion per year, its famous "Talking Can & Cap" campaign. Now Coors Canada spends 25 percent of its marketing budget on sales promotions, and 25 percent of its $4.8-million media budget is allocated to support the sales promotions. In 2001, it offered four in-case promotions in Western Canada, one in Quebec, and at least one in Ontario. Says one Coors Canada executive, "We are trying to make our in-case promotions build equity as much as they can for what they are, (but) we also have promotions that we're primarily trying to drive image with." Coors Canada's "Tracker" campaign for Coors Light in Quebec is an example of this. When a consumer opens a "tracker" bottle, the Coors Light/Musique Plus Tracker team greets the lucky winner with trip to a Los Angeles party. The opened bottle triggers a Global Positioning System transmitter that facilitates the search![17]

Part Five   Strengthen the Message

In this section, we examine the various parts of a sales promotion plan. First, we consider some objectives marketers have for sales promotion programs. Next, we illustrate why the various sales promotion decisions are strategic options. Finally, we discuss the key tactics that are critical for all sales promotions. We focus on the consumer market to illustrate these ideas. Application to the trade market is readily done once the concept is understood.

Sales Promotion Plan

Objectives of Consumer Sales Promotion

As the use of sales promotion techniques continues to increase, companies must consider what they hope to accomplish through their consumer promotions and how they interact with other promotional activities such as advertising, direct marketing, and personal selling. When marketers implement sales promotion programs without considering their long-term cumulative effect on the brand's image and position in the marketplace, they often do little more than create short-term spikes in the sales curve.

Not all sales promotion activities are designed to achieve the same objectives. As with any promotional mix element, marketers must plan consumer promotions by conducting a situation analysis and determining sales promotion's specific role in the integrated marketing communications program. They must decide what the promotion is designed to accomplish and to whom it should be targeted. Setting clearly defined objectives and measurable goals for their sales promotion programs forces managers to think beyond the short-term sales fix (although this can be one goal).

While the basic goal of most consumer sales promotion programs is to induce purchase of a brand, the marketer may have a number of different objectives for both new and established brands. We use the ideas developed in Chapter 5 to highlight how sales promotions can help achieve behavioural and communication objectives.

Trial Purchase   One of the most important uses of sales promotion techniques is to encourage consumers to try a new product or service. While thousands of new products are introduced to the market every year, as many as 90 percent of them fail within the first year. Many of these failures are due to the fact that the new product or brand lacks the promotional support needed either to encourage initial trial by enough consumers or to induce enough of those trying the brand to repurchase it. Many new brands are merely new versions of an existing product without unique benefits, so advertising alone cannot induce trial. Sales promotion tools have become an important part of new brand introduction strategies; the level of initial trial can be increased through techniques such as sampling, couponing, and refund offers.

A trial purchase objective is also relevant for an established brand that uses a sales promotion to attract nonusers of the product category. Attracting nonusers of the product category can be very difficult, as consumers may not see a need for the product. Sales promotions can appeal to nonusers by providing them with an extra incentive to try the product, but a more common strategy for increasing sales of an established brand is to attract consumers who use a competing brand. This can be done by giving them an incentive to switch, such as a coupon, premium offer, bonus pack, or price deal. Marketers can also get users of a competitor to try their brand through sampling or other types of promotional programs.

Repeat Purchase   The success of a new brand depends not only on getting initial trial but also on inducing a reasonable percentage of people who try the brand to repurchase it and establish ongoing purchase patterns. Promotional incentives such as coupons or refund offers are often included with a sample to encourage repeat purchase after trial. For example, when Lever Brothers introduced its Lever 2000 brand of bar soap, it distributed millions of free samples along with a 75-cent coupon. The samples allowed consumers to try the new soap, while the coupon provided an incentive to purchase it.

A company can use sales promotion techniques in several ways to retain its current customer base through continued repeat purchases. One way is to load them with the product, taking them out of the market for a certain time. Special price promotions, coupons, or bonus packs can encourage consumers to stock up on the brand. This not only keeps them using the company's brand but also reduces the likelihood they will switch brands in response to a competitor's promotion.

Increasing Consumption   Many marketing managers are responsible for established brands competing in mature markets, against established competitors, where consumer purchase patterns are often well set. Awareness of an established brand is generally high as a result of cumulative advertising effects, and many consumers have probably tried the brand. These factors can create a challenging situation for the brand manager. Sales promotion can generate some new interest in an established brand to help increase sales or defend market share against competitors.

Marketers attempt to increase sales for an established brand in several ways, and sales promotion can play an important role in each. One way to increase product consumption is by identifying new uses for the brand. Sales promotion tools like recipe books or calendars that show various ways of using the product often can accomplish this.

Support IMC Program/Build Brand Equity   A final objective for consumer-oriented promotions is to enhance or support the integrated marketing communications effort for a brand or company. Building brand equity and image has traditionally been done through advertising. However, sales promotion techniques such as contests or sweepstakes and premium offers are often used to draw attention to an ad, increase involvement with the message and product/service, and help build relationships with consumers.

Marketers often turn to sales promotion in the fall to reach students of all ages who are going back to school. For example, DaimlerChrysler displayed its new PT Cruiser and Neon RT to university students at nine campuses across Canada during frosh week in September 2001 as part of its "Coolest car on campus" campaign. A contest allowed students to paint a PT Cruiser with water-based paint, with the winning university receiving the car for a campus drive-safe program. In addition, students dressed up in costumes in front of the car, and photos were sent to their parents as part of the "I'll be graduating before you know it" campaign.[18]

Consumer Sales Promotion Strategy Decisions

Strategic decisions for sales promotions fall into three broad categories: sales promotion tool decision, application across product lines, and application in geographic markets.

Sales Promotion Strategy Options   Our view of sales promotions is that the options identified in Figure 12-1 are important strategic choices for a marketer. Essentially, the key strategic decision for a marketer concerns the most appropriate sales promotion option(s) that will best achieve the behavioural objective(s) for the target audience(s). Two characteristics of sales promotions help guide the strategic direction of the sales promotion plan: the degree to which the sales promotion is "franchise building" and whether the incentive of the sales promotion is immediate or delayed.

Franchise-Building Characteristic   Sales promotion activities that communicate distinctive brand attributes and contribute to the development and reinforcement of brand identity are consumer franchise-building (CFB) promotions.[19] Consumer sales promotion efforts cannot make consumers loyal to a brand that is of little value or does not provide them with a specific benefit. But they can make consumers aware of a brand and, by communicating its specific features and benefits, contribute to the development of a favourable brand attitude. Consumer franchise-building promotions are designed to build long-term brand preference and help the company achieve the ultimate goal of full-price purchases that do not depend on a promotional offer.

For years, franchise or image building was viewed as the exclusive realm of advertising, and sales promotion was used only to generate short-term sales increases. But now marketers are recognizing the image-building potential of sales promotion and paying attention to its CFB value. A survey of senior marketing executives found that 88 percent believe consumer promotions can help build a brand's equity, and 58 percent think trade promotions can contribute.[20] One sales promotion expert says:

> Today's marketers who appreciate the potential of sales promotion as an ongoing strategy that works to build a brand's franchise recognize that promotion's potential goes well beyond mere quick-fix, price-off tactics. The promotion professional is familiar with a variety of approaches to generating consumer involvement—that is, sweepstakes, special events, premiums, or rebates—and understands that the given campaign must work in harmony with long-term goals and brand positioning.[21]

Companies can also use sales promotion to contribute to franchise building by developing an offer consistent with the image of the brand. An example of a successful consumer brand-building promotion is the Search for 2000 Uses Sweepstakes promotion for WD-40, shown in Exhibit 12–4. The WD-40 Company positions its brand as the leading multipurpose problem solver that cleans, protects, penetrates, lubricates, and displaces moisture like no other product on earth. The marketing strategy for WD-40 is to continually promote the myriad of uses for the product. The Search for 2000 Uses Sweepstakes, which was launched to coincide with the new millennium, asked consumers to suggest their use for WD-40 in order to be entered for a chance to win various prizes, such as WD-40 can radios, T-shirts, baseball caps, and a grand prize of $10,000 in company stock. The sweepstakes reinforced WD-40's image as a multipurpose problem solver and also encouraged consumers to visit the company's website to enter their use.

Exhibit 12–4   WD-40's Search for 2000 Uses Sweepstakes is an excellent example of a consumer brand-building promotion

Nonfranchise-Building Characteristic   Nonfranchise-building (non FB) promotions are designed to accelerate the purchase decision process and generate an immediate increase in sales. These activities do not communicate information about a brand's unique features or the benefits of using it, so they do not contribute to the building of brand identity and image. Price-off deals, bonus packs, and rebates or refunds are examples of non-FB sales promotion techniques. Trade promotions receive the most criticism for being nonfranchise building—for good reason. First, many of the promotional discounts and allowances given to the trade are never passed on to consumers. Most trade promotions that are forwarded through the channels reach consumers in the form of lower prices or special deals and lead them to buy on the basis of price rather than brand equity.

Many specialists in the promotional area stress the need for marketers to use sales promotion tools to build a franchise and create long-term continuity in their promotional programs. Whereas non-FB promotions merely borrow customers from other brands, well-planned CFB activities can convert consumers to loyal customers. Short-term non-FB promotions have their place in a firm's promotional mix, particularly when competitive developments call for them. But their limitations must be recognized when a long-term marketing strategy for a brand is developed.

Incentive Characteristic   As noted, sales promotions provide consumers with an extra incentive or reward for engaging in a certain form of behaviour, such as purchasing a brand. For some sales promotion tools, the incentive that the consumer receives is immediate, while for others the reward is delayed and not realized immediately. Using their situation analysis as an input, marketers decide the relative balance between immediate or delayed incentives. The decision is based on the target audience(s) and

Figure 12–2 Consumer sales promotion tools for various objectives

Communication and Behavioural Objectives

Consumer Reward Incentive	Trial purchase	Repeat purchase/ customer loading	Support IMC program/ build brand equity
Immediate	• Sampling • Instant coupons • In-store coupons • In-store rebates	• Price-off deals • Bonus packs • In- and on-package free premiums • Loyalty programs	• Events • In- and on-package free premiums
Delayed	• Media- and mail-delivered coupons • Mail-in refunds and rebates • Free mail-in premiums • Scanner- and Internet-delivered coupons	• In- and on-package coupons • Mail-in refunds and rebates • Loyalty programs	• Self-liquidating premiums • Free mail-in premiums • Contests and sweepstakes • Loyalty programs

the intended behavioural objective(s). The chart in Figure 12–2 outlines which sales promotion tools can be used to accomplish various behavioural objectives and identifies whether the extra incentive or reward is immediate or delayed.[22]

It should be noted that in Figure 12–2 some of the sales promotion techniques are listed more than once because they can be used to accomplish more than one objective with both immediate and delayed incentives. For example, loyalty programs can be used to retain customers by providing both immediate and delayed rewards. Shoppers who belong to loyalty programs sponsored by supermarkets, and who receive discounts every time they make a purchase, are receiving immediate rewards that are designed to retain them as customers. Some loyalty promotions, such as frequency programs used by airlines, car rental companies, and hotels, offer delayed rewards by requiring that users accumulate points to reach a certain level or status before the points can be redeemed. Loyalty programs can also be used by marketers to help build brand equity. For example, when an airline or car rental company sends its frequent users upgrade certificates, the practice helps build relationships with these customers and thus contributes to brand equity.

Application across Product Lines Another part of the strategic sales promotion decision is the degree to which each sales promotion tool is applied to the range of sizes, varieties, models, or products. Overall, there are three important product decisions for sales promotions. The first concerns whether the sales promotion should be run on the entire line or on individual items. If the latter option is selected (i.e., selective application), the second decision concerns which specific items. The marketer could run a promotion on either the more or less popular items. Similarly, the marketer could focus on higher or lower price points. Sometimes, a sales promotion is offered on a unique product format or size instead of the regular product. For example, Kellogg's bundled three brands of cereal with plastic in one sales promotion in which each size was not the standard size typically distributed. Thus, the third strategic issue concerns whether the sales promotion is run on the "regular" stock or some other special version.

Application across Geographic Markets Sales promotions can be run nationally or in select markets. Local or regional market conditions, with respect to consumer demand and competitive intensity, tend to dictate the degree of tailoring sale promotions for each geographic market. Intuitively, it appears that many marketers would be faced with situations where offering unique sales promotions for each geographic market would achieve optimal communication and behavioural effects; however, there are three factors that marketers need to consider. First, a regional focus requires additional managerial commitment in planning and implementation. Second, achieving objectives more specifically may result in greater expense, thus necessitating a cost-benefit analysis. Finally, national accounts may not be too receptive with different types of sales promotions in one province versus another.

Consumer Sales Promotion Tactics Decisions

You can receive a coupon with a value anywhere from 50¢ to $2.00 for many consumer products, early in the year or later in the year, often or not so often, or from an number of outlets (i.e., direct mail, magazine). As this implies, for each sales promotion option, the marketer faces a number of key tactical decisions: value of the incentive, timing, and distribution. We briefly describe each of these so that you can put together a comprehensive sales promotion plan.

Value of Incentive Whether the marketer is offering some sort of price discount or a consumer franchise-building sales promotion such as a premium, eventually the marketer has to decide the value of the sales promotion. For example, should the coupon be the equivalent of a 10- or a 20-percent discount? This decision is contingent upon the threshold at which consumers will respond to a sales promotion and the number of potential consumer responses; each will contribute to the total cost of the sales promotion. Similarly, if a beer company is offering a premium, a strategic decision has to be made as to the relative value of the premium: for example, a T-shirt worth $10 to $15 or perhaps a "cozy" worth a couple of dollars.

A non-economic interpretation of value is also possible. Hostess Frito-Lay (HFL) has used various in-pack collectables (i.e., stickers) of well-known entertainment or pop-culture icons (i.e., *The Simpsons, Star Wars*) that attract young impulse-purchase consumers. The focus of these sales promotions transfer well to point-of-sale displays to attract consumer's attention and to meet retailers' need for innovative merchandising to move product off the shelves. In 2001, HFL used Marvel comic-book characters on packaging and convenience-store point-of-sale displays, and offered limited-edition comic books as part of a trivia challenge in association with Teletoon.[23]

Timing The time element of the sales promotion is important in a few directions that are mutually dependent. A marketer has to decide during which months, weeks, or days the sales promotion will be offered. Seasonal or some other consumption pattern discovered through market research, or the situation analysis, may guide this choice. Secondly, sales promotions can be offered for one day, one week, a few weeks, or even a few months. Target audience and behavioural objectives typically guide this duration decision. Finally, the frequency of the sales promotion is a final timing consideration. If coupons have been decided, the marketer needs to decide whether one will be offered every six months or perhaps two every six months.

Distribution For most sales promotions, there is a logistical consideration as to how the promotion will get to the consumer or how the consumer will get to the sales promotion. There are many choices for sales promotions such as coupons (e.g., direct mail, in-ad), while for others, such as premiums, the choices may be limited. We discuss some of the distribution options for each sales promotion in the next section, where we describe each sales promotion and their strengths and limitations.

Marketers use various sales promotion techniques to meet the objectives just discussed. Figure 12–3 shows the extent to which these consumer promotions are used by package-goods companies. We now review a number of these options.

Consumer Sales Promotion Strategy Options

Sampling

Sampling involves a variety of procedures whereby consumers are given some quantity of a product for no charge to induce trial. Sampling is generally considered

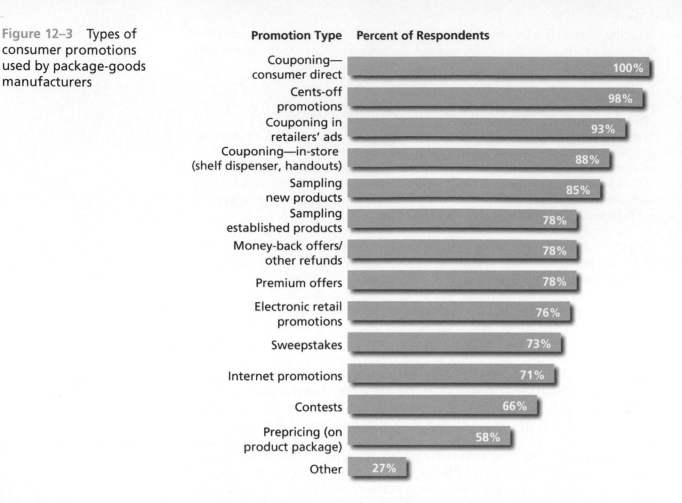

the most effective way to generate trial, although it is also the most expensive. As a sales promotion technique, sampling is often used to introduce a new product or brand to the market. However, as Figure 12–3 shows, sampling is also used for established products as well. Some companies do not use sampling for established products, reasoning that samples may not induce satisfied users of a competing brand to switch and may just go to the firm's current customers, who would buy the product anyway. This may not be true when significant changes (new and improved) are made in a brand.

Manufacturers of package-goods products such as food, health care items, cosmetics, and toiletries are heavy users of sampling since their products meet the three criteria for an effective sampling program:

1. The products are of relatively low unit value, so samples do not cost too much.
2. The products are divisible, which means they can be broken into small sample sizes that are adequate for demonstrating the brand's features and benefits to the user.
3. The purchase cycle is relatively short, so the consumer will consider an immediate purchase or will not forget about the brand before the next purchase occasion.

Strengths and Limitations of Sampling

Samples are an excellent way to induce a prospective buyer to try a product or service. One expert estimates approximately 75 percent of the households receiving a sample will try it.[24] Sampling generates much higher trial rates than advertising or other sales promotion techniques.

Getting people to try a product leads to a second benefit of sampling: consumers experience the brand directly, gaining a greater appreciation for its benefits. This can be particularly important when a product's features and benefits are difficult to describe through advertising. Many foods, beverages, and cosmetics have subtle features that are most appreciated when experienced directly.

The brand must have some unique or superior benefits for a sampling program to be worthwhile. Otherwise, the sampled consumers revert back to other brands and do not become repeat purchasers. The costs of a sampling program can be recovered only if it gets a number of consumers to become regular users of the brand at full retail price.

Another possible limitation to sampling is that the benefits of some products are difficult to gauge immediately, and the learning period required to appreciate the brand may require supplying the consumer with larger amounts of the brand than are affordable. An example would be an expensive skin cream that is promoted as preventing or reducing wrinkles but has to be used for an extended period before any effects are seen.

Sampling Methods One basic decision the sales promotion or brand manager must make is how the sample will be distributed. The sampling method chosen is important not only in terms of costs but also because it influences the type of consumer who receives the sample. The best sampling method gets the product to the best prospects for trial and subsequent repurchase. Some basic distribution methods include door-to-door, direct-mail, in-store, and on-package approaches.

Door-to-door sampling, in which the product is delivered directly to the prospect's residence, is used when it is important to control where the sample is delivered. This distribution method is very expensive because of labor costs, but it can be cost-effective if the marketer has information that helps define the target audience and/or if the prospects are located in a well-defined geographic area.

Sampling through media, some companies have samples delivered directly to consumers' homes by including them with newspapers or magazines. There are a number of newspapers that can now distribute a sample into a subscriber segment as small as 250 households with little increase in costs to marketers.[25]

Sampling through the mail is common for small, lightweight, nonperishable products such as those shown in Exhibit 12–5. A major advantage of this method is that the marketer has control over where and when the product will be distributed and can target the sample to specific market areas. Many marketers are using information from geodemographic target marketing programs such as Claritas's Prizm or Microvision to better target their sample mailings. The main drawbacks to mail sampling are postal restrictions and increasing postal rates.

In-store sampling is increasingly popular, especially for food products. The marketer hires temporary demonstrators who set up a table or booth, prepare small samples of the product, and pass them out to shoppers. The in-store sampling approach can be very effective for food products, since consumers get to taste the item and the demonstrator can give them more information about the product while it is being sampled. Demonstrators may also give consumers a cents-off coupon for the sampled item to encourage immediate trial purchase. While this sampling method can be very effective, it can also be expensive and requires a great deal of planning, as well as the cooperation of retailers.

On-package sampling, where a sample of a product is attached to another item, is another common sampling method (see Exhibit 12–6). This procedure can be very cost-effective, particularly for multiproduct firms that attach a sample of a new product to an existing brand's package. A drawback is that since the sample is distributed only to consumers who purchase the item to which it is attached, the sample will not reach nonusers of the carrier brand. Marketers can expand this sampling method by attaching the sample to multiple carrier brands and including samples with products not made by their company.

Event sampling has become one of the fastest-growing and most popular ways of distributing samples. Many marketers are using sampling programs that are part of integrated marketing programs that feature events, media tie-ins, and other activities that provide consumers with a total sense of a brand rather than just a few tastes of a food or beverage or a trial size of a package-goods product. Event sampling can take place in stores as well as at a variety of other venues such as concerts, sporting events, and other places.

Exhibit 12–5 Product samples sent through the mail

Exhibit 12–6 Armor All uses on-package samples for related products

Direct sampling is when, with the advancement of technology, marketers can deliver samples directly. Some companies send samples to consumers who call toll-free numbers to request them or mail in sample request forms. As discussed in Chapter 14, these sampling methods are becoming popular because they can help marketers build a database for direct marketing.

Location sampling allows many companies to use specialized sample distribution services who help the company identify consumers who are nonusers of a product or users of a competing brand and develop appropriate procedures for distributing a sample to them. Many college students receive sample packs at the beginning of the semester that contain trial sizes of such products as mouthwash, toothpaste, headache remedies, and deodorant.

The Internet is yet another way companies are making it possible for consumers to sample their products, and it is adding a whole new level of targeting to the mix by giving consumers the opportunity to choose the samples they want. Schick Canada created a three-page mini-site to let consumers order a free sample of its new unisex razor, Xtreme III, in the fall of 2000. The home page (www.schick.ca) showed uncluttered images of the product and a couple indicating its unisex feature. The second page described a couple of features, while the third page permitted consumers to request the sample. A link on www.canadianfreestuff.com directed users to the site in addition to a viral e-mail. In the first three months, Schick Canada had received about 9,000 requests for samples.

Creative approaches offering a combination of technology and creativity are driving new sampling methods that let marketers target more efficiently. For example, Kendall-Futuro, the marketer of Curad adhesive strips, inserted kid-size bandage sample packs and coupons into 7.5 million McDonald's Happy Meals. The sampling promotion created so much exposure for the new brand, which was decorated with images of McDonald's characters, that the subsequent retail sell-in exceeded projections by 30 percent.[26]

Coupons

The oldest, most widely used, and most effective sales promotion tool is the cents-off coupon. Coupons have been around since 1895, when the C. W. Post Co. started using the penny-off coupon to sell its new Grape-Nuts cereal. In recent years, coupons have become increasingly popular with consumers, which may explain their explosive growth among manufacturers and retailers that use them as sales promotion incentives. As Figure 12–3 showed, coupons are the most popular sales promotion technique. They are used by nearly all the package-goods firms in the Carol Wright Promotions survey.

The number of coupons distributed by consumer package-goods marketers reached 2.67 billion in 2001. After peaking at 3.3 billion in 1996, coupon distribution declined to 2.5 billion for 1999 and 2000. According to NCH Promotional Services, a company that tracks coupon distribution and redemption patterns, over 80 percent of consumers in the United States and Canada use coupons and nearly 25 percent say they always use them when they shop. Consumers generally seek out the coupons offering the highest savings, as the average face value of the 122 million coupons that were redeemed in 1998 was $1.25.[27]

Strengths and Limitations of Coupons Coupons have a number of strengths that make them popular sales promotion tools for both new and established products. First, coupons make it possible to offer a price reduction only to those consumers who are price-sensitive. Such consumers generally purchase *because* of coupons, while those who are not as concerned about price buy the brand at full value. Coupons also make it possible to reduce the retail price of a product without relying on retailers for cooperation, which can often be a problem. Coupons are generally regarded as second only to sampling as a promotional technique for generating trial. Since a coupon lowers the price of a product, it reduces the consumer's perceived risk associated with trial of a new brand. Coupons can encourage repurchase after initial trial. Many new products include a cents-off coupon inside the package to encourage repeat purchase.

Coupons can also be useful promotional devices for established products. They can encourage nonusers to try a brand, encourage repeat purchase among current users, and get users to try a new, improved version of a brand. Coupons may also help coax users of a product to trade up to more expensive brands. The product category where coupons are used most is disposable diapers, with 43 percent of purchases being made with a coupon, followed by cereal (35 percent), detergents (29 percent), and deodorant (25 percent). Some of the product categories where coupons are used the least include carbonated beverages (8 percent), candy (7 percent), and gum (2 percent).

But there are a number of problems with coupons. First, it can be difficult to estimate how many consumers will use a coupon and when. Response to a coupon is rarely immediate; it typically takes anywhere from two to six months to redeem one. A study of coupon redemption patterns by Inman and McAlister found that many coupons are redeemed just before the expiration date rather than in the period following the initial coupon drop.[28] Many marketers are attempting to expedite redemption by shortening the time period before expiration. The average length of time from issue date to expiration date for coupons in 2001 was 234 days. However, coupons remain less effective than sampling for inducing initial product trial in a short period.

A problem associated with using coupons to attract new users to an established brand is that it is difficult to prevent the coupons from being used by consumers who already use the brand. For example, General Foods decided to reduce its use of coupons for Maxwell House coffee when research revealed the coupons were being redeemed primarily by current users. Rather than attracting new users, coupons can end up reducing the company's profit margins among consumers who would probably purchase the product anyway.

Other problems with coupons include low redemption rates and high costs. Couponing program expenses include the face value of the coupon redeemed plus costs for production, distribution, and handling of the coupons. Figure 12–4 shows the calculations used to determine the costs of a couponing program using an FSI (freestanding insert) in the Saturday newspaper and a coupon with an average face value of 75 cents. The marketer should track costs closely to ensure the promotion is economically feasible.

Cost per Coupon Redeemed: An Illustration	
1. Distribution cost 5,000,000 circulation × $15/M	$75,000
2. Redemptions at 2%	100,000
3. Redemption cost 100,000 redemptions × $.75 face value	$75,000 ·
4. Retailer handling cost and processor fees 100,000 redemptions × $.10	$10,000
5. Total program cost Items 1 + 3 + 4	$160,000
6. Cost per coupon redeemed Cost divided by redemption	$1.60
7. Actual product sold on redemption (misredemption estimated at 20%) 100,000 × 80%	80,000
8. Cost per product moved Program cost divided by amount of product sold	$2.00

Figure 12–4 Calculating couponing costs

Another problem with coupon promotions is misredemption, or the cashing of a coupon without purchase of the brand. Coupon misredemption or fraud occurs in a number of ways, including:

- Redemption of coupons by consumers for a product or size not specified on the coupon.
- Redemption of coupons by salesclerks in exchange for cash.
- Gathering and redemption of coupons by store managers or owners without the accompanying sale of the product.
- Gathering or printing of coupons by criminals who sell them to unethical merchants, who in turn redeem them.

Many manufacturers hold firm in their policy to not pay retailers for questionable amounts or suspicious types of coupon submissions. However, some companies are less aggressive, and this affects their profit margins. Marketers must allow a certain percentage for misredemption when estimating the costs of a couponing program. Ways to identify and control coupon misredemption, such as improved coding, are being developed, but it still remains a problem.

Coupon Distribution   Coupons can be disseminated to consumers in a number of ways, including freestanding inserts in Saturday newspapers, direct mail, newspapers (either in individual ads or as a group of coupons in a cooperative format), magazines, and packages.

Distribution through newspaper *freestanding inserts* (FSIs) is by far the most popular method for delivering coupons to consumers, accounting for over 55 percent of all coupons distributed in 2001. There are a number of reasons why FSIs are the most popular way of delivering coupons, including their high-quality four-colour graphics, competitive distribution costs, national same-day circulation, market selectivity, and the fact that they can be competition-free due to category exclusivity (by FSI company). Because of their consumer popularity and predictable distribution, coupons distributed in FSIs are also a strong selling point with the retail trade. On the other hand, FSIs suffer from a low redemption rate of 1 percent, (see Figure 12–5) and their widespread distribution may lead to a clutter problem.

Direct mail accounts for about 5 percent of all coupons distributed. Most are sent by local retailers or through co-op mailings where a packet of coupons for many different products is sent to a household (Exhibit 12–7). Direct-mail couponing has several advantages. First, the mailing can be sent to a broad audience or targeted to specific geographic or demographic segments. Firms that mail their own coupons can be quite selective about recipients. Another important advantage of direct-mail couponing is a redemption rate of nearly 4 percent, much higher than for FSIs. Direct-mail couponing can also be combined with a sample, which makes it a very effective way to gain the attention of consumers. The major disadvantage of direct-mail coupon delivery is the expense relative to other distribution methods. The cost per thousand for distributing coupons through co-op mailings ranges from $10 to $15, and more targeted promotions can cost $20 to $25 or even more. Also, the higher redemption rate of mail-delivered coupons may result from the fact that many recipients are already users of the brand who take advantage of the coupons sent directly to them.

The use of *newspapers* and *magazines* as couponing vehicles is similar to direct mail, accounting for 6 percent of the total distributed in 2001. The advantages of newspapers as a couponing vehicle include market selectivity, shorter lead times with timing to the day, cooperative advertising opportunities that can lead to cost efficiencies, and promotional tie-ins with retailers. Other advantages of newspaper-delivered coupons are the broad exposure and consumer receptivity. Many consumers actively search the newspaper for coupons, especially on Saturdays or "food day" (when grocery stores advertise their specials). This enhances the likelihood of the consumer at least noticing the coupon. Distribution of coupons through magazines can take advantage of the selectivity of the publication to reach specific target audiences, along with enhanced production capabilities and extended copy life in the home. One feature of these print options is that the distribution cost is not a fac-

Figure 12–5 Coupon redemption rates by media

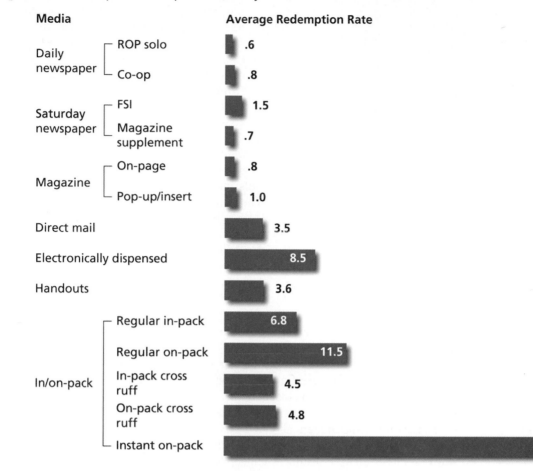

Media		Average Redemption Rate
Daily newspaper	ROP solo	.6
	Co-op	.8
Saturday newspaper	FSI	1.5
	Magazine supplement	.7
Magazine	On-page	.8
	Pop-up/insert	1.0
Direct mail		3.5
Electronically dispensed		8.5
Handouts		3.6
In/on-pack	Regular in-pack	6.8
	Regular on-pack	11.5
	In-pack cross ruff	4.5
	On-pack cross ruff	4.8
	Instant on-pack	35.6

tor if the advertiser was planning to run a print ad in the first place. However, clearly there is a significant limitation with a 1 percent redemption rate.

Placing coupons either *inside* or on the *outside* of the *package* is a distribution method that accounted for about 12 percent of the coupons distributed in 2001. The in/on package coupon has virtually no distribution costs and a much higher redemption rate than other couponing methods, averaging 9 percent. An in/on pack coupon that is redeemable for the next purchase of the same brand is known as a **bounce-back coupon.** This type of coupon gives consumers an inducement to repurchase the brand.

Bounce-back coupons are often used with product samples to encourage the consumer to purchase the product after sampling. They may be included in or on the package during the early phases of a brand's life cycle to encourage repeat purchase, or they may be a defensive manoeuvre for a mature brand that is facing competitive pressure and wants to retain its current users. The main limitation of bounce-back coupons is that they go only to purchasers of the brand and thus do not attract nonusers. A bounce-back coupon placed on the package for Kellogg's Eggo brand waffles is shown in Exhibit 12–8.

Another type of in/on pack coupon is the **cross-ruff coupon,** which is redeemable on the purchase of a different product, usually one made by the same company but occasionally through a tie-in with another manufacturer. Cross-ruff coupons have a redemption rate of 4 to 5 percent and can be effective in encouraging consumers to try other products or brands. Companies with wide product lines, such as cereal manufacturers, often use these coupons.

Yet another type of package coupon is the **instant coupon,** which is attached to the outside of the package so that the consumer can rip it off

Exhibit 12–7 Cox Target Media promotes its direct-mail couponing services

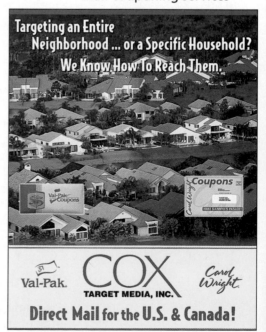

Exhibit 12–8 Kellogg's uses an on-package coupon to encourage repurchase

and redeem it immediately at the time of purchase. Instant coupons have redemption levels of around 36 percent and give consumers an immediate point-of-purchase incentive. They can be selectively placed in terms of promotion timing and market region. Some companies prefer instant coupons to price-off deals because the latter require more cooperation from retailers and can be more expensive, since every package must be reduced in price.

Another distribution method that has experienced strong growth over the past 10 years or so is **in-store couponing,** which includes all co-op couponing programs distributed in a retail store environment. This medium now accounts for around 16 percent of total coupon distribution. Coupons are distributed to consumers in stores in several ways, including tear-off pads, handouts in the store (sometimes as part of a sampling demonstration), on-shelf dispensers, and electronic dispensers, with a 7 percent redemption rate. These in-store coupons have several advantages: They can reach consumers when they are ready to make a purchase, increase brand awareness on the shelf, generate impulse buying, and encourage product trial. They also provide category exclusivity. In-store couponing removes the need for consumers to clip coupons from FSIs or print ads and then remember to bring them to the store.

Innovations for Coupons Earlier we noted that coupon distribution has dropped by about 20 percent in recent years. However, despite the growing sentiment among major marketers that coupons are inefficient and costly, very few companies are likely to abandon them entirely. Although most coupons never get used, consumers use some of them and have come to expect them. More than 80 percent of consumers use coupons and nearly one-quarter say they use them every time they shop. With so many consumers eager for coupons, marketers will continue to accommodate them. However, companies as well as the coupon industry are looking for ways to improve on their use.

Marketers are continually searching for more effective couponing techniques. General Mills, Kellogg, and Post recently replaced brand-specific coupons with universal coupons good for any of their cereal brands. For example, to make its couponing spending more efficient, Post began using universal coupons worth $1.50 off two boxes (matching the average cereal-coupon discount of 75 cents) and cut coupon distribution in half. Even though Post dropped only half as many coupons, redemption rates reached 6 percent, far exceeding the FSI average of less than 2 percent.[29]

Some marketers are broadening their use of account-specific direct-mail couponing, in which coupons are cobranded with individual retailers but can be used by consumers at any retail store. Procter & Gamble began using account-specific couponing with Tide detergent and has broadened the program to include mailings for a number of other brands.[30]

While many marketers are using the Internet for online promotions, online coupons account for less than 1 percent of all coupons distributed. One of the major problems that has kept marketers away from "e-couponing" is the risk of fraud, as it is too easy for consumers or unscrupulous retailers to mass-duplicate online coupons by printing out several, or by photocopying the black-and-white prints. There are ways to deal with this problem such as coding coupons and verifying them in-store when they are redeemed. However, this is time-consuming and not very popular with retailers. Two alternatives are now on the scene in Canada. Two websites, coupons.com and save.ca, allow consumers to print or receive coupons in the mail respectively.

Premiums

Premiums are a sales promotion device used by many marketers. A **premium** is an offer of an item of merchandise or service either free or at a low price that is an extra incentive for purchasers. Many marketers are eliminating toys and gimmicks in favor of value-added premiums that reflect the quality of the product and are consistent with its image and positioning in the market. The two basic types of offers are the free premium and the self-liquidating premium.

Free Premiums Free premiums are usually small gifts or merchandise included in the product package or sent to consumers who mail in a request along with a proof of purchase. In/on package free premiums include toys, balls, trading cards, or other items included in cereal packages, as well as samples of one product included with another. Surveys have shown that in/on package premiums are consumers' favourite type of promotion.[31]

Package-carried premiums have high impulse value and can provide an extra incentive to buy the product. However, several problems are associated with their use. First, there is the cost factor, which results from the premium itself as well as from extra packaging that may be needed. Finding desirable premiums at reasonable costs can be difficult, particularly for adult markets, and using a poor premium may do more harm than good.

Since most free mail-in premium offers require the consumer to send in more than one proof of purchase, they encourage repeat purchase and reward brand loyalty. But a major drawback of mail-in premiums is that they do not offer immediate reinforcement or reward to the purchaser, so they may not provide enough incentive to purchase the brand. Few consumers take advantage of mail-in premium offers; the average redemption rate is only 2 to 4 percent.[32]

Perhaps the most successful in-package premium in Canada in 2001 was a General Mills giveaway of six CD-ROM computer games such as Monopoly Junior and Clue. Modelled after a similar premium offer in the U.S., the Canadian division worked with only one games supplier, Hasbro, versus a couple of partners used south of the border. Hasbro was selected because both it and General Mills represent quality and heritage. The premium was so popular that store employees witnessed consumers searching through cases to find the game they wanted, as well as some consumers who left the store with only the CD-ROM, after purchasing the cereal. For competitive reasons, executives at General Mills were not willing to reveal any results but did admit that the consumer reaction was beyond belief given the empty shelves.[33]

Free premiums have become very popular in the restaurant industry, particularly among fast-food chains such as McDonald's and Burger King, which use premium offers in their kids' meals to attract children.[34] McDonald's has become the world's largest toymaker on a unit basis, commissioning about 750 million toys per year for its Happy Meals (Exhibit 12–9). Many of the premium offers used by the fast-food giants have cross-promotional tie-ins with popular movies and can be very effective at generating incremental sales. McDonald's gained a major competitive advantage in the movie tie-in premium wars in 1996 when it signed an agreement with Disney giving McDonald's exclusive rights to promotional tie-ins with Disney movies for 10 years.[35] In late 1999, McDonald's won another round of the tie-in wars by signing an exclusive promotional deal with "Teletubbies," the popular children's series which had previously partnered with Burger King for promotions.[36] Burger King's problems were compounded when its major promotion with the animated film *Pokemon: The First Movie,* had to be cancelled after several young children suffocated on the plastic balls used as part of the giveaway.[37]

One of the fastest-growing types of incentive offers being used by marketers is Air Miles, which have literally become a promotional currency. Consumers are now choosing credit-card services, phone services, hotels, and many other products and services on the

Exhibit 12–9 McDonald's Happy Meals use toys to help attract children

basis of mileage premiums for Air Miles. Even the Liquor Control Board of Ontario gives Air Miles!

Self-liquidating premiums require the consumer to pay some or all of the cost of the premium plus handling and mailing costs. The marketer usually purchases items used as self-liquidating premiums in large quantities and offers them to consumers at lower-than-retail prices. The goal is not to make a profit on the premium item but rather just to cover costs and offer a value to the consumer.

In addition to cost savings, self-liquidating premiums offer several advantages to marketers. Offering values to consumers through the premium products can create interest in the brand and goodwill that enhances the brand's image. These premiums can also encourage trade support and gain in-store displays for the brand and the premium offer. Self-liquidating premiums are often tied directly to the advertising campaign, so they extend the advertising message and contribute to consumer franchise building for a brand. General Mills Canada was at it again with a successful self-liquidating premium during Christmas of 2001. Customers received a beanbag version of the Pillsbury Doughboy for $2.99 with the purchase of two refrigerated-dough products. This marked the first time the brand icon had ever been directly merchandised! Pillsbury had the perfect opportunity because the Doughboy is the second-most recognized icon in North America, after Coca-Cola's Polar Bears. Even more impressive was the retailer participation and consumer acceptance. All retailers in Canada ran with the deal, and more than 200,000 Doughboys found a new home. And just to make sure that consumers liked the idea even more, the Doughboy came in three models: one holding a candy cane, another, a stocking, and the third, gifts.[38]

Self-liquidating premium offers have the same basic limitation as mail-in premiums: a very low redemption rate. Low redemption rates can leave the marketer with a large supply of items with a logo or some other brand identification that makes them hard to dispose of. Thus, it is important to test consumers' reaction to a premium incentive and determine whether they perceive the offer as a value. Another option is to use premiums with no brand identification, but that detracts from their consumer franchise-building value.

Contests and Sweepstakes

Contests and sweepstakes are an increasingly popular consumer sales promotion. These promotions seem to have an appeal and glamour that tools like cents-off coupons lack. Contests and sweepstakes are exciting because, as one expert has noted, many consumers have a "pot of gold at the end of the rainbow mentality" and think they can win the big prizes being offered.[39] The lure of sweepstakes and promotions has also been influenced by the "instant-millionaire syndrome" that has derived from huge cash prizes given by many state lotteries in recent years. Marketers are attracted to contests and sweepstakes as a way of generating attention and interest among a large number of consumers.

There are differences between contests and sweepstakes. A **contest** is a promotion where consumers compete for prizes or money on the basis of skills or ability. The company determines winners by judging the entries or ascertaining which entry comes closest to some predetermined criteria. Contests usually provide a purchase incentive by requiring a proof of purchase to enter or an entry form that is available from a dealer or advertisement. Some contests require consumers to read an ad or package or visit a store display to gather information needed to enter. Marketers must be careful not to make their contests too difficult to enter, as doing so might discourage participation among key prospects in the target audience.

A **sweepstakes** is a promotion where winners are determined purely by chance; it cannot require a proof of purchase as a condition for entry. Entrants need only submit their names for the prize drawing. While there is often an official entry form, handwritten entries must also be permitted. One form of sweepstakes is a **game,** which also has a chance element or odds of winning. Scratch-off cards with instant winners are a popular promotional tool. Some games occur over a longer period and require more involvement by consumers. Promotions where consumers must collect game pieces are popular among retailers and fast-food chains as a way to build store traffic and repeat purchases. For example, McDonald's has used promotions based on the game *Monopoly* several times in recent years.

Because they are easier to enter, sweepstakes attract more entries than contests. They are also easier and less expensive to administer, since every entry does not have to be checked or judged. Choosing the winning entry in a sweepstakes requires only the random selection of a winner from the pool of entries or generation of a number to match those held by sweepstakes entrants. Experts note that the costs of mounting a sweepstakes are also very predictable. Companies can buy insurance to indemnify them and protect against the expense of awarding a big prize. In general, sweepstakes present marketers with a fixed cost, which is a major advantage when budgeting for a promotion.

Contests and sweepstakes can get the consumer involved with a brand by making the promotion product relevant. For example, contests that ask consumers to suggest a name for a product or to submit recipes that use the brand can increase involvement levels. Nabisco developed an "Open a box, make up a snack," promotional contest for its three top cracker brands—Ritz, Triscuit, and Wheat Thins. Consumers sent in their favourite recipes, which were then made available on a dedicated website and at a toll-free number. Marketers can use contests and sweepstakes to build brand equity by connecting the prizes to the lifestyle, needs, or interests of the target audience. Procter & Gamble teamed up with MuchMusic for two contests to promote its Cover Girl brand of make-up. In January 2001, seven lucky winners received a live, on-air makeover with celebrity hair and makeup artists. Another contest, "Prom Night 2001," featured one winner and nine friends receiving a makeover and a limousine ride to their prom, among other prizes.[40]

Limitations of Contests and Sweepstakes While the use of contests and sweepstakes continues to increase, there are some limitations associated with these types of promotions. Many sweepstakes and/or contest promotions do little to contribute to consumer franchise building for a product or service and may even detract from it. The sweepstakes or contest often becomes the dominant focus rather than the brand, and little is accomplished other than giving away substantial amounts of money and/or prizes. Many promotional experts question the effectiveness of contests and sweepstakes. Some companies have cut back or even stopped using them because of concern over their effectiveness and fears that consumers might become dependent on them.[41]

Numerous legal considerations affect the design and administration of contests and sweepstakes.[42] But companies must still be careful in designing a contest or sweepstakes and awarding prizes. Most firms use consultants that specialize in the design and administration of contests and sweepstakes to avoid any legal problems, but they may still run into problems with promotions.

A final problem with contests and sweepstakes is participation by professionals or hobbyists who submit many entries but have no intention of purchasing the product or service. Because it is illegal to require a purchase as a qualification for a sweepstakes entry, consumers can enter as many times as they wish. Professional players sometimes enter one sweepstakes several times, depending on the nature of the prizes and the number of entries the promotion attracts. Newsletters are even available that inform them of all the contests and sweepstakes being held, the entry dates, estimated probabilities of winning for various numbers of entries, how to enter, and solutions to any puzzles or other information that might be needed. The presence of these professional entrants not only defeats the purpose of the promotion but may also discourage entries from consumers who think their chances of winning are limited.

Refunds and Rebates

Refunds (also known as rebates) are offers by the manufacturer to return a portion of the product purchase price, usually after the consumer supplies some proof of purchase. Consumers are generally very responsive to rebate offers, particularly as the size of the savings increases. Rebates are used by makers of all types of products, ranging from package goods to major appliances, cars, and computer software.

Package-goods marketers often use refund offers to induce trial of a new product or encourage users of another brand to switch. Consumers may perceive the savings offered through a cash refund as an immediate value that lowers the cost of the item, even though those savings are realized only if the consumer redeems the refund or rebate offer. Redemption rates for refund offers typically range from 1 to 3 percent for print and point-of-purchase offers and 5 percent for in/on package offers.

Refund offers can also encourage repeat purchase. Many offers require consumers to send in multiple proofs of purchase. The size of the refund offer may even increase as the number of purchases gets larger. Some package-goods companies are switching away from cash refund offers to coupons or cash/coupon combinations. Using coupons in the refund offer enhances the likelihood of repeat purchase of the brand.

Rebates have become a widely used form of promotion for consumer durables. Products such as cameras, sporting goods, appliances, televisions, audio and video equipment, computers, and cars frequently use rebate offers to appeal to price-conscious consumers. The use of rebates for expensive items like cars was begun by Chrysler Corp. in 1981 to boost sales and generate cash for the struggling company. Rebates are now common not only in the auto industry and other durable products but for package-goods products as well.

Strengths and Limitations of Refunds and Rebates   Rebates can help create new users and encourage brand switching or repeat purchase behaviour, or they can be a way to offer a temporary price reduction. The rebate may be perceived as an immediate savings even though many consumers do not follow through on the offer. This perception can influence purchase even if the consumer fails to realize the savings, so the marketer can reduce price for much less than if it used a direct price-off deal.

Some limitations are associated with refunds and rebates. Many consumers are not motivated by a refund offer because of the delay and the effort required to obtain the savings. They do not want to be bothered saving cash register receipts and proofs of purchase, filling out forms, and mailing in the offer.[43] A study of consumer perceptions found a negative relationship between the use of rebates and the perceived difficulties associated with the redemption process.[44] The study also found that consumers perceive manufacturers as offering rebates to sell products that are not faring well. Nonusers of rebates were particularly likely to perceive the redemption process as too complicated and to suspect manufacturers' motives. This implies that companies using rebates must simplify the redemption process and use other promotional elements such as advertising to retain consumer confidence in the brand.

When small refunds are being offered, marketers may find other promotional incentives such as coupons or bonus packs more effective. They must be careful not to overuse rebate offers and confuse consumers about the real price and value of a product or service. Also, consumers can become dependent on rebates and delay their purchases or purchase only brands for which a rebate is available. Many retailers have become disenchanted with rebates and the burden and expense of administering them.[45]

Bonus Packs

Bonus packs offer the consumer an extra amount of a product at the regular price by providing larger containers or extra units (Exhibit 12–10). Bonus packs result in a lower cost per unit for the consumer and provide extra value as well as more product for the money. There are several advantages to bonus pack promotions. First,

Exhibit 12–10   Bonus packs provide more value for consumers

they give marketers a direct way to provide extra value without having to get involved with complicated coupons or refund offers. The additional value of a bonus pack is generally obvious to the consumer and can have a strong impact on the purchase decision at the time of purchase.

Bonus packs can also be an effective defensive manoeuvre against a competitor's promotion or introduction of a new brand. By loading current users with large amounts of its product, a marketer can often remove these consumers from the market and make them less susceptible to a competitor's promotional efforts. Bonus packs may result in larger purchase orders and favourable display space in the store if relationships with retailers are good. They do, however, usually require additional shelf space without providing any extra profit margins for the retailer, so the marketer can encounter problems with bonus packs if trade relationships are not good. Another problem is that bonus packs may appeal primarily to current users who probably would have purchased the brand anyway or to promotion-sensitive consumers who may not become loyal to the brand.

Price-Off Deals

Another consumer sales promotion tool is the direct **price-off deal,** which reduces the price of the brand. Price-off reductions are typically offered right on the package through specially marked price packs, as shown in Exhibit 12–11. Typically, price-offs range from 10 to 25 percent off the regular price, with the reduction coming out of the manufacturer's profit margin, not the retailer's. Keeping the retailer's margin during a price-off promotion maintains its support and cooperation.

Marketers use price-off promotions for several reasons. First, since price-offs are controlled by the manufacturer, it can make sure the promotional discount reaches the consumer rather than being kept by the trade. Like bonus packs, price-off deals usually present a readily apparent value to shoppers, especially when they have a reference price point for the brand and thus recognize the value of the discount.[46] So price-offs can be a strong influence at the point of purchase when price comparisons are being made. Price-off promotions can also encourage consumers to purchase larger quantities, preempting competitors' promotions and leading to greater trade support.

Price-off promotions may not be favourably received by retailers, since they can create pricing and inventory problems. Most retailers will not accept packages with a specific price shown, so the familiar X amount off the regular price must be used. Also, like bonus packs, price-off deals appeal primarily to regular users instead of attracting nonusers. Finally, the Federal Government has regulations regarding the conditions that price-off labels must meet and the frequency and timing of their use.

Exhibit 12–11 Examples of price-off packages

Frequency Programs

One of the fastest growing areas of sales promotion is the use of **frequency programs** (also referred to as *continuity* or *loyalty programs*). Frequency programs have become commonplace in a number of product and service categories, particularly travel and hospitality, as well as among retailers. Virtually every airline, car rental company, and hotel chain has some type of frequency program. Loyalty programs are also used by a variety of retailers, including grocery stores, department stores, home centres, bookstores, and even local bagel shops.

Many package-goods companies are also developing frequency programs. Pillsbury, Nestlé, Kraft, and others have recently introduced continuity programs that offer consumers the opportunity to accumulate points for continuing to purchase their brands; the points can be redeemed for gifts and prizes. For example, Gerber Baby Foods has developed a frequency program known as Gerber Rewards, in which consumers who purchase 16 or more Gerber products at one time automatically receive a game-piece coupon carrying a unique PIN number and an 800 phone number.[47] Customers call the phone number, punch in the PIN number, and receive

Exhibit 12–12 Gerber Rewards is an example of a loyalty program that helps build a customer database and encourages consumers to purchase more Gerber baby products

points for entry into a sweepstakes giving away a $250,000 college scholarship. Consumers earn more points with subsequent purchases of Gerber products (Exhibit 12–12).

There are a number of reasons why frequency programs have become so popular. Marketers view these programs as a way of encouraging consumers to use their products or services on a continual basis and as a way of developing strong customer loyalty. Many companies are also realizing the importance of customer retention and understand that the key to retaining and growing market share is building relationships with loyal customers. Frequency programs also provide marketers with the opportunity to develop databases containing valuable information on their customers that can be used to better understand their needs, interests, and characteristics as well as to identify and track a company's most valuable customers. These databases can also be used to target specific programs and offers to customers to increase the amount they purchase and/or to build stronger relationships with them. For example, as part of the Gerber Rewards program discussed above, the company developed a database on those entering the sweepstakes that includes the ages of their children. Participants in the program periodically receive direct mail offers of discounts and deals on Gerber products that are based on the ages of their children.

As frequency programs become more common, marketers will be challenged to find ways to use them as a means of differentiating their product, service, business, or retail store. Marketers must find ways to make them true loyalty programs rather than just frequent-buyer programs. This will require the careful management of databases to identify and track valuable customers and their purchase history and the strategic use of targeted loyalty promotions.

Event Marketing

Another type of consumer sales promotion that has become very popular in recent years is the use of event marketing. It is important to make a distinction between *event marketing* and *event sponsorships,* as the two terms are often used interchangeably yet they refer to different activities. **Event marketing** is a type of promotion where a company or brand is linked to an event or where a themed activity is developed for the purpose of creating experiences for consumers and promoting a product or service. Marketers often do event marketing by associating their product with some popular activity such as a sporting event, concert, fair, or festival. However, marketers also create their own events to use for promotional purposes.

Subaru wanted to get consumers, sales consultants, and media representatives to be familiar with its new brands, Impreza WRX and Outback H6, so it developed the "2001 Subaru National Ride & Drive," its first event-marketing program. Members of each target audience in six Canadian cities (Quebec City, Montreal, Toronto, Calgary, Edmonton, and Vancouver) could test-drive the vehicles and talk to key Subaru employees.

Subaru enlisted over 5,000 candidates through auto-show response cards and their website. From that enlistment, 3,000 qualified individuals received a direct-mail invitation to the event, of which 77 percent responded positively versus a 50- to 60-percent objective. The event included a classroom-style seminar, a vehicle and course walk-around, the test-drive, and a demonstration by professional drivers with participants in the car. Subaru obtained enthusiastic written and verbal feedback on the event, especially the demonstration, and gave a thank-you card to all participants, which directed them to a dedicated website that had photos of the event.

The information received continued in the selling process. All information was passed on to the respective dealerships along with highlights of the event (i.e., statistics, photos). The program resulted in a 3 percent participant-to-sales conversion rate in the first 6 weeks; given the nature of car purchases, additional sales may be forthcoming to improve this ratio. Other statistics show the value of event marketing as post-event purchasing desires increased over the pre-event numbers, and 61 percent of all participants claimed that they would visit a Subaru dealership.[48]

An **event sponsorship** is an integrated marketing communications activity where a company develops actual sponsorship relations with a particular event and provides financial support in return for the right to display a brand name, logo, or advertising message and be identified as a supporter of the event. Event marketing often takes place as part of a company's sponsorship of activities such as concerts, the arts, social causes, and sporting events.

Event marketing has become very popular in recent years as marketers develop integrated marketing programs including a variety of promotional tools that create experiences for consumers in an effort to associate their brands with certain lifestyles and activities. Marketers use events to distribute samples as well as information about their products and services or to actually let consumers experience the product.

Trade Sales Promotion

Objectives of Trade Sales Promotion

Like consumer promotions, sales promotion programs targeted to the trade should be based on well-defined objectives and measurable goals and a consideration of what the marketer wants to accomplish. Typical objectives for promotions targeted to marketing intermediaries such as wholesalers and retailers include obtaining distribution and support for new products, maintaining support for established brands, encouraging retailers to display established brands, and building retail inventories.

Obtain Distribution for New Products
Trade promotions are often used to encourage retailers to give shelf space to new products. Essentially, this translates into a trial purchase objective like we saw with consumer promotions. Manufacturers recognize that only a limited amount of shelf space is available in supermarkets, drugstores, and other major retail outlets. Thus, they provide retailers with financial incentives to stock new products. For example, Lever Brothers used heavy sampling and high-value coupons in the successful introduction of Lever 2000 bar soap. However, in addition to these consumer promotions, the company used discounts to the trade to encourage retailers to stock and promote the new brand.

While trade discounts or other special price deals are used to encourage retailers and wholesalers to stock a new brand, marketers may use other types of promotions to get them to push the brand. Merchandising allowances can get retailers to display a new product in high-traffic areas of stores, while incentive programs or contests can encourage wholesale or retail store personnel to push a new brand.

Maintain Trade Support for Established Brands
Trade promotions are often designed to maintain distribution and trade support for established brands. Clearly, this objective is akin to a repeat purchase objective that we saw with consumer sales promotion. Brands that are in the mature phase of their product life cycle are vulnerable to losing wholesale and/or retail distribution, particularly if they are not differentiated or face competition from new products. Trade deals induce wholesalers and retailers to continue to carry weaker products because the discounts increase their profit margins. Brands with a smaller market share often rely heavily on trade promotions, since they lack the funds required to differentiate themselves from competitors through media advertising.

Even if a brand has a strong market position, trade promotions may be used as part of an overall marketing strategy. As discussed previously, Heinz has relied heavily on trade promotions to hold its market share position for many of its brands. Many consumer-package-goods companies count on trade promotions to maintain retail distribution and support.

Build Retail Inventories
Manufacturers often use trade promotions to build the inventory levels of retailers or other channel members, another form of repeat purchasing. There are several reasons manufacturers want to load retailers with their products. First, wholesalers and retailers are more likely to push a product when they have high inventory levels rather than storing it in their warehouses or back rooms. Building channel members' inventories also ensures they will not run out of stock and thus miss sales opportunities.

Some manufacturers of seasonal products offer large promotional discounts so that retailers will stock up on their products before the peak selling season begins. This enables the manufacturer to smooth out seasonal fluctuations in its production schedule and passes on some of the inventory carrying costs to retailers or wholesalers. When retailers stock up on a product before the peak selling season, they often run special promotions and offer discounts to consumers to reduce excess inventories.

Encourage Retailers to Display Established Brands
Another objective of trade-oriented promotions is to encourage retailers to display and promote an established brand. This could be analogous to increased consumption as seen with consumer sales promotion objectives since the retailer demonstrates increased commitment. Marketers recognize that many purchase decisions are made in the store and promotional displays are an excellent way of generating sales. An important goal is to obtain retail store displays of a product away from its regular shelf location. A typical supermarket has approximately 50 display areas at the ends of aisles, near checkout counters, and elsewhere. Marketers want to have their products displayed in these areas to increase the probability shoppers will come into contact with them. Even a single display can increase a brand's sales significantly during a promotion.

Manufacturers often use multifaceted promotional programs to encourage retailers to promote their products at the retail level.

Trade Sales Promotion Strategy Options

Manufacturers use a variety of trade promotion tools as inducements for wholesalers and retailers. Next we examine some of the most often used types of trade promotions and some factors marketers must consider in using them. These promotions include contests and incentives, trade allowances, displays and point-of-purchase materials, sales training programs, trade shows, and co-op advertising.

Contests and Incentives
Manufacturers may develop contests or special incentive programs to stimulate greater selling effort and support from reseller management or sales personnel. Contests or incentive programs can be directed toward managers who work for a wholesaler or distributor as well as toward store or department managers at the retail level. Manufacturers often sponsor contests for resellers and use prizes such as trips or valuable merchandise as rewards for meeting sales quotas or other goals.

Contests or special incentives are often targeted at the sales personnel of the wholesalers, distributors/dealers, or retailers. These salespeople are an important link in the distribution chain because they are likely to be very familiar with the market, more frequently in touch with the customer (whether it be another reseller or the ultimate consumer), and more numerous than the manufacturer's own sales organization. Manufacturers often devise incentives or contests for these sales personnel. These programs may involve cash payments made directly to the retailer's or wholesaler's sales staff to encourage them to promote and sell a manufacturer's product. These payments are known as **push money** (pm) or *spiffs*. For example, an appliance manufacturer may pay a $25 spiff to retail sales personnel for selling a certain

Figure 12–6 Three forms
of promotion targeted to
reseller salespeople

- **Product or Program Sales**

  Awards are tied to the selling of a product, for example:

  Selling a specified number of cases

  Selling a specified number of units

  Selling a specified number of promotional programs

- **New Account Placements**

  Awards are tied to:

  The number of new accounts opened

  The number of new accounts ordering a minimum number of cases or units

  Promotional programs placed in new accounts

- **Merchandising Efforts**

  Awards are tied to:

  Establishing promotional programs (such as theme programs)

  Placing display racks, counter displays, and the like

model or size. In sales contests, salespeople can win trips or valuable merchandise for meeting certain goals established by the manufacturer. As shown in Figure 12–6, these incentives may be tied to product sales, new account placements, or merchandising efforts.

While contests and incentive programs can generate reseller support, they can also be a source of conflict between retail sales personnel and management. Some retailers want to maintain control over the selling activities of their sales staff. They don't want their salespeople devoting an undue amount of effort to trying to win a contest or receive incentives offered by the manufacturer. Nor do they want their people becoming too aggressive in pushing products that serve their own interests instead of the product or model that is best for the customer.

Many retailers refuse to let their employees participate in manufacturer-sponsored contests or to accept incentive payments. Retailers that do allow them often have strict guidelines and require management approval of the program.

Trade Allowances Probably the most common trade promotion is some form of **trade allowance,** a discount or deal offered to retailers or wholesalers to encourage them to stock, promote, or display the manufacturer's products. Types of allowances offered to retailers include buying allowances, promotional or display allowances, and slotting allowances.

Buying Allowances A buying allowance is a deal or discount offered to resellers in the form of a price reduction on merchandise ordered during a fixed period. These discounts are often in the form of an **off-invoice allowance,** which means a certain per-case amount or percentage is deducted from the invoice. A buying allowance can also take the form of *free goods;* the reseller gets extra cases with the purchase of specific amounts (for example, 1 free case with every 10 cases purchased).

Buying allowances are used for several reasons. They are easy to implement and are well accepted, and sometimes expected, by the trade. They are also an effective way to encourage resellers to buy the manufacturer's product, since they will want to take advantage of the discounts being offered during the allowance period. Manufacturers offer trade discounts expecting wholesalers and retailers to pass the price reduction through to consumers, resulting in greater sales. However, as discussed shortly, this is often not the case.

Promotional Allowances Manufacturers often give retailers allowances or discounts for performing certain promotional or merchandising activities in support of their brands. These merchandising allowances can be given for providing special displays away from the product's regular shelf position, running in-store promotional programs, or including the product in an ad. The manufacturer generally has guidelines or a contract specifying the activity to be performed to qualify for the promotional allowance. The allowance is usually a fixed amount per case or a percentage deduction from the list price for merchandise ordered during the promotional period.

Slotting Allowances In recent years, retailers have been demanding a special allowance for agreeing to handle a new product. *Slotting allowances,* also called *stocking allowances, introductory allowances,* or *street money,* are fees retailers charge for providing a slot or position to accommodate the new product. Retailers justify these fees by pointing out the costs associated with taking on so many new products each year, such as redesigning store shelves, entering the product into their computers, finding warehouse space, and briefing store employees on the new product.[49] They also note they are assuming some risk, since so many new product introductions fail.

Slotting fees can range from a few hundred dollars per store to $50,000 or more for an entire retail chain. Manufacturers that want to get their products on the shelves nationally can face several million dollars in slotting fees. Many marketers believe slotting allowances are a form of blackmail or bribery and say some 70 percent of these fees go directly to retailers' bottom lines.

Retailers can continue charging slotting fees because of their power and the limited availability of shelf space in supermarkets relative to the large numbers of products introduced each year. Some retailers have even been demanding **failure fees** if a new product does not hit a minimum sales level within a certain time. The fee is charged to cover the costs associated with stocking, maintaining inventories, and then pulling the product.[50] Large manufacturers with popular brands are less likely to pay slotting fees than smaller companies that lack leverage in negotiating with retailers.

Problems with Trade Allowances Many companies are concerned about the abuse of trade allowances by wholesalers, retailers, and distributors. Marketers give retailers these trade allowances so that the savings will be passed through to consumers in the form of lower prices, but companies such as Procter & Gamble claim that only 30 percent of trade promotion discounts actually reach consumers because 35 percent is lost in inefficiencies and another 35 percent is pocketed by retailers and wholesalers. Moreover, many marketers believe that the trade is taking advantage of their promotional deals and misusing promotional funds.

For example, many retailers and wholesalers engage in a practice known as **forward buying,** where they stock up on a product at the lower deal or off-invoice price and resell it to consumers after the marketer's promotional period ends. Another common practice is **diverting,** where a retailer or wholesaler takes advantage of the promotional deal and then sells some of the product purchased at the low price to a store outside its area or to a middleperson who resells it to other stores.

Forward buying and diverting are widespread practices. Industry studies show that nearly 40 percent of wholesalers' and retailers' profits come from these activities. In addition to not passing discounts on to consumers, forward buying and diverting create other problems for manufacturers. They lead to huge swings in demand that cause production scheduling problems and leave manufacturers and retailers always building toward or drawing down from a promotional surge. Marketers also worry that the system leads to frequent price specials, so consumers learn to make purchases on the basis of what's on sale rather than developing any loyalty to their brands.

The problems created by retailers' abuse led Procter & Gamble, one of the country's most powerful consumer products marketers, to adopt **everyday low pricing (EDLP),** which lowers the list price of over 60 percent of its product line by 10 to 25 percent while cutting promotional allowances to the trade. The price cuts leave the overall cost of the product to retailers about the same as it would have been with the various trade allowance discounts.

P&G argues that EDLP eliminates problems such as deal buying, leads to regular low prices at the retail level, and helps build brand loyalty among consumers. Yet the EDLP strategy has caused great controversy in the trade, which depends heavily on promotions to attract consumers. Some retailers took P&G products off the shelf; others cut their ads and displays of the company's brands. Retailers prefer to operate on a *high/low strategy* of frequent price specials and argue that EDLP puts them at a disadvantage against the warehouse stores and mass merchandisers that already use everyday low pricing. They also say that some products, such as those that are bought on impulse, thrive on promotions and don't lend themselves to EDLP. Retailers rely on promotions like end-of-aisle displays and price discounts to create excitement and generate incremental sales and profits from products like soft drinks, cookies, and candy.[51]

Critics of EDLP also note that while the strategy may work well for market leaders whose brands enjoy high loyalty, it is not effective for marketers trying to build market share or prop up lagging products. Moreover, many consumers are still motivated more by promotional deals and specials than by advertising claims from retailers promoting everyday low prices.

Despite the criticism, P&G says EDLP is paying off and volume is growing faster in its brands that have switched to the new pricing strategy. And it claims that market share in two-thirds of these product categories has increased. P&G recently extended its use of everyday low pricing to international markets, including the United Kingdom and Italy.[52] IMC Perspective 12–2 discusses how P&G continues to make changes in the way sales promotions are being used by package-goods marketers.

Displays and Point-of-Purchase Materials   The next time you are in a store, take a moment to examine the various promotional materials used to display and sell products. Point-of-purchase displays are an important promotional tool because they can help a manufacturer obtain more effective in-store merchandising of products. Companies in Canada spend a lot of money on point-of-purchase materials, including end-of-aisle displays, banners, posters, shelf cards, motion pieces, and stand-up racks, among others. Exhibit 12–13 shows an award-winning point-of-purchase display for Top-Flite golf balls.

Many manufacturers help retailers use shelf space more efficiently through **planograms,** which are configurations of products that occupy a shelf section in a store. Some manufacturers are developing computer-based programs that allow retailers to input information from their scanner data and determine the best shelf layouts by experimenting with product movement, space utilization, profit yields, and other factors.[53]

Sales Training Programs   Another form of manufacturer-sponsored promotional assistance is sales training programs for reseller personnel. Many products sold at the retail level require knowledgeable salespeople who can provide consumers with information about the features, benefits, and advantages of various brands and models. Cosmetics, appliances, computers, consumer electronics, and sporting equipment are examples of products for which consumers often rely on well-informed retail sales personnel for assistance.

Manufacturers provide sales training assistance to retail salespeople in a number of ways. They may conduct classes or training sessions that retail personnel can attend to increase their knowledge of a product or a product line. These training sessions present information and ideas on how to sell the manufacturer's product and may also include motivational components. Sales training classes for retail personnel are often sponsored by companies selling high-ticket items or complex products such as personal computers, cars, or ski equipment.

Another way manufacturers provide sales training assistance to retail employees is through their own sales force. Sales reps educate retail personnel about their product line and provide selling tips and other relevant information. The reps can provide ongoing sales training as they come into contact with retail sales staff on a regular basis and can update them on changes in the product line, market developments, competitive information, and the like.

Manufacturers also give resellers detailed sales manuals, product brochures, reference manuals, and other material. Many companies provide videocassettes for

IMC Perspective 12–2
Procter & Gamble Continues to Redefine Sales Promotion Strategy

For decades, Procter & Gamble and many other consumer-package-goods marketers prospered by bombarding both shoppers and retailers with promotional offers. The marketing system that developed during the 1980s and into the early '90s was based on the assumption that the best way to move products was through bigger and better promotions and pricing. Shoppers browsed through the aisles looking for specials, as popular brands would sell at full price one week and half-off the next. They clipped coupons, saved box tops, mailed in refund or rebate offers, and looked for packages with a toy or some other premium offer inside. Marketers pushed so many specials and price changes that it became difficult for them, as well as the retailers, to keep all the paperwork straight. P&G alone made an average of 55 price changes a day across 110 brands and offered over 400 different promotions a year.

But recently P&G, considered by many to be the world's preeminent consumer products company, discovered that the marketing system that had evolved over the years had forgotten someone very important: the consumer. Today's average consumer, more often than not a woman, takes just 21 minutes to do her shopping. In that time she buys an average of 18 items out of 30,000 choices in a supermarket. She spends 25 percent less time browsing than she did five years ago, and she often doesn't bother to check prices. She wants the same product at the same price in the same row and shelf position week after week. She is willing to pay more and be loyal to a store if it makes her shopping experience pleasant.

P&G began to simplify its promotional programs in the early '90s by moving many of its brands to an everyday-low-pricing (EDLP) strategy, which vastly reduced the number of deals offered to retailers and distributors in favour of lower list prices. P&G argues that all of the allowances and deals are costly and confusing for retailers. Moreover, they cause shelf prices to fluctuate weekly and train consumers to buy on price instead of perceived value, thereby undermining the development of brand loyalty. In 1996, P&G took its drive to simplify a step further by eliminating or cutting back on 27 different types of promotions, including the traditional bonus packs, premiums, cents-off packs, and refund offers. The company also cut back on its use of coupons, noting that with redemption rates declining, they are a less efficient way of attracting customers. P&G has put the money saved from these cutbacks into lower prices and other promotions such as sampling and in-store demonstrations.

Procter & Gamble has long been a bellwether for the package-goods industry, and its actions resulted in a broad movement by marketers to reduce the complexity of their sales promotion programs. However, when the changes were made, P&G's CEO Durk Jager noted there was little time to relax, as the company's rivals were working on how to better meet shoppers' needs and make things even simpler for them. In fact, P&G did not relax at all. In early 1999 a major restructuring initiative called "Organization 2005" was begun, and it is designed to double sales to $75 billion by 2005.

Better marketing is one of the major goals of the multifaceted initiative, and it will embrace promotion from a new perspective: strategic interaction between a brand and targeted consumers. P&G hopes to accomplish this through more consumer research, deeper retail partnerships, and more account-specific/local promotions. P&G has formed market development organizations (MDOs), which are regional teams staffed by brand and marketing managers that will act as experts on local consumers and retailers for P&G's seven global business units. The MDOs will become regional and local marketing experts on consumers and work with their retail partners to develop strategic marketing programs that meet consumer needs and sell more product more profitably.

Forming the MDOs was motivated in part by P&G's desire to develop stronger relationships with powerful retailers that are acquiring control of the

SPECIAL REPORT INVESTING IN HOT OVERSEAS MARKETS

BusinessWeek

SEPTEMBER 9, 1996   A PUBLICATION OF THE McGRAW-HILL COMPANIES $3.50

MARKETING
Make It Simple

Marketers sell too much stuff in too many
different ways. Now the smart ones
are cutting the complexity.
Once again, P&G is leading the charge.
PAGE 96

IVORY

retail sales personnel that include product information, product-use demonstrations, and ideas on how to sell their product. These selling aids can often be used to provide information to customers as well.

Trade Shows   Another important promotional activity targeted to resellers is the **trade show,** a forum where manufacturers can display their products to current as well as prospective buyers. According to the Trade Show Bureau, nearly 100 million people attend the 5,000 trade shows each year in the United States and Canada, and the number of exhibiting companies exceeds 1.3 million. In many industries, trade shows are a major opportunity to display one's product lines and interact with customers. They are often attended by important management personnel from large retail chains as well as by distributors and other reseller representatives.

A number of promotional functions can be performed at trade shows, including demonstrating products, identifying new prospects, gathering customer and competitive information, and even writing orders for a product. Trade shows are particularly valuable for introducing new products, because resellers are often looking for new merchandise to stock. Shows can also be a source of valuable leads to follow up on through sales calls or direct marketing. The social aspect of trade shows is also important. Many companies use them to entertain key customers and to develop and maintain relationships with the trade. A recent academic study demonstrated that trade shows generate product awareness and interest and can have a measurable economic return.[54]

Exhibit 12–13   Spalding uses point-of-purchase displays for Top-Flite golf balls to help generate in-store sales

Cooperative Advertising   The final form of trade-oriented promotion we examine is **cooperative advertising,** where the cost of advertising is shared by more than one party. There are three types of cooperative advertising. Although the first two are not trade-oriented promotion, we should recognize their objectives and purpose.

Horizontal cooperative advertising is advertising sponsored in common by a group of retailers or other organizations providing products or services to the market. For example, automobile dealers who are located near one another in an auto park or along the same street often allocate some of their ad budgets to a cooperative advertising fund. Ads are run promoting the location of the dealerships and encouraging car buyers to take advantage of their close proximity when shopping for a new automobile.

Ingredient-sponsored cooperative advertising is supported by raw materials manufacturers; its objective is to help establish end products that include the company's materials and/or ingredients. Companies that often use this type of advertising include Du Pont, which promotes the use of its materials such as Teflon, Thinsulate, and Kevlar in a variety of consumer and industrial products, and NutraSweet, whose artificial sweetener is an ingredient in many food products and beverages. Perhaps the best-known, and most successful, example of this type of cooperative advertising is the "Intel Inside" program, sponsored by Intel Corporation.

The most common form of cooperative advertising is the trade-oriented form, **vertical cooperative advertising,** in which a manufacturer pays for a portion of the advertising a retailer runs to promote the manufacturer's product and its availability in the retailer's place of business. Manufacturers generally share the cost of advertising run by the retailer on a percentage basis (usually 50/50) up to a certain limit.

The amount of cooperative advertising the manufacturer pays for is usually based on a percentage of dollar purchases. If a retailer purchases $100,000 of product from a manufacturer, it may receive 3 percent, or $3,000, in cooperative advertising money. Large retail chains often combine their co-op budgets across all of their stores, which gives them a larger sum to work with and more media options.

Cooperative advertising can take on several forms. Retailers may advertise a manufacturer's product in, say, a newspaper ad featuring a number of different products, and the individual manufacturers reimburse the retailer for their portion of the ad. Or the ad may be prepared by the manufacturer and placed in the local media by the retailer. Exhibit 12–14 shows a cooperative ad format for New Balance athletic shoes that retailers in various market areas can use by simply inserting their store name and location.

Once a cooperative ad is run, the retailer requests reimbursement from the manufacturer for its percentage of the media costs. Manufacturers usually have specific requirements the ad must meet to qualify for co-op reimbursement, such as size, use of trademarks, content, and format. Verification that the ad was run is also required, in the form of a tearsheet (print) or an affidavit from the radio or TV station (broadcast) and an invoice.

As with other types of trade promotions, manufacturers have been increasing their cooperative advertising expenditures in recent years. Some companies have been moving money out of national advertising into cooperative advertising because they believe they can have greater impact with ad campaigns in local markets. There is also a trend toward more cooperative advertising programs initiated by retailers, which approach manufacturers with catalogues, promotional events they are planning, or advertising programs they have developed in conjunction with local media and ask them to pay a percentage of the cost. Manufacturers often go along with these requests, particularly when the retailer is large and powerful.[55]

Exhibit 12–14   This New Balance ad is an example of vertical cooperative advertising

Those involved in the promotional process must recognize that sales promotion techniques usually work best in conjunction with advertising and that the effectiveness of an ad campaign can be enhanced by consumer sales promotion efforts. Rather than separate activities competing for a firm's promotional budget, advertising and sales promotion should be viewed as complementary tools. When properly planned and executed to work together, advertising and sales promotion can have a more complete and persuasive communication effect that is much greater than that of either promotional mix element alone.

IMC Issues Related to Sales Promotion Decisions

Proper coordination of advertising and sales promotion is essential for the firm to take advantage of the opportunities offered by each tool and get the most out of its promotional budget. Successful integration of advertising and sales promotion requires decisions concerning not only the allocation of the budget to each area but also the coordination of the ad and sales promotion themes, the timing of the various promotional activities, and the strategic role of sales promotion.

Budget Allocation

While many companies are spending more money on sales promotion than on media advertising, it is difficult to say just what percentage of a firm's overall promotional budget should be allocated to advertising versus consumer- and trade-oriented promotions. This allocation depends on a number of factors, including the specific promotional objectives of the campaign, the market and competitive situation, and the brand's stage in its life cycle.

Consider, for example, how allocation of the promotional budget may vary according to a brand's stage in the product life cycle. In the introductory stage, a large amount of the budget may be allocated to sales promotion techniques such as sampling and couponing to induce trial. In the growth stage, however, promotional dollars may be used primarily for advertising to stress brand differences and keep the brand name in consumers' minds.

When a brand moves to the maturity stage, advertising is primarily a reminder to keep consumers aware of the brand. Consumer-oriented sales promotions such as coupons, price-offs, premiums, and bonus packs may be needed periodically to maintain consumer loyalty, attract new users, and protect against competition. Trade-oriented promotions are needed to maintain shelf space and accommodate retailers' demands for better margins as well as encourage them to promote the brand. A study on the synergistic effects of advertising and promotion examined a brand in the mature phase of its life cycle and found that 80 percent of its sales at this stage were due to sales promotions. When a brand enters the decline stage of the product life cycle, most of the promotional support will probably be removed and expenditures on sales promotion are unlikely.

Creative Themes

To integrate the advertising and sales promotion programs successfully, the theme of consumer promotions should be tied in with the advertising and positioning theme wherever possible. Sales promotion tools should attempt to communicate a brand's unique attributes or benefits and to reinforce the sales message or campaign theme. In this way, the sales promotion effort contributes to the consumer franchise-building effort for the brand.

At the same time, media advertising should be used to draw attention to a sales promotion program such as a contest, sweepstakes, or event or to a special promotion offer such as a price reduction or rebate program. An example of this is the ad shown in Exhibit 12–15 for WD-40, which promotes the Search for 2000 Uses Sweepstakes that was discussed earlier and shown in Exhibit 12–4. Note how both the magazine ad and the sweepstakes promotion integrate the variety-of-uses positioning theme used for WD-40.

Keeps handle from drying and cracking.

Protects metal from rust and corrosion.

Cleans and lubricates blade for next "Burly Man" Logging Competition.

Got a new use for WD-40.? Enter our Search For 2000 Uses Sweepstakes and maybe you could win $10,000 worth of WD-40 Company stock. Details at www.wd40.com. Now for that next project.

Media Support

Media support for a sales promotion program is critical and should be coordinated with the media program for the ad campaign. Media advertising is often needed to deliver such sales promotion materials as coupons, sweepstakes, contest entry forms, premium offers, and even samples. It is also needed to inform consumers of a promotional offer as well as to create awareness, interest, and favourable attitudes toward the brand.

By using advertising in conjunction with a sales promotion program, marketers can make consumers aware of the brand and its benefits and increase their responsiveness to the promotion. Consumers are more likely to redeem a coupon or respond to a price-off deal for a brand they are familiar with than one they know nothing about. Moreover, product trial created through sales promotion techniques such as sampling or high-value couponing is more likely to result in long-term use of the brand when accompanied by advertising.[56]

Using a promotion without prior or concurrent advertising can limit its effectiveness and risk damaging the brand's image. If consumers perceive the brand as being promotion dependent or of lesser quality, they are not likely to develop favourable attitudes and long-term loyalty. Conversely, the effectiveness of an ad can be enhanced by a coupon, a premium offer, or an opportunity to enter a sweepstakes or contest.

An example of the effective coordination of advertising and sales promotion is the introductory campaign Lever Brothers developed for its Lever 2000 bar soap. As noted earlier in the chapter, Lever Brothers used high-value coupons, sent samples, and offered discounts to retailers as part of its introductory marketing blitz. These sales promotion efforts were accompanied by heavy advertising in print and TV with the tagline "Presenting some of the 2000 body parts you can clean with Lever 2000" (Exhibit 12–16).

Sales promotion was important in inducing trial for Lever 2000 and continued after introduction in the form of couponing. But it was the strong positioning created through effective advertising that converted consumers to

Presenting Some Of The 2000 Body Parts You Can Clean With Lever 2000.

The Deodorant Soap That's Better For Your Skin.

- Lever 2000 has special skin-care ingredients.
- It won't dry your skin like other deodorant soaps can.
- It's been clinically proven better for your skin than any soap—not just any deodorant soap.

- You can use Lever 2000 everywhere. On hard parts. Soft parts. Tough parts. And pretty parts. All your 2000 parts.

regular users. Repeat sales of the brand were at about 40 percent even after heavy discounting ended. Just six months after its introduction, Lever 2000 became the number-two deodorant soap in dollar volume, with an estimated 8.4 percent of the $1.5 billion bar-soap market.[57]

To coordinate their advertising and sales promotion programs more effectively, many companies are getting their sales promotion agencies more involved in the advertising and promotional planning process. Rather than hiring agencies to develop individual, nonfranchise-building types of promotions with short-term goals and tactics, many firms are having their sales promotion and advertising agencies work together to develop integrated promotional strategies and programs. Figure 12–7 shows how the role of sales promotion agencies is changing.

Strategic Role

The increasing use of sales promotion in marketing programs is more than a passing fad. It is a fundamental change in strategic decisions about how companies market their products and services. The value of this increased emphasis on sales promotion has been questioned by several writers, particularly with regard to the lack of adequate planning and management of sales promotion programs.[58]

Overuse of sales promotion can be detrimental to a brand in several ways. A brand that is constantly promoted may lose perceived value. Consumers often end up purchasing a brand because it is on sale, they get a premium, or they have a coupon, rather than basing their decision on a favourable attitude they have developed. When the extra promotional incentive is not available, they switch to another brand. A recent study by Priya Raghubir and Kim Corfman examined whether price promotions affect pretrial evaluations of a brand.[59] They found that offering a price promotion is more likely to lower a brand's evaluation when the brand has not been promoted previously compared to when it has been frequently promoted; that price promotions are used as a source of information about a brand to a greater extent when the evaluator is not an expert but does have some product or industry knowledge; and that promotions are more likely to result in negative evaluations when they are uncommon in the industry. The findings from this study suggest that marketers must be careful in the use of price promotions as they may inhibit trial of a brand in certain situations.

Alan Sawyer and Peter Dickson have used the concept of *attribution theory* to examine how sales promotion may affect consumer attitude formation.[60] According to this theory, people acquire attitudes by observing their own behaviour and con-

Traditional	New and Improved
1. Primarily used to develop short-term tactics or concepts.	1. Used to develop long- and short-term promotional strategies as well as tactics.
2. Hired/compensated on a project-by-project basis.	2. Contracted on annual retainer, following formal agency reviews.
3. Many promotion agencies used a mix—each one hired for best task and/or specialty.	3. One or two exclusive promotion agencies for each division or brand group.
4. One or two contact people from agency.	4. Full team or core group on the account.
5. Promotion agency never equal to ad agency—doesn't work up front in annual planning process.	5. Promotion agency works on equal basis with ad agency—sits at planning table up front.
6. Not directly accountable for results.	6. Very much accountable—goes through a rigorous evaluation process.

Figure 12–7   The shifting role of the promotion agency

Figure 12–8 The sales promotion trap

All Other Firms	Our Firm	
	Cut back promotions	Maintain promotions
Cut back promotions	Higher profits for all	Market share goes to our firm
Maintain promotions	Market share goes to all other firms	Market share stays constant; profits stay low

sidering why they acted in a certain manner. Consumers who consistently purchase a brand because of a coupon or price-off deal may attribute their behaviour to the external promotional incentive rather than to a favourable attitude toward the brand. By contrast, when no external incentive is available, consumers are more likely to attribute their purchase behaviour to favourable underlying feelings about the brand.

Another potential problem with consumer-oriented promotions is that a **sales promotion trap** or spiral can result when several competitors use promotions extensively.[61] Often a firm begins using sales promotions to differentiate its product or service from the competition. If the promotion is successful and leads to a differential advantage (or even appears to do so), competitors may quickly copy it. When all the competitors are using sales promotions, this not only lowers profit margins for each firm but also makes it difficult for any one firm to hop off the promotional bandwagon.[62] This dilemma is shown in Figure 12–8.

A number of industries have fallen into this promotional trap. In the cosmetics industry, gift-with-purchase and purchase-with-purchase promotional offers were developed as a tactic for getting buyers to sample new products. But they have become a common, and costly, way of doing business.[63] Fast-food chains have also fallen into the trap with promotions featuring popular menu items.

Marketers must consider both the short-term impact of a promotion and its long-term effect on the brand. The ease with which competitors can develop a retaliatory promotion and the likelihood of their doing so should also be considered. Marketers must be careful not to damage the brand franchise with sales promotions or to get the firm involved in a promotional war that erodes the brand's profit margins and threatens its long-term existence. Marketers are often tempted to resort to sales promotions to deal with declining sales and other problems when they should examine such other aspects of the marketing program as channel relations, price, packaging, product quality, or advertising.

Summary

Over the past decade, marketers have been allocating more of their promotional dollars to sales promotion to influence consumers' purchase behaviour. The growing power of retailers, erosion of brand loyalty, increase in consumers' sensitivity to promotions, increase in new product introductions, fragmentation of the consumer market, short-term focus of marketing and brand managers, and increase in advertising clutter are some of the reasons for this increase.

Sales promotions can be characterized as either franchise building or nonfranchise building. The former contribute to the long-term development and reinforcement of brand identity and image; the latter are designed to accelerate the purchase process and generate immediate increases in sales.

Sales promotion techniques can be classified as either trade or consumer oriented. A number of consumer sales promotion techniques were examined in this chapter, including sampling, couponing, premiums, contests and sweepstakes, rebates and refunds, bonus packs, price-off deals, frequency programs, and event marketing. The characteristics of these promotional tools were examined, along with their advantages and limitations. Various trade promotions were also examined, including trade contests and incentives, trade allowances, displays and point-of-purchase materials, sales training programs, trade shows, and cooperative advertising.

Advertising and sales promotion should not be viewed as separate activities but rather as complementary tools. When planned and executed properly, advertising and sales promotion can produce a synergistic effect that is greater than the response generated from either promotional mix element alone. To accomplish this, marketers must coordinate budgets, advertising and promotional themes, media scheduling and timing, and target audiences.

Sales promotion abuse can result when marketers become too dependent on the use of sales promotion techniques and sacrifice long-term brand position and image for short-term sales increases. Many industries experience sales promotion traps when a number of competitors use promotions extensively and it becomes difficult for any single firm to cut back on promotion without risking a loss in sales. Overuse of sales promotion tools can lower profit margins and threaten the image and even the viability of a brand.

Key Terms

sales promotion, 308
consumer sales promotion, 309
trade sales promotion, 309
account-specific marketing, 312
consumer franchise-building (CFB) promotions, 316
nonfranchise-building (non-FB) promotions, 317

sampling, 319
bounce-back coupon, 325
cross-ruff coupon, 326
instant coupon, 326
in-store couponing, 326
premium, 327
self-liquidating premiums, 328
contest, 328
sweepstakes, 328
game, 329
refund, 330

bonus packs, 330
price-off deal, 331
frequency programs, 331
event marketing, 332
event sponsorship, 333
push money, 334
trade allowance, 335
off-invoice allowance, 335
failure fees, 336
forward buying, 336
diverting, 336
everyday low pricing (EDLP), 336

planograms, 337
trade show, 339
cooperative advertising, 339
horizontal cooperative advertising, 339
ingredient-sponsored cooperative advertising, 339
vertical cooperative advertising, 340
sales promotion trap, 344

Discussion Questions

1. What are the differences between consumer and trade sales promotion? Discuss the role of each in a marketer's IMC program.

2. Discuss how sales promotion can be used as an acceleration tool to speed up the sales process and maximize sales volume.

3. Discuss the various reasons marketers have been shifting their marketing dollars to sales promotion from media advertising. Discuss the pros and cons of this reallocation of marketers' advertising and promotion budgets.

4. What are the differences between consumer franchise-building and nonfranchise-building promotions? Find an example of a promotional offer you believe contributes to the equity of a brand and explain why.

5. Discuss how the Internet can be used for the distribution of various promotional offers such as samples, coupons, premiums, contests, and sweepstakes.

6. IMC Perspective 12–2 discusses how Procter &Gamble (P&G) continues to redefine and simplify its sales promotion strategy in recent years. Evaluate the various changes P&G has made in its promotional strategy. Do you think other consumer-package-goods marketers will follow some of the moves made by P&G?

7. What is meant by a sales promotion trap? Find an example of an industry where a promotional war is currently taking place. What are the options for a marketer involved in such a situation?

8. Canadian Tire and Pillsbury used an aspect of their brand for a sales promotion for the first time ever. Does this damage the brand at all in light of some concerns about sales promotion raised in this chapter? What other brand has a long-standing icon that could be used for a sales promotion?

Chapter Thirteen

Public Relations

Chapter Objectives

- To recognize the role of public relations in the promotional mix.

- To understand public relations and its strengths and limitations.

- To understand the reasons for corporate advertising and its advantages and disadvantages.

- To know how to compile a public relations plan.

- To understand how public relations is obtained partly through publicity generated through news media.

What's the Buzz?

Have you ever wondered why something was all of a sudden popular, like a new brand of shoes or clothing, even though you've never seen any advertising or marketing for it? Ever wonder how you came to simply agree that "this is the *in* thing" now?

This is "buzz," a strategic meshing of public relations and word of mouth that work together to create awareness and stimulate sales of a product of service. In a *Harvard Business Review* article titled "The Buzz of Buzz" (November/December 2000), author Renée Dye wrote: "Word-of-mouth promotion has become an increasingly potent force, capable of catapulting products from obscurity into runaway commercial success." Innovative companies are using the promotional and brand power of public relations as a competitive advantage to reach you, the consumer, in this cluttered marketplace. For example:

- Lingerie retailer La Senza staged fashion shows on the streets of Toronto.
- Greeting-card retailer Hallmark invited men to watch a movie marathon of *Love Story* to celebrate Father's Day.
- Orange-juice maker Tropicana launched an on-pack tie-in with the movie *Monsters Inc.* to the delight of many kids screaming like monsters.

Marketing public relations programs appears useful for all communications situations: emerging brands, public launches, brand repositioning, and the rejuvenation of mature brands. In all cases, PR can spark perceptual and attitudinal change and result in new positive consumer support for new users, current customers, and competitor's customers. One reason for the recent growth of PR appears to be the weakness of traditional media to reach their target audience effectively. Indeed, some successful PR programs are online as marketers try to attract new customers who are younger.

It seems that word of mouth is still the most trusted form of communication, and PR is the right kind of exposure to generate the kind of communication effects that marketers love: awareness and positive attitude that results in more people spreading the word and presenting the brand within a relevant context. And PR's ability to do this less expensively than other IMC tools makes it a vital part of a marketer's communications plans.

Source: Judy Lewis, "Building Buzz," *Marketing Magazine*, January 28, 2002.

The attempt to generate buzz cited in the lead-in are just some examples of the many ways organizations integrate public relations programs with other elements of the promotional mix to market their products more effectively. These efforts have become such an integral part of the IMC mix that many agencies have formed departments within the public relations area specifically for this purpose. McCann-Erickson refers to it as experiential branding, while Puris Lintas calls it idea engineering. Whatever you call it, such efforts are clearly on the increase.[1] Besides generating increased sales, the good publicity provides long-term benefits.

Public relations is an integral part of the overall promotional effort that must be managed and coordinated with the other elements of the promotional mix. However, it does not always have the specific objectives of product and service promotion, nor does it always involve the same methods you have become accustomed to as you have read this text. Typically, these activities are designed more to change attitudes toward an organization or issue than to promote specific products or affect behaviours directly (though you will see that this role is changing in some organizations). This chapter explores the role of public relations, its related topic of publicity generated by news media, corporate advertising, the strengths and limitations of each, and the process by which they are employed. Examples of such efforts—both successful and unsuccessful—are also included.

Public Relations

What is public relations? How does it differ from other elements of marketing discussed thus far? Perhaps a good starting point is to define what the term *public relations* has traditionally meant and then to introduce its new role.

The Traditional Definition of PR

A variety of books define **public relations,** but perhaps the most comprehensive definition is that offered by the *Public Relations News* (the weekly newsletter of the industry):

> the management function which evaluates public attitudes, identifies the policies and procedures of an organization with the public interest, and executes a program of action (and communication) to earn public understanding and acceptance.[2]

Public relations is indeed a management function. The term *management* should be used in its broadest sense; it is not limited to business managements but extends to other types of organizations, including nonprofit institutions.

In this definition, public relations requires a series of stages, including:

1. The determination and evaluation of public attitudes.
2. The identification of policies and procedures of an organization with a public interest.
3. The development and execution of a communications program designed to bring about public understanding and acceptance.

This definition reveals that public relations involves much more than activities designed to sell a product or service. The PR program may involve some of the promotional program elements previously discussed but use them in a different way. For example, press releases may be mailed to announce new products or changes in the organization, special events may be organized to create goodwill in the community, and advertising may be used to state the firm's position on a controversial issue.

The New Role of PR

In an increasing number of marketing-oriented companies, new responsibilities have been established for public relations. It takes on a broader focus of the organization and a marketing perspective, designed to promote specific products and/or services.

Figure 13–1 Four classes of marketing and public relations use

Marketing	Public Relations	
	Weak	**Strong**
Weak	1 Example: Small social service agencies	2 Example: Hospitals and colleges
Strong	3 Example: Small manufacturing companies	4 Example: Fortune 500 companies

Figure 13–1 demonstrates four relationships that marketing and public relations can assume in an organization. These relationships are defined by the degree of use of each function.

Class 1 relationships are characterized by a minimal use of either function. Organizations with this design typically have very small marketing and/or public relations budgets and devote little time and effort to them. Small social service agencies and nonprofit organizations are typically class 1.

Organizations characterized by a *class 2* relationship have a well-established public relations function but do very little in the way of formal marketing. Universities and hospitals typically have such a design, although in both cases marketing activities are increasing. Both of these groups have moved in the direction of class 4 organizations in recent years, though PR activities still dominate.

Many small companies are typified by a *class 3* organization, in which marketing dominates and the public relations function is minimal. Private companies (without stockholders) and small manufacturers with little or no public to appease tend to employ this design.

Class 4 enterprises have both strong marketing and strong public relations. These two departments often operate independently. For example, public relations may be responsible for the more traditional responsibilities described earlier, while marketing promotes specific products and/or services. Both groups may work together at times, and both report to top management. Many Fortune 500 companies employ multiple ad agencies and PR firms.

The new role of public relations might best be characterized as class 4, although with a slightly different relationship. Rather than each department operating independently, the two now work closely together, blending their talents to provide the best overall image of the firm and its product or service offerings. Public relations departments increasingly position themselves as a tool to both supplant and support traditional advertising and marketing efforts and as a key part of the IMC program.

Writing in *Advertising Age,* William N. Curry notes that organizations must use caution in developing class 4 relationships because PR and marketing are not the same thing, and when one becomes dominant, the balance required to operate at maximum efficiency is lost.[3] He says losing sight of the objectives and functions of public relations in an attempt to achieve marketing goals may be detrimental in the long run. Others take an even stronger view that if public relations and marketing distinctions continue to blur, the independence of the PR function will be lost and it will become much less effective.[4] In this book, we take the position that in a truly integrated marketing communications program, public relations must play an integral role. We recognize this issue in the next section when we discuss the public relations strategy.

Publicity: One Effect of Public Relations

Publicity refers to the generation of news about a person, product, service, or organization that appears in broadcast or print media. In some instances, it appears that

Exhibit 13–1   Tree Top responds to the threat of negative publicity

publicity and public relations are synonymous. A good example of this situation is one company's effort to respond to adverse publicity with public relations, as shown in Exhibit 13–1. Tree Top's problems began when the major news media reported that the chemical Alar, used by some growers to regulate the growth of apples, may cause cancer in children. Despite published statements by reliable scientific and medical authorities (including the U.S. Surgeon General) that Alar does not cause cancer, a few special-interest groups were able to generate an extraordinary amount of adverse publicity, causing concern among consumers and purchasing agents. A few school districts took apples off their menus, and even applesauce and juice were implicated. Tree Top ran the ad in Exhibit 13–1 to state its position and alleviate consumers' fears. It also sent a direct mailing to nutritionists and day care operators. The campaign was successful in assuring consumers of the product's safety and rebuilding their confidence.

In other instances, it seems that publicity is the end result or effect of the public relations effort. Because marketers like to have as much control as possible over the time and place where information is released, they often provide the news media with pre-packaged material. One way to do this is with the **video news release (VNR),** a publicity piece produced by publicists so that stations can air it as a news story. The videos almost never mention that they are produced by the subject organization, and most news stations don't mention it either.

Another example is when a firm uses the media effectively for product launches. The firm, Hill and Knowlton, was faced with the task of generating publicity for Microsoft Canada's launch of Windows 2000 through the media. A concern was that the media might treat it as a non-event because of previous reports of early reviews and the like. The solution was to focus on key customer benefits in all communications to those that would provide third-party endorsements and all media players. The launch featured a presence on *Canada AM* (i.e., interview and demonstration), a CIO breakfast in Toronto, a speech by the president of Microsoft Canada, press conferences, interviews with Microsoft representatives, and a partner/customer reception. The results over the next 6 weeks saw Microsoft receive 28 million media impressions.

There are at least three complications that contribute to these two examples. First is the fact that publicity typically lasts for a short period of time. The communication effect of an article in the newspaper about a new product may last for a few weeks. Alternatively, public relations is a concerted program with many exposures extending over a period of time that has a lasting communication effect. A second complication is that public relations is designed to provide positive information about a firm and is usually controlled by the firm or its agent. Publicity, on the other hand, is not always positive and is not always under the control of, or paid for by, the organization. One factor that distinguishes publicity from the other IMC program elements is its sheer power as a form of communication, which gives rise to the final complication. Some of the more powerful incidents of publicity are unplanned by the corporation, and the focus is on the successful and unsuccessful reactions of the organization to positive or negative events.

Perhaps the most famous example is Tylenol, which experienced a substantial drop in sales after extensive media coverage of the tampering of its products while on store shelves. The Johnson & Johnson marketing efforts (including a strong public relations emphasis) designed to aid recovery were a model in proficiency that will be studied by students of marketing (in both the classroom and the boardroom) for many years. By January 1983, almost 100 percent of the original brand share had been regained.

Strengths of Public Relations

1. *Credibility.* Because public relations communications are not perceived in the same light as advertising—that is, the public does not realize the organization either directly or indirectly paid for them—they tend to have more credibility. The fact that the media are not being compensated for providing the information may lead receivers to consider the news more truthful and credible. For example, an article in newspapers or magazines discussing the virtues of aspirin may be perceived as much more credible than an ad for a particular brand of aspirin.

Automotive awards presented in magazines such as *Motor Trend* have long been known to carry clout with potential car buyers. Now marketers have found that even lesser media mean a lot as well. General Motors' Pontiac division played up an award given to Pontiac as "the best domestic sedan" by *MotorWeek* in a 30-minute program carried by about 300 public broadcasting stations. Likewise, Chrysler trumpeted the awards given to its Jeep Cherokee by *4-Wheel & Off Road* magazine.[5] It has become a common practice for car companies to promote their achievements.

News about a product may in itself serve as the subject of an ad. Exhibit 13–2 demonstrates how Olympus used favourable publicity from a variety of sources to promote its digital camera. A number of auto manufacturers have also taken advantage in their ads of high customer satisfaction ratings reported by J. D. Powers & Associates, an independent research firm specializing in automotive research.

2. *Cost.* In both absolute and relative terms, the cost of public relations is very low, especially when the possible effects are considered. While a firm can employ public relations agencies and spend millions of dollars on PR, for smaller companies this form of communication may be the most affordable alternative available.

When Hewlett-Packard launched its new line of Pavilion PCs, the launch team was told that it would receive the $15 million advertising budget promised only if it first brought the HP name to consumers. Armed with only public relations and point-of-purchase materials, the team and its PR agency created the tagline "It's not just a PC. It's an HP," which appeared on all communications pieces, packaging, and product literature (Exhibit 13–3). Press releases and product information were then disseminated to many consumer and trade media. When it came time to seek the advertising dollars, the HP Pavilion (the name Pavilion never appeared alone) was firmly entrenched in the minds of the target market.[6]

Many public relations programs require little more than the time and expenses associated with putting the program together and getting it distributed, yet they still accomplish their objectives.

3. *Avoidance of clutter.* Because they are typically perceived as news items, public relations messages are not subject to the clutter of ads. A story regarding a new product introduction or breakthrough is treated as a news item and is likely to receive attention.

4. *Lead generation.* Information about technological innovations, medical breakthroughs, and the like results almost immediately in a multitude of inquiries. These inquiries may give the firm some quality sales leads. For example, when Tiger Woods, one of the longest drivers on the PGA tour, was seen using a Cobra

Exhibit 13–2 Olympus capitalizes on positive publicity in its advertising

golf club in the internationally televised U.S. Open, the club manufacturer received inquiries from all over the world.

5. *Ability to reach specific groups.* Because some products appeal to only small market segments, it is not feasible to engage in advertising and/or promotions to reach them. If the firm does not have the financial capabilities to engage in promotional expenditures, the best way to communicate to these groups is through public relations.

6. *Image building.* Effective public relations helps to develop a positive image for the organization. A strong image is insurance against later misfortunes. For example, in 1982, seven people in the Chicago area died after taking Extra Strength Tylenol capsules that had been laced with cyanide (after they reached the store). Within one week of the poisonings, Tylenol's market share fell from 35 to only 6.5 percent. Strong public relations efforts combined with an already strong product and corporate image helped the product rebound (despite the opinions of many experts that it had no chance of recovering). A brand or firm with a lesser image would never have been able to come back.

Limitations of Public Relations

1. *Weaker brand or corporate identification effect.* Perhaps the major disadvantage of public relations is the potential for not completing the communications process. While public relations messages can break through the clutter of commercials, the receiver may not make the connection to the source. Many firms' PR efforts are never associated with their sponsors in the public mind.

2. *Inconsistent message.* Public relations may also misfire through mismanagement and a lack of coordination with the marketing department. When marketing and PR departments operate independently, there is a danger of inconsistent communications, redundancies in efforts, and so on.

3. *Timing.* Timing of the publicity is not always completely under the control of the marketer. Unless the press thinks that the information has very high news value, the timing of a press release is entirely up to the media—if it gets released at all. Thus, the information may be released earlier than desired or too late to make an impact.

4. *Accuracy.* A major way to get publicity is the press release. Unfortunately, the information sometimes gets lost in translation—that is, it is not always reported the way the provider wishes it to be. As a result, inaccurate information, omissions, or other errors may result. Sometimes when you see a publicity piece that was written on the basis of a press release, you wonder if the two are even about the same topic.

Exhibit 13–3   The HP Pavilion launch relied heavily on public relations activities

Public Relations Plan

In a survey of 100 top and middle managers in the communications field, over 60 percent said that their PR programs involved little more than press releases, press kits for trade shows, and new product announcements.[7] Further, these tools were not designed into a formal public relations effort but rather were used only as needed. In other words, no structured program was evident in well over half of the companies surveyed!

Public relations is an ongoing process requiring formalized policies and procedures for dealing with problems and opportunities. Just as you would not develop an advertising and/or promotions program without a plan, you should not institute public relations efforts haphazardly. Moreover, the public relations plan needs to be integrated into the overall marketing communications program. A public relations plan

Figure 13–2   Ten questions for evaluating public relations plans

1. Does the plan reflect a thorough understanding of the company's business situation?
2. Has the PR program made good use of research and background sources?
3. Does the plan include full analysis of recent editorial coverage?
4. Do the PR people fully understand the product's strengths and weaknesses?
5. Does the PR program describe several cogent, relevant conclusions from the research?
6. Are the program objectives specific and measurable?
7. Does the program clearly describe what the PR activity will be and how it will benefit the company?
8. Does the program describe how its results will be measured?
9. Do the research, objectives, activities, and evaluations tie together?
10. Has the PR department communicated with marketing throughout the development of the program?

can be structured like the other IMC tools we have discussed thus far. It starts with a situation analysis and includes decisions with respect to target audiences, behavioural objectives, communication objectives, strategy, and tactics. Once the plan is written, marketers should ask themselves some of the questions in Figure 13–2 to determine whether their public relations plan is complete. Given the broad nature of public relations, there are many options for each part of the plan that we now discuss.

Situation Analysis

Some elements of the situation analysis from the marketing plan or IMC plan are reviewed. An additional key piece of information is a current assessment of people's attitudes toward the firm, its product or service, or specific issues beyond those directed at a product or service. Why are firms so concerned with the public's attitudes?

One reason is that these attitudes may affect sales of the firm's products. A number of companies have experienced sales declines as a result of consumer boycotts. Procter & Gamble, Coors, Nike, and Texaco (Exhibit 13-4) are just a few companies that responded to organized pressures. Second, no one wants to be perceived as a bad citizen. Corporations exist in communities, and their employees may both work and live there. Negative attitudes carry over to employee morale and may result in a less-than-optimal working environment internally and in the community. Due to their concerns about public perceptions, many privately held corporations, publicly held companies, utilities, and the media survey public attitudes. The reasons for conducting this research are many:

1. *It provides input into the planning process.* Once the firm has determined public attitudes, they become the starting point in the development of programs designed to maintain favourable positions or change unfavourable ones.

2. *It serves as an early warning system.* Once a problem exists, it may require substantial time and money to correct. By conducting research, the firm may be able to identify potential problems and handle them effectively before they become serious issues.

3. *It secures support internally.* If research shows that a problem or potential problem exists, it will be much easier for the public relations arm to gain the support it needs to address this problem.

Exhibit 13–4   Texaco responds to negative publicity

Where we go from here...

Texaco is facing a vital challenge. It's broader than any specific words and larger than any lawsuit.

We are committed to begin meeting this challenge swiftly through specific programs with concrete goals and measurable timetables.

Our responsibility is to eradicate discriminatory behavior wherever and however it surfaces within our company. Our challenge is to make Texaco a company of limitless opportunity for all men and women. Our goal is to broaden economic access to Texaco for women and minorities and to increase the positive impact our investments can have in communities across America.

We have started down this road by reaching out to prominent minority and religious leaders to explore ways to make Texaco a model of diversity and workplace equality.

It is essential to this urgent mission that we work together to help solve the problems we face as a company – which, after all, echo the problems faced in society as a whole.

Discrimination will be extinguished only if we tackle it together – only if we join in a unified, common effort.

Together we can take Texaco into the 21st century as a model of diversity.

We can make Texaco a company of limitless opportunity.

We can and must make Texaco a leader in according respect to every man and woman.

Peter I. Bijur
Chairman & CEO

TEXACO

Visit our Web site: http://www.texaco.com

4. *It increases the effectiveness of the communication.* The better it understands a problem, the better the firm can design communications to deal with it.[8]

Determine Relevant Target Audiences

The targets of public relations efforts may vary, with different objectives for each. Some may be directly involved in selling the product; others may affect the firm in a different way (e.g., they may be aimed at stockholders or legislators). These audiences may be internal or external to the firm.

Internal audiences may include the employees of the firm, stockholders and investors, members of the local community, suppliers, and current customers. Why are community members and customers of the firm considered internal rather than external? According to John Marston, it's because these groups are already connected with the organization in some way and the firm normally communicates with them in the ordinary routine of work.[9]

External audiences are those people who are not closely connected with the organization (e.g., the public at large). It may be necessary to communicate with these groups on an ongoing basis for a variety of reasons, ranging from ensuring goodwill to introducing new policies, procedures, or even products. A few examples may help.

Employees of the Firm   Maintaining morale and showcasing the results of employees' efforts are often prime objectives of the public relations program. Organizational newsletters, notices on bulletin boards, paycheck envelope stuffers, direct mail, and annual reports are some of the methods used to communicate with these groups. Personal methods of communicating may be as formal as an established grievance committee or as informal as an office Christmas party. Other social events, such as corporate bowling teams or picnics, are also used to create goodwill.

Stockholders and Investors   You may think an annual report like the one in Exhibit 13–5 just provides stockholders and investors with financial information regarding the firm. While this is one purpose, annual reports are also a communications channel for informing this audience about why the firm is or is not doing well, future plans, and other information that goes beyond numbers.

For example, McDonald's has successfully used annual reports to fend off potential PR problems. One year the report described McDonald's recycling efforts to alleviate consumers' concerns about waste; another report included a 12-page spread on food and nutrition. Other companies use similar strategies, employing shareholders' meetings, video presentations, and other forms of direct mail. General Motors' annual public interest report is sent to shareholders and community members to detail the company's high standards of corporate responsibility. Companies have used these approaches to generate additional investments, to bring more of their stocks "back home" (i.e., become more locally controlled and managed), and to produce funding to solve specific problems, as well as to promote goodwill.

Community Members   People who live and work in the community where a firm is located or doing business are often the target of public relations efforts. Such efforts may involve ads informing the community of activities that the organization is engaged in— for example, reducing air pollution, cleaning up water supplies, or, as shown in Exhibit 13–6, protecting turtles. (As you can see, the community can be defined very broadly.) Demonstrating to people that the organization is a good citizen with their welfare in mind

Exhibit 13–5 Annual reports serve a variety of purposes

may also be a reason for communicating to these groups.

Exhibit 13–6 Chevron demonstrates concern for the public

Racing To
The Moon.

Instinct and moonlight guide them to the ocean. For newborn sea turtles, it is a run for survival. They must quickly move past predators to the safety of deep water. That's why people working in partnership on Thevenard Island conceal the light from their oil and gas operations. So the turtles won't be drawn off-course. Which helps protect a threatened species by making certain the only light visible is the one that leads home.

People Do.
www.peopledo.com

Suppliers and Customers
An organization wishes to maintain *goodwill* with its suppliers as well as its consuming public. If consumers think a company is not socially conscious, they may take their loyalties elsewhere. Suppliers may be inclined to do the same. Indirect indications of the success of PR efforts may include more customer loyalty, less antagonism, or greater cooperation between the firm and its suppliers or consumers.

The Media
Perhaps one of the most critical external publics is the media, which determine what you will read in your newspapers or see on TV, and how this news will be presented. Because of the media's power, they should be informed of the firm's actions. Companies issue press releases and communicate through conferences, interviews, and special events. The media are generally receptive to such information so long as it is handled professionally; reporters are always interested in good stories.

Educators
A number of organizations provide educators with information regarding their activities. The Direct Marketing Association, the Promotional Products Association, and the Yellow Pages Publishers Association (YPPA), among others, keep educators informed in an attempt to generate goodwill as well as exposure for their causes. These groups and major corporations provide information regarding innovations, state-of-the-art research, and other items of interest. YPPA provides materials specifically designed for educators.

Educators are a target audience because, like the media, they control the flow of information to certain parties—in this case, people like you. *Business Week, Fortune,* and *Fast Company* magazines attempt to have professors use their magazines in their classes. In addition to selling more magazines, such usage would also lend credibility to the mediums.

Civic and Business Organizations
The local nonprofit civic organizations also serve as gatekeepers of information. Companies' financial contributions to these groups, speeches at organization functions, and sponsorships are all designed to create goodwill. Corporate executives' service on the boards of nonprofit organizations also generates positive public relations.

Governments
Public relations often attempts to influence government bodies directly at both local and national levels. Successful lobbying may mean immediate success for a product, while regulations detrimental to the firm may cost it millions.

Financial Groups
In addition to current shareholders, potential shareholders and investors may be relevant target markets. Financial advisors, lending institutions, and others must be kept abreast of new developments as well as financial information, since they offer the potential for new sources of funding. Press releases and corporate reports play an important role in providing information to these publics.

Behavioural Objectives

The framework for behavioural objectives discussed in Chapter 5 is readily applicable for public relations. Recall that behavioural objectives are trial purchase, repeat purchase, purchase-related action, or consumption. No matter what target audiences are selected in the prior step, an astute marketer will know that it is important to understand the type of behaviour desired as a result of the communication.

The idea of a "purchase" seems incongruous for some public relations situations, so the marketer may have to view this as the target audience "buying into the idea" or some other specific behaviour in order to carefully define the objectives.

Communication Objectives

Similarly, the communication objectives of Chapter 5 can be used for public relations. Communication objectives include category need, brand awareness, brand attitude, purchase intention, and purchase facilitation. Each of these can be the focus of the public relations plan, although slight modifications are needed. For example, the "brand" may in fact be the corporation itself or a new product that is talked about in a press release. In addition, the notion of a "category" has to be adjusted. Some target audiences want to be affiliated with "good corporate citizens" that are responsible to the community, the environment, or some other issue. Often then, the "category" will be related to the particular topic or focus of the public relations message.

Awareness is critical for a brand and is important for the organization. Many organizations engage in various social causes because the exposure of their name will enhance the general public's recall and recognition at a later point in time.

We started off by highlighting the importance of existing attitudes of the target audiences. Clearly then, the public relations plan should have a specific section that outlines the attitude change or modification desired. It should also illustrate the key motives addressed and what attributes or benefits of the firm or product that the message should focus on.

Strategy

The strategy decisions for public relations are twofold, as we saw with advertising: message and media. The primary message decisions concern the degree to which the message will have a marketing or corporation focus, and the creative associated with the message. We will briefly describe some issues related to this decision in this section. Like advertising, there are a number of options to disseminate the message, news media, advertising media, and events. We will discuss these in more detail in the next major section.

Focus of the Message Thomas L. Harris has referred to public relations activities designed to support marketing objectives as **marketing public relations** functions.[10] Marketing objectives that may be aided by public relations activities include raising awareness, informing and educating, gaining understanding, building trust, giving consumers a reason to buy, and generating consumer acceptance. These points are consistent with the behavioural and communication objective of our framework. One of the major threats expressed by Harris is that marketing public relations may lead to public relations becoming subservient to marketing—a concern expressed by many opponents. However, if employed properly and used in conjunction with other traditional public relations practices as well as IMC elements, marketing public relations can be used effectively in the following ways:

- *Building marketplace excitement before media advertising breaks.* A new product announcement is an opportunity to gain extra exposure, thereby increasing the effectiveness of ads or the entire IMC plan.
- *Creating advertising news where there is no product news.* Ads themselves can be the focus of publicity if they are entertaining or topical.
- *Introducing a product with little or no advertising.*
- *Influencing the influentials—that is, providing information to opinion leaders.*
- *Defending products at risk with a message of reassurance.*
- *Constructively promoting a product.* Energizer's national education campaign that urges consumers to change the batteries in their fire alarms when they reset their clocks in the fall has resulted in a strong corporate citizen image and increased sales of batteries.

A system for measuring the effectiveness of the public relations program has been developed by Lotus HAL. The criteria used in the evaluation process follow:

- Total number of impressions over time
- Total number of impressions on the target audience
- Total number of impressions on specific target audiences
- Percentage of positive articles over time
- Percentage of negative articles over time
- Ratio of positive to negative articles
- Percentage of positive/negative articles by subject
- Percentage of positive/negative articles by publication or reporter
- Percentage of positive/negative articles by target audience

Figure 13–3 Criteria for measuring the effectiveness of PR

The historic role of public relations is one of communicating a favourable image of the corporation as a whole. The domain of this image, or reputation management, concerns every facet of how the organization interacts with its many social, economic, political, and charitable constituents, in addition to the general public locally, nationally, and internationally.

Given the two broad directions of the actual message, marketing versus corporate, an organization has to decide the relative degree of the messages' impact over the course of a year or even longer, as public relations tends to have a lasting communication effect. Too much of a focus in either direction and the organization loses the opportunity to communicate fully. (Figure 13–3 shows one independent system for measuring PR's success.)

Creative of the Message We will discuss the many tools for public relations shortly; however, in deciding what message to communicate, the marketer is faced with the decision as to whether the creative strategy of advertising or other IMC tools should be adopted for public relations. On the one hand, there is the argument that all communications should have a common look and feel to them. To counter this, one could argue that unique target audiences with a specific message should have an appropriate creative associated with it.

Tactics

The tactics of public relations partly depend upon the type of media or dissemination tool used (discussed next). When using news media, a marketer would need to know how to make a media presentation, whom to contact, how to issue a press release, and what to know about each medium addressed, including TV, radio, newspapers, magazines, and direct-response advertising. In addition, decisions regarding alternative media such as news conferences, seminars, events, and personal letters, as well as insights on how to deal with government and other legislative bodies have to be made. Because this information is too extensive to include as a single chapter in this text, we suggest you peruse one of the many books available on this subject for additional insights.

As noted previously, we have grouped the strategy options under two topics: news media and advertising media.

Public Relations Strategy Options

News Media Options

A number of news media options are available for communicating with various target audiences, including press releases, press conferences, exclusives, interviews, and community involvement.

The Press Release

One of the most important publics is the press. To be used by the press, information must be factual, true, and of interest to the medium as well as to its audience. The source of the **press release** can do certain things to improve the likelihood that the "news" will be disseminated.

Jonathan Schenker of Ketchum Public Relations, New York, suggests four technological methods to make life easier for the press and to increase the likelihood that the media will use your story:

1. *Telephone press conferences.* Since reporters cannot always get to a press conference, use the telephone to call them for coverage.

2. *In-studio media tours.* Satellite communications providing a story, and a chance to interview, from a central location such as a TV studio save broadcast journalists time and money by eliminating their need to travel.

3. *Multicomponent video news releases (VNR).* A five-component package consisting of a complete script in print and on tape, a video release with a live reporter, a local contact source at which to target the video, and a silent video news release that allows the station to fill in with its own news reporter lend an advantage by saving the media money.

4. *Targeted newswire stories.* When the sender targets the public relations message, reporters are spared the need to read through volumes of news stories to select those of interest to their target audiences.

The information in a press release won't be used unless it's of interest to the readers of the medium it's sent to. For example, financial institutions may issue press releases to business trade media and to the editor of the business section of a general-interest newspaper. Information on the release of a new rock album is of more interest to radio disk jockeys than to TV newscasters; sports news also has its interested audiences.

Press Conferences

We are all familiar with **press conferences** held by political figures. While used less often by organizations and corporations, this form of delivery can be very effective. The topic must be of major interest to a specific group before it is likely to gain coverage. Usually major accomplishments (such as a profit announcement), major breakthroughs (such as medical cures), emergencies, or catastrophes warrant a national press conference. On a local level, community events, local developments, and the like may receive coverage. Companies often call press conferences when they have significant news to announce, such as the introduction of a new product or advertising campaign. Sports teams use this tool to attract fan attention and interest when a new star is signed. TV3, a Malaysian broadcast system, held an international press conference to announce its introduction of an interactive TV service.

Exclusives

Although most public relations efforts seek a variety of channels for distribution, an alternative strategy is to offer one particular medium exclusive rights to the story if that medium reaches a substantial number of people in the target audience. Offering an **exclusive** may enhance the likelihood of acceptance. As you watch television over the next few weeks, look for the various networks' and local stations' exclusives. Notice how the media actually use these exclusives to promote themselves.

Interviews

When you watch TV or read magazines, pay close attention to the personal interviews. Usually someone will raise specific questions, and a spokesperson provided by the firm will answer them. Ted Rogers often gives interviews pertaining to the many technological divisions that exist in the Rogers communications conglomerate. Microsoft's president, Steve Ballmer, appeared in a number of personal interviews to present the company's position in a legal case brought against it by the U.S. government.

Community Involvement

Many corporations enhance their public images through involvement in the local community that are often covered by the media.

Nestlé Listens to Its Customers and Does the Right Thing

Nestlé Canada's quick reversal in 2001 of its plans to stop manufacturing its chocolate bars in a peanut- and nut-free environment is a smart business decision. It was an all-too-rare instance where a company actually listened to consumer feedback and acted in a way that, in the short term, probably limits its flexibility. In the long term, though, Nestlé's bold move will likely pay off in spades in terms of consumer goodwill, and the whole experience appears to have given it a leg up in developing, and in fact cornering, an unexplored market segment and marketing proposition.

When Nestlé announced in late April 2001 that, as of January 2002, it would no longer guarantee that Smarties, Aero, Kit Kat, Coffee Crisp, and Mirage chocolates would be produced in a nut-free environment, there was an air of inevitability to it. Consumer demand for chocolate products containing nuts is, in fact, on the rise, and the company wanted the flexibility to be able to use the same facility to produce them as is used for the non-nut products. But once you have nuts running through the machinery, and nut particles floating in the air, it's virtually impossible to ensure that trace elements of nuts aren't in something. An estimated 150 to 200 people die each year in North America because of anaphylaxis, in essence of severe asthmatic reaction to foods, most notably nuts. And unlike, say, the risks of tobacco smoke, which can take decades to do its damage, contact with even a particle of a nut can trigger an attack.

So, better safe than sorry, Nestlé embarked on a PR and outreach effort to alert the public of the change. It was just one of the realities of business these days. For the sake of competitive advantage and efficiencies, the consumer loses some choices, and we're all a bit diminished by the reduction in options. But, hey, it's only a candy bar and who can argue the business logic?

But as Nestlé almost instantly began to hear in literally thousands of phone calls, letters, and e-mails that it received in the wake of its announcement, while the portion of the population directly affected by nut allergies is small—maybe 2.5 percent, or 600,000 to 700,000 Canadians—the universe of those impacted by the problem is huge and growing. It learned that just about every place where kids congregate, such as schools, day care centers, summer camps, and clubs such as Scouts and Guides, is becoming increasingly sensitized to the dangers and is restricting foods with peanuts.

Nestlé was also surprised to learn from those that were contacting it that their products had, in fact, been the only major chocolate brands still offering safety for those with nut allergies. In effect, a move in the name of internal efficiency and production flexibility was mushrooming into a situation where the company was snatching candy from allergic kids. Further, the company was contacted by people who hadn't realized that

Nestlé's products were nut-free, and now that they did know, would love to be able to buy them.

Still, the public reaction was so far under the radar that it was a surprise, albeit a pleasant one, to hear that the company was changing its plans after just 3 weeks—a decision so sudden that it was unable to keep off store shelves the new packaging warning that products were no longer nut-free.

The lobbying effort, such as it was, was more a wave of simultaneous personal reactions rather than any orchestrated assault. Yes, one Toronto man set up a website (www.savethesmarties.com) to rally opposition to the move, and spokespeople for various allergy bodies publicly urged the company to change its mind; but for the most part, the company was inundated with individuals telling stories about how the decision would impact family and friends.

"We have been truly overwhelmed by the emotional chord that our original decision struck with consumers," said Graham Lute, Nestlé's senior vice president of consumer communications, meals, beverages and dairy, corporate affairs, and market intelligence, in a May 14 release announcing the change of heart. "We've listened to consumers and moved quickly to reverse our original decision. We will pursue other options to satisfy the growing segment of consumers who want peanut/nut chocolate products."

The media reaction to the move was downright glowing. Positive pieces appeared in all the major papers and the leader of the Anaphylaxis Network could be heard on CBC Radio praising Nestlé for its sensitivity and urging people to buy its products.

Nestlé clearly will have to incur unplanned-for costs to set up a new facility to produce products with nuts, but if it can tastefully capitalize on the consumer goodwill and awareness generated by its adept handling of the peanut problem, it may well come out ahead of the game. But even if there is no huge payback, the company deserves high praise for simply doing the right thing at the right time.

Source: Adapted from Stan Sutter, "Not Just Peanuts," *Marketing Magazine,* June 11, 2001. Used with permission.

This involvement may take many forms, including membership in local organizations and contributions to or participation in community events. For example, Rogers' employees work throughout many neighbourhoods on Halloween evening to promote community safety. It also includes organizations participating in emergencies. A flood in Venezuela, which killed hundreds, brought aid from governments and businesses from around the world.

Strengths of News Media Options

1. *News media messages are highly credible.* Unlike advertising and sales promotions, publicity is not usually perceived as being sponsored by the company (in negative instances, it never is). So consumers perceive this information as more objective and place more confidence in it.

2. *Endorsement.* Publicity information may be perceived as endorsed by the medium in which it appears. For example, publicity regarding a breakthrough in the durability of golf balls will go far to promote them if it is reported by *Golf* magazine. *Car & Driver's* award for car of the year reflects the magazine's perception of the quality of the auto selected.

3. *Frequency Potential.* Still another reason for publicity's power is the frequency of exposure it generates. When Lay's introduced its campaign for Doritos Tortilla Thins featuring comedian Chevy Chase, TV reporters aired 1,734 stories about the ads using footage provided by Frito-Lay.[11]

Limitations of News Media Options

1. *Timing.* Timing of the publicity through news media is not always completely under the control of the marketer. Unless the press thinks the information has very high news value, the timing of the press release is entirely up to the media—if it gets released at all. Thus, the information may be released earlier than desired or too late to make an impact.

2. *Accuracy.* The information contained in the press release sometimes gets lost in translation—that is, it is not always reported the way the provider wishes it

to be. As a result, inaccurate information, omissions, or other errors may result. Sometimes when you see a publicity piece that was written on the basis of a press release, you wonder if the two are even about the same topic.

One of the more controversial forms of advertising is **corporate advertising.** Actually an extension of the public relations function, corporate advertising does not promote any one specific product or service. Rather, it is designed to promote the firm overall, by enhancing its image, assuming a position on a social issue or cause, or seeking direct involvement in something. Why is corporate advertising controversial? A number of reasons are offered:

Corporate Advertising Options

1. *Consumers are not interested in this form of advertising.* A Gallup and Robinson study reported in *Advertising Age* found consumers were 35 percent less interested in corporate ads than in product-oriented advertising.[12] This may be because consumers do not understand the reasons behind such ads.

2. *It's a costly form of self-indulgence.* Firms have been accused of engaging in corporate image advertising only to satisfy the egos of top management. This argument stems from the fact that corporate ads are not easy to write. The message to be communicated is not as precise and specific as one designed to position a product, so the top managers often dictate the content of the ad, and the copy reflects their ideas and images of the corporation.

3. *The firm must be in trouble.* Some critics believe the only time firms engage in corporate advertising is when they are in trouble—either in a financial sense or in the public eye—and are advertising to attempt to remedy the problem.

4. *Corporate advertising is a waste of money.* Given that the ads do not directly appeal to anyone, are not understood, and do not promote anything specific, critics say the monies could be better spent in other areas. Again, much of this argument has its foundation in the fact that corporate image ads are often intangible. They typically do not ask directly for a purchase; they do not ask for investors. Rather, they present a position or try to create an image. Because they are not specific, many critics believe their purpose is lost on the audience and these ads are not a wise investment of the firm's resources.

Since the term *corporate advertising* tends to be used as a catchall for any type of advertising run for the direct benefit of the corporation rather than its products or services, much advertising falls into this category. For purposes of this text (and to attempt to bring some perspective to the term), we use it to describe any type of advertising designed to promote the organization itself rather than its products or services. Corporate advertising is targeted at both internal and external audiences and involves the promotion of the organization as well as its ideas. Marketers seek attainment of corporate advertising's objectives by implementing image, advocacy, or cause-related advertising, as well as event sponsorships and Internet communication. Each form is designed to achieve specific goals.

Image Advertising

One form of corporate advertising is devoted to promoting the organization's overall image. **Image advertising** may accomplish a number of objectives, including creating goodwill both internally and externally, creating a position for the company, and generating resources, both human and financial. A number of methods are used:

1. *General image or positioning ads.* As shown in Exhibit 13–7, ads are often designed to create an image of the firm in the public mind. The exhibit shows how Tyco is attempting to create an image of itself as a market leader and health care expert, not a *toy* company.

Exhibit 13–7 Tyco uses image advertising to avoid confusion

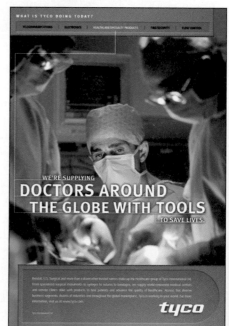

WHAT IS TYCO DOING TODAY?

WE'RE SUPPLYING
DOCTORS AROUND THE GLOBE WITH TOOLS
TO SAVE LIVES.

tyco

PR Converts Canadians to Krispy Kreme

Urban legends seem to swirl around the Krispy Kreme Doughnuts brand like steam rising from one of its Hot Original Glazed confections. Ever hear the one about the woman who was driving by a Krispy Kreme outlet and swerved across traffic, rolling her car, when she saw the "Hot Doughnuts Now" sign light up? How about the store owner in Toronto who imported dozens of Krispy Kremes from Buffalo and resold them, one at a time, at the checkout counter until someone from Krispy Kreme showed up and demanded that he cease and desist? Another one making the rounds is that Krispy Kreme, absolutely will not...never...EVER?? use anything other than public relations in its marketing. Actually, that last one is largely true. When Krispy Kreme opens a new store, such as the one in Mississauga, Ontario last December—its first in Canada and the first outside the U.S.—PR typically dominates the marketing strategy. In this case, traditional media only plays a supporting role.

Krispy Kreme is one of those rare brands to have achieved "cult brand" status, defined in an April 16, 2001, *Forbes* article as a brand that "seizes the imagination of a small group who spread the word, make converts, help turn a fringe product into a mainstream name." Yet one of the challenges facing Toronto–based KremeKo, which holds the development rights for Ontario, Quebec, and the four Atlantic provinces, is how to make this 64-year-old brand—which has deeply nostalgic American roots—relevant to Canadians who are said to consume more doughnuts per capita than the people of any other nation, and who consider doughnut brand loyalty to be an important part of their national identity.

That's why PR makes so much sense for Krispy Kreme in this market. The media buzzed about Krispy Kreme's arrival in Canada many months before it actually opened its door. Mat Wilcox, whose Vancouver–based Wilcox Group is the brand's PR agency for Canada, fielded media inquiries that resulted in more than 500 stories. Massive doughnut "drops" were an important part of the PR plan because they got the product into peoples' hands several months before the first store opened. There was also a steady stream of hot, fresh doughnuts delivered to media outlets, as well at toques emblazoned with the Krispy Kreme logo. The company plans to open a total of 50 stores in Canada.

Source: Adapted from Angela Kryhul, "The Krispy Cult," *Marketing Magazine,* January 28, 2002. Used with permission.

This type of advertising also occurs when a company changes its name. In 2001, Andersen Consulting became Accenture, while Mutual Life Insurance became Clarica. Accenture was part of a worldwide make-over of 178 offices costing $263 million with 50 separate marketing teams. The Canadian team used public relations, direct mail to clients, and consumer print and TV ads created by an American agency. Clarica is the Latin root word for "clear" and that became the focus of all advertising messages, both print and television, as consumers truly wanted clear financial choices. Naturally, Clarica created a clear image of the "new" company through its corporate advertising efforts.

2. *Television sponsorships.* A firm often runs corporate image advertising on TV programs or specials. For example, the Hallmark or IBM specials and documentaries on network TV are designed to promote the corporation as a good citizen. By associating itself with high-quality or educational programming, the firm hopes for a carryover effect that benefits its own image.

According to John Bennett, senior VP for international marketing communications, the sponsorships are designed to fulfill specific business objectives while providing support for the recipients.[13] Exhibit 13–8 shows a few organizations that decided a Juno Awards sponsorship would be good for them.

3. *Recruiting.* The promotional piece presented in Exhibit 13–9 is a good example of corporate image advertising designed to attract new employees. If you are a graduating senior considering a career in the new Internet economy, this ad, promoting a corporate image for the company, will interest you.

The employment section of most major metropolitan newspapers is an excellent place to see this form of corporate image advertising at work. Notice the ads in these papers and consider the images the firms are presenting.

4. *Generating financial support.* Some corporate advertising is designed to generate investments in the corporation. By creating a more favourable image, the firm makes itself attractive to potential stock purchasers and investors. More investments mean more working capital, more monies for research and development, and so on. In this instance, corporate image advertising is almost attempting to make a sale; the product is the firm.

While there is no concrete evidence that corporate image advertising leads directly to increased investment, at least one study shows a correlation between the price of stock and the amount of corporate advertising done.[14] Firms that spend more on corporate advertising also tend to have higher-priced stocks (though a direct relationship is very difficult to substantiate).

This thing called image is not unidimensional. Many factors affect it. Figure 13–4 shows the results of a survey conducted by Harris Interactive and the Reputation Institute on the best corporate reputations in the United States. The most admired firms did not gain their positions merely by publicity and word of mouth (nor, we guess, did the least admired).

A positive corporate image cannot be created just from a few advertisements. Quality of products and services, innovation, sound financial practices, good corporate citizenship, and wise marketing are just a few of the factors that contribute to overall image. In addition, the type of product marketed and emotional appeal also contribute. The survey mentioned above demonstrated that profits and stock performances had little to do with reputation and that once a reputation is acquired, it has lasting power (Exxon can't shake its problems with the oil spill, yet Coca-Cola weathered the European crisis rather well). The study shows that companies are ranked differently on key corporate attributes including emotional appeal, social responsibility, workplace environment, and vision and leadership (among 16 others).[15] Another study, examining the best reputations in high technology, showed that the best-regarded companies (Microsoft, Intel, and Sony) do not necessarily receive similar ratings toward their stocks (Figure 13–5).[16]

Advocacy Advertising

A second major form of corporate advertising addresses social, business, or environmental issues. Such **advocacy advertising** is concerned with propagating ideas and elucidating controversial social issues of public importance in a manner that supports the interests of the sponsor.[17]

While still portraying an image for the company or organization, advocacy advertising does so indirectly, by adopting a position on

Exhibit 13–8 Some Juno Awards sponsors

Exhibit 13–9 An ad designed to attract new employees

Figure 13–4 The best corporate reputations in America

The Leaders

Top 30 companies, based on Reputation Quotient (RQ), a standardized instrument that measures a company's reputation by examining how the public perceives companies based on 20 attributes.

Rank	Company	RQ	Rank	Company	RQ	Rank	Company	RQ
1	Johnson & Johnson	83.4	11	Dell	78.4	21	FedEx	75.7
2	Coca-Cola	81.6	12	General Electric	78.1	22	Procter & Gamble	71.9
3	Hewlett-Packard	81.2	13	Lucent	78.0	23	Nike	71.3
4	Intel	81.0	14	Anheuser-Busch	78.0	24	McDonald's	71.2
5	Ben & Jerry's	81.0	15	Microsoft	77.9	25	Southwest Airlines	70.6
6	Wal-Mart	80.5	16	amazon.com	77.8	26	America Online	69.2
7	Xerox	79.9	17	IBM	77.6	27	DaimlerChrysler	69.1
8	Home Depot	79.7	18	Sony	77.4	28	Toyota	68.6
9	Gateway	78.8	19	Yahoo!	76.9	29	Sears	67.6
10	Disney	78.7	20	AT&T	75.7	30	Boeing	67.3

The Building Blocks

Twenty corporate attributes are classified into the following six elements of reputation. Top five companies in each category:

Emotional Appeal[1]	Social Responsibility[2]	Products and Services[3]
1 Johnson & Johnson	1 Ben & Jerry's	1 Johnson & Johnson
2 Coca-Cola	2 amazon.com	2 Intel
3 Hewlett-Packard	3 Johnson & Johnson	3 Hewlett-Packard
4 Ben & Jerry's	4 Wal-Mart	4 Xerox
5 Xerox	5 Xerox	5 Ben & Jerry's

[1]How much the company is liked, admired, and respected

[2]Perceptions of the company as a good citizen in its dealings with communities, employees, and the environment

[3]Perceptions of the quality, innovation, value, and reliability of its products and services

Workplace Environment[4]	Vision and Leadership[5]	Financial Performance[6]
1 Johnson & Johnson	1 Microsoft	1 Microsoft
2 Lucent	2 Intel	2 Wal-Mart
3 Ben & Jerry's	3 Anheuser-Busch	3 Coca-Cola
4 Hewlett-Packard	4 Coca-Cola	4 Johnson & Johnson
5 Intel	5 Dell	5 Intel

[4]Perception of how well the company is managed, how it is to work for, and the quality of its employees

[5]How much the company demonstrates a clear vision and strong leadership

[6]Perceptions of its profitability, prospects, and risk

a particular issue rather than promoting the organization itself. Advocacy advertising has increased in use over the past few years and has also met with increased criticism. The ads may be sponsored by a firm or by a trade association and are designed to tell readers how the firm operates or management's position on a particular issue.

Figure 13–5 Relationship between reputation and stock purchases

Best-Regarded Companies		Attitudes toward Stocks	
Digital-technology companies that received the highest corporate reputation ratings among online computer users.		Percentage of respondents active in the stock market who said they will definitely or probably buy these stocks.	
Company	Reputation quotient*	Company	Will or may purchase stock
Microsoft	82.27	Dell	74%
Intel	81.50	Lucent	67
Sony	79.85	Gateway	63
Dell	79.62	Microsoft	63
Lucent	78.35	Sun Microsytems	62
Gateway	78.28	Intel	61
Eastman Kodak	78.23	Cisco Systems	59
Texas Instruments	77.57	IBM	54
Cisco Systems	77.23	Micron	53
Hewlett-Packard	77.20	Compaq	51
Xerox	77.17	Symantec	49
Symantec	76.73	Motorola	48
Intuit	76.70	Yahoo!	48
Sun Microsystems	76.58	Texas Instruments	47
IBM	76.02	Advanced Micro Devices	46
Motorola	75.84	Eastman Kodak	46
Red Hat	75.41	Novell	46
Yahoo!	74.91	Red Hat	46
3Com	74.89	Hewlett Packard	45
Canon	74.86	E*Trade	44

*A standardized instrument that measures a company's reputation by examining how the public perceives companies based on 20 attributes.

Sometimes the advertising is a response to negative publicity or to the firm's inability to place an important message through public relations channels. Sometimes the firm just wants to get certain ideas accepted or have society understand its concerns.

Advocacy advertising has been criticized by a number of sources. But this form of communication has been around for a long time. AT&T engaged in issues-oriented advertising way back in 1908 and continues to employ this form of communication. Critics contend that companies with large advertising budgets purchase too much ad space and time and that advocacy ads may be misleading, but the checks and balances of regular product advertising also operate in this area.

Cause-Related Advertising

An increasingly popular method of image building is **cause-related marketing,** in which companies link with charities or nonprofit organizations as contributing sponsors. The company benefits from favorable publicity, while the charity receives much-needed funds. Spending on cause-related marketing has increased considerably in the past decade. Proponents of cause marketing say that association with a cause may differentiate one brand or store from another, increase consumer acceptance of price increases, generate favourable publicity, and even win over skeptical officials who may have an impact on the company.[18] Cause marketing relationships can take a variety of forms. Making outright donations to a nonprofit cause, having companies volunteer for the cause, donating materials or supplies, running public service announcements, or even providing event refreshments are some of the ways companies get involved.

While companies receive public relations benefits from their association with causes, with 80 percent of consumers saying they have a more positive impression of companies that support a cause, they sometimes receive financial rewards as well.[19] Visa's "Reading is Fundamental" campaign led to a 17 percent increase in sales, BMW saw sales increase when it sponsored a program to eradicate breast cancer, and Wendy's International in Denver saw sales increase by more than 33 percent when a portion of purchases was contributed to Denver's Mercy Medical Center.[20]

At the same time, not all cause marketing is a guarantee of success. Cause marketing requires more than just associating with a social issue, and it takes time and effort. Companies have gotten into trouble by misleading consumers about their relationships, and others wasted money by hooking up with a cause that offered little synergism. One survey showed that over 300 companies had associated themselves with breast cancer concerns, with most becoming lost in sponsorship clutter. Others have simply picked the wrong cause—finding that their customers and potential customers either have little interest in or don't like the cause. In some cases, cause marketing is considered nothing more than shock advertising. Finally, the results of cause-marketing efforts can sometimes be hard to quantify.

Event Sponsorships

Corporate sponsorships of charities and causes has become a popular form of public relations. While some companies sponsor specific events and/or causes with primarily traditional public relations objectives in mind, a separate and more marketing-oriented use of sponsorships is also on the increase. Such **event sponsorships** take on a variety of forms, as shown in Figure 13–6. Anything from golf apparel (Mossimo sponsors golfer David Duval) and equipment to concerts (Tommy Hilfiger's sponsorship of Lilith Fair) to naming stadiums (Corel paid $20 million to change the name of the Ottawa Senators' Palladium to the Corel Centre) is now a candidate for corporate sponsorship.

Sports receives the majority of event sponsorship monies. Among the most popular sporting events for sponsorship are auto racing, golf and tennis tournaments, and running events. Professional sports leagues and teams as well as Olympic teams and competitions also receive large amounts of sponsorship money. Bicycle racing, beach volleyball, skiing, and various water sports are also attracting corporate sponsorship. Traditionally, tobacco, beer, and car companies have been among the largest sports event sponsors. Now a number of other companies have become involved in event sponsorships, including beverage companies, airlines, telecommunications and financial services companies, and high-tech firms.

Figure 13–6 Annual sponsorship spending in North America by property ($ millions)

	1996	1997	1998	1999*
Sports	$3,540	$3,840	$4,556	$5,100
Entertainment tours and attractions	566	650	680	756
Festivals, fairs, events	512	558	612	685
Causes	485	535	544	630
Arts	323	354	408	460
Total	$5,426	$5,937	$6,800	$7,631

*Projected.

Many marketers are attracted to event sponsorship because it gets their company and/or product names in front of consumers. By choosing the right events for sponsorship, companies can get visibility among their target audience. For example, Clairol Canada signed a one-year, six-figure deal with the Canadian Football League in 2001 to help launch its new hair-colouring products for men. As one executive points out, "We're using the CFL and the Grey Cup to create excitement around hair colour and to make it more appealing to men, who may look at hair colour as something completely feminine. Also, Herbal Essences is targeted at men 15 to 25, and that's very much the target audience of the CFL and the Grey Cup." The deal includes national consumer promotion with in-store and media support. Other communications include on-field signage and in-stadium commercial messages during all playoff games, including the Grey Cup.[21]

Many companies are attracted to event sponsorships because effective IMC programs can be built around them and promotional tie-ins can be made to local, regional, national, and even international markets. Companies are finding event sponsorships an excellent platform from which to build equity and gain affinity with target audiences as well as a good public relations tool.

Most companies focus their marketing efforts on specific market segments and are always looking for ways to reach these target audiences. Many marketers are finding that sales promotion tools such as event marketing, contests and sweepstakes, and sampling are very effective ways to reach specific geographic, demographic, psychographic, and ethnic markets.

Event sponsorship has become a good public relations tool for reaching specific target audiences. Golf tournaments are a popular event for sponsorship by marketers of luxury automobiles and other upscale products and services. The golf audience is affluent and highly educated, and marketers believe that golfers care passionately about the game, leading them to form emotional attachments to brands they associate with the sport.

Canadian amateur athletes and semi-pro sports organizations have been working with marketers to develop sponsorships that benefit both parties. Alpine Canada Alpin (ACA), the governing body for the Canadian alpine ski team, generated $1.9 million in sponsorship deals representing 25 percent of its annual budget, compared to 16 percent from the public sector for the 2000–01 season. It signed deals with Wrigley Canada, General Motors, and Fido cellphones. The key success factor in landing these deals is the fact that World Cup ski races had TV audiences of over 30 million.[22]

A major issue that continues to face the event sponsorship industry is incomplete research. As marketers become interested in targeted audiences, they will want more evidence that event sponsorship is effective and is a good return on their investment. Measuring the effectiveness of event sponsorships is discussed in Chapter 17.

The Internet

The Internet has become a means by which companies and organizations can disseminate corporate advertising beyond tranditional media. Companies have used the Web to establish media, government, investor, and community relationships; deal with crises; and even perform corporate image, advocacy, and cause-related advertising. Companies have used their websites to address issues as well as to provide information about products and services, archive press releases, link to other articles and sites, and provide lists of activities and events. Other Internet tools, including e-mails and e-mail newsletters, have also been used effectively.

Shel Holtz notes that while there are many similarities between public relations activities conducted in traditional media and those conducted on the Internet, three main elements account for the differences between the two:

1. The Internet offers a more limited opportunity to gain attention due to short exposure times.
2. The Internet offers the opportunity to build internal links that provide the media with instant access to additional sources of information on the issue.

3. The Internet offers the ability to provide much more substantial information. Print and broadcast materials are confined by time and space limitations, while the Internet can literally provide volumes of information at a fingertip—or click of a mouse.[23]

Holtz also notes that while public relations activities are increasing on the Internet, and will continue to do so, PR people have been some of the slowest to adopt the new technology. However, as more and more media people and PR people gain confidence, the Internet will become a major source of public relations activities.

Strengths of Corporate Advertising

1. *It is an excellent vehicle for positioning the firm.* Firms, like products, need to establish an image or position in the marketplace. Corporate image ads are one way to accomplish this objective. A well-positioned product is much more likely to achieve success than is one with a vague or no image. The same holds true of the firm. Stop and think for a moment about the image that comes to mind when you hear the name IBM, Apple, Johnson & Johnson, or Procter & Gamble.

   Now what comes to mind when you hear Unisys, USX, or Navistar? How many consumer brands can you name that fall under ConAgra's corporate umbrella? (Swiss Miss, Wesson, La Choy, and many others.) While we are not saying these latter companies are not successful—because they certainly are—we are suggesting their corporate identities (or positions) are not as well entrenched as the identities of those first cited. Companies with strong positive corporate images have an advantage over competitors that may be enhanced when they promote the company overall.

2. *It offers some control that the message will be disseminated.* As the PR efforts of firms have increased, the attention paid to these events by the media has lessened (not because they are of any less value, but because there are more events to cover). The net result is that when a company engages in a public relations effort, there is no guarantee it will receive press coverage and publicity. Corporate image advertising gets the message out, and though consumers may not perceive it as positively as information from an objective source, the fact remains that it can communicate what has been done.

3. *It reaches a select target audience.* Corporate image advertising should not be targeted to the general public. It is often targeted to investors and managers of other firms rather than to the general public. It doesn't matter if the general public does not appreciate this form of communication, as long as the target audience does. In this respect, this form of advertising may be accomplishing its objectives.

Limitations of Corporate Advertising

1. *Questionable effectiveness.* There is no strong evidence to support the belief that corporate advertising works. Many doubt the data cited earlier that demonstrated a correlation between stock prices and corporate image advertising. A study by Bozell & Jacobs Advertising of 16,000 ads concluded that corporate advertising contributed to only 4 percent of the variability in the company's stock price, compared with a 55 percent effect attributable to financial factors.[24] A second study also casts doubts on earlier studies that concluded that corporate advertising worked.[25]

2. *Constitutionality and/or ethics.* Some critics contend that since larger firms have more money, they can control public opinion unfairly. This point was resolved in the courts in favour of the advertisers. Nevertheless, many consumers still see such advertising as unfair and immediately take a negative view of the sponsor.

Summary

This chapter examined the role of the promotional elements of public relations. Public relations is typically done through publicity generated through news media and corporate advertising. We noted that these areas are all significant to the marketing and communications effort and are usually considered differently from the other promotional elements. The reasons for this special treatment stem from the facts that (1) they are typically not designed to promote a specific product or service and (2) in many instances it is harder for the consumer to make the connection between the communication and its intent.

Public relations was shown to be useful in its traditional responsibilities as well as in a more marketing-oriented role. In many firms, PR is a separate department operating independently of marketing; in others, it is considered a support system. Many large firms have an external public relations agency, just as they have an outside ad agency.

In the case of publicity, another factor enters the equation: lack of control over the communication the public will receive. In corporate advertising, the organization remains the source and retains much more control. Publicity often takes more of a reactive than a proactive approach, yet it may be more instrumental (or detrimental) to the success of a product or organization than all other forms of promotion combined.

While not all publicity can be managed, the marketer must nevertheless recognize its potential impact. Press releases and the management of information are just two of the factors under the company's control. Proper reaction and a strategy to deal with uncontrollable events are also responsibilities.

Corporate advertising was described as controversial, largely because the source of the message is top management, so the rules for other advertising and promoting forms are often not applied. This element of communication definitely has its place in the promotional mix. But to be effective, it must be used with each of the other elements, with specific communications objectives in mind.

Finally, in this chapter we tried to illustrate that the public relations plan is put together much like the advertising or sales promotion plans.

Key Terms

public relations, 348
publicity, 349
video news release
    (VNR), 350
internal audiences, 354

external audiences, 354
marketing public
    relations, 356
press release, 357
press conference, 358

exclusive, 358
corporate advertising,
    360
image advertising, 361

advocacy advertising,
    363
cause-related
    marketing, 365
event sponsorships, 366

Discussion Questions

1. Discuss the advantages that the Internet offers for those responsible for conducting public relations activities. Describe how these activities are different than traditional methods.

2. Discuss some of the advantages associated with the use of marketing public relations (MPRs). What are some of the disadvantages?

3. Explain why traditional public relations practitioners might be unhappy with the organization's use of MPRs. Take a position as to whether this criticism is justified.

4. List and describe the advantages and disadvantages of the use of public relations in an IMC program. Provide an example of an appropriate use of public relations in this mix.

5. What is a video news release (VNR)? Provide an example of a situation in which a company might employ the use of a VNR. Discuss some of the ethical implications (if any) in using this tool.

6. Give examples of companies that are pursuing traditional public relations activities and those that are employing the new role.

7. Many companies are now taking the position that their charitable contributions should lead to something in return—for example, sales or increased visibility. Discuss the pros and cons of this position.

8. Many companies are now trying to generate as much free publicity as they can. Cite some examples of this, and discuss the advantages and disadvantages associated with this strategy.

Chapter Fourteen
Direct Marketing

Chapter Objectives

- To recognize the purpose of direct marketing as a communications tool.

- To appreciate the strategies and tactics involved in direct marketing.

- To demonstrate the use of direct-marketing media.

- To determine the scope and effectiveness of direct marketing.

Direct Marketing Goes Digital

When you hear the term direct marketing, how many of you think first about direct mail? If you do, it's most likely because direct mail has been the most prolific of direct-communications tools in our marketing history. As compared to other methods of direct marketing, Canadians most welcome direct mail, and pay more attention to it than any other medium (see Canada Post statistics later on in this text).

Many of you may be surprised to find out that the first direct-marketing tool in Canada came from the T. Eaton Company. They produced the first catalogue and relied on the horse and buggy or train to get the catalogues to forts and settlements across the country. Years ago, when catalogues became popular, many people thought retail stores would become extinct! As with other mediums, such as radio and TV, there was similar skepticism at first. These predictions did not come true, of course, and in fact, mediums such as TV, radio, and newspapers have never done so well as they have now that the Internet is around! Retail stores do well because of good direct-marketing strategies, and it is a fact that our best Internet businesses—that is the ones with longevity—have started as "bricks and mortar" companies and have added on the "clicks" (e-commerce Internet sites) to grow their businesses.

However, let's put our marketing communicators' hats on for a moment. Think about what the purpose of direct marketing *actually* is. "To communicate with our customers *directly,* that is, no middleman, no tool, or piece of technology acting in between you and your customer." The most pure form of direct marketing then is personal selling!

This is true, but now let's look at how we can pick out direct marketing among our media choices. For instance, when you think of the post office, you think of *direct mail.* (And perhaps "junk mail" also comes to mind!) Now think of the telephone, and *telemarketing* (and maybe the word "annoying") comes to mind, that is, someone soliciting to you directly on the phone, perhaps to donate to a fundraiser in your community or perhaps it's a multi-national automated phone device that kicks in when you pick up the phone. How about the television? Yes, *infomercials* are very successful today and have come a long way from the 30-second commercial that "slices and dices" with the 1-800 number tagged on to the bottom of the ad, along with the various credit cards you can use. Today, infomercials can be hour-long productions, and the various shopping networks are examples of one of the most successful direct-marketing sales enterprises. So, how about magazines and newspapers? *Direct response advertising,* which uses media like these to communicate to us directly as customers about products or services and asks us to respond *directly* to the company producing the ad. These ads, just like the TV ads we discussed, will ask you to call a 1-800 number, or to log on to their website, in order to contact them directly. Radio is another medium that can be used in direct marketing, although it is not as popular as others due to its very nature. That brings us to electronic media. We use fax machines and e-mail to communicate directly to our customers as well. Think of how many times you receive messages directly from a supplier on your e-mail, informing, reminding, and persuading you to take action of some kind.

That leads us to the Internet. Chapter 15 gives you an overview of this medium and its power as a marketing device. For now, though, let's look at how one person used direct marketing on the Internet to bring his small local e-commerce company in Sooke, on Vancouver Island, up from a local story to an international, award-winning success.

In 1995, Keith Waters, then a government Web programmer, was scribbling on a notepad, thinking about how his wife Cathy often talked about how tough it was to get out-of-print books for customers at her used bookstore in Victoria. He came up with Advanced Book Exchange Inc., or abebooks.com, where a small group of booksellers started to list about 5,000 used titles for sale in 1996. Now, in 2002, abebooks has almost 10,000 international booksellers listing 36 million used-book titles on a huge searchable database accessible from its website. It's the world's largest B2B (business-to-business) exchange, and the leading source for rare, out-of-print, and collectible books. The tremendous success has even taken the founders by surprise, says Waters, now abebooks CIO. "We hoped it would grow to about 1 or 2 percent of where it's at now," he says. "Now, with 10,000 booksellers, it's still growing, and it's still fun."

Basically, abebooks gives independent booksellers the technical, marketing, and business support they need to sell their books on the Internet, in exchange for a monthly fee based on the number of books they list on the site. By using the abebooks site, these small businesses can access a worldwide market and compete with the big booksellers. In November, the company, which employs 80 people, came up big at the Canadian Information Productivity Awards, the largest business awards program in Canada for information management. Abebooks won recognition as the best of show, the best e-commerce, and for excellence in information technology. *Forbes* magazine has rated abebooks as "best of the best" in the rare book category of its Internet awards, *Maclean's* magazine has recognized the e-commerce company, and the Boston Consulting Group has named it one of the most profitable dot-coms—putting it in the minority of 1990s start-up companies. The site has thousands of loyal customers and gets 1.5 million hits a day. There's no advertising at abebooks.com, and the focus of the site is an attractive, easy-to-use search function. Clients can choose to buy the books over the Internet, with abebooks handling the transaction, or to contact the bookseller directly.

Sources: "The rare-books biz goes hi-tech," *Vancouver Sun,* Saturday, March 23, 2002; Canada Post, Direct Marketing; Canadian Facts 2000.

As the lead-in to this chapter shows, the Internet has already become a powerful direct-marketing tool. But it is also important to realize that the Internet, like advertising and direct mail, is but one of the tools used by direct marketers. In this chapter, we discuss direct marketing and its role as a communications tool. Direct marketing is one of the fastest-growing forms of promotion in terms of dollar expenditures, and for many marketers it is rapidly becoming the medium of choice for reaching consumers. Stan Rapp and Thomas Collins, in their book *Maximarketing,* propose that direct marketing be the driving force behind the overall marketing program.[1] They present a nine-step model that includes creating a database, reaching prospects, developing the sale, and developing the relationship. We begin with an overview of direct marketing and then examine direct-marketing programs. The chapter concludes with a discussion of the strengths and limitations of this marketing tool.

Direct Marketing

While most companies continue to rely primarily on the other promotional mix elements to move their products and services through intermediaries, an increasing number are going directly to the consumer. These companies believe that while the traditional promotional mix tools such as advertising, and sales promotion, are effective in creating brand image, conveying information, and/or creating awareness. However, going direct with these same tools can generate an immediate behavioural response which makes direct marketing a valuable tool in the integrated communications program.

Defining Direct Marketing

As noted in Chapter 1, **direct marketing** is a system of marketing by which organizations communicate directly with target customers to generate a response or transaction. This response may take the form of an inquiry, a purchase, or even a vote. In his *Dictionary of Marketing Terms,* Peter Bennett defines direct marketing as:

> The total of activities by which the seller, in effecting the exchange of goods and services with the buyer, directs efforts to a target audience using one or more media (direct selling, direct mail, telemarketing, direct-action advertising, catalogue selling, cable TV selling, etc.) for the purpose of soliciting a response by phone, mail, or personal visit from a prospect or customer.[2]

First we must distinguish between direct marketing and direct-marketing media. As you can see in Figure 14–1, direct marketing is an aspect of total marketing— that is, it involves marketing research, segmentation, evaluation, and the like, just as our planning model in Chapter 1 did. Direct marketing uses a set of **direct-response media,** including direct mail, telemarketing, interactive TV, print, the Internet, and other media. These media are the tools by which direct marketers implement the communications process.

The purchases of products and services through direct-response advertising $51 billion in Canada during 2000.[3] Firms that use this marketing method range from major retailers such as Victoria's Secret to publishing companies to computer retailers to financial services. Business-to-business and industrial marketers have also significantly increased their direct-marketing efforts, as noted earlier.

The Growth of Direct Marketing

Direct marketing has been around since the invention of the printing press in the 15th century. Ben Franklin was a very successful direct marketer in the early 1700s, and Warren Sears and Montgomery Ward (you may have heard of these guys) were using this medium in the 1880s.

The major impetus behind the growth of direct marketing may have been the development and expansion of the Postal Service, which made catalogues available to both urban and rural dwellers. Catalogues revolutionized North American buying habits; consumers could now shop without ever leaving their homes.

	Ad Spending ($ 000's)	Sales Impact ($ 000's)
All media	9,369,259	51,192,316
Direct mail	1,872,507	16,050,887
Telephone marketing	2,837,118	16,146,281
Newspaper	1,109,262	7,182,170
Magazine	487,503	3,048,530
Television	1,579,419	4,349,055
Radio	549,256	1,806,043
Other	934,192	2,609,349

Source: CMA 2001 Market Fact Book.

Figure 14–1   2000 Direct marketing statistics

But catalogues alone do not account for the rapid growth of direct marketing. A number of factors in our society have led to the increased attractiveness of this medium for both buyer and seller:

- *Consumer credit cards.* There are a significant number of credit cards—bank, oil company, retail, and so on—in circulation in Canada. This makes it feasible for consumers to purchase both low- and high-ticket items through direct-response channels and assures sellers that they will be paid. Of course, not all of this will be through direct marketing, but a high percentage of direct purchases do use this method of payment, and companies such as American Express, MasterCard, and Visa are among the heaviest direct advertisers.

- *Direct-marketing syndicates.* Companies specializing in list development, statement inserts, catalogues, and sweepstakes have opened many new opportunities to marketers. The number of these companies continues to expand, creating even more new users.

- *The changing structure of our North American society and the market.* One of the major factors contributing to the success of direct marketing is that so many of us are now "money-rich and time-poor."[4] The rapid increase in dual-income families (in 1999, an estimated 60 percent of women were in the work force) has meant more income.[5] At the same time, the increased popularity of physical fitness, do-it-yourself crafts and repairs, and home entertainment have reduced the time available for shopping and have increased the attractiveness of direct purchases.

- *Technological advances.* The rapid technological advancement of the electronic media and of computers has made it easier for consumers to shop and for marketers to be successful in reaching the desired target markets. The majority of the 11 million households in Canada receive home shopping programs.

- *Miscellaneous factors.* A number of other factors have contributed to the increased effectiveness of direct marketing, including changing values, more sophisticated marketing techniques, and the industry's improved image. These factors will also ensure the success of direct marketing in the future. Figure 14–2 shows us just how much direct marketing is growing in Canada.[6] Of the various advertising methods shown in this chart, all but

Figure 14–2 Direct marketing growth in Canada

Projected change in frequency of using various media (% of advertisers)				
	More	Less	About the Same	Net Projected Increase
Web site	65	4	22	+61
Addressed direct mail	37	7	41	+30
E-mail advertising/messages	33	9	30	+24
Newspapers	23	12	58	+11
Magazines	25	17	49	+ 8
Radio	21	14	54	+ 7
Television	17	12	57	+ 5
Banner ads	18	11	45	+ 7
Telemarketing	18	14	39	+ 4
Free standing inserts in newspapers	17	14	50	+ 3
Transit	10	13	49	– 3
Direct response television	5	11	47	– 6

Source: Canadian Facts, 2000.

direct-response television and transit advertising have a positive net projected increase in usage. Notice that Web site usage, direct mail, and e-mail advertising are all on a steep growth rate.

While some organizations rely on direct marketing solely to generate consumer response, in many others, direct marketing is an integral part of the IMC program. They use direct marketing to achieve goals other than sales goals and to integrate it with other program elements. We first examine the role of direct marketing in the IMC program and then consider its more *traditional* role.

The Role of Direct Marketing in the IMC Program

Long the stepchild of the promotional mix, direct marketing is now becoming an important component in the integrated marketing programs of many organizations. In fact, direct-marketing activities support and are supported by other elements of the promotional mix.

Combining Direct Marketing with Advertising
Obviously, direct marketing is in itself a form of advertising. Whether through mail, print, or TV, the direct-response offer is an ad. It usually contains a 1-800 or 1-900 number or a form that requests mailing information. Sometimes the ad supports the direct-selling effort. For example, Victoria's Secret runs image ads to support its store and catalogue sales. Direct-response ads or infomercials are also referred to in retail outlet displays.

Combining Direct Marketing with Public Relations
As you will see later in this text, public relations activities often employ direct-response techniques. Private companies may use telemarketing activities to solicit funds for charities or cosponsor charities that use these and other direct-response techniques to solicit funds. Likewise, corporations and/or organizations engaging in public relations activities may include 1-800 numbers or website addresses in their ads or promotional materials.

Combining Direct Marketing with Personal Selling
Telemarketing and direct selling are two methods of personal selling. Non-profit organizations such as charities often use telemarketing to solicit funds. For-profit companies are also using telemarketing with much greater frequency to screen and qualify prospects (which reduces selling costs) and to generate leads. Direct-mail pieces are often used to invite prospective customers to visit auto showrooms to test-drive new cars; the salesperson then assumes responsibility for the selling effort.

Combining Direct Marketing with Sales Promotions
How many times have you received a direct-mail piece notifying you of a sales promotion or event or inviting you to participate in a contest or sweepstakes? Ski shops regularly mail announcements of special end-of-season sales. Whistler Ski Resort and Intrawest constantly mail out and send e-mail promotions to their customer database

Exhibit 14–1 Direct marketers cross-promote with sales promotions

announcing promotional and seasonal vacation packages, room rates, and lift ticket specials. The Bay, Sears, and other retail outlets call their existing customers to notify them of special sales promotions. Each of these is an example of a company using direct-marketing tools to inform customers of sales promotions. In turn, the sales promotion event may support the direct-marketing effort. Databases are often built from the names and addresses acquired from a promotion, and direct mail and/or telemarketing calls follow. Exhibit 14–1 shows how Carol Wright, a direct mail promotion firm, participated with the Daytime Emmy Awards Show, combining its sales promotion with a direct marketing campaign.

Direct Marketing Program Plan

To successfully implement direct-marketing programs, companies must make a number of decisions. As in other marketing programs, they must determine (1) what the program's objectives will be; (2) which markets to target (through the use of a list or marketing database); and (3) what direct-marketing media strategy will be employed.

Direct-Marketing Objectives

Exhibit 14–2
Saskatchewan and Newfoundland encourages visits through direct mail

The direct marketer seeks a direct response. The objectives of the program are normally behaviours—for example, test-drives, votes, contributions, and/or sales. A typical objective is defined through a set response, perhaps a 2 to 3 percent response rate.

Not all direct marketing seeks a behavioural response, however. Many organizations use direct marketing to build an image, maintain customer satisfaction, and inform and/or educate customers in an attempt to lead to future actions. Exhibit 14–2 shows how the provinces of Saskatchewan and Newfoundland use direct mail to encourage travel.

Developing a Database

As we have discussed throughout this text, market segmentation and targeting are critical components of any promotional program. Direct-marketing programs employ these principles even more than others, since the success of a direct-marketing program is in large part tied to the ability to reach a very significant target audience. Research by the U.S. Postal Service showed that 65 percent of the companies surveyed rely on their internal databases for marketing purposes.[7] To segment and target their audiences, direct marketers use a **database,** a listing of

customers and/or potential customers. This database is a tool for **database market-ing**—the use of specific information about individual customers and/or prospects to implement more effective and efficient marketing communications.[8]

The database marketing effort must be an integral part of the overall IMC program. At the very least, this list contains names, addresses, and postal codes; more sophisticated databases include information on demographics and psychographics, purchase transactions and payments, personal facts, neighbourhood data, and even credit histories (see Figure 14–3). This database serves as the foundation from which the direct-marketing programs evolve. Databases are used to perform the following functions:[9]

- *Improving the selection of market segments.* Some consumers are more likely to be potential purchasers, users, voters, and so on than others. By analyzing the characteristics of the database, a marketer can target a greater potential audience. For example, catalogue companies have become very specialized. Companies such as Lands' End, Sears, and The Gap, have culled their lists and become much more efficient, targeting only those who are most likely to purchase their products.

- *Stimulate repeat purchases.* Once a purchase has been made, the customer's name and other information are entered into the database. These people are proven direct-marketing users who offer high potential for repurchase. Magazines, for example, routinely send out renewal letters and/or call subscribers before the expiration date. Blockbuster Entertainment helps its video-rental customers select movies and locate additional Blockbuster locations. Companies from window cleaners to carpet cleaners to car dealers build a base of customers and contact them when they are "due" to repurchase.

- *Cross-sell.* Customers who demonstrate a specific interest also constitute strong potential for other products of the same nature. For example, the National Geographic Society has successfully sold globes, maps, videos, travel magazines, and an assortment of other products to subscribers who obviously have an interest in geography and/or travel. Likewise, Victoria's Secret has expanded its clothing lines primarily through sales to existing customers, and Kraft–General Foods has successfully cross-sold products in its varied food line. Upon responding to the direct-mail piece sent by Hertz (Exhibit 14–3), you are asked for your permission for Hertz to provide your

Consumer Database	Business-to-Business Database
Name	Name of company/contact/decision maker(s)
Address/Postal code	Title of contact
Telephone number	Telephone number
Length of residence	Source of order/inquiry or referral
Age	Credit history
Gender	Industrial classification
Marital status	Size of business
Family data (number of children, etc.)	Revenues
Education	Number of employees
Income	Time in business
Occupation	Headquarters location
Transaction history	Multiple locations
Promotion history	Purchase history
Inquiring history	Promotion history
Unique identifier	Inquiry history
	Unique identifier

Figure 14–3 Contents for a comprehensive database

Exhibit 14–3 Hertz seeks permission to use receivers' names

name to its parent company, Ford, and others, and to allow Hertz to send you information on other products and services.

Numerous other companies have established comprehensive databases on existing and potential customers both in North America and internationally. Database marketing has become so ubiquitous that many people are concerned about invasion of privacy. Direct marketers are concerned as well. The Direct Marketing Association (DMA), the trade association for direct marketers, the Canadian Marketing Association (CMA), and the Canadian Advertising Foundation (CAF) have asked its members to adhere to ethical rules of conduct in their marketing efforts. They point out that if the industry does not police itself, the government will.

Sources of Database Information   There are many sources of information for direct-marketing databases:

- *Statistics Canada.* Census data provide information on almost every household in Canada. Data include household size, demographics, income, and other information.
- *Canada Post.* Postal codes provide information on both household and business locations.
- *List services.* Many providers of lists are available. The accuracy and timeliness of the lists vary.
- *Info Canada.* Provincial Business Directory provides information regarding business lists. Published by province, Direct Mail List Rates and Data contains thousands of list selections
- *Marketing research houses.* Large research houses conduct annual studies of customers who buy at home via mail or telephone. They compile information on total orders placed, types of products purchased, demographics, and purchase satisfaction, among others.
- *Direct Marketing Association.* The direct marketers' trade organization promotes direct marketing and provides statistical information on direct-marketing use. The DMA's *Fact Book of Direct Marketing* contains information regarding use, attitudes toward direct marketing, rules and regulations, and so forth.
- *Others.* The Canadian Marketing Association, Dunn and Bradstreet, Fortune 500, *The Book of Lists,* and other published periodicals of this nature all contain listed information that can be used for these purposes.

Consumer-goods manufacturers, banks, credit bureaus, retailers, charitable organizations, and other business operations also sell lists and other selected information. Companies can build their own databases through completed warranty cards, surveys, and so on.

Determining the Effectiveness of the Database While many companies maintain a database, many do not use them effectively. Collecting names and information is not enough; the list must be kept current, purged of old and/or inactive customers, and updated frequently. The more information about customers that can be contained in the database, the more effective it will be. The Postal Service recommends an **RFM scoring method** for this purpose.[10] RFM stands for the recency, frequency, and monetary transactions between the company and the customer. More specifically, data need to be entered each time there is a transaction so that the company can track how recently purchases have been made, how often they are made, and what amounts of money are being spent. In addition, tracking which products and/or services are used increases the ability for databases to conduct the activities previously mentioned in this section. By analyzing the database on a regular basis, the company or organization can identify trends and buying patterns that will help it establish a better relationship with its customers by more effectively meeting their needs.

Direct-Marketing Media Strategy

As with all other communications programs discussed in this text, marketers must decide the message to be conveyed, the size of the budget, and so on. Perhaps the major difference between direct-marketing programs and other promotional mix programs regards the use of media.

As shown in Figure 14–1, direct marketing employs a number of media, including direct mail, telemarketing, direct-response broadcasting, the Internet, and print. Each medium is used to perform specific functions, although they generally follow a one- or two-step approach.

In the **one-step approach,** the medium is used directly to obtain an order. You've probably seen TV commercials for products such as wrench sets, workout equipment, or magazine subscriptions in which the viewer is urged to phone a toll-free number to place an order immediately. Usually these ads accept credit cards or cash on delivery and give an address. Their goal is to generate an immediate sale when the ad is shown.

The **two-step approach** may involve the use of more than one medium. The first effort is designed to screen, or qualify, potential buyers. The second effort generates the response. For example, many companies use telemarketing to screen on the basis of interest, then follow up to interested parties with more information designed to achieve an order or use personal selling to close the sale.

Direct Mail Direct mail is often called junk mail—the unsolicited mail you receive. However, more advertising dollars continue to be spent in direct mail than in almost any other advertising medium—an estimated $1.9 billion in 2000.[11] Mail-order sales exceeded $16 billion in 2000 ($10 billion in the consumer market).[12] Statistics show that 64 percent of Canadians read addressed direct mail right away when it arrives. Another 23 percent of Canadians keep it to review later at a time more convenient to them.[13]

Direct mail is not restricted to small companies seeking our business. Respected large companies such as American Express, AOL, RBC (Royal Bank of Canada), and Air Miles have increased their expenditures in this area, as have many others. Canada 2000 Facts statistics show that the overall opinions of companies that use direct mail are more positive than for companies that use other direct marketing media. Sales through direct mail in the business-to-business market reached $6 billion in 2000.[14] Figure 14–4 shows how Canada Post views the advantages of using direct mail to promote your business.

Many advertisers shied away from direct mail in the past, fearful of the image it might create or harbouring the belief that direct mail was useful only for low-cost products. But this is no longer the case. For example, Porsche Cars North America, Inc., uses direct mail to target high-income, upscale consumers who are most likely

Figure 14–4   Canada Post
outlines the strengths of
marketing with direct mail

Market with direct mail

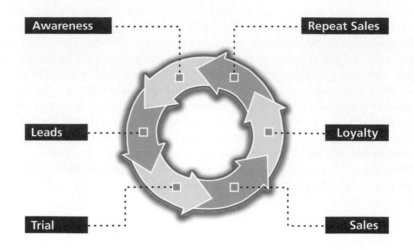

to purchase its expensive sports cars (Exhibit 14–4). In one example, Porsche developed a direct-mail piece that was sent to a precisely defined target market: physicians in specialties with the highest income levels. This list was screened to match the demographics of Porsche buyers and narrowed further to specific geographic areas. The direct-mail piece was an x-ray of a Porsche 911 Carrera 4 written in the language of the medical audience. This creative campaign generated one of the highest response rates of any mailing Porsche has done in recent years.[15] The materials shown in Exhibit 14–5 are just some of the ones sent by Mercedes to introduce its new sports

Exhibit 14–4   Porsche targets direct mail to upscale audiences

Exhibit 14–5   Mercedes used direct mail to introduce its new SUV

Consider a CD-ROM as Part of a Direct-Mail Campaign

More and more marketers who produce direct mail are leveraging the power of the Internet to employ a drive-to-Web strategy: using hard-copy direct mail as a catalyst for dialogue that takes place online. And while no one seems to disagree that online is a great place to generate dialogue, marketers continue to search for the Holy Grail of drive-to-Web. How can people move from the envelope to the keyboard?

One of the most overlooked tactics to achieve this transition is the CD-ROM. CD-ROMs came into fashion years ago. At the time, they were expensive to produce, and when consumers took to their computers, the payoff was marginal at best. And there was no Web beyond the CD to fully engage the customer. So the CD-ROM has become almost an afterthought in the wired world, conjuring up images of stick-figure animations and installation nightmares for consumers.

Nothing could be further from the truth. First, computing technology has grown exponentially, with more than 70-percent penetration rates across

Canada for consumers. For business people, it's virtually 100 percent. And the horsepower in those computers has delivered the promise of an easy-loading, fully engaging multimedia experience.

But too often marketers don't fully explore CD-ROMs, for two reasons:

1. *Too much focus on cost per piece.* Not enough focus is placed on return per piece. CD-ROMs are viewed as an expensive per-piece addition to a direct-mail campaign. The reality is that the inclusion of a CD-ROM can deliver significant lifts in response. When compared on an ROI basis, a CD-ROM can be one of the most cost-effective ways to lift response.

2. *Timeline pressure.* It takes time to think through and create a CD-ROM production. Even with existing content, the development of a CD-ROM is often longer than the relatively fast turnaround that printers are able to deliver these days.

VHS video is another method used by direct marketers to generate a lift in response, but the CD-ROM has its advantages over video. First, it has inherent interactivity that allows a customer to browse a catalogue, search for topics by interest, or make calculations. It is an easy-to-access, non-linear resource and is therefore more likely to be kept and used again. It can be easily outfitted with Web links to ensure that the dialogue continues, and those links can more easily be measured when directed to a specific URL. And it has the potential to save a bundle in postage.

Source: Adapted from John Peloza, "The CD-ROM as a Direct Tool," *Marketing Magazine,* April 29, 2002. Used with permission.

utility vehicle. Keys to the success of direct mail are the **mailing list**, which constitutes the database from which names are generated, and the ability to segment markets. Lists have become more current and more selective, eliminating waste coverage. Segmentation on the basis of geography (usually through postal codes), demographics, and lifestyles has led to increased effectiveness. The most commonly used lists are of individuals who have already purchased direct-mail products.

The importance of the list has led to a business of its own. It has been estimated that there are over 38 billion names on lists in North America, and many companies have found it profitable to sell the names of purchasers of their products and/or services to list firms. There are also a growing number of list-management companies springing up on the Internet. Canadian mailing lists by association or type of vocation are common. Companies such as www.interactdirect.com are more common now. While direct mail continues to be a favourite medium of many advertisers, and projections are that the market will continue to grow strongly over the next few years, this medium has been seriously threatened by the Internet. Between 1995 and 2000, direct-mail expenditures rose at the rate of 2.2 percent per year, while Internet expenditures increased at the rate well over 100%. Interestingly, the Internet is both a threat and an opportunity, as Internet companies have increased their expenditures in direct mail to drive potential customers to their sites. Nevertheless, the direct-mail business has experienced lower response rates from customers than in the past and has seen many advertisers shift dollars from this medium to the Net.[16] Many companies, particularly in the business-to-business market, have shifted from print to online catalogues, and legal problems have also hurt the industry.

Catalogues   Major participants in the direct-marketing business include catalogue companies. The number of catalogues mailed and the number of catalogue shoppers have increased significantly.

Many companies use catalogues in conjunction with their more traditional sales and promotional strategies. For example, companies such as Ikea, Canadian Tire, and Sears sell directly through catalogues but also use them to inform consumers of product offerings available in the stores. Some companies rely solely on catalogue sales. Others that started out exclusively as catalogue companies have branched into retail outlets, among them Lands' End and Banana Republic. L.L. Bean recently opened a superstore on the East Coast. The brand positioning statement for L.L. Bean is its "100% guarantee." The website and catalogues reach customers all over the world. The firm's computers track what each customer is buying, so new catalogues are mailed out directly to the people most interested in its products. Customers can order online 24 hours a day, or they can call the 1-800 toll-free line if they need advice. Their customer service phone line is staffed 24/7 so that the firm can solve any problem before it disrupts the CRM (customer service relationship).[17]

As you can see by the following examples, the products being offered through this medium have reached new heights as well:

- Victoria's Secret featured a $1 million Miracle Bra in its Christmas catalogue. Modelled by supermodel Claudia Schiffer, the bra contained over 100 carats of real diamonds as well as hundreds of semiprecious stones.
- Saks' Holding Co., a division of Saks Fifth Avenue, offered a pair of Mercedes-Benz convertibles in a catalogue, with bidding to start at $50,000.
- Hammacher Schlemmer featured a $43,000 taxicab and a $34,000 train set in its Christmas catalogue.

In addition to the traditional hard copies, catalogues are now available on the Internet for both consumer and business-to-business customers. In some instances in the consumer market, the catalogue merchandise is available in retail stores as well. In others, the catalogue and retail divisions are treated as separate entities. For example, if you purchase through the Eddie Bauer catalogue, you can exchange or return the merchandise to the retail stores. Victoria's Secret products, on the other hand, must be returned to the catalogue department. At the Gap, the catalogue is used to supplement the inventory in stock, and phone orders for different sizes and so on can be made from the store and shipped for free.

Broadcast Media   The success of direct marketing in the broadcast industry has been truly remarkable; over 77 percent of the U.S. population report that they have viewed a direct-response appeal on TV.[18] Direct-response TV generated around $4.4 billion in sales in 2000. Advertising expenditures amounted to $1.6 billion in 2000.[19]

Two broadcast media are available to direct marketers: television and radio. While radio was used quite extensively in the 1950s, its use and effectiveness have dwindled substantially in recent years. Thus, the majority of direct-marketing broadcast advertising now occurs on TV, which receives the bulk of our attention here. It should be pointed out, however, that the two-step approach is still very common on the radio, particularly with local companies.

Direct marketing in the broadcast industry involves both direct-response advertising and support advertising. In **direct-response advertising,** the product or service is offered and a sales response is solicited, through either the one- or two-step approach previously discussed. Examples include ads for magazine subscriptions, CDs and tapes, and tips on football or basketball betting. Toll-free phone numbers are included so that the receiver can immediately call to order. **Support advertising** is designed to do exactly that—support other forms of advertising. Ads for Publishers Clearing House or Reader's Digest or other companies telling you to look in your mailbox for a sweepstakes entry are examples of support advertising.

Direct-response TV encompasses a number of media, including direct-response TV spots like those just mentioned, infomercials, and home shopping shows (teleshopping). And Internet-TV has recently been introduced.

Infomercials   The lower cost of commercials on cable and satellite channels has led advertisers to a new form of advertising. An **infomercial** is a long commercial that ranges from 3 to 60 minutes. (Most are 30 minutes long, though the 5-minute format is gaining in popularity.) Many infomercials are produced by the advertisers and are designed to be viewed as regular TV shows. Consumers dial a 1-800 or 1-900 number to place an order. Programs such as "Liquid Luster," "Amazing Discoveries," and "Stainerator" (the so-called miracle-product shows) were the most common form of infomercial in the 1980s. While this form of show is still popular, the infomercial industry has been adopted by many big, mainstream marketers (Exhibit 14–6). Apple Computer, Microsoft, Sony, Volvo, and Philips Electronics are just some of the many others now employing this method of communication (Exhibit 14–7).

As to their effectiveness, studies indicate that infomercials get watched and sell products. Figure 14–5 shows the results of a study profiling infomercial viewers and buyers. It demonstrates that this advertising medium is indeed effective with a broad demographic base, not significantly different from the infomercial non-shopper in age, education, income, or gender.[20] There are also a number of differences between infomercial shoppers and non-shoppers, as this figure shows. Retail stores are benefiting from infomercials as well, as brand awareness leads to increased in-store purchases.[21]

TV Advertorials   In 1999, Peugeot took its first step into TV programming by developing a series of **advertorials** to show the public its entire model range. Peugeot is the first auto manufacturer to use TV advertorials. The company developed eight 5-minute films positioning the autos as "The Drive of Your Life" while providing comprehensive information on test-drives, technical specifications, and demonstrations. In addition, the auto company developed advertorials for its website, with each advertorial targeted to different target audiences.[22]

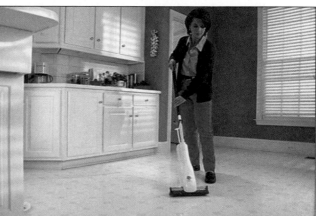

Exhibit 14–6   Dirt Devil uses infomercials to sell its products

Exhibit 14–7   Volvo uses an infomercial to attract buyers

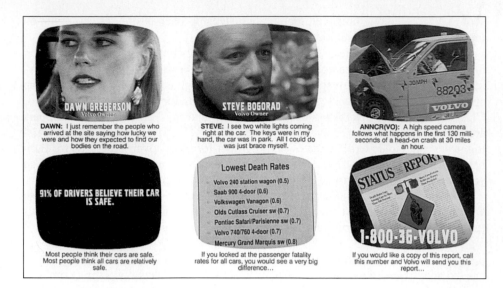

Teleshopping   The development of toll-free telephone numbers, combined with the widespread use of credit cards, has led to a dramatic increase in the number of people who shop via their TV sets. Jewellery, kitchenware, fitness products, insurance, compact discs, and a variety of items are now promoted (and sold) this way. The two major shopping channels in the United States (QVC and the Home Shopping Network [HSN]), account for over $3.4 billion worth of sales, though there are indications that this medium may have reached maturity. Sales at HSN are declining, while the sales of the others are increasing less than forecasted.

Figure 14–5   Here's who's watching (and buying from) infomercials

Hypothesis Number: Construct	Infomercial Shopper (n = 84)	Infomercial Nonshopper (n = 284)	Difference Significant at the 0.05 Level?
H1: Age[a]	2.6	2.8	N
H1: Education[b]	2.4	2.2	N
H1: Income[c]	2.8	2.7	N
H1: Gender[d]	1.4	1.5	N
H2: Importance of convenience	4.2	2.8	Y[e]
H3: Brand consciousness	3.5	3.0	Y[e]
H4: Price consciousness	4.1	3.6	Y
H5: Variety-seeking propensity	3.9	3.0	Y
H6: Impulsiveness	3.2	2.6	Y
H7: Innovativeness	3.8	3.0	Y
H8: Number of hours per week spent watching television	20	14	Y
H9: Risk aversion	2.1	3.5	Y
H10: Attitude toward shopping	1.8	3.1	Y
H11: Attitude toward direct marketing	3.1	2.1	Y
H12: Attitude toward advertising	3.5	2.9	Y

[a]Age: 1 = <20; 2 = 20–35; 3 = 36–50; 4 = 51–65; 5 = >65.
[b]Education: 1 = some school; 2 = high school diploma; 3 = some college; 4 = college degree; 5 = post-graduate degree.
[c]Income: 1 = <$15K; 2 = $15–30K; 3 = $31–45K; 4 = $46–60K; 5 = >$60K.
[d]Gender: 1 = female; 2 = male.
[e]Significant in opposite direction as hypothesized.

IMC Perspective 14-2
The ABCs of Direct-Response TV

Direct-response television (DRTV) is hot. More and more advertisers, including a large number of blue-chip companies, are using short-form DRTV and infomercials to market their products and services. That's the good news.

The bad news is that a lot of what passes for DRTV is not DRTV at all. They are more like brand commercials with a 1-900 number stuck on the end. That's fine for those who are satisfied with generating a couple of phone calls. However, for those advertisers interested in producing DRTV commercials that make the phones sit up and sing, here are some rules to making powerful, profitable direct-response commercials and infomercials.

- *The more you tell, the more you sell.* The most important thing to understand about DRTV is that each commercial needs to function as a complete, stand-alone sales presentation. That means that by the end of your spot, the viewer must have enough information to feel comfortable making a purchasing decision. It's your job to give them that information. That means presenting as many features and benefits, answering as many questions, and overcoming as many objections as possible in the allotted time. Don't cheat yourself out of a sale by leaving valuable information out of your spot.

- *The product is King, Queen, and Supreme Ruler.* Don't waste a second of precious air time talking about anything except your product or service. Creative concepts that are not about extolling the virtues of your product or service are a waste of time.

- *Focus groups will kill your commercial.* Focus groups will happily tell you what they like or don't like about your DRTV commercial. Unfortunately, what they like or don't like in a commercial has nothing to do with what makes them buy from a commercial. Never confuse what a viewer likes with what makes them pick up the phone and buy. Save your money and skip the focus groups.

- *Show your product.* TV is not a store or a show-room. The viewer can't reach up and squeeze the Charmin and then take that shiny new SUV out for a test drive. You're going to have to show how beautiful and irresistible your product really is. And by the way, with a little imagination you can also "show" intangible products or services, such as long distance, financial planning, or even political ideas.

- *Demonstrate your product.* Beauty shots are critical, but the viewer also needs to see your product or service in action. Remember this: Dynamite demonstrations have sold more products than any other DRTV technique. They captivate an audience and fuel the desire to purchase.

- *Use graphics to reinforce key selling messages.* Study after study has concluded that people understand and recall information better when they hear it *and* see it. Therefore, make sure that all the key selling points are also written on the screen as graphics at the exact same time as they are being spoken by the talent.

- *Include a powerful offer.* It is not absolutely essential to have an offer, but keep in mind that a good offer can transform an okay commercial into a runaway bestseller. Offers work because they make the viewer think about the cost of not acting, and nobody wants to miss out on a great deal. The better the offer, the better the response.

- *Value is in the mind of the viewer.* The effectiveness of your offer depends upon its *perceived* rather than its *real* value. That is why so many effective DRTV offers include inexpensive bonus items that boost the perceived value of the offer.

- *Testimonials work.* Consumers respond to hearing other consumers talk about how wonderful a product or service is and how much they love it. Especially if they happen to mention how skeptical they were before they tried it. To find out how well testimonials work, just try doing a successful infomercial without them.

- *The script is everything.* If you haven't already noticed, DRTV is a scriptwriter's medium. If the script is written properly, using proven, time-tested DR principles, the phones will sing. If the script is not written properly, your commercial will die a silent death.

Source: Adapted from Ian French, "Twenty-Four Ways to Dynamic DRTV", *Marketing Magazine,* February 11, 2002. Used with permission.

A number of reasons for the maturing of this market have been offered; many believe that the primary cause is a shift of existing customers to the World Wide Web and limited success in attracting new audiences.[23] To address this latter problem, QVC is pursuing international markets (including the United Kingdom, Canada, and Latin America) to follow up on its successes in Germany and Japan, partnerships (United signed on as official airline of the "Quest for America's Best" program), and sponsorships (for example, Geoff Bodine on the Nascar circuit).

Print Media

Magazines and newspapers are difficult media to use for direct marketing. Because these ads have to compete with the clutter of other ads and because the space is relatively expensive, response rates and profits may be lower than in other media. This does not mean these media are not used (as evidenced by the fact that expenditures total over $2 billion in 2000).[24] You're more likely to find them in specific interest areas such as financial newspapers or sports, sex, or hobby magazines.

Telemarketing

If you have a telephone, you probably do not have to be told about the rapid increase in the use of **telemarketing,** or sales by telephone. There are two types of telemarketing used by businesses. Outbound telemarketing refers to calls made by a company or its sponsor to a potential buyer or client, soliciting the sale of products, services, donations, votes, or any other "value" issue. Inbound telemarketing occurs when a company has advertised its 1-800 number or its website address, for example, asking the customer to call the number, visit the store, or log on to the website. There is usually some incentive connected with doing this, such as winning a gift, entering a contest, or receiving something for "free." Both profit and charitable organizations have employed this medium effectively in both one- and two-step approaches. Combined telemarketing sales (consumer and business-to-business) totalled over $16 billion in 2000—with $7 billion in the consumer market.[25] Telemarketing is a very big industry and employs over 156 thousand people.[26]

Business-to-business marketers such as Adobe Systems, Kaiser Permanente, and Hewlett-Packard are just a few of the many companies that use this direct-marketing medium effectively.

As telemarketing continues to expand in scope, a new dimension referred to as **audiotex** or **telemedia** has evolved. Tom Eisenhart defines telemedia as the "use of telephone and voice information services (900, 800, and 976 numbers) to market, advertise, promote, entertain, and inform."[27] Many telemedia programs are interactive. While many people still think of 900 and 976 numbers as rip-offs or "sex, lies, and phone lines," over 7,000 programs are carried on 900 numbers alone, including Tele-Lawyer, a legal information services organization; Bally's Health & Tennis Corp., the largest health-club chain in the U.S.; and NutraSweet. Figure 14–6 shows more specifically how 800/900 numbers are used as marketing tools.[28]

Problems associated with telemarketing include its potential for fraud and deception and its potential for annoyance. (Doesn't it seem as if every time you sit down to dinner you receive a phone call from someone trying to sell you something or asking for a donation?)

Those in the telemarketing and telemedia industry have responded to public criticisms. Dial-a-Porn and its ilk hold a diminishing share of 800, 900, and 976 offerings. As more and more large companies use telemedia, its tarnished image will likely brighten up.

Electronic Teleshopping

Unlike infomercials and home shopping channels, which have relied on broadcast or cable TV, **electronic teleshopping** is an online shopping and information retrieval service accessed through personal computers. While we discuss e-commerce in detail in Chapter 15, it is important to reiterate that Internet shopping is a direct-response medium that traditional direct marketers are adding to their businesses as well. For example, QVC, the home shopping channel, has started iQVC, an Internet home shopping channel that complements its cable TV channel and adds incremental sales (the cable channel drives

Figure 14–6 The use of 800, 900, and 976 numbers in marketing

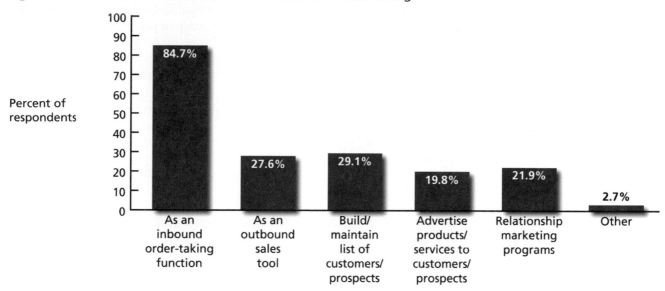

Note: *Direct* forecast survey was conducted by Jacobson Consulting Applications. The firms mailed a four-page questionnaire to direct-marketing executives, on an *n*th name basis from *Direct*'s circulation list. There were 565 responses.

customers to the website). The company was one of the first "Web department stores" to turn a profit.[29] Other direct marketers have met with less success, finding out the hard way that selling on the Internet requires different strategies. One such company, K-Tel, Inc., a highly successful direct-response TV marketer (Top 40 music, Veg-o-matic), has had much less success in adapting its traditional methods to the Web.[30] Statistics have shown that the most successful e-shopping enterprises are those that started as bricks-and-mortar companies first, and then went on to add e-commerce to their business. An article in the *National Post Business Magazine,* regarding Sears Canada and its slumping sales, says that "the last three years have proven that bricks-and-mortar retailers and cataloguers that leverage offline brands are best positioned to serve the e-commerce community." The article stated that the best strategy that Sears could adopt to recover its economic woes would be to "secure its online position and deepen relationships with its enormous customer base."[31]

E-Mail Marketing   **E-mail marketing** is one of the fastest growing forms of direct marketing over the last 5 years, showing a net projected growth rate in usage by advertisers of about 24 percent in 2001 in Canada.[32] As this form of direct marketing on the Internet is discussed in Chapter 15, we will refer you to that chapter for more information. It is important, though, to reiterate that since the growth of electronic communication through the Internet and e-commerce is projected at over 60 percent in 2002 alone, the use of e-mail for marketing messages will continue to be important in a company's marketing planning.

Many of the strengths and limitations of direct marketing have already been presented. As we have done with other media, we now summarize these factors in a concluding section.

Evaluation of Direct Marketing

Strengths of Direct Marketing

1. *Selective reach.* Direct marketing lets the advertiser reach a large number of people and reduces or eliminates waste coverage. Intensive coverage may be obtained through broadcast advertising or through the mail. While not everyone drives on highways where there are billboards or pays attention to TV commercials,

Chapter Fourteen Direct Marketing

virtually everyone receives mail. A good list allows for minimal waste, as only those consumers with the highest potential are targeted. For example, a political candidate can direct a message at a very select group of people (those living in a certain postal code, or members of McGill University Alumni, or the Royal Vancouver Yacht Club say); in the same vein, a music club can target recent purchasers of CD players, or a medical software supplier can target all M.D.s in the medical association directories.

2. *Segmentation capabilities.* Marketers can purchase lists of recent product purchasers, car buyers, bankcard holders, and so on. These lists may allow segmentation on the basis of geographic area, occupation, demographics, and job title, to mention a few. Combining this information with the geocoding capabilities of Prizm or VALS (discussed in Chapter 2), marketers can develop effective segmentation strategies.

3. *Frequency.* Depending on the medium used, it may be possible to build frequency levels. The program vehicles used for direct-response TV advertising are usually the most inexpensive available, so the marketer can afford to purchase repeat times. Frequency may not be so easily accomplished through the mail, since consumers may be annoyed to receive the same mail repeatedly. Using frequency on Internet websites is also a less expensive method, although the response rates of interstitials, banners, and pop-ups are still less than in traditional media vehicles. All information seems to indicate that this will change, however, as we develop more sophisticated advertising methods on the Net.

4. *Flexibility.* Direct marketing can take on a variety of creative forms. For example, the Discovery Network sent 17-inch TV sets to media buyers through the mail. The only message accompanying the TV sets was one on the cord that said "Plug me in" and another on a videotape that read "Play me." Upon doing so, the recipient was greeted with a 7-minute promotional video. Direct-mail pieces also allow for detailed copy that provides a great deal of information. The targeted mailing of videotapes containing product information has increased dramatically, as companies have found this a very effective way to provide potential buyers with product information. Black & Decker, Whistler Ski Resort, and a variety of auto companies such as Mercedes Benz, have successfully employed this medium.

5. *Timing.* While many media require long-range planning and have long closing dates, direct-response advertising can be much more timely. Direct mail, for example, can be put together very quickly and distributed to the target population. TV programs typically used for direct-response advertising are older, less sought programs that are likely to appear on the station's list of available spots. Another common strategy is to purchase available time at the last possible moment to get the best price.

6. *Personalization.* No other advertising medium can personalize the message as well as direct media. Parents with children at different age levels can be approached, with their child's name included in the appeal. Car owners are mailed letters congratulating them on their new purchase and offering accessories. Computer purchasers are sent software solicitations. Graduating college students receive very personalized information that recognizes their specific needs and offers solutions (such as credit cards).

7. *Costs.* While the CPM for direct mail may be very high on an absolute and a relative basis, its ability to specifically target the audience and eliminate waste coverage reduces the actual CPM. The ads used on TV are often among the lowest-priced available, and a video can be delivered for less than $1 (including postage). A second factor contributing to the cost effectiveness of direct-response advertising is the cost per customer purchasing. Because of the low cost of media, each sale generated is very inexpensive.

8. *Measures of effectiveness.* No other medium can measure the effectiveness of its advertising efforts as well as direct response. Feedback is often immediate and always accurate. It is a lot easier and more efficient to count the number of "hits" on a Web campaign or e-mail promotion, or to count the number of

coupons returned through a direct-mail campaign, or the number of 1-800 number callers.

Limitations of Direct Marketing

1. *Image factors.* As we noted earlier, the mail segment of this industry is often referred to as junk mail. Many people believe unsolicited mail promotes junk products, and others dislike being solicited. Even some senders of direct mail, including Motorola, GM, and Air Products & Chemicals, say they throw out most of the junk mail they receive. This problem is particularly relevant given the increased volume of mail being sent. (One study estimates the typical customer receives 14 pieces of junk mail per week.)[33]

   Likewise, direct-response ads on TV are often low-budget ads for lower-priced products, which contributes to the image that something less than the best products are marketed in this way. (Some of this image is being overcome by the home shopping channels, which promote some very expensive products.) Using the fax machine as a direct-response promotional media choice is unwelcome with most businesses, and the use of e-mail to promote without permission is considered SPAM and can hurt your company virally (through word of mouth).

2. *Accuracy.* One of the advantages cited for direct mail and telemarketing was targeting potential customers specifically. But the effectiveness of these methods depends on the accuracy of the lists used. People move, change occupations, and so on, and if the lists are not kept current, selectivity will decrease. Computerization has greatly improved the currency of lists and reduced the incidence of bad names; however, the ability to generate lists is becoming a problem.[34] Make sure with any list you use that it is current, with correct names, spelling, and titles, especially if using any business lists.

3. *Content support.* In our discussion of media strategy objectives in Chapter 8, we said that the ability of magazines to create mood contributes to the overall effectiveness of the ads they carry. In direct-response advertising, mood creation is limited to the surrounding program and/or editorial content. Direct mail, telephone, and online services are unlikely to create a desirable mood. Using professionals to write direct-mail copy, script writing for telemarketing, or graphics technology for Internet marketing is a wise move.

Summary

This chapter introduced you to the rapidly growing field of direct marketing, which involves a variety of methods and media beyond direct mail and telemarketing. The versatility of direct marketing offers many different types of companies and organizations a powerful promotional and selling tool.

Direct marketing continues to outpace other advertising and promotional areas in growth; many of the Fortune 500 companies now use sophisticated direct-marketing strategies. Database marketing has become a critical component of many marketing programs.

Advantages of direct marketing include its selective reach, segmentation, frequency, flexibility, and timing. Personalized and custom messages, low costs, and the ability to measure program effectiveness are also advantages of direct-marketing programs.

At the same time, a number of disadvantages are associated with the use of direct marketing. Image problems, the proliferating sale and use of databases (some of them based on inaccurate lists), lack of content support, and the intrusive nature of the medium make some marketers hesitant to use direct-marketing tools. However, self-policing of the industry and involvement by large, sophisticated companies have led to significant improvements. As a result, the use of direct marketing will continue to increase.

Key Terms

Discussion Questions

1. Identify some of the factors that have contributed to the growth of direct marketing. Do you see these factors being as relevant today? Discuss why or why not, and the impact they will have on direct marketing in the future.

2. Explain how a consumer goods company might employ database marketing. A business-to-business company? A service company?

3. The catalogue has become an important part of the shopping lives of many consumers. Describe different groups that you think might find catalogues useful in the consumer market, and explain what aspects of catalogues would attract them to this medium.

4. One of the disadvantages associated with direct-marketing media is the high cost per exposure. Some marketers feel that this cost is not really as much of a disadvantage as is claimed. Argue for or against this position.

5. Why have companies such as Volvo, Cadillac, and General Motors increased their use of infomercials? Is this a wise strategy?

6. Give an example of how companies might use direct marketing as part of an IMC program. Provide examples of both consumer and business marketers.

7. Direct marketing has been beset by a number of problems that have tarnished its image. Discuss some of these and what might be done to improve direct marketing's image.

8. How might business-to-business marketers use telemarketing effectively?

Chapter Fifteen

Internet Marketing and Interactive Media

Chapter Objectives

- To explore the different ways the Internet is used to communicate.

- To review the strengths and limitations of the Internet and interactive media.

- To understand the role of the Internet and interactive media in an IMC program.

- To evaluate the effectiveness of communications through the Internet.

"Wired Young Canadians"—Internet Use in the 21st Century

Over 30 years ago, Stanford University and UCLA connected the first two computers to begin something called the Internet by logging in with the word "log." Born on September 2, 1969, on a room-size computer at UCLA, the Internet at that time was named ARPANET (Advanced Research Projects Agency Network) by the U.S. Department of Defense, which developed the network as a way to connect research agencies across the nation. Only about 15 people were there to witness the first connection—far fewer than today, when over 90 million are connected. E-mail—which allowed person-to-person connections rather than just computer-to-computer ones—was added in 1972, and the Internet began to catch on. In 1991, when the World Wide Web enabled businesses and consumers to connect to the network, the Internet really began to grow up. And grow up it did! No one could possibly have imagined how large it would become.

Now that we are in the 21st century, it seems as though everyone is on the Internet. In the business-to-business market, almost every company has a website. You would be hard-pressed to find a Fortune 1000 company—business-to-business or consumer—that doesn't have its own website, and individuals from movie stars to teenagers have their own home pages. In July 2001, Statistics Canada released information that showed that 60 percent of Canadian households had at least one person who used the Internet. Of the 15-to-24 age group, representing 4.1 million young Canadians, 85 percent are Internet users. Of the total respondents representing 24.6 million Canadians aged 15 and over, 53 percent use the Internet. As far as shopping on the Internet is concerned, about 1.5 million families spent over $1 billion shopping on the Internet in the year 2000 in Canada. That is double the number of families, and nearly triple the amount of dollars spent, from a year earlier. Despite the rapid growth in online shopping, however, it still represented a small portion of total consumer spending in Canada last year, which reached $591 billion. In the year 2000, the use of e-mail was ranked the number one online activity for Canadians aged 15 to 19. In 1998 in the United States, more e-mails (9.4 billion per day) were sent in the United States than first-class-mail pieces.

Consider some of the following websites:

- *www.careerclick.com.* This Canadian career site helps people find jobs in their specific fields of interest. By entering a key word or job category you can look at company profiles, discover who is hiring, find career fairs, and get help with resume building.

- *www.internetwineguide.com*. Want to shop for wine? How about joining a wine club? This world-wide e-commerce site sells wine, gives information on wine tasting, offers tips on wine tours, and has its own newsletter. By entering Canada under the country code search, you can specialize your search and purchase throughout Canada.
- *www.disney.com*. This is the Walt Disney Company's Disneyland on the Web. A good example of a dynamic marketing website, with a dominant brand identity, using the latest technology for superb visual and interactive use, attracting people of all ages to the site. The Web designers have made this site not only informative but also fun to surf for information and games. And it is a full service e-commerce site for merchandise and vacations.
- *www.bmwmovies.com*. This site features short interactive video-streaming action films using known actors, created by BMW. If you wish, from this site you can go directly to the main BMW site to customize your own vehicle.
- *www.ebay.ca*. Buy and sell virtually anything you want on this Canadian partner online e-commerce auction site.
- *www.google.ca*. This Canadian search engine portal is available in both English and French.
- *www.mustardweb.com*.Do you like mustard? Then check out this site. With history, recipes, and anything commercial to do with mustard alone, this quirky yet interesting site shows how segmented and targeted (or eccentric) we can get on the net!

And this is just a sampling. Literally millions of sites are out there selling every conceivable product and service you may think of in both the consumer market and the business market. In addition to this, government agencies have discovered the Web. If you are wondering where to start with government sites, the best place to begin is with the Government of Canada's main website, www.gc.ca. You can search by subject, by province, or by type of inquiry. For instance, in the "A to Z Index" you can find everything from Aboriginal programs and business sites to young-adult resources and internship programs. Try under the "B's" and you will find information on starting a business, business programs offered, financial sources, and business accounting as well as information you may not be too eager to seek such as Revenue Canada rules and guidelines for business.

Another site that offers in-depth information on a variety of subjects through the Government of Canada is www.strategis.ic.gc.ca. For instance, if you are looking to compare banking-service packages offered in Canada, look in Canada's Office of Consumer Affairs financial services charges. A calculator helps you identify the best banking package among 100 different accounts at 15 Canadian financial institutions. And finally, one last example for students is the website www.sedar.com. This site is Canada's electronic securities document filing system. As a student, this can be very helpful to you. If you need to do some research on a public company, which must be listed on the securities administration system, information such as new company filings, company profiles, annual reports, and press releases may all be contained in this website.

The current estimate of the number of websites out there is in the billions, and it perhaps could be larger due to the fact that many websites are not tracked. There were so many websites that, according to most estimates, major portals such as like Yahoo! and Lycos contain only about 16 percent of the total number of sites. There has been such a flood of registrations for domain names that .com listings are extremely difficult to get, and the .net listings are in limited supply as well. A great many new top-level domain names are emerging now and becoming more popular, for instance, .bus, .inc, and .shop are some examples. Each country is establishing its own domain names as well. Check out www.new.net to see some 30 different new domain names being offered, in six different languages.

Because so many companies have similar names, confusion and fraud are rampant. A number of companies have changed their names to avoid confusion, while others have changed them to more accurately express what they do. For example, InfoSeek became Go.com; computer site Onsale bought Egghead, and then changed its name to Egghead.com; and the Mining Co. search engine became About.com. Companies such as TradeZone.com and GreatDomains.com have developed successful businesses by specializing in the selling of domain names. Some entrepreneurial types have purchased domain names with the idea of auctioning them off, though this is becoming harder to do now due to new legislation aimed at protecting the established names of companies and their brands. The Internet Corporation for Assigned Names and Numbers (ICANN) is having a substantial effect on this issue. In November of 2001, the .info Country Names Discussion Group considered the disposition of 327 country names in the .info top-level domain.

When will the Internet stop growing? Not very soon, according to the experts. No one could have predicted way back in the era of Woodstock (the first one) that the Internet would be where it is today. And no one knows where it will be 30 years from now.

Sources: "Internet Use on the Cusp of the 21st Century," *Canadian Social Trends,* Statistics Canada, Winter 2001; " Online Shopping Soars to $1 Billion," Business Section, *Vancouver Sun,* October 24, 2001; "Networks," *Vancouver Sun,* January 31, 2002; ICANN Public Forum, March 13, 2002; Julie Tamaki, "Taxman Is Latest to Jump into Internet Auction Craze," *Los Angeles Times,* February 7, 2000, p. A3; Bradley Johnson, "Internet Turns the Big 30," *Advertising Age,* August 30, 1999, p. 28; Laurie Freeman, "Domain-Name Dilemma Worsens," *Advertising Age,* November 8, 1999, p. 100.

By now you probably don't have to be told about the incredible variety of websites that are on the Internet offering anything from advice to products or services that are given away or sold. As the lead-in to this chapter indicates, the World Wide Web (WWW) has become the most popular component of the Internet, and its growth shows no signs of slowing. Sources estimate that 85 percent of all college students use the Internet, with over 40 percent accessing it on a daily basis.[1] For many students, it has become their first source of information for everything from school research to travel planning. Interestingly, not everyone has been able to capitalize on the market potential of the Internet, including some of the more successful "brick and mortar" companies. Procter & Gamble, for example, has experienced problems with establishing a brand identity for its products on the Web, and Levi's abandoned its attempt to sell its jeans through the Internet. Companies have learned that merely putting up a home page does not guarantee success and that the strategies that have worked effectively in traditional markets do not necessarily transfer well to the Internet.

In this chapter, we will discuss the Internet, marketers' objectives and strategies for using the Net. As you will see, the Internet is a valuable component of the integrated marketing communications program and, like other components, is most effective when used in conjunction with other IMC elements.

Defining the Internet

Before beginning our discussion, it may be useful to establish some common ground. While all of us are familiar with the Internet, the degree to which we are familiar varies. Understanding the material presented in this chapter will be easier if you are familiar with the terms used in the discussion.

The **Internet** is a worldwide means of exchanging information and communicating through a series of interconnected computers. As noted, it was started as a U.S. Defense Department project, but it is now accessible to anyone with a computer and a modem. While the most popular component of the Internet is the **World Wide Web (WWW)**, there are other features as well, as shown in Figure 15–1. For marketers, a number of these features offer potential, but it is the Web that has developed as the commercial component. For that reason, the following discussion will focus on using the Web as a communications and sales tool. Before reading further, however, please take a few minutes to examine Figure 15–2 to familiarize yourself with some of the terms that we will be using. In reality, there are many more words that have been added to our language as a result of the growth of the Internet (you can also purchase a dictionary of Internet terms), but space permits only a small inclusion here. Thus, we have stayed away from the technical jargon, concentrating primarily on marketing communications terms. If you are in need of further terminology explanations, you may want to try the website www.techweb.com/encyclopedia/, with a database of more than 20,000 information technology terms.

For our purposes in this text, it is important to define the key terms in Internet business that may be confusing to many in the industry today—even the CEOs in major companies.

Figure 15–1   Features of
the Internet

Feature	Use
Electronic mail (e-mail)	Allows users to send electronic mail anywhere in the world
Usenet	Discussion groups, newsgroups, and electronic bulletin boards, similar to those offered by online services
Telnet	Online databases, library catalogues, and electronic journals at hundreds of colleges and public libraries
File transfer protocol (ftp) or hypertext transfer protocol (http)	The ability to transfer files from one mainframe computer to another
Client server	Allows for the transfer of files from one mainframe computer to another
Gopher	A document retrieval system used to search for information
Wide Area Information Server (WAIS)	Enables one to use keywords in specific databases and retrieve full text information
World Wide Web (WWW)	Does much the same thing as gopher and WAIS, but combines sound, graphic images, video, and hypertext on a single page; the commercial arm of the Internet

E-Business

E-business encompasses all business activities conducted electronically, which can include incorporating Internet technologies but also includes other forms of electronic means. The focus of e-business is to use the technology to manage day-to-day business processes such as online sales and marketing, manufacturing, inventory control, employees, distributors, vendors and partners, to name a few. The intent is to improve communication to better manage a company's value *chain*.

E-Commerce

Many people think that electronic commerce, or **e-commerce**, is exclusively the domain of the Internet. It is not! E-Commerce is simply a term for any kind of commercial activity that is electronically facilitated. Therefore, electronic commerce may include fax machines, banking machines, credit-card readers, or point-of-sale (POS) retail systems as well as the Internet to conduct transactions. According to U.S. Federal Standard 1032C from the Institute for Telecommunication Sciences, the term electronic commerce refers to "business transactions conducted by electronic means other than conventional telephone service, e.g., facsimile or electronic mail (e-mail)."

I-Commerce

Now that you can see from the above, that if *all financial transactions,* whether buying or selling, whether focused on the business-to-consumer market (B2C) or the business-to-business market (B2B) using electronic technology is called e-commerce, we can now define **i-commerce** as all those transactions done via the Internet. Many companies use the term e-commerce to define their Internet commerce, so don't be confused. The Internet and its terminology are evolving every day; by the time you read this textbook, much more will have evolved!

Internet Marketing

Picture all of the marketing functions that you have learned so far conducted on the Internet. If you were the Internet marketing director of a company, you would be

Figure 15–2   Internet
terminology

Term	Definition
Access	Visiting a website on the Internet from an individual computer (a client with a unique IP address). For example, you may have 10,000 accesses but from only 2,000 clients, because each client accessed an average of 5 pages. Therefore, you have 2,000 unique accesses.
Ad clicks	Number of times users click on an ad banner.
Ad click rate	Often referred to as "click-through," the percentage of ad views that result in an ad click.
Ad views (impressions)	Number of times an ad banner is downloaded (and presumably seen by viewers).
Banner	An ad on a Web page that may be "hot-linked" to the advertiser's site.
Button	An advertisement smaller than a traditional banner ad. Buttons are usually square in shape and located down the left or right side of the site; sometimes referred to as "tiles."
CPC	Cost per click—a marketing formula used to price ad banners. Some advertisers pay on the basis of the number of clicks a specific ad banner gets.
CPM	Cost per thousand for a site.
Domain name	The unique name of an Internet site. There are six domains widely used in the U.S.: .com (commercial), .edu (education), .net (network operations), .gov (U.S. government), .mil (U.S. military), and .org (organization). Additional two letter domains specify a country, for example, .sp for Spain.
Hit	Each instance in which a server sends a file to a browser. Hits are used to measure the traffic on a site.
Interstitial	An advertisement that appears in a window on your screen while you are waiting for a Web page to load.
Link	An electronic connection between two websites.
Opt-in-e-mail	List of Internet users who have voluntarily signed up to receive commercial e-mail about topics of interest.
Page views	Number of times a user requests a page that contains a particular ad; used to indicate the number of times an ad was potentially seen, or "gross impressions."
Permission marketing	An e-mail communications technique that sends out an e-mail message to a prospective customer asking permission to send them future correspondence, advertising, or news items.
Rich media	Advanced technology used in Internet ads, such as streaming video, which allows interaction and special effects.
Sneezing	To verbally tell someone about a new and interesting website. (See "Viral marketing.")
Spam	An e-mail marketing technique that sends out e-mail messages to prospective customers without their permission. It is considered an unacceptable method of communications because it has not been requested by the recipient and is therefore considered "e-junk" mail.
Sponsorships	The sponsoring of a site's content by an advertiser.
Unique users	Number of different individuals who visit a site within a specific time period.
Valid hits	Number of hits that deliver all the information to a user (excludes error messages, redirects, etc.)
Viral Marketing	A marketing approach that spreads like wildfire and has nothing to do with computer viruses. The term was coined by the venture capital firm Draper Fisher Jurveston of Redwood City, California, after its investment in Hotmail grew dramatically. Hotmail automatically places an advertisement at the end of everyone's e-mail message suggesting that they sign up for the free service. In a year and a half since beginning this practice, more than 12 million people became Hotmail users.
Visits	A sequence of requests made by one user at one site.

responsible for the planning and implementation of an Internet marketing plan that would include goals for sales and market growth. This plan would have a target audience strategy, a product assortment and service strategy, pricing strategies for the various market segments, distribution strategies that maximize the Internet customer's purchasing and delivery satisfaction, and of course, a communications strategy to reach those sales and market share goals. This, in a nutshell, is what **Internet marketing** encompasses.

Internet Marketing Communications

As with other media discussed earlier in this text, businesses that have websites require the development of an IMC (integrated marketing communications) plan that uses the Internet to help fulfill their marketing communication goals. This plan should consider target audiences (users of the Net), specific objectives and strategies, and methods for measuring effectiveness. To develop a successful Internet marketing communications strategy, all of the lessons learned so far in this text apply to the Internet as well.

Web Participants

The Web, like all other media, has both customers (users) and those trying to reach these users (advertisers, sponsors, e-commerce). As with other media, there are sites that are targeted to consumers (B2C) and sites in the business-to-business (B2B) market. Let's start our discussion with the users—the target markets.

Users: Consumer Market   As noted in the lead-in, the growth of the Internet has been phenomenal. By 1998, the number of people using the net had grown to 54 million in the United States and 95 million worldwide, with projections that it would increase to 282 million by the end of 2002.[2] Every annual projection is constantly being altered as more and more users come aboard. As shown in Figure 15–3, the adoption curve of the Internet greatly outpaces that of any other medium. A number of reasons have been offered to explain this rapid adoption. A long period of economic prosperity, Internet innovation, heavy investments by companies, and changing lifestyles of the consumer (consumers are now "money rich and time poor") have all contributed.

It's suspected that 2002 saw a further increase in the number of households shopping on the Internet, despite the implosion of the high-tech sector, and a possible

Figure 15–3   Adoption curves for various media—the Web is ramping fast

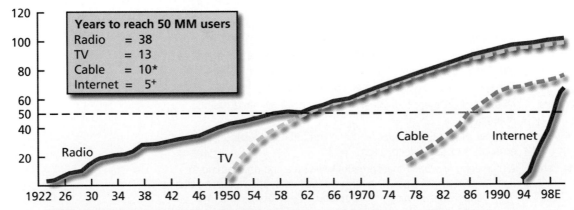

* The launch of HBO in 1976 was used to estimate the beginning of cable as an entertainment/advertising medium. Though cable technology was developed in the late 1940s, its initial use was primarily for the improvement of reception in remote areas. It was not until HBO began to distribute its pay-TV movie service via satellite in 1976 that the medium became a distinct content and advertising alternate to broadcast television.
+ Morgan Stanley Technology Research Estimate

reduction in e-retail outlets. Statistics Canada won't know for sure until the 2002 survey is complete, however, the dollar value of purchases soared despite a reduction in the number of businesses on the Net.[3]

The demographic profile of Internet users has changed as well. The principal characteristic is the well-documented fact that Internet use is greatly influenced by the socio-economic status of the household; that is, the households with higher incomes and higher levels of education are much more likely to own a computer and use the Internet.[4] For example, in Canada, only 30 percent of individuals with household incomes under $20,000 in 2000 had used the Internet, compared to 81 percent of individuals in households with incomes of $80,000 or more. Thirteen percent of adults 20 and over with less than a high school diploma used the Internet, whereas 79 percent of those with a university degree did so. Another important characteristic is that of age. Young people are far more enthusiastic surfers than people in their 60s and 70s. However, the growth of Internet use among the older population increased almost tenfold, from 1997 to 2000, with up to 77-percent use in the higher income brackets.

Shoppers   While Figures 15–4 and 15–5 reflect the profile of Internet "users" and their primary reasons for using the Net, the profile of Internet shoppers is slightly different. A study by Scarborough Research found that Internet users can be segmented into two distinct groups: (1) those 18 and over who shop on the Web, and (2) the "wired but wary"—those who use the Internet but do not shop there.[5] Those most prone to shop—who constitute approximately 25 percent of Internet users— are very upscale and have diverse Internet usage patterns. As noted by Bob Cohen, president of Scarborough Research, "E-shoppers clearly evidence a rich, active, and diverse lifestyle. The shoppers travel, attend sporting events, and engage in a variety of activities including swimming, biking, and photography. Because of their active lifestyles, they are attracted to the convenience offered by e-shopping."[6] People in the wired-but-wary segment also have active lives, and they tend to be more upscale than nonusers. Their characteristics are similar to those of the shoppers but not as pronounced. Their Internet usage is less diversified, and their primary motivation for using it is e-mail.

Whether the growth in Internet usage and e-commerce will slow or continue to grow at its current pace, it will account for a substantial amount of consumer spend-

What do you do when you go online?	1998	1997
Gather news or info	91.2%	87.8%
Send e-mail	88.2	83.2
Conduct research	79.4	80.5
Surf various sites	68.5	75.3
Shop	26.8	17.8
Post to bbs	22.7	30.0
Play games	21.8	33.7
Participate in chats	18.4	30.8
None of these	1.2	1.9
Have you purchased anything online in the past year?		
Yes	28.3%	23.5%
Have you used a credit card online?		
Yes	29.1%	

Figure 15–4   What users do online

Figure 15–5   Products purchased on the Internet; rating frequency of online buying

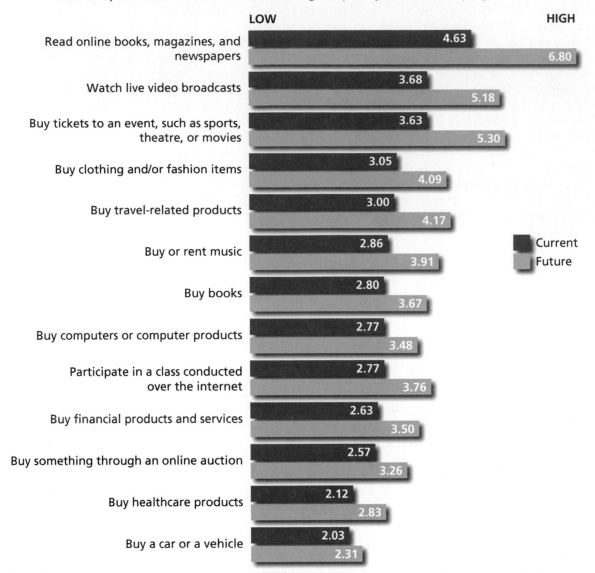

ing. The expectation is that consumer spending on the Internet will reach $184 billion by 2004.[7] These numbers make the Internet a medium to be reckoned with, and they offer strong potential to marketers.

Users: Business to Business   The consumer market figures may seem astronomical enough, but they pale in comparison to the figures on business-to-business marketing. While some consumer companies feel that a website is of little value, most business marketers consider it a necessity. A number of studies place the percentage of businesses (large and small) that have or soon will have websites at over 90 percent. The number of businesses online reached 6.3 million in 1999 and is expected to rise to 8.3 million by 2004, with over 100 million business-to-business decision makers online.[8] The revenue generated by these business sites is much higher than that generated in the consumer market—$4.7 billion in 1999, with projections of $2.7 trillion by the year 2004 (yes, that is a *t*!).[9] Businesses in the computer and electronics, shipping and warehousing, and utilities industries expect that by 2004 they will conduct over 70 percent of their transactions over the Internet. (So-called heavy industries like aerospace and defence are expected to transact less than 50 percent through this medium.)

Business-to-business marketers use the Internet in a variety of ways. Hewlett-Packard has budgeted over $100 million to target B2B users of its equipment.[10]

Cisco and Dell use the Web to track and distribute sales leads in real time, while others such as Scientific International train their sales representatives and host sales meetings via the Web as well as sell.[11] Cisco estimates that it saves $1 million per month by having sales meetings on the Web.[12] One of the main benefits for business-to-business marketers is the ability to acquire information about products and services. In today's Internet world, a company can immediately pull up the product and service offerings of a provider, without having to make a phone call or wait for a salesperson to visit. In turn, the same company can reach thousands of potential customers that it would not have been possible to reach without a website—at a significantly reduced cost. Ford and Delta Airlines may have started a new trend when they announced that all of their 350,000 and 72,000 employees, respectively, would be given free PCs for their home use. The reason? To allow them to connect to the Internet and to facilitate communications in their work as well as with other employees.[13]

Web-site Communication Objectives

When major corporations first began to conduct business on the Internet, they put up websites primarily for information purposes. Companies such as United Airlines and Maytag had sites that were really not much more than online catalogues designed for information purposes only. The role of the website quickly changed, however; sites have become much more creative, offering promotions, chat rooms, and even products and services for sale. With the introduction of Java in 1995, and now with Flash technology, it is possible to create fancier graphics, audio, and animation online.

Thus, the Internet is a communications medium, allowing companies to create awareness, provide information, and influence attitudes, as well as pursue other communications objectives. But it is also in part a direct-response medium, allowing the user to both purchase and sell products through e-commerce. We will discuss two sets of objectives pursued by companies that use the Internet. Let's first look at some of the communication objectives these companies want to achieve.

Build a Brand Image Why would Honda Motor Co., the auto giant, launch an interactive video game aimed at fickle Generation Xer's? The answer, in a word, is branding. The game, which launched in 2001, is just the latest effort by a big-name company to use online fun to build brand loyalty among tech savvy customers. Branded online games were born of the idea that companies can build consumer loyalty by associating their brands with entertainment, just as has been done with branded music videos and movies. The most popular branded gaming site is Candystand (www.candystand.com), an offshoot of Nabiscos's website, which offers more than 30 video games highlighting LifeSavers candy. During June of 2001 alone, 800,000 people visited Candystand at least once.[14]

Brand loyalty is still the most important aspect of any marketing strategy today. Look at how powerful Molson's newest Canadian pride commercial was with voters ("I AM CANADIAN"), giving it a 70 percent approval rating in the armchair critic weekly online survey![15] In pursuing brand recognition and loyalty on a website, companies are using a variety of advertising techniques that are explained further later in this chapter in the section, "Advertising on the Internet." Just as traditional advertising, company logos, brand characters, and packaging all are part of the brand strategy, the website itself should become part of the brand identity for the company. Look at any well-designed website, and chances are you will immediately know what the company brand and product line is all about. For example, check out the consumer site at www.kennethcole.com or the business-to-business site at www.xerox.com. Both of these are excellent examples of websites used for image building (Exhibit 15–1).

Disseminate Information One of the primary objectives for using the Web is to provide in-depth information about a company's products and services. In

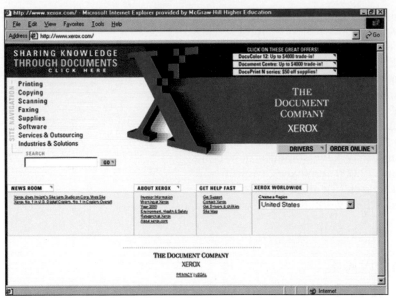

Exhibit 15–1 Xerox uses the Web to enhance their image

Exhibit 15–2 Cheerios uses their package to send users to their home page

business-to-business markets, having a website has become a necessity, as more and more buyers expect that a company will have a site providing them with detailed information about its offerings. In the government sector, contracts are often put out to bid on the Internet. Information regarding requirements, specifications, submission dates, and so on, is disseminated much quicker, to more potential candidates, and at a much lower cost via the Net than it is through other media. For many consumer companies, their websites serve as a means of communicating more information about their products and services. The Huggies site discussed earlier shows how a website can facilitate this objective, while the Cheerios box shown in Exhibit 15–2 demonstrates how General Mills refers users to its site for additional information.

Create Awareness Advertising on the Web can be useful in creating awareness of an organization as well as its specific product and service offerings. For small companies with limited budgets, the Web offers the opportunity to create awareness well beyond what might be achieved through traditional media. For example, a company in Los Angeles that distributed paper to business-to-business firms in the local market now conducts 80 percent of its business internationally as a result of posting its website. If you will recall the AIDA model covered in chapter 4 of this text, you can apply the same strategy to good website design. Here is an example of how this could work:

- Use a highly visual brand logo on your home page to get *attention.*
- Insert a vertical banner ad down one side of the page to attract the user's *interest,* perhaps a bold dollar sign, such as "$9.99—Online Trades."
- Follow with the words, "Open an account today," to create *desire.*
- Insert a bold link button at the bottom of the ad with text saying, "Click here!" to create *action.*

Gather Research Information The Web is used by marketers to gain audience profile information. This can be done through techniques such as **cookies**, which keep and store personalized information entered by a user. Companies use this information to establish and maintain relationships with their clients, to research the marketplace, and to gather competitive information. Surveys online are another example of gathering information on users and storing the data for future marketing initiatives. The amount of information collected about consumers—often without their knowledge—has become an issue for concern among many consumer and government groups. However, it must be recognized that any amount of information gathered through the Web is the same as if a consumer were filling out forms for a loyalty program, gas card, or retail-store card. In today's marketplace, the customer must be aware that anything he or she enters into a database of any kind, by hand or by using a smart card, can be stored and used for future promotional purposes.

Stimulate Trial and Re-Buy   Some websites offer electronic coupons in an attempt to stimulate trial of their products. Others, just through the frequency of their ads on the Web, encourage visits to their sites—for example, "Amazon.com" seems to appear on almost any page you access on a site (Exhibit 15–3). The ease of trying a site merely by clicking on a link is attractive to time-starved users, and items such as CDs and books have become big sellers as a result of this technique.

Exhibit 15–3   Amazon.com seems to appear everywhere on the Web

Improve Customer Service   By providing information, answering inquiries, and offering an opportunity to register complaints, many companies have found websites useful for improving customer service and building relationships. Some high-technology companies are now using their websites to present information that previously was provided in instruction manuals and by technicians at toll-free phone numbers. Other website techniques for better customer service are FAQs (frequently asked questions), e-mail response sections (many banks are now using this to answer customer queries about mortgage rate changes, balances, interest rates, RRSPs , and so on), and chat lines for easy access to a customer service representative. This last function must have dedicated personnel available on a 24/7 basis to make it effective.

Increase Distribution   While some companies use their sites to promote *i-commerce* (sales through the Internet), others use them to distribute coupons and samples. Through **affiliations**—relationships among websites in which companies cross-promote one another's products, and each is credited for sales that accrue through its site—companies have increased their exposure base by linking to other sites for purposes of creating awareness as well as distributing product. For example, some sites sell products for other companies without ever taking physical possession of the goods.

Developing and Maintaining a Website

The role of the **website** is to act as the place where information is made available by the website provider to Internet users. Developing and maintaining a successful website requires significant time and effort. To attract visitors to the site and have them return to it requires a combination of creativity, effective marketing, and continual updating of the site. As the number of sites continues to increase, the demand for service providers such as site developers, information architects, and webmasters escalates as well. Developing and maintaining a website now requires an expensive and time-intensive commitment.

Making a site work and having one work successfully are not the same thing, however, and whether a site is effective is determined by what it is that management hopes to achieve through the site. As already noted, some sites are offered for informational purposes only (this tends to be more common in the business-to-business market than the consumer market), while others approach the market much more aggressively. For example, Kimberly-Clark Corporation, the manufacturer of Huggies brand (diapers, Pull-Ups training pants, and Little Swimmers swim pants) has been extremely successful in its Internet marketing efforts. The Huggies home page (Exhibit 15–4) goes well beyond providing information. The site has additional objectives, such as *developing a relationship with parents*, *establishing a brand image* for the products through online campaigns, and *supporting sales*. For example, one campaign designed to develop one-on-one relationships offered a free sample to anyone who sent in his or her name, address, and e-mail address. Thousands of people responded to the offer, providing Kimberly-Clark with an enormous database useful for future marketing efforts. Another campaign targeted parents visiting other websites such as CTW.org (Children's Television Workshop, producer of *Sesame Street*), Women.com, iVillage.com, and BabyZone.com. In addition, anyone typing in the keywords *diapers* or *infant care* on portals Lycos and Excite was greeted with a Huggies banner ad. To bring visitors to the site, Huggies provided tips on baby care, chat with other parents, access to other baby links, and additional

Exhibit 15–4 Huggies home page

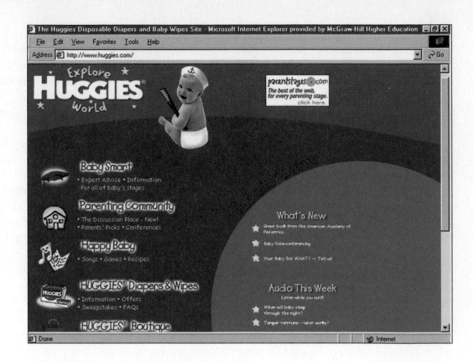

information about Huggies products. Finally, to support sales, the site directed customers to the nearest retail store that sells Huggies brands.

As the Huggies example demonstrates, a website can be an effective tool for the marketer. Depending on the nature of one's business and one's marketing objectives for the Internet, a website can range from being a very simple source of information about the company and its products to being a powerful tool for developing a brand image, sampling, and even generating sales. Following are some of the objectives sought by those marketing on the Internet.

Internet Marketing Communications and the IMC Approach

"Rumors of my demise are greatly exaggerated." This famous quote of Mark Twain can be used to describe the relationship between the Internet and traditional media quite well. As the Internet boom took off, a number of prognosticators predicted that the Internet would constitute "the end of traditional media" and "the death blow to advertisers"; they suggested that traditional media would suffer greatly as marketers moved their communications dollars to the Internet. Others suggested a moratorium on building retail stores and shopping malls, predicting that e-commerce would replace in-person shopping. In fact, the Internet may be one of the strongest arguments yet for companies to adopt an integrated marketing communications perspective. Rather than hurting traditional media and reducing the expenditures therein, the Internet both complements and relies on other media in an effective IMC program.

We must also recognize the growing number of Internet appliances now offered as competing Internet media choices. Take a look at the following examples of new gadgets out on the market today that are Internet-enabled: handheld PCs, PDAs (personal digital assistants), pen devices, palmtops, wallet PCs, Net phones and Web phones, Net printers, and more. By the year 2003, the number of handheld devices connected to the Internet will surpass the number of personal computers connected to the Internet. The prognosis is that by the year 2004 almost every appliance in your home will be Internet-enabled! Imagine having your alarm clock not only wake you up but also give you your stock quotes as well as your new e-mail and the top news items for the day. Your fridge will automatically add to your grocery list as items get used up, which you can then access from your car by using your hands-free Net phone while on your way home before you go shopping. Too much? Well, it's on the way. The arena for new developments on the Internet and the media options are growing.

A Grocer with a Difference

Mississauga, Ontario–based Grocery Gateway is a virtual grocer that allows consumers to shop online and have the goods delivered right to their front doors. The visual aspects of the website focus on the delivery man, called Jim, who is dressed in the style of the 1950s and who is rendered in Norman Rockwell fashion. A second logo that also conveys the old-fashioned values of trustworthiness and service is the Disneyesque anthropomorphic truck that stands for enthusiasm and drive.

Grocery Gateway continually updates its website, attempting to make it more user-friendly; the result is an easy-to-get-around, fair re-creation of the personal shopping experience. Once you've registered online, you log on and start shopping, prompted through aisles and categories, exactly as in a grocery store. Images of products contain nutritional information, size, and directions. Grocery Gateway carries a full line of packaged or fresh goods (about 9,000 products, compared to an estimated 12,000 in supermarkets), and is especially proud that its best-selling items are bananas— they're in half of all orders. Like all its produce, these orders are fulfilled through Grocery Gateway's alliance with high-end green grocer Longo's.

Grocery Gateway's main customer is the female head of the household, who on average orders about $120 worth of merchandise. The important question is whether there are enough customers who are willing to make the venture profitable. Predictions about the online-services share of the grocery market range from a potential of 30 percent down to what may be closer to reality, merely 1 percent. A recent study by Ipsos-Reid Corporation showed that, in Canada, 5 percent of Internet users directed some of their business to online grocery services, while 13 percent of Internet users said they were considering buying groceries online. Such variations illustrate just how uncertain the e-grocery world can be.

Sources: "Shopping online keeps cupboards full," *The Toronto Star,* March 30, 2002, p.P08; Kevin Marron, "It's a brand new game," *The Globe and Mail,* January 30, 2001, p.E1; Terry Poulton, "Grocery Gateway builds total brand personality," *Strategy,* January 15, 2001, p. 18; Raju Mudhar, "Delivering the goods," *Canadian Grocer,* April 2001, pp. 18-19.

With this in mind, let's discuss how the Internet and other IMC program elements work together.

Advertising

Online advertising has grown dramatically over the years. In 1996, about $200 million was spent globally in online advertising. In 2001, that figure rose to $9 billion! But this figure represents only 3 percent of total global advertising. Print, TV, and radio remain the biggest advertising mediums. The Internet both supports advertising and relies on advertising for its own success. On the January 2000 Super Bowl broadcast, 50 percent of the advertisements were for dot-com companies that paid as much as $2 million per spot to promote themselves.[16]

Advertising on the Internet Like broadcast or print, the Internet is also used as an advertising medium. Companies and organizations working to promote their products and services must consider this medium as they would television, magazines, outdoor, and so on. Advertising on the Internet employs a variety of forms.

Banners   Nearly every website that incorporates *third-party advertising* as part of their *revenue model* displays **banner ads.** It is the most common form of advertising on the Web, accounting for approximately 53 percent of advertising expenditures. The number of online ad impressions listed in the 4th quarter of 2000 in Canada was 172 billion. The expected average number of banner ads that online users will see per day in 2005 are 950.[17] Banner ads may be used for creating awareness or recognition or for direct-marketing objectives. Banner ads that run vertically down the side of a Web page are often called *skyscrapers,* or *inline ads*. While banner ads can be useful for driving traffic to a website, they can often be more useful for branding purposes—making Internet users aware of a brand or positioning a brand in the minds of users.

Sponsorships   The second most common form of advertising is **sponsorships,** which account for approximately 30 percent of total advertising expenditures. There are two types of sponsorships. Regular sponsorships occur when a company pays to sponsor a section of a site, for example, Clairol's sponsorship of a page on GirlsOn.com and Intuit's TurboTax sponsorship of a page on Netscape's financial section. A more involved agreement is the **content sponsorship,** in which the sponsor not only provides dollars in return for name association but also participates in providing the content itself. In some cases, the site is responsible for providing content and having it approved by the sponsor; in other instances, the sponsor may contribute all or part of the content. Due in part to the decline in the effectiveness of banner ads and to the desire for more enrolment and exposure, sponsorships have been increasing in popularity.

Text Ads   **Text ads** are short messages with embedded Web links. Text ads do not use graphics, only alphanumeric characters. This can be very important if your potential customers do not have the latest technology for audio/visual/ animation capabilities. It may be the *only* advertising they will see on their PCs!

Pop-Ups   When you access the Internet, have you ever seen a small window appear advertising AOL's "Instant Messenger"? Such windows are known as **pop-ups,** and they often appear when you access a certain site. Pop-ups are usually larger than a banner ad but smaller than a full screen.

Interstitials   **Interstitials** are ads that pop up on your screen after you have clicked on a hyperlink to go to another Web page, and you are waiting for a site's content to download. Although some advertisers believe that interstitials are irritating and more of a nuisance than a benefit, a study conducted by Grey Advertising found that only 15 percent of those surveyed felt that the ads were irritating (versus 9 percent for banner ads) and that 47 percent liked the ads (versus 38 percent for banners). Perhaps more importantly, while ad recall of banner ads was approximately 51 percent, recall of interstitials was much higher, at 76 percent. Pop-ups and interstitials account for approximately 6 percent of all advertising on the Internet.[18]

Push Technologies   **Push technologies,** or **webcasting** technologies, also called **intermercials,** allow companies to "push" a message to consumers rather than waiting for them to find it. Push technologies dispatch Web pages and news updates and may have sound and video geared to specific audiences and even individuals. For example, a manager whose job responsibilities involve corporate finance might log on to his or her computer and find that new stories are automatically there on the economy, stock updates, or a summary of a speech by Alan Greenspan. Companies such as Pointcast provide screen savers that automatically "hook" the viewer to their sites for sports, news, weather reports, and/or other information that the viewer has specified. Users can use **personalization**—that is, they can personalize their sites to request the kinds of specific information they are most interested in viewing. For example, if you are into college sports, you can have updates sent to you through sites providing college sports information. The service is paid for by advertisers who flash their messages on the screen.

Link Ads   While considered by some as not a type of advertising, **link ads** serve many of the same purposes as are served by the types discussed above. Link ads come in two types, text and logos. Link ads are good for low-key, not-in-your-face promotion. For example, a visitor to one site may click on a logo that provides additional information and/or related materials at another site. Thus someone on ESPN.com may link to Nike.com and find information on sports-related products.

Other forms of advertising, such as ads placed in chat rooms, are also available. Given the limited use of many of these alternatives, we suggest the reader consult additional resources for more information.

Advertising by Internet Companies   It's almost impossible to turn on the television, listen to the radio, or read a magazine these days without being exposed to a dot-com ad. As more and more advertisers use the Internet as a medium to promote their goods and services, the sites that they advertise on, as well as the search engines and portals that host these sites, continue to increase their advertising expenditures in traditional media. Magazines, newspapers, and outdoor have also benefited from their expenditures. In addition, a number of new print media have developed as trade magazines for the industry. For examples, look to EBIZ Business Week, Internet Week, or Wired News, for a few examples.

Sales Promotion on the Internet

The next time you log on to a website, take a minute to notice how the site attempts to get you to come back. Sales promotion has become the most frequently used (overused?) method of encouraging repeat visits. Repeat visits are one measure of audience size used to determine the price a site is able to charge advertisers and sponsors; therefore, one of the primary objectives of a site is to get you to come back. Notice that on the home page of many sites you will find "free stuff," which encourages people to come back to the site in an attempt to win prizes. Sites offer everything from free e-mail to instant messaging to telephone services. They have also offered sweepstakes, as in the following past examples: At the Virgin Atlantic Airways site, CEO Richard Branson appeared to invite the user to enter a sweepstakes; www.BMW.com offered a contest for a free BMW; and visitors to the Brita water site had a chance to win $500,000—and the list goes on (Exhibit 15–5).

As discussed in Chapter 12, delivering coupons on the Net is another rapidly growing use of sales promotion. Excite and e centives.com (a provider of sales promotions for Internet applications) have entered a marketing alliance that gives Excite users access to an online couponing system very similar to that in the real world. At www.coolsavings.com, marketers can access the site directly to update their promotion offers and to promote various products and services. In exchange

Exhibit 15–5   Sweepstakes and contests are commonly employed on the Internet

for the free coupons, consumers provide valuable database information when they complete a short survey to qualify. Each of the coupons is assigned a unique number and bar code so that when it is redeemed, the marketer can track the effectiveness of the offer. Other companies, like www.hotcoupons.com, provide coupon distribution as well. A study for NPD Online Research indicated that 30 percent of the Web user respondents had used online coupons in 1999 and that the number of users continues to increase. The study also indicated that consumers' awareness of online coupons is nearly 80 percent (among Web users).[19] Webstakes.com has taken its online sweepstakes and promotions to Japan, the United Kingdom, Ireland, Australia, and New Zealand.[20]

Good Gracious! Welcome! Here's WHAT'S NEW at the Home of the Hollow Tree

Personal Selling on the Internet

The Internet has been both a benefit and a detriment to many of those involved in personal selling—particularly those in the business-to-business market. For some, the Internet has been a threat that might take away job opportunities. Companies have found that they can remain effective—even increase effectiveness—by building a strong Web presence. The high-cost and poor-reach disadvantages of personal selling are allowing these companies to reduce new hires and even cut back on their existing sales forces.

On the positive side, websites have been used quite effectively to enhance and support the selling effort. As noted earlier, the Web has become a primary source of information for millions of customers in the consumer and business-to-business markets. Visitors to websites can gain volumes of information about a company's products and services. In return, the visitors become a valuable resource for leads that both internal and external salespersons can follow up, and they become part of a prospect database. Not only can potential customers learn about the company's offerings, but the selling organization can serve and qualify prospects more cost-effectively.

Some companies have used the Internet to improve their one-on-one relationships with customers. By providing more information in a more timely and efficient manner, a company enables customers to learn more about what it has to offer. This increases the opportunity for cross-selling and customer retention. For example, Neoforma.com links hospitals and medical supply vendors with listings of 300,000 medical products, with pages describing separate product categories.[21] For those interested in medical products, the site has become a one-stop shopping centre. In addition, by providing a website, companies can improve their response times to inquiries as well as complaints, thereby improving customer service.

Yet another use of the Internet is for sales conferences. A number of companies, including Cisco and Scientific American, have used Internet video to hold sales conferences, saving the salespeople important time and the companies millions of dollars.

In a well-designed IMC program, the Internet and personal selling are designed to be complementary tools—working together to increase sales. It appears that more and more companies are coming to this realization.

Public Relations on the Internet

As with other media, the Internet is a useful medium for conducting public relations activities. Many sites devote a portion of their content to public relations activities, including the provision of information about the company, its philanthropic activities, annual reports, and so on. Shel Holtz, in his book *Public Relations on the Internet,* notes that the public relations industry has been slow to adopt the Internet. Some of the more traditional public relations organizations do not use the Net at all, while most others use it primarily as a tool for disseminating information. Holtz notes that the Web offers a number of opportunities to public relations practitioners, including: (1) the development of media relations websites, (2) the ability to provide customized information dissemination, and (3) the development of positive e-mail relationships.

One example of the use of public relations on the Internet is provided by Chrysler. Working with reporters, Chrysler developed a one-stop information source for the media (the public could also use the site, but reporters would have to register to use the "newsroom"). News stories and other forms of content, photo images, and cross-references to other sites or media were included on the site, as were press kits and a calendar of upcoming events (Exhibit 15–6). The objective of the site was to improve relations with the press, and Chrysler was quite effective in doing so.

At the same time, many philanthropic and non-profit organizations have found the Internet to be a useful way to generate funds. Several sites have developed to perform the functions that are required in traditional fund-raising programs. For

The Dot-CA Revolution!

Marketers are increasingly reaching to the Internet to support marketing campaigns by including websites as part of the marketing mix. The selection of a domain name enabling visitors to reach a specific site is an important decision, as it has to be memorable and connected to the brand or company.

Up until the late 1990s, dot-com domain names were often chosen by default. But now, Canadian businesses have a new alternative the Canadian Internet Registration Authority (CIRA). CIRA is the not-for-profit corporation mandated to operate the dot-ca top-level domain for all Canadians. It is responsible for setting policy and managing the dot-ca domain database as well as registering domain names through its network of certified registrars. The Ottawa-based dot-ca governing body has recently experienced 500 percent growth in dot-ca registrations between December 2000 (60,000 names) and July 2002 (300,000 names).

Previously, dot-ca domain names had been registered on a volunteer basis at the University of British Columbia. With the recent usage and rapid commercialization of the Internet, the Internet community agreed that the original rules and mode of operation had to be changed. A representative committee recommended that a not-for-profit, private-sector corporation be incorporated to run the dot-ca registry. This occurred in December 1998, when the CIRA was incorporated.

In November 2001, CIRA commissioned a study by The Strategic Council, which reveals that Canadian Internet users:

- Know that dot-ca means Canada,
- Prefer visiting dot-ca sites for services and information (71 percent agreement),
- Prefer to shop online through a dot-ca web site if given a choice (77 percent agreement),

- Associate dot-com with American and international companies,
- Associate great patriotic and emotional appeal with dot-ca domain names.

An analysis carried out by Jupiter Media Metrix on behalf of CIRA corroborates the rising popularity of the dot-ca extension. Jupiter Media Metrix studied the traffic flow of ten popular websites with both dot-com and dot-ca extensions—AOL, eBay, foodtv, Ford, Google, MSN, Netscape, Sears, Ticketmaster, and Yahoo!—between January 2001 and April 2002. In eight of the ten sites, the results reveal that there is a greater traffic increase in the website with the dot-ca extension over those with dot-com.

In May 2002, another CIRA study performed by Impact Research, a member of the Cossette Communications Group—Canada's largest full service communications agency—revealed that Canadian companies perceive more value in dot-ca names for Canadian consumers and business development, and sites bearing dot-ca names are more trustworthy and honest than dot-com sites.

Marketers registering domain names for campaigns and promotions need to think of how they will manage their domain names after the campaigns or promotions have ended. Domain names can be registered for periods ranging from one to ten years. "Domain name poachers" are on the lookout for expired domain names that have been advertised and promoted. By registering expired names and directing them to other sites, poachers are able to increase their visitor traffic and charge higher advertising banner fees.

example, in just one month in 1999 during the war between Serbia and Kosovo, the American Red Cross was able to raise $1 million for aid to Kosovo citizens through its website.[22] Other sites have been formed to handle public relations activities for charitable organizations, provide information regarding the causes the charity supports, collect contributions, and so on.

Direct Marketing on the Internet

Our discussion of direct marketing and the Internet will approach the topic from two perspectives: the use of direct-marketing tools for communications objectives (as discussed in Chapter 14) and e-commerce. As we stated previously, many direct-marketing tools, such as direct mail, infomercials, and the like, have been adapted

Exhibit 15–6 Chrysler provides public relations information on its site

to the Internet, as you will see. At the same time, e-commerce—selling directly to the consumer via the Internet—has become an industry of its own.

Direct Mail   Direct mail on the Internet is essentially an electronic version of regular mail. Like regular mail it is highly targeted, relies heavily on lists, and attempts to reach consumers with specific needs through targeted messages. As we discussed earlier under personalization, consumers can opt to have specific types of e-mail sent to them and other types not sent. For example, if you permit, media firms and web portals will e-mail you information about specific promotions, articles that will appear, books on sale, and other items that you may purchase.

Sometimes, users may also receive less targeted and unwanted e-mails. The electronic equivalent of junk mail, these messages are referred to as **SPAM.** Because of the high volumes of SPAM that have been sent, and the fact that many consumers consider it a nuisance, the U.S. government has passed laws regulating its use.

Catalogue-oriented companies such as Lands' End have also increased their use of the electronic media. The company recently aired television commercials to promote the ease and efficiency of using its online catalogue, and sent customers in its existing database direct-mail pieces informing them of the same.

While many consumers don't like SPAM or other forms of e-mail, at least one study has shown the effectiveness of e-mails. In a survey of 667 online consumers, conducted by E-Buyersguide.com, 63 percent of the respondents said they first found their "e-tailers" by responding to e-mail promotions.[23]

Database Marketing   A number of database services exist on the Internet. For example, EDGAR (Electronic Data Gathering and Retrieval) contains all the documents that companies are required to file electronically with the Securities and Exchange Commission. This information includes key financials, management personnel, and so on. Hundreds of other databases exist as well. Some companies have established successful database marketing businesses on the Web. One such company, Freelotto, has a 10 million–member database available to marketers (at a price) who may want to target all types of customers, including credit card users, gardeners, and computer users, among others. The company offers a "one-stop" service that collects the names and addresses, qualifies the prospects, and e-mails the seller's messages. Many companies have developed electronic databases to be used in the same way, as described in Chapter 14.

Infomercials   Yes, even the infomercial has discovered the Net. The same people who brought you "Amazing Discoveries" infomercials on television now produce infomercials for the Internet (and they are not alone). One such infomercial, by iMall, a company based in Provo, Utah, runs marketing seminars on how to make money on the Internet.

Direct Sales   Direct sales on the Internet, has truly taken off. A study by Harris Interactive Surveys revealed that 33 percent of online users expected to purchase at least one item over the Internet during the 1999 holiday season. If they did, the results would be some $9.5 billion in expenditures in that very short time period.[24]

All indications are that this number will continue to increase in the future. While CDs, books, and travel account for most Internet purchases, a number of other items are finding their way there as well. Clothing, automobiles, and stocks and bonds are now regularly purchased through the Internet. Amazon.com, most known for its book sales, now offers a variety of other products for sale—including pharmaceuticals (Exhibit 15–7).

While more and more consumers buy online, consumer sales are only about one-sixth of those by business-to-business marketers. Cisco systems alone did $9.5 billion of e-commerce in 1999, more than 75 percent of its total sales.[25] Other business-to-business companies such as Applied Industrial Technologies, National Semiconductor, and Xerox have also found success in the world of e-commerce.

Perhaps the best way to end our discussion of how the Internet fits into an IMC program is with an example. IMC Perspective 15–3 details how IBM successfully employed an IMC program effectively utilizing the Internet.

Exhibit 15–7   Amazon.com offers more than just books

Evaluation of Internet Marketing

Strengths of Internet Marketing

1. *Target marketing.* A major advantage of the Web is the ability to target very specific groups of individuals with a minimum of waste coverage. For those in the business-to-business market, the Internet resembles a combination trade magazine and trade show, as only those most interested in the products and/or services that a site has to offer will visit the site (others have little or no reason to do so). In the consumer market, through personalization and other targeting techniques, sites are becoming more tailored to meet one's needs and wants.

2. *Message tailoring.* As a result of precise targeting, messages can be designed to appeal to the specific needs and wants of the target audience. The interactive capabilities of the Net make it possible to carry on one-to-one marketing with increased success in both the business and the consumer markets.

3. *Interactive capabilities.* Because the Internet is interactive, it provides strong potential for increasing customer involvement and satisfaction and almost immediate feedback for buyers and sellers. A study of online users found that 24 percent watched the 2000 Super Bowl while multitasking online.[26] As multitasking increases, the interactive capabilities of the Internet will make this medium even more attractive.

4. *Information access.* Perhaps the greatest advantage of the Internet is its availability as an information source. Internet users can find a plethora of information about almost any topic of their choosing merely by conducting a search through one of the search engines. Once they have visited a particular site, users can garner a wealth of information regarding product specifications, costs, purchase information, and so on. Links will direct them to even more information if it is desired.

5. *Sales potential.* The numbers provided earlier in this chapter demonstrate the incredible sales numbers being generated in both the business-to-business and the consumer segments. Forecasts are for almost exponential growth in the future.

IBM's B-to-B IMC Program Taps the Internet

These days it's hard to miss IBM's "Self-service Web sites from IBM service customers better" advertising campaign on TV. It's also hard to miss it if you pick up a magazine or newspaper around the world. What you may not have seen is the IBM campaign running on the Internet—but you should. The message promoted in the traditional media is that IBM is a solutions provider. On the Internet, the ads specifically show how.

The IMC campaign actually was developed back in 1997 and was a bit of a departure from IBM's typical way of advertising. In the past, separate advertisements might be run in a variety of media, with little or no connection between them. When the company initiated the e-business solutions campaign, it recognized that a more integrated campaign would be required, employing a variety of media but maintaining consistency across the channels and in the positioning. More importantly, the media play different and complementary roles. For example, teaser ads are run in print and on TV with the objective of gaining exposure and attention and driving the receiver to the Internet for more information. The timing of the humourous TV vignettes is simultaneous with the print ads in *The New York Times, The Wall Street Journal, USA Today, The Washington Post, Financial Times, Forbes, Business Week,* and *Information Week,* which provide more detail on how IBM helped its customers solve an e-business problem. The print ads then direct the reader to the website to acquire even more information.

In addition to using the traditional media, IBM places a high degree of emphasis on the Internet. An *e* rather than an *a* inside of the "@" mark was used for branding IBM as an Internet company. Every IBM customer could use the mark on his or her website, and IBM carried the logo on all its communications. Banner ads were placed on portals as well as other sites. Clicking on the banner took the viewer to a rich-medium "minisite" that showed how IBM helped a company solve its specific problem. Newer ads promoting its server products also use TV and print to drive viewers to the Net. Once there, they will see banner ads with Java script, which allows users to participate in the processes being advertised. For example, an ad for eSeeds.com, an online vendor of seeds, allows the user to sow seeds and then water them by holding the mouse button down. The flowers then grow while the user watches. The message explains that eSeeds is building its business on an IBM AS/400 server.

In 1998 IBM spent $45 million on Internet ads—7 percent of the total $600 million budget. By 1999 10 percent, or $60 million, will be allocated to the Net. This makes IBM the largest single online advertiser in the world. But the question is, "Is it working?"

In 1994, *Financial Times* rated IBM at the bottom of its brand value list—assigning a value of a negative $50 million to IBM due to the myriad of directions the company was going in with no apparent cohesion. The new IMC campaign was designed with three goals in mind: (1) to alert the world to the fact that e-business was transforming the way IBM would do business in the future; (2) to establish a strong brand association between IBM and e-business solutions; and (3) to convince its own 300,000 employees in 160 countries that IBM was itself a player in the e-business world. The company and its advertising agency, Ogilvy & Mather, believed that a more cohesive and integrated approach was necessary. They were right!

Sources: Peter T. Leach, "The Blue Period," *Critical Mass,* Fall 1999, pp. 86–92; "IBM E-Business," *1999 Effie Awards* (American Marketing Association, 1999), p. 24.

6. *Creativity.* Creatively designed sites can enhance a company's image, lead to repeat visits, and positively position the company or organization in the consumer's mind.

7. *Exposure.* For many smaller companies, with limited budgets, the Web enables them to gain exposure to potential customers that heretofore would have been impossible. For a fraction of the investment that would be required using traditional media, companies can gain national and even international exposure in a timely manner.

8. *Speed.* For those requesting information on a company, its products, and/or its service offerings, the Internet is the quickest means of acquiring this information.

Limitations of Internet Marketing

1. *Measurement problems.* One of the greatest disadvantages of the Internet is the lack of reliability of the research numbers generated. A quick review of forecasts, audience profiles, and other statistics offered by research providers will demonstrate a great deal of variance—leading to a serious lack of validity and reliability. One company, eMarketer, has attempted to reconcile such differences and explain the reasoning for the discrepancies (differences in methodologies employed), but the problem still exists. One of the industry's largest and most cited trade publications has written an exposé of a heavily cited Internet research company, referring to the numbers it provides as "scary."[27] Others have stressed concerns over the fact that most site's figures are not audited, which may lead to rampant cheating in respect to the numbers reported.[28]

2. *Audience characteristics.* Due in part to the accelerating growth of the Net, audience characteristics change quickly. Numbers reported may be outdated quickly and often vary from one provider to the next.

3. *Websnarl.* At times, downloading information from the Net takes a long time. When there are a number of users, the time increases and some sites may be inaccessible due to too many visitors. For many users who expect speed, this is a major disadvantage.

4. *Clutter.* As the number of ads proliferates, the likelihood of one ad's being noticed drops accordingly. The result is that some ads may not get noticed, and some consumers may become irritated by the clutter. Some studies already show that banner ads may be losing effectiveness for this very reason.

5. *Potential for deception.* The Center for Media Education has referred to the Web as "a web of deceit" in regard to attempts of advertisers to target children with subtle advertising messages. The Center, among others, has asked the U.S. government to regulate the Internet. In addition, data collection without consumers' knowledge and permission, hackers, and credit card theft are a number of problems confronting the Internet.

6. *Costs.* The costs of doing business on the Internet continue to increase. While it is possible to establish a site inexpensively, establishing a good site and maintaining it is becoming more and more costly. As noted earlier, Levi's found the cost of maintaining a site it considered "world-class" was prohibitive and one of the reasons for abandoning its e-commerce efforts. Likewise, the CPMs of advertising on the Internet are often higher than some traditional media, as shown in Figure 15–6.

7. *Limited production quality.* Although it is improving, net advertising does not offer the capabilities of many competitive media from a production standpoint. While the advent of advanced technologies and rich media is narrowing the gap, the Net still lags behind some traditional media in this area.

8. *Poor reach.* While the Internet numbers are growing in leaps and bounds, its reach is still far behind that of television. As a result, as discussed earlier, Internet companies have turned to traditional media to achieve reach and awareness goals. In addition, statistics show that only a small percentage of sites on the Internet are

Figure 15–6   Ad rate comparison across major media

Medium	Vehicle	Cost	Reach	CPM
TV	:30 network prime time	$120,000	10 million households	$12
Consumer magazine	Page, 4-color in *Cosmopolitan*	$86,155	2.5 million paid readers	35
Online service	Banner on CompuServe major-topic page	$10,000 per month	750,000 visitors	13
Website	Banner on Infoseek	$10,000 per month	500,000 page views per month	20

captured by search engines and that the top 50 sites listed account for 95 percent of the sites visited.[29]

Overall, the Internet offers marketers some very definite advantages over traditional media. At the same time, disadvantages and limitations render this medium as less than a one-stop solution. However, as part of an IMC program, the Internet is a very valuable tool.

Additional Interactive Media

While the Internet has captured most of the attention of marketers, additional interactive media are also available and can be used as a contributor to an IMC program. Interactive CD-ROMs, kiosks, and interactive phones have been used by marketers to provide information to their audiences. Interactive television advertising was recently introduced in the US a few years ago and just last year in Canada.

In the US, one of the more attention-getting and promising of the new interactive media is WebTV. A wholly owned subsidiary of Microsoft, WebTV (now called MSN TV) had more than 1 million subscribers in 2000.[30] Another interactive TV company, OpenTV, has over 300,000 subscribers.[31] Multitasking will allow television viewers to watch an event—for example, a football game—and pull up information on players, history of the matchups between the teams, and other statistics without ever leaving the couch or the game. (The numbers will appear in a window.) WebTV's "Personal TV" service allows viewers complete control over what they watch and when they watch it. In addition, viewers can pause the live program, digital video record, and instant replay. The service also allows for fast forwarding, rewinding, skipping ahead, and/or searching for one's favourite scene.

Interactive television, emerged in Canada during October of 2001 when Rogers Cable launched Enhanced Television for its 27,000 digital cable customers who have digital set-top boxes connected to the televisions. This technology, developed by Wink Communications of California, is similar to WebTV described above. Canadian consumers can now interact with programs and commercials by pushing the select button of their remote control when the flashing "i" appears periodically on the screen. If the results previously found in the US are any indication, then we may see extensive advertising dollars invested in this media. For example, Wink executives cite a financial services firm that had half its users who interacted with the ad request a new account kit.[32]

The technology behind interactive television is predicated on three important features. Addressability is achieved since each box has a unique IP address much like computers have when connecting to the Internet. Thus, the exact time and location of an advertising message is known which gives exact precision on the nature of the audience exposed to the message. Personalization software and program viewership of will allow advertisers to deliver a tailored message to a precisely defined target audience. The implication of this is that a advertiser of a children's product can reach households with children with a specific ad. Finally, consumers interact with the advertiser by requesting coupons, samples or product information (i.e., location).[33]

While interactive television is making a splash in North America the past few years, campaigns have been flourishing in Europe and Asia. For example, Procter and Gamble has adapted this technolog in the U.K. and Hong Kong as a key part of their marketing mix for some brands. In France, Honda has had success with using responses to bring consumer further along in the decision-making process of buying a car as consumers requested information or arranged a test drive.[34]

The future of interactive television in Canada appears promising. Early results show that Citytv has a 30% of the households have interacted with Enhanced TV, figure substantially higher than the average response rate found in the US. However, media industry observers note that while the technology is interesting, they will be cautious about purchasing media time until it appears to be a vital part of the media mix.[35]

Summary

This chapter introduced you to the Internet and interactive media. It explained some of the objectives for these media and how they can be used in an IMC program.

The discussion of the Internet focused on understanding the key terms used in the industry, the objectives sought when using the Internet, and Internet communications strategies. In addition, the role of the Internet in an IMC program was discussed, with an explanation of how all the IMC program elements can be used with the Internet. Advantages of the Internet—including the ability to target markets, interactive capabilities, and relationship building—were discussed. In addition, disadvantages—including high costs, unreliable measurements and statistics, and relatively low reach (compared to that of traditional media)—were reviewed. Sources of Internet measurement data were also provided.

The Internet has been the most rapidly adopted medium of our time. It holds great potential for both business-to-business and consumer marketers. However, contrary to popular belief, the Internet is not a stand-alone medium. Its role in an integrated marketing communications program strengthens the overall program as well as the effectiveness of the Internet itself.

Interactive media has not yet fulfilled its promise. While still in its infancy, the medium has not received the acceptance and use expected. Test market indications are that the medium still needs improvements—particularly in content—before reaching mass acceptance.

Key Terms

Internet, 397
World Wide Web (WWW), 397
e-business, 398
e-commerce, 398
i-commerce, 398

Internet marketing, 400
website, 403
cookies, 405
affiliations, 406
text ads, 408
banner ads, 408

sponsorships, 408
content sponsorship, 408
pop-ups, 408
interstitials, 408
push technologies, 408
webcasting, 408

intermercials, 408
personalization, 408
link ads, 409
SPAM, 412

Discussion Questions

1. While some believe that the Internet poses a threat to traditional media, others disagree, arguing that it is just another medium to marketers. Explain some of the arguments on both sides. What is your conclusion?

2. The Internet is growing at an extremely rapid pace. At the same time, there are indications that this growth will slow. Discuss some factors that may lead to decreased growth of the use of this medium.

3. Discuss the objectives marketers may be seeking in their use of the Internet. Which is the Internet best suited for?

4. Explain the different forms that advertisers might use to advertise on the Internet. Discuss some of the advantages and disadvantages associated with each.

5. What is meant by personalization? Give an example of how a consumer company might use personalization.

6. A number of Internet marketers have been criticized as engaging in unethical practices. Discuss some of the practices that might be considered unethical. What should be done to curtail these practices?

7. Discuss some of the ways that marketers attempt to measure the effectiveness of their programs on the Internet. How do these measures relate to more traditional measures? Describe the advantages and disadvantages of traditional versus Internet measures.

8. Discuss some of the advantages of using the Internet. For which types of companies is the Internet best suited? Why?

9. What is interactive TV? Explain how interactive television differs from traditional television. Give an example of how a company might employ this medium.

10. Many marketers feel that the Internet offers much more potential to business-to-business marketers than it does to consumer marketers. Detail some of the reasons they feel this way and draw a conclusion as to the merits of this argument.

Chapter Sixteen

Organizing for Integrated Marketing Communication

Chapter Objectives

- To understand how companies organize for advertising and other aspects of integrated marketing communications.

- To examine methods for selecting, compensating, and evaluating advertising agencies.

- To explain the role and functions of specialized marketing communications organizations.

- To examine various perspectives on the use of integrated services and responsibilities of advertisers versus agencies.

Get a Grip on Advertising

In November 2001, Labatt Brewing Co. fired its advertising agency of 8 years, Ammirati Puris. Citing its frustration with the agency's ability to deliver sufficient value for Labatt's advertising investments, the beer giant has decided to operate its own "in-house" agency.

In announcing the firing, Labatt criticized the agency model in general rather than its particular agency. It seems Labatt believes that the agency model is flawed in that clients pay too much money for the work and receive far too little attention. The alternative for Labatt would be a stripped-down agency that had only a few clients (i.e., four to six) where the focus is on creative and not on the account managers.

Industry participants believed the comments to be a bit off base since the type of agency that Labatt described already exists: the creative boutique. Further, even the smallest of agencies need some amount of staff to do background research, develop strategies, and take care of clients' needs, not to mention some staff to handle basic accounting and information technology services. "You can't just have a bunch of creatives running around making ads. You need some grown-ups around, too, to make sure things get done," says one advertising executive. Finally, creative people thrive on a variety of work, and many wondered how a small agency would be able to keep highly skilled creative employees fulfilled.

Labatt's vision and plan may be two different things. It announced its new agency, Grip Limited, in January of 2002. Grip's would be 100 percent employee-owned, and its sole client would be Labatt. Grip would be responsible for Labatt Blue and Blue Light for North America, and John Labatt Classic, Kokanee, and Carlsberg in Canada. Grip claimed that it would be responsible to its clients and not its shareholders and that it would have greater efficiency in the advertising development process. Curiously, the model almost sounds as if the agency is really the advertising department for Labatt. However, the plan is to have other clients eventually who will sit on the board and play an active management role. Time will tell if this is a new agency model or another version of the "in-house" agency.

Sources: "Labatt Grips Its New Agency Model," *Marketing Magazine*, January 14, 2002; "If they build it, will anyone come?" *Marketing Magazine*, December 10, 2001.

Developing and implementing an integrated marketing communications program is usually a complex and detailed process involving the efforts of many persons. As consumers, we generally give little thought to the individuals or organizations that create the clever advertisements that capture our attention or the contests or sweepstakes we hope to win. But for those involved in the marketing process, it is important to understand the nature of the industry and the structure and functions of the organizations involved. The advertising and promotions business is changing as marketers search for better ways to communicate with their customers. These changes are impacting the way marketers organize for marketing communications, as well as their relationships with advertising agencies and other communication specialists.

This chapter examines the various organizations that participate in the IMC process, their roles and responsibilities, and their relationship to one another. We discuss how companies organize internally for advertising and promotion. For most companies, advertising is planned and executed by an outside ad agency. Many large agencies offer a variety of other IMC capabilities, including public relations, sales promotion, and direct marketing. Thus, we will devote particular attention to the ad agency's role and the overall relationship between company and agency.

Other participants in the promotional process (such as direct-response, sales promotion, and interactive agencies and public relations firms) are becoming increasingly important as more companies take an integrated marketing communications approach to promotion. We examine the role of these specialized marketing communications organizations in the promotional process as well. The chapter concludes with a discussion of whether marketers are best served by using the integrated services of one large agency or the separate services of a variety of communications specialists.

Participants in the Integrated Marketing Communications Process: An Overview

Before discussing the specifics of the industry, we'll provide an overview of the entire system and identify some of the players. As shown in Figure 16–1, participants in the integrated marketing communications process can be divided into five major groups: the advertiser (or client), advertising agencies, media organizations, specialized communication services, and collateral services. Each group has specific roles in the promotional process. We discuss the first four in great detail in this chapter.

The advertisers, or **clients,** are the key participants in the process. They have the products, services, or causes to be marketed, and they provide the funds that pay for advertising and promotions. The advertisers also assume major responsibility for developing the marketing program and making the final decisions regarding the advertising and promotional program to be employed. The organization may perform most of these efforts itself, either through its own advertising department or by setting up an in-house agency.

Figure 16–1 Participants in the integrated marketing communications process

However, many organizations use an **advertising agency,** an outside firm that specializes in the creation, production, and/or placement of the communications message and that may provide other services to facilitate the marketing and promotions process. Many large advertisers retain the services of a number of agencies, particularly when they market a number of products. For example, Procter & Gamble uses 10 promotional agencies in Canada. More and more, ad agencies are acting as partners with advertisers and assuming more responsibility for developing the marketing and promotional programs.

Media organizations are another major participant in the advertising and promotions process. The primary function of most media is to provide information or entertainment to their subscribers, viewers, or readers. But from the perspective of the promotional planner, the purpose of media is to provide an environment for the firm's marketing communications message. The media must have editorial or program content that attracts consumers so advertisers and their agencies will want to buy time or space with them. Exhibit 16–1 shows an ad run in advertising trade publications promoting the value of *Link* magazine as a media vehicle for reaching college students. While the media perform many other functions that help advertisers understand their markets and their customers, a medium's primary objective is to sell itself as a way for companies to reach their target markets with their messages effectively.

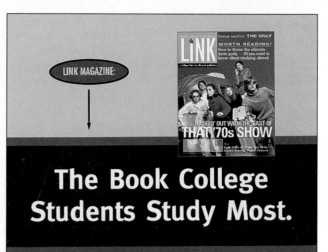

Exhibit 16–1   *Link* magazine advertises its value for reaching college students

The next group of participants are organizations that provide **specialized marketing communications services.** They include direct marketing agencies, sales promotion agencies, interactive agencies, and public relations firms. These organizations provide services in their areas of expertise. A direct-response agency develops and implements direct-marketing programs, while sales promotion agencies develop promotional programs such as contests and sweepstakes, premium offers, or sampling programs. Interactive agencies are being retained to develop websites for the Internet and help marketers as they move deeper into the realm of interactive media. Public relations firms are used to generate and manage publicity for a company and its products and services as well as to focus on its relationships and communications with its relevant publics.

The final participants shown in the promotions process of Figure 16–1 are those that provide **collateral services,** the wide range of support functions used by advertisers, agencies, media organizations, and specialized marketing communications firms. These individuals and companies perform specialized functions the other participants use in planning and executing advertising and other promotional functions. They include marketing research companies, package design firms, consultants, media buying services, photographers, printers, video production houses, and event marketing services companies.

Organizing for Advertising and Promotion in the Firm

Virtually every business organization uses some form of marketing communications. However, the way a company organizes for these efforts depends on several factors, including its size, the number of products it markets, the role of advertising and promotion in its marketing mix, the advertising and promotion budget, and its marketing organization structure. Many individuals throughout the organization may be involved in the promotions decision-making process. Marketing personnel have the most direct relationship with advertising and are often involved in many aspects of the decision process, such as providing input to the campaign plan, agency selection, and evaluation of proposed programs. Top management is usually interested in how the advertising program represents the firm, and this may also mean being involved in advertising decisions even when the decisions are not part of its day-to-day responsibilities.

While many people both inside and outside the organization have some input into the advertising and promotion process, direct responsibility for administering the program must be assumed by someone within the firm. Many companies have an advertising department headed by an advertising or communications manager operating under a marketing director. An alternative used by many large multiproduct firms is a decentralized marketing (brand management) system.

The Centralized System

In many organizations, marketing activities are divided along functional lines, with advertising placed alongside other marketing functions such as sales, marketing research, and product planning, as shown in Figure 16–2. The **advertising manager** is responsible for all promotions activities except sales. In the most common example of a **centralized system,** the advertising manager controls the entire promotions operation, including budgeting, coordinating creation and production of ads, planning media schedules, and monitoring and administering the sales promotions programs for all the company's products or services.

The specific duties of the advertising manager depend on the size of the firm and the importance it places on promotional programs. Basic functions the manager and staff perform include the following.

Planning and Budgeting   The advertising department is responsible for developing advertising and promotions plans that will be approved by management and recommending a promotions program based on the overall marketing plan, objectives, and budget. Formal plans are submitted annually or when a program is being changed significantly, as when a new campaign is developed. While the advertising department develops the promotional budget, the final decision on allocating funds is usually made by top management.

Administration and Execution   The manager must organize the advertising department and supervise and control its activities. The manager also supervises the execution of the plan by subordinates and/or the advertising agency. This requires working with such departments as production, media, art, copy, and sales promotion. If an outside agency is used, the advertising department is relieved of much of the executional responsibility; however, it must review and approve the agency's plans.

Coordination with Other Departments   The manager must coordinate the advertising department's activities with those of other departments, particularly

Figure 16–2   The advertising department under a centralized system

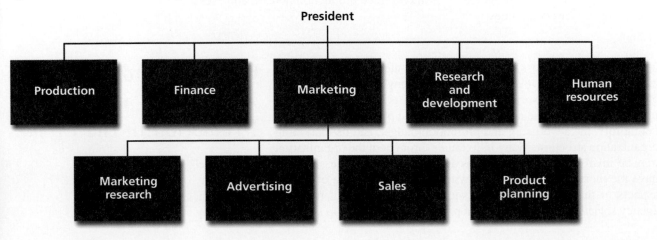

those involving other marketing functions. For example, the advertising department must communicate with marketing research and/or sales to determine which product features are important to customers and should be emphasized in the company's communications. Research may also provide profiles of product users and nonusers for the media department before it selects broadcast or print media. The advertising department may also be responsible for preparing material the sales force can use when calling on customers, such as sales promotion tools, advertising materials, and point-of-purchase displays.

Coordination with Outside Agencies and Services   Many companies have an advertising department but still use many outside services. For example, companies may develop their advertising programs in-house while employing media buying services to place their ads and/or use collateral services agencies to develop brochures, point-of-purchase materials, and so on. The department serves as liaison between the company and any outside service providers and also determines which ones to use. Once outside services are retained, the manager will work with other marketing managers to coordinate their efforts and evaluate their performances.

A centralized organizational system is often used when companies do not have many different divisions, product or service lines, or brands to advertise. Many companies prefer a centralized advertising department because developing and coordinating advertising programs from one central location facilitates communication regarding the promotions program, making it easier for top management to participate in decision making. A centralized system may also result in a more efficient operation because fewer people are involved in the program decisions, and as their experience in making such decisions increases, the process becomes easier.

At the same time, problems are inherent in a centralized operation. First, it is difficult for the advertising department to understand the overall marketing strategy for the brand. The department may also be slow in responding to specific needs and problems of a product or brand. As companies become larger and develop or acquire new products, brands, or even divisions, the centralized system may become impractical.

The Decentralized System

In large corporations with multiple divisions and many different products, it is very difficult to manage all the advertising, promotional, and other functions through a centralized department. These types of companies generally have a **decentralized system,** with separate manufacturing, research and development, sales, and marketing departments for various divisions, product lines, or businesses. Many companies that use a decentralized system, such as Procter & Gamble, Gillette Co., and Nestlé, assign each product or brand to a **brand manager** who is responsible for the total management of the brand, including planning, budgeting, sales, and profit performance. (The term *product manager* is also used to describe this position.) The brand manager, who may have one or more assistant brand managers, is also responsible for the planning, implementation, and control of the marketing program.[1]

Under this system, the responsibilities and functions associated with advertising and promotions are transferred to the brand manager, who works closely with the outside advertising agency and other marketing communications specialists as they develop the promotional program.[2] In a multiproduct firm, each brand may have its own ad agency and may compete against other brands within the company, not just against outside competitors. For example, Exhibit 16–2 shows ads for Cheer and Tide, which are both Procter & Gamble products that compete for a share of the laundry detergent market.

As shown in Figure 16–3, the advertising department is part of marketing services and provides support for the brand managers. The role of marketing services is to assist the brand managers in planning and coordinating the integrated marketing communications program. In some companies, the marketing services group may include sales promotion. The brand managers may work with sales promotion people

Figure 16–3 A decentralized brand management system

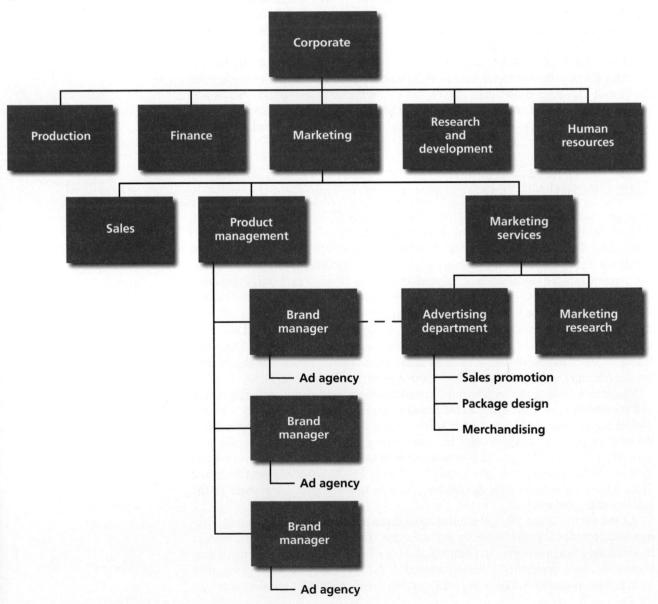

to develop budgets, define strategies, and implement tactical executions for both trade and consumer promotions. Marketing services may also provide other types of support services, such as package design and merchandising.

Some companies may have an additional layer(s) of management above the brand managers to coordinate the efforts of all the brand managers handling a related group of products. An example is the organizational structure of Procter & Gamble, shown in Figure 16–4. This system—generally referred to as a **category management system**—includes category managers as well as brand and advertising managers. The category manager oversees management of the entire product category and focuses on the strategic role of the various brands in order to build profits and market share.[3]

The advertising manager may review and evaluate the various parts of the program and advise and consult with the brand managers. This person may have the authority to override the brand manager's decisions on advertising. In some multiproduct firms that spend a lot on advertising, the advertising manager may coordinate the work of the various agencies to obtain media discounts for the firm's large volume of media purchases.

An advantage of the decentralized system is that each brand receives concentrated managerial attention, resulting in faster response to both problems and opportunities. The brand manager system is also more flexible and makes it easier to adjust various aspects of the advertising and promotional program, such as creative platforms and media and sales promotion schedules.[4]

There are some drawbacks to the decentralized approach. Brand managers often lack training and experience. The promotional strategy for a brand may be developed by a brand manager who does not really understand what advertising or sales promotion can and cannot do and how each should be used. Brand managers may focus too much on short-run planning and administrative tasks, neglecting the development of long-term programs.

Another problem is that individual brand managers often end up competing for management attention, marketing dollars, and other resources, which can lead to unproductive rivalries and potential misallocation of funds. The manager's persuasiveness may become a bigger factor in determining budgets than the long-run profit

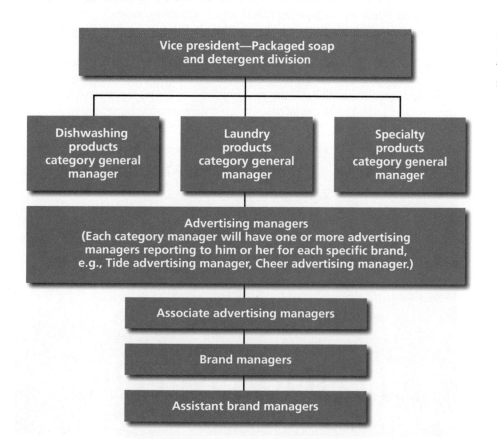

Figure 16–4   A Procter & Gamble division, using the category management system

potential of the brands. These types of problems were key factors in Procter & Gamble's decision to switch to a category management system.

Finally, the brand management system has been criticized for failing to provide brand managers with authority over the functions needed to implement and control the plans they develop.[5] Some companies have dealt with this problem by expanding the roles and responsibilities of the advertising and sales promotion managers and their staff of specialists. The staff specialists counsel the individual brand managers, and advertising or sales promotion decision making involves the advertising and/or sales promotion manager, the brand manager, and the marketing director.

Management Issues of Advertising Agencies

Advertising Agency Decision

Irrespective of whether an advertiser uses a centralized or decentralized organizational structure, there remains the choice of whether a firm will have its own in-house agency or whether it will employ an external advertising agency. We now briefly discuss the relative merits and concerns of both options.

In-House Agency Option
Some companies, in an effort to reduce costs and maintain greater control over agency activities, have set up their own advertising agencies internally. An **in-house agency** is an advertising agency that is set up, owned, and operated by the advertiser. Some in-house agencies are little more than advertising departments, but in other companies they are given a separate identity and are responsible for the expenditure of large sums of advertising dollars. Large advertisers that use in-house agencies include Calvin Klein, Avon, Revlon, and Benetton. Many companies use in-house agencies exclusively; others combine in-house efforts with those of outside agencies. For example, No Fear handles most of its advertising in-house, but it does use an outside agency for some of its creative work (Exhibit 16–3). (The specific roles performed by in-house agencies will become clearer when we discuss the functions of outside agencies.)

A major reason for using an in-house agency is to reduce advertising and promotion costs. Companies with very large advertising budgets pay a substantial amount to outside agencies in the form of media commissions. With an internal structure, these commissions go to the in-house agency. An in-house agency can also provide related work such as sales presentations and sales force materials, package design, and public relations at a lower cost than outside agencies. A study by

Exhibit 16–3 Most of the advertising for No Fear is done by an in-house agency

a passion for podiums

M. Louise Ripley found that creative and media services were the most likely functions to be performed outside, while merchandising and sales promotion were the most likely to be performed in-house.[6]

Saving money is not the only reason companies use in-house agencies. Time savings, bad experiences with outside agencies, and the increased knowledge and understanding of the market that come from working on advertising and promotion for the product or service day by day are also reasons. Companies can also maintain tighter control over the process and more easily coordinate promotions with the firm's overall marketing program. Some companies use an in-house agency simply because they believe it can do a better job than an outside agency could.[7]

Opponents of in-house agencies say they can give the advertiser neither the experience and objectivity of an outside agency nor the range of services. They argue that outside agencies have more highly skilled specialists and attract the best creative talent and that using an external firm gives a company a more varied perspective on its advertising problems and greater flexibility. In-house personnel may become narrow or grow stale while working on the same product line, but outside agencies may have different people with a variety of backgrounds and ideas working on the account. Flexibility is greater because an outside agency can be dismissed if the company is not satisfied, whereas changes in an in-house agency could be slower and more disruptive.

The cost savings of an in-house agency must be evaluated against these considerations. For many companies, high-quality advertising is critical to their marketing success and should be the major criterion in determining whether to use in-house services. Companies like Rockport and Redken Laboratories have moved their in-house work to outside agencies in recent years. Redken cited the need for a "fresh look" and objectivity as the reasons, noting that management gets too close to the product to come up with different creative ideas. Companies often hire outside agencies as they grow and their advertising budgets and needs increase. For example, the fast-growing personal computer company Gateway hired an outside agency a few years ago to handle all of its advertising.[8]

Advertising Agency Option Probably the main reason outside agencies are used is that they provide the client with the services of highly skilled individuals who are specialists in their chosen fields. An advertising agency staff may include artists, writers, media analysts, researchers, and others with specific skills, knowledge, and experience who can help market the client's products or services. Many agencies specialize in a particular type of business and use their knowledge of the industry to assist their clients.

An outside agency can also provide an objective viewpoint of the market and its business that is not subject to internal company policies, biases, or other limitations. The agency can draw on the broad range of experience it has gained while working on a diverse set of marketing problems for various clients. For example, an ad agency that is handling a travel-related account may have individuals who have worked with airlines, cruise ship companies, travel agencies, hotels, and other travel-related industries. The agency may have experience in this area or may even have previously worked on the advertising account of one of the client's competitors. Thus, the agency can provide the client with insight into the industry (and, in some cases, the competition).

Many major companies use an advertising agency to assist them in developing, preparing, and executing their promotional programs. An ad agency is a service organization that specializes in planning and executing advertising programs for its clients. As we noted, other agencies are now a key part of the IMC process. Canadian marketing communications agencies are highly concentrated. The top ten marketing communications firms have combined domestic revenue of about $683 million, while the subsequent groups of ten firms are approximately $351 million (11 to 20), $160 million (21 to 30), $105 million (31 to 40) and $65 million (41 to 50). The top ten firms represent 50 percent of revenue of the top 50 firms, while the top 20 firms have hit the one billion mark in sales. The largest firm, Cossette Communication Group Inc., has domestic revenues of $129 million and about 1,200 employees, while the 50th largest firm, Armada Advertising Agency, has $5.7 million in revenue and 40 employees.

Many of the large firms are subsidiaries of larger international conglomerates, however, a number are based in Canada, including the leading-ranked Cossette, 5th-ranked Maxxcom Inc., 9th-ranked Maritz Canada, 11th-ranked Nurun, 14th-ranked Envoy Communications Group, and 16th-ranked Carlson Marketing Group of Canada (see Figure 16–5). While Maxxcom is the fifth largest in Canada with $69 million in revenues, it has just over $200 million from international sales. Nurun and Envoy have significant international presence, as approximately half of their total revenue is obtained from sales in other countries.

As you know, agencies provide a number of different services, and the revenues can be examined on an individual service basis for all of the agencies. Figure 16–6 shows the top ten agencies by advertising creative revenue. Because this is a large part

Figure 16–5 Canada's top 20 marketing communications services companies

Ranking	Company	2001 Gross Revenues*
1	Cossette Communication Group	128,860,000
2	MacLaren McCann Canada	92,993,000
3	The Young & Rubicam Group of Companies	71,674,000
4	BBDO Canada	70,523,297
5	Maxxcom	69,128,112
6	DDB Group Canada	59,816,240
7	Publicis Canada	53,435,665
8	DraftWorldwide Canada	47,676,766
9	Maritz Canada	45,093,864
10	Ogilvy & Mather (Canada)	44,257,010
11	Nurun	42,600,000
12	FCB Worldwide (Canada)	42,286,455
13	Palmer Jarvis DDB	39,263,585
14	Envoy Communications Group	38,193,538
15	Fleishman-Hillard	36,399,925
16	Carlson Marketing Group Canada	33,830,000
17	Bensimon•Byrne D'Arcy	31,634,000
18	Leo Burnett Company	31,510,281
19	TBWA\Chait\Day	29,207,685
20	J. Walter Thompson Company	25,755,203

Figure 16–6 Advertising creative (*Based on companies that provided breakdowns*)

Ranking	Company	Main Ranking	2001 Gross Revenues*
1	Cossette Communication Group	1	47,438,000
2	DDB Group Canada	6	37,575,127
3	BBDO Canada	4	34,987,776
4	Palmer Jarvis DDB	13	25,214,941
5	FCB Worldwide (Canada)	12	24,167,716
6	Bensimon•Byrne D'Arcy	17	21,956,000
7	DraftWorldwide Canada	8	18,420,262
8	Doner Canada	26	13,493,821
9	Grey Advertising	21	11,526,000
10	Anderson DDB Health & Lifestyle	25	10,806,174

of the revenue stream for many agencies, it is not surprising to see Cossette leading here as well. And perhaps also not too surprising, Cossette leads all Canadian firms in direct marketing (Figure 16–7) and media planning and buying (Figure 16–8). Fleishman-Hillard and Nurun lead in public relations (Figure 16–9) and interactive/digital marketing (Figure 16–10), respectively, although Cossette is near the top once again. Finally, Maritz Canada is the leading sales promotion firm in Canada (Figure 16–11) which helps make it the ninth-largest marketing communications firm in Canada.

Ranking	Company	Main Ranking	2001 Gross Revenues*
1	Cossette Communication Group	1	16,659,000
2	Carlson Marketing Group Canada	16	16,335,000
3	FCB Worldwide (Canada)	12	12,807,123
4	DraftWorldwide Canada	8	7,250,089
5	DDB Group Canada**	6	4,457,419
6	Grey Advertising	21	4,009,000
7	Marketing Communication Group	37	3,899,642
8	Palmer Jarvis DDB	13	3,433,058
9	Rapp Collins	61	3,337,492
10	BBDO Canada	4	2,132,861

Figure 16–7 Direct marketing (*Based on companies that provided breakdowns*)

Ranking	Company	Main Ranking	2001 Gross Revenues*
1	Cossette Communication Group	1	14,108,000
2	BBDO Canada	4	12,141,890
3	DDB Group Canada**	6	9,466,739
4	Saint-Jacques Vallée Young & Rubicam	39	7,015,939
5	Bensimon•Byrne D'Arcy	17	5,203,000
6	PALM Publicité Marketing	30	5,049,798
7	Palmer Jarvis DDB	13	4,145,889
8	Griffin Bacal Volny	49	3,677,139
9	Groupaction Marketing	28	3,433,640
10	Amalgame-Cargo créativité stratégique	62	2,200,000

Figure 16–8 Media planning and buying (*Based on companies that provided breakdowns*)

Ranking	Company	Main Ranking	2001 Gross Revenues*
1	Fleishman-Hillard	15	33,835,329
2	Cossette Communication Group	1	11,193,000
3	BenchMark Porter Novelli	43	7,143,002
4	Strategic Objectives	48	6,200,000
5	Torchia Communications	57	4,481,966
6	Bensimon•Byrne D'Arcy	17	4,475,000
7	Thornley Fallis Group	69	2,936,438
8	Delta Media	88	1,171,964
9	Marketing Communication Group	37	1,091,501
10	Calder Bateman	71	575,000

Figure 16–9 Public relations (*Based on companies that provided breakdowns*)

Figure 16–10 Interactive/
digital marketing (*Based on
companies that provided
breakdowns*)

Ranking	Company	Main Ranking	2001 Gross Revenues*
1	Nurun	11	42,600,000
2	Blast Radius	44	18,600,000
3	Cossette Communication Group	1	10,444,000
4	Grey Advertising	21	8,810,000
5	BBDO Canada	4	4,302,106
6	Maritz Canada	9	4,206,418
7	DDB Group Canada	6	2,943,777
8	Fleishman-Hillard	15	2,564,596
9	Palmer Jarvis DDB	13	2,404,212
10	PALM Publicité Marketing	30	2,065,826

Figure 16–11 Promotion
marketing (*Based on
companies that provided
breakdowns*)

Ranking	Company	Main Ranking	2001 Gross Revenues*
1	Maritz Canada	9	32,764,762
2	Draft Worldwide Canada	8	14,419,593
3	Advantex Marketing International	35	9,029,651
4	Cossette Communication Group	1	7,133,000
5	FCB Worldwide (Canada)	12	5,311,616
6	Capital C Communications	64	3,500,000
7	BBDO Canada	4	2,958,664
8	G/Comm Marketing	58	1,869,000
9	Allard Johnson Communications	24	1,000,000
10	Hargreaves Charbonneau & Associates	75	891,800

From an international perspective, the advertising industry underwent major changes as large agencies merged with or acquired other agencies and support organizations. These **superagencies** were formed so that agencies could provide clients with integrated marketing communications services worldwide. Some advertisers became disenchanted with the superagencies and moved to smaller agencies that were flexible and more responsive.[9] However, the agency business consolidated again medium-size agencies were acquired and became part of large advertising organizations such as Omnicom Group, WPP Group, and the Interpublic Group of Cos. Many of the mid-size agencies were acquired by or forged alliances with larger agencies because their clients wanted an agency with international communications capabilities and their alignment with larger organizations gave them access to a network of agencies around the world.[10] Recent merger and acquisition activity concerns has seen major agencies acquiring companies specializing in areas such as interactive communications, direct marketing, and sales promotion so that they can offer their clients an ever-broader range of integrated marketing communication services.[11] Figure 16–12 shows the top ten international agencies and where the leading Canadian firms fit in the rankings based on global revenues. The difference in revenues for the Canadian firms is a result of different measurement systems between the two sources.

Full Service Advertising Agencies

Since ad agencies can range in size from a one- or two-person operation to large organizations with over 1,000 employees, the services offered and functions per-

Figure 16–12 World's top ad organizations

Rank				Worldwide gross income ($US M)	
2001	2000	Company	Headquarters	2001	% change
1	2	WPP	London	8,165.0	2.5
2	1	Interpublic Group of Companies	New York	7,981.4	−1.9
3	3	Omnicom Group	New York	7,404.2	6.0
4	4	Publicis Groupe (includes Bcom3 Group)	Paris	4,769.9	2.0
5	5	Dentsu	Tokyo	2,795.5	−8.9
6	6	Havas	Levallois-Peret, France	2,733.1	−2.1
7	7	Grey Global Group	New York	1,863.6	1.7
8	8	Cordiant Communications Group	London	1,174.5	−7.0
9	9	Hakuhodo	Tokyo	874.3	−13.0
10	10	Asatsu-DK	Tokyo	394.6	−8.7
Canadian-based organizations in top 100					
18	18	Maxxcom	Toronto	177.1	−0.1
24	30	Cossette Communication Group	Quebec City	95.2	12.1
48	46	Envoy Communications Group	Toronto	54.8	−8.3
51	42	Wolf Group Integrated Communications	Toronto	51.9	−20.0

Source: Reprinted with permission from the April 22, 2002, issue of *Advertising Age*. Copyright: Crain Communications 2002

formed will vary. In order to understand the variety of agencies, we focus on the largest and most complex. Many companies employ what is known as a **full-service agency,** which offers its clients a full range of marketing, communications, and promotions services, including planning, creating, and producing the advertising; performing research; and selecting media. A full-service agency may also offer non-advertising services such as strategic market planning; sales promotions, direct marketing, and interactive capabilities; package design; and public relations and publicity.

The full-service agency is made up of departments that provide the activities needed to perform the various advertising functions and serve the client, as shown in Figure 16–13.

Account Services Account services, or account management, is the link between the ad agency and its clients. Depending on the size of the client and its advertising budget, one or more account executives serve as liaison. The **account executive** is responsible for understanding the advertiser's marketing and promotions needs and interpreting them to agency personnel. He or she coordinates agency efforts in planning, creating, and producing ads. The account executive also presents agency recommendations and obtains client approval.

As the focal point of agency–client relationships, the account executive must know a great deal about the client's business and be able to communicate this to specialists in the agency working on the account.[12] The ideal account executive has a strong marketing background as well as a thorough understanding of all phases of the advertising process.

Marketing Services Over the past two decades, use of marketing services has increased dramatically. One service gaining increased attention is research, as agencies realize that to communicate effectively with their clients' customers, they must

Figure 16–13   Full-service agency organizational chart

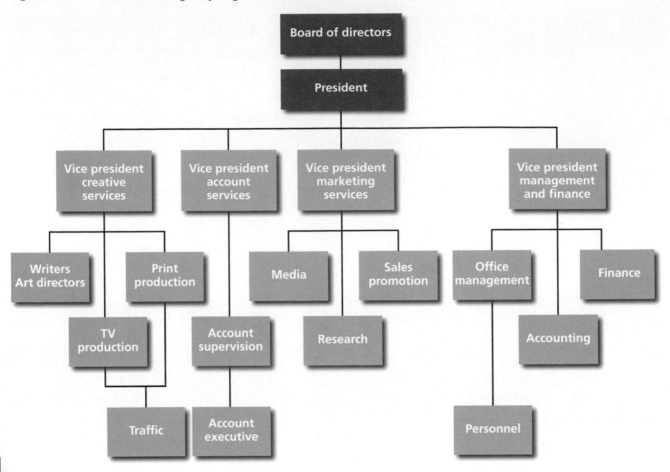

have a good understanding of the target audience. As shown in Chapter 1, the advertising planning process begins with a thorough situation analysis, which is based on research and information about the target audience.

Most full-service agencies maintain a *research department* whose function is to gather, analyze, and interpret information that will be useful in developing advertising for their clients. This can be done through primary research—where a study is designed, executed, and interpreted by the research department—or through the use of secondary (previously published) sources of information. Sometimes the research department acquires studies conducted by independent syndicated research firms or consultants. The research staff then interprets these reports and passes on the information to other agency personnel working on that account.

The research department may also design and conduct research to pretest the effectiveness of advertising the agency is considering. For example, copy testing is often conducted to determine how messages developed by the creative specialists are likely to be interpreted by the receiving audience.

The *media department* of an agency analyzes, selects, and contracts for space or time in the media that will be used to deliver the client's advertising message. The media department is expected to develop a media plan that will reach the target audience and effectively communicate the message. Since most of the client's ad budget is spent on media time and/or space, this department must develop a plan that both communicates with the right audience and is cost-effective.

Media specialists must know what audiences the media reach, their rates, and how well they match the client's target audience. The media department reviews information on demographics, magazine and newspaper readership, radio listenership, and consumers' TV viewing patterns to develop an effective media plan. The media buyer implements the media plan by purchasing the actual time and space. The media department is becoming an increasingly important part of the agency

General Motors Drives the Brand Management Road

The use of a brand management organizational system has been around since 1927, when Procter & Gamble pioneered the concept by assigning a manager to work exclusively on Camay soap. Since then the practice of making a single manager a brand's internal champion with responsibility for all of its marketing has become commonplace in most large consumer, as well as industrial product, companies. However, General Motors (GM), the largest corporation in the United States, recently adopted the same brand management techniques used to sell cereal, toothpaste, soap, and thousands of other products in hopes of selling more cars.

The goal of General Motors founder Alfred P. Sloan was to "build a car for every purse and purpose," and for many years GM created some of the strongest brand names in the auto industry, including Cadillac, Pontiac, Chevrolet, Oldsmobile, and Buick. However, over the past few decades, fuzzy advertising and marketing as well as lookalike models from competing GM divisions helped blur the identity of many of these brands. The problem was compounded by a system where dozens of managers in marketing, sales, and planning would work on various aspects of marketing for many different models. Moreover, GM's traditional divisional managers had too many responsibilities and could not give enough attention to the individual brands.

To address these problems and once again create strong identities for its 40-plus brands of cars, trucks, minivans, and sport utility vehicles, GM appointed brand managers who work under the divisional general manager but are accountable for the sales success of individual brands such as the Chevrolet Malibu or Buick Century. The GM brand managers have full responsibility for marketing their vehicles, including pricing, advertising, and promotion. They are responsible for developing target markets as well as conceiving, implementing, and managing marketing campaigns that will differentiate their brands.

General Motors implemented its brand management system in 1996 and the new system has brought common processes, practices, and systems and has helped eliminate duplicated effort by its marketing divisions. And it has played a major role in increasing sales of GM models such as the Pontiac Grand Prix and Chevy Malibu.

One concern expressed over GM's brand management system is that it defines brands down too far, as every single model is a brand, and attention needs to be given to the image and positioning of divisions such as Oldsmobile and Cadillac. One GM division where GM is addressing this issue is Cadillac, which is striving to reclaim its luxury standard status.

At the end of 1999, Cadillac began a new advertising and positioning theme for the entire Cadillac division. The new ad campaign revolves around the design and technology theme, and signals a push for distinctive styling and technological innovation for all the Cadillac models. In the past, Cadillac models had their own advertising taglines. However, now advertising for various models such as Catera, Seville, and DeVille DTS will all use the theme "The Power of &," which signifies how Cadillac is combining design and technology in inspiring new ways. The campaign's goal is to build a uniform personality around the theme and in both print and TV ads an emphasis is placed on humanizing the image of Cadillac.

As one management consultant has noted, "The cornerstone of brand management is to stop chasing your competition and start chasing your customer. GM has gotten the message." GM's goal is for its brand management system to continue to create an array of well-defined brands that even Alfred Sloan would be proud of.

Sources: Tanya Irwin, "A Brand New Cadillac," *Adweek,* September 6, 1999, p. 30; Jean Halliday, "GM's Brand Management Report Card," *Advertising Age,* March 9, 1998, pp. 1, 26; Kathleen Kerwin, "GM Warms Up the Branding Iron," *Business Week,* September 23, 1996, pp. 153–54.

business as many large advertisers consolidate their media buying with one or a few agencies to save money and improve media efficiency. An agency's strategic ability to negotiate prices and effectively use the vast array of media vehicles available is becoming as important as its ability to create ads.

The research and media departments perform most of the functions that full-service agencies need to plan and execute their clients' advertising programs. Some agencies offer additional marketing services to their clients to assist in other promotional areas. An agency may have a sales promotion department, or merchandising department, that specializes in developing contests, premiums, promotions, point-of-sale materials, and other sales materials. It may have direct-marketing specialists and package designers, as well as a PR/publicity department. Many agencies have developed interactive media departments to create websites for their clients. The growing popularity of integrated marketing communications has prompted many full-function agencies to develop capabilities and offer services in these other promotional areas.

Creative Services

The creative services department is responsible for the creation and execution of advertisements. The individuals who conceive the ideas for the ads and write the headlines, subheads, and body copy (the words constituting the message) are known as **copywriters.** They may also be involved in determining the basic appeal or theme of the ad campaign and often prepare a rough initial visual layout of the print ad or television commercial.

While copywriters are responsible for what the message says, the *art department* is responsible for how the ad looks. For print ads, the art director and graphic designers prepare *layouts,* which are drawings that show what the ad will look like and from which the final artwork will be produced. For TV commercials, the layout is known as a *storyboard,* a sequence of frames or panels that depict the commercial in still form.

Members of the creative department work together to develop ads that will communicate the key points determined to be the basis of the creative strategy for the client's product or service. Writers and artists generally work under the direction of the agency's creative director, who oversees all the advertising produced by the organization. The director sets the creative philosophy of the department and may even become directly involved in creating ads for the agency's largest clients.

Once the copy, layout, illustrations, and mechanical specifications have been completed and approved, the ad is turned over to the *production department.* Most agencies do not actually produce finished ads; they hire printers, engravers, photographers, typographers, and other suppliers to complete the finished product. For broadcast production, the approved storyboard must be turned into a finished commercial. The production department may supervise the casting of people to appear in the ad and the setting for the scenes as well as choose an independent production studio. The department may hire an outside director to turn the creative concept into a commercial. Copywriters, art directors, account managers, people from research and planning, and representatives from the client side may all participate in production decisions, particularly when large sums of money are involved.

Creating an advertisement often involves many people and takes several months. In large agencies with many clients, coordinating the creative and production processes can be a major problem. A *traffic department* coordinates all phases of production to see that the ads are completed on time and that all deadlines for submitting the ads to the media are met. The traffic department may be located in the creative services area of the agency, or be part of media or account management, or be separate.

Management and Finance

Like any other business, an advertising agency must be managed and perform basic operating and administrative functions such as accounting, finance, and human resources. It must also attempt to generate new business. Large agencies employ administrative, managerial, and clerical people to perform these functions. The bulk of an agency's income (approximately 64 percent) goes to salary and benefits for its employees. Thus, an agency must manage its personnel carefully and get maximum productivity from them.

Part Six Implement, Control, and Monitor the IMC Plan

Structure   Full-function advertising agencies must develop an organizational structure that will meet their clients' needs and serve their own internal requirements. Most medium-size and large agencies are structured under either a departmental or a group system. Under the **departmental system,** each of the agency functions shown in Figure 16–13 is set up as a separate department and is called on as needed to perform its specialty and serve all of the agency's clients. Ad layout, writing, and production are done by the creative department, marketing services is responsible for any research or media selection and purchases, and the account services department handles client contact. Some agencies prefer the departmental system because it gives employees the opportunity to develop expertise in servicing a variety of accounts.

Many large agencies use the **group system,** in which individuals from each department work together in groups to service particular accounts. Each group is headed by an account executive or supervisor and has one or more media people, including media planners and buyers; a creative team, which includes copywriters, art directors, artists, and production personnel; and one or more account executives. The group may also include individuals from other departments such as marketing research, direct marketing, or sales promotion. The size and composition of the group varies depending on the client's billings and the importance of the account to the agency. For very important accounts, the group members may be assigned exclusively to one client. In some agencies, they may serve a number of smaller clients. Many agencies prefer the group system because employees become very knowledgeable about the client's business and there is continuity in servicing the account.

Other Types of Agencies and Services

Not every agency is a large full-service agency. Many smaller agencies expect their employees to handle a variety of jobs. For example, account executives may do their own research, work out their own media schedule, and coordinate the production of ads written and designed by the creative department. Many advertisers, including some large companies, are not interested in paying for the services of a full-service agency but are interested in some of the specific services agencies have to offer. Over the past few decades, several alternatives to full-service agencies have evolved, including creative boutiques and media buying services.

Creative Boutiques   A **creative boutique** is an agency that provides only creative services. These specialized companies have developed in response to some clients' desires to use only the creative talent of an outside provider while maintaining the other functions internally. The client may seek outside creative talent because it believes an extra creative effort is required or because its own employees do not have sufficient skills in this regard. Some advertisers have been bypassing traditional agencies and tapping into the movie industry for creative ideas for their commercials.[13] For example, a few years ago Coca-Cola entered into a joint venture with Disney and three former employees of Creative Artists Agency (CAA), a Hollywood talent agency, to create an in-house agency called Edge Creative. The agency created several commercials for Coca-Cola's flagship brand, including the popular polar bears spot (Exhibit 16–4).

Full-service agencies often subcontract work to creative boutiques when they are very busy or want to avoid adding full-time employees to their payrolls. Creative boutiques are usually founded by members of the creative departments of full-service agencies who leave the firm and take with them clients who want to retain their creative talents. These boutiques usually perform the creative function on a fee basis.

Exhibit 16–4 This popular Coca-Cola spot was done by the company's in-house creative boutique

One area where Canadian agencies have worked with specialized creative firms is in the development of messages targeted to specific ethnic markets. It is very expensive and difficult for large agencies to be set up for each ethnic community that it may try to reach in a campaign, so they rely on specialists who have the expertise. With a tremendous growth of Chinese immigrants in Toronto and Vancouver, firms such as Ford have used tailored messages and ethnic media to influence the attitudes of this target audience that has very different beliefs than other consumers because of their heritage. Ford could not succeed in establishing a unique brand position with this target audience without the assistance of those more familiar. One trade-off that advertisers need in order to make this work is to put the media savings from lower cost publications or TV programming into the production of appropriate creative messages.[14]

Media Buying Services   **Media buying services** are independent companies that specialize in the buying of media, particularly radio and television time. The task of purchasing advertising media has grown more complex as specialized media proliferate, so media buying services have found a niche by specializing in the analysis and purchase of advertising time and space. Agencies and clients usually develop their own media strategies and hire the buying service to execute them. Some media buying services do help advertisers plan their media strategies. Because media buying services purchase such large amounts of time and space, they receive large discounts and can save the small agency or client money on media purchases. Media buying services are paid a fee or commission for their work.

Media buying services have been experiencing strong growth in recent years as clients seek alternatives to full-service agency relationships. Many companies have been unbundling agency services and consolidating media buying to get more clout from their advertising budgets. Nike, Bugle Boy, and Pennzoil are among those that have switched some or all of their media buying from full-service agencies to independent media buyers.

Agency Compensation

As you have seen, the type and amount of services an agency performs vary from one client to another. As a result, agencies use a variety of methods to get paid for their services. Agencies are typically compensated in three ways: commissions, some type of fee arrangement, or percentage charges.

Commissions from Media

The traditional method of compensating agencies is through a **commission system,** where the agency receives a specified commission (usually 15 percent) from the media on any advertising time or space it purchases for its client. This system provides a simple method of determining payments, as shown in the following example.

Assume an agency prepares a full-page magazine ad and arranges to place the ad on the back cover of a magazine at a cost of $100,000. The agency places the order for the space and delivers the ad to the magazine. Once the ad is run, the magazine will bill the agency for $100,000, less the 15 percent ($15,000) commission. The media will also offer a 2 percent cash discount for early payment, which the agency may pass along to the client. The agency will bill the client $100,000 less the 2 percent cash discount on the net amount, or a total of $98,300, as shown in Figure 16–14. The $15,000 commission represents the agency's compensation for its services.

Use of the commission system to compensate agencies has been quite controversial for many years. A major problem centres on whether the 15 percent commission represents equitable compensation for services performed. Two agencies may require the same amount of effort to create and produce an ad. However, one client may spend $200,000 on commissionable media, which results in a $30,000 agency income, while the other spends $2 million, generating $300,000 in commissions. Critics argue that the commission system encourages agencies to recommend high media expenditures to increase their commission level.

Figure 16–14 Example of commission system payment

Media Bills Agency		Agency Bills Advertiser	
Costs for magazine space	$100,000	Costs for magazine space	$100,000
Less 15% commission	−15,000	Less 2% cash discount	−1,700
Cost of media space	$ 85,000	Advertiser pays agency	$ 98,300
Less 2% cash discount	−1,700		
Agency pays media	$ 83,300	Agency income	$ 15,000

Another criticism of the commission system is that it ties agency compensation to media costs. In periods of media cost inflation, the agency is (according to the client) disproportionately rewarded. The commission system has also been criticized for encouraging agencies to ignore cost accounting systems to justify the expenses attributable to work on a particular account. Still others charge that this system tempts the agency to avoid noncommissionable media such as direct mail, sales promotions, or advertising specialties, unless they are requested by the client.

Defenders of the commission system argue that it is easy to administer and it keeps the emphasis in agency competition on non-price factors such as the quality of the advertising developed. Proponents argue that agency services are proportional to the size of the commission, since more time and effort are devoted to the large accounts that generate high revenue for the agency. They also say the system is more flexible than it appears because agencies often perform other services for large clients at no extra charge, justifying such actions by the large commission they receive.

The commission system has been a highly debated topic among advertisers and agencies for years. Critics of the system have argued that it provides an incentive for agencies to do the wrong thing, such as recommending mass-media advertising when other forms of communication such as direct marketing or public relations might do a better job.[15] They argue that the commission system is outdated and must be changed. This does indeed appear to be happening. A recent study of agency compensation conducted by the Association of National Advertisers (ANA) indicates that agency compensation based on the traditional 15 percent commission is becoming rare.[16] The survey found that only 9 percent of clients use a 15 percent commission, and 75 percent said their agency compensation amounts to less than a 15 percent commission. However, nearly two-thirds of the companies indicated that they use the 15 percent commission as a benchmark to evaluate their current agency compensation agreements.

While the use of the 15 percent commission is on the wane, many advertisers still use some form of media commission to compensate their agencies. Many advertisers have gone to a **negotiated commission** system to compensate their agencies. This commission structure can take the form of reduced percentage rates, variable commission rates, and commissions with minimum and maximum profit rates. Negotiated commissions are designed to consider the needs of the clients as well as the time and effort exerted by the agency, thereby avoiding some of the problems inherent in the traditional 15 percent sytem. Some of the leading agencies now receive an average commission on media of 8 to 10 percent versus the traditional 15 percent.[17] Agencies are also relying less on media commissions for their income as their clients expand their integrated marketing communications programs to include other forms of promotion and cut back on mass-media advertising. The percentage of agency income from media commissions is declining, and a greater percentage is coming through other methods such as fees and performance incentives.

Other Compensation Systems

Since many believe the commission system is not equitable to all parties, many agencies and their clients have developed some type of fee arrangement or cost-plus agreement for agency compensation. Some are using incentive-based compensation, which is a combination of a commission and a fee system, while others are experimenting with percentage charges.

Fee Arrangement

There are two basic types of fee arrangement systems. In the straight or **fixed-fee method,** the agency charges a basic monthly fee for all of its services and credits to the client any media commissions earned. Agency and client agree on the specific work to be done and the amount the agency will be paid for it. Sometimes agencies are compensated through a **fee-commission combination,** in which the media commissions received by the agency are credited against the fee. If the commissions are less than the agreed-on fee, the client must make up the difference. If the agency does much work for the client in noncommissionable media, the fee may be charged over and above the commissions received.

Both types of fee arrangements require that the agency carefully assess its costs of serving the client for the specified period, or for the project, plus its desired profit margin. To avoid any later disagreement, a fee arrangement should specify exactly what services the agency is expected to perform for the client.

Cost-Plus Agreement

Under a **cost-plus system,** the client agrees to pay the agency a fee based on the costs of its work plus some agreed-on profit margin (often a percentage of total costs). This system requires that the agency keep detailed records of the costs it incurs in working on the client's account. Direct costs (personnel time and out-of-pocket expenses) plus an allocation for overhead and a markup for profits determine the amount the agency bills the client.

Fee agreements and cost-plus systems are commonly used in conjunction with a commission system. The fee-based system can be advantageous to both the client and the agency, depending on the size of the client, advertising budget, media used, and services required. Many clients prefer fee or cost-plus systems because they receive a detailed breakdown of where and how their advertising and promotion dollars are being spent. However, these arrangements can be difficult for the agency, as they require careful cost accounting and may be difficult to estimate when bidding for an advertiser's business. Agencies are also reluctant to let clients see their internal cost figures.

Incentive-Based Compensation

Many clients these days are demanding more accountability from their agencies and tying agency compensation to performance through some type of **incentive-based system.** While there are many variations, the basic idea is that the agency's ultimate compensation level will depend on how well it meets predetermined performance goals. These goals often include objective measures such as sales or market share as well as more subjective measures such as evaluations of the quality of the agency's creative work. Companies using incentive-based systems determine agency compensation through media commissions, fees, bonuses, or some combination of these methods. Some clients use a sliding scale whereby the agency's base compensation is less than the 15 percent commission but the agency can earn extra commissions or bonuses depending on how it meets sales or other performance goals.

Percentage Charges

Another way to compensate an agency is by adding a markup of **percentage charges** to various services the agency purchases from outside providers. These may include market research, artwork, printing, photography, and other services or materials. Markups usually range from 17.65 to 20 percent and are added to the client's overall bill. Since suppliers of these services do not allow the agency a commission, percentage charges cover administrative costs while allowing a reasonable profit for the agency's efforts. (A markup of 17.65 percent of costs added to the initial cost would yield a 15 percent commission. For example, research costs of $100,000 × 17.65% = $100,000 + $17,650 = $117,650. The $17,650 markup is about 15 percent of $117,650.)

As you can see, there is no one method of compensation to which everyone subscribes. Many companies are changing their compensation systems as they move away from traditional mass media and turn to a wider array of marketing communication tools. They are also trying to make their agencies more accountable through formal evaluation.

Evaluation of Agencies

Given the substantial amounts of money being spent on advertising and promotion, demand for accountability of the expenditures has increased. Regular reviews of the agency's performance are necessary. The agency evaluation process usually involves two types of assessments, one financial and operational and the other more qualitative. The **financial audit** focuses on how the agency conducts its business. It is designed to verify costs and expenses, the number of personnel hours charged to an account, and payments to media and outside suppliers. The **qualitative audit** focuses on the agency's efforts in planning, developing, and implementing the client's advertising programs and considers the results achieved.

The agency evaluation is often done on a subjective, informal basis, particularly in smaller companies where ad budgets are low or advertising is not seen as the most critical factor in the firm's marketing performance. Some companies have developed formal, systematic evaluation systems, particularly when budgets are large and the advertising function receives much emphasis. As advertising costs continue to rise, the top management of these companies wants to be sure money is being spent efficiently and effectively.

One example of a formal agency evaluation system is that used by Borden Foods Corporation, which markets a variety of consumer products. Borden's brand teams meet once a year with the company's agencies to review their performance. Brand management completes an advertising agency performance evaluation. These reports are compiled and reviewed with the agency at each annual meeting. Borden's evaluation process covers eight areas of performance. Borden and the agency develop an action plan to correct areas of deficiency. But some companies doubt whether advertising effectiveness can be directly related to sales and have developed their own evaluation procedures.

Exhibit 16–5 Young & Rubicam has been the agency for Dr Pepper for more than three decades

Gaining and Losing Clients

The evaluation process described above provides valuable feedback to both the agency and the client, such as indicating changes that need to be made by the agency and/or the client to improve performance and make the relationship more productive. Many agencies have had very long-lasting relationships with their clients (see Exhibit 16–5); however, long-term relationships are becoming less common. There are a number of reasons why clients switch agencies. Some of the more common reasons that agencies lose clients are as follows:

- *Poor performance or service.* The client becomes dissatisfied with the quality of the advertising and/or the service provided by the agency.

- *Poor communication.* The client and agency personnel fail to develop or maintain the level of communication necessary to sustain a favourable working relationship.

- *Unrealistic demands by the client.* The client places demands on the agency that exceed the amount of compensation received and reduce the account's profitability.

- *Personality conflicts.* People working on the account on the client and agency sides do not have enough rapport to work well together.

Dr Pepper/Seven Up, Inc. congratulates Young & Rubicam on 75 years of creative excellence.

In 1999, brand Dr Pepper and Y&R will celebrate three decades of creative teamwork. From "The Most Misunderstood" to "This Is The Taste," Y&R has helped Dr Pepper become the powerful trademark brand it is today. It just goes to show, we're better together!

Dr Pepper and Y&R Better Together!

- *Personnel changes.* A change in personnel at either the agency or the advertiser can create problems. New managers may wish to use an agency with which they have established ties. Agency personnel often take accounts with them when they switch agencies or start their own.
- *Changes in size of the client or agency.* The client may outgrow the agency or decide it needs a larger agency to handle its business. If the agency gets too large, the client may represent too small a percentage of its business to command attention.
- *Conflicts of interest.* A conflict may develop when an agency merges with another agency or when a client is part of an acquisition or merger.
- *Changes in the client's corporate and/or marketing strategy.* A client may change its marketing strategy and think a new agency is needed to carry out the new program.
- *Declining sales.* When sales of the client's product or service are stagnant or declining, advertising may be seen as contributing to the problem. A new agency may be sought for a new creative approach.
- *Conflicting compensation philosophies.* Disagreement may develop over the level or method of compensation. As more companies move toward incentive-based compensation systems, disagreement over compensation is becoming more commonplace.
- *Changes in policies.* Policy changes may result when either party reevaluates the importance of the relationship, the agency acquires a new (and larger) client, or either side undergoes a merger or acquisition.

If the agency recognizes these warning signs, it can try to adapt its programs and policies to make sure the client is satisfied. Some of the situations discussed here are unavoidable, and others are beyond the agency's control. But to maintain the account, problems within the agency's control must be addressed.

The time may come when the agency decides it is no longer in its best interest to continue to work with the client. Personnel conflicts, changes in management philosophy, and/or insufficient financial incentives are just a few of the reasons for such a decision. Then the agency may terminate the account relationship.

Specialized Services

Many companies assign the development and implementation of their promotional programs to an advertising agency. But several other types of organizations provide specialized services that complement the efforts of ad agencies. Direct-response agencies, sales promotion agencies, and public relations firms are important to marketers in developing and executing IMC programs. Let us examine the functions these organizations perform.

Sales Promotion Agencies

Developing and managing sales promotion programs such as contests, sweepstakes, refunds and rebates, premium and incentive offers, and sampling programs is a very complex task. Most companies use a **sales promotion agency** to develop and administer these programs. Some large ad agencies have created their own sales promotion department or acquired a sales promotion firm. However, most sales promotion agencies are independent companies that specialize in providing the services needed to plan, develop, and execute a variety of sales promotion programs.

Sales promotion agencies often work in conjunction with the client's advertising and/or direct-response agencies to coordinate their efforts with the advertising and direct-marketing programs. Services provided by large sales promotion agencies include promotional planning, creative, research, tie-in coordination, fulfillment, premium design and manufacturing, catalogue production, and contest/sweepstakes management. Many sales promotion agencies are also developing direct/database

Women are the greatest untapped market in a marketing communications industry that is facing a chronic shortage of talent, says Stefan Danis, chief talent officer and CEO of Mandrake, the Toronto-based executive search firm. The future is one of integrated communications, and women possess the qualities needed to ensure the success of that business. Women are more intuitive and give greater attention to detail than men do, Danis says, noting studies that show women think holistically while men are more narrow and deep thinkers.

But if women are the key to success in marketing, the industry has yet to catch on and continues to treat women like chopped liver. "It's still a man's world and women adapt to it," Danis said in an interview after his keynote speech at a Le Publicité-Club de Montreal conference on careers in marketing communications. Danis says few women are heading ad agencies, and for every woman who enters the industry, another disillusioned woman leaves it. Women face many more life challenges than men, and only clued-in employers who provide them with specific benefits—such as the option to telecommute, work sharing, access to nurseries and day care, and longer maternity leaves—will benefit from their potential, he says.

Danis quoted from Ivey and Rotman business school studies showing that only 3 percent of business school graduates want careers in marketing and sales. And while the Canadian economy will grow by 2 percent annually for the next 15 years, workers ages 35 to 45 in the workforce will decline by more than 15 percent. A chronic talent shortage will worsen unless a supply chain is created and salaries are increased. Danis also painted a picture of employers who will have to constantly be on the lookout for new talent and fight to keep their best.

Danis espoused a "Jim Pattison school of management" approach to employees in which only the strong performers survive. Under that approach, for every ten employees, the top two would be promoted annually, the bottom two would be dumped, and the survivors would be given salary hikes. "You have to move out your C players—get rid of the bottom 20 percent." This tactic would not affect employee morale, he insists, if employees know what to expect in advance. "Morale is more affected when you tolerate bad performance than when you reward good performance."

Source: Adapted from Danny Kucharsky, "Women Key to Ad Industry's Success," *Marketing Magazine*, April 8, 2002. Used with permission.

marketing and telemarketing to expand their integrated marketing services capabilities. Sales promotion agencies are generally compensated on a fee basis.

Public Relations Firms

Many large companies use both an advertising agency and a PR firm. The **public relations firm** develops and implements programs to manage the organization's publicity, image, and affairs with consumers and other relevant publics, including employees, suppliers, stockholders, government, labour groups, citizen action groups, and the general public. The PR firm analyzes the relationships between the client and these various publics, determines how the client's policies and actions relate to and affect these publics, develops PR strategies and programs, implements these programs using various public relations tools, and evaluates their effectiveness.

The activities of a public relations firm include planning the PR strategy and program, generating publicity, conducting lobbying and public affairs efforts, becoming involved in community activities and events, preparing news releases and other communications, conducting research, promoting and managing special events, and managing crises. As companies adopt an IMC approach to promotional planning, they are coordinating their PR activities with advertising and other promotional areas. Many companies are integrating public relations and publicity into the marketing communications mix to increase message credibility and save media costs.[18]

Direct-Response Agencies

One of the fastest-growing areas of IMC is direct marketing, where companies communicate with consumers through telemarketing, direct mail, and other forms of direct-response advertising. As this industry has grown, numerous direct-response agencies have evolved that offer companies their specialized skills in both consumer and business markets.

Direct-response agencies provide a variety of services, including database management, direct mail, research, media services, and creative and production capabilities. While direct mail is their primary weapon, many direct-response agencies are expanding their services to include such areas as infomercial production and database management. Database development and management is becoming one of the most important services provided by direct-response agencies. Many companies are using database marketing to pinpoint new customers and build relationships and loyalty among existing customers.[19]

A typical direct-response agency is divided into three main departments: account management, creative, and media. Some agencies also have a department whose function is to develop and manage databases for their clients. The account managers work with their clients to plan direct-marketing programs and determine their role in the overall integrated marketing communications process. The creative department consists of copywriters, artists, and producers. Creative is responsible for developing the direct-response message, while the media department is concerned with its placement.

Like advertising agencies, direct-response agencies must solicit new business and have their performance reviewed by their existing clients, often through formal assessment programs. Most direct-response agencies are compensated on a fee basis, although some large advertisers still prefer the commission system.

Interactive Agencies

With the rapid growth of the Internet and other forms of interactive media, a new type of specialized marketing communications organization has evolved—the interactive agency. Many marketers are using **interactive agencies** that specialize in the development and strategic use of various interactive marketing tools such as websites for the Internet, banner ads, CD-ROMs, and kiosks.[20] Many traditional advertising agencies have established interactive capabilities, ranging from a few specialists within the agency to an entire interactive division. For example, some of the largest interactive agencies such as Ogilvy Interactive, Grey Interactive, and Euro RSCG Interactive are affiliates of major agencies. Ogilvy Interactive has developed websites and major interactive campaigns for a number of clients, including the award winning e-business campaign for IBM.

While many agencies have or are developing interactive capabilities, a number of marketers are turning to more specialized interactive agencies to develop websites and interactive media. They feel these companies have more expertise in designing and developing websites as well as managing and supporting them (see Exhibit 16–6). Interactive agencies range from smaller companies that specialize in website design and creation to full-service interactive agencies that provide all the elements needed for a successful Internet/interactive marketing program. These services include strategic consulting regarding the use of the Internet and online brand-

Exhibit 16–6 AGENCY.COM developed the website and various online promotions that support the global branding strategy for British Airways

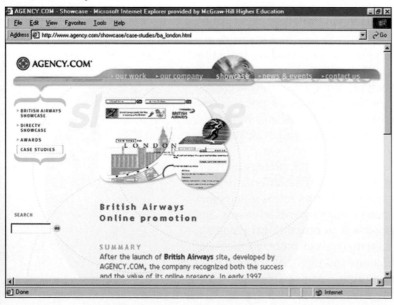

ing, technical knowledge, systems integration, and the development of electronic commerce capabilities.

As the Internet becomes an increasingly important marketing tool, more companies will be turning to interactive agencies to help them develop successful interactive marketing programs. The number of interactive agencies will continue to grow, as will their importance in the development and implementation of Internet-based strategies and initiatives.

You have seen that marketers can choose from a variety of specialized organizations to assist them in planning, developing, and implementing an integrated marketing communications program. But companies must decide whether to use a different organization for each marketing communications function or consolidate them with a large advertising agency that offers all of these services under one roof.

Integrated Marketing Communications Services

As noted in Chapter 1, during the 1980s many of the large agencies began developing IMC capabilities when they realized that their clients were shifting their promotional dollars away from traditional advertising to other forms of promotion. Some did this through mergers and acquisitions and became superagencies consisting of advertising, public relations, sales promotion, and direct-response agencies. Many large agencies are continuing to expand their IMC capabilities by acquiring specialists in various fields. All the major agency holding companies either own or have substantial investments in interactive and direct-response agencies.

While some agencies are expanding their IMC capabilities by acquiring specialized firms and services, others are doing so internally. For example, Foote, Cone & Belding (FCB) recently reorganized and absorbed its sales promotion and direct marketing agencies into the general agency Marketing Drive, which is a global integrated marketing services company supporting all clients of FCB. FCB assigns individuals from various departments to "brand groups" that include account planning and creative members as well as staffers from the various IMC disciplines FCB handles for that client. The brand groups for whom FCB's primary responsibility is advertising are led by ad staffers. A brand group for whom the agency's primary responsibility is sales promotion will be led by someone from Marketing Drive staff. Under this structure, brand building relies on a whole range of IMC tools rather than just advertising.[21] FCB has used the approach in successful brand building efforts for a number of clients such as Amazon.com, Dockers, and Taylor Made golf equipment (Exhibit 16–7).

The Foote, Cone & Belding approach to IMC is an example of what Ander Gronstedt and Esther Thorson call a *matrix organization design,* where an agency combines functional division and cross-functional task force teams.[22] In such an organization, planning and execution of integrated marketing communications programs are collaborative efforts by an interdepartmental account team. The members of the team come from different disciplines and bring a diversity of backgrounds, specialties, and perspectives that can be valuable in creating the IMC program for the client.

Exhibit 16–7 The Foote, Cone & Belding agency uses a variety of IMC tools to build brand identity for clients such as Taylor Made

Pros and Cons of Integrated Services

It has been argued that the concept of integrated marketing is nothing new, particularly in smaller companies and communication agencies that have been coordinating a variety of promotional tools for years. And larger advertising agencies have been trying to gain more of their clients' promotional business for over 20 years. However, in the past, the various services were run as separate profit centres. Each was motivated to push its own expertise and pursue its own goals rather than develop truly integrated marketing programs. Moreover, the creative specialists in many agencies resisted becoming involved in sales promotion or direct marketing. They preferred to concentrate on developing magazine ads or television commercials rather than designing coupons or direct-mail pieces.

Proponents of the integrated marketing services agency (the one-stop shop) contend that past problems are being solved and the various individuals in the agencies and subsidiaries are learning to work together to deliver a consistent message to the client's customers. They argue that maintaining control of the entire promotional process achieves greater synergy among each of the communications program elements. They also note that it is more convenient for the client to coordinate all of its marketing efforts—media advertising, direct mail, special events, sales promotions, and public relations—through one agency. An agency with integrated marketing capabilities can create a single image for the product or service and address everyone, from wholesalers to consumers, with one voice.

But not everyone wants to turn the entire IMC program over to one agency. Opponents say the providers become involved in political wrangling over budgets, do not communicate with each other as well and as often as they should, and do not achieve synergy. They also claim that agencies' efforts to control all aspects of the promotional program are nothing more than an attempt to hold on to business that might otherwise be lost to independent providers. They note that synergy and economies of scale, while nice in theory, have been difficult to achieve and competition and conflict among agency subsidiaries have been a major problem.[23]

Many companies use a variety of vendors for communication functions, choosing the specialist they believe is best suited for each promotional task, be it advertising, sales promotion, or public relations. Many marketers agree with the vice president of advertising at Reebok, who noted, "Why should I limit myself to one resource when there is a tremendous pool of fresh ideas available?"[24]

Responsibility for IMC: Agency versus Client

Surveys of advertisers and agency executives have shown that both groups believe integrated marketing is important to their organizations' success and that it will be even more important in the future.[25] However, marketers and agency executives have very different opinions regarding who should be in charge of the integrated marketing communications process. Many advertisers prefer to set strategy for and coordinate their own IMC campaigns, but most agency executives see this as their domain.

While agency executives believe their shops are capable of handling the various elements an integrated campaign requires, many marketers, particularly larger firms, disagree. Marketing executives say the biggest obstacle to implementing IMC is the lack of people with the broad perspective and skills to make it work. Agencies are felt to lack expertise in database marketing, marketing research, and information technology. Internal turf battles, agency egos, and fear of budget reductions are also cited as major barriers to successful integrated marketing campaigns.[26]

Many ad agencies are adding more resources to offer their clients a full line of services. They are expanding their agencies' capabilities in interactive and multimedia advertising, database management, direct marketing, public relations, and sales promotion. However, many marketers still want to set the strategy for their IMC campaigns and seek specialized expertise, more quality and creativity, and greater control and cost efficiency by using multiple providers.

Most marketers do recognize that ad agencies will no longer stick primarily to advertising and will continue to expand their IMC capabilities. There is an opportunity for agencies to broaden their services beyond advertising—but they will have to develop true expertise in a variety of integrated marketing communications areas. They will also have to create organizational structures that make it possible for individuals with expertise in a variety of communications areas to work well together both internally and externally. One thing is certain: as companies continue to shift their promotional dollars away from media advertising to other IMC tools, agencies will continue to explore ways to keep these monies under their roofs.

Summary

The development, execution, and administration of an advertising and promotions program involve the efforts of many individuals, both within the company and outside it. Participants in the integrated marketing communications process include the advertiser or client, ad agencies, media organizations, specialized marketing communications firms, and providers of collateral services.

Companies use two basic systems to organize internally for advertising and promotion. Centralized systems offer the advantages of facilitated communications, lower personnel requirements, continuity in staff, and more top-management involvement. Disadvantages include a lower involvement with overall marketing goals, longer response times, and difficulties in handling multiple product lines.

Decentralized systems offer the advantages of concentrated managerial attention, more rapid responses to problems, and increased flexibility, though they may be limited by ineffective deci-sion making, internal conflicts, misallocation of funds, and a lack of authority. Firms have to decide if they will hire an external advertising agency or use an in-house service to create their ads and purchase media. In-house agencies, while offering the advantages of cost savings, control, and increased coordination, have the disadvantage of less experience, objectivity, and flexibility.

Many firms use advertising agencies to help develop and execute their programs. These agencies may take on a variety of forms, including full-service agencies, creative boutiques, and media buying services. The first offers the client a full range of services (including creative, account, marketing, and financial and management services); the other two specialize in creative services and media buying, respectively. Agencies are compensated through commission systems, percentage charges, and fee- and cost-based systems. Recently, the emphasis on agency accountability has increased. Agencies are being evaluated on both financial and qualitative aspects, and some clients are using incentive-based compensation systems that tie agency compensation to performance measures such as sales and market share.

In addition to using ad agencies, marketers use the services of other marketing communication specialists, including direct marketing agencies, sales promotion agencies, public relations firms, and interactive agencies. A marketer must decide whether to use a different specialist for each promotional function or have all of its integrated marketing communications done by an advertising agency that offers all of these services under one roof.

Recent studies have found that most marketers believe it is their responsibility, not the ad agency's, to set strategy for and coordinate IMC campaigns. The lack of a broad perspective and specialized skills in nonadvertising areas is seen as the major barrier to agencies' increased involvement in integrated marketing communications.

Key Terms

clients, 422
advertising agency, 423
media organizations, 423
specialized marketing
    communications
    services, 423
collateral services, 423
advertising manager, 424
centralized system, 424
decentralized
    system, 425

brand manager, 425
category management
    system, 427
in-house agency, 428
superagencies, 432
full-service agency, 433
account executive, 433
copywriters, 436
departmental
    system, 437
group system, 437

creative boutique, 437
media buying
    services, 438
commission
    system, 438
negotiated commission,
    439
fixed-fee method, 440
fee-commission
    combination, 440
cost-plus system, 440

incentive-based
    system, 440
percentage charges, 440
financial audit, 441
qualitative audit, 441
sales promotion
    agency, 442
public relations firm, 443
direct-response
    agency, 444
interactive agencies, 444

Discussion Questions

1. Identify the various organizations that participate in the integrated marketing communications process and briefly discuss their roles and responsibilities.

2. What are some of the specific responsibilities and duties of an advertising manager under a centralized advertising department structure? Why is an advertising manager needed if a company uses an outside agency?

3. What is a product or brand manager? Discuss how a brand manager would be involved with the integrated marketing communications program.

4. Discuss the pros and cons of using an in-house advertising agency. What are some of the reasons why companies might change from using an in-house agency and hire an outside agency?

5. Discuss the various functions a full-service advertising agency performs for its clients. Might any one of these functions be more important than another?

6. Discuss the various methods by which advertising agencies are compensated. What factors will determine the type of compensation arrangement a company uses with an agency?

7. Why are many companies moving away from the traditional commission system and using incentive-based compensation for their advertising agencies? Why might an ad agency be reluctant to accept an incentive-based compensation system?

8. Discuss the various reasons why marketers often choose to switch advertising agencies. Find an example of a company that has recently changed advertising agencies and analyze the reasons given for the change.

9. What is an interactive agency? Discuss the reason why a marketer might choose to use an interactive agency rather than have a full-service agency develop its interactive marketing tools such as website design.

10. Discuss the reasons why a company might want to have all its integrated marketing communication activities performed versus having these activities performed by several different agencies who specialize in various areas of IMC.

Chapter Seventeen

Measuring the Effectiveness of Integrated Marketing Communications

Chapter Objectives

- To understand reasons for measuring promotional program effectiveness.

- To know the various measures used in assessing promotional program effectiveness.

- To evaluate alternative methods for measuring promotional program effectiveness.

- To understand the requirements of proper effectiveness research.

Does Your Campaign Measure Up?

Measuring the outcomes of a promotional program can be a daunting and sometimes overlooked part of the planning process. A recent study, Performance by Results (PBR), commissioned by the Association of Canadian Advertisers highlights the importance of clearly identifying the objectives of the promotional plan and measuring the performance of the plan based on these objectives.

One focus of the study is to investigate and define an advertising remuneration process where the basic advertising agency fee is adjusted by a reward based on the degree of achieving mutually agreed upon objectives between the client and the agency. Another focus of the study is to view the remuneration as a part of a system of linking performance, its measurement, and reward within the client-agency relationship, something that has been characteristic of supply relationships in other industries. The benefits of the PBR system are:

- Greater efficiency and accountability
- Achievement of cost efficiencies
- Higher productivity
- Fewer barriers of self-interest
- Stronger mutual understanding
- Improved retention of creative talent
- Increased agency strategic input
- Improved client-agency communication

Performance measures are a key element of the PBR system, and the study highlights three general groups that should comprise the evaluation: overall business performance, marketing communication effectiveness, and agency process evaluation. Measures from the first two groups are familiar to us (see Chapter 5). Business measures include sales, market share, profitability, and margins. Marketing communication effectiveness measures include brand awareness and brand image ratings (i.e., brand attitude). This group also includes likeability of advertising and advertising impact (i.e., emotional responses), two measures that are more process-related. And this group also includes four measures that are more behavioural objectives: intent to purchase, trial, repeat purchase, and brand loyalty.

The PBR system recognizes that there is no standard formula in applying these measures. The relative importance of each measure needs to be investigated for each brand and its marketing situation. Furthermore, the measures should take into account the role of promotion in the marketing mix and how promotion contributes to business results for the brand and within the product category or industry. In addition, the PBR study provides the following suggestions:

- Objectives can be short term and long term.
- An appropriate number of objectives should be used to focus the organization.
- The objectives should be consistent with other performance measures used in the organization.
- Objectives should be periodically re-evaluated by the client and the agency.

Although some of these recommendations may be intuitive, it should be noted that the Canadian PBR study is the most thorough published examination of the PBR system in the world. Another remarkable achievement for our marketing communication industry!

Sources: "The Benefits of PBR," *Marketing Magazine*, July 9, 2001; "Executive Summary," *Marketing Magazine*, July 9, 2001; "Finding the Right PBR Performance Measures," *Marketing Magazine*, July 16, 2001.

As marketers spend their communications dollars in diverse areas, the need to determine the effectiveness of these expenditures becomes increasingly important. As you can see by the lead-in to this chapter, several methods for evaluating the effectiveness of these programs are used. Both clients and agencies are continually striving to determine whether their communications are working and how well they are working relative to other options. Measuring the effectiveness of the promotional program is a critical element in the promotional planning process. Research allows the marketing manager to evaluate the performance of specific program elements and provides input into the next period's situation analysis. It is a necessary ingredient to a continuing planning process, yet it is often not carried out.

In this chapter, we discuss some reasons firms should measure the effectiveness of their IMC programs, as well as why many decide not to. We also examine how, when, and where such measurements can be conducted. Most of our attention is devoted to measuring the effects of advertising because much more time and effort have been expended developing evaluation measures in advertising than in the other promotional areas. Furthermore, since most other promotional tools have an advertisement-like message, most of these research techniques can be applied. However, we will note a few unique characteristics for measuring the effectiveness of other tools.

It is important to understand that in this chapter we are concerned with research that is conducted in an evaluative role—that is, to measure the effectiveness of advertising and promotion and/or to assess various strategies before implementing them. This is not to be confused with research discussed earlier in the text to help develop the promotional program, although the two can (and should) be used together. While evaluative research may occur at various times throughout the promotional process (including the development stage), it is conducted specifically to assess the effects of various strategies. We begin our discussion with the reasons effectiveness should be measured as well as some of the reasons firms do not do so.

The Measuring Advertising Effectiveness Debate

Almost any time one engages in a project or activity, whether for work or fun, some measure of performance occurs. In sports you may compare your golf score against par or your time on a ski course to other skiers' performance. In business, employees are generally given objectives to accomplish, and their job evaluations are based on their ability to achieve these objectives. Advertising and promotion should not be an exception. It is important to determine how well the communications program is working and to measure this performance against some standards.

Reasons for Measuring Advertising Effectiveness

Assessing the effectiveness of ads both before they are implemented and after the final versions have been completed and fielded offers a number of advantages:

1. *Avoiding costly mistakes.* Total advertising topped $10 billion in 2000. This is a lot of money to be throwing around without some understanding of how well it is being spent. If the program is not achieving its objectives, the marketing manager needs to know so he or she can stop spending (wasting) money on it.

Just as important as the out-of-pocket costs is the opportunity loss due to poor communications. If the advertising and promotions program is not accomplishing its objectives, not only is the money spent lost but so too is the potential gain that could result from an effective program. Thus, measuring the effects of advertising does not just save money. It also helps the firm maximize its investment. For example, one mass merchant discovered that promoting Tide detergent generated more cross-selling opportunities than did promotions of nonpremium brands like Purex (Exhibit 17–1). At the same time, promotions of motor oil had no cross-selling impact.[1]

Exhibit 17–1 Tide has been shown to be an effective promotional draw

2. *Evaluating alternative strategies.* Typically a firm has a number of strategies under consideration. For example, there may be some question as to which medium should be used or whether one message is more effective than another. Or the decision may be between two promotional program elements. For example, should research be spent on sponsorships or on advertising? One retailer found that advertising do-it-yourself products on the radio was effective in rural areas but not in urban locales.[2] Research may be designed to help the manager determine which strategy is most likely to be effective. Companies often test alternate versions of their advertising in different cities to determine which ad communicates most effectively. They may also explore different forms of couponing.

3. *Increasing the efficiency of advertising in general.* You may have heard the expression "can't see the forest for the trees." Sometimes advertisers get so close to the project they lose sight of what they are seeking, and because they know what they are trying to say, they expect their audience will also understand. They may use technical jargon that not everyone is familiar with. Or the creative department may get too creative or too sophisticated and lose the meaning that needs to be communicated. How many times have you seen an ad and asked yourself what it was trying to say, or how often have you seen an ad that you really like, but you can't remember the brand name? Conducting research helps companies develop more efficient and effective communications. An increasing number of clients are demanding accountability for their promotional programs and putting more pressure on the agencies to produce. As IMC Perspective 17–1 demonstrates, effective research can be used for both of these purposes.

Reasons for Not Measuring Advertising Effectiveness

Companies give a number of reasons for not measuring the effectiveness of advertising and promotions strategies:

1. *Cost.* Perhaps the most commonly cited reason for not testing (particularly among smaller firms) is the expense. Good research can be expensive, in terms of both time and money. Many managers decide that time is critical and they must implement the program while the opportunity is available. Many believe the monies spent on research could be better spent on improved production of the ad, additional media buys, and the like.

While the first argument may have some merit, the second does not. Imagine what would happen if a poor campaign were developed or the incentive program did not motivate the target audience. Not only would you be spending money without the desired effects, but the effort could do more harm than good. Spending

Checking In Early with Consumers

Ten years ago, the debate over whether to listen to consumers often created an adversarial stance between client and agency. On the agency side, "consumer testing" was often seen as an impediment to the creative development process. It was a practice thought to interfere with creativity, especially in the free-spending 1980s. Even in the more sober 1990s, a feeling still existed that research meant putting too much of the decision making with the consumer.

To many clients, the solution was "copy testing" of commercials that were already concrete ideas. The best way to provide the required reassurance was seen by many clients as elaborately quantitative techniques with banks of normative data, and ideally, proven marketplace predictive validity. The other side of the argument from agencies has been the "trust me" approach, which means no pretesting with consumers. Many agencies continue to feel this is the only way that truly breakthrough creative can be produced.

In fact, both sides have valid points. Clients need an insurance policy, and agencies want to produce effective breakthrough creative that may defy conventional wisdom and traditional techniques. Consumers are not always the best judges of advertising executions, and should not be expected to be. However, if new ideas don't somehow resonate, there can be a great deal of client and agency discomfort with the huge expenditures of money.

Consumers are the experts in one critical area—their relationships with a brand and how any particular campaign will fit with their system of beliefs about the brand. Only by knowing how consumers feel about a brand at the outset, can advertising and marketing professionals see how new information fits in and, therefore, be able to develop exciting and meaningful creative.

This change of emphasis to gain a better understanding of the consumer's relationship with the brand early on in the development process, and before executions are created, is causing a shift to a different thinking process. As a result, a distinct and often much more fruitful and less adversarial research process is evident.

The research process is changing. More work is being done up front, which feeds into the positioning-development process. It also provides greater insights into the consumer's "truths" about a brand, and allows for more imaginative approaches to build on these truths and to appeal to the constantly evolving consumer in an ever-changing world. When this type of research is done up front, it means marketers have a more solid foundation on which to build new ideas.

Source: Adapted from Marion Plunkett, "Checking In Early with Consumers," *Marketing Magazine*, February 22, 1999. Used with permission.

more money to buy media does not remedy a poor message or substitute for an improper promotional mix. For example, one firm watched its test-market sales for a new brand of beer fall short of expectations. The solution, it decided, was to buy all the TV time available that matched its target audience. After two months, sales had not improved, and the product was abandoned in the test market. Analysis showed the problem was not in the media but rather in the message, which communicated no reason to buy. Research would have identified the problem, and millions of dollars and a brand might have been saved. The moral: spending research monies to gain increased exposure to the wrong message is not a sound management decision.

2. *Research problems.* A second reason cited for not measuring effectiveness is that it is difficult to isolate the effects of promotional elements. Each variable in the marketing mix affects the success of a product or service. Because it is rarely possible to measure the contribution of each marketing element directly, some managers become frustrated and decide not to test at all. They say, "If I can't determine the specific effects, why spend the money?"

This argument also suffers from weak logic. While we agree that it is not always possible to determine the dollar amount of sales contributed by promotions, research can provide useful results. Communications effectiveness can be measured and may carry over to sales.

3. *Disagreement on what to test.* The objectives sought in the promotional program may differ by industry, by stage of the product life cycle, or even for different people within the firm. The sales manager may want to see the impact of promotions on sales, top management may wish to know the impact on corporate image, and those involved in the creative process may wish to assess recall and/or recognition of the ad. Lack of agreement on what to test often results in no testing.

Again, there is little rationale for this position. With the proper design, many or even all of the above might be measured. Since every promotional element is designed to accomplish its own objectives, research can be used to measure its effectiveness in doing so.

4. *The objections of creative.* It has been argued by many (and denied by others) that the creative department does not want its work to be tested and many agencies are reluctant to submit their work for testing. This is sometimes true. Ad agencies' creative departments argue that tests are not true measures of the creativity and effectiveness of ads; applying measures stifles their creativity; and the more creative the ad, the more likely it is to be successful. They want permission to be creative without the limiting guidelines marketing may impose.

At the same time, the marketing manager is ultimately responsible for the success of the product or brand. Given the substantial sums being allocated to advertising and promotion, it is the manager's right, and responsibility, to know how well a specific program—or a specific ad—will perform in the market.

Decisions for Measuring Advertising Effectiveness

We now identify some broad issues for measuring the communication effects of advertising. This section considers what elements to evaluate, as well as when and where such evaluations should occur. The issue of how to measure is covered in the next section.

What to Test

The focus of the testing is mostly on the key decisions that the advertiser makes while putting a campaign together. As shown in this book, we consider creative decisions, media decisions, and budgeting decisions.

Creative Decisions
Both the message and the means by which it is communicated are bases for evaluation. For example, in the beer example discussed earlier, the message never provided a reason for consumers to try the new product. In other instances, the message may not be strong enough to pull readers into the ad by attracting their attention, or it may not be clear enough to help them evaluate the product. Sometimes the message is memorable but doesn't achieve the other goals set by management. One study showed that 7 of the 25 products that scored highest on interest and memorability in Video Storyboard Tests' ad test had flat or declining sales.[3] A number of the creative strategy and creative tactics decisions regarding the message can be tested.

The primary creative strategy decision, **creative theme/idea,** can be tested. When a company decides to change its theme or is planning to launch an unusual attention-getting approach, it may want to see the reactions of the target audience prior to investing in the media placement. Similarly, different message appeals can be tested (i.e., rational versus emotional), or different versions of one appeal can be tested. Finally, another important question is whether the spokesperson being used is effective and how the target audience will respond to him or her. A product spokesperson may be an excellent source initially but, owing to a variety of reasons, may lose impact over time in terms of attractiveness or likeability. Thus, all major creative strategy decisions can be tested.

Continuing with creative tactics, different execution styles displayed on storyboards can be presented to members of the target audience in focus groups for their reaction. The message structure can be looked at as reading body-copy in an interview or some other method. Specific design elements, such as the music in a television ad or the headline of a print ad, can also be the focus or research. Overall, advertisers use a variety of research methods to test essentially any creative tactic that they are unsure about or that require confirmation.

Many of the other tools we have discussed in this book have a creative or message associated with it. Many sales promotions have a visual as well as some advertising-like message that reinforces the brand position in the target audience's mind. Similarly, firms use many creative tactics to gain the attention of media personnel so that their story will get picked up by the media in order to get publicity exposure. Thus, while we have examined the creative in the context of advertising in the book, as we noted previously, all the decisions are relevant in the other promotional tools, and as expected, the same research is possible if the advertiser believes it necessary.

Media Decisions   Research may be designed to determine which media class (for example, broadcast versus print), subclass (newspaper versus magazines), or specific vehicles (which newspapers or magazines) generate the most effective results. The location within a particular medium (front page versus back page) and size of ad or length of commercial also merit examination. For example, research has demonstrated that readers pay more attention to larger ads.[4] One successful direct marketer found that old TV shows yield more responses than first runs:

> The fifth rerun of "Leave It to Beaver" will generate much more response than will the first run of a prime-time television program. Who cares if you miss something you have seen four times before? But you do care when it's the first time you've seen it.[5]

Another factor is the **vehicle option source effect,** "the differential impact that the advertising exposure will have on the same audience member if the exposure occurs in one media option rather than another."[6] People perceive ads differently depending on their context.[7]

A final factor in media decisions involves scheduling. The evaluation of flighting versus pulsing or continuous schedules is important, particularly given the increasing costs of media time. As discussed in Chapter 8, there is evidence to support the fact that continuity may lead to a more effective media schedule than does flighting. Likewise, there may be opportunities associated with increasing advertising weights in periods of downward sales cycles or recessions. The manager experimenting with these alternative schedules and/or budget outlays should attempt to measure their differential impact.[8]

Budgeting Decisions   A number of studies have examined the effects of budget size on advertising effectiveness and the effects of various ad expenditures on sales. Many companies have also attempted to determine whether increasing their ad budget directly increases sales. This relationship is often hard to determine, perhaps because using sales as an indicator of effectiveness ignores the impact of other marketing mix elements. More definitive conclusions may be possible if other dependent variables, such as the communications objectives stated earlier, are used.

When to Test

Virtually all test measures can be classified according to when they are conducted. **Pretests** are measures taken before the campaign is implemented; **posttests** occur after the ad or commercial has been in the field. A variety of pretests and posttests are available to the marketer, each with its own methodology designed to measure some aspect of the advertising program. Figure 17–1 classifies these testing methods.

Pretesting   Pretests may occur at a number of points, from as early on as idea generation to rough execution to testing the final version before implementing it. More than one type of pretest may be used. For example, concept testing (which is discussed later in this chapter) may take place at the earliest development of the ad or commercial, when little more than an idea, basic concept, or positioning state-

Pretests		
Laboratory Methods		
Consumer juries	Theatre tests	Readability tests
Portfolio tests	Rough tests	Comprehension and reaction tests
Physiological measures	Concept tests	
Field Methods		
Dummy advertising vehicles	On-air tests	

Posttests		
Field Methods		
Recall tests	Single-source systems	Recognition tests
Association measures	Inquiry tests	Tracking studies

Figure 17–1 Classification of testing methods

ment is under consideration. GM used focus groups to derive the concepts to promote its new minivan. In other instances, layouts of the ad campaign that include headlines, some body copy, and rough illustrations are used. For TV commercials, storyboards and animatics may be tested. The GM minivan research also involved the evaluation of six animatics. In these tests specific shortcomings were identified, and the ads were changed to enhance certain executional elements.

The methodologies employed to conduct pretests vary. In focus groups, participants freely discuss the meanings they get from the ads, consider the relative advantages of alternatives, and even suggest improvements or additional themes. In addition to or instead of the focus groups, consumers are asked to evaluate the ad on a series of rating scales. (Different agencies use different measures.) In-home interviews, mall intercept, or laboratory methods may be used to gather the data.

The advantage of pretesting at this stage is that feedback is relatively inexpensive. Any problems with the concept or the way it is to be delivered are identified before large amounts of money are spent in development. Sometimes more than one version of the ad is evaluated to determine which is most likely to be effective.

A study of 4,637 on-air commercials designed to build normative intelligence conducted by McCollum Spielman Worldwide (MSW) found that only 19 percent were considered outstanding or really good. Nearly twice as many (34 percent) were failures. On the other hand, of those spots that were pretested before the final form was aired, the share of good to outstanding rose to 37 percent, while the failure rate fell to 9 percent.[9] This is certainly a testimonial to the value of pretesting.

The disadvantage is that mock-ups, storyboards, or animatics may not communicate nearly as effectively as the final product. The mood-enhancing and/or emotional aspects of the message are very difficult to communicate in this format. Another disadvantage is time delays. Many marketers believe being first in the market offers them a distinct advantage over competitors, so they forgo research to save time and ensure this position.

Posttesting   Posttesting is also common among both advertisers and ad agencies (with the exception of testing commercials for wearout). Figure 17–2 presents the results of a study that examined ad agencies' and advertisers' use of various advertising research methods. The percentage of organizations that evaluate finished commercials and TV campaigns is very high. Posttesting is designed to (1) determine if the campaign is accomplishing the objectives sought and (2) serve as input into the next period's situation analysis. An excellent example of using research to guide future advertising strategies is reflected in an experiment conducted by Lowes, a home improvement retailer in the U.S. In a study designed to test 36 different versions of covers for its catalogues (which are sent to between

Figure 17–2   General findings about copy research

	Total		Agencies		Advertisers	
	Number	Percent	Number	Percent	Number	Percent
Total respondents	112	100.0	39	100.0	73	100.0
Undertake preliminary, background, or strategic research in preparation for advertising campaigns	104	92.9	39	100.0	65	89.0
Evaluate copy ideas, storyboards, other formats before rough commercial	85	75.9	34	87.2	51	69.9
Evaluate rough commercial execution of other formats before finished commercial	102	91.1	38	97.4	64	87.7
Evaluate finished commercials	105	93.8	35	89.7	70	95.9
Evaluate TV campaigns	98	87.5	37	94.9	61	83.6
Test competitive commercials	73	65.2	27	69.2	46	63.0
Test commercials for wearout	29	25.9	9	23.1	20	27.4

30 and 40 million homes per year), the company determined that by putting more products on the covers, using real pictures rather than cartoons, and reducing the size of the catalogue, the catalogues were more effective. Other tests varying the number of TV spots, newspaper ads, and sports sponsorships led to increases in advertising spending and affirmation of the company's sponsorship of NASCAR auto racing.[10] A variety of posttest measures are available, most of which involve survey research methods.

Where to Test

In addition to when to test, decisions must be made as to *where*. These tests may take place in either laboratory or field settings.

Laboratory Tests   In **laboratory tests,** people are brought to a particular location where they are shown ads and/or commercials. The testers either ask questions about them or measure participants' responses by other methods—for example, pupil dilation, eye tracking, or galvanic skin response.

The major advantage of the lab setting is the *control* it affords the researcher. Changes in copy, illustration, formats, colours, and the like can be manipulated inexpensively and the differential impact of each assessed. This makes it much easier for the researcher to isolate the contribution of each factor.

The major disadvantage is the lack of *realism*. Perhaps the greatest effect of this lack of realism is a **testing bias.** When people are brought into a lab (even if it has been designed to look like a living room), they may scrutinize the ads much more closely than they would at home. A second problem with this lack of realism is that it cannot duplicate the natural viewing situation, complete with the distractions or comforts of home. Looking at ads in a lab setting may not be the same as viewing at home on the couch, with the spouse, kids, dog, cat, and parakeet chirping in the background. (A bit later you will see that some testing techniques have made progress in correcting this deficiency. No, they did not bring in the dogs and the parakeets.) Overall, however, the control offered by this method probably outweighs the disadvantages, which accounts for the frequent use of lab methods.

Field Tests   **Field tests** are tests of the ad or commercial under natural viewing situations, complete with the realism of noise, distractions, and the comforts of home. Field tests take into account the effects of repetition, program content, and even the presence of competitive messages.

The major disadvantage of field tests is the lack of control. It may be impossible to isolate causes of viewers' evaluations. If atypical events occur during the test, they may bias the results. Competitors may attempt to sabotage the research. And field tests usually take more time and money to conduct, so the results are not available to be acted on quickly. Thus, realism is gained at the expense of other important factors. It is up to the researcher to determine which trade-offs to make.

Methods of Measuring Advertising Effectiveness

Our discussion of what should be tested, when, and where was general and designed to establish a basic understanding of the overall process as well as some key terms. In this section, we discuss more specifically some of the methods commonly used at each stage. First, however, it is important to establish some criteria by which to judge ads and commercials.

Conducting evaluative research is not easy. In 1982, 21 of the largest U.S. ad agencies endorsed a set of principles aimed at "improving the research used in preparing and testing ads, providing a better creative product for clients, and controlling the cost of TV commercials."[11] This set of nine principles, called **PACT (Positioning Advertising Copy Testing),** defines *copy testing* as research "which is undertaken when a decision is to be made about whether advertising should run in the marketplace. Whether this stage utilizes a single test or a combination of tests, its purpose is to aid in the judgment of specific advertising executions."[12] The nine principles of good copy testing are shown in Figure 17–3.

As you can see, advertisers and their clients are concerned about developing *appropriate* testing methods. Adherence to these principles may not make for perfect testing, but it goes a long way toward improving the state of the art and alleviates at least one of the testing problems cited earlier. Testing may occur at various points throughout the development of an ad or a campaign: (1) concept generation research, (2) rough, prefinished art, copy, and/or commercial testing, (3) finished art or commercial pretesting, and (4) market testing of ads or commercials (posttesting).

Concept Generation and Testing

Figure 17–4 describes the process involved in advertising **concept testing,** which is conducted very early in the campaign development process in order to explore the targeted consumer's response to a potential ad or campaign or have the consumer

1. Provide measurements that are relevant to the objectives of the advertising.
2. Require agreement about how the results will be used in advance of each specific test.
3. Provide multiple measurements (because single measurements are not adequate to assess ad performance).
4. Be based on a model of human response to communications—the reception of a stimulus, the comprehension of the stimulus, and the response to the stimulus.
5. Allow for consideration of whether the advertising stimulus should be exposed more than once.
6. Require that the more finished a piece of copy is, the more soundly it can be evaluated and require, as a minimum, that alternative executions be tested in the same degree of finish.
7. Provide controls to avoid the biasing effects of the exposure context.
8. Take into account basic considerations of sample definition.
9. Demonstrate reliability and validity.

Figure 17–3 Positioning Advertising Copy Testing (PACT)

Figure 17–4 Concept
testing

Objective:	Explores consumers' responses to various ad concepts as expressed in words, pictures, or symbols.
Method:	Alternative concepts are exposed to consumers who match the characteristics of the target audience. Reactions and evaluations of each are sought through a variety of methods, including focus groups, direct questioning, and survey completion. Sample sizes vary depending on the number of concepts to be presented and the consensus of responses.
Output:	Qualitative and/or quantitative data evaluating and comparing alternative concepts.

evaluate advertising alternatives. Positioning statements, copy, headlines, and/or illustrations may all be under scrutiny. The material to be evaluated may be just a headline or a rough sketch of the ad. The colours used, typeface, package designs, and even point-of-purchase materials may be evaluated.

One of the more commonly used methods for concept testing is focus groups, which usually consist of 8 to 10 people in the target market for the product. Companies have tested everything from product concepts to advertising concepts using focus groups. For most companies, the focus group is the first step in the research process. The number of focus groups used varies depending on group consensus, strength of response, and/or the degree to which participants like or dislike the concepts. In general, about 10 are usually needed to test a concept sufficiently.

While focus groups continue to be a favourite of marketers, they are often over-used. The methodology is attractive in that results are easily obtained, directly observable, and immediate. A variety of issues can be examined, and consumers are free to go into depth in areas they consider important. Also, focus groups don't require quantitative analysis. Unfortunately, many managers are uncertain about research methods that require statistics, and focus groups, being qualitative in nature, don't demand much skill in interpretation. Weaknesses with focus groups are shown in Figure 17–5. Clearly, there are appropriate and inappropriate circumstances for employing this methodology.

Another way to gather consumers' opinions of concepts is mall intercepts, where consumers in shopping malls are approached and asked to evaluate rough ads and/or copy. Rather than participating in a group discussion, individuals assess the ads via questionnaires, rating scales, and/or rankings. New technologies allow for concept testing over the Internet, where advertisers can show concepts simultaneously to consumers throughout Canada, garnering feedback and analyzing the results almost instantaneously.

Rough Art, Copy, and Commercial Testing

Because of the high cost associated with the production of an ad or commercial (many network commercials cost hundreds of thousands of dollars to produce),

Figure 17–5 Weaknesses associated with focus group research

- The results are not quantifiable.
- Sample sizes are too small to generalize to larger populations.
- Group influences may bias participants' responses.
- One or two members of the group may steer the conversation or dominate the discussion.
- Consumers become instant "experts."
- Members may not represent the target market. (Are focus group participants a certain type of person?)
- Results may be taken to be more representative and/or definitive than they really are.

Figure 17–6   Rough testing
terminology

A rough commercial is an unfinished execution that may fall into three broad categories:

Animatic Rough

Succession of drawings/cartoons

Rendered artwork

Still frames

Simulated movement: Panning/zooming of frame/rapid sequence

Photomatic Rough

Succession of photographs

Real people/scenery

Still frames

Simulated movements: Panning/zooming of frame/rapid sequence

Live-Action Rough

Live motion

Stand-in/nonunion talent

Nonunion crew

Limited props/minimal opticals

Location settings

A Finished Commercial Uses

Live motion/animation

Highly paid union talent

Full union crew

Exotic props/studio sets/special effects

advertisers are increasingly spending more monies testing a rendering of the final ad at early stages. Slides of the artwork posted on a screen or animatic and photomatic roughs may be used to test at this stage. (See Figure 17–6 for an explanation of terminology.) Because such tests can be conducted for about $3,000 to $5,000, research at this stage is becoming ever more popular.

But cost is only one factor. The test is of little value if it does not provide relevant, accurate information. Rough tests must indicate how the finished commercial would perform. Some studies have demonstrated that these testing methods are reliable and the results typically correlate well with the finished ad.[13]

Most of the tests conducted at the rough stage involve lab settings, although some on-air field tests are also available. Popular tests include comprehension and reaction tests and consumer juries: Again, the Internet allows field settings to be employed.

1. *Comprehension and reaction tests.* One key concern for the advertiser is whether the ad or commercial conveys the meaning intended. The second concern is the reaction the ad generates. Obviously, the advertiser does not want an ad that evokes a negative reaction or offends someone. **Comprehension and reaction tests** are designed to assess these responses (which makes you wonder why some ads are ever brought to the marketplace).

Tests of comprehension and reaction employ no one standard procedure. Personal interviews, group interviews, and focus groups have all been used for this purpose, and sample sizes vary according to the needs of the client; they typically range from 50 to 200 respondents.

2. *Consumer juries.* This method uses consumers representative of the target market to evaluate the probable success of an ad. **Consumer juries** may be asked to rate a selection of layouts or copy versions presented in pasteups on separate sheets. The objectives sought and methods employed in consumer juries are shown in Figure 17–7.[14] Sample questions asked of jurists are shown in Figure 17–8.

While the jury method offers the advantages of control and cost effectiveness, serious flaws in the methodology limit its usefulness:

- *The consumer may become a self-appointed expert.* One of the benefits sought from the jury method is the objectivity and involvement in the product or service that the targeted consumer can bring to the evaluation process. Sometimes, however, knowing they are being asked to critique ads, participants try to become more *expert* in their evaluations, paying more attention and being more critical than usual. The result may be a less than objective evaluation or an evaluation on elements other than those intended.

- *The number of ads that can be evaluated is limited.* Whether *order of merit* or *paired comparison* methods are used, the ranking procedure becomes tedious as the number of alternatives increases. Consider the ranking of 10 ads.

Figure 17–7 Consumer juries

Objective:	Potential viewers (consumers) are asked to evaluate ads and give their reactions to and evaluation of them. When two or more ads are tested, viewers are usually asked to rate or rank order the ads according to their preferences.
Method:	Respondents are asked to view ads and rate them according to either (1) the order of merit method or (2) the paired comparison method. In the former, the respondent is asked to view the ads, then rank them from one to *n* according to their perceived merit. In the latter, ads are compared only two at a time. Each ad is compared to every other ad in the group, and the winner is listed. The best ad is that which wins the most times. Consumer juries typically employ 50 to 100 participants.
Output:	An overall reaction to each ad under construction as well as a rank ordering of the ads based on the viewers' perceptions.

Figure 17–8 Questions asked in a consumer jury test

1. Which of these ads would you most likely read if you saw it in a magazine?
2. Which of these headlines would interest you the most in reading the ad further?
3. Which ad convinces you most of the quality or superiority of the product?
4. Which layout do you think would be most effective in causing you to buy?
5. Which ad did you like best?
6. Which ad did you find most interesting?

While the top two and the bottom two may very well reveal differences, those ranked in the middle may not yield much useful information.

In the paired comparison method, the number of evaluations required is calculated by the formula

$$\frac{n(n-1)}{2}$$

If six alternatives are considered, 15 evaluations must be made. As the number of ads increases, the task becomes even more unmanageable.

- *A halo effect is possible.* Sometimes participants rate an ad good on all characteristics because they like a few and overlook specific weaknesses. This tendency, called the **halo effect,** distorts the ratings and defeats the ability to control for specific components. (Of course, the reverse may also occur—rating an ad bad overall due to only a few bad attributes.)

- *Preferences for specific types of advertising may overshadow objectivity.* Ads that involve emotions or pictures may receive higher ratings or rankings than those employing copy, facts, and/or rational criteria. Even though the latter are often more effective in the marketplace, they may be judged less favourably by jurists who prefer emotional appeals.

Some of the problems noted here can be remedied by the use of ratings scales instead of rankings. But ratings are not always valid either. Thus, while consumer juries have been used for years, questions of bias have led researchers to doubt their validity. As a result, a variety of other methods (discussed later in this chapter) are more commonly employed.

Pretesting of Finished Ads

Figure 17–2 showed that pretesting finished ads receives the most attention and participation among marketing researchers and their agencies. At this stage, a finished advertisement or commercial is used; since it has not been presented to the market, changes can still be made.

Many researchers believe testing the ad in final form provides better information. Several test procedures are available for print and broadcast ads, including both laboratory and field methodologies.

Print methods include portfolio tests, analyses of readability, and dummy advertising vehicles. Broadcast tests include theatre tests and on-air tests. Both print and broadcast may use physiological measures.

Pretesting Finished Print Messages A number of methods for pretesting finished print ads are available. The most common of these methods are portfolio tests, readability tests, and dummy advertising vehicles.

Portfolio Tests **Portfolio tests** are a laboratory methodology designed to expose a group of respondents to a portfolio consisting of both control and test ads. Respondents are then asked what information they recall from the ads. The assumption is that the ads that yield the *highest recall* are the most effective.

While portfolio tests offer the opportunity to compare alternative ads directly, a number of weaknesses limit their applicability:

1. Factors other than advertising creativity and/or presentation may affect recall. Interest in the product or product category, the fact that respondents know they are participating in a test, or interviewer instructions (among others) may account for more differences than the ad itself.

2. Recall may not be the best test. Some researchers argue that for certain types of products (those of low involvement) ability to recognize the ad when shown may be a better measure than recall.

One way to determine the validity of the portfolio method is to correlate its results with readership scores once the ad is placed in the field. Whether such validity tests are being conducted or not is not readily known, although the portfolio method remains popular in the industry.

Readability Tests The communications efficiency of the copy in a print ad can be tested without reader interviews. This test uses the **Flesch formula,** named after its developer, Rudolph Flesch, to assess readability of the copy by determining the average number of syllables per 100 words. Human interest appeal of the material, length of sentences, and familiarity with certain words are also considered and correlated with the educational background of target audiences. Test results are compared to previously established norms for various target audiences. The test suggests that copy is best comprehended when sentences are short, words are concrete and familiar, and personal references are drawn.

This method eliminates many of the interviewee biases associated with other tests and avoids gross errors in understanding. The norms offer an attractive standard for comparison.

Disadvantages are also inherent, however. The copy may become too mechanical, and direct input from the receiver is not available. Without this input, contributing elements like creativity cannot be addressed. To be effective, this test should be used only in conjunction with other pretesting methods.

Dummy Advertising Vehicles In an improvement on the portfolio test, ads are placed in "dummy" magazines developed by an agency or research firm. The magazines contain regular editorial features of interest to the reader, as well as the test ads, and are distributed to a *random sample* of homes in predetermined geographic areas. Readers are told the magazine publisher is interested in evaluations of editorial content and asked to read the magazines as they normally would. Then they are interviewed on their reactions to both editorial content and ads. Recall, readership, and interest-generating capabilities of the ad are assessed.

The advantage of this method is that it provides a more natural setting than the portfolio test. Readership occurs in the participant's own home, the test more closely approximates a natural reading situation, and the reader may go back to the magazine, as people typically do.

But the dummy magazine shares the other disadvantages associated with portfolio tests. The testing effect is not eliminated, and product interest may still bias the results. Thus, while this test offers some advantages over the portfolio method, it is not a guaranteed measure of the advertising's impact.

While all the previously described measures are available, the most popular form of pretesting of print ads now involves a series of measures that account for the shortcomings cited above. The tests can be used for rough and/or finished ads and are most commonly conducted in the respondents' homes enabling the researcher to collect multiple measures from many samples.

Pretesting Finished Broadcast Ads A variety of methods for pretesting broadcast ads are available. The most popular are theatre tests, on-air tests, and physiological measures.

Theatre Tests In the past, one of the most popular laboratory methods for pretesting finished commercials was **theatre testing.** In tests, participants are invited by telephone, mall intercepts, and/or tickets in the mail to view pilots of proposed TV programs. In some instances, the show is actually being tested, but more commonly a standard program is used so that audience responses can be compared with normative responses established by previous viewers. Sample sizes range from 250 to 600 participants.

On entering the theatre, viewers are told a drawing will be held for gifts and asked to complete a product preference questionnaire asking which products they would prefer if they win. This form also requests demographic data. Participants may be seated in specific locations in the theatre to allow observation by age, sex, and so on. They view the program and commercials, and a form asking for evaluations is distributed. Participants are then asked to complete a second form for a drawing so that changes in product preference can be noted. In addition to product/brand preference, the form may request other information:

1. Interest in and reaction to the commercial.
2. Overall reaction to the commercial as measured by an adjective checklist.
3. Recall of various aspects of the commercial.
4. Interest in the brand under consideration.
5. Continuous (frame-by-frame) reactions throughout the commercial.

The methods of theatre testing operations vary, though all measure brand preference changes. For example, many of the services now use videotaped programs with the commercials embedded for viewing in one's office rather than in a theatre. Others establish viewing rooms in malls and/or hotel conference rooms. Some do not take all the measures listed here; others ask the consumers to turn dials or push buttons on a keypad to provide the continual responses. An example of one methodology is shown in Figure 17–9.

Those opposed to theatre tests cite a number of disadvantages. First, they say the environment is too artificial. The lab setting is bad enough, but asking respondents to turn dials or, as one service does, wiring people for physiological responses takes

Figure 17–9 The ACT theatre methodology

Advertising Control for Television (ACT), a lab procedure of McCollum Spielman Worldwide, uses about 400 respondents representing four cities. It measures initial brand preference by asking participants which brands they most recently purchased. Respondents are then divided into groups of 25 to view a 30-minute program with seven commercials inserted in the middle. Four are test commercials; the other three are control commercials with established viewing norms. After viewing the program, respondents are given a recall test of the commercials. After the recall test, a second 30-minute program is shown, with each test commercial shown again. The second measure of brand preference is taken at this time, with persuasion measured by the percentage of viewers who switched preferences from their most recently purchased brand to one shown in the test commercials.

them too far from a natural viewing situation. Second, the contrived measure of brand preference change seems too phony to believe. Critics contend that participants will see through it and make changes just because they think they are supposed to. Finally, the group effect of having others present and overtly exhibiting their reactions may influence viewers who did not have any reactions themselves.

Proponents argue that theatre tests offer distinct advantages. In addition to control, the established norms (averages of commercials' performances) indicate how one's commercial will fare against others in the same product class that were already tested. Further, advocates say the brand preference measure is supported by actual sales results.

Despite the limitations of theatre testing, most major consumer product companies have used it to evaluate their commercials. This method may have shortcomings, but it allows them to identify strong or weak commercials and to compare them to other ads.

On-Air Tests   Some of the firms conducting theatre tests also insert the commercials into actual TV programs in certain test markets. Typically, the commercials are in finished form, although the testing of ads earlier in the developmental process is becoming more common. This is referred to as an **on-air test** and often includes single-source ad research (discussed later in this chapter).

On-air testing techniques offer all the advantages of field methodologies, as well as all the disadvantages. Further, there are negative aspects to the specific measures taken through the on-air systems. One concern is associated with **day-after recall scores,** the primary measure used in these tests. Lyman Ostlund notes that measurement errors may result from the natural environment—the position of the ad in the series of commercials shown, the adjacent program content, and/or the number of commercials shown.[15] While the testing services believe their methods overcome many of these criticisms, each still uses recall as one of the primary measures of effectiveness. Since recall tests best reflect the degree of attention and interest in an ad, claims that the tests predict the ad's impact on sales may be going too far. (In 28 studies reviewed by Jack Haskins, only two demonstrated that factual recall could be related to sales.)[16] Joel Dubow's research indicates that recall is a necessary but not sufficient measure, while research by Jones and Blair was even more demonstrative, noting that "it is unwise to look to recall for an accurate assessment of a commercial's sales effect."[17]

On the plus side, most of the testing services have offered evidence of both validity and reliability for on-air pretesting of commercials. Some firms claim their pretest and posttest results yield the same recall scores 9 out of 10 times—a strong indication of reliability and a good predictor of the effect the ad is likely to have when shown to the population as a whole.

In summary, on-air pretesting of finished or rough commercials offers some distinct advantages over lab methods and some indications of the ad's likely success. Whether the measures used are as strong an indication as the providers say still remains in question.

Physiological Measures   A less common method of pretesting finished commercials involves a laboratory setting in which physiological responses are measured. These measures indicate the receiver's *involuntary* response to the ad, theoretically eliminating biases associated with the voluntary measures reviewed to this point. (Involuntary responses are those over which the individual has no control, such as heartbeat and reflexes.) Physiological measures used to test both print and broadcast ads include pupil dilation, galvanic skin response, eye tracking, and brain waves:

1. *Pupil dilation.* Research in **pupillometrics** is designed to measure dilation and constriction of the pupils of the eyes in response to stimuli. Dilation is associated with action; constriction involves the body's conservation of energy.

Advertisers have used pupillometrics to evaluate product and package design as well as to test ads. Pupil dilation suggests a stronger interest in (or preference for) an ad or implies arousal or attention-getting capabilities. Other attempts to determine the affective (liking or disliking) responses created by ads have met with less success.

Because of high costs and some methodological problems, the use of pupillometrics has waned over the past decade. But it can be useful in evaluating certain aspects of advertising.

2. *Galvanic skin response.* Also known as **electrodermal response,** GSR measures the skin's resistance or conductance to a small amount of current passed between two electrodes. Response to a stimulus activates sweat glands, which in turn increases the conductance of the electrical current. Thus, GSR/EDR activity might reflect a reaction to advertising. In their review of the research in this area, Paul Watson and Robert Gatchel concluded that GSR/EDR (1) is sensitive to affective stimuli, (2) may present a picture of attention, (3) may be useful to measure long-term advertising recall, and (4) is useful in measuring ad effectiveness.[18] In interviews with practitioners and reviews of case studies, Priscilla LaBarbera and Joel Tucciarone also concluded that GSR is an effective measure and is useful for measuring affect, or liking, for ads.[19] While a number of companies have offered skin response measures, this research methodology is not commonly used now, and LaBarbera and Tucciarone believe that it is underused, given its potential.

3. *Eye tracking.* A methodology that is more commonly employed is **eye tracking** (Figure 17–10), in which viewers are asked to view an ad while a sensor aims a beam of infrared light at the eye. The beam follows the movement of the eye and shows the exact spot on which the viewer is focusing. The continuous reading of responses demonstrates which elements of the ad are attracting attention, how long the viewer is focusing on them, and the sequence in which they are being viewed.

Eye tracking can identify strengths and weaknesses in an ad. For example, attractive models or background action may distract the viewer's attention away from the brand or product being advertised. The advertiser can remedy this distraction before fielding the ad. In other instances, colours or illustrations may attract attention and create viewer interest in the ad.

4. *Brain waves.* **Electroencephalographic (EEG) measures** can be taken from the skull to determine electrical frequencies in the brain. These electrical impulses are used in two areas of research, alpha waves and hemispheric lateralization.

- **Alpha activity** refers to the degree of brain activation. People are in an alpha state when they are inactive, resting, or sleeping. The theory is that a person in an alpha state is less likely to be processing information (recall correlates negatively with alpha levels) and that attention and processing require moving from this state. By measuring a subject's alpha level while viewing a commercial, researchers can assess the degree to which attention and processing are likely to occur.

- **Hemispheric lateralization** distinguishes between alpha activity in the left and right sides of the brain. It has been hypothesized that the right side of the brain processes visual stimuli and the left processes verbal stimuli. The right hemisphere is thought to respond more to emotional stimuli, while the left responds to logic. The right determines recognition, while the left is responsible for recall.[20] If these hypotheses are correct, advertisers could design ads to increase learning and memory by creating stimuli to appeal to each hemi-

Figure 17–10   Eye movement research

Objective:	Tracks viewers' eye movements to determine what viewers read or view in print ads and where their attention is focused in TV commercials or billboards.
Method:	Fibre optics, digital data processing, and advanced electronics are used to follow eye movements of viewers and/or readers as they process an ad.
Output:	Relationship among what readers see, recall, and comprehend. Scan paths on print ads, billboards, commercials, and print materials. (Can also be used to evaluate package designs.)

sphere. However, some researchers believe the brain does not function laterally and an ad cannot be designed to appeal to one side or the other.

While EEG research has engaged the attention of academic researchers, it has been much less successful in attracting the interest of practitioners.

Market Testing of Ads

The fact that the ad and/or campaign has been implemented does not mean there is no longer a need for testing. The pretests were conducted on smaller samples and may in some instances have questionable merit, so the marketer must find out how the ad is doing in the field. In this section, we discuss methods for posttesting an ad. Some of the tests are similar to the pretests discussed in the previous section and are provided by the same companies.

Posttests of Print Ads
A variety of print posttests are available, including inquiry tests, recognition tests, and recall tests.

Inquiry Tests Used in both consumer and business-to-business market testing, **inquiry tests** are designed to measure advertising effectiveness on the basis of inquiries generated from ads appearing in various print media, often referred to as "bingo cards." The inquiry may take the form of the number of coupons returned, phone calls generated, or direct inquiries through reader cards. Figure 17–11 shows that the reader response card is still the most commonly employed response to trade ads. For example, if you called in a response to an ad in a local medium recently, perhaps you were asked how you found out about the company or product or where you saw the ad. This is a very simple measure of the ad's or medium's effectiveness.

More complex methods of measuring effectiveness through inquiries may involve (1) running the ad in successive issues of the same medium, (2) running

Figure 17–11 Ad response methods

Despite the rise in popularity of electronic response mechanisms, the traditional reader service, or "bingo card," remains the most common way to respond to trade publication advertising.

Ad Response Methods Used Frequently or Very Frequently*	
Indirect Methods	
Return reader service cards	41%
Save ads for reference	35
Discuss advertised products with others	30
Pass ads on to others for possible action	26
Direct Methods	
Send back reply cards/coupons	31%
Contact vendors' websites	28
Telephone manufacturers	23
Telephone local distributors/reps	22
Go to magazine websites	21
Stop at vendors' trade show exhibits	20
Discuss products with sales reps	20
Send faxes to vendors	17
Contact distributors' websites	15
Send e-mail messages	10
Mail notes to vendors	6

*The 2,705 respondents could name more than one method.

split-run tests, in which variations of the ad appear in different copies of the same newspaper or magazine, and/or (3) running the same ad in different media. Each of these methods yields information on different aspects of the strategy. The first measures the *cumulative* effects of the campaign; the second examines specific elements of the ad or variations on it. The final method measures the effectiveness of the medium rather than the ad itself.

While inquiry tests may yield useful information, weaknesses in this methodology limit its effectiveness. For example, inquiries may not be a true measure of the attention-getting or information-providing aspects of the ad. The reader may be attracted to an ad, read it, and even store the information but not be motivated to inquire at that particular time. Time constraints, lack of a need for the product or service at the time the ad is run, and other factors may limit the number of inquiries. But receiving a small number of inquiries doesn't mean the ad was not effective; attention, attitude change, awareness, and recall of copy points may all have been achieved. At the other extreme, a person with a particular need for the product may respond to any ad for it, regardless of specific qualities of the ad.

Major advantages of inquiry tests are that they are inexpensive to implement and they provide some feedback with respect to the general effectiveness of the ad or medium used. But they are usually not very effective for comparing different versions or specific creative aspects of an ad.

Recognition Tests   Perhaps the most common posttest of print ads is the **recognition method,** most closely associated with Roper Starch Worldwide. The *Starch Readership Report* lets the advertiser assess the impact of an ad in a single issue of a magazine, over time, and/or across different magazines (see Figure 17–12). Starch measures over 75,000 ads in more than 1,000 issues representing more than 100 consumer, farm, and business magazines and newspapers per year and provides a number of measures of the ad's effectiveness. An example of a Starch-scored ad is shown in Exhibit 17–2.

Starch also offers the *Starch Impression Study* and the *Starch Ballot Readership Study.* The impression study provides consumers' qualitative impressions of ads (for example, company image and important features); the readership study measures readership in business magazines.

Starch claims that (1) the pulling power of various aspects of the ad can be assessed through the control offered, (2) the effectiveness of competitors' ads can be compared through the norms provided, (3) alternative ad executions can be tested, and (4) readership scores are a useful indication of consumers' *involvement* in the ad or campaign. (The theory is that a reader must read and become involved in the ad before the ad can communicate. To the degree that this readership can be shown, it is a direct indication of effectiveness.)

Figure 17–12   The *Starch Readership Report*

Objective:	Determining recognition of print ads and comparing them to other ads of the same variety or in the same magazine.
Method:	Samples are drawn from 20 to 30 urban areas reflecting the geographic circulation of the magazine. Personal interviewers screen readers for qualifications and determine exposure and readership. Samples include a minimum of 200 males and females, as well as specific audiences where required. Participants are asked to go through the magazines, looking at the ads, and provide specific responses.
Output:	*Starch Readership Reports* generate three recognition scores:

- Noted score—the percentage of readers who remember seeing the ad.
- Seen-associated score—the percentage of readers who recall seeing or reading any part of the ad identifying the product or brand.
- Read-most score—the percentage of readers who report reading at least half of the copy portion of the ad.

Of these claims, perhaps the most valid is the ability to judge specific aspects of the ad. Many researchers have criticized other aspects of the Starch recognition method (as well as other recognition measures) on the basis of problems of false claiming, interviewer sensitivities, and unreliable scores:

1. *False claiming.* Research shows that in recognition tests, respondents may claim to have seen an ad when they did not. False claims may be a result of having seen similar ads elsewhere, expecting that such an ad would appear in the medium, or wanting to please the questioner. Interest in the product category also increases reporting of ad readership. Whether this false claiming is deliberate or not, it leads to an overreporting of effectiveness. On the flip side, factors such as interview fatigue may lead to an underreporting bias—that is, respondents not reporting an ad they did see.

2. *Interviewer sensitivities.* Any time research involves interviewers, there is a potential for bias. Respondents may want to impress the interviewer or fear looking unknowledgeable if they continually claim not to recognize an ad. There may also be variances associated with interviewer instructions, recordings, and so on, regardless of the amount of training and sophistication involved.

3. *Reliability of recognition scores.* Starch admits that the reliability and validity of its readership scores increase with the number of insertions tested, which essentially means that to test just one ad on a single exposure may not produce valid or reliable results.

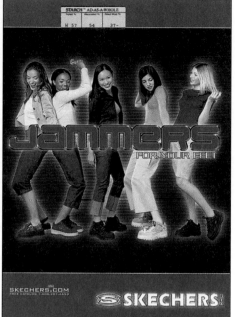

Exhibit 17–2 Example of a Starch-scored ad

In sum, despite critics, the Starch readership studies continue to dominate the posttesting of print ads. The value provided by norms and the fact that multiple exposures can improve reliability and validity may underlie the decisions to employ this methodology.

Recall Tests There are several tests to measure recall of print ads. Perhaps the best known of these are the Ipsos-ASI Next*Print test and the Gallup & Robinson Magazine Impact Research Service (MIRS) (described in Figure 17–13). These **recall tests** are similar to those discussed in the section on pretesting broadcast ads in that they attempt to measure recall of specific ads.

In addition to having the same interviewer problems as recognition tests, recall tests have other disadvantages. The reader's degree of involvement with the product and/or the distinctiveness of the appeals and visuals may lead to higher-than-accurate recall scores, although in general the method may lead to lower levels of recall than actually exist (an error the advertiser would be happy with). Critics contend the test is not strong enough to reflect recall accurately, so many ads may score as less effective than they really are, and advertisers may abandon or modify them needlessly.

Objective:	Tracking recall of advertising (and client's ads) appearing in magazines to assess performance and effectiveness.
Method:	Test magazines are placed in participants' homes and respondents are asked to read the magazine that day. A telephone interview is conducted the second day to assess recall of ads, recall of copy points, and consumers' impressions of the ads. Sample size is 150 people.
Output:	Three measurement scores are provided: • Proven name registration—the percentage of respondents who can accurately recall the ad. • Idea communication—the number of sales points the respondents can recall. • Favourable buying attitude—the extent of favourable purchase reaction to the brand or corporation.

Figure 17–13 Gallup & Robinson Magazine Impact Research Service

On the plus side, it is thought that recall tests can assess the ad's impact on memory. Proponents of recall tests say the major concern is not the results themselves but how they are interpreted. In one very interesting study of the effects of brand name suggestiveness on recall, Kevin Keller, Susan Heckler, and Michael Houston found that suggestive brand names (those that convey relevant attribute or benefit information about the product) facilitate the initial recall of the brand's benefits but inhibit recall of subsequently advertised claims. These results would seem to indicate that a suggestive brand name could facilitate initial positioning of the brand but make it more difficult to introduce new attributes at a later time. The authors suggest that these results might be useful in explaining why Jack in the Box has had trouble developing a more adult image and why Old Spice and Oldsmobile have had difficulty with younger audiences.[21]

A very extensive longitudinal study was conducted by the Netherlands Institute of Public Opinion (NIPO) to assess the relationship between recall and recognition. The results indicated that the average correlation between recall and recognition in both newspapers and magazines was very high ($r = .96$ and $.95$, respectively). The study concluded that recall actually stems from recognition, in that 99 percent of 3,632 cases of recall also had recorded recognition. In addition, likable and interesting ads doubled the recall scores and increased the recall share of recognition. Creative advertising was much more effective for creating perceptions and recall than was the size of the ad.[22]

Posttests of Broadcast Commercials

A variety of methods exist for posttesting broadcast commercials. The most common provide a combination of day-after recall tests, persuasion measures, and diagnostics. Test marketing and tracking studies, including single-source methods, are also employed.

Day-After Recall Tests   The most popular method of posttesting employed in the broadcasting industry for decades was the *Burke Day-After Recall test*. While a number of companies offered day-after recall methodologies, the "Burke test" for all intents and purposes became the generic name attached to these tests. While popular, day-after recall tests also had problems, including limited samples, high costs, and security issues (ads shown in test markets could be seen by competitors). In addition, the following disadvantages with recall tests were also suggested:

1. *DAR tests may favour unemotional appeals because respondents are asked to verbalize the message.* Thinking messages may be easier to recall than emotional communications, so recall scores for emotional ads may be lower.[23] A number of other studies have also indicated that emotional ads may be processed differently from thinking ones; some ad agencies, for example, Leo Burnett and BBDO Worldwide, have gone so far as to develop their own methods of determining emotional response to ads.[24]

2. *Program content may influence recall.* The programs in which the ad appears may lead to different recall scores for the same brand. The net result is a potential inaccuracy in the recall score and in the norms used to establish comparisons.[25]

3. *A prerecruited sample may pay increased attention to the program and the ads contained therein because the respondents know they will be tested the next day.* This effect would lead to a higher level of recall than really exists.

The major advantage of day-after recall tests is that they are field tests. The natural setting is supposed to provide a more realistic response profile. These tests are also popular because they provide norms that give advertisers a standard for comparing how well their ads are performing. In addition to recall, a number of different measures of the commercial's effectiveness are now offered, including persuasive measures and diagnostics. (The Burke test itself no longer exists.)

Comprehensive Measures

As noted earlier in our discussion of pretesting broadcast commercials, a measure of a commercial's persuasive effectiveness is gathered by asking consumers to choose a brand that they would want to win in a

Objectives:	To assist advertisers in copy testing of their commercials through multiple measures to determine (1) the potential of the commercial for impacting sales, (2) how the ad contributes to brand equity, (3) how well it is in line with existing advertising strategies and objectives, and (4) how to optimize effectiveness.
Method:	Consumers are recruited to evaluate a TV program, with ads embedded into the program as they would be on local prime-time television. Consumers view the program on a videotape in their homes to simulate actual field conditions. (The option to use local cable television programs with commercial inserts is also provided.)
Output:	Related recall (day-after recall) scores; persuasion scores, including brand preference shifts, purchase intent and frequency, brand equity differentiation, and relevance and communication; and reaction diagnostics to determine what viewers take away from the ad and how creative elements contribute to or distract from advertising effectiveness.

Figure 17–14 Ipsos-ASI's Next*TV

drawing and then—after exposure to the ad—ask the question again. In theatre settings, this is accomplished by announcing a series of prize drawings, with viewers indicating which of the brands they would choose if they won. In field settings, it is accomplished by taking a brand preference measure when the video is delivered and then again the next day. Some of the services offer additional persuasion measures, including purchase-intent and frequency-of-purchase criteria.

In addition to measuring recall and persuasion, copy testing firms also provide diagnostic measures. These measures are designed to garner viewers' evaluations of the ads, as well as how clearly the creative idea is understood and how well the proposition is communicated. Rational and emotional reactions to the ads are also examined. While each of the measures just described provides specific input into the effectiveness of a commercial, many advertisers are interested in more than just one specific input. Thus, some companies provide comprehensive approaches in which each of the three measures just described can be obtained through one testing program. Figure 17–14 describes one such comprehensive program, Ipsos-ASI's Next*TV test (Exhibit 17–3).

Exhibit 17–3 Ipsos-ASI offers a comprehensive testing measure

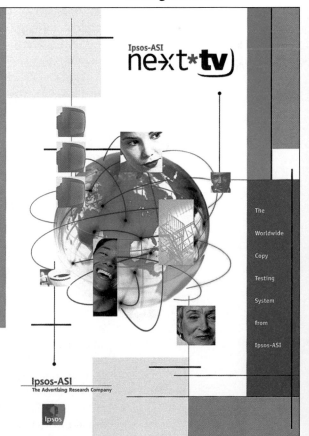

Test Marketing Many companies conduct tests designed to measure their advertising effects in specific test markets before releasing them nationally. The markets chosen are representative of the target market. For example, a company may test its ads in London, Ontario; Peterborough, Ontario; or Winnipeg, Manitoba, if the demographic and socioeconomic profiles of these cities match the product's market. A variety of factors may be tested, including reactions to the ads (for example, alternative copy points), the effects of various budget sizes, or special offers. The ads run in finished form in the media where they might normally appear, and effectiveness is measured after the ads run.

The advantage of test marketing of ads is realism. Regular viewing environments are used and the testing effects are minimized. A high degree of control can be attained if the test is designed successfully. For example, an extensive test market study was designed and conducted by Seagram and Time, Inc., over three years to measure the effects of advertising frequency on consumers' buying habits. This study demonstrated just how much could be learned from research conducted in a field setting but with some experimental controls. It also showed that proper research can provide strong insights into the impact of ad campaigns. (Many advertising researchers consider this study one of the most conclusive ever conducted in the attempt to demonstrate the effects of advertising on sales.)

The Seagram study also reveals some of the disadvantages associated with test market measures, not the least of which are cost and time. Few firms have the luxury to spend three years and hundreds of thousands of dollars on such a test. In addition, there is always the fear that competitors may discover and intervene in the research process. Test marketing can provide substantial insight into the effectiveness of advertising if care is taken to minimize the negative aspects of such tests.

Single-Source Tracking Studies   Since the 1980s, the focus of many research efforts has been on single-source tracking methods. **Single-source tracking methods** track the behaviours of consumers from the television set to the supermarket checkout counter. Participants in a designated area who have cable TV and agree to participate in the studies are given a card (similar to a credit card) that identifies their household and gives the research company their demographics. The households are split into matched groups; one group receives an ad while the other does not, or alternate ads are sent to each. Their purchases are recorded from the bar codes of the products bought. Commercial exposures are then correlated with purchase behaviours.

Earlier we mentioned the use of single-source ad research in pretesting commercials. One study demonstrated that the single-source method can also be used effectively to posttest ads, allowing for a variety of dependent measures and tracking the effects of increased ad budgets and different versions of ad copy—and even ad effects on sales.[26]

A 10-year study conducted by Information Resources' BehaviorScan service demonstrated long-term effects of advertising on sales. The study examined copy, media schedules, ad budgets, and the impact of trade promotions on sales in 10 markets throughout the United States and concluded that advertising can produce sales growth as long as two years after a campaign ends.[27] (The study also concluded that results of copy recall and persuasion tests were unlikely to predict sales reliably.) A number of single-source methods have been used, among them BehaviorScan (Information Resources) and MarketSource. The A.C. Nielsen company's Scantrack is another commonly employed single-source tracking system.

Many advertisers believe these single-source measures will change the way research is conducted due to the advantages of control and the ability to measure directly the ads' effects on sales. A number of major corporations and ad agencies are now employing this method, including Campbell Soup, Colgate-Palmolive, Nestlé, General Foods, P&G, Pepsi-Cola, Leo Burnett, and J. Walter Thompson. After using scanner data to review the advertising/sales relationship for 78 brands, John Jones concluded that single-source data are beginning to fulfill their promise now that more measurements are available.[28]

While single-source testing is a valuable tool, it still has some problems. One researcher says, "Scanner data focus on short-term sales effects, and as a result capture only 10 to 30 percent of what advertising does."[29] Others complain that the data are too complicated to deal with, as an overabundance of information is available. Still another disadvantage is the high cost of collecting single-source data. While the complexity of single-source data resulted in a slow adoption rate, this method of tracking advertising effectiveness became widely adopted in the 1990s.

Tracking Print/Broadcast Ads   One of the more useful and adaptable forms of posttesting involves tracking the effects of the ad campaign by taking measurements at regular intervals. **Tracking studies** have been used to measure the effects of advertising on awareness, recall, interest, and attitudes toward the ad and/or brand as well as purchase intentions. (Ad tracking may be applied to both print and broadcast ads but is much more common with the latter.) Personal interviews, phone surveys, mall intercepts, and even mail surveys have been used. Sample sizes typically range from 250 to 500 cases per period (usually quarterly or semiannually). Tracking studies yield perhaps the most valuable information available to the marketing manager for assessing current programs and planning for the future.

1. Properly defined objectives

2. Alignment with sales objectives

3. Properly designed measures (e.g., adequate sample size, maximum control over interviewing process, adequate time between tracking periods)

4. Consistency through replication of the sampling plan

5. Random samples

6. Continuous interviewing (that is, not seasonal)

7. Evaluate measures related to behaviour (attitudes meet this criterion; recall of ads does not)

8. Critical evaluative questions asked early to eliminate bias

9. Measurement of competitors' performance

10. Skepticism about questions that ask where the advertising was seen or heard (TV always wins)

11. Building of news value into the study

12. "Moving averages" used to spot long-term trends and avoid seasonality

13. Data reported in terms of relationships rather than as isolated facts

14. Integration of key marketplace events with tracking results (e.g., advertising expenditures of self and competitors, promotional activities associated with price changes in ad campaigns, introductions of new brands, government announcements, changes in economic conditions)

Figure 17–15 Factors that make or break tracking studies

The major advantage of tracking studies is that they can be tailored to each specific campaign and/or situation. A standard set of questions can track effects of the campaign over time. The effects of various media can also be determined, although with much less effectiveness. Tracking studies have also been used to measure the differential impact of different budget sizes, the effects of flighting, brand or corporate image, and recall of specific copy points. Finally, when designed properly, as shown in Figure 17–15, tracking studies offer a high degree of reliability and validity.[30]

Some of the problems of recall and recognition measures are inherent in tracking studies, since many other factors may affect both brand and advertising recall. Despite these limitations, however, tracking studies are a very effective way to assess the effects of advertising campaigns.

In summary, you can see that each of the testing methods considered in this chapter has its strengths and its limitations. You may wonder: Can we actually test advertising effectiveness? What can be done to ensure a valid, reliable test? The next section of this chapter suggests some answers.

There is no surefire way to test advertising effectiveness. However, in reponse to pressures to determine the contribution of ads to the overall marketing effort, steps are being taken to improve this measurement task. Let's begin by reviewing the major problems with some existing methods and then examine possible improvements.

Establishing a Program for Measuring Advertising Effectiveness

Problems with Current Research Methods

When current testing methods are compared to the criteria established by PACT (see Figure 17–3), it is clear that some of the principles important to good copy testing can be accomplished readily, whereas others require substantially more effort. For example, principle 6 (providing equivalent test ads) should require a minimum of effort. The researcher can easily control the state of completion of the test communications. Also fairly easy are principles 1 and 2 (providing measurements relative to the objectives sought and determining a priori how the results will be used).

We have seen throughout this text that each promotional medium, the message, and the budget all consider the marketing and communications objectives sought. The integrated marketing communications planning model establishes the roles of these elements. So by the time one gets to the measurement phase, the criteria by which these programs will be evaluated should simply fall into place.

Slightly more difficult are principles 3, 5, and 8, although again these factors are largely in the control of the researcher. Principle 3 (providing multiple measurements) may require little more than budgeting to make sure more than one test is conducted. At the most, it may require considering two similar measures to ensure reliability. Likewise, principle 5 (exposing the test ad more than once) can be accomplished with a proper research design. Finally, principle 8 (sample definition) requires little more than sound research methodology; any test should use the target audience to assess an ad's effectiveness. You would not use a sample of nondrinkers to evaluate new liquor commercials.

The most difficult factors to control—and the principles that may best differentiate between good and bad testing procedures—are PACT requirements 4, 7, and 9. Fortunately, however, addressing each of these contributes to the attainment of the others.

The best starting point is principle 4, which states the research should be guided by a model of human response to communications that encompasses reception, comprehension, and behavioural response. It is the best starting point, in our opinion, because it is the principle least addressed by practicing researchers. If you recall, Chapter 4 proposed a number of models that could fulfill this principle's requirements. Yet even though these models have existed for quite some time, few if any common research methods attempt to integrate them into their methodologies. Most current methods do little more than provide recall scores, despite the fact many researchers have shown that recall is a poor measure of effectiveness. Models that do claim to measure such factors as attitude change or brand preference change are often fraught with problems that severely limit their reliability. An effective measure must include some relationship to the communications process.

It might seem at first glance that principle 7 (providing a nonbiasing exposure) would be easy to accomplish. But lab measures, while offering control, are artificial and vulnerable to testing effects. And field measures, while more realistic, often lose control. The Seagram and Time study may have the best of both worlds, but it is too large a task for most firms to undertake. Some of the improvements associated with the single-source systems help to solve this problem. In addition, properly designed ad tracking studies provide truer measures of the impact of the communication. As technology develops and more attention is paid to this principle, we expect to see improvements in methodologies soon.

Last but not least is principle 9, the concern for reliability and validity. Most of the measures discussed are lacking in at least one of these criteria, yet these are two of the most critical distinctions between good and bad research. If a study is properly designed, and by that we mean it addresses principles 1 through 8, it should be both reliable and valid.

Essentials of Effective Testing

Simply put, good tests of advertising effectiveness must address the nine principles established by PACT. One of the easiest ways to accomplish this is by following the decision sequence model in formulating promotional plans.

- *Establish communications objectives.* It is nearly impossible to show the direct impact of advertising on sales. The marketing objectives established for the promotional program are not good measures of communication effectiveness. On the other hand, attainment of communications objectives can be measured and leads to the accomplishment of marketing objectives.

- *Use a consumer response model.* Early in this text we reviewed hierarchy of effects models and cognitive response models, which provide an understanding of the effects of communications and lend themselves to achieving communications goals. We also presented Rossiter and Percy's model for stating communication objectives which could also be a basis for measurement.

- *Use both pretests and posttests.* From a cost standpoint—both actual cost outlays and opportunity costs—pretesting makes sense. It may mean the difference between success or failure of the campaign or the product. But it should work in conjunction with posttests, which avoid the limitations of pretests, use much larger samples, and take place in more natural settings. Posttesting may be required to determine the true effectiveness of the ad or campaign.

- *Use multiple measures.* Many attempts to measure the effectiveness of advertising focus on one major dependent variable—perhaps sales, recall, or recognition. As noted earlier in this chapter, advertising may have a variety of effects on the consumer, some of which can be measured through traditional methods, others that require updated thinking (recall the discussion on physiological responses). For a true assessment of advertising effectiveness, a number of measures may be required.

- *Understand and implement proper research.* It is critical to understand research methodology. What constitutes a good design? Is it valid and reliable? Does it measure what we need it to? There is no shortcut to this criterion, and there is no way to avoid it if you truly want to measure the effects of advertising.

A major study sponsored by the Advertising Research Foundation (ARF), involving interviews with 12,000 to 15,000 people, addressed some of these issues.[31] While we do not have the space to analyze this study here, note that the research was designed to evaluate measures of copy tests, compare copy testing procedures, and examine some of the PACT principles. Information on this study has been published in a number of academic and trade journals and by the ARF.

All the advertising effectiveness measures discussed in the previous section have their inherent strengths and weaknesses. At the start of this chapter, we noted that the effectiveness of other promotional tools are measured with the same methods. Since all promotional tools require both communication and behavioural objectives, the measurement of their effectiveness can be generalized from advertising. However, each tool has unique characteristics that require specialized measurement to fully assess their effectiveness. We now briefly summarize some these measurements.

Measuring the Effectiveness of Other IMC Tools

Sales Promotion Effectiveness

Elizabeth Gardener and Minakshi Trivedi offer a communications framework to allow managers to evaluate sales promotion strategies over a given set of specific criteria. Borrowing from advertising applications, and using four communications goals—attention, comprehension (understanding), persuasion, and purchase—the researchers show the impact of four promotional tools and everyday low pricing (EDLP) on each goal (Figure 17–16). In addition, the impact of everyday low pricing, Procter & Gamble's strategy for discontinuing the use of sales promotions, is also discussed in the article.[32]

The implication of this study is that sales promotions can be evaluated with a framework similar to the one we summarized in Chapter 5. Much of the advertising research methods and measures discussed thus far can be used in the context of sales promotions. For example, pre- or post-surveys can be used to assess brand awareness or brand attitude (i.e., attribute or benefit beliefs) associated with the sales promotion. Furthermore, assessment of attention, cognitive, and emotional responses of the promotional offer can also be measured with the appropriate method. From a

Figure 17–16   Conceptual framework analysis

		Communication Factors			
		Attention/ Impression	Communication/ Understanding	Persuasion	Purchase
Sales Promotions	FSI coupons	✓✓	✓✓✓	✓✓	✓✓
	On-shelf coupons	✓✓✓	✓✓✓	✓✓✓	✓✓✓
	On-pack promotions	✓	✓	✓✓	✓
	Bonus packs	✓✓✓	✓✓	✓✓	✓✓
	EDLP	✓	✓✓	✓✓	✓

Promotional tendency to fulfill factor: ✓✓✓ = Strong; ✓✓ = Moderate; ✓ = Weak

behavioural standpoint, measurement of switching and loyalty is assessed with scanner data. Other aspects of behaviour can be measured by counting the number of inquiries, coupon redemptions, and contest entries.

Public Relations Effectiveness

As with the other promotional program elements, it is important to evaluate the effectiveness of the public relations efforts. In addition to determining the contribution of this program element to attaining communications objectives, the evaluation tells management:

1. How to assess what has been achieved through public relations activities;
2. How to measure public relations achievements quantitatively;
3. How to judge the quality of public relations achievements and activities.

As discussed in Chapter 13 (Figure 13–3), a number of criteria may be used to measure the effects of PR programs through news media. Raymond Simon suggests additional managerial approaches and research methods for accomplishing this evaluation process, including the following:[33]

- *Management by objectives.* Executives and their managers act together to identify communication objectives to be attained and the responsibilities of the managers. These objectives are then used as a standard to measure accomplishments.
- *Matching objectives and results.* Specific communications objectives should be related to actions, activities, or media coverage.
- *Personal observation and reaction.* Personal observation and evaluation by one's superiors should occur at all levels of the organization.
- *Public opinion and surveys.* Research in the form of public opinion surveys may be used to gather data to evaluate program goal attainment.
- *Internal and external audits.* Internal audits involve evaluations by superiors or peers within the firm to determine the performance of the employee (or his or her programs). External audits are conducted by consultants or other parties outside the organization.

Others suggest comprehensive approaches like we have seen with advertising. Walter Lindenmann says three levels of measures are involved: (1) the basic, which measures the actual PR activities undertaken; (2) the intermediate, which measures audience reception and understanding of the message; and (3) the advanced, which measures the perceptual and behavioral changes that result.[34] A similar approach is

Figure 17-17 The Ketchum Effectiveness Yardstick (KEY); a strategic approach to the measurement of public relations results

At Ketchum, we believe strongly that it is possible to measure public relations effectiveness. We also believe strongly that measuring public relations results can be done in a timely and cost-efficient manner.

Our strategic approach to public relations measurement involves a two-step process:

1. Setting in advance very specific and clearly defined public relations goals and objectives, and,

2. Pinpointing those levels of measurement that are crucial to the organization in determining to what extent those specific public relations goals and objectives have been met.

In the model, there are three levels for measuring PR effectiveness:

- Level #1—the Basic level for measuring public relations OUTPUTS. This measures the amount of exposure an organization receives in the media, the total number of placements, the total number of impressions, and/or the likelihood of having reached specific target audience groups. Research tools often used when conducting Level #1 measurement include content analysis or publicity tracking studies, secondary analysis, segmentation analysis, and basic public opinion polls.

- Level #2—the Intermediate level for measuring public relations OUTGROWTHS. Outgrowths measure whether or not target audience groups actually received the messages directed at them, paid attention to them, understood the messages, and retained those messages in any shape or form. Research tools often used when conducting Level #2 measurement include focus groups; in-depth interviews; telephone, mail, face-to-face, or mall intercept surveys; testing techniques; and recall studies.

- Level #3—the Advanced level for measuring public relations OUTCOMES. This measures opinion, attitude, and/or behaviour change to determine if there has been a shift in views and/or how people act when it comes to an organization, its products, or its services. Research tools often used when conducting Level #3 measurement include before-and-after studies, experimental and quasi-experimental research, ethnographic studies, communications audits, and multivariate analyses of data.

- The different levels of measuring public relations impact can be plotted on a yardstick in a hierarchial fashion. Here is a graphic displaying the KETCHUM EFFECTIVENESS YARDSTICK (KEY), which summarizes from left to right these levels of public relations measurement:

KETCHUM EFFECTIVENESS YARDSTICK

Level #1	Level #2	Level #3
Basic—Measuring	Intermediate—Measuring	Advanced—Measuring
OUTPUTS	OUTGROWTHS	OUTCOMES
Media placements	Receptivity	Opinion change
Impressions	Awareness	Attitude change
Targeted	Comprehension	Behaviour change
Audiences	Retention	

More detailed information about Ketchum's strategic approach to measuring public relations effectiveness may be obtained by contacting Graham Hueber, Vice President and Director of Research at Ketchum.

shown in Figure 17–17, which is a model developed by Ketchum Public Relations for tracking the effects of public relations. Some organizations may use a combination of measures, depending on their specific needs. For example, Hewlett-Packard uses impression counts, awareness and preference studies, in-house assessments, press clippings counts, and tracking studies.[35]

The effectiveness of corporate advertising can be measured with the methods used to measure product-specific advertising. Some research has tried to link corporate advertising with stock prices, but this research has proven to suffer from methodological concerns. The methods most typically used are the following:

- *Focus group research.* Focus groups have been used to find out what investors want to see in ads and how they react after the ads are developed.
- *Attitude surveys.* Corporate advertising effectiveness measurement often involves attitude surveys to understand both the public's and investors' reactions to ads.

The growth in sponsorship investments has led to a corresponding emergence of measuring the effectiveness of sponsorships. Essentially, measures of sponsorship effectiveness can be categorized as exposure-based methods or tracking measures:[36]

- *Exposure methods.* Exposure methods can be classified as those that monitor the quantity and nature of the media coverage obtained for the sponsored event and those that estimate direct and indirect audiences. While commonly employed by corporations, scholars have heavily criticized these measures. Pham argues that media coverage is not the objective of sponsorships and should not be considered as a measure of effectiveness. He argues that the measures provide no indication of perceptions, attitude change, or behavioural change and should therefore not be considered as measures of effectiveness.[37]
- *Tracking measures.* These measures are designed to evaluate the awareness, familiarity, and preferences engendered by sponsorship based on surveys. A number of empirical studies have measured recall of sponsors' ads, awareness of and attitudes toward the sponsors and their products, and image effect including brand and corporate images.

While each of these measures has its advantages and disadvantages, we suggest using several in assessing the impact of sponsorships. In addition to those mentioned here, the eight-step process suggested in Figure 17–18 could be used to guide these evaluations.

Direct Marketing Effectiveness

For direct-marketing programs that do not have an objective of generating an immediate behavioural response, traditional measures of advertising effectiveness can be applied. In those situations requiring a direct response, measuring the effectiveness should include some specific behavioural measure in addition to the communication measures. Using the cost per order (CPO), advertisers can evaluate the relative effectiveness of an ad in only a few minutes based on the number of calls generated. By running the same ad on different stations, a direct marketer can determine the rel-

Figure 17–18 Eight steps to measuring event sponsorship

1. Narrowly define objectives with specifics.
2. Establish solid strategies against which programming will be benchmarked and measure your programming and effectiveness against the benchmark.
3. Set measurable and realistic goals; make sure everything you do supports them.
4. Enhance, rather than just change, other marketing variables.
5. Don't pull Marketing Plan 101 off the shelf. Programming should be crafted to reflect the particulars of your company's constituencies and target audiences.
6. Define the scope of your involvement. Will it involve multiple areas within the company? Who internally and externally comprises the team?
7. Think "long term." It takes time to build brand equity. Also, think of leveraging your sponsorship through programming for as long as possible, before and after the event.
8. Build evaluation and a related budget into your overall sponsoring program. Include items such as pre- and post-event attitude surveys, media analysis, and sales results.

ative effectiveness of the medium itself. For example, if the advertiser targets a $5 return per order and a broadcast commercial (production and print) costs $2,500, the ad is considered effective if it generates 500 orders. Similar measures have been developed for print and direct-mail ads.

Internet Marketing Effectiveness

Measuring the effectiveness of the Internet is done by variety of methods, most of which can be done electronically. Audience information (demographics, psychographics, and so on) and exposure were the initial measures of effectiveness; however, fully measuring communication effects is an emerging trend.

Exposure Measures   The following commonly used measures assess the amount of exposure of the Web content through their interaction. While these are important, they do not account for any processing or communication effects in terms of awareness or attitude.

- *Hits.* The number of times that a specific component of a site is requested. Hits could represent 100 people making one request or one person making 100 requests. As a result, hits have been criticized. The primary value of hits is to let the website owner know which part(s) of the site are most and least popular.
- *Viewers.* The number of viewers to a site.
- *Unique visitors.* The number of different visitors to a site within a specified period of time.
- *Clicks (click-throughs).* The number of visitors to a site that click on a banner ad to retrieve more information. Some companies bill clients on the number of clicks their ad generates, contending that this is the most effective way of providing value for the expenditure. Others, like P&G, have found clicks to be less than accurate and place less emphasis on this measure.
- *Click-through rate.* The ratio of click-throughs from an ad to a page within the advertiser's website. For example, a successful ad might entice 2 percent of those who see it to click to acquire more information.
- *Impressions/page views.* The number of times viewers view a page.

This information is typically collected by a cookie, an electronic device attached to your file (usually without your knowing it) that collects information on where you visit, how many times you visit, where you click, and the like. A new technology goes beyond "cookies" by tracking what sites are on the Internet and where, as well as who, goes to them. The technology collects data on all Web activity by any user who signs up for it and measures how much traffic a site gets, where they go next are all reported. The limitation of these measures (i.e., exposure only) and the need of advertisers' desire for additional information have resulted in further investigation for comprehensive effective measures.

Processing and Communication Effects Measures   The movement for comprehensive communication effects measurement reveals that the Internet has its own set of criteria for measuring effectiveness and it is also borrowing from traditional measures—for example, brand recall is becoming a major area of focus.[38] Many companies that provide research information in traditional media are now extending their reach into the Internet world. Academics are also beginning to publish articles related to measuring effectiveness on the Internet. Studies on consumers' attitudes toward a site, response variations in e-mail surveys, and similarities between brick-and-mortar retailing and e-commerce are just a few of the many articles being published in academic journals to advance the measurement of the Internet.[39] We now summarize a few emerging communication effects measures.

Online Measuring   Firms are developing methods similar to those found in other media (i.e. PMB study) to measure demographics, psychographics, location of Web access, media usage, and buying habits. Clients can determine who saw their ads, determine reach, and ascertain whether the right target audience was reached. Advertisers can test the impact of their messages, receiving a report detailing impressions and clicks by time of day and day of the week.

Recall and Retention   Traditional interviews with Web users help determine recall and whether viewers remember the ads they see, as well as whether there is a "halo-effect" among ads.

Non-response   Measures are being developed to determine where consumers go once they have been exposed to an advertisement but decide not to click on it.

Surveys   Survey research, conducted both online and through traditional methods, is employed to determine everything from site usage to attitudes toward a site.

Panels   Adapting traditional panel research is the focus of some firms that provide information on demographics, unique users, frequency of visitors, pages viewed, and how long a viewer stays at a site ("stickiness").

Sales   Of course, for the e-commerce marketers, a prime indicator of effectiveness is the number of sales generated. Adding information regarding demographics, user behaviours, and so on, can increase the effectiveness of this measure.

Tracking   Some companies now provide information regarding site performance (downtime, speed, and so on) as well as analyze shopping patterns, tying demographic information to site activities, frequency of hits, number of repeat visitors, and the like, over time to assist advertisers in developing more targeted and effective messages. The information can also be used to measure the effectiveness of site content by determining how many visitors access the content, how long they stay there, and how many pages are read.

Sources of Measurement Data   The number of sources available that provide information about the Internet is enormous. Below we provide a partial list just to give you some indication of the types of information available. Most of the companies listed are the largest and/or most cited sources, and the list is by no means intended to be exhaustive:

- *Arbitron.* Arbitron provides demographic, media usage, and lifestyle data on users of the Internet as well as other interactive media.
- *MRI and SMRB.* Both of these companies now provide information regarding viewership profiles for the Internet and other interactive media. Nielsen offers similar data.
- *Audit Bureau of Circulations.* This print agency is developing a product called WebFacts to certify web counts.
- *Internet Advertising Bureau (IAB).* A trade organization of the Internet, IAB provides information on statistics, usage, and strategies regarding the Internet.
- *iVALS.* The same VALS discussed in Chapter 2, iVALS provides value and lifestyle information about Internet users.
- *PC-Meter.* This is a metering service that measures how much time computer users spend at their machines, what software and services they access, and how long they spend online.
- *eMarketer.* This company publishes comparative data from various research sources and explains the different methods used to arrive at the projections. It also publishes its own projections.
- *eAdvertiser.* A joint venture between eMarketer and *Advertising Age,* eAdvertiser publishes a series of reports combining the former's projections but geared more specifically to the advertising community.
- *DoubleClick.* DoubleClick is a seller of advertising space on websites and a provider of tracking and reporting for advertisers. It purchased NetGravity,

Marketing Research Profession in Trouble

There is a perception that marketing research is in trouble. The pessimists claim that others are usurping the position of marketing research as the "principal suppliers of credible intelligence to marketing decision-makers," and a result, research budgets are waning.

The European Society for Medical Research Annual Congress, held in Paris in 1999, warned that the research industry will not exist in 2010 unless it understands the influences on it. This may well be the case for marketing unless marketing research providers redefine what they do.

Researchers tend to play the role of translator, turning what marketers need to make their decisions into questions that consumers can answer, and then translating the consumer feedback into actionable directions for the marketer. Their job is to bridge the gap between the two players. Unfortunately, the job can be a passive one. Clients give them research objectives, and researchers deliver a report—often with little input into the strategic decision making that follows.

Researchers are losing ground because of several factors:

- *A variety of other intelligence suppliers are now providing information to the strategists.* Data miners delve into existing databases to uncover truths that might have come from market research in an earlier era. Increasingly sophisticated analysis tools, broader databases, and the often lower cost of analyzing data already in-house give them a solid base of operations. Additionally, competitive intelligence and insight managers use a broader range of methods to collect different types of strategic information.

- *Management consultants can be better at communicating insights to strategists than are researchers.* "Numbers" and methodological justification can submerge succinct, action-oriented insights, even when they are present in a market-research presentation.

- *While many researchers are increasingly using the Internet as one more methodology, it can also be seen as a competitor.* If you know how to search, you can find just about anything on the Internet, its proponents will insist. The accessibility of the Internet allows just about anyone to do his or her own survey.

- *Client expectations are changing.* The pressure of business in the first decade of the 21st century requires quick, succinct, and to-the-point insights. A month is a year in the online world.

Canada's market researchers can gain new ground by defining a new, broader profession of marketing intelligence. The Futures Committee of the Professional Marketing Research Society has recommended that the society expand its focus and its membership to include other occupations, such as data mining, management consultants, and competitive intelligence practitioners.

Source: Adapted from Jordan A. Levitin, "Redefining Research," *Marketing Magazine,* July 16, 2001. Used with permission.

---

a provider of in-house ad tracking software, so that it could offer advertisers a more complete package.

- *24/7.* This firm provides many of the services offered by DoubleClick, such as the ability to place an advertiser's ad on a variety of sites, targeted or run-of-site.

- *Jupiter, Forrester, and MediaMetrics.* These are three of the largest providers of statistics and website information, including data on users, projections, trends, and so on.

- Business 2.0, The Industry Standard, *and* Fast Company. Each of these business-to-business magazines targets those interested in the Internet, from a technological as well as a business perspective, with emphasis on the latter.

- *Internet Advertising Report and Individual.com.* Both these organizations provide an online newsletter containing information on trends, statistics, and other articles of interest to Internet users in the business community.

Summary

This chapter introduced you to issues involved in measuring the effects of advertising and promotions. These issues include reasons for testing, reasons companies do not test, and the review and evaluation of various research methodologies. We arrived at a number of conclusions: (1) advertising research to measure effectiveness is important to the promotional program, (2) not enough companies test their ads, and (3) problems exist with current research methodologies. In addition, we reviewed the criteria for sound research and suggested some ways to accomplish effective studies.

All marketing managers want to know how well their promotional programs are working. This information is critical to planning for the next period, since program adjustments and/or maintenance are based on evaluation of current strategies. Problems often result when the measures taken to determine such effects are inaccurate or improperly used.

This chapter demonstrated that testing must meet a number of criteria (defined by PACT) to be successful. These evaluations should occur both before and after the campaigns are implemented.

A variety of research methods were discussed, many provided by syndicated research firms such as Ipsos-ASI, MSW, Arbitron, and A. C. Nielsen. Many companies have developed their own testing systems.

Single-source research data such as BehaviorScan, Scantrack, and Market Source were discussed for measuring the effects of advertising. These single-source systems offer strong potential for improving the effectiveness of ad measures in the future, since commercial exposures and reactions may be correlated to actual purchase behaviours.

It is important to recognize that different measures of effectiveness may lead to different results. Depending on the criteria used, one measure may show that an ad or promotion is effective while another states that it is not. This is why clearly defined objectives and the use of multiple measures are critical to determining the true effects of an IMC program.

Key Terms

creative theme/idea, 455
vehicle option source effect, 456
pretests, 456
posttests, 456
laboratory tests, 458
testing bias, 458
field tests, 458
PACT (Positioning Advertising Copy Testing), 459

concept testing, 459
comprehension and reaction tests, 461
consumer juries, 461
halo effect, 462
portfolio tests, 463
Flesch formula, 463
theatre testing, 464
on-air test, 465

day-after recall scores, 465
pupillometrics, 465
electrodermal response, 466
eye tracking, 466
electroencephalographic (EEG) measures, 466
alpha activity, 466

hemispheric lateralization, 466
inquiry tests, 467
split-run tests, 468
recognition method, 468
recall tests, 469
single-source tracking methods, 472
tracking studies, 472

Discussion Questions

1. Discuss some of the reasons why some companies decide not to measure the effectiveness of their promotional programs. Explain why this may or may not be a good strategy.

2. Discuss the differences between pretesting and posttesting. Give examples of each.

3. What is the difference between a lab test and a field test? When should each be employed?

4. Give examples of the various types of rough testing methodologies. Describe why a company might wish to test at this phase of the process. When might they wish to test only completed ads?

5. Major changes have taken place in the way that theatre tests are conducted. Describe some of these changes and the changes in measures that have also occurred in this testing method.

6. Discuss some of the reasons copywriters and researchers are often at odds regarding the creative aspects of the campaign. What steps might be taken to reduce this conflict?

7. A great deal of money is being spent on sponsorships. Discuss why organizations are increasing their expenditures in this area and how they can measure the effectiveness of these investments.

8. The bottom line for advertisers is to evoke some behaviour—for example, sales. Explain why it may be difficult to use sales to measure advertising effectiveness.

9. Describe some of the effectiveness measures that might be used to get at nonquantifiable aspects of advertising and promotions.

10. Describe some of the methods used to test other elements of the promotional mix.

Chapter Eighteen

Advertising Regulation and Ethical, Social, and Economic Effects of Advertising

Chapter Objectives

- To be familiar with the advertising regulation system in Canada.

- To evaluate the ethical perspectives of advertising.

- To understand the social effects of advertising.

- To examine the economic role of advertising and its effects on consumer choice, competition, and product costs and prices.

Tastes Great—Can't Wait

What do you get when you combine a VIA Rail train, some kids, and the fun marketing of Kool-Aid? How about the "Kool-Train," an award-winning campaign that won the Best of Show at *Marketing Magazine's* Media Innovation Awards and a spot in the Media Lions competition at the International Advertising Festival in Cannes.

In 1998 and 1999, Kraft Canada launched the "Face" campaign, where the Kool-Aid Smile was seen on interesting and non-traditional venues like the Toronto Island Ferry and the bottom of public swimming pools. The success of the campaign presented a challenge for the media team that was looking for the next "wow!" idea for spring/summer 2000. The idea had to be fresh and captivating for kids, one that would build on the unique "Pointable Media" theme, and yet not alienate the moms with purchasing power.

The result of strategic media thinking and creativity was the "Kool-Train" concept, ten VIA train engines wrapped in fun and wacky Kool-Aid imagery. The Media Edge developed the concept of the Kool-Train and approached various partners to incorporate integrated campaigns to build on the theme. VIA Rail Canada, *Kidsworld Magazine, TV Guide*, and YTV all jumped on board. So, Kool-Aid and its partners created a totally integrated campaign that was completely relevant for kids and moms alike in giving them an ethical and socially responsible brand experience.

Kidsworld Magazine developed a Kool-Train curriculum. It provided teachers and students with an original and fun learning experience through a history-based program. YTV tied in and featured a Kool-Train contest that asked kids to use visual arts to show how the railroad affected Canada. It was communicated nicely with the help of two popular YTV hosts, Sam and Aaron. *TV Guide*, in the meantime, was approached with a unique contest idea to "Spot the Kool-Train" within its listing pages over a 4-week period, integrating VIA Rail and Holiday Inn prizes to attract the mom as another key target audience.

From Kool-Aid's perspective, the campaign was a success with increased awareness and a 3-year record-high volume share during a cool and rainy summer. From a kids consumer behaviour perspective, it appears Kool-Aid hit the mark too. It offered an IMC program that spoke to kids of a certain age with the media and sales promotion that fits them precisely.

Sources: Helen Kang, "A Kool Way to Target Kids/Moms," *Marketing Magazine*, July 30, 2001; Kraft Foods Newsroom, "All Aboard the Kool-Train," *Kraft Foods*, May 1, 2000, *www.kraft.com/newsroom*.

If I were to name the deadliest subversive force within capitalism, the single greatest source of its waning morality—I would without hesitation name advertising. How else should one identify a force that debases language, drains thought, and undoes dignity?[1]

The primary focus of this text has been on the role of advertising and other promotional variables as marketing activities used to convey information to, and influence the behaviour of, consumers. We have been concerned with examining the advertising and promotion function in the context of a business and marketing environment and from a perspective that assumes these activities are appropriate. However, as you can see in this quote from economist Robert Heilbroner, not everyone shares this viewpoint. Advertising and promotion are the most visible of all business activities and are prone to scrutiny by those who are concerned about the methods marketers use to sell their products and services.

Proponents of advertising argue that it is the lifeblood of business—it provides consumers with information about products and services and encourages them to improve their standard of living. They say advertising produces jobs and helps new firms enter the marketplace. Companies employ people who make the products and provide the services that advertising sells. Free market economic systems are based on competition, which revolves around information, and nothing delivers information better and at less cost than advertising.

Not everyone, however, is sold on the value of advertising. Critics argue that most advertising is more propaganda than information; it creates needs and faults consumers never knew they had. Ads suggest that children won't succeed without a computer, that our bodies should be leaner, our faces younger, and our houses cleaner. They point to the sultry, scantily clad bodies used in ads to sell everything from perfume to beer to power tools and argue that advertising promotes materialism, insecurity, and greed.

One of the reasons advertising and other forms of integrated marketing communications are becoming increasingly criticized is because they are so prevalent. Not only are there more magazine, newspaper, outdoor, TV, and radio ads than ever, but more and more public space is becoming commercialized. Advertising professor David Helm notes: "Between the stickered bananas and the ads over the urinals and the ones on the floor of the supermarkets, we're exposed to 3,000 commercial messages a day. That's one every 15 seconds, assuming we sleep for 8 hours, and I'd guess right now there's someone figuring out how to get us while our eyes are closed."[2]

Because of its high visibility and pervasiveness, along with its persuasive character, advertising has been the subject of a great deal of controversy and criticism. Numerous books are critical of not only advertising's methods and techniques but also its social consequences. Various parties—including scholars, economists, politicians, sociologists, government agencies, social critics, special-interest groups, and consumers—have attacked advertising for a variety of reasons, including its excessiveness, the way it influences society, the methods it uses, its exploitation of consumers, and its effect on our economic system.

Advertising is a very powerful force, and this text would not be complete without a look at the criticisms regarding its ethical, social, and economic effects as well as some defences against these charges. Before we entertain this debate, we will review the regulations affecting advertising in Canada. As you read this chapter, remember that the various perspectives presented reflect judgments of people with different backgrounds, values, and interests. You may see nothing wrong with the ads for cigarettes or beer or sexually suggestive ads. Other students, however, may oppose these actions on moral and ethical grounds. While we attempt to present the arguments on both sides of these controversial issues, you will have to draw your own conclusions as to who is right or wrong.

Advertising Regulation in Canada

Regulation of advertising in Canada occurs through both government regulation and self-regulation. In this section, we review both of these topics. With respect to government regulation, we focus on three prevalent domains. The Canadian Radio-television and Telecommunications Commission (CRTC) is responsible for laws and regulations concerning broadcasting and telecommunications, so its role in advertising is relevant. Health Canada has placed stringent laws for tobacco promotion. Finally, the Quebec government has strong regulations with respect to advertising to children. In the other direction, the Advertising Standards Council (ASC) acts as the self-regulation body for the advertising industry. Responsibility for many of the federal laws regarding the content of advertising messages for specific product categories has been transferred to ASC by the request of the Federal Government.

Canadian Radio-television and Telecommunications Commission (CRTC)

The mandate of the CRTC is to ensure that the *Broadcasting Act of 1991* and the *Telecommunications Act of 1993* are upheld throughout Canada. The broad objective of both acts is to make certain that all Canadians can receive broadcasting and telecommunications services. In attaining its mandate, the CRTC is required to delicately balance the needs of citizens, industries, and various interest groups with respect to programming and costs. For purposes of advertising, we will concentrate on the broadcasting side.

The CRTC regulates over 5,900 media organizations (i.e., television, cable distribution, AM and FM radio, pay and specialty television, direct-to-home satellite systems, multipoint distribution systems, subscription television and pay audio). The CRTC is responsible for granting the licences for these media and ensuring that they comply with the *Broadcasting Act*. Within the context of the *Broadcasting Act,* the CRTC focuses on a number of relevant issues (i.e., content, competition, technology). As you may expect, advertising is one area in which the CRTC plays a role. We now turn to a few of the more topical or interesting aspects of advertising that are regulated by the CRTC:

- *Advertising limits.* The CRTC ensures that TV stations and specialty services carry 12 minutes of advertising during the broadcast day, which lasts 18 hours beginning at 6:00 a.m. However, public service announcements or "ads" for Canadian TV shows are not counted in this total.
- *Infomercials.* An infomercial is a program lasting more than 12 minutes that combines the promotion of a product in an engaging entertainment-like style. The CRTC approves all informercials for any television station, network, or specialty service.
- *900 numbers.* The CRTC has guidelines for advertising adult-oriented phone services by restricting the number of times they are advertised and the hour in which they are aired. Implementation of this occurs through the Television Bureau of Canada.
- *Alcohol and drugs.* There are regulations for advertising these products, but the CRTC has disbanded the screening process of the ads. This is now the responsibility of the ASC, and we will summarize this later in this section.

There are two areas for which you might expect the CRC to be involved in, but thus far, it has no responsibility:

- *False or misleading ads.* The CRTC does not address complaints of these types of ads and refers complaints to the Competition Bureau of the Federal Government. The CRTC has left this for the ASC as well.
- *Internet.* For the time being, the CRTC has not provided any regulations on the content of the Internet, although the Federal Government provides extensive guideline booklets.

Regulation of Tobacco Advertising

Tobacco products are severely restricted by Health Canada regulations on their use of traditional advertising media. One avenue that tobacco companies turned to fairly quickly when the restrictions were enacted many years ago was to sponsor various arts, cultural, and sporting events; however, this option will be discontinued in 2003. Print ads communicating these sponsorships were the only permitted advertising, so the new restriction appears to present even greater limits. Presently, tobacco firms also face significant packaging requirements such as presenting graphic images of the consequences of tobacco use, disallowing any reference to "light," and including a full list of ingredients. With such limited options to attract new users or retain existing consumers, the tobacco companies have been very creative with interesting media choices recently.

Underground marketing has emerged where communication of the brands occurs through exclusive distribution in select bars, pubs, and nightclubs. Through mechanisms such as these, the tobacco companies can get customers to register so that direct marketing techniques can take place, such as contest offers. And 1-800 numbers on tobacco packaging get customers to engage with the tobacco firms directly using creative angles. Point-of-sale communication has also been a competitive tactic that the companies aggressively pursue. Some companies have begun to use the Internet, but thus far, mostly as a means of communicating sponsorship deals. Currently, all of these IMC tools are legal, and we will find out whether the future looks bright for tobacco manufacturers, as they continue to innovate, or cloudy if the government steps in even further.[3]

Quebec Regulations on Advertising to Children

According to the *Consumer Protection Act of Quebec,* it is illegal to direct commercial advertising messages to persons younger than 13 years of age. Provisions are in place to determine whether or not an ad is directed to children. Specifically, the provisions concern the product, the way the ad is presented, and the time and place the ad is shown. One exception to the law is a regularly published magazine that is for sale. These magazines, however, have 16 guidelines with respect to their advertising claims; the types of products; the portrayal of people's behaviour, motivation, or attitude reflected in the ad; and the source of the message (i.e., person or character).

To apply the law, the Quebec government provides summary guidelines for advertisers to follow, and it also provides screening services for advertisers if they are uncertain whether it contravenes the law. The purpose of the guidelines is to ensure that advertisers fully understand and correctly interpret the law. The guidelines pertain to precisely describing the types of advertising appeals that are not permitted, clearly defining what is meant by a children's TV program, and exactly stating the percentage of children in the audience that constitutes a children's TV program. The guidelines include the degree to which messages can be directed towards children depending upon whether the product is exclusively for children (i.e., candy), partially for children (i.e., cereal), or not for children. There are also specific guidelines for public service announcements directed to children, even though there is no commercial message.

Advertising Standards Council (ASC)

The ASC is a not-for-profit, self-regulatory, industry body with a mandate to create and maintain community confidence in advertising. The ASC represents advertisers, media organizations, and advertising industry suppliers and has more than 200 corporate members. Its Standards Division administers the industry's self-regulatory codes (i.e., *Canadian Code of Advertising Standards, Gender Portrayal Guidelines*), handles complaints about advertising, and administers any disputes that arise between advertisers. Its Advertising Clearance Division previews advertisements in five industry categories, as well as ads directed towards children, ensuring that advertisers will follow applicable legislation, regulatory codes, and industry standards.

Canadian Code of Advertising Standards
The Code, as it is known, describes what is not acceptable advertising. According to the ASC, "Advertising is defined as any message (the content of which is controlled directly or indirectly by

the advertiser) expressed in any language and communicated in any medium to Canadians with the intent to influence their choice, opinion or behaviour." The Code pertains to the content of ads only. It does not limit the promotion of legal products or the demonstration of products for their intended purpose. The intention of the Code is to provide standards so that responsible and effective adverting results without minimizing the right of firms to advertise. It does not supersede any other laws or regulations.

The Code is used as the criteria to assess whether a complaint is legitimate or not, and the ASC is very clear in how it uses the Code to resolve complaints. "The context and content of the advertisement and the audience actually, or likely to be, or intended to be, reached by the advertisement, and the medium/media used to deliver the advertisement, are relevant factors in assessing its conformity with the Code."

The Code is supported by all member organizations as it sets the standard for advertising with respect to honesty, truth, accuracy, fairness, and propriety. Members are expected to follow the Code both in letter and in spirit and are expected to substantiate any advertised claims when requested. The Code contains fourteen clauses.

1. Accuracy and Clarity
2. Disguised Advertising Techniques
3. Price Claims
4. Bait and Switch
5. Guarantees
6. Comparative Advertising
7. Testimonials
8. Professional or Scientific Claims
9. Imitation
10. Safety
11. Superstitions and Fears
12. Advertising to Children
13. Advertising to Minors
14. Unacceptable Depictions and Portrayals

Gender Portrayal Guidelines   The Guidelines, based on a previous CRTC task force, attempts to ensure that women and men are portrayed appropriately in advertising. The ASC presents the Guidelines as the direction of areas or topics from which complaints or issues have arisen over the past 30 years. Overall, there are six clauses, and each essentially suggests that men and women should be presented as equals in all of these domains: authority, decision making, sexuality, violence, diversity, and language.

When interpreting the Guidelines, ASC has four suggestions that advertisers should consider. The overall impression of the ad should not violate the spirit of gender equality. There are clauses specifically addressed towards women, as men are at less risk of being negatively portrayed. History and art should not be used as an excuse for violating a clause. Finally, certain products and how they are advertised are amenable to more appropriate media.

Complaint Process   The Standards Division handles complaints in three streams. **Consumer complaints** are those from ordinary citizens who believe that an ad is unacceptable. The ASC receives these complaints directly as well as through government departments and agencies of all levels, the Better Business Bureau, the CRTC, and the Canadian Broadcast Standards Council. **Special interest group complaints** are those from a demonstrated organization that expresses a unified viewpoint. This is a new stream first recognized in the spring of 2002. Complaints from other advertisers are known as **trade disputes.** While there is a distinct complaint process for consumers and special interest groups, the general procedures for each have a degree of similarity that we will touch upon. A summary of all consumer complaints is published in an annual report.

The initial complaint is authenticated to make sure that it is, in fact, a consumer or special interest group complaint and not a trade dispute. From there, the complaint is evaluated to determine whether it legitimately violates a Code provision. This initial assessment occurs at the national (i.e., Toronto) or regional (i.e., Alberta, Atlantic, British Columbia) Consumer Response Councils for English ads, and le Conseil des normes in Montreal for French ads. If the complaint is valid, the advertiser is contacted and has an opportunity to respond to the complaint before the Council makes a formal ruling. On the other hand, the advertiser can take an appropriate action to remedy the complaint as part of the response. In these cases, the advertiser would not be identified in the ASC complaints report. An advertiser who responds and does not remedy the situation can be identified in the report if the Council upholds the complaint.

Complaints Report   The ASC has published a more comprehensive annual report since 1997. This format includes the identification of advertisers and the details of all complaints. Previously the annual report provided global statistics. Figure 18–1 shows a capsule summary of the past 3 years, in which the number of complaints and ads has stabilized. The ratio of the number of complaints to the number of ads indicates that the number of complaints per ad is less than two. This underscores the fact that the number of complaints is not a factor, but rather the content of the complaint is justification for investigating an ad. The percentage of complaints upheld has seen some modest movement, as it ranges from 14 percent to 17 percent. Interestingly, the vast minority of complaints concern issues with respect to gender. In general, about half of all complaints originate from television, but 2001 saw an interesting change with the second highest number of complaints coming from out-of-home media. Finally, the complaints-by-product category does not seem to indicate a discernable pattern.

In 2001, a few complaints stood out as having substantially more complaints than the average. A magazine ad for an Yves Saint Laurent fragrance allegedly had a photo that was sexually exploitive of women, showing a woman apparently in the throes of ecstasy. This ad received 12 complaints, and the Council upheld the com-

Figure 18–1   Summary of complaints from the Advertising Standards Council's annual Complaints Report

	1999	2000	2001
Number of complaints (ads)			
Received	1,075 (813)	1,143 (815)	1,164 (815)
Pursued	802 (552)	817 (521)	833 (540)
Evaluated by Council	248 (123)	289 (139)	321 (155)
Code	203 (106)	255 (123)	285 (133)
Guideline	45 (17)	34 (16)	36 (22)
Upheld by Council	181 (67)	180 (71)	161 (75)
Code	152 (59)	152 (60)	139 (66)
Guideline	29 (8)	28 (11)	22 (9)
Upheld Complaints %	17%	16%	14%
Leading *Code* Clause	Clause 14 Clause 1	Clause 14 Clause 1	Clause 14 Clause 1
Leading Product Category	Food/Supermarkets Automotive Personal/Proprietary	Food Alcohol Retail	Personal/Proprietary Food/Supermarkets
Leading Media	Television Newspaper	Television Newspaper	Television Out-of-Home

plaint, citing Clause 14 of the *Code* and principles of the *Guideline*. It seems while some amount of sensuality is acceptable for advertising fragrances, this ad had crossed the line a bit too far.

A Ford Motor Company TV ad showed a young female shoving a male store clerk into the hatchback of her car and driving away with him. This ad received nine complaints, and the Council upheld the complaint, citing Clause 14 as the ad depicted an abduction, which is an unlawful activity. Ford appealed the decision; however, the Appeal Panel confirmed the original decision. Ford's post-appeal statement makes this example an interesting debate:

> "Ford of Canada did not intend to offend any segment of the population in this particular advertisement; rather the aim of the ad was to show the attributes of the Focus. The identical advertisement shown in Quebec (both in English and in French) was determined not to contravene the *Code* by the Consumer Response Council and Appeal Panel in Quebec. Particulars of this complaint were provided to the press by a consumer complainant even though this process is intended to be confidential. Subsequent to the Appeal Decision, Margaret Wente, in a lengthy *Globe and Mail* article dated January 31, 2002, gave strong positive support for the ad. However, in light of the decision of the ASC Appeal Panel, Ford of Canada will withdraw the current English advertisement."

Clearance Process   The ASC provides clearance services for ads for many product categories and ads directed towards children for all jurisdictions except Quebec.

- *Alcohol.* The ASC adheres to the CRTC *Code for Broadcast Advertising of Alcoholic Beverages.* The CRTC disbanded the clearance services in 1997. This code gives 17 precise guidelines on what is not permitted in alcohol ads. Some of the guidelines pertain to not attracting under-age drinkers, non-drinkers, or problem drinkers. Many other guidelines focus on the message with respect to the type of consumption motivation, consumption situation, source, and appeal. The ASC will review all TV and radio ads across the country as well as print and out-of-home ads in British Columbia.

- *Cosmetics.* Health Canada transferred the clearance for cosmetic products ads to the ASC in 1992, although clearance is not an absolute requirement. The ASC follows the *Guidelines for Cosmetic Advertising and Labelling Claims.* The most recent version is a joint publication of the ASC, Health Canada, and the Canadian Cosmetic, Toiletry and Fragrance Association, and was published in 2000. The guidelines list acceptable and unacceptable claims for two types of hair care products, nail products, and five types of skin care products. Another set of guidelines list unacceptable and acceptable claims for toothpaste, deodorant, mouthwash, perfumes/fragrances/colognes, sun-care products, vitamins, and aromatherapy products. Finally, the same is done for different benefit claims such as anti-wrinkle, healthy, ingredients, nourishment, relaxation, respiration, revitalization, therapy/treatment and lifting.

- *Non-prescription drugs.* Health Canada also transferred the clearance of non-therapeutic aspects of non-prescription drug ads directed towards consumers to the ASC in 1992. The ASC ensures that broadcast and print copy comply with Health Canada's *Consumer Drug Advertising Guidelines* and *The Food and Drugs Act and Regulations.* Health Canada has also given to the ASC the responsibility for resolving any complaints of advertising for this category. To facilitate this change, Health Canada has published a document that describes its role, the ASC's role, and the claims that can be made in ads directed to consumers. Most of the guidelines in this document focus on the need for advertisers to provide factual information of the product's attributes and benefits and that the claims are scientifically valid.

- *Ads directed to children.* The ASC uses the *Broadcast Code for Advertising to Children (Children's Code)*, published by the Canadian Association of Broadcasters in cooperation with the ASC, to assess whether ads directed towards children are appropriate. The code takes into account the unique characteristics of children to ensure adequate safety and has nine guidelines concerning factual presentation, product prohibitions, avoiding undue pressure, scheduling, source or endorser of the message, price, comparison claims, safety, and social values. The code also gives seven instructions on clearance procedures, such as when clearance is required or not, when ads can be directed to children, and during which programs ads can be directed to children.

- *Food.* The ASC evaluates broadcast ads with respect to *The Food and Drugs Act and Regulations* and the *Guide to Food Labelling and Advertising.* Its policy guidelines make a distinction between food claims that are exempt from clearance and those that require clearance in four categories: general advertising, occasion-greeting advertising (i.e., Christmas), promotional advertising, and sponsorship advertising. In addition, the ASC guidelines for the use of comparative advertising in food commercials outline six principles of appropriate executions of this presentation style. Finally, the ASC guidelines on claims based on research and survey data have requirements pertaining to all aspects of the research design (i.e., sample, data collection).

Ethical Effects of Advertising

While many laws and regulations determine what advertisers can and cannot do, not every issue is covered by a rule. Marketers must often make decisions regarding appropriate and responsible actions on the basis of ethical considerations rather than on what is legal or within industry guidelines. **Ethics** are moral principles and values that govern the actions and decisions of an individual or group.[4]

Ethical issues must be considered in integrated marketing communications decisions. And advertising and promotion are areas where a lapse in ethical standards or judgment can result in actions that are highly visible and often very damaging to a company. For example, many organizations and individuals have been critical of advertisers such as Calvin Klein for promoting sexual permissiveness and objectifying women in their ads (Exhibit 18–1). The company was heavily criticized and even boycotted over the controversial "kiddie porn" ads it ran a few years ago featuring intimate snapshots of teenagers in provocative states of undress.[5]

Recently Nike has been criticized over a campaign for its Air Cross Trainer II shoes that directs consumers from their televisions to their computers to learn how a commercial ends.[6] The ads feature celebrities such as sprinter Marion Jones and baseball star Mark McGwire in dramatic situations, and as each spot ends, the words "Continued at Whatever.Nike.com" appear on the screen (Exhibit 18–2). At the website, consumers may select various endings to the commercials. In the endings for one of the spots, the viewer dies. In three others, the viewer has an arm severed, gets teeth knocked out, or suffers a facial injury that sends a nurse screaming out of the emergency room. Nike's vice president of marketing explains that the strategy is to intrigue people with the endings so that they will be motivated to linger on the website. He defends the ads by saying, "Most companies don't give teens enough credit for having perspective. Their ability to have a sense of humour about things and be sarcastic without losing perspective is really high." The campaign has been one of Nike's most successful in years and has helped make the Air Cross Trainer II Nike's best-selling shoe. It also has been recognized as an excellent example of combining television advertising with the Internet. Originally, CBS and NBC asked

Exhibit 18–1 Ads by Calvin Klein have been the target of criticism by women's groups and others

Nike to cut the words "Continued at" from the spots, as they were concerned viewers would turn off the TV and log onto their computers. NBC reversed its decision a few weeks after the campaign began. However, despite the creative marriage of TV and the Internet, Nike's use of grisly outcomes to the spots on its website has been questioned.[7]

Much of the controversy over advertising stems from the ways many companies use it as a selling tool and from its impact on society's tastes, values, and lifestyles. Specific techniques used by advertisers are criticized as deceptive or untruthful, offensive or in bad taste, and exploitative of certain groups, such as children. We discuss each of these criticisms, along with advertisers' responses.

Exhibit 18–2 Some Nike TV commercials direct viewers to a website where they can select their own ending to the spot

Advertising as Untruthful or Deceptive

One of the major complaints against advertising is that many ads are misleading or untruthful and deceive consumers. A number of studies have shown a general mistrust of advertising among consumers.[8] A study by Banwari Mittal found that consumers felt that less than one-quarter of TV commercials are honest and believable.[9] Sharon Shavitt, Pamela Lowery, and James Haefner recently conducted a major national survey of over 1,000 adult consumers to determine the general public's current attitudes toward and confidence in advertising. They found that Americans generally do not trust advertising, although they tend to feel more confidence in advertising claims when focused on their actual purchase decisions.[10]

Advertisers should have a reasonable basis for making a claim about product performance and may be required to provide evidence to support their claims. However, deception can occur more subtly as a result of how consumers perceive the ad and its impact on their beliefs.[11] The difficulty of determining just what constitutes deception, along with the fact that advertisers have the right to use puffery and make subjective claims about their products, tends to complicate the issue. **Puffery** has been legally defined as "advertising or other sales presentations which praise the item to be sold with subjective opinions, superlatives, or exaggerations, vaguely and generally, stating no specific facts."[12] The use of puffery in advertising is common. For example, Bayer aspirin calls itself the "wonder drug that works wonders," Nestlé claims "Nestlé makes the very best chocolate," and Healthy Choice foods tell consumers "Never settle for less." Superlatives such as *greatest, best,* and *finest* are puffs that are often used. But a concern of many critics is the extent to which advertisers are *deliberately* untruthful or misleading.

Sometimes advertisers have made overtly false or misleading claims or failed to award prizes promoted in a contest or sweepstakes. However, these cases usually involve smaller companies and a tiny portion of the hundreds of billions of dollars spent on advertising and promotion each year. Most advertisers do not design their messages with the intention to mislead or deceive consumers or run sweepstakes with no intention of awarding prizes. Not only are such practices unethical, but the culprits would damage their reputation and risk prosecution by regulatory groups or government agencies. National advertisers in particular invest large sums of money to develop loyalty to, and enhance the image of, their brands. These companies are not likely to risk hard-won consumer trust and confidence by intentionally deceiving consumers.

The problem of untruthful or fraudulent advertising and promotion exists more at the local level and in specific areas such as mail order, telemarketing, and other forms of direct marketing. Yet there have been many cases where large companies were accused of misleading consumers with their ads or promotions. Some companies test the limits of industry and government rules and regulations to make claims that will give their brands an advantage in highly competitive markets.

While many critics of advertising would probably agree that most advertisers are not out to deceive consumers deliberately, they are still concerned that consumers may not be receiving enough information to make an informed choice. They say advertisers usually present only information that is favourable to their position and do not always tell consumers the whole truth about a product or service.

Many believe advertising should be primarily informative in nature and should not be permitted to use puffery or embellished messages. Others argue that advertisers have the right to present the most favourable case for their products and services and should not be restricted to just objective, verifiable information.[13] They note that consumers can protect themselves from being persuaded against their will and that the various industry and government regulations suffice to keep advertisers from misleading consumers. Figure 18–2 shows the advertising principles of the Association of Canadian Advertisers which advertisers may use as a guideline in preparing and evaluating their ads.

Figure 18–2 Advertising principles of the Association of Canadian Advertisers

1. *Advertisers must behave responsibly.* ACA believes:
   - Industry self-regulation is in the best interests of all Canadians. Self-regulatory policy exists to ensure that Canadians' fundamental rights and social values are not only acknowledged, but also protected.
   - Advertisers already demonstrate their responsibility by endorsing the Canadian Code of Advertising Standards—the principal instrument of self-regulation for the advertising industry in Canada.
   - The Code of Advertising Standards is only one of many industry codes and guidelines. For example, there are guidelines for gender portrayal, advertising to children, and food labelling, to name just a few.

2. *Advertisers have a right to freedom of speech.* Specifically:
   - The ACA does not believe it is reasonable for a government to allow companies to manufacture and sell legal products, and collect taxes, and then restrict them from telling anyone about it.
   - The ACA remains vigilant in ensuring advertisers' commercial freedom of speech.
   - Advertising, including advertising of products we may not like, is an aspect of free speech, and that free speech is one of society's highest values.

3. *Advertisers make an important contribution to the Canadian economy and culture.* Specifically:
   - Advertising is important to the economic and cultural life of Canadians.
   - In all its forms, advertising is estimated to represent an annual $10-billion investment in the Canadian economy.
   - Advertising revenues fuel the Canadian broadcasting system. Advertisers pay for the production and delivery into Canadian homes of programs that entertain, inform, and educate. It also funds newspapers, magazines, and even movies and Internet sites.
   - Commercials reflect our life. They are a powerful tool and means of passing along our values, traditions, and lifestyles to new citizens and the next generation.
   - Locally produced commercials contribute to our sense of identity and promote national unity.

4. *Advertisers support a vibrant, competitive economy.* The ACA believes:
   - An increased reliance on market forces does not mean that a strong and enriched local and Canadian identity cannot be maintained.
   - Our ability to protect culture by limiting access to communications vehicles is becoming increasingly difficult. A prime example is the Internet.
   - In the rapidly changing world of communications, market conditions, not protectionism, should prevail.

Source: The Association of Canadian Advertisers, www.aca-online.com.

Advertising as Offensive or in Bad Taste

Another common criticism of advertising, particularly by consumers, is that ads are offensive, tasteless, irritating, boring, obnoxious, and so on. In the recent study by Shavitt and her colleagues, about half of the respondents reported feeling offended by advertising at least sometimes. A number of other studies have found that consumers feel most advertising insults their intelligence and that many ads are in poor taste.[14] Consumers can be offended or irritated by advertising in a number of ways. Some object when a product or service like contraceptives or personal hygiene products is advertised at all. Only in the last few years have media begun accepting ads for condoms, as the AIDS crisis forced them to reconsider their restrictions (Exhibit 18–3).

A study of prime-time TV commercials found a strong product class effect with respect to the types of ads consumers perceived as distasteful or irritating. The most irritating commercials were for feminine hygiene products; ads for women's undergarments and hemorrhoid products were close behind.[15] Another study found that consumers are more likely to dislike ads for products they do not use and for brands they would not buy.[16] Ads for personal products have become more common on television and in print, and the public is more accepting of them.[17] However, advertisers must still be careful of how these products are presented and the language and terminology used. There are still many rules, regulations, and taboos advertisers must deal with to have their TV commercials approved by the networks.[18]

Exhibit 18–3 Many magazines and TV stations now accept ads for condoms

Another way advertising can offend consumers is by the type of appeal or the manner of presentation. For example, many people object to appeals that exploit consumer anxieties. Fear appeal ads, especially for products such as deodorants, mouthwash, and dandruff shampoos, are criticized for attempting to create anxiety and using a fear of social rejection to sell these products. Some ads for home computers were also criticized for attempting to make parents think that if their young children couldn't use a computer, they would fail in school.

The advertising appeals that have received the most criticism for being in poor taste are those using sexual appeals and/or nudity. These techniques are often used to gain consumers' attention and may not even be appropriate to the product being advertised. Even if the sexual appeal relates to the product, people may be offended by it. Many people object to both nudity in advertising and sexually suggestive ads.

Advertising critics are particularly concerned about the use of sexual appeals to glorify the image of cigarettes, liquor, and beer or to suggest they can enhance one's own attractiveness. Some women's groups criticized the Airwalk ad shown in Exhibit 18–4, arguing that it showed a submissive and sexually available woman. A critic argued that the ad contains a number of symbolic cues that are sexually suggestive and combine to reinforce an image of the woman's sexual submission to the man.[19]

Another common criticism of sexual appeals is that they can demean women (or men) by depicting them as sex objects (Exhibit 18–5). This was clearly the reason the ASC upheld the complaint for the Yves Saint Laurent fragrance discussed in the previous section.

Some advertisers complain about the double standard: even the most suggestive commercials are bland compared with the content of many TV programs. The networks say they have to scrutinize commercials more carefully because ads

Exhibit 18–4   This Airwalk ad was criticized for being suggestive and symbolizing sexual submission

Exhibit 18–5   Sexual appeals are often criticized for portraying women as sex objects

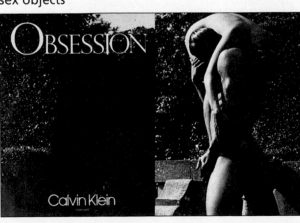

encourage people to imitate behaviours, while programs are merely meant to entertain. Network executives also note the complaints of parents who are concerned about their children seeing these ads since they cannot always be there to change the channel or turn off the TV.

Because of the increasing clutter in the advertising environment, advertisers will probably continue to use sexual appeals and other techniques that offend many people but catch the attention of consumers in their target audience. How far the advertisers can go with these appeals will probably depend on the public's reactions. When consumers think they have gone too far, they are likely to pressure the advertisers to change their ads and the media to stop accepting them. Ethical Perspective 18–1 discusses how many marketers are using gender stereotypes to draw consumers' attention to their ads.

Advertising and Children

One of the most controversial topics advertisers must deal with is the issue of advertising to children. TV is a vehicle through which advertisers can reach children easily. Children between the ages of 2 and 11 watch an average of 15.5 hours of TV a week. Studies show that television is an important source of information for children about products.[20] Concern has also been expressed about marketers' use of other promotional vehicles and techniques such as radio ads, point-of-purchase displays, premiums in packages, and the use of commercial characters as the basis for TV shows.

Critics argue that children, particularly young ones, are especially vulnerable to advertising because they lack the experience and knowledge to understand and evaluate critically the purpose of persuasive advertising appeals. Research has shown that preschool children cannot differentiate between commercials and programs, do not perceive the selling intent of commercials, and cannot distinguish between reality and fantasy.[21] Research has also shown that children need more than a skeptical attitude toward advertising; they must understand how advertising works in order to use their cognitive defenses against it effectively.[22] Because of children's limited ability to interpret the selling intent of a message or identify a commercial, critics charge that advertising to them is inherently unfair and deceptive and should be banned or severely restricted.

At the other extreme are those who argue that advertising is a part of life and children must learn to deal with it in the **consumer socialization process** of acquiring the skills needed to function in the marketplace.[23] They say existing restrictions are adequate for controlling children's advertising. A recent study by Tamara Mangleburg and Terry Bristol provided support for the socialization argument. They found that adolescents developed skeptical attitudes toward advertising that were learned through interactions with socialization agents such as parents, peers, and television. They also found that marketplace knowledge plays an important role in adolescents' skepticism toward advertising. Greater knowledge of the marketplace appears to give teens a basis by which to evaluate ads and makes them more likely to recognize the persuasion techniques used by advertisers.[24]

The *Children's Code* discussed earlier recognizes the above debate explicitly, in the background section, to find a balance between these two points of view. A study comparing the attitudes of business executives and consumers

Sex Role Stereotypes Still Alive and Well

It is, apparently, a particularly dirty fork. It is not just dirty, but dirty and compelling, attracting the attention of both the woman and her young daughter. "I hate leftovers!" declares the woman. "Yuck!" adds the daughter. Then the male voice-over for Dual Action Electrasol speaks, and we learn that with Electrasol the woman's problems will be solved. In fact, that same fork, now clean, powerfully draws mother and daughter back into the kitchen. The daughter triumphantly holds the fork and exclaims, "Hey! No more leftovers!"

It is an unimaginative television ad at best, one created years ago and being rerun now to promote the Reckitt Benckiser–owned brand. It is an ad, however, that illustrates what still plagues many advertisements for cleaning products: the notion that women are obsessed with dirt, or the notion that if anyone was to be obsessed with dirt, it would be a woman. The Electrasol ad is notable because it shows not one, but two generations, suggesting that either the mother is training her daughter to worry about dirt, or this worry is innate in all females, manifesting itself even at a young age.

While some advertisers are making attempts to portray men in more domestic roles, the fact that, in the 21st century, we are still seeing advertisements that primarily continue to target women as the cleaners and caretakers (think "Dr. Mom") says little about how hard women and men, although women in particular, have worked to break down these stereotypes. And, although historically pigeonholing women in the "homemaker" role was a hot button for those angry about how women are portrayed in the media, it has become a lesser evil, explains Melanie Cishecki, executive director for MediaWatch, a Toronto–based organization that works to improve the portrayal of women and girls in the media. There are now, after all, other serious issues to contend with.

"Advertisers have made some changes in that kind of (domestic) portrayal of women," Cishecki notes. "Now, it may be a question of there being other issues that have emerged that seem to be more pressing in the public mind like violence, like sexualization of women, like the body image issue."

You don't have to look far to find examples of the latter issues. They're everywhere, from the recent breast-obsessed campaign in Toronto promoting the MOJO radio station to the controversial global ad created in-house by Yves Saint Laurent (YSL) to promote its Opium perfume, which features a naked woman (save high-heeled sandals and some jewelry) lying on a black satin cloth with her back arched, her mouth open, her left hand holding her left breast, her knees bent, and her thighs spread apart. Both are examples of the current trend towards "porno chic" that's causing a stir in Europe.

The buzz about the Opium ad in Canada, according to Leanne Delap, the editor of Toronto–based *Fashion* magazine, is that the model is a size 12, so "she pleases those who want to see more realistic dimensions of female beauty, but offends those who object to the nudity." Indeed, it caused enough of a flap that poster versions of it were banned in Britain late last year, although the magazine campaign is ongoing.

Though YSL's model may please those who look for more "realistic" female images, the Opium ad is certainly open to more disturbing interpretations: Not only is the model—Sophie Dahl, interestingly enough, the granddaughter of children's author Roald Dahl—nude, but she is presented as sexually available. She is clearly passive, despite her hand on her breast. And she sports a green circle around her eye that bears a much more striking resemblance to a bruise than to any eye-shadow/eye-liner combination. This could lead some consumers to see a connection between the clear sexual imagery in the ad and a subtle hint at violence toward women.

There are reasons why ads such as the Opium ad are created. "I don't believe that any male ad executive gets up on a Wednesday morning and says, 'I'm going to go into work today and make life hell for women,'" says Louise Ripley, a professor of marketing, women's studies, and environmental studies at York University in Toronto. "But they are so deeply socialized in anti-women thinking that it comes through without thinking about it."

Source: Adapted from Kathleen Martin, "How Far Really?" *Marketing Magazine,* July 2, 2001. Used with permission.

regarding children's advertising found that marketers of products targeted to children believe advertising to them provides useful information on new products and does not disrupt the parent–child relationship. However, the general public did not have such a favourable opinion. Older consumers and those from households with children had particularly negative attitudes toward children's advertising.[25]

It is important to many companies to communicate directly with children. However, only by being sensitive to the naiveté of children as consumers will they be able to do so freely and avoid potential conflict with those who believe children should be protected from advertising.

Social Effects of Advertising

Concern is often expressed over the impact of advertising on society, particularly on values and lifestyles. While a number of factors influence the cultural values, lifestyles, and behaviour of a society, the overwhelming amount of advertising and its prevalence in the mass media lead many critics to argue that advertising plays a major role in influencing and transmitting social values. In his book *Advertising and Social Change,* Ronald Berman says:

> The institutions of family, religion, and education have grown noticeably weaker over each of the past three generations. The world itself seems to have grown more complex. In the absence of traditional authority, advertising has become a kind of social guide. It depicts us in all the myriad situations possible to a life of free choice. It provides ideas about style, morality, behavior.[26]

While there is general agreement that advertising is an important social influence agent, opinions as to the value of its contribution are often negative. Advertising is criticized for encouraging materialism, manipulating consumers to buy things they do not really need, perpetuating stereotypes, and controlling the media.

Advertising Encourages Materialism

Many critics claim advertising has an adverse effect on consumer values by encouraging **materialism,** a preoccupation with material things rather than intellectual or spiritual concerns. Many critics believe that advertising:

- Seeks to create needs rather than merely showing how a product or service fulfills them.
- Surrounds consumers with images of the good life and suggests the acquisition of material possessions leads to contentment and happiness and adds to the joy of living.
- Suggests material possessions are symbols of status, success, and accomplishment and/or will lead to greater social acceptance, popularity, sex appeal, and so on.

Exhibit 18–6 Rolls-Royce appeals to consumers' materialism

The ad shown in Exhibit 18–6 for Rolls-Royce automobiles is an example of how advertising can promote materialistic values.

This criticism of advertising assumes that materialism is undesirable and is sought at the expense of other goals. But many believe materialism is an acceptable part of the **Protestant ethic,** which stresses hard work and individual effort and initiative and views the accumulation of material possessions as evidence of success. Others argue that the acquisition of material possessions has positive economic impact by encouraging consumers to keep consuming after their basic needs are met. Many believe economic growth is essential and materialism is both a necessity and an inevitable part of this progress.

Economist John Kenneth Galbraith, often a vocal critic of advertising, describes the role advertising plays in industrialized economies by encouraging consumption:

> Advertising and its related arts thus help develop the kind of man the goals of the industrial system require—one that reliably spends his income and works reliably because he is always in need of more. In the absence of the massive and artful persuasion that accompanies the management of demand, increasing abundance might well have reduced the interest of people in acquiring more goods. Being not pressed by the need for these things, they would have spent less reliably to get more. The consequence—a lower and less reliable propensity to consume—would have been awkward for the industrial system.[27]

It has also been argued that an emphasis on material possessions does not rule out interest in intellectual, spiritual, or cultural values. Defenders of advertising say consumers can be more interested in higher-order goals when basic needs have been met. Raymond Bauer and Stephen Greyser point out that consumers may purchase material things in the pursuit of nonmaterial goals.[28] For example, a person may buy an expensive stereo system to enjoy music rather than simply to impress someone or acquire a material possession.

Even if we assume materialism is undesirable, there is still the question of whether advertising is responsible for creating and encouraging it. While many critics argue that advertising is a major contributing force to materialistic values, others say advertising merely reflects the values of society rather than shaping them.[29] They argue that consumers' values are defined by the society in which they live and are the results of extensive, long-term socialization or acculturation.

The argument that advertising is responsible for creating a materialistic and hedonistic society is addressed by Stephen Fox in his book *The Mirror Makers: A History of American Advertising and Its Creators*. Fox concludes advertising has become a prime scapegoat for our times and merely reflects society. Regarding the effect of advertising on cultural values, he says:

> To blame advertising now for those most basic tendencies in American history is to miss the point. It is too obvious, too easy, a matter of killing the messenger instead of dealing with the bad news. The people who have created modern advertising are not hidden persuaders pushing our buttons in the service of some malevolent purpose. They are just producing an especially visible manifestation, good and bad, of the American way of life.[30]

The ad shown in Exhibit 18–7 was developed by the American Association of Advertising Agencies and suggests that advertising is a reflection of society's tastes and values, not vice versa. The ad was part of a campaign that addressed criticisms of advertising.

Advertising does contribute to our materialism by portraying products and services as symbols of status, success, and achievement and by encouraging consumption. As Richard Pollay says, "While it may be true that advertising reflects cultural values, it does so on a very selective basis, echoing and reinforcing certain attitudes, behaviours, and values far more frequently than others."[31]

Advertising Makes People Buy Things They Don't Need

A common criticism of advertising is that it manipulates consumers into buying things they do not need. Many critics say advertising should just provide information useful in making purchase decisions and should not persuade. They view information advertising (which reports price, performance, and other objective criteria) as desirable but persuasive advertising (which plays on consumers' emotions, anxieties, and psychological needs and desires such as status, self-esteem, and attractiveness) as unacceptable. Persuasive advertising is criticized for fostering discontent among consumers and encouraging them to purchase products and services to solve deeper problems. Critics say advertising exploits consumers and persuades them to buy things they don't need.

Defenders of advertising offer a number of rebuttals to these criticisms. First, they point out that a substantial amount of advertising is essentially informational in nature.[32] Also, it is difficult to separate desirable informational advertising from undesirable persuasive advertising. Shelby Hunt, in examining the *information-persuasion dichotomy,* points out that even advertising that most observers would categorize as very informative is often very persuasive.[33] He says, "If advertising critics really believe that persuasive advertising should not be permitted, they

Exhibit 18–7 The advertising industry argues that advertising reflects society

Exhibit 18–8 The AAAA responds to the claim that advertising makes consumers buy things they do not need

are actually proposing that no advertising be allowed, since the purpose of all advertising is to persuade."[34]

Defenders of advertising also take issue with the argument that it should be limited to dealing with basic functional needs. In our society, most lower-level needs recognized in Maslow's hierarchy, such as the need for food, clothing, and shelter, are satisfied for most people. It is natural to move from basic needs to higher-order ones such as self-esteem and status or self-actualization. Consumers are free to choose the degree to which they attempt to satisfy their desires, and wise advertisers associate their products and services with the satisfaction of higher-order needs.

Proponents of advertising offer two other defences against the charge that advertising makes people buy things they do not really need. First, this criticism attributes too much power to advertising and assumes consumers have no ability to defend themselves against it.

Second, it ignores the fact that consumers have the freedom to make their own choices when confronted with persuasive advertising. While they readily admit the persuasive intent of their business, advertisers are quick to note it is extremely difficult to make consumers purchase a product they do not want or for which they do not see a personal benefit. For example, the "green" marketing movement has not gotten consumers to forgo low prices in favour of products that make environmental claims. The market research firm of Roper Starch Worldwide conducted an extensive study of 300 green ads that appeared in magazines between 1991 and 1994 and found that most were not effective. The study concluded that too many green ads failed to make the connection between what the company is doing for the environment and how it affects individual consumers.[35]

If advertising were as powerful as the critics claim, we would not see products with multimillion-dollar advertising budgets failing in the marketplace. The reality is that consumers do have a choice, and they are not being forced to buy. Consumers ignore ads for products and services they do not really need or that fail to interest them (see Exhibit 18–8).

Advertising and Stereotyping

Advertising is often accused of creating and perpetuating stereotypes through its portrayal of women and ethnic minorities.

Women The portrayal of women in advertising is an issue that has received a great deal of attention through the years.[36] Advertising has received much criticism for stereotyping women and failing to recognize the changing role of women in our society. Critics have argued that advertising often depicts women as preoccupied with beauty, household duties, and motherhood or shows them as decorative objects or sexually provocative figures. The various research studies conducted through the years show a consistent picture of gender stereotyping that has varied little over time. Portrayals of adult women in American television and print advertising have emphasized passivity, deference, lack of intelligence and credibility, and punishment for high levels of efforts. In contrast, men have been portrayed as constructive, powerful, autonomous, and achieving.[37]

Research on gender stereotyping in advertising targeted to children has found a pattern of results similar to that reported for adults. A recent study found sex-role stereotyping in television advertising targeted at children in the United States as well as in Australia.[38] Boys are generally shown as being more knowledgeable, active, aggressive, and instrumental than girls. Nonverbal behaviours involving dominance and control are associated more with boys than girls. Advertising directed toward children has also been shown to feature more boys than girls, to position boys in more dominant, active roles, and to use male voiceovers more frequently than female ones.[39]

Feminist groups such as MediaWatch argue that advertising that portrays women as sex objects contributes to violence against women. MediaWatch and its supporters often communicate to advertisers and their agencies about ads they find insulting to women and have even called for boycotts against offending advertisers. MediaWatch has also been critical of advertisers for the way they portray women in advertising for clothing, cosmetics, and other products. The organization feels that many of these ads contribute to the epidemic of eating disorders and smoking among women and girls who hope such means will help them control their weight.[40]

While sexism and stereotyping still exist, advertising's portrayal of women is improving in many areas. Many advertisers have begun to recognize the importance of portraying women realistically. The increase in the number of working women has resulted not only in women having more influence in family decision making but also in more single-female households, which mean more independent purchasers.

In its most recent annual report, MediaWatch gave "thumbs-down awards" to Vichy, Browns Shoes, Calvin Klein, and Kahlúa Black Russian. Positive recognition went to "Cam's Breast Exam," a TV ad showing eager lads ready to do a breast exam for women to prevent cancer, and Body Shop for realistically portraying women.

Researchers Steven Kates and Glenda Shaw-Garlock argue that the transformed social positioning of women in North American society is perhaps the most important social development of this century.[41] They note that as women have crossed the boundary from the domestic sphere to the professional arena, expectations and representations of women have changed as well. For example, a number of magazines, such as *MS* and *Working Woman,* now incorporate and appeal to the sociocultural shifts in women's lives. Many advertisers are now depicting women in a diversity of roles that reflect their changing place in society. In many ads, the stereotypic character traits attributed to women have shifted from weak and dependent to strong and autonomous.[42]

Some advertisers have found that being more sensitive to women customers can influence their purchase behaviour. For example, a few years ago Maidenform began a campaign critical of negative stereotyping of women that significantly increased sales (Exhibit 18–9). Nike saw its sales to women increase 28 percent as

Exhibit 18–9 Maidenform's campaign lamenting the stereotyping of women resulted in a significant increase in sales

Somehow, women always seem
   to be portrayed like this.
Or like this.
Like this.

Or like this.
Like this.
Or like this.
While there are many stereotypes
   of women . . .

there aren't many women who
   fit them.
A simple truth known by all
   women . . . most men . . .
   and one lingerie company.

a result of its "Empathy" campaign, which directly targeted women and issues that are relevant to them.[43]

Visible Minorities Several U.S. academic studies in the late 1980s and early 90s examined the incidence of visible minorities in advertising. A study conducted in 1987 found that 11 percent of the people appearing in commercials were African-Americans.[44] Another study conducted two years later found that African-Americans appeared in 26 percent of all ads on network TV that used live models but Hispanics appeared in only 6 percent of the commercials with live models. The researchers also found that TV ads in which blacks appeared were overwhelmingly integrated (Exhibit 18–10) and the blacks were likely to have played either minor or background roles in the majority of the ads.[45] A study conducted in 1995 found that 17 percent of prime-time network TV ads featured African-Americans as dominant characters and the majority of commercials featured them in minor roles.[46] A recent study by Corliss L. Green found that ads targeting African-Americans through racially targeted media, especially with race-based products, benefit from featuring African-American models with a dominant presence in the ad.[47]

Exhibit 18–10 Ikea broke new ground with this ad showing an interracial couple shopping for furniture

A recent study of U.S. prime-time TV commercials found that Asian male and female models are overrepresented in terms of their proportion of the U.S. population (3.6 percent), appearing in 8.4 percent of the commercials. However, Asian models were more likely than members of other minority groups to appear in background roles, and Asian women were rarely depicted in major roles. The study also found that portrayals of Asian-Americans put more emphasis on the work ethic and less on other aspects of their lives.[48]

It may be difficult to generalize these findings to Canada, however; we should keep in mind that Canadians are exposed to these ads when watching U.S. television programs that do not simulcast Canadian commercials or when reading American magazines. So to a degree, Canadian consumers will experience and perceive some amount of imbalance through this exposure.

Visible minorities comprise about 18 percent of Canada's population, of which 23 percent are Chinese, 19 percent are South Asians, and 19 percent are black. Recent Canadian trends and commentary by practitioners suggest that the portrayal of visible minorities can be improved in Canadian advertising, even though there has been significant improvement over the past 5 years. For example, a recent study suggests that 45 percent of all Canadians feel that advertising is directed to whites, and 48 percent feel that visible minorities are under-represented.

Perhaps following on the success of Budweiser's award-winning "Whassup" campaign, many Canadian beer companies were including many visible minorities in their ads in 2001. Although the beer companies do not have specific guidelines, they encourage the casting of their TV commercials to have a full representative selection of actors. However, there are some who contend that the casting does not always specify that visible minorities are welcome and that this problem carries over to other media such as print, Internet, and direct mail.[49]

Advertising and the Media

The fact that advertising plays such an important role in financing the media has led to concern that advertisers may influence or even control the media (Exhibit 18–11). It is well documented that *economic censorship* occurs, whereby the media avoid certain topics or even present biased news coverage, in acquiescence to advertiser demands.[50] In fact, Professors Lawrence Soley and Robert Craig say, "The assertion that advertisers attempt to influence what the public sees, hears, and reads in the mass media is perhaps the most damning of all criticisms of advertising, but this criticism isn't acknowledged in most advertising textbooks."[51] We will address this important issue in this book by considering arguments on both sides.

Arguments Supporting Advertiser Control

Some critics charge the media's dependence on advertisers' support makes them susceptible to various forms of influence, including exerting control over the editorial content of magazines and newspapers; biasing editorial opinions to favour the position of an advertiser; limiting coverage of a controversial story that might reflect negatively on a company; and influencing the program content of television.

Newspapers and magazines receive nearly 70 percent of their revenue from advertising; commercial TV and radio derive virtually all their income from advertisers. Small, financially insecure newspapers, magazines, or broadcast stations are the most susceptible to pressure from advertisers, particularly companies that account for a large amount of the media outlet's advertising revenue. A local newspaper may be reluctant to print an unfavourable story about a car dealer or supermarket chain on whose advertising it depends. For example, a few years ago more than 40 car dealers cancelled their ads in the *San Jose Mercury News* when the paper printed an article titled "A Car Buyer's Guide to Sanity." The dealers objected to the tone of the article, which they felt implied consumers should consider car dealers unethical adversaries in the negotiation process.[52] A survey of 147 daily newspapers found that more than 90 percent of editors have been pressured by advertisers and more than one-third of them said advertisers had succeeded in influencing news at their papers.[53]

Individual TV stations and even the major networks also can be influenced by advertisers. Programming decisions are made largely on the basis of what shows will attract the most viewers and thus be most desirable to advertisers. Critics say this often results in lower-quality television as educational, cultural, and informative programming is usually sacrificed for shows that get high ratings and appeal to the mass markets.

Arguments against Advertiser Control

The commercial media's dependence on advertising means advertisers can exert influence on their character, content, and coverage of certain issues. However, media executives offer several reasons why advertisers do not exert undue influence over the media.

First, they point out it is in the best interest of the media not to be influenced too much by advertisers. To retain public confidence, they must report the news fairly and accurately without showing bias or attempting to avoid controversial issues. Media executives point to the vast array of topics they cover and the investigative reporting they often do as evidence of their objectivity. They want to build a large audience for their publications or stations so that they can charge more for advertising space and time.

Media executives also note that an advertiser needs the media more than they need any individual advertiser, particularly when the medium has a large audience or does a good job of reaching a specific market segment. Many publications and stations have a very broad base of advertising support and can afford to lose an advertiser that attempts to exert too much influence. This is particularly true for the

"You're GAY!!!... Well, I'm feeling quite happy myself."

LOG ON FOR A MORE WELCOMING FINANCIAL WORLD.

gfn.com
▶THE GAY FINANCIAL NETWORK

Welcome to gfn.com, the Gay Financial Network. With free daily news and information, plus the best in online trading, home mortgages, online banking, insurance and more from top-name financial partners, gfn.com is empowering the gay community toward realizing our American dream.

free daily financial news and information | banking ▸ mortgages ▸ insurance ▸ investing

Exhibit 18–11 The Gay Financial Network broke barriers by becoming the first gay-oriented company to advertise in the mainstream media

larger, more established, financially secure media. For example, a consumer products company would find it difficult to reach its target audience without network TV and could not afford to boycott a network if it disagreed with a station's editorial policy or program content. Even the local advertiser in a small community may be dependent on the local newspaper, since it may be the most cost-effective media option available.

The media in Canada are basically supported by advertising; this means we can enjoy them for free or for a fraction of what they would cost without advertising. The alternative to an advertiser-supported media system is support by users through higher subscription costs for the print media and a fee or pay-per-view system with TV. The ad in Exhibit 18–12, part of a campaign by the International Advertising Association, explains how advertising lowers the cost of print media for consumers. Another alternative is government-supported media like those in many other countries, but this runs counter to most people's desire for freedom of the press. Although not perfect, our system of advertising-supported media provides the best option for receiving information and entertainment.

Summarizing Social Effects

We have examined a number of issues and have attempted to analyze the arguments for and against them. Many people have reservations about the impact of advertising and promotion on society. The numerous rules, regulations, policies, and guidelines marketers comply with do not cover every advertising and promotional situation. Moreover, what one individual views as distasteful or unethical may be acceptable to another.

Exhibit 18–12 This ad points out how advertising lowers the cost of newspapers for consumers

WITHOUT ADVERTISING, YOUR NEWSPAPER WOULD COST YOU A BUNDLE.

Did you know that every ad in your newspaper helps pay for the rest of the essential pages? The fact is, your paper would cost you about $5.00 a day without advertisements. A price that would make news indeed.

Advertising. That's the way it works.

The global partnership of advertisers, agencies and media

Negative opinions regarding advertising and other forms of promotion have been around almost as long as the field itself, and it is unlikely they will ever disappear. However, the industry must address the various concerns about the effects of advertising and other forms of promotion on society. Advertising is a very powerful institution, but it will remain so only as long as consumers have faith in the ads they see and hear every day. Many of the problems discussed here can be avoided if individual decision makers make ethics an important element of the IMC planning process.

The primary focus of this discussion of social effects has been on the way advertising is used (or abused) in the marketing of products and services. It is important to note that advertising and other IMC tools, such as direct marketing and public relations, are also used to promote worthy causes and to deal with problems facing society (drunk driving, drug abuse, and the AIDS crisis, among others). Campaigns for nonprofit organizations and worthy causes are often developed pro bono by advertising agencies, and free advertising time and space are donated by the media.

Economic Effects of Advertising

Advertising plays an important role in a free-market system like ours by making consumers aware of products and services and providing them with information for decision making. Advertising's economic role goes beyond this basic function, however. It is a powerful force that can affect the functioning of our entire economic system.

Advertising can encourage consumption and foster economic growth. It not only informs customers of available goods and services but also facilitates entry into markets for a firm or a new product or brand; leads to economies of scale in production, marketing, and distribution, which in turn lead to lower prices; and hastens the acceptance of new products and the rejection of inferior products.

Critics of advertising view it as a detrimental force that not only fails to perform its basic function of information provision adequately but also adds to the cost of products and services and discourages competition and market entry, leading to industrial concentration and higher prices for consumers.

In their analysis of advertising, economists generally take a macroeconomic perspective: they consider the economic impact of advertising on an entire industry or on the economy as a whole rather than its effect on an individual company or brand. Our examination of the economic impact of advertising focuses on these broader macro-level issues. We consider its effects on consumer choice, competition, and product costs and prices.

Effects on Consumer Choice

Some critics say advertising hampers consumer choice, as large advertisers use their power to limit our options to a few well-advertised brands. Economists argue that advertising is used to achieve (1) **differentiation,** whereby the products or services of large advertisers are perceived as unique or better than competitors', and (2) brand loyalty, which enables large national advertisers to gain control of the market, usually at the expense of smaller brands.

Larger companies often end up charging a higher price and achieve a more dominant position in the market than smaller firms that cannot compete against them and their large advertising budgets. When this occurs, advertising not only restricts the choice alternatives to a few well-known, heavily advertised brands but also becomes a substitute for competition based on price or product improvements.

Heavily advertised brands dominate the market in certain product categories, such as soft drinks, beer, and cereals.[54] But advertising generally does not create brand monopolies and reduce the opportunities for new products to be introduced to consumers. In most product categories, a number of different brands are on the store shelves and thousands of new products are introduced every year. The opportunity to advertise gives companies the incentive to develop new brands and improve their existing ones. When a successful new product such as a personal computer is introduced, competitors quickly follow and use advertising to inform consumers about

Exhibit 18–13 Virgin Atlantic Airways chair Richard Branson acknowledges the importance of advertising

their brand and attempt to convince them it is superior to the original. Companies like Virgin Atlantic Airways recognize that advertising has been an important part of their success (Exhibit 18–13).

Effects on Competition

One of the most common criticisms economists have about advertising concerns its effects on competition. They argue that power in the hands of large firms with huge advertising budgets creates a **barrier to entry,** which makes it difficult for other firms to enter the market. This results in less competition and higher prices. Economists note that smaller firms already in the market find it difficult to compete against the large advertising budgets of the industry leaders and are often driven out of business. For example, the Canadian beer industry is dominated by two national brewers, Molson and Labatts, who account for over 90 percent of the market. With their high advertising and promotion expenditures, these companies are spending much less per barrel than smaller firms, making it very difficult for the latter to compete.

Large advertisers clearly enjoy certain competitive advantages. First, there are **economies of scale** in advertising, particularly with respect to factors such as media costs. Firms such as Procter & Gamble, which spends millions of dollars per year on advertising and promotion, are able to make large media buys at a reduced rate and allocate them to their various products.

Large advertisers usually sell more of a product or service, which means they may have lower production costs and can allocate more monies to advertising, so they can afford the costly but more efficient media like network television. Their large advertising outlays also give them more opportunity to differentiate their products and develop brand loyalty. To the extent that these factors occur, smaller competitors are at a disadvantage and new competitors are deterred from entering the market.

While advertising may have an anticompetitive effect on a market, there is no clear evidence that advertising alone reduces competition, creates barriers to entry, and thus increases market concentration. Lester Telser noted that high levels of advertising are not always found in industries where firms have a large market share. He found an inverse relationship between intensity of product class advertising and stability of market share for the leading brands.[55] These findings run contrary to many economists' belief that industries controlled by a few firms have high advertising expenditures, resulting in stable brand shares for market leaders.

Defenders of advertising say it is unrealistic to attribute a firm's market dominance and barriers to entry solely to advertising. There are a number of other factors, such as price, product quality, distribution effectiveness, production efficiencies, and competitive strategies. For many years, Hershey chocolate bar was a dominant brand even though it spent little on advertising. Hershey did not advertise at all until 1970. For 66 years, the company relied on the quality of its products, its favourable reputation and image among consumers, and its extensive channels of distribution to market its brands. Industry leaders often tend to dominate markets because they have superior product quality and the best management and competitive strategies, not simply the biggest advertising budgets.[56]

Effects on Product Costs and Prices

A major area of debate among economists, advertisers, consumer advocates, and policymakers concerns the effects of advertising on product costs and prices. Critics argue that advertising increases the prices consumers pay for products and services. First, they say the large sums of money spent advertising a brand constitute an expense that must be covered and the consumer ends up paying for it through higher prices. This is a common criticism from consumer advocates. Several studies show that firms with higher relative prices advertise their products more intensely than do those with lower relative prices.[57]

A second way advertising can result in higher prices is by increasing product differentiation and adding to the perceived value of the product in consumers' minds. Paul Farris and Mark Albion note that product differentiation occupies a central position in theories of advertising's economic effects.[58] The fundamental premise is that advertising increases the perceived differences between physically homogeneous products and enables advertised brands to command a premium price without an increase in quality.

Critics of advertising generally point to the differences in prices between national brands and private-label brands that are physically similar, such as aspirin or tea bags, as evidence of the added value created by advertising. They see consumers' willingness to pay more for heavily advertised national brands rather than purchasing the lower-priced, nonadvertised brand as wasteful and irrational. However, consumers do not always buy for rational, functional reasons. The emotional, psychological, and social benefits derived from purchasing a national brand are important to many people. Moreover, say Albion and Farris,

> Unfortunately there seems to be no single way to measure product differentiation, let alone determine how much is excessive or attributable to the effects of advertising . . . Both price insensitivity and brand loyalty could be created by a number of factors such as higher product quality, better packaging, favorable use experience and market position. They are probably related to each other but need not be the result of advertising.[59]

Proponents of advertising offer several other counterarguments to the claim that advertising increases prices. They acknowledge that advertising costs are at least partly paid for by consumers. But advertising may help lower the overall cost of a product more than enough to offset them. For example, advertising may help firms achieve economies of scale in production and distribution by providing information to and stimulating demand among mass markets. These economies of scale help cut the cost of producing and marketing the product, which can lead to lower prices—if the advertiser chooses to pass the cost savings on to the consumer. The ad in Exhibit 18–14, from a campaign sponsored by the American Association of Advertising Agencies, emphasizes this point.

Advertising can also lower prices by making a market more competitive, which usually leads to greater price competition. A study by Lee Benham found that prices of eyeglasses were 25 to 30 percent higher in states that banned eyeglass advertising than in those that permitted it.[60] Robert Steiner analyzed the toy industry and concluded that advertising resulted in lower consumer prices. He argued that curtailment of TV advertising would drive up consumer prices for toys.[61] Finally, advertising is a means to market entry rather than a deterrent and helps stimulate product innovation, which makes markets more competitive and helps keep prices down.

Overall, it is difficult to reach any firm conclusions regarding the relationship between advertising and prices. After an extensive review of this area, Farris and Albion concluded, "The evidence connecting manufacturer advertising to prices is neither complete nor definitive . . . consequently, we cannot say whether advertising is a tool of market efficiency or market power without further research."[62]

Economist James Ferguson argues that advertising cannot increase the cost per unit of quality to consumers because if it did, consumers would not continue to respond positively to advertising.[63] He believes advertising lowers the costs of information about brand qualities, leads to increases in brand quality, and lowers the average price per unit of quality.

Exhibit 18–14 This ad refutes the argument that reducing advertising expenditures will lead to lower prices

Figure 18–3 Two schools of thought on advertising's role in the economy

Advertising = Market Power		Advertising = Information
Advertising affects consumer preferences and tastes, changes product attributes, and differentiates the product from competitive offerings.	Advertising	Advertising informs consumers about product attributes but does not change the way they value those attributes.
Consumers become brand loyal and less price sensitive and perceive fewer substitutes for advertised brands.	Consumer buying behaviour	Consumers become more price sensitive and buy best "value." Only the relationship between price and quality affects elasticity for a given product.
Potential entrants must overcome established brand loyalty and spend relatively more on advertising.	Barriers to entry	Advertising makes entry possible for new brands because it can communicate product attributes to consumers.
Firms are insulated from market competition and potential rivals; concentration increases, leaving firms with more discretionary power.	Industry structure and market power	Consumers can compare competitive offerings easily and competitive rivalry increases. Efficient firms remain, and as the inefficient leave, new entrants appear; the effect on concentration is ambiguous.
Firms can charge higher prices and are not as likely to compete on quality or price dimensions. Innovation may be reduced.	Market conduct	More informed consumers pressure firms to lower prices and improve quality; new entrants facilitate innovation.
High prices and excessive profits accrue to advertisers and give them even more incentive to advertise their products. Output is restricted compared with conditions of perfect competition.	Market performance	Industry prices decrease. The effect on profits due to increased competition and increased efficiency is ambiguous.

Summarizing Economic Effects

Albion and Farris suggest that economists' perspectives can be divided into two principal schools of thought that make different assumptions regarding the influence of advertising on the economy.[64] Figure 18–3 summarizes the main points of the "advertising equals market power" and "advertising equals information" perspectives.

Advertising Equals Market Power The belief that advertising equals market power reflects traditional economic thinking and views advertising as a way to change consumers' tastes, lower their sensitivity to price, and build brand loyalty among buyers of advertised brands. This results in higher profits and market power for large advertisers, reduces competition in the market, and leads to higher prices and fewer choices for consumers. Proponents of this viewpoint generally have negative attitudes regarding the economic impact of advertising.

Advertising Equals Information The belief that advertising equals information takes a more positive view of advertising's economic effects. This model sees advertising as providing consumers with useful information, increasing their price sensitivity (which moves them toward lower-priced products), and increasing competition in the market. Advertising is viewed as a way to communicate with consumers and tell them about a product and its major features and attributes. More informed and knowledgeable consumers pressure companies to provide high-quality products at lower prices. Efficient firms remain in the market, whereas inefficient firms leave as new entrants appear. Proponents of this model believe the economic effects of advertising are favourable and think it contributes to more efficient and competitive markets.

To me it means that if we believe to any degree whatsoever in the economic system under which we live, in a high standard of living and in high employment, advertising is the most efficient known way of moving goods in practically every product class.

My proof is that millions of businessmen have chosen advertising over and over again in the operations of their business. Some of their decisions may have been wrong, but they must have thought they were right or they wouldn't go back to be stung twice by the same kind of bee.

It's a pretty safe bet that in the next 10 years many Americans will be using products and devices that no one in this room has even heard of. Judging purely by past performance, American advertising can be relied on to make them known and accepted overnight at the lowest possible prices.

Advertising, of course, makes possible our unparalleled variety of magazines, newspapers, business publications, and radio and television stations.

It must be said that without advertising we would have a far different nation, and one that would be much the poorer—not merely in material commodities, but in the life of the spirit.

Leo Burnett

These excerpts are from a speech given by Leo Burnett on the American Association of Advertising Agencies' 50th anniversary, April 20, 1967.

It is unlikely the debate over the economic effects and value of advertising will be resolved soon. Many economists will continue to take a negative view of advertising and its effects on the functioning of the economy, while advertisers will continue to view it as an efficient way for companies to communicate with their customers and an essential component of our economic system. The International Advertising Association has been running a campaign for several years to convince consumers around the world of the economic value of advertising. Ads like the one shown in Exhibit 18–15 are used in countries such as China and Russia, where consumers are unfamiliar with the concept of advertising. The goal of the campaign is to get consumers in these countries to recognize the role advertising plays in contributing to their economic well-being.[65]

Figure 18–4, excerpts from a speech given by famous adman Leo Burnett, summarizes the perspective of most advertising people on the economic effects of advertising. While many advertising and marketing experts agree that advertising and promotion play an important role in helping to expand consumer demand for new products, not everyone would agree that this is desirable.

WHEN ADVERTISING DOES ITS JOB, MILLIONS OF PEOPLE KEEP THEIRS.

Good advertising doesn't just inform. It sells. It helps move product and keep businesses in business. Every time an ad arouses a consumer's interest enough to result in a purchase, it keeps a company going strong. And it helps secure the jobs of the people who work there.

Advertising. That's the way it works.

INTERNATIONAL ADVERTISING ASSOCIATION

The global partnership of advertisers, agencies and media

Exhibit 18–15 This ad is part of a global campaign by the International Advertising Association to educate consumers about the economic value of advertising

Summary

Various levels of government regulate different aspects of Canadian advertising; however, self-regulation of these laws is quite prominent in Canada. This self-regulation occurs through the Advertising Standards Council (ASC), a non-profit organization of advertising industry members. The ASC responds to all complaints with respect to advertising and publishes an annual report that summarizes the complaints it receives each year. The ASC is also responsible for clearing ads prior to their airing for a number of products. Some of the ASC's responsibilities have been given to it as the Federal Government has withdrawn services with the belief that industry is sufficiently responsible.

Even though there appears to be sufficient control of advertising, it is a very powerful institution that has been the target of considerable criticism regarding its ethical, social, and economic impact. The criticism of advertising concerns the specific techniques and methods used as well as its effect on societal values, tastes, lifestyles, and behaviour. Critics argue that advertising is deceptive and untruthful; that it is often offensive, irritating, or in poor taste; and that it exploits certain groups. Many people believe advertising should be informative only and advertisers should not use subjective claims, puffery, embellishment, or persuasive techniques.

Advertising often offends consumers by the type of appeal or man-ner of presentation used; sexually suggestive ads and nudity receive the most criticism. Advertisers say their ads are consistent with contemporary values and lifestyles and are appropriate for the target audiences they are attempting to reach. Advertising to children is an area of particular concern, since critics argue that children lack the experience, knowledge, and ability to process and evaluate persuasive advertising messages rationally.

The pervasiveness of advertising and its prevalence in the mass media have led critics to argue that it plays a major role in influencing and transmitting social values. Advertising has been charged with encouraging materialism, manipulating consumers to buy things they do not really want or need, perpetuating stereotypes through its portrayal of certain groups such as women and visible minorities.

Advertising has also been scrutinized with regard to its economic effects. The basic economic role of advertising is to give consumers information that helps them make consumption decisions. Some people view advertising as a detrimental force that has a negative effect on competition, product costs, and consumer prices. Economists' perspectives regarding the effects of advertising follow two basic schools of thought: the advertising equals market power model and the advertising equals information model. Arguments consistent with each perspective were considered in analyzing the economic effects of advertising.

Key Terms

consumer complaints, 489

special interest group complaints, 489

trade disputes, 489

ethics, 492

puffery, 493

consumer socialization process, 496

materialism, 498

Protestant ethic, 498

differentiation, 505

barrier to entry, 506

economies of scale, 506

Discussion Questions

1. Explain why you agree or disagree with the rulings of the ASC presented in this chapter regarding the Yves Saint Laurent fragrance ad and the Ford Focus automobile ad?

2. Discuss the role of ethics in advertising and promotion. How do ethical considerations differ from legal considerations?

3. Nike has received some criticism for the violence in the ending to the commercials for the Air Cross Trainer II that appear on its "Whatever.Nike.com" website. Do you think these commercial endings are too violent or do you agree with the company's vice president of marketing who argues that teens can keep them in perspective?

4. Evaluate the arguments for and against advertising to children. Do you feel restrictions are needed for advertising and other forms of promotion targeted to children?

5. A common criticism of advertising is that it stereotypes women. Discuss the ways this might occur. Do you think the Airwalk ad shown in Exhibit 18–4 is suggestive and symbolizes sexual submission?

6. With which position do you agree: "Advertising determines Canadian consumers' tastes and values and is responsible for creating a materialistic society," or "Advertising is a reflection of society and mirrors its tastes and values"?

7. Discuss how advertising can impact consumer choice, as well as its impact on product costs and the prices paid for products and services.

8. Discuss the two major perspectives of the economic impact of advertising: "advertising equals market power" versus "advertising equals information."

Glossary of Advertising and Promotion Terms

80/20 rule (2)   The principle that 80 percent of sales volume for a product or service is generated by 20 percent of the customers.

5-W's model of communication (4)   A model of the communications process that contains five basics elements: who? (source), says what? (message), in what way? (channel), to whom? (receiver), and with what effect? (feedback).

A

absolute costs (8)   The actual total cost of placing an ad in a particular media vehicle.

account executive (16)   The individual who serves as the liaison between the advertising agency and the client. The account executive is responsible for managing all of the services the agency provides to the client and representing the agency's point of view to the client.

account-specific marketing (12)   Development of customized promotional programs for individual retail accounts by marketers.

ad execution-related thoughts (4)   A type of thought or cognitive response that a message recipient has concerning factors related to the execution of the ad such as creativity, usual effects, colour, and style.

advertising (1)   Any paid form of non-personal communication about an organization, product, service, or idea by an identified sponsor.

advertising agency (16)   A firm that specializes in the creation, production, and placement of advertising messages and may provide other services that facilitate the marketing communications process.

advertising appeal (7)   The basis or approach used in an advertising message to attract the attention or interest of consumers and/or influence their feelings toward the product, service, or cause.

advertising campaign (6)   A comprehensive advertising plan that consists of a series of messages in a variety of media that centre on a single theme or idea.

advertising creativity (6)   The ability to generate fresh, unique, and appropriate ideas that can be used as solutions to communication problems.

advertising manager (16)   The individual in an organization who is responsible for the planning, coordinating, budgeting, and implementing of the advertising program.

advertising specialties (11)   Items used as giveaways to serve as a reminder or stimulate remembrance of a company or brand such as calendars, T-shirts, pens, key tags, and the like. Specialties are usually imprinted with a company or brand name and other identifying marks such as an address and phone number.

advocacy advertising (13)   Advertising that is concerned with the propagation of ideas and elucidation of social issues of public importance in a manner that supports the position and interest of the sponsor.

aerial advertising (11)   A form of outdoor advertising where messages appear in the sky in the form of banners pulled by airplanes, skywriting, and on blimps.

affect referral decision rule (3)   A type of decision rule where selections are made on the basis of an overall impression or affective summary evaluation of the various alternatives under consideration.

affiliates (9)   Local television stations that are associated with a major network. Affiliates agree to pre-empt time during specified hours for programming provided by the network and carry the advertising contained in the program.

affiliation (15)   A relationship with other websites in which a company can cross-promote and is credited for sales that accrue through their site.

affordable method (8)   A method of determining the budget for advertising and promotion where all other budget areas are covered and remaining monies are available for allocation.

agate line (10)   Unit of newspaper space measurement, 1 column wide by 1/14 inch deep. (Thus, 14 agate lines = 1 column inch.)

agency evaluation process (16)   The process by which a company evaluates the performance of its advertising agency. This process includes both financial and qualitative aspects.

AIDA model (4)   A model that depicts the successive stages a buyer passes through in the personal selling process including: attention, interest, desire, and action.

alpha activity (17)   A measure of the degree of brain activity that can be used to assess an individual's reactions to an advertisement.

animatic (6)   A preliminary version of a commercial whereby a videotape of the frames of a storyboard is produced along with an audio soundtrack.

arbitrary allocation (8)   A method for determining the budget for advertising and promotion based on arbitrary decisions of executives.

attitude toward the ad (4)   A message recipient's affective feelings of favourability or unfavourability toward an advertisement.

attractiveness (6)   A source characteristic that makes him or her appealing to a message recipient. Source attractiveness can be based on similarity, familiarity, or likeability.

audimeter (9) An electric measurement device that is hooked to a television set to record when the set is turned on and the channel to which it is tuned.

audiotex (14) The use of telephone and voice information services to market, advertise, promote, entertain, and inform consumers.

average frequency (8) The number of times the average household reached by a media schedule is exposed to a media vehicle over a specified period.

average quarter-hour figure (AQH) (9) The average number of persons listening to a particular station for at least 5 minutes during a 15-minute period. Used by Arbitron in measuring the size of radio audiences.

average quarter-hour rating (9) The average quarter-hour figure estimate expressed as a percentage of the population being measured. Used by Arbitron in measuring the size of radio audiences.

average quarter-hour share (9) The percentage of the total listening audience tuned to each station as a percentage of the total listening audience in the survey area. Used by Arbitron in measuring the size of radio audiences.

B

banner (15) An ad on a Web page that may be "hot-linked" to the advertiser's site.

barrier to entry (18) Conditions that make it difficult for a firm to enter the market in a particular industry, such as high advertising budgets.

behaviouristic segmentation (2) A method of segmenting a market by dividing customers into groups based on their usage, loyalties, or buying responses to a product or service.

benchmark measures (5) Measures of a target audience's status concerning response hierarchy variables such as awareness, knowledge, image, attitudes, preferences, intentions, or behaviour. These measures are taken at the beginning of an advertising or promotional campaign to determine the degree to which a target audience must be changed or moved by a promotional campaign.

benefit segmentation (2) A method of segmenting markets on the basis of the major benefits consumers seek in a product or service.

billings (16) The amount of client money agencies spend on media purchases and other equivalent activities. Billings are often used as a way of measuring the size of advertising agencies.

bleed pages (10) Magazine advertisements where the printed area extends to the edge of the page, eliminating any white margin or border around the ad.

body copy (7) The main text portion of a print ad. Also often referred to as copy.

bonus packs (12) Special packaging that provides consumers with extra quantity of merchandise at no extra charge over the regular price.

bottom-up approach (8) A method of determining the budget for advertising and promotion by determining the specific tasks that have to be performed and estimating the costs of performing them. See objective and task method.

bounce-back coupon (12) A coupon offer made to consumers as an inducement to repurchase the brand.

brand attitude (5) Target audience overall evalutaion of the brand in relation to its ability to satisfy the reason they want it.

brand awareness (5) Target audience ability to recognize and/or recall the brand within the category in sufficient detail to make a purchase.

brand development index (BDI) (8) An index that is calculated by taking the percentage of a brand's total sales that occur in a given market as compared to the percentage of the total population in the market.

brand equity (2) The intangible asset of added value or goodwill that results from the favourable image, impressions of differentiation, and/or the strength of consumer attachment of a company name, brand name, or trademark.

brand loyal customers (5) Consumers that regularly purchase a company's branded product.

brand loyalty (3) Preference by a consumer for a particular brand that results in continual purchase of it.

brand manager (16) The person responsible for the planning, implementation, and control of the marketing program for an individual brand.

brand purchase facilitation (5) Target audience perception that a marketing factor could affect their purchase or use of the brand.

brand purchase intention (5) Target audience self-instruction to respond (purchase, purchase-related action) to the brand.

brand re-trial objective (5) A behavioural objective aimed at encouraging consumers to make a brand re-trial purchase, that is, their first purchase of a focal brand after some time delay.

brand-switching objective (5) A behavioural objective aimed at encouraging consumers to make a brand-switching purchase, that is, a purchase of a focal brand instead of a competing brand.

brand trial objective (5) A behavioural objective aimed at encouraging consumers to make a brand trial purchase, that is, their first purchase of a focal brand.

business-to-business advertising (17) Advertising used by one business to promote the products and/or services it sells to another business.

C

cable television (9) A form of television where signals are carried to households by wire rather than through the airways.

campaign theme (6) The central message that is communicated in all advertising and other promotional activities.

carryover effect (5) A delayed or lagged effect whereby the impact of advertising on sales can occur during a subsequent time period.

category development index (CDI) (8) An index that is calculated by taking the percentage of a product category's total sales that occur in a given market area as compared to the percentage of the total population in the market.

category extension (2) The strategy of applying an existing brand name to a new product category.

category need (5) Target audience perception of requiring a product to satisfy a need.

category trial objective (5) A behavioural objective aimed at encouraging consumers to make a category trial purchase, that is, their first purchase in a product category.

category management system (16) An organizational system whereby managers have responsibility for the marketing programs for a particular category or line of products.

cause-related marketing (13) A method of image building in which companies link with charities or non-profit organizations as contributing sponsors.

central route to persuasion (4) One of two routes to persuasion recognized by the elaboration likelihood model. The central route to persuasion views a message recipient as very active and involved in the communications process and as having the ability and motivation to attend to and process a message.

centralized system (16) An organizational system whereby advertising along with other marketing activities such as sales, marketing research, and planning are divided along functional lines and are run from one central marketing department.

channel (4) The method or medium by which communication travels from a source or sender to a receiver.

city zone (10) A category used for newspaper circulation figures that refers to a market area composed of the city where the paper is published and contiguous areas similar in character to the city.

classified advertising (10) Advertising that runs in newspapers and magazines that generally contains text only and is arranged under subheadings according to the product, service, or offering. Employment, real estate, and automotive ads are the major forms of classified advertising.

clicks (click-throughs) (17) Number of times users click on a banner ad.

click-through rate (17) The percentage of ad views that resulted in a click.

clients (16) The organizations with the products, services, or causes to be marketed and for which advertising agencies and other marketing promotional firms provide services.

clipping service (8) A service which clips competitors' advertising from local print media allowing the company to monitor the types of advertising that are running or to estimate their advertising expenditures.

clutter (9, 10, 12) The nonprogram material that appears in a broadcast environment, including commercials, promotional messages for shows, public service announcements, and the like.

cognitive dissonance (3) A state of psychological tension or post-purchase doubt that a consumer may experience after making a purchase decision. This tension often leads the consumer to try to reduce it by seeking supportive information.

cognitive responses (4) Thoughts that occur to a message recipient while reading, viewing, and/or hearing a communication.

commission system (16) A method of compensating advertising agencies whereby the agency receives a specified commission (traditionally 15 percent) from the media on any advertising time or space it purchases.

communication (4) The passing of information, exchange of ideas, or process of establishing shared meaning between a sender and a receiver.

communication objectives (1, 5) Goals that an organization seeks to achieve through its promotional program in terms of communication effects such as creating awareness, knowledge, image, attitudes, preferences, or purchase intentions.

communication task (5) Under the DAGMAR approach to setting advertising goals and objectives, something that can be performed by and attributed to advertising such as awareness, comprehension, conviction, and action.

comparative advertising (6, 7) The practice of either directly or indirectly naming one or more competitors in an advertising message and usually making a comparison on one or more specific attributes or characteristics.

competitive advantage (2) Something unique or special that a firm does or possesses that provides an advantage over its competitors.

competitive parity method (8) A method of setting the advertising and promotion budget based on matching the absolute level of percentage of sales expenditures of the competition.

compliance (6) A type of influence process where a receiver accepts the position advocated by a source to obtain favourable outcomes or to avoid punishment.

comprehension and reaction tests (17) Advertising effectiveness tests that are designed to assess whether the ad conveyed the desired meaning and is not reacted to negatively.

concave-downward function (8) An advertising/sales response function that views the incremental effects of advertising on sales as decreasing.

concentrated marketing (2) A type of marketing strategy whereby a firm chooses to focus its marketing efforts on one particular market segment.

concept testing (17) A method of pretesting alternative ideas for an advertisement or campaign by having consumers provide their responses and/or reactions to the creative concept.

consumer behaviour (3) The process and activities that people engage in when searching for, selecting, purchasing, using, evaluating, and disposing of products and services so as to satisfy their needs and desires.

consumer complaints (18) Complaints to the Advertising Standards Council from ordinary citizens who believe that an ad is unacceptable.

consumer franchise-building (CFB) promotions (12) Sales promotion activities that communicate distinctive brand attributes and contribute to the development and reinforcement of brand identity.

consumer juries (17) A method of pretesting advertisements by using a panel of consumers who are representative of the target audience and provide ratings, rankings, and/or evaluations of advertisements.

consumer sales promotion (12) Sales promotion techniques that are targeted to the ultimate consumer such as coupons, samples, contests, rebates, sweepstakes, and premium offers.

consumer socialization process (18) The process by which an individual acquires the skills needed to function in the marketplace as a consumer.

content sponsorship (15) The sponsor not only provides dollars in return for name association on the Internet but participates in the provision of content itself.

contest (12) A promotion whereby consumers compete for prizes or money on the basis of skills or ability, and winners are determined by judging the entries or ascertaining which entry comes closest to some predetermined criteria.

continuity (8) A media scheduling strategy where a continuous pattern of advertising is used over the time span of the advertising campaign.

controlled-circulation basis (10) Distribution of a publication free to individuals a publisher believes are of importance and responsible for making purchase decisions or are pre-screened for qualification on some other basis.

cookie (15) An identifying string of text attached to a website visitor's computer for information-gathering purposes, such as how often they visit the site, what is looked at, and in what sequence.

cooperative advertising (12) Advertising program in which a manufacturer pays a certain percentage of the expenses a retailer or distributor incurs for advertising the manufacturer's product in a local market area.

copy platform (6) A document that specifies the basic elements of the creative strategy such as the basic problem or issue the advertising must address, the advertising and communications objectives, target audience, major selling idea or key benefits to communicate, campaign theme or appeal, and supportive information or requirements.

copywriter (16) Individual who helps conceive the ideas for ads and commercials and writes the words or copy for them.

corporate advertising (13) Advertising designed to promote overall awareness of a company or enhance its image among a target audience.

cost per customer purchasing (14) A cost effectiveness measure used in direct marketing based on the cost per sale generated.

cost per order (CPO) (14) A measure used in direct marketing to determine the number of orders generated relative to the cost of running the advertisement.

cost per ratings point (8) A computation used by media buyers to compare the cost efficiency of broadcast programs that divides the cost of commercial time on a program by the audience rating.

cost per thousand (8) A computation used in evaluating the relative cost of various media vehicles that represents the cost of exposing 1,000 members of a target audience to an advertising message.

cost-plus system (16) A method of compensating advertising agencies whereby the agency receives a fee based on the cost of the work it performs plus an agreed-on amount for profit.

counterargument (4) A type of thought or cognitive response a receiver has that is counter or opposed to the position advocated in a message.

coverage (8) A measure of the potential audience that might receive an advertising message through a media vehicle.

CPC (15) Cost-per-click is a marketing formula used to price ad banners. Some advertisers pay based on the number of clicks a specific banner gets.

creative boutique (16) An advertising agency that specializes in and provides only services related to the creative aspects of advertising.

creative execution style (7) The manner or way in which a particular advertising appeal is transformed into a message.

creative strategy (6) A determination of what an advertising message will say or communicate to a target audience.

creative tactics (6) A determination of how an advertising message will be implemented so as to execute the creative strategy.

creative theme/idea (17) The primary creative strategy decision of an IMC campaign.

creativity (6) A quality possessed by persons that enables them to generate novel approaches, generally reflected in new and improved solutions to problems.

credibility (6) The extent to which a source is perceived as having knowledge, skill, or experience relevant to a communication topic and can be trusted to give an unbiased opinion or present objective information on the issue.

cross-ruff coupon (12) A coupon offer delivered on one product that is redeemable for the purchase of another product. The other product is usually one made by the same company but may involve a tie-in with another manufacturer.

culture (3) The complexity of learned meanings, values, norms, and customs shared by members of a society.

cume (9) A term used for cumulative audience, which is the estimated total number of different people who listened to a radio station for a minimum of 5 minutes during a particular daypart.

D

DAGMAR (5) An acronym that stands for defining advertising goals for measured advertising results. An approach to setting advertising goals and objectives developed by Russell Colley.

daily inch rate (8) A cost figure used in periodicals based on an advertisement placed one inch deep and one column wide (whatever the column inch).

database (14) A listing of current and/or potential customers for a company's product or service that can be used for direct-marketing purposes.

database marketing (14) The use of specific information about individual customers and/or prospects to implement more effective and efficient marketing communications.

day-after recall scores (17) A measure used in on-air testing of television commercials by various marketing research companies. The day-after recall score represents the percentage of viewers surveyed who can remember seeing a particular commercial.

dayparts (9) The time segments into which a day is divided by radio and television networks and stations for selling advertising time.

decentralized system (16) An organizational system whereby planning and decision-making responsibility for marketing, advertising, and promotion lies with a product/brand manager or management team rather than a centralized department.

decoding (4) The process by which a message recipient transforms and interprets a message.

demographic segmentation (2) A method of segmenting a market based on the demographic characteristics of consumers.

departmental system (16) The organization of an advertising agency into departments based on functions such as account services, creative, media, marketing services, and administration.

differentiated marketing (2) A type of marketing strategy whereby a firm offers products or services to a number of market segments and develops separate marketing strategies for each.

differentiation (18) A situation where a particular company or brand is perceived as unique or better than its competitors.

direct headline (7) A headline that is very straightforward and informative in terms of the message it is presenting and the target audience it is directed toward. Direct headlines often include a specific benefit, promise, or reason for a consumer to be interested in a product or service.

directional medium (11) Advertising media that are not used to create awareness or demand for products or services but rather to inform customers as to where purchases can be made once they have decided to buy. The Yellow Pages are an example of a directional medium.

direct marketing (1, 14) A system of marketing by which an organization communicates directly with customers to generate a response and/or transaction.

direct-response advertising (1, 14) A form of advertising for a product or service that elicits a sales response directly from the advertiser.

direct-response agency (16) A company that provides a variety of direct-marketing services to their clients including database management, direct mail, research, media service, and creative and production capabilities.

direct-response media (14) Media that are used for direct-marketing purposes including direct mail, telemarketing, print, and broadcast.

direct selling (1, 14) The direct personal presentation, demonstration, and sale of products and services to consumers usually in their homes or at their jobs.

display advertising (10) Advertising in newspapers and magazines that uses illustrations, photos, headlines, and other visual elements in addition to copy text.

dissonance/attribution model (4) A type of response hierarchy where consumers first behave, then develop attitudes or feelings as a result of that behaviour, and then learn or process information that supports the attitude and behaviour.

diverting (12) A practice whereby a retailer or wholesaler takes advantage of a promotional deal and then sells some of the product purchased at the low price to a store outside of their area or to a middleman who will resell it to other stores.

domain name (15) The unique name of an Internet site. The six domains most widely used in the U.S. are .com (commercial), .edu (education), .net (network operations), .gov (U.S. government), .mil (U.S. military), and .org (organization). Additional two letter domains specify a country, for example, .sp for Spain.

duplicated reach (8) Audience members' exposure to a message as a result of messages having appeared in two or more different media vehicles.

E

e-commerce (15) Direct selling of goods and services through the Internet.

economies of scale (8, 18) A decline in costs with accumulated sales or production. In advertising, economies of scale often occur in media purchases as the relative costs of advertising time and/or space may decline as the size of the media budget increases.

effective reach (8) A measure of the percentage of a media vehicle's audience reached at each effective frequency increment.

elaboration likelihood model (ELM) (4) A model that identifies two processes by which communications can lead to persuasion—central and peripheral routes.

electrodermal response (17) A measure of the resistance the skin offers to a small amount of current passed between two electrodes. Used as a measure of consumers' reaction level to an advertisement.

electroencephalographic (EEG) measures (17) Measures of the electrical impulses in the brain that are sometimes used as a measure of reactions to advertising.

electronic teleshopping (14) Online shopping and information retrieval service that is accessed through a personal computer.

emotional appeals (7) Advertising messages that appeal to consumers' feelings and emotions.

encoding (4) The process of putting thoughts, ideas, or information into a symbolic form.

ethics (18) Moral principles and values that govern the actions and decisions of an individual or group.

evaluative criteria (3) The dimensions or attributes of a product or service that are used to compare different alternatives.

event marketing (12) A type of promotion where a company or brand is linked to an event, or where a themed activity is developed for the purpose of creating experiences for consumers and promoting a product or service.

event sponsorship (12, 13) A type of promotion whereby a company develops sponsorship relations with a particular event such as a concert, sporting event, or other activity.

evoked set (3) The various brands identified by a consumer as purchase options and that are actively considered during the alternative evaluation process.

exclusive (13) A public relations tactic whereby one particular medium is offered exclusive rights to a story.

external analysis (1) The phase of the promotional planning process that focuses on factors such as the characteristics of an organization's customers, market segments, positioning strategies, competitors, and marketing environment.

external audiences (13) In public relations, a term used in reference to individuals who are outside of or not closely connected to the organization such as the general public.

external audits (13) Evaluations performed by outside agencies to determine the effectiveness of an organization's public relations program.

external search (3) The search process whereby consumers seek and acquire information from external sources such as advertising, other people, or public sources.

eye tracking (17) A method for following the movement of a person's eyes as he or she views an ad or commercial. Eye tracking is used for determining which portions or sections of an ad attract a viewer's attention and/or interest.

F

failure fee (12) A trade promotion arrangement whereby a marketer agrees to pay a penalty fee if a product stocked by a retailer does not meet agreed-upon sales levels.

favourable brand switchers (5) Customers that buy a focal brand but also buy other brands within a given time period for the same product category. For some product categories, consumers habitually purchase from a few favourites or those brands within their evoked set.

fear appeal (6) An advertising message that creates anxiety in a receiver by showing negative consequences that can result from engaging in (or not engaging in) a particular behaviour.

fee-commission combination (16) A type of compensation system whereby an advertising agency establishes a fixed monthly fee for its services to a client and media commissions received by the agency are credited against the fee.

feedback (4) Part of message recipient's response that is communicated back to the sender. Feedback can take a variety of forms and provides a sender with a way of monitoring how an intended message is decoded and received.

field of experience (4) The experiences, perceptions, attitudes, and values that senders and receivers of a message bring to a communication situation.

field tests (17) Tests of consumer reactions to an advertisement that are taken under natural viewing situations rather than in a laboratory.

financial audit (16) An aspect of the advertising agency evaluation process that focuses on how the agency conducts financial affairs related to serving a client.

fixed-fee method (16) A method of agency compensation whereby the agency and client agree on the work to be done and the amount of money the agency will be paid for its services.

Flesch formula (17) A test used to assess the difficulty level of writing based on the number of syllables and sentences per 100 words.

flighting (8) A media scheduling pattern in which periods of advertising are alternated with periods of no advertising.

focus groups (6) A qualitative marketing research method whereby a group of 10–12 consumers from the target audience are led through a discussion regarding a particular topic such as a product, service, or advertising campaign.

forward buying (12) A practice whereby retailers and wholesalers stock up on a product being offered by a manufacturer at a lower deal or off-invoice price and resell it to consumers once the marketer's promotional period has ended.

frequency (8) The number of times a target audience is exposed to a media vehicle(s) in a specified period.

frequency programs (12) A type of promotional program that rewards customers for continuing to purchase the same brand of a product or service over time (also referred to as continuity or loyalty programs).

full-service agency (16) An advertising agency that offers clients a full range of marketing and communications services including the planning, creating, producing, and placing of advertising messages and other forms of promotion.

functional consequences (3) Outcomes of product or service usage that are tangible and can be directly experienced by a consumer.

G

game (12) A promotion that is a form of sweepstakes because it has a chance element or odds of winning associated with it. Games usually involve game card devices that can be rubbed or opened to unveil a winning number or prize description.

gatefolds (10) An oversize magazine page or cover that is extended and folded over to fit into the publication. Gatefolds are used to extend the size of a magazine advertisement and are always sold at a premium.

general preplanning input (6) Information gathering and/or market research studies on trends, developments, and happenings in the marketplace that can be used to assist in the initial stages of the creative process of advertising.

geographical weighting (8) A media scheduling strategy where certain geographic areas or regions are allocated higher levels of advertising because they have greater sales potential.

geographic segmentation (2) A method of segmenting a market on the basis of different geographic units or areas.

green marketing (18) The marketing and promotion of products on the basis of environmental sensitivity.

gross ratings points (GRPs) (8) A measure that represents the total delivery or weight of a media schedule during a specified time period. GRPs are calculated by multiplying the reach of the media schedule by the average frequency.

group system (16) The organization of an advertising agency by dividing it into groups consisting of specialists from various departments such as creative, media, marketing services, and other areas. These groups work together to service particular accounts.

H

halo effect (17) The tendency for evaluations of one attribute or aspect of a stimulus to distort reactions to its other attributes or properties.

headline (7) Words in the leading position of the advertisement; the words that will be read first or are positioned to draw the most attention.

hemispheric lateralization (17) The notion that the human brain has two relatively distinct halves or hemispheres with each being responsible for a specific type of function. The right side is responsible for visual processing while the left side conducts verbal processing.

heuristics (3) Simplified or basic decision rules that can be used by a consumer to make a purchase choice, such as buy the cheapest brand.

hierarchy of effects model (4) A model of the process by which advertising works that assumes a consumer must pass through a sequence of steps from initial awareness to eventual action. The stages include awareness, interest, evaluation, trial, and adoption.

hierarchy of needs (3) Abraham Maslow's theory that human needs are arranged in an order or hierarchy based on their importance. The need hierarchy includes physiological, safety, social/love and belonging, esteem, and self-actualization needs.

hit (17) Each time a server sends a file to a browser it is recorded as a "hit." Hits are used to measure the traffic on a website.

horizontal cooperative advertising (12) A cooperative advertising arrangement where advertising is sponsored in common by a group of retailers or other organizations providing products or services to a market.

households using television (HUT) (9) The percentage of homes in a given area that are watching television during a specific time period.

I

identification (6) The process by which an attractive source influences a message recipient. Identification occurs when the receiver is motivated to seek some type of relationship with the source and adopt a similar position in terms of beliefs, attitudes, preferences, or behaviour.

image advertising (13) Advertising that creates an identity for a product or service by emphasizing psychological meaning or symbolic association with certain values, lifestyles, and the like.

image transfer (9) A radio advertising technique whereby the images of a television commercial are implanted into a radio spot.

incentive-based system (16) A form of compensation whereby an advertising agency's compensation level depends on how well it meets predetermined performance goals such as sales or market share.

indirect headlines (7) Headlines that are not straightforward with respect to identifying a product or service or providing information regarding the point of an advertising message.

in-flight advertising (11) A variety of advertising media targeting air travellers while they are in flight.

infomercials (9, 14) Television commercials that are very long, ranging from several minutes to an hour. Infomercials are designed to provide consumers with detailed information about a product or service.

informational/rational appeals (7) Advertising appeals that focus on the practical, functional, or utilitarian need for a product or service and emphasize features, benefits, or reasons for owning or using the brand.

information processing model (4) A model of advertising effects developed by William McGuire that views the receiver of a message as an information processor and problem solver. The model views the receiver as passing through a response hierarchy that includes a series of stages including message presentation, attention, comprehension, acceptance or yielding, retention, and behaviour.

ingredient-sponsored cooperative advertising (12) Advertising supported by raw material manufacturers with the objective being to help establish end products that include materials and/or ingredients supplied by the company.

inherent drama (6) An approach to advertising that focuses on the benefits or characteristics that lead a consumer to purchase a product or service and uses dramatic elements to emphasize them.

in-house agency (16) An advertising agency set up, owned, and operated by an advertiser that is responsible for planning and executing the company's advertising program.

ink-jet imaging (10) A printing process where a message is reproduced by projecting ink onto paper rather than mechanical plates. Ink-jet imaging is being offered by many magazines to allow advertisers to personalize their messages.

innovation-adoption model (4) A model that represents the stages a consumer passes through in the adoption process for an innovation such as a new product. The series of steps includes awareness, interest, evaluation, trial, and adoption.

inquiry tests (17) Tests designed to measure advertising effectiveness on the basis of inquiries or responses generated from the ad such as requests for information, number of phone calls, or number of coupons redeemed.

inside cards (11) A form of transit advertising where messages appear on cards or boards inside of vehicles such as buses, subways, or trolleys.

instant coupon (12) Coupons attached to a package that can be removed and redeemed at the time of purchase.

in-store couponing (12) The distribution of coupons in retail stores through various methods such as tear-off pads, handouts, and on-shelf or electronic dispensers.

in-store media (11) Advertising and promotional media that are used inside of a retail store such as point-of-purchase displays, ads on shopping carts, coupon dispensers, and display boards.

integrated information response model (4) A model of the response process or sequence advertising message recipients go through which integrates concepts from the traditional and low-involvement response hierarchy perspectives.

integrated marketing communication objectives (5) Statements of what various aspects of the integrated marketing communications program will accomplish with respect to factors such as communication tasks, sales, market share, and the like.

integrated marketing communications (IMC) (1) A concept of marketing communications planning that recognizes the added value of a comprehensive plan that evaluates the strategic roles of a variety of communication disciplines—for example, general advertising, direct response, sales promotion, and public relations—and combines these disciplines to provide clarity, consistency, and maximum communications impact.

integration processes (3) The way information such as product knowledge, meanings, and beliefs is combined to evaluate two or more alternatives.

interactive agency (16) An organization that specializes in the creation of interactive media such as CD-ROMs, kiosks, and websites.

interactive media (1, 15) A variety of media that allows the consumer to interact with the source of the message, actively receiving information and altering images, responding to questions, and so on.

internal analysis (1) The phase of the promotional planning process that focuses on the product/service offering and the firm itself including the capabilities of the firm and its ability to develop and implement a successful integrated marketing communications program.

internal audiences (13) In public relations, a term used to refer to individuals or groups inside of the organization or with a close connection to it.

internal audits (13) Evaluations by individuals within the organization to determine the effectiveness of a public relations program.

internalization (6) The process by which a credible source influences a message recipient. Internalization occurs when the receiver is motivated to have an objectively correct position on an issue and the receiver will adopt the opinion or attitude of the credible communicator if he or she believes the information from this source represents an accurate position on the issue.

internal search (3) The process by which a consumer acquires information by accessing past experiences or knowledge stored in memory.

Internet (15) A worldwide means of exchanging information and communicating through a series of interconnected computers.

interstitial (15) An advertisement that appears in a window on your computer screen while you are waiting for a Web page to load.

J

jingles (7) Songs about a product or service that usually carry the advertising theme and a simple message.

L

laboratory tests (17) Tests of consumer reactions to advertising under controlled conditions.

layout (7) The physical arrangement of the various parts of an advertisement including the headline, subheads, illustrations, body copy, and any identifying marks.

link (15) An electronic connection between two websites.

low-involvement hierarchy (4) A response hierarchy whereby a message recipient is viewed as passing from cognition to behaviour to attitude change.

M

mailing list (14) A type of database containing names and addresses of present and/or potential customers who can be reached through a direct-mail campaign.

marginal analysis (8) A principle of resource allocation that balances incremental revenues against incremental costs.

marketing (1, 2) The process of planning and executing the conception, pricing, promotion, and distribution of ideas, goods, and services to create exchanges that satisfy individual and organizational objectives.

marketing channels (2) The set of interdependent organizations involved in the process of making a product or service available to customers.

marketing mix (1, 2) The controllable elements of a marketing program including product, price, promotion, and place.

marketing objectives (1, 5) Goals to be accomplished by an organization's overall marketing program such as sales, market share, or profitability.

marketing plan (1) A written document that describes the overall marketing strategy and programs developed for an organization, a particular product line, or a brand.

marketing public relations (13) Public relations activities designed to support marketing objectives and programs.

market opportunities (2) Areas where a company believes there are favourable demand trends, needs, and/or wants that are not being satisfied, and where it can compete effectively.

market segmentation (2) The process of dividing a market into distinct groups that have common needs and will respond similarly to a marketing action.

market segments (2) Identifiable groups of customers sharing similar needs, wants, or other characteristics that make them likely to respond in a similar fashion to a marketing program.

mass media (4) Non-personal channels of communication that allow a message to be sent to many individuals at one time.

materialism (18) A preoccupation with material things rather than intellectual or spiritual concerns.

media buying services (16) Independent companies that specialize in the buying of media, particularly radio and television time.

media objectives (8) The specific goals an advertiser has for the media portion of the advertising program.

media organizations (16) One of the four major participants in the integrated marketing communications process whose function is to provide information or entertainment to subscribers, viewers, or readers while offering marketers an environment for reaching audiences with print and broadcast messages.

media plan (8) A document consisting of objectives, strategies, and tactics for reaching a target audience through various media vehicles.

media planning (8) The series of decisions involved in the delivery of an advertising message to prospective purchasers and/or users of a product or service.

media strategies (8) Plans of action for achieving stated media objectives such as which media will be used for reaching a target audience, how the media budget will be allocated, and how advertisements will be scheduled.

media vehicle (8) The specific program, publication, or promotional piece used to carry an advertising message.

medium (8) The general category of communication vehicles that are available for communicating with a target audience such as broadcast, print, direct mail, and outdoor.

message (4) A communication containing information or meaning that a source wants to convey to a receiver.

mnemonics (3) Basic cues such as symbols, rhymes, and associations that facilitate the learning and memory process.

mobile billboards (11) An out-of-home medium in which advertisements are able to be transported to different locations (signs painted on automobiles, trailers pulling billboards, and the like).

motivation research (3) Qualitative research designed to probe the consumer's subconscious and discover deeply rooted motives for purchasing a product.

motive (3) Something that compels or drives a consumer to take a particular action.

multiattribute attitude model (3) A model of attitudes that views an individual's evaluation of an object as being a function of the beliefs that he or she has toward the object on various attributes and the importance of these attributes.

N

need recognition (3) The first stage in the consumer's decision-making process in which the consumer perceives a need and becomes motivated to satisfy it.

negotiated commission (16) A method of compensating advertising agencies whereby the client and agency negotiate the commission structure rather than relying on the traditional 15 percent media commission.

new category users (5) Consumers that are not purchasing within a product category, such as university graduates who are purchasing in new categories because they now have the money to do so.

noise (4) Extraneous factors that create unplanned distortion or interference in the communications process.

nonfranchise-building (non-FB) promotions (12) Sales promotion activities that are designed to accelerate the purchase decision process and generate an immediate increase in sales but do little or nothing to communicate information about a brand and contribute to its identity and image.

O

objective and task method (8) A bottom-up approach to budget setting involving a three-step process: (1) determining objectives, (2) determining the strategies and tasks required to attain these objectives, and (3) estimating the costs associated with these strategies and tasks.

off-invoice allowance (12) A promotional discount offered to retailers or wholesalers whereby a certain per-case amount or percentage is deducted from the invoice.

on-air tests (17) Testing the effectiveness of television commercials by inserting test ads into actual TV programs in certain test markets.

one-step approach (14) A direct-marketing strategy in which the medium is used directly to obtain an order (for example, television direct-response ads).

open-rate structure (10) A rate charged by newspapers in which discounts are available based on frequency or bulk purchases of space.

other brand loyals (5) Consumers that are loyal to a brand other than the company's brand within a product category.

other brand switchers (5) Consumers that regularly purchase from a number of a company's competing brands within a product category.

out-of-home media (11) The variety of advertising forms including outdoor, transit, skywriting, and other media viewed outside the home.

outside posters (11) Outdoor transit posters appearing on buses, taxis, trains, subways, and trolley cars.

P

PACT (Positioning Advertising Copy Testing) (17) A set of principles endorsed by 21 of the largest U.S. ad agencies aimed at improving the research used in preparing and testing ads, providing a better creative product for clients, and controlling the cost of TV commercials.

page views (17) Number of times a user requests a page that contains a particular ad. Used to indicate the number of times an ad was potentially seen, or "gross impressions."

pass-along rate (8) An estimate of the number of readers of a magazine in addition to the original subscriber or purchaser.

pass-along readership (10) The audience that results when the primary subscriber or purchaser of a magazine gives the publication to another person to read, or when the magazine is read in places such as waiting rooms in doctors' offices, etc.

payout plan (8) A budgeting plan that determines the investment value of the advertising and promotion appropriation.

people meter (9) An electronic device that automatically records a household's television viewing, including channels watched, number of minutes of viewing, and members of the household who are watching.

percentage charges (16) The markups charged by advertising agencies for services provided to clients.

percentage-of-sales method (8) A budget method in which the advertising and/or promotions budget is set based on a percentage of sales of the product.

perception (3) The process by which an individual receives, selects, organizes, and interprets information to create a meaningful picture of the world.

peripheral route to persuasion (4) In the elaboration likelihood model, one of two routes to persuasion in which the receiver is viewed as lacking the ability or motivation to process information and is not likely to be engaging in detailed cognitive processing.

personalization (15) Individuals can request that specific information they are interested in viewing be sent to their computers.

personal selling (1) Person-to-person communication in which the seller attempts to assist and/or persuade prospective buyers to purchase the company's product or service or to act on an idea.

planograms (12) A planning configuration of products that occupy a shelf section in a store that is used to provide more efficient shelf space utilization.

pop-ups (15) Advertisement windows on the Internet usually larger than a banner ad and smaller than a full screen.

portfolio tests (17) A laboratory methodology designed to expose a group of respondents to a portfolio consisting of both control and test print ads.

positioning (2) The art and science of fitting the product or service to one or more segments of the market in such a way as to set it meaningfully apart from competition.

positioning strategies (2) The strategies used in positioning a brand or product.

posttests (17) Ad effectiveness measures that are taken after the ad has appeared in the marketplace.

preferred position rate (10) A rate charged by newspapers that ensures the advertiser the ad will appear in the position required and/or in a specific section of the newspaper.

premium (12) An offer of an item of merchandise or service either free or at a low price that is used as an extra incentive for purchasers.

preprinted inserts (10) Advertising distributed through newspapers that is not part of the newspaper itself, but is printed by the advertiser and then taken to the newspaper to be inserted.

press release (13) Factual and interesting information released to the press.

pretests (17) Advertising effectiveness measures that are taken before the implementation of the advertising campaign.

price elasticity (2) The responsiveness of the market to change in price.

price-off deal (12) A promotional strategy in which the consumer receives a reduction in the regular price of the brand.

primacy effect (7) A theory that the first information presented in the message will be the most likely to be remembered.

primary circulation (10) The number of copies of a magazine distributed to original subscribers.

problem detection (6) A creative research approach in which consumers familiar with a product (or service) are asked to generate an exhaustive list of problems encountered in its use.

product manager (16) The person responsible for the planning, implementation, and control of the marketing program for an individual brand.

product placement (11) A form of advertising and promotion in which products are placed in television shows and/or movies to gain exposure.

product/service-specific preplanning input (6) Specific studies provided to the creative department on the product or service, the target audience, or a combination of the two.

product symbolism (2) The meaning that a product or brand has to consumers.

program rating (9) The percentage of TV households in an area that are tuned to a program during a specific time period.

promotion (1) The coordination of all seller-initiated efforts to set up channels of information and persuasion to sell goods and services or to promote an idea.

promotional management (1) The process of coordinating the promotional mix elements.

promotional mix (1) The tools used to accomplish an organization's communications objective. The promotional mix includes advertising, direct marketing, sales promotion, publicity/public relations, and personal selling.

promotional plan (1) The framework for developing, implementing, and controlling the organization's communications program.

promotional products marketing (11) The advertising or promotional medium or method that uses promotional products such as ad specialties, premiums, business gifts, awards, prizes, or commemoratives.

promotional pull strategy (2) A strategy in which advertising and promotion efforts are targeted at the ultimate consumers to encourage them to purchase the manufacturer's brand.

promotional push strategy (2) A strategy in which advertising and promotional efforts are targeted to the trade to attempt to get them to promote and sell the product to the ultimate consumer.

Protestant ethic (18) A perspective of life which stresses hard work and individual effort and initiative and views the accumulation of material possessions as evidence of success.

psychographic segmentation (2) Dividing the product on the basis of personality and/or lifestyles.

psychosocial consequences (3) Purchase decision consequences that are intangible, subjective, and personal.

public relations (1, 13) The management function that evaluates public attitudes, identifies the policies and procedures of an individual or organization with the public interest, and executes a program to earn public understanding and acceptance.

public relations firm (16) An organization that develops and implements programs to manage a company's publicity, image, and affairs with consumers and other relevant publics.

publicity (1, 13) Communications regarding an organization, product, service, or idea that is not directly paid for or run under identified sponsorship.

puffery (18) Advertising or other sales presentations that praise the item to be sold using subjective opinions, superlatives, or exaggerations, vaguely and generally, stating no specific facts.

pulsing (8) A media scheduling method that combines flighting and continuous scheduling.

pupillometrics (17) An advertising effectiveness methodology designed to measure dilation and constriction of the pupils of the eye in response to stimuli.

purchase intention (3) The predisposition to buy a certain brand or product.

purchase-related behaviour objective (5) A behavioural objective related to consumer actions that will lead to a higher probability of purchasing a particular focal brand.

push money (12) Cash payments made directly to the retailers' or wholesalers' sales force to encourage them to promote and sell a manufacturer's product.

push technology (15) Allows a company to "push" a message to the consumer through the Internet rather than waiting for them to find it.

Q

qualitative audit (16) An audit of the advertising agency's efforts in planning, developing, and implementing the client's communications programs.

qualitative media effect (7) The positive or negative influence the medium may contribute to the message.

R

ratings point (9) A measurement used to determine television viewing audiences in which one ratings point is the equivalent of 1 percent of all of the television households in a particular area tuned to a specific program.

rational appeal (7) Communications in which features and/or benefits are directly presented in a logical, rational method.

reach (8) The number of different audience members exposed at least once to a media vehicle (or vehicles) in a given period.

readers per copy (8) A cost comparison figure used for magazines that estimates audience size based on pass-along readership.

recall tests (17) Advertising effectiveness tests designed to measure advertising recall.

receiver (4) The person or persons with whom the sender of a message shares thoughts or information.

recency effect (7) The theory that arguments presented at the end of the message are considered to be stronger and therefore are more likely to be remembered.

recognition method (17) An advertising effectiveness measure of print ads that allows the advertiser to assess the impact of an ad in a single issue of a magazine over time and/or across alternative magazines.

reference group (3) A group whose perspectives, values, or behaviour is used by an individual as the basis for his or her judgments, opinions, and actions.

refutational appeal (7) A type of message in which both sides of the issue are presented in the communication, with arguments offered to refute the opposing viewpoint.

relationship marketing (1) An organization's effort to develop a long-term, cost-effective link with individual customers for mutual benefit.

relative cost (8) The relationship between the price paid for advertising time or space and the size of the audience delivered; it is used to compare the prices of various media vehicles.

reminder advertising (7) Advertising designed to keep the name of the product or brand in the mind of the receiver.

repeat-consumption objective (5) Communicating with current customers who have previously purchased the brand and have the product at their home or work.

repeat-purchase objective (5) A behavioural objective aimed at encouraging consumers to make a repeat purchase, that is, to continue buying a particular focal brand.

repositioning (2) The changing of a product or brand's positioning.

resellers (2) Intermediaries in the marketing channel such as wholesalers, distributors, and retailers.

response (4) The set of reactions the receiver has after seeing, hearing, or reading a message.

retail trading zone (10) The market outside the city zone whose residents regularly trade with merchants within the city zone.

ROI (return on investment) budgeting method (8) A budgeting method in which advertising and promotions are considered investments, and thus measurements are made in an attempt to determine the returns achieved by these investments.

run of paper (ROP) (10) A rate quoted by newspapers that allows the ad to appear on any page or in any position desired by the medium.

S

sales promotion (1, 12) Marketing activities that provide extra value or incentives to the sales force, distributors, or the ultimate consumer and can stimulate immediate sales.

sales promotion agency (16) An organization that specializes in the planning and implementation of promotional programs such as contests, sweepstakes, sampling, premiums, and incentive offers for its clients.

sales promotion trap (12) A spiral that results when a number of competitors extensively use promotions. One firm uses sales promotions to differentiate its product or service and other competitors copy the strategy, resulting in no differential advantage and a loss of profit margins to all.

salient attributes (2) A product's attributes and/or benefits that are important to consumers and are the basis for making a purchase decision.

salient beliefs (3) Beliefs concerning specific attributes or consequences that are activated and form the basis of an attitude.

sampling (12) A variety of procedures whereby consumers are given some quantity of a product for no charge to induce trial.

satisfaction (3) A result that occurs when a consumer's expectations about a product are either met or exceeded.

scatter market (9) A period for purchasing television advertising time that runs throughout the TV season.

script (7) A written version of the commercial that provides a detailed description of its video and audio content.

selective attention (3) A perceptual process in which consumers choose to attend to some stimuli and not others.

selective binding (10) A computerized production process that allows the creation of hundreds of copies of a magazine in one continuous sequence.

selective comprehension (3) The perceptual process whereby consumers interpret information based on their own attitudes, beliefs, motives, and experiences.

selective demand advertising (2) Advertising that focuses on stimulating demand for a specific manufacturer's product or brand.

selective exposure (3) A process whereby consumers choose whether or not to make themselves available to media and message information.

selective learning (4) The process whereby consumers seek information that supports the choice made and avoid information that fails to bolster the wisdom of a purchase decision.

selective perception (3) The perceptual process involving the filtering or screening of exposure, attention, comprehension, and retention.

selective retention (3) The perceptual process whereby consumers remember some information but not all.

selectivity (10) The ability of a medium to reach a specific target audience.

self-liquidating premiums (12) Premiums that require the consumer to pay some or all of the cost of the premium plus handling and mailing costs.

self-regulation (18) The practice by the advertising industry of regulating and controlling advertising to avoid interference by outside agencies such as the government.

semiotics (4) The study of the nature of meaning.

sensation (3) The immediate and direct response of the senses (taste, smell, sight, touch, and hearing) to a stimulus such as an advertisement, package, brand name, or point-of-purchase display.

share of audience (9) The percentage of households watching television in a special time period that are tuned to a specific program.

showing (11) The percentage of supplicated audience exposed to an outdoor poster daily.

single-source tracking (17) A research method designed to track the behaviours of consumers from the television set to the supermarket checkout counter.

situational determinants (3) Influences originating from the specific situation in which consumers are to use the product or brand.

sleeper effect (6) A phenomenon in which the persuasiveness of a message increases over time.

slotting allowance (12) Fees that must be paid to retailers to provide a "slot" or position to accommodate a new product on the store shelves.

social class (3) Relatively homogeneous divisions of society into which people are grouped based on similar lifestyles, values, norms, interests, and behaviours.

source (4, 6) The sender—person, group, or organization—of the message.

source bolsters (4) Favourable cognitive thoughts generated toward the source of a message.

source derogations (4) Negative thoughts generated about the source of a communication.

source power (6) The power of a source as a result of his or her ability to administer rewards and/or punishments to the receiver.

SPAM (15) Unsolicited commercial e-mail.

special interest group complaints (18) Complaints about an ad to the Advertising Standards Council from a demonstrated organization that expresses a unified viewpoint.

specialized marketing communication services (16) Organizations that provide marketing communication services in their areas of expertise including direct marketing, public relations, and sales promotion firms.

specialty advertising (11) An advertising, sales promotion, and motivational communications medium that employs useful articles of merchandise imprinted with an advertiser's name, message, or logo.

split-30s (9) 30-second TV spots in which the advertiser promotes two different products with two different messages during a 30-second commercial.

split-run test (17) An advertising effectiveness measure in which different versions of an ad are run in alternate copies of the same newspaper and/or magazine.

sponsorship (9) When the advertiser assumes responsibility for the production and usually the content of a television program as well as the advertising that appears within it.

sponsorships (15) When advertisers sponsor content on a website, it is considered a sponsorship.

spot advertising (9) Commercials shown on local television stations, with the negotiation and purchase of time being made directly from the individual stations.

S-shaped response curve (8) A sales response model that attempts to show sales responses to various levels of advertising and promotional expenditures.

standard learning model (4) Progression by the consumers through a learn-feel-do hierarchical response.

storyboard (6) A series of drawings used to present the visual plan or layout of a proposed commercial.

strategic marketing plan (2) The planning framework for specific marketing activities.

subcultures (3) Smaller groups within a culture that possess similar beliefs, values, norms, and patterns of behaviour that differentiate them from the larger cultural mainstream.

subheads (7) Secondary headlines in a print ad.

subliminal perception (3) The ability of an individual to perceive a stimulus below the level of conscious awareness.

superagencies (16) Large external agencies that offer integrated marketing communications on a worldwide basis.

superstations (9) Independent local stations that send their signals via satellite to cable operators that, in turn, make them available to subscribers (WWOR, WPIX, WGN, WSBK, WTBS).

support advertising (14) A form of direct marketing in which the ad is designed to support other forms of advertising appearing in other media.

support argument (4) Consumers' thoughts that support or affirm the claims being make by a message.

support media (11) Those media used to support or reinforce messages sent to the target audience through other more "dominant" and/or more traditional media.

sweepstakes (12) A promotion whereby consumers submit their names for consideration in the drawing or selection of prizes and winners are determined purely by chance. Sweepstakes cannot require a proof of purchase as a condition for entry.

T

target market process (2) The process of identifying the specific needs of segments, selecting one or more of these segments as a target, and developing marketing programs directed to each.

target ratings points (TRPs) (8) The number of persons in the primary target audience that the media buy will reach—and the number of times.

team approach (13) A method of measuring the effectiveness of public relations programs whereby evaluators are actually involved in the campaign.

teaser advertising (7) An ad designed to create curiosity and build excitement and interest in a product or brand without showing it.

telemarketing (14) Selling products and services by using the telephone to contact prospective customers.

telemedia (14) The use of telephone and voice information services (800, 900, 976 numbers) to market, advertise, promote, entertain, and inform.

television households (9) The number of households in a market that own a television set.

television network (9) The provider of news and programming to a series of affiliated local television stations.

terminal posters (11) Floor displays, island showcases, electronic signs, and other forms of advertisements that appear in train or subway stations, airline terminals, etc.

testing bias (17) A bias that occurs in advertising effectiveness measures because respondents know they are being tested and thus alter their responses.

theatre testing (17) An advertising effectiveness pretest in which consumers view ads in a theatre setting and evaluate these ads on a variety of dimensions.

top-down approaches (8) Budgeting approaches in which the budgetary amount is established at the executive level and monies are passed down to the various departments.

total audience/readership (10) A combination of the total number of primary and pass-along readers multiplied by the circulation of an average issue of a magazine.

total audience (television) (9) The total number of homes viewing any 5-minute part of a television program.

tracking studies (17) Advertising effectiveness measures designed to assess the effects of advertising on awareness, recall, interest, and attitudes toward the ad as well as purchase intentions.

trade advertising (2) Advertising targeted to wholesalers and retailers.

trade allowance (12) A discount or deal offered to retailers or wholesalers to encourage them to stock, promote, or display a manufacturer's products.

trade disputes (18) Complaints about an ad to the Advertising Standards Council from other advertisers.

trademark (2) An identifying name, symbol, or other device that gives a company the legal and exclusive rights to use.

trade sales promotion (12) A sales promotion designed to motivate distributors and retailers to carry a product and make an extra effort to promote or "push" it to their customers.

trade show (12) A type of exhibition or forum where manufacturers can display their products to current as well as prospective buyers.

transformational advertising (7) An ad that associates the experience of using the advertised brand with a unique set of psychological characteristics that would not typically be associated with the brand experience to the same degree without exposure to the advertisement.

transit advertising (11) Advertising targeted to target audiences exposed to commercial transportation facilities, including buses, taxis, trains, elevators, trolleys, airplanes, and subways.

two-step approach (14) A direct-marketing strategy in which the first effort is designed to screen or qualify potential buyers, while the second effort has the responsibility of generating the response.

U

undifferentiated marketing (2) A strategy in which market segment differences are ignored and one product or service is offered to the entire market.

unduplicated reach (8) The number of persons reached once with a media exposure.

unique selling proposition (6) An advertising strategy that focuses on a product or service attribute that is distinctive to a particular brand and offers an important benefit to the customer.

unique visitors (17) The number of different individuals who visit a website within a specific time period.

V

values and lifestyles program (VALS) (2) Stanford Research Institute's method for applying lifestyle segmentation.

vehicle option source effect (17) The differential impact the advertising exposure will have on the same audience member if the exposure occurs in one media option rather than another.

vertical cooperative advertising (12) A cooperative arrangement under which a manufacturer pays for a portion of the advertising a retailer runs to promote the manufacturer's product and its availability in the retailer's place of business.

video advertising (11) Advertisements appearing in movie theatres and on videotapes.

video news release (13) News stories produced by publicists so that television stations may air them as news.

visits (17) A sequence of requests made by one user at one site.

voiceover (7) Action on the screen in a commercial that is narrated or described by a narrator who is not visible.

W

want (3) A felt need shaped by a person's knowledge, culture, and personality.

waste coverage (8) A situation where the coverage of the media exceeds the target audience.

webcasting (15) A system for pushing out site information to Web users rather than waiting for them to find the site on their own. (Often referred to as push technologies.)

website (15) The information made available to users of the Internet by the provider.

word-of-mouth communications (5) Social channels of communication such as friends, neighbours, associates, co-workers, or family members.

World Wide Web (WWW) (15) Commonly referred to as the Web, the commercial component of the Internet.

Y

Yellow Pages advertising (11) Advertisements that appear in the various Yellow Pages-type phone directories.

Z

zapping (9) The use of a remote control device to change channels and switch away from commercials.

zero-based communications planning (5) An approach to planning the integrated marketing communications program that involves determining what tasks need to be done and what marketing communication functions should be used to accomplish them and to what extent.

zipping (9) Fast-forwarding through commercials during the playback of a program previously recorded on a VCR.

Endnotes

Chapter One

1. Brent Armstrong, "The First Meal's Not Enough," *Marketing Magazine,* September 10, 2001.
2. Peter Widdis, "Bringing Brands to Life," *Marketing Magazine,* January 15, 2001.
3. "AMA Board Approves New Marketing Definition," *Marketing News,* March 1, 1985, p. 1.
4. Michael L. Ray, *Advertising and Communication Management* (Englewood Cliffs, NJ: Prentice Hall, 1982).
5. Ralph S. Alexander, ed., *Marketing Definitions* (Chicago: American Marketing Association, 1965), p. 9.
6. "Trends in Media," Television Bureau of Advertising, New York.
7. Richard Lewis, "Absolut Vodka Case History," *A Celebration of Effective Advertising: 30 Years of Winning EFFIE Campaigns* (New York: American Marketing Association, 1999), pp. 20–23.
8. The 1999 Annual Report of the U.S. Promotion Industry, *Promo,* July 1999, p. S3.
9. *Cox Direct 20th Annual Survey of Promotional Practices* (Largo Lakes, FL: Cox Direct, 1998).
10. H. Frazier Moore and Bertrand R. Canfield, *Public Relations: Principles, Cases, and Problems,* 7th ed. (Burr Ridge, IL: Irwin, 1977), p. 5.
11. Art Kleiner, "The Public Relations Coup," *Adweek's Marketing Week,* January 16, 1989, pp. 20–23.
12. Adrienne Ward Fawcett, "Integrated Marketing—Marketers Convinced: Its Time Has Arrived," *Advertising Age,* November 6, 1993, pp. S1–2.
13. "Do Your Ads Need a SuperAgency?" *Fortune,* April 27, 1991, pp. 81–85; Faye Rice, "A Cure for What Ails Advertising?" *Fortune,* December 16, 1991, pp. 119–22.

14. Don E. Schultz, "Integrated Marketing Communications: Maybe Definition Is in the Point of View," *Marketing News,* January 18, 1993, p. 17.
15. Ibid.
16. Tom Duncan and Sandra E. Moriarty, "A Communication-Based Model for Managing Relationships," *Journal of Marketing* 62 (April 1998), pp. 1–13.
17. Louise Lee, "Can Nike Still Do It?" *Business Week,* February 21, 2000, pp. 121–28.
18. Harlan E. Spotts, David R. Lambert, and Mary L. Joyce, "Marketing Déjà Vu: The Discovery of Integrated Marketing Communications," *Journal of Marketing Education* 20, no. 3 (December 1998), pp. 210–18.
19. Kate Fitzgerald, "Beyond Advertising," *Advertising Age,* August 3, 1998, pp. 1, 14; Jane Smith, "Integrated Marketing," *Marketing Tools,* November/December 1995, pp. 63–70; Thomas R. Duncan and Stephen E. Everett, "Client Perception of Integrated Marketing Communications," *Journal of Advertising Research,* May/June 1993, pp. 30–39.
20. Lesley Young, "A Marketing Tale," *Marketing Magazine,* July 30, 2001.
21. Anthony J. Tortorici, "Maximizing Marketing Communications through Horizontal and Vertical Orchestration," *Public Relations Quarterly* 36, no. 1 (1991), pp. 20–22.
22. Robert H. Ducoffe, Dennis Sandler, and Eugene Secunda, "A Survey of Senior Agency, Advertiser, and Media Executives on the Future of Advertising," *Journal of Current Issues and Research in Advertising* 18, no. 1 (Spring 1996).
23. Dave Guilford and Hillary Chura, "BMW Loads Up Bond Push to Precede Film Premiere," *Advertising Age,* November 1, 1999, p. 12.

24. Sergio Zyman, *The End of Marketing As We Know It* (New York: HarperBusiness, 1999); Joe Cappo, "Agencies: Change or Die," *Advertising Age,* December 7, 1992, p. 26.
25. Don E. Schultz, "Be Careful Picking Database for IMC Efforts," *Marketing News,* March 11, 1996, p. 14.
26. Leonard L. Berry, "Relationship Marketing of Services—Growing Interest, Emerging Perspectives," *Journal of the Academy of Marketing Science* 23, no. 4, 1995, pp. 236–45; Jonathan R. Capulsky and Michael J. Wolfe, "Relationship Marketing: Positioning for the Future," *Journal of Business Strategy,* July–August 1991, pp. 16–26.
27. B. Joseph Pine II, Don Peppers, and Martha Rogers, "Do You Want to Keep Your Customers Forever?" *Harvard Business Review,* March–April 1995, p. 103–14.

Chapter Two

1. Spencer L. Hapoinen, "The Rise of Micromarketing," *The Journal of Business Strategy,* November/December 1990, pp. 37–42.
2. Dan Fost, "Growing Older, but Not Up," *American Demographics,* September 1998, pp. 58–65.
3. "What Happened to Advertising?" *Business Week,* September 23, 1991, pp. 66–72.
4. Edward M. Tauber, "Research on Food Consumption Values Finds Four Market Segments: Good Taste Still Tops," *Marketing News,* May 15, 1981, p. 17; Rebecca C. Quarles, "Shopping Centers Use Fashion Lifestyle Research to Make Marketing Decisions," *Marketing News,* January 22, 1982, p. 18; and "Our Auto, Ourselves," *Consumer Reports,* June 1985, p. 375.

5. Judith Graham, "New VALS 2 Takes Psychological Route," *Advertising Age,* February 13, 1989, p. 24.

6. "WestJet Fuels Up Advertising Effort," *Marketing Magazine,* March 12, 2001; "Flying the Cluttered Skies," *Marketing Magazine,* April 9, 2001.

7. J. Paul Peter and Jerry C. Olson, *Consumer Behavior* (Burr Ridge, IL: Richard D. Irwin, 1987), p. 505.

8. Michael R. Solomon, "The Role of Products as Social Stimuli: A Symbolic Interactionism Perspective," *Journal of Consumer Research,* December 1983, pp. 319–29.

9. Don E. Schultz, Stanley I. Tannenbaum, and Robert F. Lauterborn, *Integrated Marketing Communications: Putting It Together and Making It Work* (Lincolnwood, IL: NTC Publishing Group), p. 72.

10. "The Message Is in the Bottle," *Marketing Magazine,* October 8, 2001.

11. Peter and Olson, *Consumer Behavior,* p. 571.

12. Paul W. Farris and David J. Reibstein, "How Prices, Ad Expenditures, and Profits Are Linked," *Harvard Business Review,* November–December 1979, pp. 172–84.

13. Eric N. Berkowitz, Roger A. Kerin, and William Rudelius, *Marketing,* 6th ed. (Burr Ridge, IL: Irwin/ McGraw-Hill, 2000).

14. David W. Stewart, Gary L. Frazier, and Ingrid Martin, "Integrated Channel Management: Merging the Communication and Distribution Functions of the Firm," in *Integrated Communication: Synergy of Persuasive Voices,* pp. 185–215, Esther Thorson & Jeri Moore (eds), Lawrence Earlbaum Associates, 1996, Mahwah, NJ.

15. *Ayer's Dictionary of Advertising Terms* (Philadelphia: Ayer Press, 1976).

16. Davis A. Aaker and John G. Myers, *Advertising Management,* 3rd ed. (Englewood Cliffs, NJ: Prentice Hall, 1987), p. 125.

17. Jack Trout and Al Ries, "Positioning Cuts through Chaos in the Marketplace," *Advertising Age,* May 1, 1972, pp. 51–53.

18. David A. Aaker and J. Gary Shansby, "Positioning Your Product," *Business Horizons,* May–June 1982, pp. 56–62.

19. Trout and Ries, "Positioning Cuts through Chaos."

20. Aaker and Myers, *Advertising Management.*

Chapter Three

1. Russell W. Belk, "Possessions and the Extended Self," *Journal of Consumer Research,* September 1988, pp. 139–68.

2. Leon G. Schiffman and Leslie Lazar Kannuk, *Consumer Behavior,* 4th ed. (Englewood Cliffs, NJ: Prentice Hall, 1991), p. 192.

3. Eric N. Berkowitz, Roger A. Kerin, Steven W. Hartley, and William Rudelius, *Marketing,* 6th ed. (Burr Ridge, IL: Irwin/McGraw-Hill, 2000), p. 14.

4. A. H. Maslow, "'Higher' and 'Lower' Needs," *Journal of Psychology* 25 (1948), pp. 433–36.

5. Jeffrey Ball, "But How Does It Make You Feel?" *The Wall Street Journal,* May 3, 1999, p. B1.

6. Jagdish N. Sheth, "The Role of Motivation Research in Consumer Psychology" (Faculty Working Paper, University of Illinois, Champaign: 1974); Bill Abrams, "Charles of the Ritz Discovers What Women Want," *The Wall Street Journal,* August 20, 1981, p. 29; and Ernest Dichter, *Getting Motivated* (New York: Pergamon Press, 1979).

7. Ronald Alsop, "Advertisers Put Consumers on the Couch," *The Wall Street Journal,* May 13, 1988, p. 19.

8. Ball, "But How Does It Make You Feel?"

9. For an excellent discussion of memory and consumer behaviour, see James R. Bettman, "Memory Factors in Consumer Choice: A Review," *Journal of Marketing* 43 (Spring 1979), pp. 37–53.

10. Gilbert Harrell, *Consumer Behavior* (San Diego: Harcourt Brace Jovanovich, 1986), p. 66.

11. Raymond A. Bauer and Stephen A. Greyser, *Advertising in America: The Consumer View* (Boston: Harvard Business School, 1968).

12. Neal Santelmann, "Color That Yells 'Buy Me'," *Forbes,* May 2, 1988, p. 110.

13. J. Paul Peter and Jerry C. Olson, *Consumer Behavior,* 2nd ed. (Burr Ridge, IL: Irwin/McGraw-Hill, 1990), p. 73.

14. Gordon W. Allport, "Attitudes," in *Handbook of Social Psychology,* ed. C. M. Murchison (Winchester, MA: Clark University Press, 1935), p. 810.

15. Robert B. Zajonc and Hazel Markus, "Affective and Cognitive Factors in Preferences," *Journal of Consumer Research* 9 (1982), pp. 123–31.

16. Alvin Achenbaum, "Advertising Doesn't Manipulate Consumers," *Journal of Advertising Research,* April 2, 1970, pp. 3–13.

17. William D. Wells, "Attitudes and Behavior: Lessons from the Needham Lifestyle Study," *Journal of Advertising Research,* February–March 1985, pp. 40–44; and Icek Ajzen and Martin Fishbein, "Attitude-Behavior Relations: A Theoretical Analysis and Review of Empirical Research," *Psychological Bulletin,* September 1977, pp. 888–918.

18. For a review of multiattribute models, see William L. Wilkie and Edgar A. Pessemier, "Issues in Marketing's Use of Multiattribute Models," *Journal of Marketing Research* 10 (November 1983), pp. 428–41.

19. Joel B. Cohen, Paul W. Minniard, and Peter R. Dickson, "Information Integration: An Information Processing Perspective," in *Advances in Consumer Research,* vol. 7, ed. Jerry C. Olson (Ann Arbor, MI: Association for Consumer Research, 1980), pp. 161–70.

20. Peter and Olson, *Consumer Behavior,* p. 182.

21. Peter L. Wright and Fredric Barbour, "The Relevance of Decision Process Models in Structuring Persuasive Messages," *Communications Research,* July 1975, pp. 246–59.

22. James F. Engel, "The Psychological Consequences of a Major Purchase Decision," in *Marketing in Transition,* ed. William S. Decker (Chicago: American Marketing Association, 1963), pp. 462–75.

23. Richard L. Oliver, *Satisfaction: A Behavioral Perspective on the Consumer* (New York: McGraw-Hill, 1997).

24. John A. Howard and Jagdish N. Sheth, *The Theory of Consumer Behavior* (New York: John Wiley & Sons, 1969).

25. Gerald J. Gorn, "The Effects of Music in Advertising on Choice: A Classical Conditioning Approach," *Journal of Marketing* 46 (Winter 1982), pp. 94–101.

26. James J. Kellaris, Anthony D. Cox, and Dena Cox, "The Effect of Background Music on Ad Processing: A Contingency Explanation," *Journal of Marketing,* 57, no. 4 (Fall 1993), p. 114.

27. Brian C. Deslauries and Peter B. Everett, "The Effects of Intermittent and Continuous Token Reinforcement on Bus Ridership," *Journal of Applied Psychology* 62 (August 1977), pp. 369–75.

28. Michael L. Rothschild and William C. Gaidis, "Behavioral Learning

Theory: Its Relevance to Marketing and Promotions," *Journal of Marketing Research* 45, no. 2 (Spring 1981), pp. 70–78.

29. For an excellent discussion of social class and consumer behaviour, see Richard P. Coleman, "The Continuing Significance of Social Class to Marketing," *Journal of Consumer Research* 10, no. 3 (December 1983), pp. 265–80.

30. Lyman E. Ostlund, *Role Theory and Group Dynamics in Consumer Behavior: Theoretical Sources,* ed. Scott Ward and Thomas S. Robertson (Englewood Cliffs, NJ: Prentice Hall, 1973), pp. 230–75.

31. James Stafford and Benton Cocanougher, "Reference Group Theory," in *Perspective in Consumer Behavior,* ed. H. H. Kassarjian and T. S. Robertson (Glenview, IL: Scott, Foresman, 1981), pp. 329–43.

32. Jagdish N. Sheth, "A Theory of Family Buying Decisions," in *Models of Buying Behavior,* ed. Jagdish N. Sheth (New York: Harper & Row, 1974), pp. 17–33.

33. Russell Belk, "Situational Variables and Consumer Behavior," *Journal of Consumer Research,* December 1975, pp. 157–64.

Chapter Four

1. Wilbur Schram, *The Process and Effects of Mass Communications* (Urbana: University of Illinois Press, 1955).

2. Ibid.

3. Joseph Ransdell, "Some Leading Ideas of Peirce's Semiotic," *Semiotica* 19 (1977), pp. 157–78.

4. Michael Solomon, *Consumer Behavior,* 4th ed. (Upper Saddle River, NJ: Prentice-Hall, 1999), p. 17.

5. Nina Munk, "Levi's Ongoing Quest for Street Cred," *Fortune,* February 1, 1999, p. 40.

6. For an excellent article on the application of semiotics to consumer behaviour and advertising, see David G. Mick, "Consumer Research and Semiotics: Exploring the Morphology of Signs, Symbols, and Significance," *Journal of Consumer Research* 13, no. 2 (September 1986), pp. 196–213; see also Edward F. McQuarrie and David Glen Mick, "Figures of Rhetoric in Advertising Language," *Journal of Consumer Research* 22 (March 1996), pp. 424–38.

7. Barry L. Bayus, "Word of Mouth: The Indirect Effect of Marketing Efforts," *Journal of Advertising Research,* June/July 1985, pp. 31–39.

8. Jacob Jacoby and Wayne D. Hoyer, "Viewer Miscomprehension of Televised Communication: Selected Findings," *Journal of Marketing,* Fall 1982, pp. 12–26; Jacoby and Hoyer, "The Comprehension and Miscomprehension of Print Communications: An Investigation of Mass Media Magazines," Advertising Education Foundation study, New York, 1987.

9. E. K. Strong, *The Psychology of Selling* (New York: McGraw-Hill, 1925), p. 9.

10. Robert J. Lavidge and Gary A. Steiner, "A Model for Predictive Measurements of Advertising Effectiveness," *Journal of Marketing* 24 (October 1961), pp. 59–62.

11. Everett M. Rogers, *Diffusion of Innovations* (New York: Free Press, 1962), pp. 79–86.

12. William J. McGuire, "An Information Processing Model of Advertising Effectiveness," in *Behavioral and Management Science in Marketing,* ed. Harry J. Davis and Alvin J. Silk (New York: Ronald Press, 1978), pp. 156–80.

13. Michael L. Ray, "Communication and the Hierarchy of Effects," in *New Models for Mass Communication Research,* ed. P. Clarke (Beverly Hills, CA: Sage, 1973), pp. 147–75.

14. Herbert E. Krugman, "The Impact of Television Advertising: Learning without Involvement," *Public Opinion Quarterly* 29 (Fall 1965), pp. 349–56.

15. Scott A. Hawkins and Stephen J. Hoch, "Low-Involvement Learning: Memory without Evaluation," *Journal of Consumer Research* 19, no. 2 (September 1992), pp. 212–25.

16. Harry W. McMahan, "Do Your Ads Have VIP?" *Advertising Age,* July 14, 1980, pp. 50–51.

17. Harold H. Kassarjian, "Low Involvement: A Second Look," in *Advances in Consumer Research,* vol. 8 (Ann Arbor: Association for Consumer Research, 1981), pp. 31–34; also see Anthony G. Greenwald and Clark Leavitt, "Audience Involvement in Advertising: Four Levels," *Journal of Consumer Research* 11, no. 1 (June 1984), pp. 581–92.

18. Judith L. Zaichkowsky, "Conceptualizing Involvement," *Journal of Advertising* 15, no. 2 (1986), pp. 4–14.

19. Robert E. Smith and William R. Swinyard, "Information Response Models: An Integrated Approach," *Journal of Marketing* 46, no. 2 (Winter 1982), pp. 81–93.

20. Ibid., p. 90.

21. Ibid., p. 86.

22. Robert E. Smith, "Integrating Information from Advertising and Trial: Processes and Effects on Consumer Response to Product Information," *Journal of Marketing Research* 30 (May 1993), pp. 204–19.

23. Jerry C. Olson, Daniel R. Toy, and Phillip A. Dover, "Mediating Effects of Cognitive Responses to Advertising on Cognitive Structure," in *Advances in Consumer Research,* vol. 5, ed. H. Keith Hunt (Ann Arbor, MI: Association for Consumer Research, 1978), pp. 72–78.

24. Anthony A. Greenwald, "Cognitive Learning, Cognitive Response to Persuasion and Attitude Change," in *Psychological Foundations of Attitudes,* ed. A. G. Greenwald, T. C. Brock, and T. W. Ostrom (New York: Academic Press, 1968); Peter L. Wright, "The Cognitive Processes Mediating Acceptance of Advertising," *Journal of Marketing Research* 10 (February 1973), pp. 53–62; Brian Wansink, Michael L. Ray, and Rajeev Batra, "Increasing Cognitive Response Sensitivity," *Journal of Advertising* 23, no. 2 (June 1994), pp. 65–76.

25. Peter Wright, "Message Evoked Thoughts, Persuasion Research Using Thought Verbalizations," *Journal of Consumer Research* 7, no. 2 (September 1980), pp. 151–75.

26. Scott B. Mackenzie, Richard J. Lutz, and George E. Belch, "The Role of Attitude toward the Ad as a Mediator of Advertising Effectiveness: A Test of Competing Explanations," *Journal of Marketing Research* 23 (May 1986), pp. 130–43; and Rajeev Batra and Michael L. Ray, "Affective Responses Mediating Acceptance of Advertising," *Journal of Consumer Research* 13 (September 1986), pp. 234–49.

27. Tim Ambler and Tom Burne, "The Impact of Affect on Memory of Advertising," *Journal of Advertising Research* 29, no. 3 (March/April 1999), pp. 25–34; Ronald Alsop, "TV Ads That Are Likeable Get Plus Rating for Persuasiveness," *The Wall Street Journal,* February 20, 1986, p. 23.

28. David J. Moore and William D. Harris, "Affect Intensity and the Consumer's Attitude toward High

Endnotes

524

Impact Emotional Advertising Appeals," *Journal of Advertising* 25, no. 2 (Summer 1996), pp. 37–50; Andrew A. Mitchell and Jerry C. Olson, "Are Product Attribute Beliefs the Only Mediator of Advertising Effects on Brand Attitude?" *Journal of Marketing Research* 18 (August 1981), pp. 318–32.

29. David J. Moore, William D. Harris, and Hong C. Chen, "Affect Intensity: An Individual Difference Response to Advertising Appeals," *Journal of Consumer Research* 22 (September 1995), pp. 154–64; Julie Edell and Marian C. Burke, "The Power of Feelings in Understanding Advertising Effects," *Journal of Consumer Research* 14 (December 1987), pp. 421–33.

30. Richard E. Petty and John T. Cacioppo, "Central and Peripheral Routes to Persuasion: Application to Advertising," in *Advertising and Consumer Psychology,* ed. Larry Percy and Arch Woodside (Lexington, MA: Lexington Books, 1983), pp. 3–23.

31. David A. Aaker, Rajeev Batra, and John G. Myers, *Advertising Management,* 5th ed. (Upper Saddle River, NJ: Prentice Hall, 1996).

32. Richard E. Petty, John T. Cacioppo, and David Schumann, "Central and Peripheral Routes to Advertising Effectiveness: The Moderating Role of Involvement," *Journal of Consumer Research* 10 (September 1983), pp. 135–46.

33. Demetrios Vakratsas and Tim Ambler, "How Advertising Works: What Do We Really Know?" *Journal of Marketing* 63 (January 1999), pp. 26–43.

Chapter Five

1. Robert A. Kriegel, "How to Choose the Right Communications Objectives," *Business Marketing,* April 1986, pp. 94–106.

2. Donald S. Tull, "The Carry-Over Effect of Advertising," *Journal of Marketing,* April 1965, pp. 46–53.

3. Darral G. Clarke, "Econometric Measurement of the Duration of Advertising Effect on Sales," *Journal of Marketing Research* 23 (November 1976), pp. 345–57.

4. Philip Kotler, *Marketing Decision Making: A Model Building Approach* (New York: Holt, Rinehart & Winston, 1971), ch. 5.

5. For a more detailed discussion of this, see William M. Weilbacher,

Advertising, 2nd ed. (New York: Macmillan, 1984), p. 112.

6. Russell H. Colley, *Defining Advertising Goals for Measured Advertising Results* (New York: Association of National Advertisers, 1961).

7. Ibid., p. 21.

8. Michael L. Ray, "Consumer Initial Processing: Definitions, Issues, Applications," in *Buyer/Consumer Information Processing,* ed. G. David Hughes (Chapel Hill: University of North Carolina Press, 1974); David A. Aaker and John G. Myers, *Advertising Management,* 2nd ed. (Englewood Cliffs, NJ: Prentice Hall, 1982), pp. 122–23.

9. Sandra Ernst Moriarty, "Beyond the Hierarchy of Effects: A Conceptual Framework," in *Current Issues and Research in Advertising,* ed. Claude R. Martin, Jr., and James H. Leigh (Ann Arbor, MI: University of Michigan, 1983), pp. 45–55.

10. Don E. Schultz, Dennis Martin, and William Brown, *Strategic Advertising Campaigns,* 2nd ed. (Lincolnwood, IL: Crain Books, 1984).

11. Courtland I. Bovee and William F. Arens, *Advertising,* 3rd ed. (Burr Ridge, IL: Richard D. Irwin, 1989).

12. Stewart H. Britt, "Are So-Called Successful Advertising Campaigns Really Successful?" *Journal of Advertising Research* 9, no. 2 (1969), pp. 3–9.

13. Steven W. Hartley and Charles H. Patti, "Evaluating Business-to-Business Advertising: A Comparison of Objectives and Results," *Journal of Advertising Research* 28 (April/May 1988), pp. 21–27.

14. Ibid., p. 25.

15. Study cited in Robert F. Lauterborn, "How to Know If Your Advertising Is Working," *Journal of Advertising Research* 25 (February/March 1985), pp. RC 9–11.

16. Don E. Schultz, "Integration Helps You Plan Communications from Outside-In," *Marketing News,* March 15, 1993, p. 12.

17. Thomas R. Duncan, "To Fathom Integrated Marketing, Dive!" *Advertising Age,* October 11, 1993, p. 18.

18. John Rossiter and Larry Percy, *Advertising Communications and Promotion Management* (New York: McGraw Hill, 1996).

19. Marla Lampert, "One less worry for the trip," *Marketing Magazine,* June 18, 2001.

20. Eve Lazarus, "Taking on Goliath," *Marketing Magazine,* March 4, 2002.

21. Mark Higgins, "Smart Marketing," *Marketing Magazine,* April 2, 2001.

22. Lesley Young, "It Pays to Get aggressive," *Marketing Magazine,* February 12, 2001.

Chapter Six

1. Lara Mills, "Campaigns with Legs," *Marketing Magazine,* May 15, 2000.

2. "Cows Cheer Olympic Athletes," *Marketing Magazine,* February 4, 2002.

3. Jeanne Whalen, "BK Caters to Franchisees with New Review," *Advertising Age,* October 25, 1993, p. 3.

4. "Burger King Corporation Unveils New Advertising," PR Newswire, August 4, 1999.

5. Joshua Levine, "Fizz, Fizz—Plop, Plop," *Fortune,* June 21, 1993, p. 139.

6. Jean Halliday and Alice Z. Cuneo, "Nissan Reverses Course to Focus on the Product," *Advertising Age,* February 16, 1998, pp. 1, 39.

7. Bill Abrams, "What Do Effie, Clio, Addy, Andy and Ace Have in Common?" *The Wall Street Journal,* July 16, 1983, p. 1; Jennifer Pendleton, "Awards—Creatives Defend Pursuit of Prizes," *Advertising Age,* April 25, 1988, p. 1; David Herzbrun, "The Awards Awards," *Advertising Age,* May 2, 1988, p. 18.

8. Elizabeth C. Hirschman, "Role-Based Models of Advertising Creation and Production," *Journal of Advertising* 18, no. 4 (1989), pp. 42–53.

9. Ibid., p. 51.

10. Cyndee Miller, "Study Says 'Likability' Surfaces as Measure of TV Ad Success," *Marketing News,* January 7, 1991, pp. 6, 14; and Ronald Alsop, "TV Ads That Are Likeable Get Plus Rating for Persuasiveness," *The Wall Street Journal,* February 20, 1986, p. 23.

11. For an interesting discussion on the embellishment of advertising messages, see William M. Weilbacher, *Advertising,* 2nd ed. (New York: Macmillan, 1984), pp. 180–82.

12. David Ogilvy, *Confessions of an Advertising Man* (New York: Atheneum, 1963); and Hanley Norins, *The Compleat Copywriter* (New York: McGraw-Hill, 1966).

13. Hank Sneiden, *Advertising Pure and Simple* (New York: ANACOM, 1977).

14. Quoted in Valerie H. Free, "Absolut Original," *Marketing Insights,* Summer 1991, p. 65.

15. Jon Steel, *Truth, Lies & Advertising: The Art of Account Planning* (New York: Wiley, 1998).

16. James Webb Young, *A Technique for Producing Ideas,* 3rd ed. (Chicago: Crain Books, 1975), p. 42.

17. Sandra E. Moriarty, *Creative Advertising: Theory and Practice* (Englewood Cliffs, NJ: Prentice Hall, 1986).

18. Brian Mills, "The Egg Man Cometh," *Marketing Magazine,* February 26, 2001.

19. Thomas L. Greenbaum, "Focus Groups Can Play a Part in Evaluating Ad Copy," *Marketing News,* September 13, 1993, pp. 24–25.

20. "Sleemans brings out the truth," *Marketing Magazine,* May 28, 2001; "Sleeman shifts its target," *Marketing Magazine,* April 16, 2001; "Sleeman ads bow without brewery boss," *Marketing Magazine,* April 4, 2001; "Sleeman touts label-free band," *Marketing Magazine,* April 15, 2002.

21. Nancy Vonk, "People Just Love It," *Marketing Magazine,* October 15, 2001.

22. Chris Daniels, "Canucks vs. Yanks," *Marketing Magazine,* May 22, 2000.

23. Danny Kucharsky, "CTC ads selling dreams of Canada," *Marketing Magazine,* February 26, 2001.

24. John O'Toole, *The Trouble with Advertising,* 2nd ed. (New York: Random House, 1985), p. 131.

25. David Ogilvy, *Ogilvy on Advertising* (New York: Crown, 1983), p. 16.

26. Rosser Reeves, *Reality in Advertising* (New York: Knopf, 1961), pp. 47, 48.

27. Ogilvy, *Confessions.*

28. Martin Mayer, *Madison Avenue, U.S.A.* (New York: Pocket Books, 1958).

29. Jack Trout and Al Ries, "The Positioning Era Cometh," *Advertising Age,* April 24, 1972, pp. 35–38; May 1, 1972, pp. 51–54; May 8, 1972, pp. 114–16.

30. Ingrid Button, "Turning the Export Ship Around," *Marketing Magazine,* August 27, 2001.

31. Sandra E. Moriarty, *Creative Advertising: Theory and Practice,* 2nd ed. (Englewood Cliffs, NJ: Prentice Hall, 1991), p. 76.

32. William M. Weilbacher, *Advertising,* 2nd ed. (New York: Macmillan, 1984), p. 197.

33. William Wells, John Burnett, and Sandra Moriarty, *Advertising* (Englewood Cliffs, NJ: Prentice Hall, 1989), p. 330.

34. William L. Wilkie and Paul W. Farris, "Comparative Advertising: Problems and Potential," *Journal of Marketing* 39 (1975), pp. 7–15.

35. For a review of comparative advertising studies, see Cornelia Pechmann and David W. Stewart, "The Psychology of Comparative Advertising," in *Attention, Attitude and Affect in Response to Advertising,* ed. E. M. Clark, T. C. Brock, and D. W. Stewart (Hillsdale, NJ: Lawrence Erlbaum, 1994), pp. 79–96; and Thomas S. Barry, "Comparative Advertising: What Have We Learned in Two Decades?" *Journal of Advertising Research* 33, no. 2 (1993), pp. 19–29.

36. Stuart J. Agres, "Emotion in Advertising: An Agency Point of View," in *Emotion in Advertising: Theoretical and Practical Explanations,* ed. Stuart J. Agres, Julie A. Edell, and Tony M. Dubitsky (Westport, CT: Quorom Books, 1991).

37. Edward Kamp and Deborah J. Macinnis, "Characteristics of Portrayed Emotions in Commercials: When Does What Is Shown in Ads Affect Viewers?" *Journal of Advertising Research,* November/December 1995, pp. 19–28.

38. For a review of research on the effect of mood states on consumer behaviour, see Meryl Paula Gardner, "Mood States and Consumer Behavior: A Critical Review," *Journal of Consumer Research* 12, no. 3 (December 1985), pp. 281–300.

39. Cathy Madison, "Researchers Work Advertising into an Emotional State," *Adweek,* November 5, 1990, p. 30.

40. Louise Kramer, "McDonald's Ad Goal: 'Touch People,'" *Advertising Age,* November 15, 1999, p. 22.

41. Michael L. Ray and William L. Wilkie, "Fear: The Potential of an Appeal Neglected by Marketing," *Journal of Marketing* 34 (January 1970), pp. 54–62.

42. Brian Sternthal and C. Samuel Craig, "Fear Appeals Revisited and Revised," *Journal of Consumer Research* 1 (December 1974), pp. 22–34.

43. Punam Anand Keller and Lauren Goldberg Block, "Increasing the Persuasiveness of Fear Appeals: The Effect of Arousal and Elaboration," *Journal of Consumer Research* 22, no. 4 (March 1996), pp. 448–60.

44. John F. Tanner, Jr., James B. Hunt, and David R. Eppright, "The Protec-tion Motivation Model: A Normative Mode of Fear Appeals," *Journal of Marketing* 55 (July 1991), pp. 36–45.

45. Ibid.

46. Sternthal and Craig, "Fear Appeals Revisited and Revised."

47. Herbert Jack Rotfeld, "The Textbook Effect: Coventional Wisdom, Myth and Error in Marketing," *Journal of Marketing* 64 (April 2000), pp. 122–27.

48. For a discussion of the use of humour in advertising, see C. Samuel Craig and Brian Sternthal, "Humor in Advertising," *Journal of Marketing* 37 (October 1973), pp. 12–18.

49. Yong Zhang, "Response to Humorous Advertising: The Moderating Effect of Need for Cognition," *Journal of Advertising* 25, no. 1 (Spring 1996), pp. 15–32; Marc G. Weinberger and Charles S. Gulas, "The Impact of Humor in Advertising: A Review," *Journal of Advertising* 21 (December 1992), pp. 35–59.

50. Marc G. Weinberger and Leland Campbell, "The Use of Humor in Radio Advertising," *Journal of Advertising Research* 31 (December/January 1990–91), pp. 44–52.

51. Thomas J. Madden and Marc C. Weinberger, "Humor in Advertising: A Practitioner View," *Journal of Advertising Research* 24, no. 4 (August/September 1984), pp. 23–26.

52. David Ogilvy and Joel Raphaelson, "Research on Advertising Techniques That Work and Don't Work," *Harvard Business Review,* July/August 1982, p. 18.

53. *Topline,* no. 4 (September 1989), McCann-Erickson, New York.

54. Eric Schmuckler, "Plan of the Year: Best Campaign Spending between $10 Million and $25 Million," *MediaWeek,* May 24, 1999.

55. Dottie Enrico, "Teaser Ads Grab Spotlight on Madison Ave.," *USA Today,* July 6, 1995, pp.1, 2B.

56. "Infiniti Ads Trigger Auto Debate," *Advertising Age,* January 22, 1990, p. 49.

57. Quote by Irwin Warren, cited in Enrico, "Teaser Ads Grab Spotlight."

58. Herbert C. Kelman, "Processes of Opinion Change," *Public Opinion Quarterly* 25 (Spring 1961), pp. 57–78.

59. William J. McGuire, "The Nature of Attitudes and Attitude Change," in *Handbook of Social Psychology,* 2nd

ed., ed. G. Lindzey and E. Aronson (Cambridge, MA: Addison-Wesley, 1969), pp. 135–214; Daniel J. O'Keefe, "The Persuasive Effects of Delaying Identification of High- and Low-Credibility Communicators: A Meta-Analytic Review," *Central States Speech Journal* 38 (1987), pp. 63–72.

60. Roobina Ohanian, "The Impact of Celebrity Spokespersons' Image on Consumers' Intention to Purchase," *Journal of Advertising Research,* February/March 1991, pp. 46–54.

61. Erick Reidenback and Robert Pitts, "Not All CEOs Are Created Equal as Advertising Spokespersons: Evaluating the Effective CEO Spokesperson," *Journal of Advertising* 20, no. 3 (1986), pp. 35–50; Roger Kerin and Thomas E. Barry, "The CEO Spokesperson in Consumer Advertising: An Experimental Investigation," in *Current Issues in Research in Advertising,* ed. J. H. Leigh and C. R. Martin (Ann Arbor: University of Michigan, 1981), pp. 135–48; and J. Poindexter, "Voices of Authority," *Psychology Today,* August 1983.

62. A. Eagly and S. Chaiken, "An Attribution Analysis of the Effect of Communicator Characteristics on Opinion Change," *Journal of Personality and Social Psychology* 32 (1975), pp. 136–44.

63. For a review of these studies, see Brian Sternthal, Lynn Phillips, and Ruby Dholakia, "The Persuasive Effect of Source Credibility: A Situational Analysis," *Public Opinion Quarterly* 42 (Fall 1978), pp. 285–314.

64. Brian Sternthal, Ruby Dholakia, and Clark Leavitt, "The Persuasive Effects of Source Credibility: Tests of Cognitive Response," *Journal of Consumer Research* 4, no. 4 (March 1978), pp. 252–60; and Robert R. Harmon and Kenneth A. Coney, "The Persuasive Effects of Source Credibility in Buy and Lease Situations," *Journal of Marketing Research* 19 (May 1982), pp. 255–60.

65. For a review, see Noel Capon and James Hulbert, "The Sleeper Effect: An Awakening," *Public Opinion Quarterly* 37 (1973), pp. 333–58.

66. Darlene B. Hannah and Brian Sternthal, "Detecting and Explaining the Sleeper Effect," *Journal of Consumer Research* 11, no. 2 (September 1984), pp. 632–42.

67. H. C. Triandis, *Attitudes and Attitude Change* (New York: Wiley, 1971).

68. Lise Laguerre, "It's Respect in Either Language," *Marketing Magazine,* May 6, 2002.

69. J. Mills and J. Jellison, "Effect on Opinion Change Similarity between the Communicator and the Audience He Addresses," *Journal of Personality and Social Psychology* 9, no. 2 (1969), pp. 153–56.

70. Sam Walker, "Michael Jordan Isn't Retiring from Hot Deals," *The Wall Street Journal,* February 15, 1999, pp. B1, 4.

71. "P&G smiles with Sale and Pelletier," *Marketing Magazine,* March 4, 2002.

72. Valerie Folkes, "Recent Attribution Research in Consumer Behavior: A Review and New Directions," *Journal of Consumer Research* 14 (March 1988), pp. 548–65; John C. Mowen and Stephen W. Brown, "On Explaining and Predicting the Effectiveness of Celebrity Endorsers," in *Advances in Consumer Research,* vol. 8 (Ann Arbor, MI: Association for Consumer Research, 1981), pp. 437–41.

73. Charles Atkin and M. Block, "Effectiveness of Celebrity Endorsers," *Journal of Advertising Research* 23, no. 1 (February/March 1983), pp. 57–61.

74. Ellen Neuborne, "Generation Y," *Business Week,* February 15, 1999, pp. 81–88.

75. Study by Total Research Corp. cited in Bruce Horowitz, "Wishing on a Star," *Los Angeles Times,* November 7, 1993, pp. D1, 7.

76. Jeff Jensen, "Performance, Shoe Tech Take Ad Stage for '98," *Advertising Age,* January 12, 1998, pp. 3, 36.

77. Michael A. Kamins, "An Investigation into the 'Match-Up' Hypothesis in Celebrity Advertising," *Journal of Advertising* 19, no. 1 (1990), pp. 4–13.

78. Grant McCracken, "Who Is the Celebrity Endorser? Cultural Foundations of the Endorsement Process," *Journal of Consumer Research* 16, no. 3 (December 1989), pp. 310–21.

79. Ibid., p. 315.

80. Raymond Serafin, "Subaru Outback Taps 'Crocodile Dundee,'" *Advertising Age,* September 15, 1995, p. 38; Steve Geisi, "'Dundee' Returns to Extend Outback into Entry Level," *Brandweek,* September 2, 1996, pp. 1, 6.

81. For an excellent review of these studies, see Marilyn Y. Jones, Andrea J. S. Stanaland, and Betsy D. Gelb, "Beefcake and Cheesecake: Insights for Advertisers," *Journal of Advertising* 27, no. 2 (Summer 1998), pp. 32–51; and W. B. Joseph, "The Credibility of Physically Attractive Communicators," *Journal of Advertising* 11, no. 3 (1982), pp. 13–23.

82. Michael Solomon, Richard Ashmore, and Laura Longo, "The Beauty Match-Up Hypothesis: Congruence between Types of Beauty and Product Images in Advertising," *Journal of Advertising* 21, no. 4, pp. 23–34; M. J. Baker and Gilbert A. Churchill, Jr., "The Impact of Physically Attractive Models on Advertising Evaluations," *Journal of Marketing Research* 14 (November 1977), pp. 538–55.

83. Robert W. Chestnut, C. C. La Chance, and A. Lubitz, "The Decorative Female Model: Sexual Stimuli and the Recognition of the Advertisements," *Journal of Advertising* 6 (Fall 1977), pp. 11–14; and Leonard N. Reid and Lawrence C. Soley, "Decorative Models and Readership of Magazine Ads," Journal of *Advertising Research* 23, no. 2 (April/May 1983), pp. 27–32.

Chapter Seven

1. Martin Mayer, *Madison Avenue, U.S.A.* (New York: Pocket Books, 1958), p. 64.

2. "Dove revives soap litmus test," *Marketing Magazine,* January 15, 2001.

3. Sally Beatty, "P&G to Ad Agencies: Please Rewrite Our Old Formulas," *The Wall Street Journal,* November 5, 1998, pp. B1, 10; Alecia Swasy, "P&G Tries Bolder Ads—With Caution," *The Wall Street Journal,* May 7, 1990, pp. B1, 7.

4. Lynn Coleman, "Advertisers Put Fear into the Hearts of Their Prospects," *Marketing News,* August 15, 1988, p. 1.

5. Kevin Goldman, "Chips Ahoy! Ad Uses Spin on Claymation," *The Wall Street Journal,* February 9, 1994, p. B5.

6. Marla Matzer, "Alcohol Activists Want to Cage Bud's Lizards," *Los Angeles Times,* May 5, 1998, pp. D1, 17.

7. Barbara B. Stern, "Classical and Vignette Television Advertising: Structural Models, Formal Analysis, and Consumer Effects," *Journal of Consumer Research* 20, no. 4 (March 1994), pp. 601–15; and John Deighton, Daniel Romer, and Josh

McQueen, "Using Drama to Persuade," *Journal of Consumer Research* 15, no. 3 (December 1989), pp. 335–43.

8. Sandra E. Moriarty, *Creative Advertising: Theory and Practice,* 2nd ed. (Englewood Cliffs, NJ: Prentice Hall, 1991), p. 77.

9. Herbert E. Krugman, "On Application of Learning Theory to TV Copy Testing," *Public Opinion Quarterly* 26 (1962), pp. 626–39.

10. C. I. Hovland and W. Mandell, "An Experimental Comparison of Conclusion Drawing by the Communicator and by the Audience," *Journal of Abnormal and Social Psychology* 47 (July 1952), pp. 581–88.

11. Alan G. Sawyer and Daniel J. Howard, "Effects of Omitting Conclusions in Advertisements to Involved and Uninvolved Audiences," *Journal of Marketing Research* 28 (November 1991), pp. 467–74.

12. George E. Belch, "The Effects of Message Modality on One- and Two-Sided Advertising Messages," in *Advances in Consumer Research,* vol. 10, ed. Richard P. Bagozzi and Alice M. Tybout (Ann Arbor, MI: Association for Consumer Research, 1983), pp. 21–26.

13. Robert E. Settle and Linda L. Golden, "Attribution Theory and Advertiser Credibility," *Journal of Marketing Research* 11 (May 1974), pp. 181–85; and Edmund J. Faison, "Effectiveness of One-Sided and Two-Sided Mass Communications in Advertising," *Public Opinion Quarterly* 25 (Fall 1961), pp. 468–69.

14. "Campaigns with Legs," *Marketing Magazine,* May 15, 2000.

15. Alan G. Sawyer, "The Effects of Repetition of Refutational and Supportive Advertising Appeals," *Journal of Marketing Research* 10 (February 1973), pp. 23–37; and George J. Szybillo and Richard Heslin, "Resistance to Persuasion: Inoculation Theory in a Marketing Context," *Journal of Marketing Research* 10 (November 1973), pp. 396–403.

16. Andrew A. Mitchell, "The Effect of Verbal and Visual Components of Advertisements on Brand Attitudes and Attitude toward the Advertisement," *Journal of Consumer Research* 13 (June 1986), pp. 12–24; and Julie A. Edell and Richard Staelin, "The Information Processing of Pictures in Advertisements," *Journal of Consumer Research* 10, no. 1 (June 1983), pp. 45–60; Elizabeth C. Hirschmann, "The Effects of Verbal and Pictorial Advertising Stimuli on Aesthetic, Utilitarian and Familiarity Perceptions," *Journal of Advertising* 15, no. 2 (1986), pp. 27–34.

17. Jolita Kisielius and Brian Sternthal, "Detecting and Explaining Vividness Effects in Attitudinal Judgments," *Journal of Marketing Research* 21, no. 1 (1984), pp. 54–64.

18. H. Rao Unnava and Robert E. Burnkrant, "An Imagery-Processing View of the Role of Pictures in Print Advertisements," *Journal of Marketing Research* 28 (May 1991), pp. 226–31.

19. Susan E. Heckler and Terry L. Childers, "The Role of Expectancy and Relevancy in Memory for Verbal and Visual Information: What Is Incongruency?" *Journal of Consumer Research* 18, no. 4 (March 1992), pp. 475–92.

20. Michael J. Houston, Terry L. Childers, and Susan E. Heckler, "Picture-Word Consistency and the Elaborative Processing of Advertisements," *Journal of Marketing Research,* November 1987, pp. 359–69.

21. William F. Arens, *Contemporary Advertising,* 6th ed. (Burr Ridge, IL: Irwin/McGraw-Hill, 1998), p. 284.

22. W. Keith Hafer and Gordon E. White, *Advertising Writing,* 3rd ed. (St. Paul, MN: West Publishing, 1989), p. 98.

23. Janet Kestin, "Reality Rules," *Marketing Magazine,* February 26, 2001.

24. Carol Marie Cooper, "Who Says Talk Is Cheap," *New York Times,* October 22, 1998, pp. C1, 5; and Wendy Brandes, "Star Power Leaves Some Voice-Over Artists Speechless," *The Wall Street Journal,* June 2, 1995, p. B6.

25. Linda M. Scott, "Understanding Jingles and Needledrop: A Rhetorical Approach to Music in Advertising," *Journal of Consumer Research* 17, no. 2 (September 1990), pp. 223–36.

26. Ibid., p. 223.

27. Russell I. Haley, Jack Richardson, and Beth Baldwin, "The Effects of Nonverbal Communications in Television Advertising," *Journal of Advertising* Research 24, no. 4, pp. 11–18.

28. Gerald J. Gorn, "The Effects of Music in Advertising on Choice Behavior: A Classical Conditioning Approach," *Journal of Marketing* 46 (Winter 1982), pp. 94–100.

29. "A Few Rockers Give Ad Makers No Satisfaction," *The Wall Street Journal,* August 25, 1995, p. B1.

30. Stephanie N. Mehta, "Northern Telecom Plays Down Phone Roots, Embraces 'I Word,'" *The Wall Street Journal,* April 14, 1999, p. B10.

31. "Bud Light sells spoof soundtrack," *Marketing Magazine,* February 21, 2002.

32. Eleftheria Parpis, "Creative: Best Campaign," *Adweek,* January 24, 2000, p. 1.

33. Christopher P. Puto and William D. Wells, "Informational and Transformational Advertising: The Different Effects of Time," in *Advances in Consumer Research,* Vol. 11, ed. Thomas C. Kinnear (Ann Arbor, MI: Association for Consumer Research, 1984), p. 638.

34. Eric LeBlanc and Kate Tutly, "The Heart of the Matter," *Marketing Magazine,* July 16, 2001.

35. Richard Vaughn, "How Advertising Works: A Planning Model," *Journal of Advertising Research* 20, no. 5 (October 1980), pp. 27–33.

36. Richard Vaughn, "How Advertising Works: A Planning Model Revisited," *Journal of Advertising Research* 26, no. 1 (February/March 1986), pp. 57–66.

37. Beatty, "P&G to Ad Agencies."

Chapter Eight

1. Frank M. Bass, "A Simultaneous Equation Regression Study of Advertising and Sales of Cigarettes," *Journal of Marketing Research* 6, no. 3 (August 1969), p. 291; David A. Aaker and James M. Carman, "Are You Overadvertising?" *Journal of Advertising Research* 22, no. 4 (August/September 1982), pp. 57–70.

2. Julian A. Simon and Johan Arndt, "The Shape of the Advertising Response Function," *Journal of Advertising Research* 20, no. 4 (1980), pp. 11–28.

3. Paul B. Luchsinger, Vernan S. Mullen, and Paul T. Jannuzzo, "How Many Advertising Dollars Are Enough?" *Media Decisions* 12 (1977), p. 59.

4. Paul W. Farris, *Determinants of Advertising Intensity: A Review of the Marketing Literature* (Report no. 77–109, Marketing Science Institute, Cambridge, MA, 1977).

5. John P. Jones, "Ad Spending: Maintaining Market Share," *Harvard Business Review,* January/February

1990, pp. 38–42; and James C. Schroer, "Ad Spending: Growing Market Share," *Harvard Business Review,* January/February 1990, pp. 44–48.

6. Randall S. Brown, "Estimating Advantages to Large-Scale Advertising," *Review of Economics and Statistics* 60 (August 1978), pp. 428–37.

7. Kent M. Lancaster, "Are There Scale Economies in Advertising?" *Journal of Business* 59, no. 3 (1986), pp. 509–26.

8. Johan Arndt and Julian Simon, "Advertising and Economics of Scale: Critical Comments on the Evidence," *Journal of Industrial Economics* 32, no. 2 (December 1983), pp. 229–41; Aaker and Carman, "Are You Overadvertising?"

9. George S. Low and Jakki J. Mohr, "The Budget Allocation between Advertising and Sales Promotion: Understanding the Decision Process," 1991 AMA Educators' Proceedings, Chicago, Summer 1991, pp. 448–57.

10. Melvin E. Salveson, "Management's Criteria for Advertising Effectiveness" (Proceedings 5th Annual Conference, Advertising Research Foundation, New York, 1959), p. 25.

11. Robert Settle and Pamela Alreck, "Positive Moves for Negative Times," *Marketing Communications,* January 1988, pp. 19–23.

12. James O. Peckham, "Can We Relate Advertising Dollars to Market Share Objectives?" in *How Much to Spend for Advertising,* ed. M. A. McNiven (New York: Association of National Advertisers, 1969), p. 30.

13. George S. Low and Jakki Mohr, "Setting Advertising and Promotion Budgets in Multi-Brand Companies," *Journal of Advertising Research,* January/February 1999, pp. 667–78.

14. Chuck Ross, "Study Finds for Continuity vs. Flights," *Advertising Age,* April 19, 1999, p. 2.

15. Michael J. Naples, *Effective Frequency: The Relationship between Frequency and Advertising Effectiveness* (New York: Association of National Advertisers, 1979).

16. Joseph W. Ostrow, "Setting Frequency Levels: An Art or a Science?" *Journal of Advertising Research* 24 (August/September 1984), pp. 9–11.

17. Naples, *Effective Frequency.*

18. Joseph W. Ostrow, "What Level Frequency?" *Advertising Age,* November 1981, pp. 13–18.

19. Jack Myers, "More Is Indeed Better," *Media Week,* September 6, 1993, pp. 14–18; and Jim Surmanek, "One-Hit or Miss: Is a Frequency of One Frequently Wrong?" *Advertising Age,* November 27, 1995, p. 46.

20. Ostrow, "What Level Frequency?"

Chapter Nine

1. Television Bureau of Canada website (www.tvb.ca).

2. 2001 Fall Survey, BBM Canada.

3. "Making the Most of Magazines," *Marketing Magazine,* October 15, 2001.

4. Lex van Meurs, "Zapp! A Study on Switching Behavior during Commercial Breaks," *Journal of Advertising Research,* January/February 1998, pp. 43–53; John J. Cronin, "In-Home Observations of Commercial Zapping Behavior," *Journal of Current Issues and Research in Advertising* 17, no. 2 (Fall 1995), pp. 69–75.

5. Laura Petrecca, "4A's: Production Costs for TV Spots Up by 6%," *Advertising Age,* August 18, 1997, p. 30.

6. Joe Flint, "Commercial Clutter on TV Networks Rises to Record," *The Wall Street Journal,* March 2, 2000, p. B18.

7. Dennis Kneal, "Zapping of TV Ads Appears Pervasive," *The Wall Street Journal,* April 25, 1988, p. 27.

8. John J. Cronin and Nancy Menelly, "Discrimination vs. Avoidance: 'Zipping' of Television Commercials," *Journal of Advertising* 21, no. 2 (June 1992), pp. 1–7.

9. Cronin, "In-Home Observations of Commercial Zapping Behavior."

10. Carrie Heeter and Bradley S. Greenberg, "Profiling the Zappers," *Journal of Advertising Research,* April/May 1985, pp. 9–12; Fred S. Zufryden, James H. Pedrick, and Avu Sandaralingham, "Zapping and Its Impact on Brand Purchase Behavior," *Journal of Advertising Research* 33 (January/February 1993), pp. 58–66; and Patricia Orsini, "Zapping: A Man's World," Spring Television Report, *Adweek's Marketing Week,* April 8, 1991, p. 3.

11. Lex van Meurs, "Zapp! A Study on Switching Behavior during Commercial Breaks," *Journal of Advertising Research,* January/February 1998, pp. 43–53.

12. Linda F. Alwitt and Parul R. Prabhaker, "Identifying Who Dislikes Television Advertising: Not by Demographics Alone," *Journal of Advertising Research* 32, no. 5 (1992), pp. 30–42.

13. Banwari Mittal, "Public Assessment of TV Advertising: Faint Praise and Harsh Criticism," *Journal of Advertising Research* no. 34, 1 (1994), pp. 35–53; Ernest F. Larkin, "Consumer Perceptions of the Media and Their Advertising Content," *Journal of Advertising* 8 (1979), pp. 5–7.

14. Lucy L. Henke, "Young Children's Perceptions of Cigarette Brand Advertising Symbols: Awareness, Affect, and Target Market Identification," *Journal of Advertising* 24, no. 4 (Winter 1995), pp. 13–28.

15. Bruce Grondin, "No More BBM vs. Nielsen," *Marketing Magazine,* October 15, 2001; Chris Powell, "CanWest picks BBM over Nielsen," *Marketing Magazine,* June 3, 2002; www.bbm.ca; www.nielsenmedia.ca; www.tvb.ca.

16. Suein L. Hwang, "Old Media Get a Web Windfall," *The Wall Street Journal,* September 17, 1999, p. B1.

17. Verne Gay, "Image Transfer: Radio Ads Make Aural History," *Advertising Age,* January 24, 1985, p. 1.

18. Avery Abernethy, "Differences Between Advertising and Program Exposure for Car Radio Listening," *Journal of Advertising Research* 31, no. 2 (April/May 1991), pp. 33–42.

19. Martin Peers, "Radio Produces Both Gains and Skeptics," *The Wall Street Journal,* January 1, 1999, p. B6.

20. Ibid.

Chapter Ten

1. Herbert E. Krugman, "The Measurement of Advertising Involvement," *Public Opinion Quarterly* 30 (Winter 1966–67), pp. 583–96.

2. *The Magazine Handbook* (New York: Magazine Publishers of America, 1999).

3. *The Magazine Handbook.*

4. Ibid.

5. *A Study of Media Involvement,* Vol. 7 (New York: Magazine Publishers of America, 1996).

6. Christine Larson, "Made to Order," *Adweek,* October 25, 1999, pp. 64–70.

7. Sally Goll Beatty, "Philip Morris Starts Lifestyle Magazine," *The Wall Street Journal,* September 16, 1996, pp. B1, 8.

8. Study cited in Jim Surmanek, *Media Planning: A Practical Guide* (Lincolnwood, IL: Crain Books, 1985).

9. *How Advertising Readership Is Influenced by Ad Size,* Report no. 110.1, Cahners Advertising Research, Newton, MA; and *Larger Advertisements Get Higher Readership,* LAP Report no. 3102, McGraw-Hill Research, New York.

10. *Effect of Size, Color and Position on Number of Responses to Recruitment Advertising,* LAP Report no. 3116, McGraw-Hill Research, New York.

11. Junu Bryan Kim, "Cracking the Barrier of Two Dimensions," *Advertising Age,* October 6, 1991, pp. 32, 34.

12. Ann Marie Kerwin, "Print's Power Play," *Advertising Age: The Next Century,* special issue, 1999.

Chapter Eleven

1. Maritz AmeriPoll, August 1998.

2. *Adweek,* August 25, 1997, p. 3.

3. Mukesh Bhargava and Naveen Donthu, "Sales Response to Outdoor Advertising," *Journal of Advertising Research,* August 1999, pp. 7–18.

4. *Advertisers Take the City Bus to Work* (New York: Winston Network, 1988), p. 13.

5. Jennifer Lawrence, "In-Flight Gets above Turbulence," *Advertising Age,* August 19, 1991, p. 32.

6. David Kalish, "Supermarket Sweepstakes," *Marketing & Media Decisions,* November 1988, p. 34.

7. "Cinema Advertising Comes of Age," *Marketing Magazine,* May 6, 2002.

8. Betsy Baurer, "New Quick Flicks: Ads at the Movies," *USA Today,* March 13, 1986, p. D1.

9. Ibid.

10. Michael A. Belch and Don Sciglimpaglia, "Viewers' Evaluations of Cinema Advertising," *Proceedings of the American Institute for Decision Sciences,* March 1979, pp. 39–43.

11. Adam Snyder, "Are Spots on Home Video Badvertising?" *Brandweek,* January 29, 1996, p. 40.

12. Alice Cuneo, "Now Playing: Gap, Target Take Retail to the Movies," *Advertising Age,* June 9, 1997, p. 14.

13. Promotional Products Association International (Irving, TX), 1996.

14. Promotional Products Association International, 2000.

15. George L. Herpel and Steve Slack, *Specialty Advertising: New Dimensions in Creative Marketing* (Irving, TX: Specialty Advertising Association, 1983), pp. 76, 79–80.

16. Ibid., p. 78.

17. M. J. Caballero and J. B. Hunt, *Smilin' Jack: Measuring Goodwill,* unpublished research report from the Center for Professional Selling, Baylor University, 1989; M. J. Cooper and J. B. Hunt, *How Specialty Advertising Affects Goodwill,* research report of Specialty Advertising Association International (now PPAI), Irving, TX, 1992.

18. Herpel and Slack, *Specialty Advertising,* p. 75.

19. Carol Hall, "Branding the Yellow Pages," *Marketing & Media Decisions,* April 1989, p. 3.

20. Ibid., p. 5.

21. Yellow Pages Publishers Association, 2000.

22. J. D. Reed, "Plugging Away in Hollywood," Time, January 2, 1998, p. 103.

23. Pola Gupta and Kenneth Lord, "Product Placement in Movies: The Effect of Prominence and Mode on Audience Recall," *Journal of Current Issues and Research in Advertising* 20, no. 1 (Spring 1998), pp. 1–29.

24. Pola B. Gupta and Stephen J. Gould, "Consumers' Perceptions of the Ethics and Acceptability of Product Placements in Movies: Product Category and Individual Differences," *Journal of Current Issues and Research in Advertising* 19, no. 1 (Spring 1997), pp. 40–49.

25. Randall Rothenberg, "Is It a Film? Is It an Ad? Harder to Tell," *The New York Times,* March 13, 1990, p. D23.

26. Laurie Mazur, "Screenland's Dirty Little Secret," *E magazine,* May/June 1996, p. 38.

27. "Consumer Products Become Movie Stars," *The Wall Street Journal,* February 29, 1988, p. 23.

28. Damon Darlin, "Highbrow Hype," *Forbes,* April 12, 1993, pp. 126–27.

Chapter Twelve

1. Louis J. Haugh, "Defining and Redefining," *Advertising Age,* February 14, 1983, p. M44.

2. Scott A. Nielsen, John Quelch, and Caroline Henderson, "Consumer Promotions and the Acceleration of Product Purchases," in *Research on Sales Promotion: Collected Papers,* ed. Katherine E. Jocz (Cambridge, MA: Marketing Science Institute, 1984).

3. J. Jeffrey Inman and Leigh McAlister, "Do Coupon Expiration Dates Affect Consumer Behavior?" *Journal of Marketing* Research 31, August 1994, pp. 423–28.

4. "Promotion Trends 2000," *Promo Magazine,* May 2000, p. A5.

5. Richard Sale, "Evaluation in Evolution," *Promo Magazine,* September 1998, pp. 63–68.

6. Richard Sale, "Attack," *Promo Magazine,* September 1999, pp. 79–84.

7. "The Effects of Promotion Stimuli on Consumer Purchase Behavior" (Glenview, IL: FSI Council, 1999).

8. "1996 Trend Report," Actmedia, Inc., Anaheim, CA.

9. Leigh McAlister, "A Model of Consumer Behavior," *Marketing Communications,* April 1987.

10. Betsy Spethmann, "Trading Newsprint for Pepperoni," *Promo Magazine,* August 1999, pp. 51–52.

11. Al Urbanski, "Techno Promo," *Promo Magazine,* August 1998, pp. 48–52, 146, 147.

12. NCH Reporter, no. 1 (Nielsen Clearing House, 1983).

13. *The Magazine Handbook,* no. 59 (New York: Magazine Publishers of America, 1991).

14. Judann Dagnoli, "Jordan Hits Ad Execs for Damaging Brands," *Advertising Age,* November 4, 1991, p. 47.

15. Judan Pollack, "Heinz to Pare Products While It Boosts Ads," *Advertising Age,* March 3, 1997, pp. 3, 37.

16. Judann Pollack, "Charlie Rejoins Frenzied Tuna Wars," *Advertising Age,* May 31, 1999, p. 32.

17. "Promo's New Prominence," *Marketing Magazine,* September 3, 2001.

18. "It's Elementary," *Marketing Magazine,* December 3, 2001.

19. R. M. Prentice, "How to Split Your Marketing Funds Between Advertising and Promotion Dollars," *Advertising Age,* January 10, 1977, pp. 41–42, 44.

20. Betsy Spethmann, "Money and Power," *Brandweek,* March 15, 1993, p. 21.

21. Quote by Vincent Sottosanti, president of Council of Sales Promotion Agencies, in "Promotions That Build Brand Image," *Marketing Communications,* April 1988, p. 54.

22. Adapted from Terrence A. Shimp, *Advertising, Promotion, and Supplemental Aspect of Integrated Marketing Communication,* 4th ed. (Fort Worth, TX: Dryden Press, 1997), p. 487.

23. "Hostess' Heroes," *Marketing Magazine,* August 6, 2001.

24. Reference cited in John P. Rossiter and Larry Percy, *Advertising and Promotion Management* (New York: McGraw-Hill, 1987), p. 360.

25. Peter Breen, "Sophisticated Sampling," *Promo Magazine,* September 1999, pp. 63–68.

26. Glenn Heitsmith, "Something for Nothing," *Promo Magazine,* September 1993, pp. 30–36.

27. *Worldwide Coupon Distribution & Redemption Trends,* (Lincolnshire, IL: NCH Promotional Services, 1999).

28. J. Jeffrey Inman and Leigh McAlister, "Do Coupon Expiration Dates Affect Consumer Behavior?"

29. Betsy Spethmann, "A Wake-Up Call at Breakfastime," *Promo Magazine,* December 1996, pp. 27–28.

30. Jack Neff, "P&G Extends Co-branded Coupons," *Advertising Age,* June 3, 1996, p. 9.

31. Survey by Oxtoby-Smith, Inc., cited in "Many Consumers View Rebates as a Bother," *The Wall Street Journal,* April 13, 1989, p. B1.

32. William R. Dean, "Irresistable but Not Free of Problems," *Advertising Age,* October 6, 1980, pp. S1–12.

33. "Cereal Killer," *Marketing Magazine,* May 14, 2001.

34. Eric Schmuckler, "Two Action Figures to Go, Hold the Burger," *Brandweek,* April 1, 1996, pp. 38–39.

35. "Mickey May Be the Big Winner in Disney–McDonald's Alliance," *The Wall Street Journal,* May 24, 1996, p. B5.

36. Louise Kramer, "McD's Steals Another Toy from BK," *Advertising Age,* November 15, 1999, pp. 1, 74.

37. "In Wake of Second Death, CPSC and Burger King Again Urge Consumers to Destroy and Discard Pokemon Balls," Burger King Press Release, January 27, 2000.

38. "Doughboy promo pops off the shelf," *Marketing Magazine,* January 14, 2002.

39. "Sweepstakes Fever," *Forbes,* October 3, 1988, pp. 164–66.

40. "P&G and MuchMusic head to the prom," *Marketing Magazine,* February 23, 2001; "Much, P&G team up to target teens," *Marketing Magazine,* March 5, 2001.

41. Bob Woods, "Picking a Winner," *Promo Magazine,* August 1998, pp. 57–62.

42. Maxine S. Lans, "Legal Hurdles Big Part of Promotions Game," *Marketing News,* October 24, 1994, pp. 15–16.

43. Survey by Oxtoby-Smith, Inc., "Many Consumers View Rebates."

44. Peter Tat, William A. Cunningham III, and Emin Babakus, "Consumer Perceptions of Rebates," *Journal of Advertising Research,* August/September 1988, pp. 45–50.

45. Martha Graves, "Mail-In Rebates Stirring Shopper, Retailer Backlash," *Los Angeles Times,* January 11, 1989, pt. IV, p. 1.

46. Edward A. Blair and E. Lair Landon, "The Effects of Reference Prices in Retail Advertisements," *Journal of Marketing* 45, no. 2 (Spring 1981), pp. 61–69.

47. Richard Sale, "Not Your Mother's Coupon," *Promo Magazine,* April 1999, pp. 56–61.

48. "Takin' it to the streets," *Marketing Magazine,* September 10, 2001.

49. Frank Green, "Battling for Shelf Control," *San Diego Union,* November 19, 1996, pp. C1, 6, 7.

50. "Want Shelf Space at the Supermarket? Ante Up," *Business Week,* August 7, 1989, pp. 60–61.

51. Melissa Campanelli, "What's in Store for EDLP?" *Sales & Marketing Management,* August 1993, pp. 56–59; "Procter & Gamble Hits Back," *Business Week,* July 19, 1993, pp. 20–22.

52. Amy Barone and Laurel Wentz, "Artzt Steering Barilla into EDLP Strategy," *Advertising Age,* February 26, 1996, p. 10.

53. Tom Steinhagen, "Space Management Shapes Up with Planograms," *Marketing News,* November 12, 1990, p. 7.

54. Srinath Gopalakrishna, Gary L. Lilien, Jerome D. Williams, and Ian K. Sequeria, "Do Trade Shows Pay Off?" *Journal of Marketing* 59, July 1995, pp. 75–83.

55. Cynthia Rigg, "Hard Times Means Growth for Co-op Ads," *Advertising Age,* November 12, 1990, p. 24.

56. Edwin L. Artzt, "The Lifeblood of Brands," *Advertising Age,* November 4, 1991, p. 32.

57. "Everyone Is Bellying Up to This Bar," *Business Week,* January 27, 1992, p. 84.

58. Jack Neff, "The New Brand Management," *Advertising Age,* November 8, 1999, pp. S2, 18; Benson P. Shapiro, "Improved Distribution with Your Promotional Mix," *Harvard Business Review,* March/April 1977, p. 116; and Roger A. Strang, "Sales Promotion—Fast Growth, Faulty Management," *Harvard Business Review,* July/August 1976, p. 119.

59. Priya Raghubir and Kim Corfman, "When Do Price Promotions Affect Pretrial Brand Evaluations?" *Journal of Marketing Research* 36 (May 1999), pp. 211–22.

60. Alan G. Sawyer and Peter H. Dickson, "Psychological Perspectives on Consumer Response to Sales Promotion," in *Research on Sales Promotion: Collected Papers,* ed. Katherine E. Jocz (Cambridge, MA: Marketing Science Institute, 1984).

61. William E. Myers, "Trying to Get Out of the Discounting Box," *Adweek,* November 11, 1985, p. 2.

62. Leigh McAlister, "Managing the Dynamics of Promotional Change," in *Looking at the Retail Kaleidoscope,* Forum IX (Stamford, CT: Donnelley Marketing, April 1988).

63. "Promotions Blemish Cosmetic Industry," *Advertising Age,* May 10, 1984, pp. 22–23, 26.

Chapter Thirteen

1. Judann Pollack, "New Marketing Spin: The PR 'Experience,'" *Advertising Age,* August 5, 1996, p. 33.

2. Raymond Simon, *Public Relations, Concept and Practices,* 2nd ed. (Columbus, OH: Grid Publishing, 1980), p. 8.

3. William N. Curry, "PR Isn't Marketing," *Advertising Age,* December 18, 1991, p. 18.

4. Martha M. Lauzen, "Imperialism and Encroachment in Public Relations," *Public Relations Review* 17, no. 3 (Fall 1991), pp. 245–55.

5. Raymond Serafin, "Cars Squeeze Mileage from Awards," *Advertising Age,* June 4, 1990, p. 36.

6. Jeffrey M. O'Brien, "H-P Heads for Home," *Marketing Computers,* July/August 1996, pp. 55–58.

7. Bob Donath, "Corporate Communications," *Industrial Marketing,* July 1980, pp. 53–57.

8. Simon, *Public Relations,* p. 164.

9. John E. Marston, *Modern Public Relations* (New York: McGraw-Hill, 1979).

10. Thomas L. Harris, "How MPR Adds Value to Integrated Marketing Communications," *Public Relations Quarterly,* Summer 1993, pp. 13–18.

11. J. Lawrence, "New Doritos Gets the Star Treatment," *Advertising Age,* March 29, 1993, p. 64.

12. Jaye S. Niefeld, "Corporate Advertising," *Industrial Marketing,* July 1980, pp. 64–74.

13. John Burnett, "Shopping for Sponsorships? Integration Is Paramount," *Brandweek,* February 14, 1994, p. 18.

14. Ed Zotti, "An Expert Weighs the Prose and Yawns," *Advertising Age,* January 24, 1983, p. M-11.

15. Ronald Alsop, "The Best Corporate Reputations in America," *The Wall Street Journal,* September 29, 1999, p. B1.

16. Ronald Alsop, "The Best Reputations in High Tech," *The Wall Street Journal,* November 18, 1999, p. B1.

17. Prakash Sethi, *Advertising and Large Corporations* (Lexington, MA: Lexington Books, 1977), pp. 7–8.

18. Harvey Meyer, "When the Cause Is Just," *Journal of Business Strategy,* November/December 1999, pp. 27–31.

19. Ibid., p. 28.

20. Ibid., p. 29.

21. "Clairol expands CFL sponsor roster," *Marketing Magazine,* July 30, 2001.

22. "The 'Bush Leagues,'" *Marketing Magazine,* May 14, 2001.

23. Shel Holtz, *Public Relations on the Internet* (New York: American Management Association, 1998).

24. Karen Benezra, "Cause and Effects Marketing," *Brandweek,* April 22, 1996, p. 38.

25. Donath, "Corporate Communications," p. 52.

Chapter Fourteen

1. Stan Rapp and Thomas I. Collins, *Maximarketing* (New York: McGraw-Hill, 1987).

2. Peter D. Bennett, ed., *Dictionary of Marketing Terms* (Chicago: American Marketing Association, 1988), p. 58.

3. *Canadian Marketing Association 2001 Fact Book.* (Don Mills: Canadian Marketing Association, 2001).

4. Jagdish N. Sheth, "Marketing Megatrends," *Journal of Consumer Marketing* 1, no. 1 (June 1983), pp. 5–13.

5. "Ladies First," *Life Insurance International,* August 31, 1999, www.Ads.com.

6. Canadian Facts 2000, Canada Post website, March 25, 2002.

7. "Direct Mail by the Numbers," U.S. Postal Service, 1999.

8. "A Potent New Tool for Selling: Database Marketing," *Business Week,* September 5, 1994, pp. 56–59.

9. Herbert Kanzenstein and William S. Sachs, *Direct Marketing,* 2nd ed. (New York: Macmillan, 1992).

10. "Direct Mail by the Numbers."

11. *Canadian Marketing Association 2001 Fact Book,* 2001.

12. Ibid.

13. Canadian Facts 2000, Canada Post website, March 25, 2002.

14. *Direct Marketing Association Economic Impact,* 2000.

15. Cleveland Horton, "Porsche 300,000: The New Elite," *Advertising Age,* February 5, 1990, p. 8.

16. *Direct Marketing Association Economic Impact,* 2000.

17. Patricia O'Dell, "Mail's Last Call?" *Direct,* January 2000, pp. 63–64.

18. L.L. Bean website (www.llbean.com).

19. Elaine Underwood, "Is There a Future for the TV Mall?" *Brandweek,* March 25, 1996, pp. 24–26.

20. *Canadian Marketing Association 2001 Fact Book,* 2001.

21. Profiling study by Naveen Donthu and David Gilliland.

22. "Average Sales Figures for Infomercial products," *Response Magazine,* September 1999.

23. Chad Rubel, "Infomercials Evolve as Major Firms Join Successful Format," *Marketing News,* January 2, 1995, p. 1.

24. Anne-Marie Crawford, "Peugeot Develops First TV Advertorials for Cars," *Marketing,* December 9, 1999, p. 9.

25. Underwood, "Is There a Future for the TV Mall?"

26. *Canadian Marketing Association 2001 Fact Book,* 2001.

27. Ibid.

28. Direct Marketing Association, 2000.

29. Tom Eisenhart, "Tele-media: Marketing's New Dimension," *Business Marketing,* February 1991, pp. 50–53.

30. Direct Marketing Association 2000.

31. Dana Blakenhorn, "Infomercial Sire Is QVC Leverages Its TV Brand," *Advertising Age,* March 1998, www.AdAge.com.

32. Bob Howard, "Successful K-Tel TV Strategy Doesn't Translate to Net," *Los Angeles Times,* January 31, 2000, p. C1.

33. "Case Study Response to Sears Canada," *National Post Business Magazine,* January 2002.

34. Canada Facts 2000.

35. Direct Selling Association, 2000, www.DSA.com.

36. Paul Hughes, "Profits Due," *Entrepreneur,* February 1994, pp. 74–78.

37. "Bear Market," *Direct,* December 1999, p. 1+.

Chapter Fifteen

1. "Life on Campus: More Than Half of College Students Surf the Internet from Their Room," *Media Center,* August 25, 1999.

2. "Who's Online," *Business 2.0,* January 2000, p. 251.

3. Eric Beauchesne, "Online Shopping Soars to $1 Billion in 2000," *Ottawa Citizen,* October 24, 2001.

4. For more information see "General Social Survey: Internet Use, 2000 "The Daily," March, 26, 2001. http://www.statcan.ca/Daily/English/010326/d010326a.htm.

5. "The Lifestyles of Online Shoppers," www.cyberatlas.com, 2000.

6. Ibid.

7. Cecile B. Corral, "Clicks & Mortar: Category Leaders in Cyber Retailing," *Discount Store News,* December 13, 1999, pp. 10–13.

8. Tom Hyland, "Web Advertising: A Year of Growth," *Internet Advertising Bureau,* February 9, 2000, pp. 1–4.

9. Michael Shirer, "eMarket Places Will Lead U.S. Business eCommerce to $2.7 Trillion in 2004, According to Forrester," www.individual.com, February 8, 2000.

10. Laurie Freeman, "HP Gambles $100 M on Securing Its Net Position," *Business Marketing,* June 1999, pp. 1+.

11. Melinda Ligos, "Point, Click, Sell," *Sales and Marketing Management,* May 1999, pp. 51–55.

12. Ibid.

13. William Holstein, "Let Them Have PC's," *U.S. News & World Report,* February 14, 2000.

14. Nichola Groom, "U.S. Firms Use Online Games to Build Brands," *Reuters News Service,* August 12, 2001.

15. Peter Brieger, *The Financial Post,* April 23, 2001.

16. Kipp Cheng, "Online Ads on Superbowl.com: The Good, the Bad, and the Ugly," *Adweek,* February 7, 2000, pp. 52–54.

17. Jupiter Media Metrix.

18. "Online Media Strategies for Advertising," Internet Advertising Bureau, Spring 1999.

19. Helen D'Antoni, "NPD Online Research Finds More Individuals Are Pointing and Clipping with On-

Endnotes

line Coupons," www.individual.com, November 11, 1999.

20. Pamela Parker, "Webstakes, TKAI, Partner to Take Online Promotions to Japan," www.individual.com, February 2, 2000.

21. Chad Kaydo, "You've Got Sales," *Sales and Marketing Management,* October 1999, pp. 29–39.

22. Sean Donahue, "Hassle-Free Philanthropy," *Business 2.0,* October 1999, pp. 47–51.

23. Pamela Parker, "Direct E-Mail Promotions Best at Attracting Buyers," Internet News.com, December 22, 1999.

24. *Business Wire,* August 26, 1999, p. 1.

25. Ligos, "Point, Click, Sell."

26. Leslie Singer, "NPD Study Finds Internet Users Multi-tasking during the Superbowl," www.individual.com, February 9, 2000.

27. San Brekke, "Jumpin' Jupiter," *Business 2.0,* October 1999, pp. 154–61.

28. Joseph Menn, "Web Firms May Vastly Inflate Claims of 'Hits'," *Los Angeles Times,* April 17, 2000, pp. 1–8.

29. Beth Cox, "Top 50 Web Sites Get 95 Percent of All Ad Dollars," Internet News.com, June 17, 1999.

30. Teresa Buyikan and Angela Dawson, "Dropping RPA, Web TV Puts Account in Play—Adweek," Adweek.com, May 10, 1999.

31. Patrick Seitz, "Open TV Eyes an Opening in Interactive TV Market," *Investors Business Daily,* February 10, 2000, p. A6.

32. Chris Powell, "The Flashing 'i' ", *Marketing Magazine*, December 10, 2001.

33. Mark Sherman, "TV Gets Personal," *Marketing Magazine*, May 7, 2001.

34. Carey Toane, "Tune In, Turn On, Buy Lots," *Marketing Magazine,* April 16, 2001.

35. Chris Powell, "Media Cautious about Enhanced TV," *Marketing Magazine*, May 20, 2002.

Chapter Sixteen

1. Jack Neff, "P&G Redefines the Brand Manager," *Advertising Age,* October 13, 1997, pp. 1, 18, 20.

2. Thomas J. Cosse and John E. Swan, "Strategic Marketing Planning by Product Managers—Room for Improvement?" *Journal of Marketing* 47 (Summer 1983), pp. 92–102.

3. "Behind the Tumult at P&G," Fortune, March 7, 1994, pp. 74–82; "Category Management: New Tools

changing Life for Manufacturers, Retailers," *Marketing News,* September 25, 1989, pp. 2, 19.

4. Cosse and Swan, "Strategic Marketing Planning by Product Managers—Room for Improvement?"

5. Victor P. Buell, *Organizing for Marketing/Advertising Success* (New York: Association of National Advertisers, 1982).

6. M. Louise Ripley, "What Kind of Companies Take Their Advertising In-House?" *Journal of Advertising Research,* October/November 1991, pp. 73–80.

7. Bruce Horovitz, "Some Companies Say the Best Ad Agency Is No Ad Agency at All," *Los Angeles Times,* July 19, 1989, Sec IV, p. 5.

8. Bradley Johnson and Alice Z. Cuneo, "Gatey 2000 Taps DMB&B," *Advertising Age,* March 24, 1997, p. 2.

9. "Do Your Ads Need a Superagency?" *Fortune,* April 27, 1987, p. 81.

10. Sally Goll Beatty, "Global Needs Challenge Midsize Agencies," *The Wall Street Journal,* December 14, 1995, p. B9.

11. Gordon Fairclough, "Pace of Ad Mergers Is Expected to Continue," *The Wall Street Journal,* April 23, 1999, p. B2.

12. Bob Lammons, "A Good Account Exec Makes a Big Difference," *Marketing News,* June 3, 1996, p. 12.

13. Sally Goll Beatty, "Spike Lee, DDB Join to Create New Ad Agency," *The Wall Street Journal,* December 5, 1996, pp. B1, 13; Robert Frank, "Coca Cola Disney Venture Mines Creative Artists Agency Talent," *The Wall Street Journal,* November 10, 1995, p. B8.

14. "Call in the Specialists," *Marketing Magazine,* June 4, 2001.

15. Patricia Sellers, "Do You Need Your Ad Agency?" *Fortune,* November 15, 1993, pp. 47–61.

16. Judann Pollack, "ANA Survey: Under 50% Pay Agency Commissions," *Advertising Age,* June 15, 1998.

17. Ibid.

18. Prema Nakra, "The Changing Role of Public Relations in Marketing Communications," *Public Relations Quarterly,* 1 (1991) pp. 42–45.

19. "A Potent New Tool For Selling: Database Marketing," *Business Week,* September 5, 1994, pp. 56–62.

20. Mark Gleason and Debra Aho Williamson, "The New Interactive

Agency," *Advertising Age,* February 2, 1996, pp. S1–11.

21. Betsy Spethmann, "Sudden Impact," *Promo Magazine,* April 1999, pp. 42–48.

22. Anders Gronstedt and Esther Thorson, "Five Approaches to Organize an Integrated Marketing Communications Agency," *Journal of Advertising Research,* March/April 1996, pp. 48–58.

23. "Ad Firms Falter on One-Stop Shopping," *The Wall Street Journal,* December 1, 1988, p. 81; and "Do Your Ads Need a Superagency?" *Fortune,* April 27, 1987, p. 81.

23. Faye Rice, "A Cure for What Ails Advertising?" *Fortune,* December 16, 1991, pp. 119–22.

25. Philip J. Kitchen and Don E. Schultz, "A Multi-Country Comparison of the Drive for IMC," *Journal of Advertising Research,* January/February 1999, pp. 21–38.

26. David N. McArthur and Tom Griffin, "A Marketing Management View of Integrated Marketing Communications," *Journal of Advertising Research,* 37, no. 5 (September/ October) 1997, pp. 19–26; and Adrienne Ward Fawcett, "Integrated Marketing—Marketers Convinced: Its Time Has Arrived," *Advertising Age,* November 6, 1993, pp. S1–2.

Chapter Seventeen

1. Mary Tolan, "Holidays Are Here and So Is Ad Puzzle," *Advertising Age,* November 16, 1998, p. 36.

2. Ibid.

3. Laura Bird, "Loved the Ad. May (or May Not) Buy the Product," *The Wall Street Journal,* April 7, 1994, p. B1.

4. *McGraw-Hill Lap Report* no. 3151 (New York: McGraw-Hill, 1988); Alan D. Fletcher, *Target Marketing through the Yellow Pages* (Troy, MI: Yellow Pages Publishers Association, 1991), p. 23.

5. Personal interview with Jay Khoulos, president of World Communications, Inc., 1988.

6. David A. Aaker and John G. Myers, *Advertising Management,* 3rd ed. (Englewood Cliffs, NJ: Prentice Hall, 1987), p. 474.

7. Joel N. Axelrod, "Induced Moods and Attitudes toward Products," *Journal of Advertising Research* 3 (June 1963), pp. 19–24; Lauren E. Crane, "How Product, Appeal, and Program Affect Attitudes

toward Commercials," *Journal of Advertising Research* 4 (March 1964), p. 15.

8. Robert Settle, "Marketing in Tight Times," *Marketing Communications* 13, no. 1 (January 1988), pp. 19–23.

9. "What Is Good Creative?" *Topline,* no. 41 (New York: McCollum Spielman Worldwide, 1994), p. 4.

10. James R. Hagerty, "Tests Lead Lowe's to Revamp Strategy," *The Wall Street Journal,* March 11, 1999, p. B18.

11. "21 Ad Agencies Endorse Copy-Testing Principles," *Marketing News* 15, no. 17 (February 19, 1982), p. 1.

12. Ibid.

13. John M. Caffyn, "Telepex Testing of TV Commercials," *Journal of Advertising Research* 5, no. 2 (June 1965), pp. 29-37; Thomas J. Reynolds and Charles Gengler, "A Strategic Framework for Assessing Advertising: The Animatic vs. Finished Issue," *Journal of Advertising Research,* October/ November 1991, pp. 61–71; Nigel A. Brown and Ronald Gatty, "Rough vs. Finished TV Commercials in Telepex Tests," *Journal of Advertising Research* 7, no. 4 (December 1967), p. 21.

14. Charles H. Sandage, Vernon Fryburger, and Kim Rotzoll, *Advertising Theory and Practice,* 10th ed. (Burr Ridge, IL: Richard D. Irwin, 1979).

15. Lyman E. Ostlund, "Advertising Copy Testing: A Review of Current Practices, Problems and Prospects," *Current Issues and Research in Advertising,* 1978, pp. 87–105.

16. Jack B. Haskins, "Factual Recall as a Measure of Advertising Effectiveness," *Journal of Advertising Research* 4, no. 1 (March 1964), pp. 2–7.

17. John Philip Jones and Margaret H. Blair, "Examining 'Conventional Wisdoms' about Advertising Effects with Evidence from Independent Sources," *Journal of Advertising Research,* November/December 1996, pp. 37–52.

18. Paul J. Watson and Robert J. Gatchel, "Autonomic Measures of Advertising," *Journal of Advertising Research* 19 (June 1979), pp. 15–26.

19. Priscilla A. LaBarbera and Joel D. Tucciarone, "GSR Reconsidered: A Behavior-based Approach to Evaluating and Improving the Sales Potency of Advertising," *Journal*

of *Advertising Research,* September/ October 1995, pp. 33–40.

20. Flemming Hansen, "Hemispheric Lateralization: Implications for Understanding Consumer Behavior," *Journal of Consumer Research* 8 (1988), pp. 23–36.

21. Kevin Lane Keller, Susan E. Heckler, and Michael J. Houston, "The Effects of Brand Name Suggestiveness on Advertising Recall," *Journal of Marketing,* January 1998, pp. 48–57.

22. Jan Stapel, "Recall and Recognition: A Very Close Relationship," *Journal of Advertising Research,* July/August 1998, pp. 41–45.

23. Hubert A. Zielske, "Does Day-after Recall Penalize 'Feeling Ads'?" *Journal of Advertising Research* 22, no. 1 (1982), pp. 19–22.

24. Arthur J. Kover, "Why Copywriters Don't Like Advertising Research— and What Kind of Research Might They Accept," *Journal of Advertising Research,* March/April 1996, pp. RC8-RC10; Gary Levin, "Emotion Guides BBDO's Ad Tests," *Advertising Age,* January 29, 1990, p.12.

25. Terry Haller, "Day-after Recall to Persist Despite JWT Study; Other Criteria Looming," *Marketing News,* May 18, 1979, p. 4.

26. Dave Kruegel, "Television Advertising Effectiveness and Research Innovations," *Journal of Consumer Marketing* 5, no. 3 (Summer 1988), pp. 43–52.

27. Gary Levin, "Tracing Ads' Impact," *Advertising Age,* November 12, 1990, p. 49.

28. John Philip Jones, "Single-source Research Begins to Fulfill Its Promise," *Journal of Advertising Research,* May/June 1995, pp. 9–16.

29. Jeffrey L. Seglin, "The New Era of Ad Measurement," *Adweek's Marketing Week,* January 23, 1988, p. 24.

30. James F. Donius, "Marketing Tracking: A Strategic Reassessment and Planning Tool," *Journal of Advertising Research* 25, no. 1 (February/ March 1985), pp. 15–19.

31. Russell I. Haley and Allan L. Baldinger, "The ARF Copy Research Validity Project," *Journal of Advertising Research,* April/May 1991, pp. 11–32.

32. Elizabeth Gardener and Minakshi Trivedi, "A Communications Framework to Evaluate Sales Promotion Strategies," *Journal of Advertising Research,* May/June 1998, pp. 67–71.

33. Raymond Simon, *Public Relations, Concepts and Practices,* 3rd ed. (New York: John Wiley & Sons, 1984), p. 291.

34. Walter K. Lindenmann, "An Effectiveness Yardstick to Measure Public Relations Success," *Public Relations Quarterly* 38, no. 1 (Spring 1993), pp. 7–10.

35. Deborah Holloway, "How to Select a Measurement System That's Right for You," *Public Relations Quarterly* 37, no. 3 (Fall 1992), pp. 15–18.

36. Bettina Cornwell and Isabelle Maignan, "An International Review of Sponsorship Research," *Journal of Advertising,* March 1998.

37. Michel Tuan Pham, "The Evaluation of Sponsorship Effectiveness: A Model and Some Methodological Considerations," *Gestion 2000,* pp. 47–65.

38. Ellen Neuborne and Robert D. Hof, "Branding on the Net," *Business Week,* November 9, 1998, pp. 76–86.

39. Alexa Bezjian-Avery, "New Media Interactive Advertising vs. Traditional Advertising," *Journal of Advertising Research,* August 1998, pp. 23–32; Qimel Chen and William D. Wells, "Attitude toward the Site," *Journal of Advertising Research,* September 1999, pp. 27–38; Kim Bartel Sheehan and Sally J. McMillan, "Response Variation in E-Mail Surveys," *Journal of Advertising Research,* July 1999, pp. 45–54; and John Eighmey, "Profiling User Responses to Commercial Websites," *Journal of Advertising Research,* May 1997, pp. 59–66.

Chapter Eighteen

1. Robert L. Heilbroner, "Demand for the Supply Side," *New York Review of Books* 38 (June 11, 1981), p. 40.

2. David Helm, "Advertising's Overdue Revolution," speech given to the Adweek creative conference, October 1, 1999.

3. "Fanning the Embers," *Marketing Magazine,* September 10, 2001.

4. Eric N. Berkowitz, Roger A. Kerin, Steven W. Hartley, William Rudedius, et al., *Marketing,* 5th ed. (Burr Ridge, IL: Irwin/McGraw-Hill, 1997), p. 102.

5. "Calvin's World," *Newsweek,* September 11, 1995, pp. 60–66.

6. Louise Lee, "Take Our Swoosh. Please," *Business Week,* February 21, 2000, p. 128.

Endnotes

7. John Walters, "Nike Gets Kinky," *Sports Illustrated,* February 7, 2000, p. 24.

8. Stephanie O'Donohoe, "Attitudes to Advertising: A Review of British and American Research," *International Journal of Advertising* 14 (1995), pp. 245–61.

9. Banwari Mittal, "Public Assessment of TV Advertising: Faint Praise and Harsh Criticism," *Journal of Advertising Research* 34, no. 1 (1994), pp. 35–53.

10. Sharon Shavitt, Pamela Lowery, and James Haefner, "Public Attitudes toward Advertising; More Favorable Than You Might Think," *Journal of Advertising Research,* July/August 1998, pp. 7–22.

11. Gita Venkataramini Johar, "Consumer Involvement and Deception from Implied Advertising Claims," *Journal of Marketing Research* 32 (August 1995), pp. 267–79; J. Edward Russo, Barbara L. Metcalf, and Debra Stephens, "Identifying Misleading Advertising," *Journal of Consumer Research* 8 (September 1981), pp. 119–31.

12. Ivan L. Preston, *The Great American Blow-Up: Puffery in Advertising and Selling* (Madison: University of Wisconsin Press, 1975), p. 3.

13. Shelby D. Hunt, "Informational vs. Persuasive Advertising: An Appraisal," *Journal of Advertising,* Summer 1976, pp. 5–8.

14. Banwari Mittal, "Public Assessment of TV Advertising: Faint Praise and Harsh Criticism"; J. C. Andrews, "The Dimensionality of Beliefs toward Advertising in General," *Journal of Advertising* 18, no. 1 (1989), pp. 26–35; Ron Alsop, "Advertisers Find the Climate Less Hostile Outside the U.S.," *The Wall Street Journal,* December 10, 1987, p. 29.

15. David A. Aaker and Donald E. Bruzzone, "Causes of Irritation in Advertising," *Journal of Marketing,* Spring 1985, p. 47–57.

16. Stephen A. Greyser, "Irritation in Advertising," *Journal of Advertising Research* 13 (February 1973), pp. 3–10.

17. Ron Alsop, "Personal Product Ads Abound as Public Gets More Tolerant," *The Wall Street Journal,* April 14, 1986, p. 19.

18. Joanne Lipman, "Censored Scenes: Why You Rarely See Some Things in Television Ads," *The Wall Street Journal,* August 17, 1987, p. 17.

19. For an interesting analysis of an interpretation of this ad from a literary theory perspective see Aaron C. Ahuvia, "Social Criticism of Advertising: On the Role of Literary Theory and the Use of Data," *Journal of Advertising* 27, no. 1 (Spring 1998), pp. 143–62.

20. Scott Ward, Daniel B. Wackman, and Ellen Wartella, *How Children Learn to Buy: The Development of Consumer Information Processing Skills* (Beverly Hills, CA: Sage, 1979).

21. Thomas S. Robertson and John R. Rossiter, "Children and Commercial Persuasion: An Attribution Theory Analysis," *Journal of Consumer Research* 1, no. 1 (June 1974), pp. 13–20; and Scott Ward and Daniel B. Wackman, "Children's Information Processing of Television Advertising," in *New Models for Communications Research,* ed. G. Kline and P. Clark (Beverly Hills, CA: Sage, 1974), pp. 81–119.

22. Merrie Brucks, Gary M. Armstrong, and Marvin E. Goldberg, "Children's Use of Cognitive Defenses against Television Advertising: A Cognitive Response Approach," *Journal of Consumer Research* 14, no. 4 (March 1988), pp. 471–82.

23. For a discussion on consumer socialization, see Scott Ward, "Consumer Socialization," *Journal of Consumer Research* 1, no. 2 (September 1974), pp. 1–14.

24. Tamara F. Mangleburg and Terry Bristol, "Socialization and Adolescents' Skepticism toward Advertising," *Journal of Advertising* 27, no. 3 (Fall 1998), pp. 11–21.

25. Robert E. Hite and Randy Eck, "Advertising to Children: Attitudes of Business vs. Consumers," *Journal of Advertising Research,* October/November 1987, pp. 40–53; Ann D. Walsh, Russell N. Laczniak, and Les Carlson, "Mother's Preferences for Regulating Children's Television," *Journal of Advertising,* 27, no. 3 (Fall 1998), pp. 23–36.

26. Ronald Berman, *Advertising and Social Change* (Beverly Hills, CA: Sage, 1981), p. 13.

27. John K. Galbraith, *The New Industrial State* (Boston: Houghton Mifflin, 1967), cited in Richard W. Pollay, "The Distorted Mirror: Reflections on the Unintended Consequences of Advertising," *Journal of Marketing,* August 1986, p. 25.

28. Raymond A. Bauer and Stephen A. Greyser, "The Dialogue That Never Happens," *Harvard Business Review,* January/February 1969, pp. 122–28.

29. Morris B. Holbrook, "Mirror Mirror on the Wall, What's Unfair in the Reflections on Advertising," *Journal of Marketing* 5 (July 1987), pp. 95–103; and Theodore Levitt, "The Morality of Advertising," *Harvard Business Review,* July/August 1970, pp. 84–92.

30. Stephen Fox, *The Mirror Makers: A History of American Advertising and Its Creators* (New York: Morrow, 1984), p. 330.

31. Richard W. Pollay, "The Distorted Mirror: Reflections on the Unintended Consequences of Advertising," *Journal of Marketing* 50 (April 1986), p. 33.

32. Jules Backman, "Is Advertising Wasteful?" *Journal of Marketing* 32 (January 1968), pp. 2–8.

33. Hunt, "Informational vs. Persuasive Advertising."

34. Ibid., p. 6.

35. Kevin Goldman, "Survey Asks Which 'Green' Ads Are Read," *The Wall Street Journal,* April 11, 1994, p. B5.

36. Alice E. Courtney and Thomas W. Whipple, *Sex Stereotyping in Advertising* (Lexington, MA: Lexington Books, 1984).

37. Daniel J. Brett and Joanne Cantor, "The Portrayal of Men and Women in U.S. Television Commercials: A Recent Content Analysis and Trends of 15 Years," *Sex Roles* 18, no. 9/10 (1998), pp. 595–608; John B. Ford and Michael La Tour, "Contemporary Perspectives of Female Role Portrayals in Advertising," *Journal of Current Issues and Research in Advertising* 28, no. 1 (1996), pp. 81–93; "Body Shop, Zig Ad Lauded by Report," *Marketing Magazine,* March 18, 2002; "How Far Really?" *Marketing Magazine,* July 2, 2001.

38. Beverly A. Browne, "Gender Stereotypes in Advertising on Children's Television in the 1990s: A Cross-National Analysis," *Journal of Advertising* 27, no. 1 (Spring 1998), pp. 83–96.

39. Richard H. Kolbe, "Gender Roles in Children's Advertising: A Longitudinal Content Analysis," in *Current Issues and Research in Advertising,* ed. James H. Leigh and Claude R. Martin, Jr. (Ann Arbor: University of Michigan, 1990), pp. 197–206.

40. "Body Shop, Zig Ad Lauded by Report," *Marketing Magazine,* March 18, 2002; "How Far Really?" *Marketing Magazine,* July 2, 2001.

41. Steven M. Kates and Glenda Shaw-Garlock, "The Ever Entangling Web: A Study of Ideologies and Discourses in Advertising to Women," *Journal of Advertising* 28, no. 2 (Summer 1999), pp. 33–49.

42. Basil Englis, Michael Solomon, and Richard Ashmore, "Beauty before the Eyes of Beholders: The Cultural Encoding of Beauty Types in Magazine Advertising and Music Television," *Journal of Advertising,* June 1994, pp. 49–64.

43. Cyndee Miller, "Liberation for Women in Ads," *Marketing News,* August 17, 1992, p. 1; Adrienne Ward-Fawcett, "Narrowcast in Past, Women Earn Revised Role in Advertising," *Advertising Age,* October 4, 1993, p. S1.

44. James Stearns, Lynette S. Unger, and Steven G. Luebkeman, "The Portrayal of Blacks in Magazine and Television Advertising," in *AMA Educator's Proceedings,* ed. Susan P. Douglas and Michael R. Solomon (Chicago: American Marketing Association, 1987).

45. Robert E. Wilkes and Humberto Valencia, "Hispanics and Blacks in Television Commercials," *Journal of Advertising* 18, no. 1 (1989), pp. 19–26.

46. Julia Bristor, Renee Gravois Lee, and Michelle Hunt, "Race and Ideology: African American Images in Television Advertising," *Journal of Public Policy and Marketing* 14 (Spring 1995), pp. 48–59.

47. Corliss Green, "Ethnic Evaluations of Advertising: Interaction Effects of Strength of Ethnic Identification, Media Placement, and Degree of Racial Composition," *Journal of Advertising* 28, no. 1 (Spring 1999), pp. 49–64.

48. Charles R. Taylor and Barbara B. Stern, "Asian-Americans: Television Advertising and the 'Model Minority' Stereotype," *Journal of Advertising* 26, no. 2 (Summer 1997), pp. 47–61.

49. "Including Visible Minorities," *Marketing Magazine,* June 4, 2001; "Counting Ethnic Canadians in," *Marketing Magazine,* June 4, 2001; "A Toast to More Colour in Beer Ads," *Marketing Magazine,* June 4, 2001.

50. Jef I. Richards and John H. Murphy, II, "Economic Censorship and Free Speech: The Circle of Communication between Advertisers, Media and Consumers," *Journal of Current Issues and Research in Advertising* 18, no. 1 (Spring 1996), pp. 21–33.

51. Lawrence C. Soley and Robert L. Craig, "Advertising Pressure on Newspapers: A Survey," *Journal of Advertising,* December 1992, pp. 1–10.

52. Mark Simon, "Mercury News Ad Dispute Cooling Off: Advertisers Return While Reporters Stew," *San Francisco Business Chronicle,* July 15, 1994, p. B1.

53. Soley and Craig, "Advertising Pressure on Newspapers."

54. For a discussion of monopolies in the cereal industry, see Paul N. Bloom, "The Cereal Industry: Monopolists or Super Marketers?" *MSU Business Topics,* Summer 1978, pp. 41–49.

55. Lester G. Telser, "Advertising and Competition," *Journal of Political Economy,* December 1964, pp. 537–62.

56. Robert D. Buzzell, Bradley T. Gale, and Ralph G. M. Sultan, "Market Share—A Key to Profitability," *Harvard Business Review,* January/February 1975, pp. 97–106.

57. Robert D. Buzzell and Paul W. Farris, *Advertising Cost in Consumer Goods Industries,* Marketing Science Institute, Report no. 76, August 1976, p. 111; and Paul W. Farris and David J. Reibstein, "How Prices, Ad Expenditures, and Profits Are Linked," *Harvard Business Review,* November/December 1979, pp. 173–84.

58. Paul W. Farris and Mark S. Albion, "The Impact of Advertising on the Price of Consumer Products," *Journal of Marketing* 44, no. 3 (Summer 1980), pp. 17–35.

59. Ibid., p. 19.

60. Lee Benham, "The Effect of Advertising on the Price of Eyeglasses," *Journal of Law and Economics* 15 (October 1972), pp. 337–52.

61. Robert L. Steiner, "Does Advertising Lower Consumer Price?" *Journal of Marketing* 37, no. 4 (October 1973), pp. 19–26.

62. Farris and Albion, "The Impact of Advertising," p. 30.

63. James M. Ferguson, "Comments on 'The Impact of Advertising on the Price of Consumer Products,'" *Journal of Marketing* 46, no. 1 (Winter 1982), pp. 102–5.

64. Farris and Albion, "The Impact of Advertising."

65. Cyndee Miller, "The Marketing of Advertising," *Marketing News,* December 7, 1992, pp. 1, 2.

Credits and Acknowledgements

Chapter 1

IMC Perspective 1-1: Adapted from Sarah Smith, "Go Kicks Off Bell National Campaign," October 1, 2001, Marketing Magazine; Stan Sutter, "Going Too Big," October 8, 2001, Marketing Magazine; Chris Daniels, "From the Word Go," December 17, 2001, Marketing Magazine. **Exhibit 1-1:** Courtesy of WestJet. **Exhibit 1-2:** Canadian Blood Services. 1/800 Alta Vista, Ottawa ON K1G 4J5. **Exhibit 1-3:** Courtesy of Dell Computer Corporation. **Exhibit 1-4:** Courtesy V&S and Spirit AB. Imported by the House of Seagram, New York, NY. **Exhibit: 1-5:** Used by permission of Eveready Battery Company, Inc. **Exhibit 1-6:** Courtesy of Dairy Farmers of Ontario. Photography: Joaquin Rivas. **Exhibit 1-7:** Reprinted with permission by Lands' End, Inc. **Global Perspective 1-2:** Adapted from Chris Daniels, "A Room for All Seasons", Marketing Magazine, Feb 4, 2002. Reprinted with permission of Marketing Magazine; (photo left): Milan property—Photography by Robert Miller. Istanbul property—Photography by Jaime Ardiles-Arce; (photo right). Milan property—Photography by Robert Miller. Istanbul property—Photography by Jaime Ardiles-Arce. **Exhibit 1-8:** Courtesy of WestJet. **Exhibit 1-9:** Courtesy Johnson & Johnson Consumer Products, Inc. **Exhibit 1-10:** Courtesy E.I. du Pont de Nemours and Company.

Chapter 2

Exhibit 2-1: Courtesy Michelin North America. **Global Perspective 2-1:** Nikhil Deogun, "Pepsi Unveils New Advertising Effort, Scraps 'Generation Next' Campaign," The Wall Street Journal, March 5, 1999, P.B5; Betsy McKay, "New Look for the Top Pop Aims to Infuse Some Fizz into a Nostalgic Image," The Wall Street Journal, October 13, 1999, P.B1; Nikhil Doeogun, "Aggressive Push Abroad Dilutes Coke's Strength as Big Markets Stumble,"The Wall Street Jounal, February 8, 1999, P.A1; Patricia Sellers, "How Coke Is Kicking Pepsi's Can," Fortune, October 28, 1996, pp. 70-84; (photo): "Coca-Cola" trademarks appear courtesy of The Coca-Cola Company. **Exhibit 2-2:** Reproduced with the permission of McDonald's Restaurants of Canada Limited. **Exhibit 2-3:** Courtesy of Cosmar Corporation, a division of Renaisssance Cosmetics, Inc. **IMC Perspective 2-2:** Based on David Chilton, "Redefining Olay", Marketing Magazine, October 20, 1997. Erica Zlomislic, "What Went wrong? Tip Top Repositions to far too Fast", Strategy, May 25, 1998. p.1. Craig Saunders, "Holt Renfrew Reaches out to New Shoppers," Strategy, Sept 27, 1999, p.1; (photo): Courtesy of Procter & Gamble. **Exhibit 2-4:** Courtesy Den-Mat Corporation. **Exhibit 2-5:** Courtesy of American Eagle Outfitters. **Exhibit 2-6:** Courtesy of Rado Watch Co., Ltd. **Exhibit 2-7:** Courtesy Duracell. **Exhibit 2-8:** Designs copyrighted by Tiffany and Company. **Exhibit 2-9:** Courtesy of McNeil Consumer Healthcare, 1999. **Exhibit 2-10:** Acushnet Company ©. Photography © Francine Zaslow. **Exhibit 2-11:** Courtesy Kimberly-Clark Corporation. **Exhibit 2-12:** Courtesy Oneida Ltd. All rights reserved. **Exhibit 2-13:** Courtesy Black & Decker. **Exhibit 2-14:** Courtesy The Valvoline Company, a division of Ashland Inc. **Exhibit 2-15:** Courtesy Fallon-McElligott for Rolling Stone. **Exhibit 2-16:** Courtesy America's Dairy Farmers, National Dairy Board.

Chapter 3

Exhibit 3-1: Courtesy New Balance Athletic Shoe, Inc. **Exhibit 3-2:** Courtesy John Paul Mitchell Systems. **Exhibit 3-3:** Courtesy of Del Pharmaceuticals, Inc. a subsidiary of Del Laboratories, Inc. **Exhibit 3-4:** Courtesy Ericsson Inc. **Exhibit 3-5:** © The Procter & Gamble Company. Used with Permission. **Exhibit 3-6:** Courtesy Toyota Motor Sales, U.S.A. **Exhibit 3-7:** Courtesy Tropicana Products, Inc. **Global Perspective 3-1:** Adapted from Sharon Younger, "Marketing Overseas? Keep it Canadian," Strategy Magazine, Feb 11, 2002, p.23. © 2002 Brunico Communications Inc. Reprinted with permission STRATEGY and "The Canadian Marketing Report" are trademarks of Brunico Communications Inc. **Exhibit 3-8:**

Courtesy Spalding & Evenflo Companies, Inc. **Exhibit 3-9:** The ad for JEEP GRAND CHEROKEE, with use of the QUADRA DRIVE name is used with permission from Daimler Chrysler Corporation. **Exhibit 3-10:** Courtesy The Pillsbury Company. **Exhibit 3-11:** Reprinted with permission from Labatt Brewing Company Limited. **Exhibit 3-12:** Courtesy of International Business Machines Corporation. **Exhibit 3-13:** Courtesy of the Brita Products Company. **Exhibit 3-14:** Used by permission of Eveready Battery Company, Inc. Eveready ® is a registered trademark of Eveready Battery Company. **Ethical Perspective 3-2:** "Hypnosis Reveals Ad Effects," Adweek Asia, Jan 29, 1999, p.4; "Breaking French Connection," Ad Age, March 22, 1999, p.52; "Blink of an Ad," Time, Aug 3, 1998, p.51; Jack Haberstroh, "Ice Cube Sex: The Truth about Subliminal Advertising," New York Times Publishing, 1996; Kathryn Theus, "Subliming Advertising and the Psychology of Processing Unconscious Stimuli: A Review of Research," Psychology & marketing 11", no.3, 1994, pp.271-90; Timothy Moore, "Subliminal Advertising: What you See is What You Get," Journal of Marketing 46, no.2, (Spring 1982), pp.38-47; Timothy Moore, "The Case Against Subliminal Manipulation," Psychology and Marketing 5, no. 4 (Winter 1988), pp.297-316. **Exhibit 3-5:** Director General Public Affairs, Department of National Defence.

Chapter 4

Global Perspective 4-1: Kevin Reagan, "In Asia, Think Globally, Communicate Locally," Marketing News, July 19, 199, pp.12-14; Yumiko Ono, "Will Good Housekeeping Translate into Japanese?" The Wall Street Journal, Dec 30, 1997, p.B1; Greg Johnson, "Fast-Food Firms Learn Lessons of El Mercado," Los Angeles Times, Oct 8, 1996, pp.A1, 16; (photo): Reproduced with permission of AT&T. **Exhibit 4-1:** Courtesy Estee Lauder. **Exhibit 4-2:** © 1999 Time Inc. Reprinted by permission. **IMC Perspective 4-2:** Adapted from James Careless, " Re-evaluating the 50 plus Sector," Marketing Magazine, Oct 18, 1999. Reprinted with permission of Marketing Magazine; (photo left): CARP News Fifty Plus Magazine; (photo right): Courtesy of Forever Young Magazine. **Exhibit 4-3:** Courtesy Johnson & Johnson Consumer Products, Inc. **Exhibit 4-4:** Courtesy Panasonic Electronics Company. **Exhibit 4-5:** Courtesy of Canon. **Exhibit 4-6:** Courtesy Michelin North America. **Exhibit 4-7:** Courtesy Heinz U.S.A. **Exhibit 4-8:** © The Procter & Gamble Company. Used by Permission. Exhibit 4-9: Tom Sandler Photography.

Chapter 5

Exhibit 5-1: Courtesy of FPAC. **Exhibit 5-2:** Courtesy Ford Motor. **IMC Perspective 5-1:** Adapted from Ron Szekely, "L'Oreal Generates Buzz," Marketing Magazine, Jan 7, 2002. Reprinted with permission of Marketing Magazine. **Exhibit 5-3:** CP/PA STRPA/Yui Mok Pa. **Exhibit 5-4:** Courtesy Del Monte Foods. **Exhibit 5-5:** Courtesy Waterford Wedgewood USA, Inc. **Exhibit 5-6:** Courtesy Palm, Inc. Photography by Timothy Greenfield-Sanders. **IMC Perspective 5-2:** Adapted from Eve Lazarus, "Not Playing Around,: March 5, 2001, Marketing Magazine; Eve Lazarus, "What a Long, Strange Ride It's Been," March 5, 2001, Marketing Magazine.

Chapter 6

Exhibit 6-1: Courtesy Fallon McElligot for BMW of North America. **Exhibit 6-2:** Courtesy Nissan North America. **IMC Perspective 6-1:** Adapted from Margaret Nearing "Cannes-ada," July 3, 2000, Marketing Magazine; "Cannes 2001," July 2, 2001, Marketing Magazine; "Cannes Ad Festival can be a Real Eye-Opener for Marketers," July 2, 2001, Marketing Magazine; Angela Kryhul "The Bashful Beaver," Nov 26, 2001, Marketing Magazine; "More Canuk Work Entered at Cannes," May 29, 2002, Marketing Magazine. **IMC Perspective 6-2:** Adapted from Jean-Marc Leger and Dave Scholz, "The Last Laugh," Marketing Magazine,

April 15, 2002. Reprinted with permission of Marketing Magazine. **Exhibit 6-3:** Courtesy Westin Hotels & Resorts. **IMC Perspective 6-3:** Based on David Hayes, "The Boys in the Brand," National Post Business Magazine, March 2002, P.46; "The Artist as a Young Brand" Marketing Magazine, March 4, 2002; "Krall Has the Look of Love," Marketing Magazine, Feb 25, 2002; (photo): CP/Paul Chiasson. **Exhibit 6-4:** Courtesy Polaroid Corporation. **Exhibit 6-5:** Courtesy of Pfizer Canada Inc., Adams Division. **Exhibit 6-6:** Courtesy No Fear. **Exhibit 6-7:** Courtesy Leo Burnette Company, Inc. as agent for Hallmark Cards, Incorporated. **Exhibit 6-8:** Courtesy 3M. Exhibit 6-9: Courtesy The Quaker Oats Company. **Exhibit 6-10:** Courtesy Singapore Airlines. **Exhibit 6-11:** Casey's is a registered trade-mark of PRC Trademarks Inc. **Exhibit 6-12:** Courtesy Bristo-Myers Squibb Co. **Exhibit 6-13:** Courtesy SmithKline Beecham. **Exhibit 6-14:** PayDay is a registered trademark. Used with permission of Hershey Foods Corporation. Photography © Howard Berman. **Exhibit 6-15:** Courtesy Team One Advertising for LEXUS. **Exhibit 6-16:** Courtesy MasterCard International Incorporated. **Exhibit 6-18:** Courtesy of Lever Brothers Company. **Exhibit 6-19:** American Isuzu Motors, Inc. and Goodby, Silverman & Partners. **Exhibit 6-20:** Copyright 1998— GM Corp. Used with permission of GM Media Archives. All rights reserved. **Exhibit 6-21:** Courtesy The Coca-Cola Company. **Exhibit 6-22:** Courtesy Subaru of America and Temerlin McClain. **Exhibit 6-23:** Courtesy Revlon Consumer Products Corporation.

Chapter 7

IMC Perspective 7-1: Adapted from Angela Kryhul, "The Great Canadian Icon," Marketing Magazine, June 26, 2000. pp.11-15. Reprinted with permission of Marketing Magazine. **Exhibit 7-1:** © 1999 Castrol North America Inc. **Exhibit 7-2:** The DERMASIL print ad was reproduced courtesy Chesebrough-Pond's USA Co. **Exhibit 7-3:** Courtesy DuPont. Teflon® is a registered trademark of DuPont. **Exhibit 7-4:** Courtesy Sybase, Inc. **Exhibit 7-5:** Courtesy Maytag Company. **IMC Perspective 7-2:** Anita Lahey, "What the Eye Sees," March 12, 2001, Marketing Magazine. Reprinted with permission of Marketing Magazine. **Exhibit 7-6:** Courtesy of Hewlett-Packard Company. **Exhibit 7-7:** Courtesy W.K. Buckley Limited. **Exhibit 7-8:** Courtesy CamelBak Products, Inc. **Exhibit 7-9:** Courtesy Thomson Multimedia. Product photography by Thomas Card. Model photography by Dominik Guillemot. **Exhibit 7-10:** Courtesy AT&T Corp. Copyright 1997 AT&T Copr. All rights reserved. **Exhibit 7-11:** Courtesy Sims. **Exhibit 7-12:** Courtesy Volkswagen of America, Inc. and Arnold Communications. **Exhibit 7-13:** Kenmore Elite ™ ad, courtesy of Sears, Roebuck and Co.

Chapter 8

Figure 8-1: Media Digest, 200-1-2002, Canadian Market Data: "Net Advertising Revenues. As compiled by the TVB from Statistics Canada, CRTC, CAN, CCNA/Les Hebdos du Quebec, Magazines Canada/LNA, CARD, Mediacom/CAN, TeleDirect, Canada Post, IAB/Ernst & Young and industry estimates" Used with permission of Marketing Magazine. **Ethical Perspective 8-1:** Based on Astrid Van Den Broek, "A Toast to More Colour in Beer Ads," Marketing Magazine, June 4, 2001; Tony Pigott and Michael Sullivan, "Including Visible Minorities," Marketing Magazine, June 4, 2001; Astrid Van den Broek, "Canada's Advertising Still too White," Marketing Magazine, June 5, 2000; (photo): © 2001 Molson Canada. **IMC Perspective 8-2:** "General Mills Outsells Kellogg's Cereals," Tulsa World, Tulsa, OK, Dec 30, 1999, p.2: Judann Pollack, "Price Cuts Unsettling to Cereal Business," Advertising Age, Sept 28, 1998, p.510; "Kellogg Marketing Strategies under Revision," PR Newswire, Sept 4, 1998, p.1087. John Greenwald, "Cereal Showdown," Time, April 29, 1996, pp.60-61; Judann Pollack, "Cereals to Pare Ad Plans," Advertising Age, June 24, 1996, p.1; Rance Crain, "Cereals Shouldn't Squeeze Ad Bucks," Advertising Age, July 1, 1996, p.15; (photo): Stone/David Young Wolff.

Chapter 9

Exhibit 9-1: Courtesy Porsche Cars North America, Inc. **Exhibit 9-2:** Courtesy The Discovery Channel. **IMC Perspective 9-1:** Based on Sherry O'Neil, "Digital TV Winners" Marketing Magazine, May 6, 2002; James Careless, "A Rough Start for the Diginets", Marketing Magazine, Dec 10, 2001. **IMC Perspective 9-2:** Thomas Kupper, "TV Ads May be Doomed, Expert Says," San Diego Union-Tribune, Nov 2, 1999, pp.C1, 4; James Poniewozik, "Here Come PVRs, Is Network TV Doomed?," Time, Sept 27, 1999, pp.62-63; J.William Gurley, "How The Web Will Warp Advertising," Fortune, Nov 9, 1998, pp.119-120. Used with permission of Marketing Magazine; (photo): Courtesy Tivo Inc. **Figure 9-2:** Media Digest, Sept 24, 2001. Estimated Cost of Network Commercials. **Exhibit 9-3:** © 2000 National Broadcasting Company, Inc. Used by permission. **Exhibit 9-4:** © 1996 Cable News Network, Inc. A Time Warner Company. All rights reserved. **Exhibit 9-5:** Courtesy A.C. Neilsen Company. **Figure 9-6:** 2000-2001 BBM Television Data Book. Television Summer Drop-off. Used with permission. **Exhibit 9-6:** Courtesy Radio Advertising Bureau. **Exhibit 9-7:** Banana Boat of California, Inc. **Figure 9-12:** Weekly Reach & Share of Total Hours Turned by Major Demographic. BBM Fall 2000. Used with permission. **Figure 9-14:** Weekly Ratio FM Listening (12+): % Reach. BBM Fall 2000. Used with permission.

Chapter 10

Exhibit 10-1: Courtesy of Outpost Magazine. **Exhibit 10-2:** Courtesy Alberta Beef Magazine. **Figure 10-3:** Media Digest, Sept 24, 2001. Top U.S. magazines with paid Canadian circulation. Used with permission of Marketing Magazine. **IMC Perspective 10-1:** Adapted from Chris Daniels, "Missing the Target," Marketing Magazine, Sept 18, 2000. Reprinted with permission of Marketing Magazine. **Exhibit 10-3:** Courtesy of Toronto Life Magazine. **Exhibit 10-4:** Photography by Sharon Hoogstraten. **Exhibit 10-5:** Used by permission of WD-40 Company. **Exhibit 10-6:** Courtesy of Bausch & Lomb Healthcare and Optics Worldwide. **Exhibit 10-7:** Courtesy Newsweek, Inc. All rights reserved. **Exhibit 10-8:** Reprinted from 5/1/2000 Business Week Online by special permission, copyright © 2000 by the McGraw-Hill Companies, Inc. **IMC Perspective 10-2:** Wendy Bounds, "Magazine's Seek to Demonstrate Efficacy of Ads," The Wall Street Journal, April 12, 1999. pp.B1,3. **Exhibit 10-9:** Copyright © 2000 by the New York Times Co. Reprinted with permission. **Exhibit 10-11:** Courtesy Cathay Pacific Airways and McCann-Erickson. **Figure 10-4:** Readership by Gender, All Markets—2002 Interim Report. Used with permission of NADbank. **Figure 10-5:** Readership by Region, All Markets—2002 Interim Report. Used with permission of NADbank. **Figure 10-6:** Readership by Age, All Markets—2002 Interim Report. Used with permission of NADbank.

Chapter 11

Exhibit 11-1: Courtesy of Outdoor Advertising Association of America, Inc. **Figure 11-2:** 2001 Rate Cards. "Outdoor: Rates by Weekly GRP Delivery." **Exhibit 11-2:** Right—Courtesy Outdoor Advertising Association of America, Inc. **Exhibit 11-3:** http://www.ppa/org/industry_resources/sales_volume_98.html Reprinted with permission of Promotional Products Association International. **Figure 11-3:** Transit Advertising: Rates for Selected Buys (All cost in 000's). March 2001, CARD. **Exhibit 11-4:** National Yellow Pages Monitor, a division of NFD Research, Inc. **Exhibit 11-5:** Courtesy of WestJet. **IMC Perspective 11-1:** Adapted from Angela Kryhul, "When Faking it Doesn't work," Marketing Magazine, July 31, 2000. Reprinted with permission of Marketing Magazine. **Exhibit 11-6:** Courtesy Promotional Products Association International. **Global Perspective 11-2:** Peter Wonacott, "Chinese TV is an Eager Medium for (Lots of) Product Placements," The Wall Street Journal, Jan 26, 2000, p.B12; Bob Ortega, "Extreme Skiing Meets Extreme Product Placement," The Wall Street Journal, Dec 28, 1998, p.B1; (photo): Warren Miller Films/Photo by Mark Weaver. **Exhibit 11-7:** AP Photo/BMW, Stuart Ramson. **Exhibit 11-8:** AP photo/Adam Butler.

Chapter 12

Exhibit 12-1: © Procter & Gamble Company. Used with permission. **Exhibit 12-2:** KELLOGG'S POP TARTS PASTRY SWIRLS ™ and POP-TARTS SNACK-STIX ™ are trademarks of Kellogg Company. All rights reserved. Used with permission. **Exhibit 12-3:** Courtesy Cox Targe Media, Inc. **IMC Perspective 12-1:** Adapted from Scott Gardiner, "A Truly Awesome Database," Marketing Magazine, April 29, 2002. Reprinted with permission of Marketing Magazine. **Exhibit 12-4:** Courtesy WD-40 Company. **Exhibit 12-5:** Sharon Hoogstraten. **Exhibit 12-6:** ArmorAll Products Corporation. **Exhibit 12-7:** Courtesy Cox Targe Media, Inc. **Exhibit 12-8:** Courtesy Kellogg Company. Eggo ®, Common Sense ®, and Kellogg's ® are registered trademarks of Kellogg Company. All rights reserved. **Exhibit 12-9:** Courtesy McDonald's Corporation. **Exhibit 12-10:** ArmorAll Products Corporation. **Exhibit 12-11:** Courtesy Bristol-Myers Company. **Exhibit 12-12:** Courtesy Gerber Products Company. **IMC Perspective 12-2:** Kerry J. Smith, "Procter Moves the Market, Again," Promo Magazine, July 1999, p.6; Betsy Spethmann, "Procter's Gamble," Promo Magazine, July 1999, p.6; "Make it Simple," Business Week, Sept 6, 1996, pp.96-104; (photo): Reprinted from September 9, 1996 issue of Business Week by special permission, copyright © 1996 by The McGraw-Hill Companies, Inc. **Exhibit 12-13:** Courtesy Spalding Sports Worldwide. **Exhibit 12-14:** Courtesy New Balance Athletic Shoes, Inc. **Exhibit 12-15:** Courtesy WD-40 Company. **Exhibit 12-16:** Courtesy Lever Brothers Company.

Chapter 13

Exhibit 13-1: Used by permission of Tree Top, Inc. **Exhibit 13-2:** CLIENT: Olympus America, Inc. AGENCY: McCaffrey & Ratner Gottlieb Lane. **Exhibit 13-3:** Courtesy HP—Home Products Division. **Exhibit 13-4:** Courtesy Texaco. **Exhibit 13-5:** Courtesy McGraw-Hill Ryerson. **Exhibit 13-6:** Reprinted with permission of Chevron Corporation. **Ethical Perspective 13-1:** Adapted from Stan Sutter, "Not Just Peanuts" Marketing Magazine, June 11, 2001. Reprinted with permission of Marketing Magazine; (photo): © Nestle Canada Inc. **Exhibit 13-7:** Courtesy Tyco International. **IMC Perspective 13-2:** Adapted from Angela Kryhul, "The Krispy Cult," Marketing Magazine, Jan 28, 2002. Reprinted with

Credits and Acknowledgements

permission of Marketing Magazine. **Exhibit 13-8:** Design: Alana Roso/Silver Samba Design Co. **Exhibit 13-9:** Courtesy Cunningham Communications.

Chapter 14

Exhibit 14-1: Courtesy Cox Direct. **Exhibit 14-2:** Courtesy Tourism Saskatchewan www.sasktourism.com. Courtesy Newfoundland and Labrador Tourism. **Exhibit 14-3:** © 1999 Hertz System, Inc. Hertz is a registered service mark and trademark of Hertz System, Inc. **Exhibit 14-4:** Courtesy Porsche Cars North America, Inc. **Exhibit 14-5:** Photograph by Sharon Hoogstraten. **IMC Perspective 14-1:** Adapted from John Peloza, "The CD-ROM as a Direct Tool," Marketing Magazine, April 29, 2002. Reprinted with permission of Marketing Magazine; (photo): Alison Derry. **Exhibit 14-6:** Courtesy Bennett Kuhn Varner, Inc. **Exhibit 14-7:** Courtesy Volvo Cars of North America. **IMC Perspective 14-2:** Adapted from Ian French, "Twenty-Four Ways to Dynamic DRTV" Marketing Magazine, Feb 11, 2002. Reprinted with permission of Marketing Magazine.

Chapter 15

Exhibit 15-1: Courtesy Kimberly-Clark Corporation. **Exhibit 15-2:** Courtesy Xerox Corporation. **Exhibit 15-3:** Courtesy General Mills, Inc. "Cheerios" is a registered trademark of General Mills. Used with permission. **Exhibit 15-4:** Amazon.com is a registered trademark or trademark of Amazon.com, Inc. in the U.S. and/or other countries. © 2000 Amazon.com. All rights reserved. **IMC Perspective 15-1:** Based on "Shopping Online keeps Cupboards Full," Toronto Star, March 30, 2002; Kevin Marron, "It's a Brand New Game," The Globe and Mail, Jan 30, 2001, P.E1; Terry Poulton, "Grocery Gateway Builds Total Brand Personality," Strategy, Jan 15, 2001, P.18; Raju Mudhar, "Delivering the Goods," Canadian Grocer, April 2001, pp.18-19; (photo): Courtesy of Grocery Gateway. **Exhibit 15-5:** © Keebler Company. **IMC Perspective 15-2:** From materials provided by Director of Communications, Gabriel Ahad, CIRA. **Exhibit 15-6:** Courtesy DaimlerChrysler Corporation. **Exhibit 15-7:** Amazon.com is a registered trademark or trademark of Amazon.com, Inc. in the U.S. and/or other countries. © 2000 Amazon.com. All rights reserved.

Chapter 16

Exhibit 16-1: Courtesy of Link Magazine. **Exhibit 16-2:** © The Procter & Gamble Company. Used with permission. **Exhibit 16-3:** Courtesy No Fear. **IMC Perspective 16-1:** Tanya Irwin, "A Brand New Cadillac," Adweek, Sept 6, 1999, p.30; Jean Halliday, "GM's Brand Management Report Card," Advertising Age, March 9, 1998, pp.1, 26; Kathleen Kerwin, "GM Warms Up the Branding Iron,"

Business Week, Sept 23, 1996, pp.153-4; (photo): Copyright 1998—GM Corp. Used with permission of GM Media Archives. All rights reserved. **Exhibit 16-4:** Courtesy The Coca-Cola Company. "Coca-Cola" and the Dynamic Ribbon device are registered trademarks of The Coca-Cola Company. **Exhibit 16-5:** DR PEPPER ® is a registered trademark of Dr Pepper/Seven Up, Inc. © 2000 Dr. Pepper/Seven Up Inc. **IMC Perspective 16-2:** Adapted from Danny Kucharsky, "Women Key to Ad Industry's Success", Marketing Magazine, April 8, 2002. Reprinted with permission of Marketing Magazine. **Exhibit 16-6:** Reprinted with permission from the July 26, 1999 issue of Advertising Age. Copyright, Crain Communications, Inc. 1999. **Exhibit 16-7:** Courtesy Taylor Made.

Chapter 17

Exhibit 17-1: Churchill & Klehr/Liason Agency Inc. **IMC Perspective 17-1:** Adapted from Marion Plunkett, "Checking in Early with Consumers," Marketing Magazine, Feb 22, 1999. Reprinted with permission of Marketing Magazine. **Exhibit 17-2:** Courtesy Roper Starch Worldwide. **Exhibit 17-3:** Courtesy Ipsos-ASI, Inc. **IMC Perspective 17-2:** Adapted from Jordan Al Levitin, "Redefining Research," Marketing Magazine, July 16, 2001. Reprinted with permission of Marketing Magazine.

Chapter 18

Exhibit 18-1: Courtesy of Calvin Klein. **Exhibit 18-2:** Courtesy NIKE Inc. **Exhibit 18-3:** Courtesy Ansell. **Exhibit 18-4:** Courtesy Airwalk. **Exhibit 18-5:** Used by permission of Calvin Klein. **Ethical Perspective 18-1:** Adapted from Kathleen Martin, "How Far Really?", Marketing Magazine, July 2, 2001. Reprinted with permission of Marketing Magazine. **Exhibit 18-6:** Reprinted by permission of Rolls Royce Motor Cars Inc. **Exhibit 18-7:** © American Association of Advertising Agencies. **Exhibit 18-8:** © American Association of Advertising Agencies. **Exhibit 18-9:** Courtesy Maidenform Inc./Agency—Levine, Huntley, Schmidt & Beaver; Creative—Rochell Klein, Michael Vitello; Director—Mark Coppos, Copos Films. **Exhibit 18-10:** Courtesy IKEA and Deutsch Inc. **Exhibit 18-11:** Courtesy gfn.com, the Gay Financial Network, Inc. **Ethical Perspective 18-2:** Based on Gillian Shaw, "Regulators Clamp Down on Ab-machine Ads" Vancouver Sun, May 10, 2002; Cheri Hanson, "Health Canada Weighs in with product Safety Probe," Calgary Herald, May 16, 2002; "It's Grunt and Sweat to a Longer Life," Cape Breton Post, May 17, 2002; "Health Canada Investigates Stomach 'Exercise' Belts after U.S. Lawsuits," Canadian Press, May 15, 2002. **Exhibit 18-13:** © American Association of Advertising Agencies. **Exhibit 18-14:** © American Association of Advertising Agencies. **Exhibit 18-15:** Courtesy International Advertising Agency.

Name and Company Index

Name and Company Index

Subject Index

A

ability, 100
absolute cost, 224
account executive, 431
account planning, 139
account services, 431
account-specific marketing, 312
accountability, 17–18, 312
ACT theatre methodology, 462
ad execution-related thoughts, 98
advertiser control, 501–503
advertising
  advocacy, 363–365
  and brand equity, 42
  business-to-business, 8
  carryover effect, 109, 110
  cause-related, 365–366
  classified, 275
  communication task, 113
  and competitive advantage, 32
  cooperative, 339–340
  corporate. *See* corporate advertising
  creative strategy. *See* creative
    strategy
  creative tactics. *See* creative tactics
  definition, 5–6
  and direct marketing, 375
  direct-response advertising, 12, 383
  display, 275
  economies of scale, 204
  effects of, 101–102
  features of, 6–7
  feedback, measurement of, 85
  general, 275
  humour, 141
  image, 147–148, 361–363
  importance of, 6
  in-flight, 293
  by Internet companies, 407
  limits, 485
  local, 8, 275
  magazines. *See* magazine advertising
  and market type, 20
  media strategy, 25
  movement away from, 17
  mystery ads, 156–157
  national, 8, 275
  nature and purpose, 7–8
  network, 239–240
  nonpersonal component, 6
  paid component, 5–6
  primary demand, 8
  print. *See* print advertising
  professional, 8
  radio. *See* radio advertising
  reminder, 62
  retail, 8
  vs. sales promotion, 314–315
  selective demand, 8
  slice-of-death, 171
  specialty, 297
  sponsorship, 240–242, 362–363
  spot, 240
  subliminal perception, 62
  support, 383
  teaser, 156–157
  television. *See* television advertising
  third-party, 406
  trade, 8, 45
  transit, 290–293
  universal advertising standards, 137
  visual image personality, 93
advertising agencies
  accountability, 17–18
  compensation, 17–18, 436–438
  creative boutiques, 435–436
  definition, 421
  evaluation of, 439
  financial audit, 439
  full service, 430–435
  IMC services. *See* IMC services
  in-house agency, 426–427
  long-term relationships, 439
  losing clients, 439–440
  management issues. *See*
    management issues
  matrix organization design, 443
  media buying services, 436
  option, 427–430
  qualitative audit, 439
  responsibility for IMC, 444
  services offered, 428–429
  as subsidiaries, 428
  superagencies, 430
advertising appeal, 149
advertising campaign, 145
advertising creativity
  see also creative strategy; creative
    tactics
  definition, 135–138
  importance of, 133–135
  objections to testing, 453
advertising effectiveness
  budgeting decisions, 454
  costs of measurement, 451
  creative decisions, 453–454
  creative theme/idea, 453
  current research methods, 471–472
  decisions for measurement, 454–457
  essentials of effective testing,
    472–473
  field tests, 456–457
  laboratory tests, 456
  measurement debate, 450–453
  measurement methods. *See*
    measurement methods
  media decisions, 454
  PACT (Positioning Advertising
    Copy Testing), 457, 472–473
  posttests, 454, 455–457
  pretests, 454–455
  program for, 471–473
  reasons for measurement, 450–451
  reasons for non-measurement,
    451–453
  research problems, 452
  testing bias, 456
  vehicle option source effect, 454
  what to test, 453–454
  when to test, 455–456
  where to test, 456–457
advertising manager, 422
advertising regulations
  Advertising Standards Council,
    486–490
  in Canada, 484–490
  CRTC (Canadian Radio-television
    and Telecommunications
    Commission), 485
  Internet, 485
  Quebec regulations on children's
    advertising, 486
  tobacco advertising, 485–486
Advertising Standards Council
  alcohol, 489
  Canadian Code of Advertising
    Standards, 486–487
  children's advertising, 489–490
  clearance process, 489–490
  complaints process, 487–488
  complaints report, 488–489
  cosmetics, 489
  food, 490
  Gender Portrayal Guidelines,
    486, 487
  non-prescription drugs, 489
advertorials, 383
advocacy advertising, 363–365
affect referral decision rule, 67, 101
affective stage, 91
affective strategy, 182
affiliates, 239
affiliations, 403
affordable method, 205–206
agate line, 281
agencies. *See* advertising agencies
agency compensation
  commission system, 436–437
  cost-plus system, 438
  fee arrangement systems, 438
  fee-commission combination, 438
  fixed-fee method, 438
  incentive-based system, 438
  negotiated commission, 437
  percentage charges, 438–439
AIDA model, 88
airline transit media, 292–293
alcohol, 485, 489
"all-you-can-afford" method, 205–206
alpha activity, 464
alternative evaluation process
  evaluative criteria, 62–64
  evoked set, 62
  functional consequences, 63
  implications, 96–97
  integrated information response
    model, 94–97
  psychosocial consequences, 63–64
alternative response hierarchies
  dissonance/attribution model, 92
  low-involvement hierarchy, 92–94
  standard learning model, 91–92
alternative strategies, 451
animatic, 142
animation, 171
arbitrary allocation, 206
ARPANET, 393
art department, 434
aspirational reference groups, 74
associative process, 69
attitude surveys, 476
attitude toward the ad, 98
attitudes
  brand attitude, 125
  change strategies, 65–66
  importance of, 64
  influence on, 65–66
  multiattribute attitude model, 64–65
  salient beliefs, 65
  study of, 64
attractiveness
  described, 159
  familiarity, 159
  identification, 159
  likeability, 159, 160
  similarity, 159–160
attribution theory, 343
audience
  airline transit media, 293
  external, 354
  internal, 354
  Internet marketing, 413
  magazine readership, 269–270
  share of, 247
  target, 113, 118–120
  target audience coverage, 213–214
  total, 270

Subject Index

Subject Index